MACROECONOMICS

First Canadian Edition

DAVID C. COLANDER
Middlebury College

PETER S. SEPHTON
University of New Brunswick

Represented in Canada by:

 **Times Mirror**
Professional Publishing Ltd.

IRWIN

Toronto • Chicago • Bogotá • Boston • Buenos Aires
Caracas • London • Madrid • Mexico City • Sydney

Dedicated to the memory of Frank Knight and Thorstein Veblen, both of whose economics have significantly influenced the contents of this book.

Part opener photos

Part 1: Reuters/Bettmann
Part 2: Robin Smith/Tony Stone Images

Irwin Book Team

Publisher: *Roderick T. Banister*
Developmental Editor: *Sabira Hussain*
Marketing manager: Murray Moman
Production supervisor: *Bob Lange*
Assistant manager, graphics: *Charlene R. Perez*
Coordinator, graphics & desktop services: *Keri Johnson*
Photo researcher: *Michelle Oberhoffer*
Project editor: *Lynne Basler*
Senior designer: *Heidi J. Baughman*
Compositor: *Better Graphics, Inc.*
Typeface: *10/12 Times Roman*
Printer: *Webcrafters, Inc.*

Times Mirror
Higher Education Group

ISBN: 0-256-17512-1
Library of Congress Catalog Number: 95-78245

Printed in the United States of America
1 2 3 4 5 6 7 8 9 0 WEB 2 1 0 9 8 7 6 5

Preface

One of the first lessons of writing is: Know for whom you are writing. This book is written for students; this preface, however, is written for professors. Why? The answer is simple—the students for whom this book was written don't read prefaces; they don't read anything in a textbook unless it is assigned (and sometimes they don't even read that). Their interests lie in the real world, not texts. The style and structure of the body of this text is made to turn on such students, as much as they can be turned on, to economic ideas. Alas, we recognize that we will fail with many, but we sincerely believe that our success rate of actually getting students to read this textbook will likely be higher than will be the success rate for other economic textbooks written in standard professorial style.

We also recognize that students will never get a chance to read this text unless the professor chooses the book, which is why we write this preface for professors—they read prefaces. (If you're one of those rare students who read textbook prefaces, read on; it will give you a sense of what will be coming in the course.)

The Canadian edition keeps most of the distinctive components and style of the American editions, so we begin this preface with the key elements of those earlier prefaces.

Why Write another Book?

Why write a new introductory economics textbook? Since we are economists, the answer must be that the expected benefits outweighed the expected costs. But that doesn't mean we had our bank balances in mind when we decided to write this book. Quite honestly, there are easier ways of earning money. There had to be some other benefits out there. For us, those other benefits had to do with a belief about how economics should be taught—what was important and what was not.

Before we started writing this book we had done quite a bit of research on economic education. As part of that research, graduate students in a number of top graduate programs were surveyed and interviewed. Two of the most disturbing things we discovered were that economic institutions and economic literature were being given short shrift in graduate economics education. For example, in response to the question, "How important is a knowledge of economic literature to being successful as an economist?" only 10 percent of the students responded that it was very important, while 43 percent said it was unimportant. In response to the question, "How important to achieving success as an economist is having a thorough

knowledge of the economy?" only 3 percent said it was very important, while 68 percent said it was unimportant.

We believe that the majority of the profession is concerned with these results. Certainly the students we interviewed were concerned. They said they believed that institutions and literature were very important. Their survey responses simply indicated their perception of how people succeed in the profession, but the current situation was not the way it should be. Almost all economists we know believe that students need to know economic literature and have a thorough knowledge of the institutions. Without the appropriate background knowledge of institutions and literature, all the technical skills in the world aren't going to provide one with the economic sensibility necessary to understand what's going on in the economy or to decide whether or not a model is relevant.

As we thought about these results and considered our own teaching, we realized that the problem was not only in graduate schools; it had filtered down to undergraduate texts. As we looked through the texts, we saw excellent discussions of technical issues and of models, but little discussion of economic sensibility. These books didn't even try to provide the intellectual context within which those models developed or the institutional context to which those models were to be applied. The standard texts had settled into teaching technique for the sake of technique and had shifted away from teaching economic sensibility.

We decided that if we were serious about playing a role in reinstituting economic sensibility and a knowledge of institutions and literature in economic education, we would have to write an introductory textbook that did that. We took it as a challenge. Meeting that challenge was what drove us to write this book.

Teaching Economic Sensibility

The question we faced was: How do you incorporate economic sensibility into a textbook? Economic sensibility is more than a knowledge of modelling techniques; it is a mindset in which one's lens of the world is a latticework of ascending cost/benefit frameworks in which one is deciding on the optimal degree of rationality. Economic sensibility is an enforced reasonableness that provides insight into complicated issues; it is a perspective, not a technique. The argument we heard in favour of teaching technique was that economic sensibility could not be taught. We reject that argument. Economic sensibility may be hard to teach because it does not come naturally for most people, but it can and must be taught. The question is: How do you teach it? The answer we came to: Enthusiastically.

Economics with Passion

We are first and foremost economics teachers; we are excited by economics. We find economic ideas relevant, challenging, and exciting. In our lectures, we try to convey that excitement, and if the lecture is going right, we can feel the excitement in our students. Then off they go to read the text. All too often when they return to class, the fire in their eyes is gone; the textbook has lulled them into complacency. Those who know us know that we can put up with many things (not quietly, but nonetheless put up with), but one of those things isn't complacency. We want students to think, to argue, to challenge, to get passionate about the ideas. We encourage this reaction from students not just because economists' ideas deserve to be treated passionately, but also because, through a combination of passion and reason, eventually students achieve economic sensibility. We decided what was missing from most textbooks was the passion. We promised ourselves our book would retain the passion.

Now there's no way we're going to get passionate about Slutsky equations, phase diagrams, indifference curves, or an AS/AD model. Mathematicians may get passionate about such things, we don't. We do get passionate about the insight economics gives one into the problems, we, as individuals and as society, must face: the budget deficit, TANSTAAFL, the environment, and agricultural subsidies. If the techniques help in understanding the ideas, fine, but if they don't, goodbye to the techniques.

Passion without Bias

While not all textbooks are written by passionless people, the conventional wisdom is that authors should hide their passion to make their books more marketable. In some ways this makes sense—often passion and ideological bias go together. Many economists' passions are ideologically linked, and if you remove the ideology, you remove the passion. Good economic sensibility cannot be—and cannot even appear to be—biased; if passion is purged in maintaining neutrality, it is purged for a good cause.

But passion and ideological bias need not go together. We believe it is possible for a passionate textbook to be reasonably objective and unbiased. And we set out to write a book that would be as unbiased as possible (but not more so) and to do so without masking our passion for economic ideas. Various techniques allow us to do this. For example, to keep the students interested in the ideas rather than focusing on technique, we present some ideas in a debate format with two passionate believers on both sides arguing the points. The debate format makes the arguments come alive; they are no longer technical issues that must be memorized, they are passionate ideas.

A Conversational Tone

To transmit that sense of passion to the students, we needed a writing style that allowed it to come through. Quite honestly, textbookese douses passion faster than a cold shower. So this book is not written in textbookese. It's written in conversational English—we're talking to the students.

The conversational tone is not a monotone; it ebbs and flows depending on the nature of the material. Sometimes, in the analytic parts, the style approaches textbookese; the important technical aspects of economics require technical writing. When we hit those parts, we tell the students and encourage them to stick with us. But, even here we try to provide intuitive explanations that students can relate to.

The use of conversational style has two effects. First, it eliminates the sense some students have that textbooks provide the "truth." When the textbook authors are real people with peccadilloes and warts, the students won't accept what he or she says unless it makes sense to them. Approaching a textbook with a "show me" attitude stimulates true learning. Second, the conversational style keeps the students awake. If students' heads are nodding as they read a chapter, they're not learning. Now we know this book is not *Catcher in the Rye;* it's a textbook conveying sometimes complex ideas. But the excitement about economic ideas and the real world comes through.

The approach we take allows us to deal simply with complicated ideas. For example, in the book we discuss modern interpretations of Keynesian and Classical economics, real business cycles, strategic pricing, the theory of the second best, rent-seeking, Pareto optimality, and challenges to Pareto optimality. The conversational style conveys the essence of these complex topics to students in a nontechnical fashion without tying the student's brains up in technical tourniquets.

Models in Historical and Institutional Context

Discussing only the minimum of techniques necessary for the students to understand the ideas allows us more leeway to get into, and discuss, institutional and historical issues as they relate to current policy. Models without context are meaningless, and you'll find more historical and institutional issues in this book than in other principles books. The book has numerous maps; the discussion conveys the sense that geography, history, and psychology are important, even though it touches on them only tangentially.

One of the ways in which this historical and institutional approach shows up is in the complete coverage of the changing nature of economic systems. Socialism is undergoing enormous changes, and students are interested in what is happening and why it is happening. Their questions cannot be answered with technical models, but they can be discussed informally in a historical context. And that's what this book does.

The Invisible Forces

We've incorporated in the book a pedagogical device we've found useful where we want to include the social and political forces that affect reality. That device is to convey to students a picture of reality being controlled not only by the invisible hand, but also by the invisible foot (politics) and the invisible handshake (social and cultural forces). This *invisible forces* imagery lets us relate economists' abstract models to the real world; it allows us to discuss the real-world interface between economics, politics, and social forces. What makes this device effective is that students can picture these three invisible forces fighting each other to direct real world events; that image allows them to put economic models into perspective.

Some Short Prefatory Comments on the Canadian Edition

A question the reader might have, and one that we asked ourselves long and hard, is: "If the American editions were so good, why not just use the U.S. book in Canada? Why write a Canadian edition?" The most important reason is that Canadian economic history and Canadian institutions differ significantly from those in the United States. To turn on Canadian students to economics—to teach economic sensibility in Canada—we've got to take advantage of Canada's unique institutional and cultural heritage.

In our view, the existing Canadian textbooks just didn't foster the economic sensibility we wanted of our students. We knew we could provide a passionate alternative that would nurture Canadian students—particularly those whose background in quantitative methods was limited and who believed that economics was a course in technique. And, yes, while we do tell our students that "math is fun, math is our friend"—we also tell them that math is just a tool; it's not the essence of economics. We really do believe that models without context are meaningless and that students *need* to understand how Canadian social and political forces affect real world events.

Macroeconomics for the 90s

Macroeconomics is a young discipline—and the last 30 years have seen fundamental changes in how economists think about the macroeconomy. We've tried to capture that change, and many readers will, we suspect, be a bit surprised when they first look at the macro theory chapters. Those chapters develop curves that look very much like the standard AS/AD analysis, but which have different names, and which are developed in a way so that the analysis is compatible with the modern macro-thinking of the mid 1990s, not a way that is compatible with the neoclassical synthesis of the 1960s and 1970s. When you first look at these chapters you may find them difficult—because the old ways of presenting the material have been around for so long. But don't think that it will be harder for the students; remember; they aren't saddled with the earlier macro models.

There's been a positive acceptance of this new approach in the U.S. edition, and it makes the Keynesian AE/AP model fit with the modified AS/AD model—what we call the macro policy model.

To facilitate understanding of our approach, we've put in extensive appendixes. These appendixes are written in large part for the faculty, so please take a look at them.

The macro policy model moves the discussion quickly into policy issues. We think that economic sensibility and economic intuition will come much faster if students see directly how economic policy affects the macroeconomy. We think this approach takes this text beyond the macro stories of the 1960s and 1970s. It truly is a textbook for the 1990s and beyond.

Our Colloquial Writing Style

It's pretty clear that our writing style (and our style in general) isn't professorial. We agree; it isn't. But in our view, students would learn a lot more if professors were a lot less professorial. If students see us as people, they will be encouraged to think through what we have to say, and to challenge us when they think we're wrong. That's the purpose of education—to get students to think. True, it would be nice if students had a love of learning and were thirsting for knowledge. Unfortunately, the reality is that 99% of them don't. It's our job as teachers to make learning fun and exciting for students who don't want to learn, and either get them to learn, or to flunk them out. Being less professional makes us more real to students and makes learning more fun.

We see the course and the book as an entry point to an enormous store of information, not as the ultimate source. We want to motivate students to learn on their own, to read on their own, to think on their own. These desires have to be taught, and they can only be taught in a language that students can relate to. We believe in going in steps with students, not in leaps. The traditional textbookese is too much a leap for most students to make. It's not a step from the stuff they normally read; it's a leap that most of them aren't willing to make—the same type of leap it is for most of us teachers of economics to read the *Journal of Economic Theory*. There may be some relevant information in those articles, but most of us teachers aren't going to find out because the language the ideas are presented in is incomprehensible to us. So too with a text; it has to talk to students, otherwise they won't read it.

People to Thank

A book this size is not the work of two people, despite the fact that only two are listed as authors. So many people have contributed so much to this book that it is hard to know where to begin thanking them. But we must begin somewhere, so let us begin by thanking the innumerable referees who went through the various versions of the text and kept us on track:

Gary Berman
Humber College

Aurelia Best
Centennial College

Samuel Boutilier
*University College of
Cape Breton*

Chris Clark
*British Columbia Institute of
Technology*

Campion Dormuth
Palliser Institute SIAST

Sam Fefferman
*The Northern Alberta Institute
of Technology*

Peter Fortura
Algonquin College

Donald Garrie
Georgian College

Michael Hare
University of Toronto

Matlub Hussain
Dawson College

Ernie Jacobson
*The Northern Alberta
Institute of Technology*

Cheryl Jenkins
John Abbott College

Susan Kamp
University of Alberta

Gregg Levis
Georgian College

Sonja Novkovic
Saint Mary's University

Don Reddick
Kwantlen College

Michael Rushton
University of Regina

Balbir Sahni
Concordia University

Marlyce Searcy
Palliser Institute SIAST

Annie Spears
*University of Prince Edward
Island*

We cannot thank these reviewers enough. They corrected many of our mistakes, they explained to us how a text can contribute to good teaching, and they kept us focused on combining teaching economic sensibility with economic models. They provided us with page upon page of detailed comments and suggestions for improvement. The book strongly reflects their input and is much more usable because of that input.

There were many faculty and students who have informally pointed out aspects of the book that they liked, or did not like. There are so many that we can't remember them all, but those who especially deserve thanks include John Brander, Beverly Cook, Vaughan Dickson, Stephen Law, Heather Lebrecque, Maurice Tugwell, Linda Williams, and Weiqui Yu. We especially want to thank Maurice Tugwell of Acadia University for providing us with problems and exercises for inclusion in the textbook.

Massaging the Manuscript into a Book

In this edition we had immense help from Brad Mullin, Jim MacGee, and Helen Reiff. They all did great jobs, and we thank them.

In this entire process many people at Times Mirror Professional Publishing (TMPP) are extremely important and helpful. One is Milt Vacon, a sales rep at TMPP, who convinced us that we should work on this project. Another is Rod Banister, the publisher at TMPP. He believed in the project early on, and has seen to it that the book has gone forward and prospered. Then there's Sabira Hussain, our development editor. To understand Sabira's role, you have to understand a bit about us. We're difficult to work with. We're outlandish perfectionists, sticklers about deadlines, and rather blunt in our assessments. We don't like excuses or bureaucracy. We want things done perfectly, yesterday. Given these characteristics, the fact that we coexist with publishing houses is unexplainable—except for the existence of people like Sabira within the publishing houses. Sabira is superb. She almost always gets things done perfectly, yesterday, and when she doesn't, she offers no excuses—she simply gets them done today. She operates in a bureaucracy without losing sight of her main duty—to get the job done competently and professionally. She's a gem, and we thank her.

The actual production process of a four-color introductory book is complicated. It requires enormous efforts. Luckily, we had Lynne Basler, project editor, directing the manuscript through the process. She did a superb job, as did all the players in the production process: Tom Serb, the copy editor; Heidi Baughman, the designer who made the book look good; Bob Lange, the production supervisor, who worked with Better Graphics, Inc., the typesetter, and Webcrafters, Inc., the printer.

Of course, as they did their superb job, they created more work for us, reading the galley proofs, the page proofs, and doing all the final checking that must be done in an effort to eliminate those pesky errors that occur out of nowhere. Helen Reiff went over the manuscript with her fine-tooth comb and discerning eyes, and we went over it with our rake and 20/400 vision, and together we caught things overlooked until then. We thank her enormously for doing what we cannot do, and apologize to her for complaining that she is so picky.

Then, there are the sales reps who are the core of a textbook publishing company. As we traveled around the country giving lectures, we met with many of the TMPP (Times Mirror Professional Publishing) sales reps, discussing the book and learning to see it through their eyes. There are a number we remember very well; they sent us books, comments, and talked with us for hours about publishing and TMPP. We thank them

sincerely. TMPP has one great set of sales representatives out there, and we thank them for getting behind the book.

Creating the Package

These days an introductory economics book is much more than a single book; it is an entire package, and numerous people have worked on the package. The supplements and their authors include:

Instructor's Manual prepared by Peter Sephton and Paul Estenson. Includes *Experiments in Teaching and In Understanding Economics* by David Colander and Andreas Ortman.
Study Guide: Macroeconomics prepared by Susan Kamp, Richard Trieff, and Benjamin Shlaes.
Testbank to Accompany Macroeconomics prepared by Susan Kamp and Susan Dadres.
Classic Readings in Economics, edited by David Colander and Harry Landreth.
Economics: An Honors Companion, by Sunder Ramaswamy, Kailash Khandke, Jenifer Gamber and David Colander.
Case Studies in Macroeconomics, selections from *The Wall Street Journal,* edited by David Colander and Jenifer Gamber.
Macro-interactive Software prepared by Peter Sephton and Paul Estenson.

We want to say thank you to all the supplements authors for making a high-quality and innovative supplements package to the text.

Then there's our wives, Pat and Sue, and our children, who gave us the time we needed to work on this edition. Only after it was finished did we realize how absolutely necessary to getting this book out their sacrifices were.

As you can see, although our names are on the book, many people besides us deserve the credit. We thank them all.

Data Acknowledgements

All Statistics Canada sources are reproduced by authority of the Minister of Industry, 1995, and are adopted from the following sources:

Canadian Economic Observer, Catalogue 11–010
Canada Year Book 1994, Catalogue 11–402E
Historical Statistics of Canada, 2nd Edition, Catalogue 11–516E
The Labour Force, Catalogue 71–001
Consumer Prices and Price Index, Catalogue 62–010
National Income and Expenditure Accounts, Catalogue 13–001
National Balance Sheet Accounts, Catalogue 13–214
Unemployment Insurance Statistics, Catalogue 73–001
Selected Income Statistics, Catalogue 93–331
Employment Income by Occupation, Catalogue 93–332
Income Distributions by Size in Canada, Catalogue 13–207
Income After Tax Distributions by Size in Canada, Catalogue 13–210
Annual Report of the Minister of Industry, Science, and Technology under The Corporations and Labours Unions Act, Part 1, Corporations, Catalogue 61–210

Readers wishing additional information on data provided through the cooperation of Statistics Canada may obtain copies of related publications by mail from:

Publications Sales, Statistics Canada, Ottawa, Ontario, K1A0T6, by calling (613) 951–7277, or toll-free 800–267–6677. Readers may also facsimile their order by dialing (613) 951–1584.

Brief Contents

PART 1
Introduction

1 Economics and Economic Reasoning   5

   Appendix A: Economics in Perspective   28
   Appendix B: Graphish: The Language
   of Graphs   29

2 Supply and Demand   *34*

3 The Economic Organization of Society   *61*

4 Canadian Economic Institutions   *79*

   Appendix A: Trading in Stocks   102

5 An Introduction to the World Economy   *103*

PART 2
Macroeconomics

I
Macroeconomic Problems

6 Economic Growth, Business Cycles, Unemployment, and Inflation   *131*

7 National Income Accounting   *161*

II
Macroeconomics: The Basics

8 The Macroeconomic Debate   *184*

   Appendix: The Analytic Macro Model   208

9 The Keynesian Aggregate Production/Aggregate Expenditures Model   *217*

   Appendix A: The Macro Policy Model, the
   AS/AD Model, and the AP/AE Model   245
   Appendix B: Wage and Price-Level Flexibility
   and Macroeconomic Theory   249

10 Fiscal Policy and the Debate about Activist Macroeconomic Policy   *252*

   Appendix A: The Algebraic Keynesian
   Model   276
   Appendix B: The Circular Spiral, Real Business
   Cycles, and Dynamic Externalities   278

III
Monetary and Financial Institutions

11   Financial Institutions   *280*

12   Money and Banking   *301*

     Appendix A: Precise Calculations of the Money Multiplier When People Hold Cash   *320*

13   Central Banks, the Bank of Canada, and Monetary Policy   *322*

     Appendix A: Keynesian and Classical Theories of Interest and Their Implications for Monetary Policy   *343*

14   Money, Inflation, and Macroeconomic Policy   *345*

IV
International Dimensions of Economic Problems

15   International Trade   *366*

16   International Finance: The Basics   *391*

17   International Dimensions of Monetary and Fiscal Policies   *414*

V
Macroeconomic Policy Debates

18   Deficits and Debt   *428*

19   The Art of Macro Policy   *449*

20   Growth and the Macroeconomics of Developing and Transitional Economies   *478*

     Glossary   *G1*

     Index   *I1*

Contents

PART 1

Introduction

1 Economics and Economic Reasoning 5

What Economics Is About 6
  Economic Reasoning 6
  Economic Terminology 7
  Economic Insights 7
  Economic Institutions 7
  Economic Policy Options 8
A REMINDER: Five Important Things to Learn in
    Economics 8
A Guide to Economic Reasoning 8
  Marginal Costs and Marginal Benefits 8
A REMINDER: Economic Knowledge in One Sentence:
    TANSTAAFL 9
  Economics and Passion 10
  Opportunity Cost 10
  The Production Possibility Table 11
ADDED DIMENSION: Dealing with Math
    Anxiety 12
  The Production Possibility Curve 12
ADDED DIMENSION: Resources, Inputs, Technology,
    and Output 16
  The Production Possibility Curve and Tough
    Choices 17
  Economics and the Invisible Forces 17
ADDED DIMENSION: The Invisible Forces 19
Economic Terminology 19
A REMINDER: Winston Churchill and
    Lady Astor 20
Economic Insights 20
  The Invisible Hand Theory 20
  Economic Theory and Stories 21
  Microeconomics and Macroeconomics 21

Economic Institutions 22
Economic Policy Options 23
  Objective Policy Analysis 24
  Policy and the Invisible Forces 24
Conclusion 25
Chapter Summary 25
Key Terms 26
Questions for Thought and Review 26
Problems and Exercises 26
Appendix A: Economics in Perspective 28
Appendix B: Graphish: The Language of
    Graphs 29

2 Supply and Demand 34

Demand 35
  The Law of Demand 35
  The Demand Table 36
  From a Demand Table to a Demand
    Curve 39
  Individual and Market Demand Curves 39
  Shifts in Demand versus Movement along a
    Given Demand Curve 40
A REMINDER: Six Things to Remember when
    Considering a Demand Curve 42
Supply 42
  The Law of Supply 43
  The Supply Table 45
  From a Supply Table to a Supply Curve 45
  Individual and Market Supply Curves 45
ADDED DIMENSION: Supply, Production, and
    Profit 46
  Shifts in Supply versus Movement along a
    Given Supply Curve 46
A REMINDER: Six Things to Remember when
    Considering a Supply Curve 48
The Marriage of Supply and Demand 48

The First Dynamic Law of Supply and
    Demand   48
The Second Dynamic Law of Supply and
    Demand   49
The Third Dynamic Law of Supply and
    Demand   49
A REMINDER: The Dynamic Laws of Supply and
    Demand   50
The Graphical Marriage of Demand and
    Supply   50
Equilibrium   50
ADDED DIMENSION: Public Choice and
    Rent-Seeking Economic Models   50
Changes in Supply and Demand   52
Supply and Demand in Action: Oil Price
    Fluctuations   54
ADDED DIMENSION: Historical Time, Historeses,
    and "Tendency toward Equilibrium"
    Analysis   54
Conclusion   57
Chapter Summary   58
Key Terms   58
Questions for Thought and Review   58
Problems and Exercises   59

3   The Economic Organization of Society   61

Economic Systems: Capitalism and
    Socialism   62
Planning, Politics, and Markets   62
Capitalism   63
Socialism in Theory   64
Socialism in Practice   64
Differences between Soviet-Style Socialism and
    Capitalism   66
Evolving Economic Systems   67
The History of Economic Systems   68
Feudal Society: Rule of the Invisible
    Handshake   68
ADDED DIMENSION: Milestones in
    Economics   69
From Feudalism to Mercantilism   70
From Mercantilism to Capitalism   70
ADDED DIMENSION: Tradition and Today's
    Economy   71
ADDED DIMENSION: The Rise of Markets in
    Perspective   72
ADDED DIMENSION: The Role of Economists in
    Economic Transitions   73
From Capitalism to Socialism-Welfare
    Capitalism   73
From Feudalism to Socialism   75
ADDED DIMENSION: Shareholders and
    Stakeholders   76
From Socialism to ?   76
Economic Systems of the Future   76

Chapter Summary   77
Key Terms   77
Questions for Thought and Review   77
Problems and Exercises   77

4   Canadian Economic Institutions   79

A Bird's-Eye View of the Canadian
    Economy   80
The Importance of Geographic Economic
    Information   80
Diagram of the Canadian Economy   80
Business   82
Entrepreneurship and Business   82
A REMINDER: Economic Geography of Canada   83
Trials and Tribulations of Starting a Business
    83
Consumer Sovereignty and Business   84
Categories of Business   84
Stages of Business   84
ADDED DIMENSION: Balance Sheet and Income
    Statement   86
ADDED DIMENSION: Is Canada a Postindustrial
    Society?   87
Sizes of Business   87
Goals of Business   87
Forms of Business   89
Households   90
Household Types and Income   90
Households as Suppliers of Labour   91
People Power   92
The Social, Cultural, and Ideological
    Sensibilities of Canadian People   92
Government   94
Government as an Actor   94
Government as a Referee   94
ADDED DIMENSION: Finding More Information
    about the Economy   99
The Limits of Government Action   99
Chapter Summary   100
Key Terms   100
Questions for Thought and Review   100
Problems and Exercises   101
Appendix A: Trading in Stocks   102

5   An Introduction to the World Economy   103

International Economic Statistics:
    An Overview   105
Economic Geography   106
Differing Economic Problems   106
Comparative Advantage and Trade   106
How International Trade Differs from Domestic
    Trade   108

A REMINDER: A World Economic Geography Quiz 109
The Canadian International Trade Balance *111*
   Debtor and Creditor Nations *111*
   Determinants of the Trade Balance *112*
***ADDED DIMENSION: Black and Grey Markets in Currency* 112**
   Economists' View of Trade Restrictions *113*
International Economic Policy and Institutions *114*
   Government International Institutions *114*
   Global Corporations *115*
***A REMINDER: International Economic Institutions* 115**
Who Are Our International Competitors? *117*
   The European Union *119*
***ADDED DIMENSION: The North American Free Trade Agreement* 120**
***ADDED DIMENSION: Germany: The Leading EU Country* 122**
   "Japan, Inc." *121*
***ADDED DIMENSION: Economies that Don't Work So Well* 123**
   Japan, Inc., versus Canada *124*
   Don't Overestimate the Differences *124*
   The Developing Countries of the World as Competitors *125*
Conclusion *125*
Chapter Summary *125*
Key Terms *126*
Questions for Thought and Review *126*
Problems and Exercises *126*

PART

2

Macroeconomics

I

Macroeconomic Theory: The Basics

6 Economic Growth, Business Cycles, Unemployment, and Inflation *131*

Growth *132*
   The Benefits and Costs of Growth *132*
   The Causes of Growth *133*
***A REMINDER: Your Consumption and Average Consumption* 134**
***ADDED DIMENSION: Interpreting Empirical Evidence* 135**
Business Cycles *136*

   The Phases of the Business Cycle *137*
   Leading and Coincidental Indicators *138*
***ADDED DIMENSION: Business Cycles and the Stock Market* 140**
Unemployment *140*
***ADDED DIMENSION: Capitalism, the Fear of Hunger, and the Dutch Disease* 141**
   Whose Responsibility Is Unemployment? *143*
***ADDED DIMENSION: Categories of Unemployment* 144**
   How Is Unemployment Measured? *145*
   Full Employment and the Target Rate of Unemployment *147*
   Unemployment and Potential Income *147*
***ADDED DIMENSION: From Full Employment to the Target Rate of Unemployment* 148**
   Microeconomic Categories of Unemployment *147*
Inflation *150*
   Measurement of Inflation *151*
***ADDED DIMENSION: Index Numbers and the Consumer Price Index* 153**
   Real and Nominal Concepts *154*
   Why Does Inflation Occur? *155*
   Expected and Unexpected Inflation *157*
   Costs of Inflation *157*
***A REMINDER: The Costs of Inflation* 158**
The Interrelationship of Growth, Inflation, and Unemployment *159*
Chapter Summary *159*
Key Terms *159*
Questions for Thought and Review *160*
Problems and Exercises *160*

7 National Income Accounting *161*

National Income Accounting *162*
   Measuring Total Economic Output of Goods and Services *162*
   Calculating GDP *163*
Two Methods of Calculating GDP *166*
   The National Income Accounting Identity *166*
***ADDED DIMENSION: National Income Accounting and Double-Entry Bookkeeping* 168**
   The Expenditures Approach *168*
   The Income Approach *175*
   How Do We Get GDP from Net Domestic Income at Factor Cost? *176*
***A REMINDER: A Review of the Expenditures and Factor Income Approaches* 176**
Using GDP Figures *177*
   Comparing GDP among Countries *177*
   Economic Welfare over Time *178*
   Real and Nominal GDP *178*
Some Limitations of National Income Accounting *178*
***ADDED DIMENSION: The Happiness Index* 179**

GDP Measures Market Activity,
    Not Welfare   *180*
***ADDED DIMENSION: The Underground
    Economy   180***
  Measurement Errors   *180*
  Misinterpretation of Subcategories   *181*
  GDP Is Worth Using Despite Its
    Limitations   *181*
Chapter Summary   *181*
Key Terms   *182*
Questions for Thought and Review   *182*
Problems and Exercises   *182*

II

Macroeconomics: The Basics

8 The Macroeconomic Debate   *184*

The Historical Development of Modern
    Macroeconomics   *185*
  The Emergence of Classical Economics   *186*
  Say's Law   *187*
  The Quantity Theory of Money   *188*
  Classicals' View of the Great Depression   *188*
  The Emergence of Keynesian Economics   *189*
***ADDED DIMENSION: The Treasury View, Lloyd
    George, and Keynes   189***
***ADDED DIMENSION: In the Long Run, We're All
    Dead   191***
The Macro Policy Model and Its Aggregate
    Supply/Aggregate Demand
    Foundations   *192*
  The Rudiments of the AS/AD Model   *192*
  The Macro Policy Model   *195*
  Using the Macro Policy Model   *200*
Some Practice Using the Macro Policy
    Model   *202*
Why Macro Policy Is More Complicated than This
    Model Makes It Look   *203*
Conclusion and a Look Ahead   *205*
Chapter Summary   *206*
Key Terms   *206*
Questions for Thought and Review   *206*
Problems and Exercises   *207*
Appendix: The Analytic Macro Model   208
***ADDED DIMENSION: In Defense of Those Professors
    Who Assign the Appendix   210***

9 The Keynesian Aggregate Production/Aggregate
Expenditures Model   *217*

The Textbook Keynesian Model   *218*
  Aggregate Production in the Keynesian
    Model   *219*
  Aggregate Expenditures in the Keynesian
    Model   *220*

Determining the Level of Aggregate Income   *228*
  Solving for Equilibrium Graphically   *229*
  Determining the Level of Aggregate Income
    with the Keynesian Equation   *229*
***ADDED DIMENSION: A More General
    Formula   230***
  The Multiplier   *230*
  A Closer Look at the Income Adjustment
    Mechanism   *231*
Shifts in Autonomous Expenditures   *233*
  Shifts in Autonomous Consumption   *233*
  Shifts in the Investment Function   *233*
  Shifts in Government Expenditures   *234*
  Shifts in Autonomous Imports and
    Exports   *234*
  Shifts in Autonomous Expenditures and
    Keynes's Model   *234*
Further Examples of the Keynesian Model   *236*
The Relationship between the *AP/AE* Model and
    the Last Chapter's Macro Policy
    Model   *237*
  The AS/AD Model and the *AP/AE* Model   *237*
  The *AP/AE* Model and the Macro Policy
    Model   *239*
  The Keynesian Model as an Historical "Model
    in Time"   *240*
  Mechanistic and Interpretive Keynesians   *241*
  Mechanistic and Interpretive Classicals   *242*
  A Final Word   *242*
Chapter Summary   *243*
Key Terms   *243*
Questions for Thought and Review   *243*
Problems and Exercises   *244*
*Appendix A: The Macro Policy Model, the AS/AD
    Model, and the AP/AE Model   245*
*Appendix B: Wage and Price-Level Flexibility and
    Macroeconomic Theory   249*
***ADDED DIMENSION: Wormholes and the Classical
    Adjustment Story   250***

10 Fiscal Policy and the Debate about Activist
Macroeconomic Policy   *252*

Fiscal Policy and Aggregate Demand
    Management   *253*
  The Story of Keynesian Fiscal Policy   *253*
***ADDED DIMENSION: The Economic Steering
    Wheel   254***
***ADDED DIMENSION: Keynes and Keynesian
    Policy   255***
  Aggregate Demand Management   *255*
  The Tax/Transfer Multiplier and the Government
    Spending Multiplier   *256*
  Fiscal Policy in Graphs   *257*
  Applying the Models and the Questionable
    Effectiveness of Fiscal Policy   *259*

Alternatives to Fiscal Policy   *261*
  Directed Investment Policies: Policy Affecting
      Expectations   *262*
ADDED DIMENSION: Government Demand
      Management Policies   *263*
  Trade Policy and Export-Led Growth   *263*
  Autonomous Consumption Policy   *264*
  Structural versus Passive Government Budget
      and Trade Deficits   *264*
ADDED DIMENSION: Regional Multipliers   *265*
  Some Real-World Examples   *266*
ADDED DIMENSION: Shifting Terms of the
      Keynesian/Classical Truce   *266*
Problems with Fiscal and Other Activist Keynesian
      Policy   *268*
  Financing the Deficit Doesn't Have Offsetting
      Effects   *268*
  Knowing What the Situation Is   *269*
  Knowing the Level of Potential Income   *270*
  The Government's Flexibility in Changing Taxes
      and Spending   *271*
  Size of the Government Debt Doesn't
      Matter   *271*
  Fiscal Policy Doesn't Negatively Affect Other
      Government Goals   *271*
  Fiscal Policy in Practice: Summary of the
      Problems   *272*
  Building Keynesian Policies into
      Institutions   *272*
  Fiscal Policy in Perspective   *272*
  The Keynesian Model and the Practice of Fiscal
      Policy in the 1990s   *273*
Chapter Summary   *274*
Key Terms   *274*
Questions for Thought and Review   *275*
Problems and Exercises   *275*
Appendix A: The Algebraic Keynesian Model   *276*
Appendix B: The Circular Spiral, Real Business
      Cycles, and Dynamic Externalities   *278*

III

Monetary and Financial Institutions

11   Financial Institutions   *280*

Financial Assets and Financial Liabilities   *281*
Financial Institutions   *282*
  Depository Institutions   *282*
  Contractual Intermediaries   *284*
ADDED DIMENSION: Do Financial Assets Make
      Society Richer?   *284*
A REMINDER: Financial Institutions   *285*
  Investment Intermediaries   *285*
Financial Markets   *286*
  Primary and Secondary Financial Markets   *286*

Money Markets and Capital Markets   *287*
Types of Financial Assets   *288*
  Money Market Assets   *288*
  Capital Market Assets   *289*
ADDED DIMENSION: The TSE 300   *291*
ADDED DIMENSION: Capital Gains and
      Losses   *293*
The Value of a Financial Asset   *294*
ADDED DIMENSION: What Will a Bond
      Sell for?   *294*
  Present Value and Interest Rate   *294*
  Asset Prices, Interest Rates, and the
      Economy   *295*
Leading You through Two Financial
      Transactions   *296*
  Insuring Your Car   *296*
  Buying a House   *296*
  Summary   *297*
Why Financial Institutions Are Important for
      Macroeconomics   *297*
  The Classical View of the Financial
      Sector   *297*
  The Keynesian View of the Financial
      Sector   *297*
Chapter Summary   *298*
Key Terms   *299*
Questions for Thought and Review   *299*
Problems and Exercises   *299*

12   Money and Banking   *301*

The Definition and Functions of Money   *302*
  Functions of Money   *302*
ADDED DIMENSION: Characteristics of a Good
      Money   *304*
  Alternative Definitions of Money   *305*
Banks and the Creation of Money   *308*
  How Banks Create Money   *308*
  The Money Multiplier   *310*
  Faith as the Backing of Our Money
      Supply   *311*
ADDED DIMENSION: The Complex Money Multiplier
      and Reforms in Banking   *312*
  Creation of Money Using T-Accounts   *311*
Regulation of Banks and the Financial Sector
      315
  Anatomy of a Financial Panic   *315*
  Government Policy to Prevent Panic   *316*
  The Benefits and Problems of Guarantees   *316*
Chapter Summary   *318*
Key Terms   *318*
Questions for Thought and Review   *318*
Problems and Exercises   *319*
Appendix A: A Precise Calculation of the Money
      Multiplier When People Hold Cash   *320*

13 Central Banks, the Bank of Canada, and Monetary Policy 322

History and Structure of the Bank of Canada   *323*
  The Bank of Canada Is a Central Bank   *324*
  Central Bank Independence   *324*
ADDED DIMENSION: Central Banks in Other
    Countries   325
  International Considerations   *326*
Monetary Policy   *327*
  Tools of Monetary Policy   *328*
ADDED DIMENSION: Fancy Lingo   330
A REMINDER: Monetary Policy Rules   333
  How Monetary Policy Works   *333*
ADDED DIMENSION: Three Letters   339
  Problems in the Conduct of Monetary
    Policy   *339*
Conclusion and a Look Ahead   *341*
Chapter Summary   *341*
Key Terms   *341*
Questions for Thought and Review   *342*
Problems and Exercises   *342*
Appendix A: Keynesian and Classical Theories of
    Interest and Their Implications for
    Monetary Policy   343

14 Money, Inflation, and Macroeconomic Policy 345

Inflation   *346*
  The Money Supply and Inflation   *346*
  Inflation and Expectations of Inflation   *346*
  Inflation and Unemployment: The Phillips Curve
    Trade-Off   *347*
ADDED DIMENSION: Examples of Cost-Push and
    Demand-Pull Inflation   348
  The Phillips Curve and the Price-Level
    Flexibility Curve   *351*
Theories of Inflation and the Phillips Curve
    Trade-Off   *352*
  The Classical Theory of Inflation   *352*
ADDED DIMENSION: The Keeper of the Classical
    Faith: Milton Friedman   355
  The Keynesian Theory of Inflation   *356*
ADDED DIMENSION: The Distributional Effects of
    Inflation   358
  Similarities and Differences between Keynesian
    and Classical Theories   *360*
Keynesian and Classical Policies to Fight
    Stagflation   *361*
  The Classical Approach to Fighting
    Stagflation   *361*
ADDED DIMENSION: Dieting and Fighting
    Inflation   362

  The Keynesian Approach to Fighting
    Stagflation   *362*
Conclusion   *363*
Chapter Summary   *364*
Key Terms   *364*
Questions for Thought and Review   *364*
Problems and Exercises   *364*

IV
—
International Dimensions of Economic Problems

15 International Trade 366

Patterns of Trade   *367*
  Increasing but Fluctuating World Trade   *367*
  Differences in Importance of Trade   *367*
Why Do Nations Trade?   *368*
  The Principle of Absolute Advantage   *368*
  The Principle of Comparative Advantage   *371*
  Competitiveness, Exchange Rates, and
    Comparative Advantage   *372*
ADDED DIMENSION: Who Formulated the Principle
    of Comparative Advantage?   373
ADDED DIMENSION: Trade Allows Countries
    to Consume Outside Their Production
    Possibility Curves   374
  Dividing Up the Gains from Trade   *373*
ADDED DIMENSION: Countertrade   375
Trade Restrictions   *375*
  Varieties of Trade Restrictions   *375*
ADDED DIMENSION: Hormones and
    Economics   377
  Reasons for Trade Restrictions   *378*
  Why Economists Generally Oppose Trade
    Restrictions   *382*
ADDED DIMENSION: Strategic Trade Policies   388
ADDED DIMENSION: Dumping   387
  Free Trade Associations   *383*
  The World Trade Organization   *387*
Conclusion   *387*
Chapter Summary   *388*
Key Terms   *389*
Questions for Thought and Review   *389*
Problems and Exercises   *389*

16 International Finance: The Basics 391

The Balance of Payments   *392*
  The Current Account   *392*
  The Capital Account   *394*
  The Official Settlements Account   *394*

Exchange Rates   *396*
  Supply, Demand, and Fundamental Analysis of
    Exchange Rates   *396*
ADDED DIMENSION: Determining the Causes of
Fluctuations in the Dollar's Value   398
  Stability and Instability in Foreign Exchange
    Markets   *399*
ADDED DIMENSION: Arbitrage   400
  Government's Role in Determining Exchange
    Rates   *401*
Flexible, Partially Flexible, and Fixed Exchange
  Rates   *405*
  History of Exchange Rate Systems   *405*
  Advantages and Disadvantages of Alternative
    Exchange Rate Systems   *409*
ADDED DIMENSION: Turmoil within the European
Exchange Rate Mechanism   409
ADDED DIMENSION: International Trade Problems
from Shifting Values of Currencies   410
Conclusion   *412*
Chapter Summary   *412*
Key Terms   *413*
Questions for Thought and Review   *413*
Problems and Exercises   *413*

17   International Dimensions of Monetary and Fiscal
Policies   *414*

The Ambiguous International Goals of
  Macroeconomic Policy   *415*
  The Exchange Rate Goal   *415*
  The Trade Balance Goal   *416*
  International versus Domestic Goals   *416*
The Effects of Monetary and Fiscal Policies on
  International Goals   *417*
  Monetary Policy's Effect on Exchange
    Rates   *417*
  Monetary Policy's Effect on the Trade
    Balance   *419*
  Fiscal Policy's Effect on Exchange Rates   *421*
  Fiscal Policy's Effect on the Trade Deficit   *422*
International Phenomena and Domestic
  Goals   *423*
  International Monetary and Fiscal
    Coordination   *423*
  Coordination Is a Two-Way Street   *424*
  Crowding Out and International
    Considerations   *424*
Conclusion: Selecting Policies to Achieve
  Goals   *426*
Chapter Summary   *426*
Key Terms   *426*
Questions for Thought and Review   *427*
Problems and Exercises   *427*

V

Macroeconomic Policy Debates

18   Deficits and Debt   *428*

Canadian Government Deficits and Debt:
  The Historical Record   *429*
  Policy Regimes, the Deficit, and the Debt   *429*
  Politics and the Deficit   *431*
Economists' Way of Looking at Deficits and
  Debt   *432*
  Arbitrariness in Defining Deficits   *432*
  Deficits as a Summary Measure   *433*
  The Need to Judge Debt Relative to
    Assets   *433*
  Arbitrariness in Defining Debt   *404*
  Difference between Individual and Government
    Debt   *434*
  Deficits, Debt, and Debt Service Relative to
    GDP   *434*
  Two Ways GDP Growth Reduces Problems
    Posed by Deficits   *436*
ADDED DIMENSION: Inflation and Indexed
Bonds   439
  With Full Adjustment in Expectations, Creditors
    Don't Lose   *440*
  Summary to This Point   *441*
Some Reasons for Concern about Canada's
  Government Budget Deficits and
  Debt   *441*
  The Federal Deficit and Debt Are Only Part of
    the Picture   *441*
  A Different Type of Crowding Out   *443*
  Does It Matter Who Holds Government
    Debt   *444*
  Is the Deficit a Good Measure of the Stance of
    Fiscal Policy?   *445*
Conclusion   *446*
Chapter Summary   *447*
Key Terms   *447*
Questions for Thought and Review   *447*
Problems and Exercises   *448*

19   The Art of Macro Policy   *449*

The Limits of Macroeconomic Theory and
  Policy   *450*
  The Limits of Macroeconomic Policy   *450*
  The Difference between Theoretical Models and
    Policy Models   *452*
  The Interface between Theoretical and Policy
    Models   *453*

People Aren't Stupid   *453*
Credibility and Macro Policy   *454*
The Keynesian/Classical Policy Debate   *454*
The Classical View of Government Policy   *455*
The Keynesian View of Government
    Policy   *455*
Who's Right on Policy?   *455*
Flip-Flopping Views of the Deficit   *455*
Similarities and Differences between Keynesians
    and Classicals on Macro Policy   *457*
Agreement about Macroeconomic Policy   *459*
Recent History of Macroeconomic Policy   *460*
The 1990 Recession   *460*
The Sort-Of Recovery, 1992— and the Debate
    about Supply-Side Macro Policies   *461*
The Allure of Supply-Side Policies   *461*
ADDED DIMENSION: Distinguishing the Keynesian
    and Classical Supply-Side Arguments   463
Topical Issues in Canadian Macro Policy   *464*
ADDED DIMENSION: The Monetary Conditions
    Index   465
Price Stability, Full Employment, or
    Both?   *465*
ADDED DIMENSION: Does Price Stability Mean Zero
    Inflation?   468
Reforming Unemployment Insurance and Social
    Assistance Programs   *470*
Is the Solution a Return to Fixed Exchange
    Rates?   *472*
ADDED DIMENSION: New Brunswick Begins
    Reweaving Social Safety Net   473
Congratulations! You Are Now a Policy
    Advisor   *475*
Conclusion   *476*
Chapter Summary   *476*
Key Terms   *476*
Questions for Thought and Review   *477*
Problems and Exercises   *477*

Differing Goals of Developed, Developing, and
    Transitional Countries   *479*
ADDED DIMENSION: The North/South
    Conflict   480
Growth and Basic Needs   *480*
Economic Growth as an Appropriate Goal for
    Developing Countries   *480*
Institutional Differences   *481*
ADDED DIMENSION: Classical Economists and
    Long-Run Growth   482
Political Differences and Laissez-Faire   *482*
The Dual Economy   *483*
Fiscal Structure of Developing and Transitional
    Economies   *484*
Financial Institutions of Developing and
    Transitional Economies   *484*
An Example of the Different Roles of
    Financial Institutions in Transitional
    Economies   *485*
Monetary Policy in Developing and Transitional
    Countries   *486*
Focus on the International Sector and the
    Exchange Rate Constraint   *489*
Macro Institutional Policy in Developing
    Countries   *490*
Generating Saving and Investment and the
    Lingering Shadow of the Debt Crisis   *491*
The Debt Repudiation Strategy   *491*
Generating Domestic Savings   *492*
ADDED DIMENSION: The Sixteen Decisions   494
Conclusion   *495*
Chapter Summary   *495*
Key Terms   *496*
Questions for Thought and Review   *496*
Problems and Exercises   *496*

Glossary   *G1*

Index   *I1*

20   Growth and the Macroeconomics of Developing
       and Transitional Economies   *478*

About the Authors

David Colander is the Christian A. Johnson Distinguished Professor of Economics at Middlebury College. He has authored, coauthored, or edited 30 books and over 90 articles on a wide range of economic topics.

He earned his B.A. at Columbia College and his M.Phil and Ph.D. at Columbia University. He also studied at the University of Birmingham in England and at Wilhelmsburg Gymnasium in Germany. Professor Colander has taught at Columbia College, Vassar College, and the University of Miami, as well as having been a consultant to Time-Life Films, a consultant to Congress, a Brookings Policy Fellow, and Visiting Scholar at Nuffield College, Oxford. Recently, he spent two months in Bulgaria, where he worked with former professors of political economy on how to teach Western economics.

He belongs to a variety of professional associations and has served on the Board of Directors and as vice president of the History of Economic Thought Society, the Eastern Economics Association, and is on the Board of Advisors of the *Journal of Economic Perspectives*. He is also on the Editorial Board of *The Journal of Economic Methodology* and *The Eastern Economics Journal*. He is currently the president of the Eastern Economic Association.

Peter Sephton is a Professor of Economics at the University of New Brunswick in Fredericton. He has authored and coauthored over 30 journal articles on a wide variety of topics.

He earned his B.A. at McMaster University, and both his M.A. and Ph.D. at Queen's University. Professor Sephton has taught at Queen's University, the University of Regina, the University of New Brunswick, and Saint Thomas University. He has also been a consultant to the International Monetary Fund, to Provincial governments, to environmental engineering firms, and in legal cases. He has also held positions at the Bank of Canada, the Ontario Ministry of Treasury and Economics, and the Federal Business Development Bank.

Professor Sephton has written a large number of instructional materials. Most recently, he wrote materials for use in the open access distance learning course in International Finance at Athabasca University.

He is married to Sue, and together they have two children: Bill, 10, and Jenny, 8. In his spare time, he coaches both of their soccer teams.

1

Introduction

Chapter 1 Economics and Economic Reasoning

Chapter 2 Supply and Demand

Chapter 3 The Economic Organization of Society

Chapter 4 Canadian Economic Institutions

Chapter 5 An Introduction to the World Economy

Section I is an introduction, and an introduction to an introduction sounds a little funny. But other sections have introductions, so it seemed a bit funny not to have an introduction to Section I and besides, as you will see, we're a little funny ourselves (which, in turn, has two interpretations; you will, we're sure, decide which of the two is appropriate). It will, however, be a very brief introduction, consisting of questions you probably have and some answers to those questions.

SOME QUESTIONS AND ANSWERS

Why study economics?
Because it's neat and interesting and helps provide insight into events that are constantly going on around you.

Why is this book so big?
Because there's lots of important information in it and because the book is designed so your teacher can pick and choose. You'll likely not be required to read all of it, but once you start, you'll probably read it all anyhow (Would you believe?)

Why does this book cost so much?

To answer this question you'll have to read the book.

Will this book make me rich?
No.

Will this book make me happy?
It depends.

This book doesn't seem to be written in normal textbook style. Is this book really written by two professors?
Yes, but they are really different, as you'll soon see.

Will the entire book be like this?
No, the introduction is just trying to rope you in. Much of the book will be hard going. Learning happens to be a difficult process: no pain, no gain. But the authors aren't sadists; they try to make learning as pleasantly painful as possible.

What do the authors' students think of them?
Weird—definitely weird—and hard. But fair, interesting, and sincerely interested in getting us to learn. (Answer written by our students.)

So there you have it. Answers to the questions that you might never have thought of if they hadn't been put in front of you. We hope they give you a sense of us and the approach we'll use in the book. There are some neat ideas in it. Let's now briefly consider what's in the first five chapters.

A SURVEY OF THE FIRST FIVE CHAPTERS

This first section is really an introduction to the rest of the book. It gives you the background necessary to have the latter chapters make sense. Chapter 1 gives you an overview of the entire field of economics as well as an introduction to our style. Chapter 2 introduces you to supply and demand, and shows you not only the power of those two concepts, but also the limitations.

Chapter 3 tries to put supply and demand in context. It discusses evolving economic systems and how economic forces interact with political and social forces. In it you'll see how the power of supply and demand analysis is strengthened when it's interpreted with a knowledge of economic institutions. Chapters 4 and 5 then introduce you to some of those economic institutions. Chapter 4 concentrates on domestic institutions; Chapter 5 concentrates on international institutions. Now let's get on with the show.

1

Economics and Economic Reasoning

In my vacations, I visited the poorest quarters of several cities and walked through one street after another, looking at the faces of the poorest people. Next I resolved to make as thorough a study as I could of Political Economy.

~ Alfred Marshall

After reading this chapter, you should be able to:

1 State five important things to learn in economics.

2 Explain how to make decisions by comparing marginal costs and marginal benefits.

3 Define opportunity cost, and explain its relationship to economic reasoning.

4 Demonstrate opportunity cost with a production possibility curve.

5 State the principle of increasing opportunity cost.

6 Explain real-world events in terms of three "invisible forces."

7 Differentiate between microeconomics and macroeconomics.

8 Distinguish among positive economics, normative economics, and the art of economics.

When an artist looks at the world, he sees colour. When a musician looks at the world, she hears music. When an economist looks at the world, she sees a symphony of costs and benefits.[1] The economist's world might not be as colourful or as melodic as the others' worlds, but it's more practical. If you want to understand what's going on in the world that's really out there, you need to know economics.

We hardly have to convince you of this fact if you keep up with the news. Unemployment is up; inflation is down; the dollar is down; interest rates are up; businesses are going bankrupt. . . . The list is endless. So let's say you grant us that economics is important. That still doesn't mean that it's worth studying. The real question then is: How much will you learn? Most of what you learn depends on you, but part depends on the teacher and another part depends on the textbook. On both these counts, you're in luck; since your teacher chose this book for your course, you must have a super teacher.[2]

WHAT ECONOMICS IS ABOUT

1 Five important things to learn in economics are:
1. Economic reasoning
2. Economic terminology
3. Economic insights
4. Economic institutions
5. Economic policy options.

Five important things to learn in economics are:

1. Economic reasoning.
2. Economic terminology.
3. Insights economists have about economic issues, and theories that lead to those insights.
4. Information about economic institutions.
5. Information about the economic policy options facing society today.

By no coincidence, this book discusses economic reasoning, economic terminology, economic insights, economic institutions, and economic policy options.

Let's consider each in turn.

Economic Reasoning

Economic reasoning Making decisions on the basis of costs and benefits.

The most important thing you'll learn is **economic reasoning**—how to think like an economist. People trained in economics think in a certain way. They analyze everything critically; they compare the costs and the benefits of every issue and make decisions based, in part, on those costs and benefits. As we'll see later in this chapter, economists are human beings, and when they *make* choices, their decisions are coloured by their own views of how to deal with scarcity. As we'll see, part of good decision making is being able first to explain observed choices without taking sides on any issue: economists are trained to *explain* observed choices. For example, say you're trying to decide whether protecting baby seals is a good policy or not. Economists are trained to put their emotions aside and ask: What are the costs of protecting baby seals, and what are the benefits? Thus, they are open to the argument that the benefits of allowing baby seals to be killed might exceed the costs. To think like an economist is to address almost all issues using a cost/benefit approach.

Economic reasoning, once learned, is infectious. If you're susceptible, being exposed to it will change your life. It will influence your analysis of everything, including issues normally considered outside the scope of economics. For example,

---

[1] Authors are presented with a problem today. Our language has certain ambiguous words that can be interpreted as affording unequal treatment to women. For example, we use the term *man* both to describe all human beings and to describe a specific group of human beings. Similarly, we use the pronoun *he* when we mean all people. One can avoid such usage by writing *he and she* and *men and women* or *human beings,* and in much of this book these terms will be used, although every so often either the masculine or feminine term will appear. This is to see if you notice and to encourage you to think of possible sexist aspects in your own usage.

If you are wondering whether you are sexist, consider the following riddle: A father and son are in a car accident. The father is killed and the boy is injured. When the boy is brought to the hospital, the doctor on emergency room duty says, "I can't operate on him—he's my son." How can this be? If it doesn't seem like a riddle, good; if it does, whenever you see an occupation that is not gender-specific, think *man or woman* until the riddle is no longer a riddle.

[2] This book is written by two people, not a machine. That means that we have our quirks, our odd senses of humour, and our biases. All textbook writers do. Most textbooks have the quirks and eccentricities edited out so that all the books read and sound alike—professional, but dull. We choose to sound like ourselves—sometimes professional, sometimes playful, and sometimes stubborn. In our view, that makes the book more human and less dull. So forgive us our quirks—don't always take us too seriously—and we'll try to keep you awake when you're reading this book at 3 a.m., on the morning of the exam. If you think it's a killer to read a book this long, you ought to try writing one.

you will likely use economic reasoning to decide the possibility of getting a date for Saturday night, and who will pay for dinner. You will likely use it to decide whether to read this book, whether to attend class, whom to marry, and what kind of work to go into after you graduate. This is not to say that economic reasoning will provide all the answers. As you will see throughout this book, real-world questions are inevitably complicated, and economic reasoning simply provides a framework within which to approach a question.

Second, there's economic terminology, which is tossed around by the general public with increasing frequency. *GDP, corporations,* and *money supply* are just a few of the terms whose meaning any educated person in modern society needs to know. If you go to a party, don't know these terms, and want to seem intelligent, you'll have to nod knowingly. It's much better to actually *know* when you nod knowingly.

Economic Terminology

Two terms we want to introduce to you immediately are the *economy* and *economics.* The **economy** is the institutional structure through which individuals in a society coordinate their diverse wants or desires. **Economics** is the study of the economy. That is, economics is the study of how human beings in a society *coordinate* their wants and desires.

Economy   The institutional structure through which individuals in a society coordinate their diverse wants or desires.

Economics   The study of how human beings coordinate their wants.

One of society's largest problems is that individuals want more than is available, given the work they're willing to do. If individuals can be encouraged to work more and consume less, that problem can be reduced. Coordination often involves coercion; it involves limiting people's wants and increasing the amount of work individuals are willing to do to fulfill those wants.

Many of society's coordination problems involve scarcity. Therefore, economics is sometimes defined as the study of the allocation of scarce resources to satisfy individuals' wants or desires. We focus the definition on coordination rather than on scarcity to emphasize that the quantity of goods and services available depends on human action: individuals' imaginations, innovativeness, and willingness to do what needs to be done.

The reality of our society is that many people would rather play than help solve society's problems. So the basic economic problem involves inspiring people to do things that other people want them to do, and not to do things that other people don't want them to do. Thus, economics is the study of how to get people to do things they're not wild about doing (such as studying) and not to do things they *are* wild about doing (such as eating all the lobster they like), so that the things some people want to do are consistent with the things other people want them to do.

Third, you'll learn about some general insights economists have gained into how the economy functions—how an economy seems to proceed or progress without any overall plan or coordinating agency. It's almost as if an invisible hand were directing economic traffic. These insights are often based on **economic theory**—generalizations about the workings of an abstract economy. Theory ties together economists' terminology and knowledge about economic institutions and leads to economic insights.

Economic Insights

Economic theory   Generalizations about the working of an abstract economy.

We're so used to the economy's functioning that we may not realize how amazing it is that the economy works as well as it does. Imagine for a moment that you're a visitor from Mars. You see the Canadian economy functioning relatively well. Stores are filled with goods. Most people have jobs. So you ask, "Who's in charge of organizing and coordinating the economic activities of the 30 million people in Canada?" The answer you get is mind boggling: "No one. The invisible hand of the market does it all." Economic theory helps explain such mind-boggling phenomena.

Economic Institutions

Economic institution   Physical or mental stuctures that significantly influence economic decisions.

Fourth, you'll learn about economic institutions: how they work, and why they sometimes don't work. An **economic institution** is a physical or mental structure that significantly influences economic decisions. Corporations, governments, and cultural norms are all economic institutions. Many economic institutions have social, political, and religious dimensions. For example, your job often influences your social standing. In addition, many social institutions, such as the family, have economic functions. If

Cultural norms Standards people use when they determine whether a particular activity or behaviour is acceptable.

any institution significantly affects economic decisions, we include it as an economic institution because you must understand that institution if you are to understand how the economy functions.

Since **cultural norms** may be an unfamiliar concept to you, let's consider how such norms affect economies. A cultural norm is a standard people use when they determine whether a particular activity or behaviour is acceptable. For example, religious rules once held that Catholics shouldn't eat meat on Friday, so Friday became a day to eat fish. The prohibition ended in the 1960s, but the tendency to eat fish on Friday has endured. In North America today, more fish is consumed on Fridays than on any other day of the week. This fact can be understood only if you understand the cultural norm that lies behind it. Similarly, in Canada more hams are bought in April and more turkeys are bought in October and December than in other months; more pork is consumed per capita in Sweden than in Israel. Can you explain why?

Economic institutions differ significantly among countries. For example, in Germany banks are allowed to own companies; in the United States they cannot. This causes a difference in the flow of resources into investment. Or alternatively, in Japan, antitrust laws (laws under which companies can combine or coordinate their activities) are loose; in Canada they are restrictive. This causes differences in the nature of competition in the two countries.

Besides helping you understand the economy, knowledge of economic institutions also directly benefits you. How do firms decide whom to hire? How do banks work? How does unemployment insurance work? What determines how much a Japanese car will cost you? How much does the government require your boss to deduct from your paycheque? Knowing the answers to these real-world questions will make your life easier.

Economic Policy Options

Economic policy An action (or inaction) taken, usually by government, to influence economic events.

Fifth, you'll learn about economic policy options facing our country. An **economic policy** is an action (or inaction) taken, usually by government, to influence economic events. Examples of economic policy questions are: How should the government deal with the next recession? (Alas, we can be sure that there will be a next recession.) What should the government do about the budget deficit? Will lowering interest rates stimulate the economy? Should government allow two large companies to merge? You won't get specific answers to these questions; instead, you'll simply learn what some of the policy options are, and what advantages and disadvantages each option offers.

A GUIDE TO ECONOMIC REASONING

2 If the benefits of doing something exceed the costs, do it. If the costs of doing something exceed the benefits, don't do it.

Let's now look at each of these five issues more carefully. We'll start with economic reasoning. In the economic way of thinking, every choice has costs and benefits, and decisions are made by comparing the two. The rules are simple:

If the benefits of doing something exceed the costs, do it.
If the costs of doing something exceed the benefits, don't do it.

Marginal Costs and Marginal Benefits

Economists have found that, when one is considering a choice among a variety of alternatives, often it's unnecessary to look at total benefits and total costs. All one need look at are marginal costs and marginal benefits. These are key concepts in economics, and it pays to learn them early on.

ECONOMIC KNOWLEDGE IN ONE SENTENCE: TANSTAAFL

Once upon a time, Tanstaafl was made king of all the lands. His first act was to call his economic advisors and tell them to write up all the economic knowledge the society possessed. After years of work, they presented their monumental effort: 25 volumes, each about 400 pages long. But in the interim, King Tanstaafl had become a very busy man, what with running a kingdom of all the lands and everything. Looking at the lengthy volumes, he told his advisors to summarize their findings in one volume.

Despondently, the economists returned to their desks, wondering how they could summarize what they'd been so careful to spell out. After many more years of rewriting, they were finally satisfied with their one-volume effort, and tried to make an appointment to see the king. Unfortunately, affairs of state had become even more pressing than before, and the king couldn't take the time to see them. Instead he sent word to them that he couldn't be bothered with a whole volume, and ordered them, under threat of death (for he had become a tyrant), to reduce the work to one sentence.

The economists returned to their desks, shivering in their sandals and pondering their impossible task. Thinking about their fate if they were not successful, they decided to send out for one last meal. Unfortunately, when they were collecting money to pay for the meal, they discovered they were broke. The disgusted delivery man took the last meal back to the cook, and the economists started down the path to the beheading station. On the way, the delivery man's parting words echoed in their ears. They looked at each other and suddenly they realized the truth. "We're saved!" they screamed. "That's it! That's economic knowledge in one sentence!" They wrote the sentence down and presented it to the king, who thereafter fully understood all economic problems. (He also gave them a good meal.) The sentence?

There Ain't No Such Thing As A Free Lunch— TANSTAAFL.

Marginal means additional or incremental. So a **marginal cost** is the additional cost to you over and above the costs you have already incurred. Consider, for example, attending class. You've already paid your tuition, so the marginal (or additional) cost of going to class does not include tuition.

Similarly, with marginal benefit. The **marginal benefit** of reading this chapter is the *additional* knowledge you get from reading it. If you already knew everything in this chapter before you picked up the book, the marginal benefit of reading it now is zero, except that you now know you are prepared for class, whereas before you might only have suspected you were prepared.

Comparing marginal (additional) costs with marginal (additional) benefits will often tell you how you should adjust your activities to be as well off as possible. If the marginal benefit of engaging in an activity exceeds the marginal cost of doing so, you should do it. But if the marginal benefit is less than the marginal cost, you should do something else.

As an example, let's consider a discussion we might have with a student who tells us that she is too busy to attend class. We respond, "Think about the tuition you've spent for this class—it works out to about $10 a lecture." She answers that the book she reads for class is a book that we wrote, and that we wrote it so clearly she fully understands everything. She goes on:

> I've already paid the tuition and, whether I go to class or not, I can't get any of the tuition back, so the tuition doesn't enter into my marginal cost decision. The marginal cost to me isn't the tuition; it's what I could be doing with the hour instead of spending it in class. Because I value my time at $75 an hour [people who understand everything value their time highly], and even though I've heard that your lectures are super, I estimate that the marginal benefit of your class is only $50. The marginal cost, $75, exceeds the marginal benefit, $50, so I don't attend class.

We would congratulate her on her diplomacy and her economic reasoning, but tell her that we give a quiz every week, that students who miss a quiz fail the quiz, that those who fail all the quizzes fail the course, and that those who fail the course do not graduate. In short, she is underestimating the marginal benefits of attending the course. Correctly estimated, the marginal benefits of attending class exceed the marginal costs of cutting class. So she should attend class.

There's much more to be said about economic reasoning, but that will come later. For now, all you need remember is that, in economic thinking, *all things have a cost*—

Marginal cost   The change in cost associated with a change in quantity.

Marginal benefit   Additional benefit above what you've already derived.

Economic decision rule If benefits exceed costs, do it. If costs exceed benefits, don't do it.

Economics and Passion

and a benefit. Decisions are made on the basis of the **economic decision rule:** If benefits exceed costs, do it. If costs exceed benefits, don't do it.

Recognizing that everything has a cost is reasonable, but it's a reasonableness that many people don't like. It takes some of the passion out of life. It leads you to consider possibilities such as these:

- Saving some peoples' lives with liver transplants might not be worth the cost. The money might be better spent on nutritional programs that would save 20 lives for every 2 lives you might save with transplants.
- Maybe we shouldn't try to eliminate all pollution, because the cost of doing so may be too high. To eliminate all pollution would be to forgo too much of some other good activity.
- Buying a stock that went up 20 percent wasn't necessarily the greatest investment if in doing so you had to forgo some other investment that would have paid you a 30 percent return.
- It might make sense for the automobile industry to save $12 per car by not installing a safety device, even though without the safety device some people will be killed.

You get the idea. This kind of reasonableness is often criticized for being cold-blooded. But, not surprisingly, economists first reason economically; the social and moral implications of their conclusions are integrated later.

Economists' reasonableness isn't universally appreciated. Businesses love the result; others aren't so sure, as one of us discovered some years back when a girlfriend said she was leaving. "Why?" I asked. "Because," she responded, "you're so, so . . . reasonable." It took me many years after she left to learn what she already knew: There are many types of reasonableness, and not everyone thinks an economist's reasonableness is a virtue. We'll discuss such issues later; for now, let us simply warn you that, for better or worse, studying economics will lead you to view questions in a cost/benefit framework.

Opportunity Cost

Opportunity cost The benefit forgone, or the cost, of the best alternative to the activity you've chosen. In economic reasoning, the cost is less than the benefit

3 Opportunity cost is the basis of cost-benefit economic reasoning: it is the benefit forgone, or the cost of the best alternative to the activity you've chosen. In economic reasoning, that cost is less than the benefit of what you've chosen.

Putting economists' cost/benefit rules into practice isn't easy. To do so, you have to be able to choose and measure the costs and benefits correctly. Economists have devised the concept of opportunity cost to help you do that. The **opportunity cost** of undertaking an activity is the benefit forgone by undertaking that activity. The benefit forgone is the benefit that you might have gained from choosing the next-best alternative. To obtain the benefit of something, you must give up (forgo) something else—namely, the next-best alternative. All activities that have a next-best alternative have an opportunity cost.

Let's consider some examples. The opportunity cost of going out once with Natalia (or Nathaniel), the most beautiful woman (attractive man) in the world, might well be losing your solid steady, Margo (Mike). The opportunity cost of cleaning up the environment might be a reduction in the money available to assist low-income individuals. The opportunity cost of having a child might be two boats, three cars, and a two-week vacation each year for five years.

Examples are endless, but let's consider two that are particularly relevant to you: your choice of courses and your decision about how much to study. Let's say you're a full-time student and at the beginning of the term you had to choose four or five courses to take. Taking one precluded taking some other, and the opportunity cost of taking an economics course may well have been not taking a course on theatre. Similarly with studying: you have a limited amount of time to spend studying economics, studying some other subject, sleeping, or partying. The more time you spend on one activity, the less time you have for another. That's opportunity cost.

Notice how neatly the opportunity cost concept takes into account costs and benefits of all other options, and converts these alternative benefits into costs of the decision you're now making. This conversion helps you to compare costs and benefits and to select the activity with the largest difference between benefits and costs.

Opportunity costs have always made choice difficult, as we see in the early 19th-century engraving, "One or the Other." *Bleichroeder Print Collection, Baker Library, Harvard Business School.*

The relevance of opportunity cost isn't limited to your individual decisions. Opportunity costs are also relevant to government's decisions, which affect everyone in society. A common example is the guns-versus-butter debate. The resources that a society has are limited; therefore, its decision to use those resources to have more guns (more weapons) means that it must have less butter (fewer consumer goods). Thus, when society decides to spend $10 billion more on improved military hardware, the opportunity cost of that decision is $10 billion not spent on helping the homeless, paying off some of the national debt, or spending $10 billion on health care.

The opportunity cost concept has endless implications. It can even be turned upon itself. For instance, it takes time to think about alternatives; that means that there's a cost to being reasonable, so it's only reasonable to be somewhat unreasonable. If you followed that argument, you've caught the economic bug. If you didn't, don't worry. Just remember the opportunity cost concept for now. We'll infect you with economic thinking in the rest of the book.

The Production Possibility Table

We've just gone over opportunity cost. We're now going to review the same concept—only this time numerically and graphically. Opportunity cost can be seen numerically with a **production possibility table,** which lists a choice's opportunity cost by summarizing what alternative outputs you can achieve with your inputs. An **output** is simply a result of an activity—your grade in a course is an output. An **input** is what you put in to achieve that output. In this example, study time is an input.

Production possibility table   Table that lists a choice's opportunity costs.

Output   The result of an activity.

Input   What you put in to achieve output.

Let's present the study time/grades example numerically. To do so we must be more precise. Say you have exactly 20 hours a week to devote to two courses: economics and history. (So, maybe we're a bit optimistic.) Grades are given numerically and you know that the following relationships exist: if you study 20 hours in economics, you'll get a grade of 100, 18 hours—94, and so forth.[3]

Let's say that the best you can do in history is a 98 with 20 hours of study a week; 19 hours of study guarantee you a 96, and so on. The production possibility table in Exhibit 1 (a) shows the highest combination of grades you can get with various allocations of the 20 hours available for studying the two subjects. One possibility is getting 100 in economics and 58 in history. Another is getting 70 in economics and 78 in history.

Notice that the opportunity cost of studying one subject rather than the other is embodied in the production possibility table. The information in the table comes from experience; we are assuming that you've discovered that if you transfer an hour of

---

[3]Throughout the book we'll be presenting numerical examples to help you understand the concepts. The numbers we choose are often arbitrary. After all, we have to choose something. As an exercise, you might choose different numbers that apply to your own life and work out the argument using those numbers. For those who don't want to make up their own numbers, the study guide has examples with different numbers.

study from economics to history, you'll lose 3 points on your grade in economics and gain 2 points in history. Thus, the opportunity cost of a 2-point rise in your history grade is a 3-point decrease in your economics grade.

The Production Possibility Curve

Production possibility curve A curve measuring the maximum combination of outputs that can be obtained from a given number of inputs.

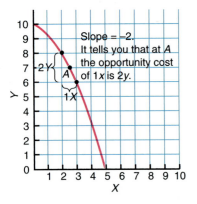

4 Remember this graph: The slope tells you the opportunity cost of good *X* in terms of good *Y.* You have to give up 2*Y* to get 1*X* when you're around point *A.*

The information in the production possibility table can also be presented graphically in a diagram. This graphical presentation of the opportunity cost concept is called the **production possibility curve.** This curve indicates the maximum combination of outputs you can obtain from a given number of inputs.

A production possibility curve is created from a production possibility table by mapping the table in a two-dimensional graph. We've taken the information from the table in Exhibit 1 (a) and mapped it into Exhibit 1 (b). The history grade is mapped, or plotted, on the horizontal axis; the economics grade is on the vertical axis.

As you can see from the bottom row of Exhibit 1 (a), if you study economics for all 20 hours and study history for 0 hours, you'll get grades of 100 in economics and 58 in history. Point *A* in Exhibit 1 (b) represents that choice. If you study history for all 20 hours and study economics for 0 hours, you'll get a 98 in history and a 40 in economics. Point *E* represents that choice. Points *B, C,* and *D* represent three possible choices between these two extremes.

Notice that the production possibility curve slopes downward from left to right. That means that there is an inverse relationship (a trade-off) between grades in economics and grades in history. The better the grade in economics, the worse the grade in history, and vice versa. That downward slope represents the opportunity cost concept—you get more of one benefit only if you get less of another benefit.

The production possibility curve not only represents the opportunity cost concept; it also measures the opportunity cost. For example, in Exhibit 1 (b), say you want to raise your grade in history from a 94 to a 98 (move from point *D* to point *E*). The opportunity cost of that 4-point increase would be a 6-point decrease in your economics grade, from 46 to 40.

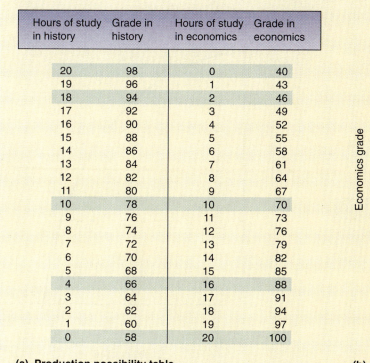

Hours of study in history	Grade in history	Hours of study in economics	Grade in economics
20	98	0	40
19	96	1	43
18	94	2	46
17	92	3	49
16	90	4	52
15	88	5	55
14	86	6	58
13	84	7	61
12	82	8	64
11	80	9	67
10	78	10	70
9	76	11	73
8	74	12	76
7	72	13	79
6	70	14	82
5	68	15	85
4	66	16	88
3	64	17	91
2	62	18	94
1	60	19	97
0	58	20	100

(a) Production possibility table

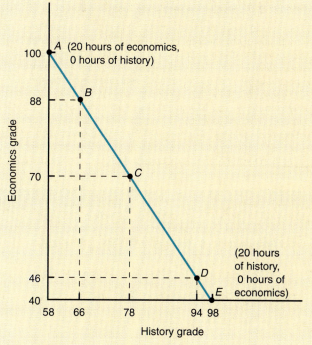

(b) Production possibility curve

EXHIBIT 1   A Production Possibility Table and Curve for Grades in Economics and History

The production possibility table (a) shows the highest combination of grades you can get with only 20 hours available for studying economics and history.

The information in the production possibility table in (a) can be plotted on a graph, as is done in (b). The grade received in economics is on the vertical axis, and the grade received in history is on the horizontal axis.

To summarize, the production possibility curve demonstrates that:

1. There is a limit to what you can achieve, given the existing institutions, resources, and technology.
2. Every choice you make has an opportunity cost. You can get more of something only by giving up something else.

Increasing Marginal Opportunity Cost   We chose an unchanging trade-off in the study time/grade example because it made the initial presentation of the production possibility curve easier. Since, by assumption, you could always trade two points on your history grade for three points on your economics grade, the production possibility curve was a straight line. But is that the way we'd expect reality to be? Probably not. The production possibility curve is generally bowed outward, as in Exhibit 2 (b).

Why? To make the answer more concrete, let's talk specifically about society's choice between eating (cheeseburgers) and spending on entertainment (CDs). The information in Exhibit 2 (b) is derived from the table in Exhibit 2 (a).

Let's see what the shape of the curve means in terms of numbers. Let's start with society producing only CDs (point *A*). Giving up a CD initially gains us a lot of cheeseburgers (4), moving us to point *B*. The next two CDs we give up gains us slightly fewer cheeseburgers (point *C*). If we continue to trade cheeseburgers for CDs, we find that at point *D* we gain almost no cheeseburgers from giving up a CD. The opportunity cost of choosing cheeseburgers over CDs increases as we increase the production of cheeseburgers.

The reason the opportunity cost of cheeseburgers increases as we consume more cheeseburgers is that some resources are relatively better suited to producing cheese-

The table in (**a**) contains information on the trade-off between the production of cheeseburgers and CDs. This information has been plotted on the graph in (**b**). Notice in (**b**) that as we move along the production possibility curve from *A* to *F*, trading CDs for cheeseburgers, we get fewer and fewer cheeseburgers for each CD given up. That is, the opportunity cost of choosing cheeseburgers over CDs increases as we increase the production of cheeseburgers. This concept is called the principle of increasing marginal opportunity cost. The phenomenon occurs because some resources are better suited for the production of CDs than for the production of cheeseburgers, and we use the better ones first.

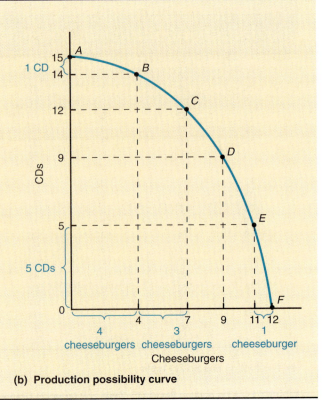

% resources devoted to production of cheeseburgers	Number of cheeseburgers	% resources devoted to production of CDs	CDs	Row
0	0	100	15	A
20	4	80	14	B
40	7	60	12	C
60	9	40	9	D
80	11	20	5	E
100	12	0	0	F

(a) Production possibility table

(b) Production possibility curve

Comparative advantage The ability to produce a good at a lower opportunity cost (forgone production of another good) than another country or resource can.

burgers, while others are relatively better suited to producing CDs. Put in economists' terminology, some resources have a comparative advantage over other resources in the production of CDs, while other resources have a comparative advantage in the production of cheeseburgers. A resource has a **comparative advantage** in the production of a good when, compared to other resources, it's relatively better suited to producing that good than to producing another good.

When making small amounts of cheeseburgers and large amounts of CDs, in the production of those cheeseburgers we use the resources whose comparative advantage is in the production of cheeseburgers. All other resources are devoted to producing CDs. Because the resources used in producing cheeseburgers aren't good at producing CDs, we're not giving up many CDs to get those cheeseburgers. As we produce more and more of a good, we must use resources whose comparative advantage is in the production of the other good—in this case, more suitable for producing CDs than for producing cheeseburgers. As we remove resources from the production of CDs to get the same additional amount of cheeseburgers, we must give up increasing numbers of CDs. An alternative way of saying this is that the opportunity cost of producing cheeseburgers becomes greater as the production of CDs increases. As we continue to increase the production of cheeseburgers, the opportunity cost of more cheeseburgers becomes very high because we're using resources to produce cheeseburgers that have a strong comparative advantage for producing CDs.

Let's consider two more specific examples. Say Canada suddenly decides it needs more wheat. To get additional wheat, we must devote additional land to growing it. This land is less fertile than the land we're already using, so our additional output of wheat per acre of land devoted to wheat will be less. Alternatively, consider the use of relief pitchers in a baseball game. If only one relief pitcher is needed, the manager sends in the best; if he must send in a second one, then a third, and even a fourth, the likelihood of winning the game decreases.

For many of the choices society must make, opportunity costs tend to increase as we choose more and more of an item. The reason is that resources are not easily adapt-

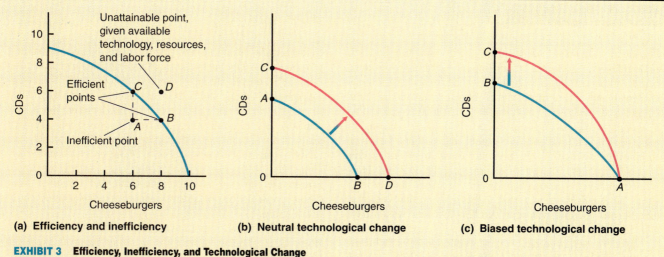

EXHIBIT 3   Efficiency, Inefficiency, and Technological Change

The production possibility curve helps us see what is meant by efficiency. At point *A*, in (**a**), all inputs are used to make 6 cheeseburgers and 4 CDs. This is inefficient since there is a way to obtain more of one without giving up any of the other; that is, to obtain 6 cheeseburgers and 6 CDs (point *C*) or 4 CDs and 8 cheeseburgers (point *B*). All points inside the production possibility curve are inefficient. With fixed inputs and given technology, we cannot go beyond the production possibility curve. For example, point *D* is unattainable.

A technological change that improves production techniques will shift the production possibility curve outward, as shown in both (**b**) and (**c**). How the curve shifts outward depends on how technology improves. For example, if we become more efficient in the production of both CDs and cheeseburgers, the curve will shift out as in (**b**). If we become more efficient in producing CDs, but not in producing cheeseburgers, then the curve will shift as in (**c**).

able from the production of one good to the production of another. Such a phenomenon about choice is so common, in fact, that it has acquired a name: the **principle of increasing marginal opportunity cost.** That principle states:

> *In order to get more of something, one must give up ever-increasing quantities of something else.*

In other words, initially the opportunity costs of an activity are low, but they increase the more we concentrate on that activity. Sometimes this law is called the flowerpot law because, if it didn't hold, all the world's food could be grown in a flowerpot. But it can't be. As we add more seeds to a fixed amount of soil, there won't be enough nutrients or room for the roots, so output per seed decreases.

Efficiency   We like, if possible, to get as much output as possible from a given amount of inputs or resources. That's how **productive efficiency** is defined: achieving as much output as possible from a given amount of inputs or resources. We would like to be efficient. The production possibility curve helps us see what is meant by productive efficiency. Consider point *A* in Exhibit 3 (a), which is inside the production possibility curve. If we are producing at point *A*, we are using all our resources to produce 6 cheeseburgers and 4 CDs. Point *A* represents **inefficiency,** since with the same inputs we could be getting either 8 cheeseburgers and 4 CDs (point *B*) or 6 CDs and 6 cheeseburgers (point *C*). Both points *B* and *C* represent efficiency, as long as we prefer more to less. We always want to move our production out to a point on the production possibility curve.

Why not move out farther, say to point *D*? If we could, we would, but by definition the production possibility curve represents the most output we can get from a certain combination of inputs. So point *D* is unattainable, given our resources and technology.

When technology improves, when more resources are discovered, or when the economic institutions get better at fulfilling our wants, we can get more output with the same inputs. What this means is that when technology or an economic institution

Principle of increasing marginal opportunity cost   In order to get more of something, one must give up ever-increasing quantities of something else.

5   The principle of increasing marginal opportunity cost states that opportunity costs increase the more you concentrate on the activity. In order to get more of something, one must give up ever-increasing quantities of something else.

Productive efficiency   Getting as much output for as few inputs as possible.

Inefficiency   Getting less output from inputs which, if devoted to some other activity, would produce more output.

Production involves transforming inputs into outputs. For example, seeds, soil, and labour (inputs) combine to produce wheat (output). Many introductory economics texts call inputs *resources* and divide those inputs into three resources: land, labour, and capital. Economists in the 1800s, often called *Classical economists,* discussed production as a means of transforming land, labour, and capital into outputs. Classical economists divided all inputs into those three categories because they were interested in answering the question: How is income divided among landowners, workers, and capitalists? The three divisions helped them focus on that question: landowners' income was rent, workers' income was wages, and capitalists' income was profit.

Modern advanced analysis of production doesn't follow this threefold division. Instead, the modern analysis is more abstract and tells how inputs in general are transformed into outputs in general. Modern economic theory has moved away from the traditional division because the division of income among these three groups isn't central to the questions economists are now asking.

But that leaves open the problem: What division of resources makes the most sense? The answer depends on what question you're asking. For example, in the grade example in this chapter, your time was the input, while in the CDs-and-

cheeseburgers example the inputs were machines, natural resources, and labour. In the most abstract categorization, the ultimate resources are space (represented by land), time (represented by labour), and matter (represented by capital). Thus, in one way of looking at it, the traditional distinction is still relevant. But in another way, it isn't. It directs our focus of analysis away from some important inputs. For example, one of the inputs that economists now focus on is *entrepreneurship,* the ability to organize and get something done. Entrepreneurship is an important input that's distinct from labour. Most listings of general resources today include entrepreneurship.

Here's another important point about resources. The term *resource* is often used with the qualifier *natural,* as in the phrase *natural resources.* Coal, oil, and iron are all *called natural resources.* Be careful about that qualifier *natural.* Whether something is or isn't a natural resource depends on the available technology. And technology is unnatural. For example, at one time a certain black gooey stuff was not a resource—it was something that made land unusable. When people learned that the black gooey stuff could be burned as a fuel, oil became a resource. What's considered a resource depends on technology. If solar technology is ever perfected, oil will go back to being black gooey stuff.

improves, the entire production possibility curve shifts outward from *AB* to *CD* in Exhibit 3 (b). How the production possibility curve shifts outward depends on how the technology improves. For example, say we become more efficient in producing CDs, but not more efficient in producing cheeseburgers. Then the production possibility curve shifts outward to *AC* in Exhibit 3 (c).

Policies that costlessly shift the production possibility curve outward are the most desirable policies because they don't require us to decrease our consumption of one good to get more of another. Alas, they are the most infrequent. Improving technology and institutions and discovering more resources are not costless; generally there's an opportunity cost of doing so that must be taken into account.

Economics, Institutions, and the Production Possibility Curve   One of the important lessons one learns in economics is that *decisions are made in context:* What makes sense in one context may not make sense in another. For example, say you're answering the question: Would society be better off if students were taught literature or if they were taught agriculture? The answer depends on the institutional context. In a developing country whose goal is large increases in material output, teaching agriculture may make sense. In a developed country, where growth in material output is less important, literature may make sense.

Recognizing the contextual nature of decisions is important in interpreting the production possibility curve. Because decisions are contextual, what the production possibility curve looks like depends on the existing institutions, and the analysis can only be applied in institutional context. The production possibility curve is not a purely technical phenomenon. The curve is an *engine of analysis* to make contextual choices, not a definitive tool to decide what one should do in all cases.

Distribution and Productive Efficiency   In discussing the production possibility curve, we avoided questions of distribution: Who gets what? But such questions cannot be ignored in real-world situations. Specifically, if the method of production is tied to a particular

In the 1990s, oil has remained an important natural resource. *Bettman Newsphotos.*

income distribution and choosing one method will help some people but hurt others, we can't say that one method of production is efficient and the other inefficient, even if one method produces more total output than the other. The term **efficiency** involves achieving a goal as cheaply as possible. The term has meaning only in regard to a specified goal. Say, for example, that we have a society of ascetics who believe that consumption above some minimum is immoral. For such a society, producing more for less (productive efficiency) would not be efficient since consumption is not its goal. Or say that we have a society that cares that what is produced is fairly distributed. An increase in output that goes to only one person and not to anyone else would not necessarily be efficient.

Efficiency   Achieving a goal as cheaply as possible. (16)

In our society, however, most people prefer more to less, and many policies have relatively small distributional consequences. On the basis of the assumption that more is better than less, economists use their own kind of shorthand for such policies and talk about efficiency as identical to productive efficiency—increasing total output. But it's important to remember the assumption under which that shorthand is used: that the distributional effects that accompany the policy aren't undesirable and that we, as a society, prefer more output.

The production possibility curve represents the tough choices society must make. Not everyone recognizes these choices. For example, politicians often talk as if the production possibility curve were nonexistent. They promise voters the world, telling them, "If you elect me, you can have more of everything." When they say that, they obscure the hard choices and increase their probability of getting elected.

The Production Possibility Curve and Tough Choices

Economists do the opposite. They promise little except that life is tough, and they continually point out that seemingly free lunches often involve significant hidden costs. Alas, political candidates who exhibit such reasonableness seldom get elected. Economists' reasonableness has earned economics the nickname, *the dismal science.*

The opportunity cost concept applies to all aspects of life. It embodies *economic forces.* **Economic forces** are the forces of scarcity; when there isn't enough to go around, goods must be rationed. **Rationing** is a structural mechanism for determining who gets what. For example, dormitory rooms are often rationed by lottery, and permission to register in popular classes is often rationed by a first-come, first-registered

Economics and the Invisible Forces

Economic forces The forces of scarcity (when there isn't enough to go around, goods must be rationed).

Rationing Structural mechanism for determining who gets what.

Market force Economic force to which society has given relatively free rein so that it has been able to work through the market.

Invisible hand Economic forces, that is, the price mechanism; the rise and fall of prices that guides our actions in a market.

6 Economic reality is controlled by three invisible forces:
1. The invisible hand (economic forces);
2. The invisible handshake (social and historical forces); and
3. The invisible foot (political and legal forces).

Invisible handshake Social and historical forces that play a role in deciding whether to let market forces operate.

Invisible foot Political and legal forces that play a role in deciding whether to let market forces operate.

rule. The same with food: If food weren't rationed, there wouldn't be enough to go around, so it must be rationed—by charging a price for it. All scarce goods or rights must be rationed in some fashion.

Rationing reflects scarcity and economic forces. One of the important choices that a society must make is whether to allow these economic forces to operate freely and openly or to try to rein them in. When society gives an economic force relatively free rein so that an economic force works through the market, it's called a **market force.**

Market forces ration by changing prices. When there's a shortage, the price goes up. When there's a surplus, the price goes down. Much of this book will be devoted to analyzing how the market works like an invisible hand, guiding economic forces to coordinate individual actions and allocate scarce resources. The **invisible hand** is the price mechanism, the rise and fall of prices that guides our actions in a market.

Societies can't choose whether or not to allow economic forces to operate—economic forces are always operating. However, societies may choose whether to allow market forces to predominate. Other forces play a major role in deciding whether to let market forces operate. We'll call these other forces the **invisible handshake** (social and historical forces) and the **invisible foot** (political and legal forces). Economic reality is determined by a contest among these three invisible forces.

Let's consider an example in which the invisible handshake prevents an economic force from becoming a market force: the problem of getting a date for Saturday night. If a school (or a society) has significantly more people of one sex than the other (let's say more men than women), some men may well find themselves without a date—that is, men will be in excess supply—and will have to find something else to do, say study or go to a movie by themselves. An "excess supply" person could solve the problem by paying someone to go out with him or her, but that would probably change the nature of the date in unacceptable ways. It would be revolting to the person who offered payment and to the person who was offered payment. That unacceptability is an example of the invisible handshake in action—the complex of social and cultural norms that guides and limits our activities. People don't try to buy dates because the invisible handshake prevents them from doing so. The invisible handshake makes the market solution for dating inappropriate.

Now let's consider another example in which it's the invisible foot—political and legal influences—that stops economic forces from becoming market forces. Say you decide that you can make some money by producing and selling your own brand of beer from your basement apartment. You try to establish a small business, but suddenly you experience the invisible foot in action. Alcoholic beverages can only be sold by government license, so you'll be prohibited from selling your beer. Economic forces—the desire to make money—led you to want to enter the business, but in this case the invisible foot squashes the invisible hand.

Often the invisible foot and invisible handshake work together against the invisible hand. For example, in Canada there aren't enough babies to satisfy all the couples who desire them. Babies born to particular sets of parents are rationed—by luck. Consider a group of parents, all of whom want babies. Those who can, have a baby; those who can't have one, but want one, try to adopt. Adoption agencies ration the available babies. Who gets a baby depends on whom people know at the adoption agency and on the desires of the birth mother, who can often specify the socioeconomic background (and many other characteristics) of the family in which she wants her baby to grow up. That's the economic force in action; it gives more power to the supplier of something that's in short supply.

If our society allowed individuals to buy and sell babies, that economic force would be translated into a market force. The invisible hand would see to it that the quantity of babies supplied would equal the quantity of babies demanded at some price. The market, not the adoption agencies, would do the rationing.[4]

---

[4]Even though it's against the law, some babies are nonetheless "sold" on a semilegal, or what is called a gray, market. In the United States in the early 1990s, "market price" for a healthy baby was about U.S. $30,000. If it were legal to sell babies (and if people didn't find having babies in order to sell them morally repugnant), the price would be much lower, since there would be a larger supply of babies.

THE INVISIBLE FORCES

Ideas are encapsulated in metaphors, and Adam Smith's "invisible hand" metaphor has been a central one in economics since 1776. It's a neat metaphor, but it sometimes makes economic forces seem to be the only forces guiding the direction of society. And that just ain't so.

In the 1970s and 1980s, a number of modern-day economists attempted to broaden the dimensions of economic analysis. To explain what they were doing, they introduced metaphors for two other invisible forces. The term *invisible handshake* was coined by Arthur Okun, an American economist working at an economic "think tank". Okun argued that social and historical forces—the invisible handshake—often prevented the invisible hand from working.

The term *invisible foot* was coined by Stephen Magee. Magee summarized the argument of a large number of economists that individuals often use politics to get what they want, expressing this phenomenon with the invisible foot metaphor. Government action to benefit particular pressure groups is the invisible foot. By the late 1980s, these two additional terms were commonly used by the group of economists who were struggling to integrate economic insights with social and political insights.

Most people, including us, find the idea of selling babies repugnant. But why? It's the strength of the invisible handshake backed up and strengthened by the invisible foot.

What is and isn't allowable differs from one society to another. For example, in Russia, until recently, private businesses were against the law, so not many people started their own businesses. In the United States, until the 1970s, it was against the law to hold gold except in jewelry, so most people refrained from holding gold. Ultimately a country's laws and social norms determine whether the invisible hand will be allowed to work.

The invisible foot and invisible handshake are active in all parts of your life. The invisible foot influences many of your everyday actions. You don't practice medicine without a license; you don't sell body parts or certain addictive drugs. These actions are all against the law. But many people do sell alcohol; that's not against the law if you have a permit. The invisible handshake also influences us. You don't make profitable loans to your friends (you don't charge your friends interest); you don't charge your children for their food (parents are supposed to feed their children); many sports and media stars don't sell their autographs (some do, but many consider the practice tacky); you don't lower the wage you'll accept in order to get a job away from someone else. The list is long. You cannot understand economics without understanding the limitations that political and social forces—the invisible foot and the invisible handshake—place on economic actions.

In summary, what happens in a society can be seen as the reaction and interaction of these three forces: the invisible hand (economic forces), the invisible foot (political and legal forces), and the invisible handshake (social and historical forces). Economics has a role to play in sociology, history, and politics, just as sociology, history, and politics have roles to play in economics. While different branches of economics attempt to offer an explanation for political forces (public choice theory), legal forces (law and economics), and social forces (institutional economics), it is important to remember that good economic theory must take into account how these forces interact with decision making.

Economics is about the real world. Throughout this book we'll use the invisible forces analogy to talk about real-world events and the interrelationships of economics, history, sociology, and politics.

ECONOMIC TERMINOLOGY

Economic terminology needs little discussion. It simply needs learning. As terms come up in discussion, you'll begin to recognize them. Soon you'll begin to understand them, and finally you'll begin to feel comfortable using them. In this book we're trying to describe how economics works in the real world, so we introduce you to many of the terms that occur in business and in discussions of the economy. Learning economic vocabulary, like learning German or French vocabulary, isn't fun. It's not

A REMINDER WINSTON CHURCHILL AND LADY ASTOR

There are many stories about Nancy Astor, the first woman elected to Britain's Parliament. A vivacious, fearless American woman, she married into the English aristocracy and, during the 1930s and 1940s, became a bright light on the English social and political scenes, which were already quite bright.

One story told about Lady Astor is that she and Winston Churchill, the unorthodox genius who had a long and distinguished political career and who was Britain's prime minister during World War II, were sitting in a pub having a theoretical discussion about morality. Churchill suggested that as a thought experiment Lady Astor ponder the question: If a man were to promise her a huge amount of money—say £1 million—for the privilege, would she sleep with him? Lady Astor did ponder the question for a while and finally answered,

yes, she would, if the money were guaranteed. Churchill then asked her if she would sleep with him for £5. Her response was sharp: "Of course not. What do you think I am—a prostitute?" This time Churchill won the battle of wits by answering, "We have already established that fact; we are now simply negotiating about price."

One moral that economists might draw from this story is that economic incentives, if high enough, can have a powerful influence on behaviour. An equally important moral of the story is that noneconomic incentives can also be very strong. Why do most people feel it's wrong to sell sex for money, even if they would be willing to do so if the price were high enough? Keeping this second moral in mind will significantly increase your economic understanding of real-world events.

---

something that's easily taught in classes. It's something that's learned by study and repetition outside the class. Learning vocabulary takes repetition and memorization, but no one ever said all learning is fun.

Whenever possible we'll integrate the introduction of new terminology into the discussion so that learning it will seem painless. In fact we've already introduced you to a number of economic terms: *opportunity cost, the invisible hand, market forces,* and *economic forces,* just to name a few. By the end of the book we'll have introduced you to hundreds more.

ECONOMIC INSIGHTS

Economists have thought about the economy for a long time, so it's not surprising that they've developed some insights into the way it works.

General insights are often embodied in a *particular economic theory*—a formulation of highly abstract, deductive relationships that capture inherent empirically-observed tendencies of economies. Theories are inevitably too abstract to apply in specific cases and, thus, these theories are often embodied, in turn, in economic models and economic principles that place the generalized insights of the theory in a more specific contextual setting. Then these theories, models, and principles are empirically tested (as best one can) to ensure that they correspond to reality. While these models and principles are less general than theories, they are still usually too general to apply in specific cases. Theories, models, and principles must be combined with a knowledge of real-world economic institutions to arrive at specific policy recommendations.

You've already been introduced to one economic principle, the principle of increasing marginal opportunity cost, which is an insight about the relationship among outputs: In order to get more of one output, you must give up ever-increasing quantities of another output. That principle can be applied to a wide variety of examples, so you need to learn only the principle, not each specific example.

To see the importance of principles, think back to grade school when you learned to add. You didn't memorize the sum of 147 and 138; instead you learned a principle of addition. The principle says that when adding 147 and 138, you first add 7 + 8, which you memorized was 15. You write down the 5 and carry the 1, which you add to 4 + 3 to get 8. Then add 1 + 1 = 2. So the answer is 285. When you know that one principle, you know how to add millions of combinations of numbers.

The Invisible Hand Theory

In the same way, knowing a theory gives you insight into a wide variety of economic phenomena, even though you don't know the particulars of each phenomenon. For example, much of economic theory deals with the *pricing mechanism* and how the market operates to coordinate *individuals' decisions*. Economists have come to the following insights:

> When the quantity supplied is greater than the quantity demanded, price has a tendency to fall.
>
> When the quantity demanded is greater than the quantity supplied, price has a tendency to rise.

Using these generalized insights, economists have developed a theory of markets that leads to the further insight that, under certain conditions, the market will coordinate individuals' decisions, allocating scarce resources *efficiently* so society moves out to its production possibility curve, not inside it. An efficient economy is one that reaps the maximum amount of outputs from the available inputs. Economists call the insight that a market economy will allocate resources efficiently the **invisible hand theory.**

Invisible hand theory The insight that a market economy will allocate resources efficiently.

Theories and the models used to represent them are enormously efficient methods of conveying information, but they're also necessarily abstract. They rely upon simplifying assumptions, and *if you don't know the assumptions, you don't know the theory.* The result of forgetting assumptions could be similar to what happens if you forget that you're supposed to add numbers in columns. Forgetting that, yet remembering all the steps, can lead to a wildly incorrect answer. For example,

$$\begin{array}{r} 471 \\ + \ 327 \\ \hline 5037 \end{array} \text{ is wrong.}$$

Knowing the assumptions of theories and models allows you to progress beyond gut reaction and better understand the strengths and weaknesses of various economic systems. Let's consider a central economic assumption: The assumption that individuals behave rationally—that what they choose reflects what makes them happiest, given the constraints. If that assumption doesn't hold, the invisible hand theory doesn't hold.

Presenting the invisible hand theory in its full beauty is an important part of any economics course. Presenting the assumptions upon which it is based and the limitations of the invisible hand is likewise an important part of the course. We'll do both throughout the book.

Economic Theory and Stories

Economic theory, and the models in which that theory is presented, often developed as a shorthand way of telling a story. These stories are important; they make the theory come alive and convey the insights that give economic theory its power. In this book we present plenty of theories and models, but they're accompanied by stories that provide the context that makes them relevant.

At times, because there's much new terminology, discussing models and theories takes up much of the presentation time and becomes a bit oppressive. That's the nature of the beast. As Albert Einstein said, "Theories should be as simple as possible, but not more so." When a theory or a model becomes oppressive, pause and think about the underlying story that the theory is meant to convey. That story should make sense and be concrete. If you can't translate the theory into a story, you don't understand the theory.

Microeconomics and Macroeconomics

Economic theory is divided into two parts: microeconomic theory and macroeconomic theory. Microeconomic theory considers economic reasoning from the viewpoint of individuals and firms and builds up from there to an analysis of the whole economy. We'll define **microeconomics** as *the study of individual choice, and how that choice is influenced by economic forces.* Microeconomics studies such things as the pricing policies of firms, households' decisions on what to buy, and how markets allocate resources among alternative ends. Our discussions of opportunity cost and the production possibility curve were based on microeconomic theory. It is from microeconomics that the invisible hand theory comes.

Microeconomics The study of individual choice, and how that choice is influenced by economic forces.

As one builds up from microeconomic analysis to an analysis of the entire society,

7 Microeconomic theory considers economic reasoning from the viewpoint of individuals and builds up; macroeconomics considers economic reasoning from the aggregate and builds down.

Macroeconomics The study of inflation, unemployment, business cycles, and growth primarily from the whole to the parts, focusing on aggregate relationships and supplementing its analysis with microeconomic insights.

everything gets rather complicated. Many economists try to simplify matters by taking a different approach—a macroeconomic approach—first looking at the aggregate, or whole, and then breaking it down into components. A micro approach would analyze a person by looking first at each individual cell and then building up. A macro approach would start with the person and then go on to his or her components—arms, legs, fingernails, feelings, and so on. Put simply, microeconomics analyzes from the parts to the whole; macroeconomics analyzes from the whole to the parts.

In recent years the analysis of macroeconomic issues—inflation, unemployment, business cycles, and growth—has used more and more microeconomic analysis to supplement it. Thus, many economists now define macroeconomics as the study of inflation, unemployment, business cycles, and growth. We'll compromise and define **macroeconomics** as *the study of inflation, unemployment, business cycles, and growth primarily from the whole to the parts—focusing on aggregate relationships and supplementing that analysis with microeconomic insights.*

To demonstrate the relationship between micro and macro analysis, let's consider again the production possibility curve, which is based on microeconomic principles. If unemployment is high, the economy is operating inside the production possibility curve and hence may be operating inefficiently. In that case, reducing unemployment can be costless. But it might also be that current institutions require such a high level of unemployment in order to prevent other problems like inflation. In that case, reducing unemployment is not costless; it involves significant, and probably costly, institutional changes. Similarly, macroeconomic growth shifts the production possibility curve outward, but that growth may be best explained by changes in microeconomic factors, such as technological change and resource endowments. Thus, even though the production possibility curve is derived from microeconomic principles, it can be used to discuss macroeconomic issues.

Neither macro nor micro is prior to the other. Clearly, macro results follow from micro decisions, but micro decisions are formed with a macro context, and can only be understood within that context. We need to be able to simultaneously develop a microfoundation of macro, and a macrofoundation of micro. The macro foundation of micro provides the institutional context within which micro decisions are made, and the micro foundation of macro provides the contextual relationship between individual decisions and aggregate outcomes.

ECONOMIC INSTITUTIONS

To know whether you can apply economic theory to reality, you must know about economic institutions. Economic institutions are complicated combinations of historical circumstance and economic, cultural, social, and political pressures. Economic institutions are all around you and affect your everyday life. For example, let's consider three economic institutions: schools, corporations, and cultural norms. Where you go to school determines the kind of job you'll get. Corporations determine what products are available to buy. Cultural norms determine what you identify as legitimate business activities. Understanding economic institutions requires the wisdom of experience, tempered with common sense—all combined with a desire to understand rather than to accept without question.

Economic institutions sometimes seem to operate in quite different manners than economic theory says they do. For example, economic theory says that prices are determined by supply and demand. However, a knowledge of economic institutions says that prices are set by rules of thumb—often by what are called cost-plus-markup rules. (That is, you determine what your costs are, multiply by 1.4 or 1.5, and the result is the price you set.) Economic theory says that supply and demand determine who's hired; a knowledge of economic institutions says that hiring is often done on the basis of whom you know, not by economic forces.

These apparent contradictions have two complementary explanations. First, economic theory abstracts from many issues. These issues may account for the differences. Second, there's no contradiction; economic principles often affect decisions from behind the scenes. For instance, supply and demand pressures determine what the price markup over cost will be. In this case, the invisible handshake is guided by the invisible hand. In all cases, however, to apply economic theory to reality—to gain the full value of economic insights—you've got to have a sense of economic institutions.

The final goal of the course is to present the economic policy options facing our society today. For example, should the government restrict mergers between firms? Should it run a budget deficit? Should it do something about the international trade deficit? Should it decrease taxes?

ECONOMIC POLICY OPTIONS

We saved our discussion of this goal for last because there's no sense talking about policy options unless you know some economic terminology, some economic theory, and something about economic institutions. Once you know something about those, you're in a position to consider the policy options available for dealing with the economic problems our society faces.

The first thing to note about policies is that they have many dimensions. Some policies operate within existing institutions without affecting them. Others indirectly change institutions. Still others are designed to change institutions directly. Policies that affect institutions are much more difficult to analyze (because their effects on institutions are generally indirect and nebulous) and to implement (since existing institutions often create benefits for specific individuals who don't want them changed) than are policies that don't affect institutions. For example, consider establishing a government program to promote research. Seems like a good thing—right? But such a policy might undermine the role of existing institutions already promoting research, and the net result of the program might be less, not more, research. When analyzing such policies, we need to take this effect on institutions into account.

On the other hand, policies that directly change institutions, while much more difficult to implement than policies that don't, also offer the largest potential for gain. They shift the production possibilities curve, whereas policies that operate within existing institutions simply move society closer to the frontier.

Let's consider an example. In the 1990s, a number of countries decided to abandon socialist institutions and put market economies in place. The result: output in those countries fell enormously as the old institutions fell. Eventually, these countries hope, once the new market institutions are predominant, output will bounce back and further gains will be made. But the temporary hardships these countries are experiencing show the enormous difficulty of implementing policies involving major institutional changes.

We have found it helpful in thinking about institutions to make an analogy to the computer, which has an operating system, software which works within that operating system, and what might be called nested software—software that only works within other software. What's efficient within one software package or operating system may be totally inefficient within another. To use a computer effectively, you must understand the interaction of the different levels of the software. To carry out economic policy effectively, one must understand the interaction and the various levels of institutions.

Let's consider an example: unemployment insurance and seasonal workers. In 1956 the Canadian Unemployment Assistance Act was introduced to protect workers during short periods of unemployment. The program has evolved to the point where it now provides benefits for workers leaving the labour force temporarily because of illness, pregnancy, work-sharing, and job-training programs. A recent study suggests that as many as 80 percent of the 1,800,000 claimants in 1989 were people who had previously received benefits. Critics argue that workers in seasonal industries abuse the unemployment insurance program since it is being used, year after year, to stabilize income. Critics argue that seasonal workers should search for jobs that offer employment year-round. This is not to say that we should not have programs to protect seasonal workers against unemployment; it is only to say that we must build into our policies their effect on institutions.

Objective Policy Analysis

Objective   Term applied to "analysis," meaning that the analysis keeps your subjective views—your value judgements—separate.

Subjective   Term applied to "analysis," meaning that the analysis reflects the analyst's views of how things should be.

Positive economics   The study of what is. and how the economy works.

Normative economics   The study of what the goals of the economy should be.

8   *Positive economics* is the study of what is, and how the economy works.
Normative economics is the study of what the goals of the economy should be.
The *art of economics* is the application of the knowledge learned in positive economics to the achievement of the goals determined in normative economics.

In thinking about policy, we must keep a number of points in mind. The most important is that good economic policy analysis is **objective.** Objective analysis does not say, "This is the way things should be," reflecting a goal established by the analyst. That would be **subjective** analysis. Instead it says, "This is the way the economy works, and if society (or the individual or firm for whom you're doing the analysis) wants to achieve a particular goal, this is how it might go about doing so." Objective analysis keeps your subjective views—your value judgements—separate.

To make clear the distinction between objective and subjective analysis, economists have divided economics into three categories: *positive economics, normative economics,* and the *art of economics.* **Positive economics** is the study of what is, and how the economy works. It asks such questions as: How does the market for hog bellies work? How do price restrictions affect market forces? These questions fall under the heading of economic theory. **Normative economics** is the study of what the goals of the economy should be. In discussing such questions, economists must carefully delineate whose goals they are discussing. One cannot simply assume that one's own goals for society are society's goals. Normative economics asks such questions as: What should the distribution of income be? What should tax policy be designed to achieve?

The **art of economics** relates positive economics to normative economics; it is the application of the knowledge learned in positive economics to the achievement of the goals one has determined in normative economics. It looks at such questions as: To achieve a certain distribution of income, how would you go about it, given the way the economy works?[5] Most policy discussions fall under the art of economics.

In each of these three branches of economics, economists separate their own value judgements from their objective analysis as much as possible. The qualifier "as much as possible" is important, since some value judgements inevitably sneak in. We are products of our environment, and the questions we ask, the framework we use, and the way we interpret empirical evidence all embody value judgements and reflect our background.

Maintaining objectivity is easiest in positive economics, where one is simply trying to understand how the economy works. In positive economics, one is working with abstract models. Maintaining objectivity is harder in normative economics. It's easy to jump from the way you think the world should be to believing that society agrees with you, and hence not to be objective about whose normative values you are using.

It's hardest to maintain objectivity in the art of economics because it embodies all the problems of both positive and normative economics. It's about how to achieve certain normative ends given the way the economy works, but it also adds more problems. Because noneconomic forces affect policy, to practice the art of economics one must make judgements about how these noneconomic forces work. These judgements are likely to embody one's own value judgements. So one must be exceedingly careful to be as objective as possible in practicing the art of economics.

One of the best ways to find out about feasible economic policy options is to consider how other countries do something and compare their approach to ours. For example, health care is supplied quite differently in various countries. To decide how to improve health care policy in Canada, policy makers study how the United States and Britain do it, and make judgements about whether the approaches those countries take will fit existing Canadian institutions. Comparative institutional analysis is an important part of the art of economics.

Policy and the Invisible Forces

When you think about the policy options facing society, you'll quickly discover that the choice of policy options depends on much more than economic theory. One must take into account historical precedent plus social, cultural, and political forces. In an

---

[5]This three-part distinction was made back in 1896 by a famous economist, John Neville Keynes, father of John Maynard Keynes, the economist who developed macroeconomics. This distinction was instilled into modern economics by Milton Friedman, among others, in the 1950s. They, however, downplayed the art of economics, which J. N. Keynes had seen as central to understanding the economists' role in policy.

economics course, we don't have time to analyze these forces in as much depth as we'd like. That's one reason there are separate history, political science, sociology, and anthropology courses.

But we don't want to pretend that these forces don't play an important role in policy decisions. They do. That's why we use the invisible force terminology when we cover these other issues. It allows us to integrate the other forces without explaining in depth how they work. We'll use this terminology when discussing policy and applying economic insights to policy questions. In economics, we focus the analysis on the invisible hand, and much of economic theory is devoted to how the economy would operate if the invisible hand were the only force operating. But as soon as we apply theory to reality and policy, we must take into account the other invisible forces.

An example will make our point more concrete. Most economists agree that holding down or eliminating tariffs (taxes on imports) and quotas (numerical limitations on imports) makes good economic sense. They strongly advise governments to follow a policy of free trade. Do governments follow free trade policies? Almost invariably they do not. The invisible foot—politics—leads society in a different direction. If you're advising a policy maker, you need to point out that these other forces must be taken into account, and how other forces should (if they should) and can (if they can) be integrated with your recommendations.

Here's another example. Economic analysis devoid of institutional content would say that the world would be more efficient if we allowed Canadian citizenship to be bought and sold. But to advise policies that would legally allow a market for buying and selling Canadian citizenship would be to recommend a kind of efficiency that goes against historical, cultural, and social norms. The invisible handshake and the invisible foot would prevent the policies from being introduced, and any economist who proposed them would probably be banished to an ivory or other type of tower.

Students will find that *Canadian Business Economics* contains useful articles on topical economic issues.

CONCLUSION

There's tons more that could be said by way of introducing you to economics, but an introduction must remain an introduction. As it is, this chapter should have:

1. Introduced you to economic reasoning.
2. Surveyed what we're going to cover in this book.
3. Given you an idea of our writing style and approach.

We'll be spending long hours together over the coming term, and before entering into such a commitment it's best to know your partner. While we won't know you, by the end of this book you'll know us. Maybe you won't love us as our mothers do, but you'll know us.

This introduction was our opening line. We hope it also conveyed the importance and relevance that belong to economics. If it did, it has served its intended purpose. Economics is tough, but tough can be fun.

CHAPTER SUMMARY

- Learning economics consists of learning: economic reasoning, economic terminology, economic insights, economic institutions, and economic policy options.

- Economic reasoning structures all questions in a cost/benefit frame: If the benefits of doing something exceed the costs, do it. If the costs exceed the benefits, don't.

- Often economic decisions can be made by comparing marginal costs and marginal benefits.

- "There ain't no such thing as a free lunch" (TANSTAAFL) embodies the opportunity cost concept.

- The production possibility curve embodies the opportunity cost concept.

- Economic reality is controlled and directed by three invisible forces: the invisible hand, the invisible foot, and the invisible handshake.

- Economics can be divided into microeconomics and macroeconomics.

- Economics also can be subdivided into positive economics, normative economics, and the art of economics.

KEY TERMS

art of economics   *(24)*

comparative advantage   *(14)*

cultural norm   *(8)*

economic decision rule   *(10)*

economic forces   *(17)*

economic institution   *(7)*

economic policy   *(8)*

economic reasoning   *(6)*

economic theory   *(7)*

economics   *(7)*

economy   *(7)*

efficiency   *(17)*

inefficiency   *(15)*

input   *(11)*

invisible foot   *(18)*

invisible hand   *(18)*

invisible hand theory   *(21)*

invisible handshake   *(18)*

macroeconomics   *(22)*

marginal benefit   *(9)*

marginal cost   *(9)*

market force   *(18)*

microeconomics   *(21)*

normative economics   *(24)*

objective   *(24)*

opportunity cost   *(10)*

output   *(11)*

positive economics   *(24)*

principle of increasing marginal
   opportunity cost   *(15)*

production possibility curve   *(12)*

production possibility table   *(11)*

productive efficiency   *(15)*

rationing   *(17)*

subjective   *(24)*

QUESTIONS FOR THOUGHT AND REVIEW

The number after each question represents the estimated degree of critical thinking required. (1 = almost none; 10 = deep thought.)

1. Design a grade production possibility table and curve that embody the principle of increasing marginal opportunity cost.   *(4)*

2. What would the production possibility curve look like if there were decreasing marginal opportunity costs? Explain. Think of an example of decreasing marginal opportunity costs.   *(8)*

3. Show how a production possibility curve would shift if a society became more productive in its output of widgets but less productive in its output of wadgets.   *(5)*

4. List two microeconomic and two macroeconomic problems.   *(2)*

5. Does economic theory prove that the free market system is best? Why?   *(4)*

6. Calculate, using the best estimates you can make:
   a. Your opportunity cost of attending your next class.
   b. Your opportunity cost of taking this course.
   c. Your opportunity cost of attending yesterday's lecture in this course.   *(6)*

7. List two recent choices you made and explain why you made those choices in terms of marginal benefits and marginal costs.   *(5)*

8. Individuals have two kidneys but most of us need only one. People who have lost both kidneys through accident or disease must be hooked up to a dialysis machine, which cleanses waste from their bodies. Say a person who has two good kidneys offers to sell one of them to someone whose kidney function has been totally destroyed. The seller asks $30,000 for the kidney, and the person who has lost both kidneys accepts the offer. Who benefits from the deal? Who is hurt? Should a society allow such market transactions? Why?   *(9)*

9. Is a good economist always objective? Why?   *(4)*

10. When all people use economic reasoning, inefficiency is impossible, because if the cost of reducing that inefficiency were greater than the benefits, the efficiency would be eliminated. Thus, if people use economic reasoning, it's impossible to be on the interior of a production possibility curve. Is this statement true or false? Why?   *(8)*

PROBLEMS AND EXERCISES

1. A country has the following production possibility table:

Resources devoted to clothing	Output of clothing	Resources devoted to food	Output of food
100%	20	0	0
80	16	20	5
60	12	40	9
40	8	60	12
20	4	80	14
0	0	100	15

a. Draw the country's production possibility curve.

b. What's happening to marginal opportunity costs as output of food increases?

c. Say the country gets better at the production of food. What will happen to the production possibility curve?

d. Say the country gets equally better at producing food and producing clothing. What will happen to the production possibility curve?

2. Go to two stores: a supermarket and a convenience store.

a. Write down the cost of a litre of milk in each.

b. The prices are most likely different. Using the terminology used in this chapter, explain why that is the case and why anyone would buy milk in the store with the higher price.

c. Do the same exercise with shirts or dresses in Wal-Mart (or its equivalent) and Eaton's (or its equivalent).

3. Suppose we learn that lawns occupy more land in Canada than any single crop, such as corn. This means that Canada is operating inefficiently and hence is at a point inside the production possibility frontier. Right? If not, what does it mean?

4. Groucho Marx is reported to have said that "The secret of success is honest and fair dealing. If you can fake those, you've got it made." What would likely happen to society's production possibility curve if everyone could fake honesty? Why? (Hint: Remember that society's production possibility curve reflects more than just technical relationships.)

5. Adam Smith, who wrote *The Wealth of Nations* and is seen as the father of modern economics, also wrote *The Theory of Moral Sentiments* in which he argued that society would be better off if people weren't so selfish and were more considerate of others. How does this view fit with the discussion of economic reasoning presented in the chapter?

6. Trade agreements like the North American Free Trade Agreement (NAFTA) attempt to eliminate trade barriers and encourage economic growth. Using production possibility curves for Canada, Mexico, and the United States, show how you think the trade agreement will affect each economy. Is there any reason for you to expect that one country will benefit more than the others? How could you illustrate that on your figures?

7. In 1995, Newfoundland fishermen wanted to hunt seals for meat. Suppose you were hired by the fishermen to lobby the government. What would you argue? If you were hired by an animal rights group to oppose the hunt, what arguments would you use?

8. In 1995, Canada and the European Union had a fight about overfishing in the waters surrounding Canada. Canada argued that excessive fishing with new technologies would decrease the future catch. In terms of the production possibility curve for fish, what were they arguing? How would your answer differ if it were the production possibility curve for fish and beef?

Economics in Perspective

All too often, students study economics out of context. They're presented with sterile analysis and boring facts to memorize, and are never shown how economics fits into the large scheme of things. That's bad; it makes economics seem boring—but economics is not boring. Every so often throughout this book, sometimes in the appendixes and sometimes in boxes, we'll step back and put the analysis in perspective, giving you an idea from whence the analysis sprang and its historical context. In educational jargon, this is called *enrichment.*

We begin here with economics itself.

First, its history: In the 1500s there were few universities. Those that existed taught religion, Latin, Greek, philosophy, history, and mathematics. No economics. Then came the *Enlightenment* (about 1700) in which reasoning replaced God as the explanation of why things were the way they were. Pre-Enlightenment thinkers would answer the question, "Why am I poor?" with, "Because God wills it." Enlightenment scholars looked for a different explanation. "Because of the nature of land ownership" is one answer they found.

Such reasoned explanations required more knowledge of the way things were, and the amount of information expanded so rapidly that it had to be divided or categorized for an individual to have hope of knowing a subject. Soon philosophy was subdivided into science and philosophy. In the 1700s, the sciences were split into natural sciences and social sciences. The amount of knowledge kept increasing, and in the late 1800s and early 1900s social science itself split into subdivisions: economics, political science, history, geography, sociology, anthropology, and psychology. Many of the insights about how the economic system worked were codified in Adam Smith's *The Wealth of Nations,* written in 1776. Notice that this is before economics as a subdiscipline developed, and Adam Smith could also be classified as an anthropologist, a sociologist, a political scientist, and a social philosopher.

Throughout the 18th and 19th centuries, economists such as Adam Smith, Thomas Malthus, John Stuart Mill, David Ricardo, and Karl Marx were more than econo-mists; they were social philosophers who covered all aspects of social science. These writers were subsequently called *Classical economists.* Alfred Marshall continued in that classical tradition, and his book, *Principles of Economics,* published in the late 1800s, was written with the other social sciences much in evidence. But Marshall also changed the questions economists ask; he focused on those questions that could be asked in a graphical supply/demand framework. In doing so he began what is called *neoclassical economics.* Marshall's analysis forms the basis of much of what's currently taught in undergraduate microeconomics courses.

In the 1930s, as economists formalized Marshall's insights, many other social science insights were removed. By the 1950s, these social sciences were cemented into college curricula and organized into college departments. Economists learned economics; sociologists learned sociology.

For a while economics got lost in itself, and economists learned little else. Marshall's analysis was downplayed, and the work of more formal economists of the 1800s (such as Leon Walras, Francis Edgeworth, and Antoine Cournot) was seen as the basis of the science of economics. Economic analysis that focuses only on formal interrelationships is called *Walrasian economics.*

Thus, in the 1990s, there are two branches of neoclassical economics: Marshallian and Walrasian. The Marshallian branch sees economics as a way of thinking and integrates insights from other disciplines. The Walrasian branch sees economics as a logical science and excludes other social sciences. This book falls solidly in the Marshallian tradition. It sees economics as a way of thinking—as an engine of analysis used to understand real-world phenomena, not as a logical exercise in deductive reasoning. Our strong belief is that in undergraduate school one should learn Marshallian economics; in graduate school one can learn Walrasian economics.

Marshallian economics is both an art and a science. It sees institutions as well as political and social dimensions of reality as important, and it shows you how economics ties into those dimensions.

Graphish
The Language of Graphs

A picture is worth 1,000 words. Economists, being efficient, like to present ideas in graphs, which are a type of picture. But a graph is worth 1,000 words only if the person looking at the graph knows the graphical language—Graphish, we'll call it. (It's a bit like English.) Graphish is usually written on graph paper. If the person doesn't know *Graphish*, the picture isn't worth any words and Graphish can be babble.

We have enormous sympathy for students who don't understand Graphish. A number of our students get thrown for a loop by graphs. They understand the idea, but Graphish confuses them. This appendix is for them, and for those of you like them. It's a primer in Graphish.

Two Ways to Use Graphs

In this book we use graphs in two ways:

1. To present an economic model or theory visually; to show how two variables interrelate.
2. To present real-world data visually. To do this, we use primarily bar charts, line charts, and pie charts.

Actually, these two ways of using graphs are related. They are both ways of presenting visually the *relationship* between two things.

Graphs are built around a number line, or axis, like the one in Exhibit B1 (a). The numbers are generally placed in order, equal distances from one another. That number line allows us to represent a number at an appropriate point on the line. For example, point *A* represents the number 4.

The number line in Exhibit B1 (a) is drawn horizontally, but it doesn't have to be; it can also be drawn vertically, as in Exhibit B1 (b).

How we divide our axes, or number lines, into intervals, is up to us. In Exhibit B1 (a), we called each interval 1; in Exhibit B1 (b), we called each interval 10. Point *A* appears after 4 intervals of 1 (starting at 0 and reading from left to right), so it represents 4. In Exhibit B1 (b), where each interval represents 10, to represent 5, we place point *B* halfway in the interval between 0 and 10.

So far, so good. Graphish developed when a vertical and a horizontal number line were combined, as in Exhibit B1 (c). When the number lines are put together they're called *axes*. (Each line is an axis. *Axes* is the plural of *axis*.) We now have a two-dimensional space in which *one point can represent two numbers*. (This two-dimensional space is called a *coordinate space*.) For example, point *A* in Exhibit B1 (c) represents the numbers (4, 5)—4 on the horizontal number line and 5 on

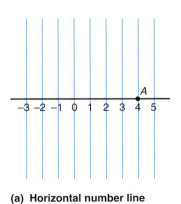

(a) Horizontal number line

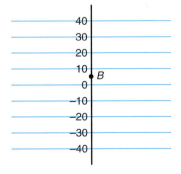

(b) Vertical number line

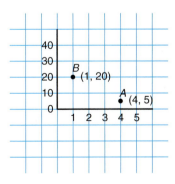

(c) Coordinate system

EXHIBIT B1   **Horizontal and Vertical Number Lines and a Coordinate System**

the vertical number line. Point *B* represents the numbers (1, 20). (By convention, the horizontal numbers are written first.)

Being able to represent two numbers with one point is neat because it allows the relationships between two numbers to be presented visually instead of having to be expressed verbally, which is often cumbersome. For example, say the cost of producing 6 units of something is $4 per unit and the cost of producing 10 units is $3 per unit. By putting both these points on a graph, we can visually see that producing 10 costs less per unit than does producing 6.

Another way to use graphs to present real-world data visually is to use the horizontal line to represent time. Say that we let each horizontal interval equal a year, and each vertical interval equal $100 in income. By graphing your income each year, you can obtain a visual representation of how your income has changed over time.

Graphs can be used to show any relationship between two variables. (*Variables* are what economists call the units that are measured on the horizontal and vertical axes.) As long as you remember that graphs are simply a way of presenting a relationship visually, you can keep graphs in perspective.

Using Graphs in Economic Modelling We use graphs throughout the book as we present economic models, or simplifications of reality. A few terms are often used in describing these graphs, and we'll now go over them. Consider Exhibit B2 (a), which lists the number of pens bought per day (column 2) at various prices (column 1).

We can present the table's information in a graph by combining the pairs of numbers in the two columns of the table and representing, or plotting, them on two axes. We do that in Exhibit B2 (b).

By convention, when graphing a relationship between price and quantity, economists place price on the vertical axis and quantity on the horizontal axis.

EXHIBIT B2   A Table and Graphs Showing the Relationships between Price and Quantity

Price of pens (in dollars)	Quantity of pens bought per day	Row
3.00	4	A
2.50	5	B
2.00	6	C
1.50	7	D
1.00	8	E

(a) Price quantity table

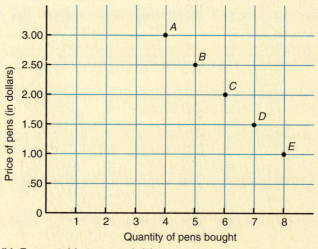

(b) From a table to a graph (1)

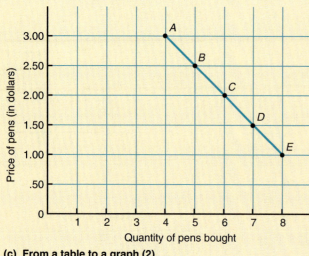

(c) From a table to a graph (2)

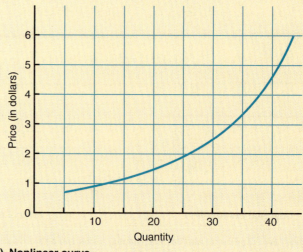

(d) Nonlinear curve

We can now connect the points, producing a line like the one in Exhibit B2 (c). With this line, we interpolate the numbers between the points. That is, we make the reasonable assumption (which makes for a nice visual presentation) that the relationship between the variables is the same *between* the points as it is at the points. This assumption is called the *interpolation assumption.* It allows us to think of a line as a collection of points and therefore to connect the points into a line.

Even though the line in Exhibit B2 (c) is straight, economists call any such line drawn on a graph a *curve.* Because it's straight, the curve in Exhibit B2 (c) is called a *linear curve.* Notice that this curve starts high on the left-hand side and goes down to the right. Economists say any curve that looks like that is downward-sloping. They also say that a *downward-sloping* curve represents an *inverse* relationship between the two variables: When one goes up, the other goes down. In this example, the line demonstrates an inverse relationship between price and quantity—that is, when the price of pens goes up, the quantity bought goes down.

Exhibit B2 (d) presents a curve that really is curved. It starts low on the left-hand side and goes up to the right. Such curves are called *nonlinear curves.* Economists say any curve that goes up to the right is upward-sloping. An *upward-sloping* curve represents a direct relationship between the two variables (what's measured on the horizontal and vertical lines). In a direct relationship, when one variable goes up, the other goes up too. *Downward-sloping* and *upward-sloping* are terms you need to memorize if you want to read, write, and speak Graphish, keeping graphically in your mind the image of the relationships they represent.

Slope   One can, of course, be far more explicit about how much the curve is sloping upward or downward. To be more explicit, mathematicians define the term slope as the change in the value on the vertical axis divided by the change in the value on the horizontal axis. Sometimes it's presented as "rise over run":

$$\text{Slope} = \frac{\text{Rise}}{\text{Run}} = \frac{\text{Change in value on vertical axis}}{\text{Change in value on horizontal axis}}$$

Slopes of Linear Curves   In Exhibit B3, we present five linear curves and measure their slopes. Let's go through an example to show how we can measure slope. To do so, we must pick two points. Let's use points *A* (6, 8) and *B* (7, 4) on curve *a.* Looking at these points, we see that as we move from 6 to 7 on the horizontal axis, we move from 8 to 4 on the vertical axis. So when the number on the vertical axis falls by 4, the number on the horizontal axis increases by 1. That means the slope is −4 divided by 1, or −4.

Notice that the inverse relationships represented by the two downward-sloping curves, *a* and *b,* have negative slopes, and that the direct relationships represented by the

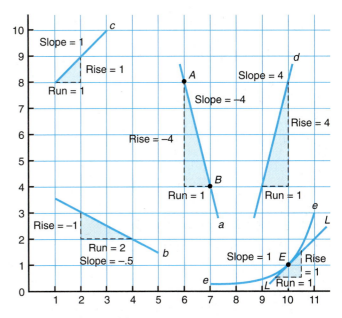

EXHIBIT B3   Slopes of Curves

two upward-sloping curves, *c* and *d,* have positive slopes. Notice also that the flatter the curve, the smaller the numerical value of the slope; and the more vertical, or steeper, the curve, the larger the numerical value of the slope. There are two extreme cases:

1. When the curve is horizontal (flat), the slope is zero.
2. When the curve is vertical (straight up and down), the slope is infinite (larger than large).

Knowing the term *slope* and how it's measured lets us describe verbally the pictures we see visually. For example, if we say a curve has a slope of zero, you should picture in your mind a flat line; if we say "a curve with a slope of minus one," you should picture a falling line that makes a 45-degree angle with the horizontal and vertical axes. (It's the hypotenuse of an equilateral triangle with the axes as the other two sides.)

Slopes of Nonlinear Curves   The preceding examples were of linear (straight) curves. With nonlinear curves—the ones that really do curve—the slope of the curve is constantly changing. As a result, we must talk about the slope of the curve at a particular point, rather than the slope of the whole curve. How can a point have a slope? Well, it can't really, but it can almost, and if that's good enough for mathematicians, it's good enough for us.

Defining the slope of a nonlinear curve is a bit more difficult. The slope at a given point on a nonlinear curve is determined by the slope of a linear (or straight) line that's tangent to that curve. (A line that's tangent to a curve is a line that just touches the curve, and touches it only at one point in the immediate vicinity of the given point.) In Exhibit B3, the line *LL* is tangent to the curve *ee* **at** point *E.* The slope of that line, and hence the slope

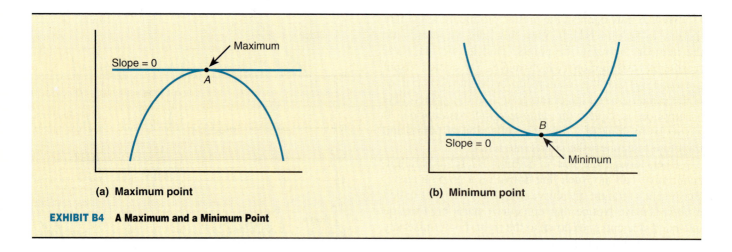

(a) Maximum point   (b) Minimum point

EXHIBIT B4   A Maximum and a Minimum Point

of the curve at the one point where the line touches the curve, is +1.

Maximum and Minimum Points Two points on a nonlinear curve deserve special mention. These points are the ones for which the slope of the curve is zero. We demonstrate those in Exhibit B4 (a) and (b). (At point *A*, we're at the top of the curve so it's at a maximum point; at point *B*, we're at the bottom of the curve so it's at a minimum point.) These maximum and minimum points are often referred to by economists, and it's important to realize that the value of the slope of the curve at each of these points is zero.

There are, of course, many other types of curves, and much more can be said about the curves we've talked about. We won't do so because, for purposes of this course, we won't need to get into those refinements.

We've presented as much Graphish as you need to know for this book.

Presenting Real-World Data in Graphs
The previous discussion treated the Graphish terms that economists use in presenting models which focus on hypothetical relationships. Economists also use graphs in presenting actual economic data. Say, for example, that you want to show how exports have changed over time. Then you would place years on the horizontal axis (by convention) and exports on the vertical axis, as in Exhibit B5 (a) and (b). Having done so, you can either connect the data, as in (a), or fill in the areas under the points for that year, as in (b). The first is called a *line graph;* the second is called a *bar graph.*

Another type of graph is a *pie chart,* such as the one presented in Exhibit B5 (c). A pie chart is useful in visu-

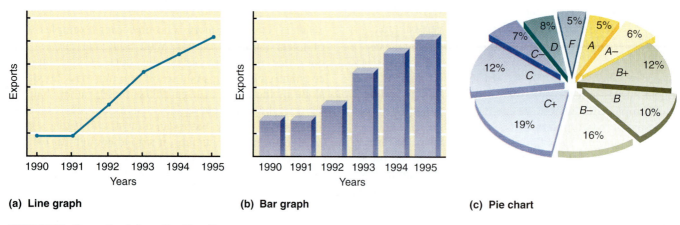

(a) Line graph   (b) Bar graph   (c) Pie chart

EXHIBIT B5   Presenting Information Visually

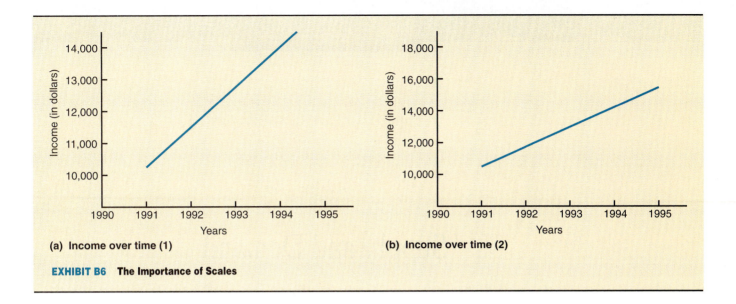

(a) **Income over time (1)**

(b) **Income over time (2)**

EXHIBIT B6   The Importance of Scales

ally presenting how a total amount is divided. The uncut pie is the total amount, and the pie pieces reflect the percentage of the whole pie that the various components make up. Exhibit B5 (c) shows the division of grades on a test we gave. Notice that 5 percent of the students got As.

There are other types of graphs, but they're all variations on line and bar graphs and pie charts. Once you understand these three basic types of graphs, you shouldn't have any trouble understanding the other types.

Interpreting Graphs about the Real World   Understanding Graphish is important, because if you don't, you can easily misinterpret the meanings of graphs. For example, consider the two graphs in Exhibit B6 (a) and (b). Which graph demonstrates the larger rise in income? If you said (a), you're wrong. The intervals in the vertical axes differ, and if you look carefully you'll see that the curves in both graphs represent the same combination of points. So when considering graphs, always make sure you understand the markings on the axes. Only then can you interpret the graph.

Let's now review what we've covered.

- A graph is a picture of points on a coordinate system in which the points denote relationships between numbers.
- A downward-sloping line represents an inverse relationship or a negative slope.
- An upward-sloping line represents a direct relationship or a positive slope.
- Slope is measured by rise over run, or a change of y (the number measured on the vertical axis) over a change in x (the number measured on the horizontal axis).
- The slope of a point on a nonlinear curve is measured by the rise over run of a line tangent to that point.
- At the maximum and minimum points of a nonlinear curve, the value of the slope is zero.
- In reading graphs, one must be careful to understand what's being measured on the vertical and horizontal axes.

2

Supply and Demand

Teach a parrot the terms supply and demand and you've got an economist.

~Thomas Carlyle

After reading this chapter, you should be able to:

1 State the law of demand.

2 Explain the importance of opportunity cost and substitution to the laws of supply and demand.

3 Draw a demand curve from a demand table.

4 Distinguish a shift in demand from a movement along the demand curve.

5 State the law of supply.

6 Draw a supply curve from a supply table.

7 Distinguish a shift in supply from a movement along the supply curve.

8 State the three dynamic laws of supply and demand.

9 Demonstrate the effect of a price ceiling and a price floor on a market.

Supply and demand. Supply and demand. Roll the phrase around your mouth, savour it like a good wine. *Supply* and *demand* are the most-used words in economics. And for good reason. They provide a good off-the-cuff answer for any economic question. Try it.

Why are bacon and oranges so expensive this winter? *Supply and demand.*

Why are interest rates falling? *Supply and demand.*

Why can't I find decent wool socks any more? *Supply and demand.*

The importance of the interplay of supply and demand makes it only natural that, early in any economics course, you must learn about supply and demand. Let's start with demand.

DEMAND

Poets and songwriters use literary license. Take the classic song by the Rolling Stones entitled "You Can't Always Get What You Want." Whether the statement is or isn't true depends on how you define *want.* If you define *want* as "being sufficiently desirous of something so that you do what's necessary to buy the good," then in a market in which prices are flexible, you *can* always get what you want. The reason: what you want depends on what the price is. If, however, you define *want* as simply "being desirous of something," then there are many unfulfilled "wants," such as our wanting expensive sports cars. We want to own Maseratis. But, we must admit, we're not willing to do what's necessary to own one. If we really wanted to own one, we'd mortgage everything we own, increase our income by doubling the number of hours we work, not buy anything else, and get that car. But we don't do any of those things, so there's a question of whether we really want the car. Sure, we'd want one if it cost $10,000, but from our actions it's clear that, at $290,000, we don't really want it. If *want* is defined as "being sufficiently desirous of something that you will do what's necessary to buy the good," you can always get what you want, because your willingness to pay the going price for something is the only way to tell whether you really want it. What you want at a low price differs from what you want at a high price. The quantity you demand varies inversely—in the opposite direction—with the price.

Prices are the tool by which the invisible hand—the market—coordinates individuals' desires and limits how much people are willing to buy—how much they really want. When goods are scarce, the market reduces people's desires for those scarce goods; as their prices go up, people buy fewer of them. As goods become abundant, their prices go down, and people want more of them. The invisible hand sees to it that what people want (do what's necessary to get) matches what's available. In doing so, the invisible hand coordinates individuals' wants. While you can't always get what you want at a low price, you can get it at some price—maybe a super-high price. It isn't surprising that the Stones chose the other definition of *want;* it's unlikely that their song would have become a hit had they put in the appropriate qualifier. You can't dance to "You Can't Always Get What You Want at the Price You Want."

The Law of Demand

What makes the qualifier appropriate is the **law of demand:**

> *More of a good will be demanded the lower its price, other things constant.*

Or alternatively:

> *Less of a good will be demanded the higher its price, other things constant.*

1 The law of demand states that the quantity of a good demanded is inversely related to the good's price. When price goes up, quantity demanded goes down.

This law is fundamental to the invisible hand's ability to coordinate individuals' desires: as prices change, people change how much of a particular good they're willing to buy.

To be clear about the meaning of the law of demand, economists differentiate the concepts *demand* and *quantity demanded.* **Demand** refers to a schedule of quantities of a good that will be bought per unit of time at various prices. **Quantity demanded** refers to a specific amount that will be demanded per unit of time at a specific price.

In graphical terms, *demand* refers to the entire **demand curve** which tells how much of a good will be bought at various prices. *Quantity demanded* refers to a point

Demand   Schedule of quantities of a good that will be bought per unit of time at various prices.

Quantity demanded   A specific amount that will be demanded per unit of time at a specific price. Refers to a point on a demand curve.

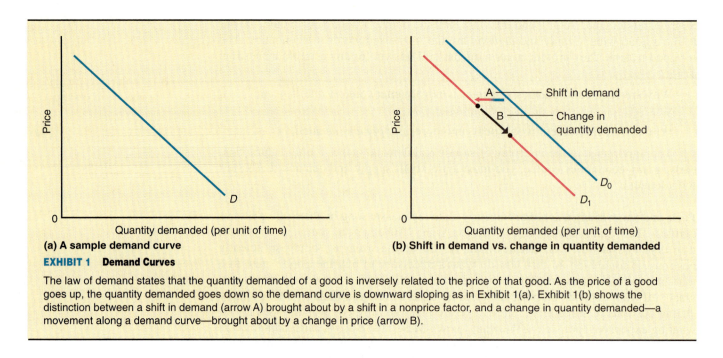

(a) A sample demand curve

(b) Shift in demand vs. change in quantity demanded

EXHIBIT 1   Demand Curves

The law of demand states that the quantity demanded of a good is inversely related to the price of that good. As the price of a good goes up, the quantity demanded goes down so the demand curve is downward sloping as in Exhibit 1(a). Exhibit 1(b) shows the distinction between a shift in demand (arrow A) brought about by a shift in a nonprice factor, and a change in quantity demanded—a movement along a demand curve—brought about by a change in price (arrow B).

Demand curve   Curve that tells how much of a good will be bought at various prices.

on a demand curve, so when economists talk about movements along a demand curve, they mean changes in quantity demanded.

Exhibit 1 (a) shows a demand curve. In graphical terms, the law of demand states that the quantity demanded of a good is inversely related to that good's price, other things constant. As the price goes up, the quantity demanded goes down. As you can see in Exhibit 1 (a), price and quantity are inversely related, so the demand curve slopes downward to the right. Exhibit 1 (b) distinguishes between a shift in demand— a shift of the entire demand curve as shown by Arrow A—and a change in quantity demanded—a movement along a demand curve as shown by Arrow B.

Just think of something you'd really like but can't afford. If the price is cut in half, you—and other consumers—become more likely to buy it. Quantity demanded goes up as price goes down.

Just to be sure you've got it, let's consider a real-world example: scalpers and the demand for hockey tickets. Standing outside a sold-out game between Montreal and Pittsburgh in Montreal, we saw tickets that normally cost $15 sell for $75. There were few takers—that is, there was little demand at that price. We figured that as soon as the game started, prices would drop and the quantity demanded (at a lower price) would rise, but this didn't happen until well after the start of the game. As the price dropped to $60, then $50, quantity demanded increased; when the price dropped to $35, the quantity demanded soared. That's the law of demand in action.

Other Things Constant   To understand the law of demand, you must understand the terminology used to discuss that law and the assumptions upon which that law is based. Let's first consider the phrase, "Other things constant."

Other things constant   An assumption that places a limitation on the implications that can be drawn from any supply/demand analysis. The elements of the particular analysis are considered under the assumption that all other elements that could affect the analysis remain constant (whether they actually remain constant or not).

Notice that in stating the law of demand, we put in a qualification: **other things constant.**[1] That's three extra words, and unless they were important we wouldn't have put them in. But what does "other things constant" mean? Say that over a period of two years, the price of cars rises as the number of cars sold likewise rises. That seems to violate the law of demand, since the number of cars sold should have fallen in response to the rise in price. Looking at the data more closely, however, we see that a third factor has also changed: individuals' income has increased overall. As income increases, people buy more cars, increasing the demand for cars.

---

[1]*Other things constant* is a translation of the Latin phrase *ceteris paribus.* Sometimes economists just use *ceteris paribus* without translating it.

The increase in price works as the law of demand states—it decreases the number of cars bought. But in this case, income doesn't remain constant; it increases. That rise in income increases the demand for cars. That increase in demand outweighs the decrease in quantity demanded that results from a rise in price, so ultimately more cars are sold. If you want to study the effect of price alone—which is what the law of demand refers to—you must make adjustments to hold income constant when you make your study. That's why the qualifying phrase *other things constant* is an important part of the law of demand.

This qualifying phrase, "other things constant," places a limitation on the implications that can be drawn from any analysis based on the law of demand. Alfred Marshall, one of the originators of this law, emphasized these limitations, arguing that it is as much of a mistake to apply supply/demand analysis to areas where these assumptions do not hold as it is not to apply it to those areas where it does apply. To emphasize this point he argued that the law of demand is directly applicable to *partial equilibrium* issues—issues in which other things can reasonably be assumed to remain constant—and that supply/demand analysis should be called **partial equilibrium analysis** (we'll explain just what we mean by *equilibrium* in a moment). He admonished his students to remember that partial equilibrium analysis is incomplete because it assumes other things equal. That it is incomplete does not mean that it cannot be used for other issues, but when applied to issues where other things do not remain constant, it must be used with an educated common sense and one must keep in the back of one's mind what does not remain constant.

Partial equilibrium analysis
Analysis of a part of a whole; it initially assumes all other things remain equal.

How much somebody wants to buy a good depends on many other things besides its price. These include individuals' tastes, prices of other goods, and even the weather. Those other factors must remain constant if you're to make a valid study of the effect of an increase in the price of a good on the quantity demanded of it. In practice it's impossible to keep all other things constant, so you have to be careful when you say that when price goes up, quantity demanded goes down. It's likely to go down, but it's always possible that something besides price has changed.

Economists recognize that many things besides price affect demand. They call them **shift factors of demand.** A shift factor of demand is something, other than the good's price, that affects how much of the good is demanded. Important shift factors of demand include:

Shift factors of demand
Something, other than the good's price, that affects how much of the good is demanded.

1. Society's income.
2. The prices of other goods.
3. Tastes.
4. Expectations.

These aren't the only shift factors. In fact anything—except the good's price changes—that affects demand (and many things do) is a shift factor. This includes changes in the income of our trading partners, changes in exchange rates, and changes in population, just to name a few. While economists agree these shift factors are important, they believe that no shift factor influences how much is demanded as consistently as the price of the specific item does. That's what makes economists focus first on price as they try to understand the world. That's why economists make the law of demand central to their analysis.

Relative Price   A second qualification is that the law of demand refers to a good's **relative price.** The relative price of a good is the price of that good compared to the price of another good or combination of goods. For example, if the price of a compact disc is $11 and the price of an apple is 50 cents, the relative price of CDs compared to the price of apples is $11/ $0.50 = 22. In other words, you can buy 22 apples with one CD or one CD with 22 apples.

Relative price   The price of a good relative to the price level.

The actual price you pay for the goods you buy is called *the money price.* You don't say that a CD has a price of 22 apples; you say that a CD has a price of $11. But don't let that fool you. While the $11 may not look like a relative price, it is. It is the price of the CD compared to a composite price for all other goods. That composite price for all other goods is the price of money. What's the price of money? It's simply how much you'll pay for money. Most people will pay $1 for $1, so the price of $1 is $1. The money price of $11 means that you can trade one CD for 11 "loonies."

Money is not desired for its own sake. You want dollar coins only because you can trade them for something else. You have in the back of your mind a good sense of what else you could do with that $11—what the opportunity cost of spending it on a CD is. You could buy, say, three Big Macs, a double order of fries, and a vanilla shake for $11. The opportunity cost of buying the CD is that big tray of fast food. Thus the money price of an item represents the price of that item relative to the prices of all other goods.

As long as your sense of what that opportunity cost is doesn't change, money price is a good representation of relative price. Over short periods the opportunity cost of $1 doesn't change. Over longer periods, though, because of inflation, money prices are not a good representation of relative prices. Say, for instance, that money prices (including your wage) on average go up 10 percent. (When this happens, economists say the price level has gone up by 10 percent.) Also say the money price of a CD goes up by 2 percent. Has the relative price of CDs gone up or down? Since the *average* money price has gone up 10 percent and the money price of a CD has risen by 2 percent, the relative price of a CD has fallen by 8 percent. The law of demand would say that the quantity of CDs demanded would increase because the relative price has gone down, even though the money price has gone up.

The use of money prices makes life easier for members of society, but it makes life harder for economics students, who must remember that, even though they see the money price of an item as an absolute number, it is actually a relative price.

2   The law of demand is based upon individuals' ability to substitute.

We emphasize that the law of demand refers to relative price because the explanation for it involves demanders' ability to *substitute* some other good for that good. If a good's relative price goes up, some people will substitute some other good for it because that substitute's relative price goes down. For example, if the money price of compact discs rises and the money price of music tapes doesn't rise, individuals will substitute music tapes for CDs.

The Demand Table

As we emphasized in Chapter 1, introductory economics depends heavily on graphs and graphical analysis—translating ideas into graphs and back again into words. So let's graph the demand curve.

Exhibit 2 (a) describes Alice's demand for renting videocassettes. In this example, the demand is for the temporary use of a videocassette. For example, at a price of $2, Alice will buy the use of six cassettes per week.

There are a number of points about the relationship between the number of videos Alice rents and the price of renting them that are worth mentioning. First, the relationship follows the law of demand: as the rental price rises, quantity demanded decreases. Second, quantity demanded has a specific *time dimension* to it. In this example it is the number of cassette rentals per week that is referred to, not the number of cassettes rented per day, hour, or year. Without the time dimension, the table wouldn't provide us with any useful information. Nine cassette rentals per year is quite a different concept from nine cassette rentals per week. Third, the cassette rentals that Alice buys are interchangeable—the ninth cassette rental doesn't significantly differ from the first, third, or any other cassette rental.

The concept of interchangeable goods causes economists significant problems in discussing real-world demand schedules because the quality of goods often differs in the real world. A pink Volkswagen is quite different from a gray Aston Martin, yet they're both cars. Luckily, in textbooks interchangeable goods cause few problems because we can pick and choose among examples. Textbook authors simply avoid examples that raise significant quality problems. However, it's only fair to point out that in the real world economists spend a great deal of time adjusting their analyses for differences in quality among goods.

EXHIBIT 2   From a Demand Table to a Demand Curve

The demand table in (a) is translated into a demand curve in (b). Each point on the table corresponds to a point on the curve. For example, point A on the graph represents row A in the table: Alice demands 9 videocassette rentals at a price of 50 cents. A demand curve is constructed by plotting all points from the demand table and connecting the points by a line.

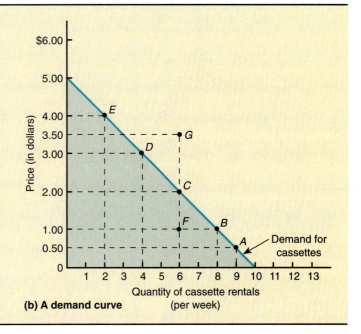

	Price (in dollars)	Cassette rentals demanded per week
A	0.50	9
B	1.00	8
C	2.00	6
D	3.00	4
E	4.00	2

(a) A demand table

(b) A demand curve

Two final points are already familiar to you. They are, fourth, the price the table refers to is a relative price even though it is expressed as a money price, and fifth, the schedule assumes that everything else is held constant.

Exhibit 2 (b) translates Exhibit 2 (a)'s information into a graph. Point A (quantity = 9, price = $.50) is graphed first at the (9, $.50) coordinates. Next we plot points B, C, D, and E in the same manner and connect the resulting dots with a solid line. The result is the demand curve, which graphically conveys the same information that's in the demand table. Notice that the demand curve is downward sloping (from left to right), indicating that the law of demand holds in the example. When a curve slopes downward to the right, we say that there is an inverse relationship between the price and the quantity demanded.

The demand curve represents the *maximum price* that an individual will pay for various quantities of a good; the individual will happily pay less. For example, say someone offers Alice six cassette rentals at a price of $1 each (point F of Exhibit 2 (b)). Will she accept? Sure; she'll pay any price within the shaded area to the left of the demand curve. But if someone offers her six rentals at $3.50 each (point G), she won't accept. At a rental price of $3.50, she's willing to buy only three cassette rentals.

Normally, economists talk about market demand curves rather than individual demand curves. A **market demand curve** is the horizontal sum of all individual demand curves. Market demand curves are what most firms are interested in. Firms don't care whether individual A or individual B buys their good; they care that *someone* buys their good.

It's a good graphical exercise to add the individual demand curves together to create a market demand curve. We do that in Exhibit 3. In it we assume that the market consists of three buyers, Alice, Pierre, and Jonas, whose demand tables are given in Exhibit 3 (a). Alice and Pierre have demand tables similar to the demand tables discussed previously. At a price of $3, Alice rents four cassettes; at a price of $2, she rents six. Jonas is an all-or-nothing individual. He rents one cassette as long as the price is equal to or below $1; otherwise he rents nothing. If you plot Jonas's demand curve, it's a vertical line. However, the law of demand still holds: as price increases, quantity demanded decreases.

From a Demand Table to a Demand Curve

Demand table

Q	P
2	5
4	3

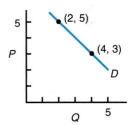

Individual and Market Demand Curves

Market demand curve
The horizontal sum of all individual demand curves.

EXHIBIT 3   From Individual Demands to a Market Demand Curve

The table (**a**) shows the demand schedules for Alice, Pierre, and Jonas. Together they make up the market for videocassette rentals. Their total quantity demanded (market demand) for videocassette rentals at each price is given in column 5. As you can see in (**b**), Alice's, Pierre's, and Jonas' demand curves can be added together to get the total market demand curve. For example, at a price of $2, Jonas demands 0, Pierre demands 3, and Alice demands 6, for a market demand of 9 (point *D*).

	(1) Price (in dollars)	(2) Alice	(3) Pierre	(4) Jonas	(5) Market demand
A	0.50	9	6	1	16
B	1.00	8	5	1	14
C	1.50	7	4	0	11
D	2.00	6	3	0	9
E	2.50	5	2	0	7
F	3.00	4	1	0	5
G	3.50	3	0	0	3
H	4.00	2	0	0	2

(a) A demand table

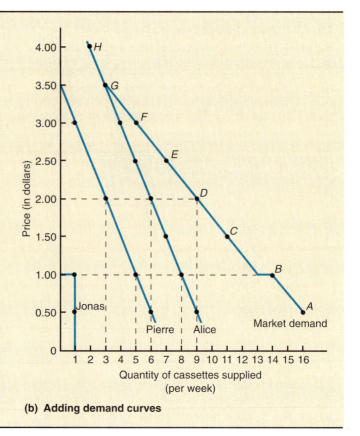

(b) Adding demand curves

---

3 To derive a demand curve from a demand table, you plot each point on the demand table on a graph and connect the points. For example:

The quantity demanded by each demander is listed in columns 2, 3, and 4 of Exhibit 3 (a). Column 5 gives total market demand; each entry is the sum of the entries in columns 2, 3, and 4. For example, at a price of $3 (row *F*), Alice demands four cassette rentals, Pierre demands one, and Jonas demands zero, for a total market demand of five cassette rentals.

Exhibit 3 (b) shows three demand curves: one each for Alice, Pierre, and Jonas. The market, or total, demand curve is the horizontal sum of the individual demand curves. To see that this is the case, notice that if we take the quantity demanded at $1 by Alice (8), Pierre (5), and Jonas (1) (row *B*, columns 2, 3, and 4), they sum to 14, which is point *B* (14, $1) on the market demand curve. We can do that for each level of price. Alternatively, we can simply add the individual quantities demanded prior to graphing (which we do in column 5 of Exhibit 3 (a)) and graph that total in relation to price. Not surprisingly, we get the same total market demand curve.

In practice, of course, firms don't measure individual demand curves, so they don't sum them up in this fashion. Instead, they estimate total demand. Still, summing up individual demand curves is a useful exercise because it shows you how the market demand curve is made up of the sum (the horizontal sum, graphically speaking) of the individual demand curves, and it gives you a good sense of where market demand curves come from. It also shows you that, even if individuals don't respond to small changes in price, the market demand curve can still be smooth and downward sloping. That's because for the market, the law of demand is based on two phenomena:

1. At lower prices, existing demanders buy more.
2. At lower prices, new demanders (some all-or-nothing demanders like Jonas) enter the market.

Shifts in Demand versus Movement along a Given Demand Curve

As we have emphasized already, the demand curves we draw assume other things are held constant. That is, we assume the price of the good, not shift factors, is causing the demand curve to be downward sloping. To distinguish between the effects of price and

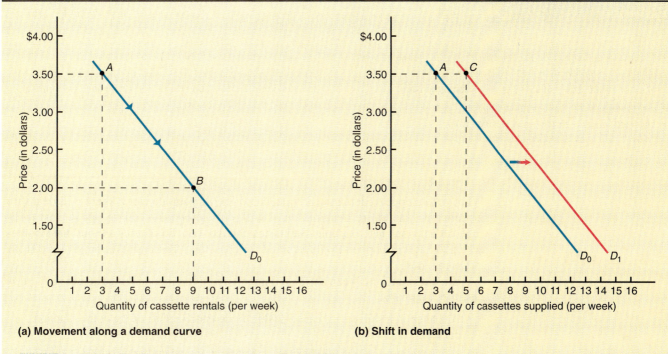

(a) Movement along a demand curve

(b) Shift in demand

EXHIBIT 4   Shifts in Demand versus Movement along a Demand Curve

A change in price causes a movement along the demand curve. For example, in (**a**), if the price of videocassette rentals is $3.50, 3 rentals will be demanded (point A). If the price falls to $2, the quantity of rentals demanded will be 9 (point B). Thus, the fall in price brings about a movement along the demand curve, from point A to point B.

A shift factor change causes a shift in demand. For example, in (**b**), at the price of $3.50, 3 cassette rentals will be demanded (point A), but if income rises while price remains the same, people are willing to buy 5 cassette rentals for $3.50 (point C) instead of only 3. An increase in income causes the entire demand curve to shift outward from D_0 to D_1.

the effects of shift factors on how much of a good is demanded, we need some terminology.

As we stated above, if how much is demanded is affected by price, we call that effect a change in the quantity demanded. Since a demand curve tells us how much is demanded at different prices, a change in the quantity demanded is represented graphically by a **movement along the demand curve.** If how much is demanded is affected by a shift factor, there is said to be a **shift in demand.** Since a change in a shift factor changes how much would be bought at each different price, a change in demand means that the entire demand curve shifts, to either the right or the left. Thus, a change in a shift factor causes a *shift* in demand; a change in price causes a *movement* along the demand curve. Differentiating between a shift in demand and movement along the demand curve is important but difficult, so it's useful to differentiate the two types of change graphically. We do so for this example in Exhibit 4.

Exhibit 4 (a) shows the effect of a change in the price of cassettes from $3.50 to $2. Point A (quantity demanded 3, price $3.50) represents the starting point. Now the price falls to $2 and the quantity demanded rises from 3 to 9, so we move along the demand curve to point B. Notice the demand curve (D_0) has already been drawn to demonstrate the effect that price has on quantity.

Now let's say that the price of $3.50 doesn't change but income rises and, as it does, quantity demanded rises to 5. Thus, at a price of $3.50, 5 cassette rentals are demanded rather than only 3. That point is represented by point C in Exhibit 4 (b). But if income causes a rise in quantity demanded at a price of $3.50, it will also likely cause an increase in the quantity demanded at all other prices. The demand curve will not remain where it was, but will shift to D_1 to the right of D_0. Because of the change in income, the entire demand curve has shifted. Thus, we say a change in this shift factor has caused a shift in demand.

Movement along a demand curve Method of representing a change in the quantity demanded. Graphically, a change in quantity demanded will cause a movement along the demand curve.

Shift in demand   If how much of a good is demanded is affected by a shift factor, there is said to be a shift in demand. Graphically, a shift in demand will cause the entire demand curve to shift.

4   Changes in quantity demanded are shown by movements along a demand curve. Shifts in demand are shown by a shift of the entire demand curve.

To see if you understand, say the local theatre decides to let everyone in for free. What will happen to demand for videocassettes? If your answer is there will be a shift in demand—the entire demand curve will shift leftward—you've got it. Just to be sure, let's try one last example. Say tastes change: couch potatoes are out, hard bodies are in. What will happen to the demand for cassettes? The entire demand curve shifts left some more.

The difference between shifts in demand and movements along the demand curve deserves emphasis:

- A change in a shift factor causes a shift in demand (a shift of the entire demand curve).
- A change in price of a good causes a change in the quantity demanded (a movement along an existing demand curve).

SUPPLY

Factors of production   Resources, or inputs, necessary to produce goods.

In one sense, supply is the mirror image of demand. Individuals control the inputs, or resources, necessary to produce goods. Such resources are often called **factors of production.** Individuals' supply of these factors to the market mirrors other individuals' demand for those factors. For example, say you decide you want to rest rather than weed your garden. You hire someone to do the weeding; you demand labour. Someone else decides she would prefer more income instead of more rest; she supplies labour to you. You trade money for labour; she trades labour for money. Here supply is the mirror image of demand.

For a large number of goods, however, the supply process is more complicated than demand. As Exhibit 5 shows, for a large number of goods, there's an intermediate step in supply. Individuals supply factors of production to firms. **Firms** are organizations of individuals that transform factors of production into consumable goods.

Firm   Economic institution that transforms factors of production into consumer goods.

Let's consider a simple example. Say you're a taco technician. You supply your labour to the factor market. The taco company demands your labour (hires you). The taco company combines your labour with other inputs like meat, cheese, beans, and tables, and produces many tacos (production) which it supplies to customers in the goods market. For produced goods, supply depends not only on individuals' decisions to supply factors of production; it also depends on firms' ability to produce—to transform those factors of production into consumable goods.

The supply process of produced goods can be much more complicated. Often there are many layers of firms—production firms, wholesale firms, distribution firms, and retailing firms—each of which passes on in-process goods to the next-layer firm. Real-world production and supply of produced goods is a multistage process.

The supply of nonproduced goods is more direct. Individuals supply their labour in the form of services directly to the goods market. For example, an independent contractor may repair your washing machine. That contractor supplies his labour directly to you.

Thus, the analysis of the supply of produced goods has two parts: an analysis of the supply of factors of production to households and to firms, and an analysis of why firms transform those factors of production into consumable goods and services.

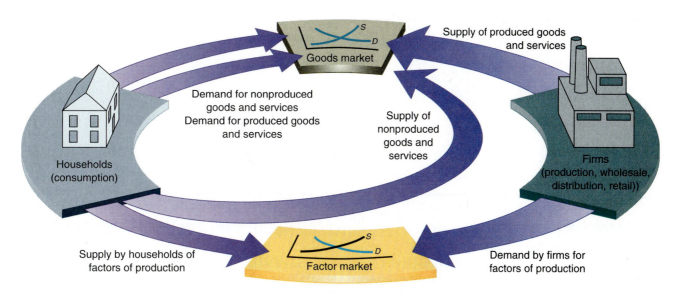

EXHIBIT 5   Transformation of Factors of Production into Consumable Goods and Services

Supply refers to the quantities that will be bought at various prices. When goods are simply traded, supply and demand both come from households. One household supplies the good; another household demands the good. When you mow a neighbour's yard for a fee, you are supplying a nonproduced good.

  With produced goods and services, such as a television and insurance, the supply process is more complicated. Households supply factors; firms demand factors and use those factors to produce goods and services. These produced goods are then supplied to households.

In talking about supply, the same convention exists that we used for demand. **Supply** refers to the various quantities offered for sale at various prices. **Quantity supplied** refers to a specific quantity offered for sale at a specific price.

There's also a law of supply that corresponds to the law of demand. The **law of supply** states that the quantity supplied of a good is positively related to that good's price, other things constant. Specifically:

Law of supply: More of a good will be supplied the higher its price, other things constant.

Or:

Law of supply: Less of a good will be supplied the lower its price, other things constant.

Price regulates quantity supplied just as it regulates quantity demanded. Like the law of demand, the law of supply is fundamental to the invisible hand's (the market's) ability to coordinate individuals' actions. Notice how the supply curve in Exhibit 6 (a) slopes upward to the right. That upward slope captures the law of supply. It tells us that the quantity supplied varies directly—in the same direction—with the price.

The same graphical distinction holds for the terms *supply* and *quantity supplied* as for the terms *demand* and *quantity demanded*. In graphical terms, supply refers to the entire supply curve because a supply curve tells us how much will be offered for sale at various prices. *Quantity supplied* refers to a point on a supply curve, so if you refer to movements along a supply curve, you're talking about changes in the quantity supplied. The distinction between a shift in supply and a change in quantity supplied is shown in Exhibit 6 (b). A shift in supply—a shift of the entire supply curve—is shown by Arrow A. A change in the quantity supplied—a movement along the entire supply curve—is shown by Arrow B.

What accounts for the law of supply? When the price of a good rises, individuals and firms can rearrange their activities in order to supply more of that good to the market, substituting production of that good for production of other goods. Thus, the same psychological tendency of individuals that underlies the law of demand—their

The Law of Supply

Supply   A schedule of quantities of goods that will be offered to the market at various prices.

Quantity supplied   A specific quantity of a good offered for sale at a specific price. Refers to a point on a supply curve.

Law of supply   More of a good will be supplied the higher its price, other things constant. Also can be stated as: Less of a good will be supplied the lower its price, other things constant.

5   The law of supply states that the quantity supplied of a good is directly related to the good's price. When prices go up, quantity supplied goes up.

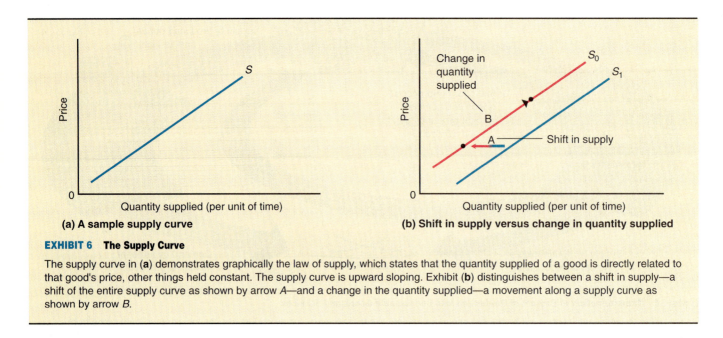

(a) A sample supply curve

(b) Shift in supply versus change in quantity supplied

EXHIBIT 6   The Supply Curve

The supply curve in (**a**) demonstrates graphically the law of supply, which states that the quantity supplied of a good is directly related to that good's price, other things held constant. The supply curve is upward sloping. Exhibit (**b**) distinguishes between a shift in supply—a shift of the entire supply curve as shown by arrow *A*—and a change in the quantity supplied—a movement along a supply curve as shown by arrow *B*.

determination to want more for less—underlies the law of supply. Individuals and firms want the highest price they can get for the smallest possible quantity they can supply.

With firms, there's a second explanation of the law of supply. Assuming firms' costs are constant, a higher price means higher profits (the difference between a firm's revenues and its costs). The expectation of those higher profits leads it to increase output as price rises, which is what the law of supply states.

Other Things Constant   As with the law of demand, the first qualification of the law of supply is that it assumes other things are held constant. Thus, if the price of wheat rises and quantity supplied falls, you'll look for something else that changed—for example, a drought might have caused the drop in quantity supplied. Your expectations would go as follows: Had there been no drought, the quantity supplied would have increased in response to the rise in price, but because there was a drought, the supply decreased, which caused prices to rise.

As with the law of demand, the law of supply represents economists' off-the-cuff response to the question: What happens to quantity supplied if price rises? If the law seems to be violated, economists search for some other variable that has changed. As was the case with demand, these other variables that might change are called *shift factors*.

This "other things constant" assumption is as important to the law of supply as it is to the law of demand. It limits the direct application of supply/demand analysis to microeconomics. To see why, consider a macroeconomic example (one which affects the entire economy). Say that all firms in an economy cut output—decrease supply— by 10 percent. Is it reasonable to assume that other things remain constant? In answering this question, think about the demand for a firm's product. As all firms cut production, peoples' income will fall and their demand for goods will fall (income is a shift factor). So when considering the aggregate economy, when considering macro issues, changes in aggregate supply and changes in the quantity of aggregate supply will likely be interrelated with changes in aggregate demand. This interaction is one of the primary reasons economists separate the micro analysis presented in this chapter from macro analysis.

Relative Price   A second qualification is that the law of supply refers to *relative price*. The reason is that, like the law of demand, the law of supply is based on individuals' and firms' ability to substitute production of this good for another, or vice versa. If the

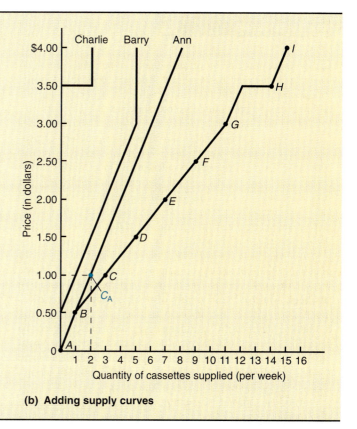

EXHIBIT 7   From a Supply Table to a Supply Curve

As with market demand, market supply is determined by adding all individual supplies at a given price. Three suppliers—Ann, Barry, and Charlie—make up the market of videocassette suppliers. The total market supply is the sum of their individual supplies at each price (shown in column 5 of (**a**)).

Each of the individual supply curves and the market supply curve have been plotted in (**b**). Notice how the market supply curve is the horizontal sum of the individual supply curves.

	(1)	(2)	(3)	(4)	(5)
Row	Price (in dollars)	Ann's supply	Barry's supply	Charlie's supply	Market supply
A	0.00	0	0	0	0
B	0.50	1	0	0	1
C	1.00	2	1	0	3
D	1.50	3	2	0	5
E	2.00	4	3	0	7
F	2.50	5	4	0	9
G	3.00	6	5	0	11
H	3.50	7	5	2	14
I	4.00	8	5	2	15

(a) A supply table

(b) Adding supply curves

---

price of corn rises relative to the price of wheat, farmers will grow less wheat and more corn. If both prices rise by equal percentages, the relative price won't change and it won't be worthwhile to substitute one good for another.

Remember Exhibit 3 (a)'s demand table for cassette rentals. In Exhibit 7 (a), columns 2 (Ann), 3 (Barry), and 4 (Charlie), we follow the same reasoning to construct a supply table for three hypothetical cassette suppliers. Each supplier follows the law of supply: when price rises, they supply more, or at least as much as they did at a lower price.

The Supply Table

Exhibit 7 (b) takes the information in Exhibit 7 (a)'s supply table and translates it into a graph of Ann's supply curve. For instance, point C_A on Ann's supply curve corresponds to the information in column 2, row C. Point C_A is at a price of $1 and a quantity of 2. Notice that Ann's supply curve is upward sloping, meaning that price is positively related to quantity. Charlie's and Barry's supply curves are similarly derived.

From a Supply Table to a Supply Curve

The supply curve represents the set of *minimum prices* an individual seller will accept for various quantities of a good. The market's invisible hand stops suppliers from charging more than the market price. If suppliers could escape the market's invisible hand and charge a higher price, they would gladly do so. Unfortunately for them, and fortunately for consumers, a higher price encourages other suppliers to begin selling cassettes. Competing suppliers' entry into the market places a limit on the price any supplier can charge.

6   To derive a supply curve from a supply table, you plot each point on the supply table on a graph and connect the points.

The market supply curve is derived from individual supply curves in precisely the same way that the demand curve was. To emphasize the symmetry in reasoning, we've made the three suppliers quite similar to the three demanders. Ann (column 2) will supply 2 at $1; if price goes up to $2 she increases her supply to 4. Barry (column 3) begins supplying at $1, and at $3 supplies 5, the most he'll supply, regardless of how

Individual and Market Supply Curves

SUPPLY, PRODUCTION, AND PROFIT

 any goods must be produced—that is, inputs must be physically transformed before they become desirable goods. Production is complicated and requires a separate analysis before it can be integrated into our analysis.

In what's called *Walrasian economics* (named after famous Swiss economist Leon Walras), the problem of production is assumed away; his is an analysis of a trading economy. This is important to recognize since it's Walrasian economics that provides the logical underpinnings for supply/demand analysis. In Walrasian economics, individuals have certain goods they trade; at some prices they sell, at some (lower) prices they buy. It is in this sense that supply is simply the mirror image of demand.

An easy way to see that supply is a mirror image of demand is to think about your supply of hours of work. When we talk of work, we say you're supplying hours of work at $6 per hour. But that same supply of work can be thought of as demand for leisure time. If, at $6 an hour, you choose to work 8 hours a day, you're simultaneously choosing to keep 16 hours for yourself (24 hours a day minus the 8 hours spent working). If we talk in terms of leisure, we speak of demand for leisure; if we talk of work, we speak of supply of labour. One is simply the mirror image of the other.

Another approach to economics is *Marshallian economics* (named after Alfred Marshall, a famous English economist). Marshallian economics does include an analysis of production. It relates costs of production with what firms are willing to sell. The reason production is difficult to integrate with an analysis of supply is that, with many production processes, per-unit costs fall as production increases. For example, in the 1920s Henry Ford produced a lot more model T cars than he had produced before; he even produced more of his cars than any of his competitors produced of their cars. As he produced more, costs per unit fell and the price of cars fell. Even today many businesses will tell you that if they can increase demand for their good, their per-unit costs and their price will go down. Such examples don't violate the law of supply. Costs per unit fall because of the nature of production. As the nature of production changes, the upward-sloping supply curve shifts outward.

There's another point we should mention about supply. Sometimes students get the impression from textbooks that supply and demand simply exist—that firms can go out, find demand curves, and start supplying. That's not a realistic picture of how the economy works. Demand curves aren't there for students or firms to see. Producing goods and supplying them inevitably involves risk and uncertainty. A company like General Motors may spend $1 billion designing a certain type of car, only to find that consumers don't like its style, or that another company has produced a car consumers like better. In that case, GM suffers a large loss.

To compensate for the potential for losses, suppliers also have the potential to make a profit on goods they sell. When the price of a good is high compared to costs of the resources used in production, expected profits are high, so more producers are encouraged to take the risk. When the price of a good is low compared to the costs, fewer firms take the risk because expected profits are low. Thus, profit is a motivating force of supply in a market economy.

---

high price rises. Charlie (column 4) has only two units to supply. At a price of $3.50 he'll supply that quantity, but higher prices won't get him to supply any more.

We sum horizontally the individual supply curves to get the market supply curve. In Exhibit 7 (a) (column 5), we add together Ann's, Barry's, and Charlie's supply to arrive at the market supply curve, which is graphed in Exhibit 7 (b). Notice each point on it corresponds to the information in columns 1 and 5 for a particular row. For example, point *H* corresponds to a price of $3.50 and a quantity of 14.

The market supply curve's upward slope is determined by two different sources: by existing suppliers supplying more and by new suppliers entering the market. Sometimes existing suppliers may not be willing to increase their quantity supplied in response to an increase in prices, but a rise in price often brings brand new suppliers into the market. For example, a rise in teachers' salaries will have little effect on the amount of teaching current teachers do, but it will increase the number of people choosing to be teachers.

Shifts in Supply versus Movement along a Given Supply Curve

Just as there can be shifts in the demand curve resulting from shift factors, so too can there be shifts in the supply curve caused by shift factors. Important shift factors of supply include:

1. Changes in the prices of inputs used in the production of a good.
2. Changes in technology.
3. Changes in suppliers' expectations.
4. Changes in taxes and subsidies.

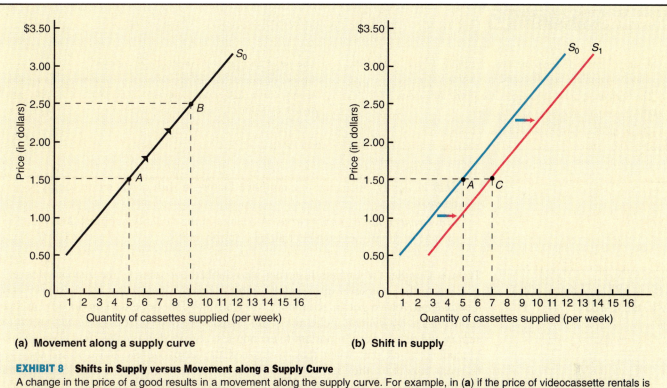

(a) Movement along a supply curve

(b) Shift in supply

EXHIBIT 8   Shifts in Supply versus Movement along a Supply Curve
A change in the price of a good results in a movement along the supply curve. For example, in (a) if the price of videocassette rentals is $1.50, 5 cassettes would be supplied (point A). But if the price of cassette rentals increases for some reason, say to $2.50, suppliers would increase supply to 9 (point B). The change in price results in a movement along the supply curve from point A to point B.

Shift factors cause a shift in the supply curve. For example, in (b), at the price of $1.50, 5 cassettes would be supplied (point A). If some new technology were introduced, lowering the cost of producing the cassette, then suppliers would supply 7 cassettes at the price of $1.50 (point C). An improvement in technology results in a shift in the supply curve from S_0 to S_1.

These aren't all the shift factors; as was the case with demand, anything that affects supply other than the good's own price is a shift factor. Each of these shift factors will cause a **shift in supply,** whereas a change in the price causes a **movement along the supply curve.**

As with demand, it's useful to graph an example of a shift in supply and to differentiate that from a movement along the supply curve. Exhibit 8 does this for our example. Exhibit 8 (a) shows the effect of a change in the price of cassettes from $1.50 to $2.50. Point A (5, $1.50) represents the starting point. Now, for some reason, price rises to $2.50 and the quantity supplied rises to 9 (point B). Because of the price increase, there's a movement along the supply curve.

Now, however, let's say that there's an improvement in technology: a new type of cassette that's cheaper to make than the existing cassette. Such an advance in technology shifts the supply curve outward to the right. Why? Because it lowers costs for each unit sold, enabling suppliers to offer more for sale at each price. An improvement in technology is shown in Exhibit 8 (b). Notice that the entire supply curve shifts from S_0 to S_1, showing that for each price, the quantity supplied will be greater. For example, at price $1.50, 5 cassettes are supplied; but after the technological improvement, at price $1.50, 7 cassettes are supplied. The same reasoning holds for any price.

Do we see such shifts in the supply curve often? Yes. A good example is computers. For the past 30 years, technological changes have continually shifted computers' supply curve to the right.

This should give you an idea of factors that shift supply, and should cement for you the difference between a shift in supply and a movement along a supply curve. But in case it didn't, here it is one more time:

Shift in supply   If how much of a good is supplied is affected by a shift factor, there is said to be a shift in supply. Graphically, a shift in supply will cause the entire supply curve to shift.

Movement along the supply curve
Method of representing a change in the quantity supplied. Graphically, a change in quantity demanded will cause a movement along the supply curve.

7   Just as with demand, it is important to distinguish between a shift in supply (a shift of the entire supply curve) and a movement along a supply curve (a change in the quantity supplied due to a change in price).

Shift in supply: A change in a nonprice factor—a shift of the entire supply curve.

Movement along a supply curve: A change in the quantity supplied due to a change in price—a movement along a supply curve.

THE MARRIAGE OF SUPPLY AND DEMAND

Thomas Carlyle, the English historian who dubbed economics "the dismal science," also wrote this chapter's introductory tidbit, "Teach a parrot the words *supply* and *demand* and you've got an economist." In Chapter 1, we hope we convinced you that economics is not dismal. In the rest of this chapter, we hope to convince you that while supply and demand are important to economics, parrots don't make good economists. If students think that when they've learned the terms *supply* and *demand* they've learned economics, they're mistaken. Those terms are just labels for the ideas behind supply and demand, and it's the ideas that are important. What's relevant about supply and demand isn't the labels but how the concepts interact. For instance, what happens if quantity supplied doesn't equal quantity demanded? It's in understanding the interaction of supply and demand that economics becomes interesting *and relevant.*

The First Dynamic Law of Supply and Demand

Excess supply   Quantity supplied is greater than quantity demanded.

When you have a market in which neither suppliers nor demanders can organize and in which prices are free to adjust, economists have a good answer for the question: What happens if quantity supplied doesn't equal quantity demanded? If quantity supplied is greater than quantity demanded (that is, if there is **excess supply,** a surplus), some suppliers won't be able to sell all their goods. Each supplier will think: "Gee, if I offer to sell it for a bit less, I'll be the lucky one who sells my good; someone else will be stuck with not selling their good." But because all suppliers with excess goods will be thinking the same thing, the price in the market will fall. As that happens, demanders will increase their quantity demanded. So the movement toward equilibrium caused by excess supply is on both the supply and demand sides.

Excess demand   Quantity demanded is greater than quantity supplied.

The reverse is also true. Say that instead of excess supply, there's **excess demand** (a shortage): quantity demanded is greater than quantity supplied. There are more demanders who want the good than there are suppliers selling the good. Let's consider what's likely to go through demanders' minds. They'll likely call long-lost friends who just happen to be sellers of that good and tell them it's good to talk to them and, by the way, don't they want to sell that . . .? Suppliers will be rather pleased that so many of their old friends have remembered them, but they'll also likely see the connection between excess demand and their friends' thoughtfulness. To stop their phones from ringing all the time, they'll likely raise their price. The reverse is true for excess supply. It's amazing how friendly suppliers become to potential demanders when there's excess supply.

8   The three dynamic laws of supply and demand are:
1. If Qd > Qs, P increases; if Qs > Qd, P decreases.
2. The larger Qs − Qd, the faster P falls; the larger Qd − Qs, the faster P rises.
3. If Qd = Qs, P does not change.

This tendency for prices to rise when demand exceeds supply and for prices to fall when supply exceeds demand is a phenomenon economists call the **first dynamic law of supply and demand:**

First dynamic law of supply and demand   When quantity demanded is greater than quantity supplied, prices tend to rise; when quantity supplied is greater than quantity demanded, prices tend to fall.

When quantity demanded is greater than quantity supplied, prices tend to rise; when quantity supplied is greater than quantity demanded, prices tend to fall.

Exhibit 9 shows the first dynamic law of supply and demand by the arrows

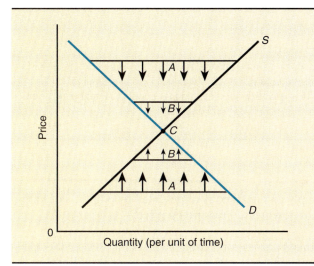

EXHIBIT 9   The Dynamic Laws of Supply and Demand

The dynamic laws of supply and demand tell us what forces will be set in motion when the quantity supplied does not equal the quantity demanded.

In this example, supply (line S) and demand (line D) are in balance at point C. When supply is greater than demand, there is downward pressure on price; when demand is greater than supply, there is upward pressure on price. The greater the difference between supply and demand, the greater the pressure on price, as indicated by the larger arrows at A and smaller arrows at B.

labelled *A*. With excess supply the arrows push price down; with excess demand the arrows push price up. It's called a *dynamic law* because *dynamic* refers to change and this law refers to how prices change, not to what prices will be.

How much pressure will there be for prices to rise or fall? That too will likely depend on differences between quantity supplied and quantity demanded. The greater the difference, the more pressure there is on individuals to raise or lower prices. If you're a seller (supplier) and all your old friends are calling you (there's major excess demand), you'll simply put a message on your answering machine saying, "The price has gone up 200 percent or 300 percent. If you're still interested in talking about old times, stay on the line. Otherwise, it was nice knowing you." If, however, only a couple of old friends call you (there's only minor excess demand), you'll probably raise your price only slightly. Or if you're a buyer (demander) and there's major excess supply, you'll leave the following message: "If you're trying to sell me anything, I'm broke and can only pay less than what you ask."

Thus, the **second dynamic law of supply and demand is:**

In a market, the larger the difference between quantity supplied and quantity demanded, the greater the pressure on prices to rise (if there is excess demand) or fall (if there is excess supply).

The second dynamic law of supply and demand is demonstrated by the smaller *B* arrows in Exhibit 9. Because the difference between quantity supplied and quantity demanded is less than before, the upward and downward pressures aren't as strong.

People's tendencies to change prices exist as long as there's some difference between quantity supplied and quantity demanded. But the change in price brings the laws of supply and demand into play. As price falls, quantity supplied decreases as some suppliers leave the business (the law of supply); and as some people who originally weren't really interested in buying the good think, "Well, at this low price, maybe I do want to buy," quantity demanded increases (the law of demand). Similarly, when price rises, quantity supplied will increase (the law of supply) and quantity demanded will decrease (the law of demand).

Whenever quantity supplied and quantity demanded are unequal, price tends to change. If, however, quantity supplied and quantity demanded are equal, price will stay the same because no one will have an incentive to change it. This observation leads to the **third dynamic law of supply and demand:**

When quantity supplied equals quantity demanded, prices have no tendency to change.

The Second Dynamic Law of Supply and Demand

Second dynamic law of supply and demand   In a market, the larger the difference between quantity supplied and quantity demanded, the greater the pressure on prices to rise (if there is excess demand) or fall (if there is excess supply).

The Third Dynamic Law of Supply and Demand

Third dynamic law of supply and demand   When quantity supplied equals quantity demanded, prices have no tendency to change.

The third dynamic law of supply and demand is represented by point *C* in Exhibit 9. At point *C* there's no upward or downward pressure on price.

The Graphical Marriage of Demand and Supply

Exhibit 10 shows supply and demand curves for cassettes and demonstrates the operation of the dynamic laws of supply and demand. Let's consider what will happen to the price of cassettes in four cases:

1. When the price is $3;
2. When the price is $2.50;
3. When the price is $1.50; and
4. When the price is $2.25.

1. When price is $3, quantity supplied is 11 and quantity demanded is only 5. Excess supply is 6. At a price of $3, individual demanders can get all they want, but most suppliers can't sell all they wish; they'll be stuck with cassettes that they'd like to sell. Suppliers will tend to offer their goods at a lower price and demanders, who see plenty of suppliers out there, will bargain harder for an even lower price. Both these forces will push the price down as indicated by the *A* arrows in Exhibit 10.
2. When price falls from $3 to $2.50, the pressures are the same kind as in (1), only they're weaker, because excess supply is smaller. There aren't as many dissatisfied suppliers searching for ways to sell their cassettes. Generally, the rate at which prices fall depends on the size of the gap between quantity supplied and quantity demanded. This smaller pressure is shown by the *B* arrows in Exhibit 10.

Now let's start from the other side.

3. Say price is $1.50. The situation is now reversed. Quantity supplied is 5 and quantity demanded is 11. Excess demand is 6. Now it's demanders who can't get what they want and suppliers who are in the strong bargaining position. The pressures will be on price to rise in the direction of the *C* arrows in Exhibit 10.
4. At $2.25, price is at its equilibrium: quantity supplied equals quantity demanded. Suppliers offer to sell 8 and demanders want to buy 8, so there's no pressure on price to rise or fall. Price will tend to remain where it is (point *E* in Exhibit 10).

Equilibrium

Equilibrium A concept in which the dynamic forces cancel each other out.

Equilibrium price The price toward which the invisible hand (economic forces) drives the market.

The concept of equilibrium appears often throughout this text. You need to understand what equilibrium is and what it isn't. The concept itself comes from physics—classical mechanics. To say something is in **equilibrium** is to say that the dynamic forces pushing on it cancel each other out. For example, a book on a desk is in equilibrium because the upward force exerted on the book by the desk equals the downward pressure exerted on the book by gravity. In supply and demand analysis, equilibrium means that the upward pressure on price is exactly offset by the downward pressure on price. **Equilibrium price** is the price toward which the invisible hand drives the market.

So much for what equilibrium is. Now let's consider what it isn't.

First, equilibrium isn't inherently good or bad. It's simply a state in which dynamic pressures offset each other. Some equilibria are awful. Say two countries are

EXHIBIT 10   The Marriage of Supply and Demand

Combining supply and demand lets us see the dynamic laws of supply and demand. These laws tell us the pressures on price when there is excess demand (there is upward pressure on price) or excess supply (there is downward pressure on price). Understanding these pressures is essential to understanding how to apply economics to reality.

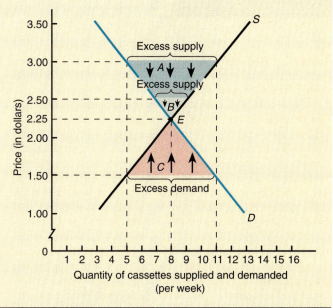

engaged in a poison gas war against each other and both sides are snuffed out. An equilibrium will have been reached, but there's nothing good about it.

Second, equilibrium isn't a state of the world. It's a characteristic of the framework you use to look at the world. A framework for looking at the world is called a **model.** The same situation could be seen as an equilibrium in one framework and as a disequilibrium in another. Say you're describing a car that's speeding along at 100 kilometres an hour. That car is changing position relative to objects on the ground. Its movement could be, and generally is, described as if it were in disequilibrium. However, if you consider this car relative to another car going 100 kilometres an hour, the cars could be modeled as being in equilibrium because their positions relative to each other aren't changing.

Model   Framework for looking at the world.

Understanding that equilibrium is a characteristic of the framework of analysis, not of the real world, is important in applying economic models to reality. For example, in the preceding description we said equilibrium occurs where supply equals demand. In a model where the invisible hand is the only force operating, that's true. In the real world, however, other forces—political and social forces—are operating. These will likely push price away from that supply/demand equilibrium. Were we to consider a model that included all these forces—political, social, and economic—equilibrium would be likely to exist where supply isn't equal to demand. In the real world, the invisible hand, foot, and handshake often work in different directions and vary in strength. For example:

- In agricultural markets, farmers use political pressure (the invisible foot) to obtain higher-than-supply/demand-equilibrium prices. Generally they succeed, so agricultural prices rise above the supply/demand-equilibrium price. The laws of supply and demand assume no political pressures on prices.

- In labour markets, social pressures often offset economic pressures and prevent unemployed individuals from accepting work at lower wages than currently employed workers (the invisible handshake). Similarly, when there's a strike, social pressures prevent people who don't have jobs from taking jobs strikers have left. People who do take those jobs are called names like *scab* or *strike-breaker,* and they don't like those names. A pure supply and demand model, though, assumes everyone who wants a job will try to become a scab.

E conomics is a developing discipline, so the models used in one time period aren't necessarily the models used in another. In their research, economists debate which models are best and how to integrate more insights into their existing models.

Two groups of economists who've recently pushed back the frontiers of economics are the *public choice economists* and the *neoclassical political economists*. Public choice economists, led by Gordon Tullock and James Buchanan, argue that the political dimension must be part of economists' models. To integrate the political dimension, they apply economic analysis to politics and consider how economic forces affect the laws that are enacted and how, in turn, those laws affect economics. Their work was instrumental in leading to the invisible foot metaphor discussed in Chapter 1, and won James Buchanan a Nobel prize in 1986.

Neoclassical political economists share with public choice economists the view that the political dimension must be part of economists' models, and have developed a variety of formal models that significantly modify earlier models' predictions. Many of their models focus on rent seeking (how suppliers can restrict supply and thereby create rents for themselves). *Rent* is defined as an income earned when supply is restricted. For example, say a carpenter's union limits the number of people who can do carpentry. The supply of carpenters will decrease and existing carpenters will earn a higher wage that includes a rent component. Rents can be created either by using politics (the invisible foot) or by special agreements (the invisible handshake). Hence, neoclassical political economists are at the forefront of the movement to broaden economic analysis.

Although the formal analyses of both these groups haven't been adopted by the majority of economists, other economists often use their informal results and insights. Throughout this book we'll discuss these and other groups' views, but we'll focus on the mainstream model that the majority of economists use.

- In product markets, suppliers conspire to limit entry by other suppliers. They work hard to get Parliament to establish tariffs and make restrictive regulations (the invisible foot). They also devise pricing strategies that scare off other suppliers and allow them to hold their prices higher than a supply/demand equilibrium. A pure supply and demand model assumes no conspiring at all.
- In the housing rental markets, consumers often organize politically and get local government to enact rent controls (ceilings on rents that can be charged for apartments). Here's an example of government (the invisible foot) putting downward pressure on price.

If social and political forces were included in the analysis, they'd provide a counterpressure to the dynamic forces of supply and demand. The result would be an equilibrium with continual excess supply or excess demand. The invisible hand pushing toward a supply/demand equilibrium would be thwarted by other invisible forces pushing in the other direction.

A formal political/social/economic model that included all these forces simultaneously would be complicated, and economists are still working on perfecting one. Meanwhile economists, in their formal analysis, focus on a pure supply and demand model in which only the invisible hand is operating. That model lets you see clearly the economic forces at work. When economists apply the pure supply/demand model to reality, however, they discuss the effects of these other forces.

In this book we'll introduce you to both the formal model (in which only market forces are operating) and the informal model (in which all forces are operating).

Changes in Supply and Demand

To ensure that you understand the supply and demand graphs throughout the book and can apply them, let's go through three examples. Exhibit 11 (a) deals with an increase in demand; Exhibit 11 (b) deals with a decrease in supply.

Let's consider again the supply and demand for cassette rentals. In Exhibit 11 (a), the supply is S_0 and initial demand is D_0. They meet at an equilibrium price of $2.25 and a quantity demanded of 8 (point A). Now say demand for cassette rentals increases from D_0 to D_1. At a price of $2.25, the quantity of cassette rentals supplied will be 8 and the quantity demanded will be 10; excess demand of 2 exists.

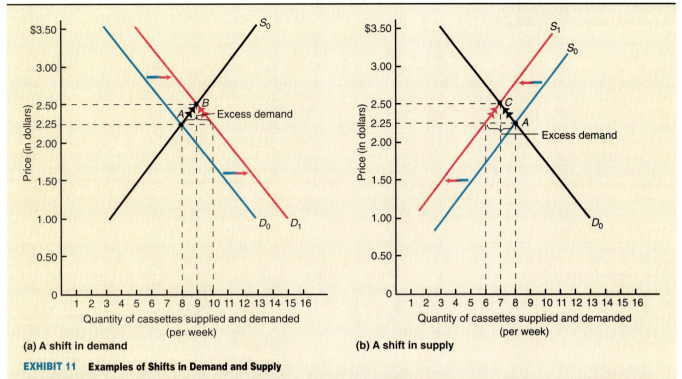

(a) A shift in demand

(b) A shift in supply

EXHIBIT 11   Examples of Shifts in Demand and Supply

When there is an increase in demand (the demand curve shifts outward), there is upward pressure on the price, as shown in (a). If there is an increase in demand from D_0 to D_1, the quantity of cassette rentals that was demanded at a price of $2.25, 8, increases to 10, but the quantity supplied remains at 8. This excess demand tends to cause prices to rise. Eventually, a new equilibrium is reached at the price of $2.50, where the quantity supplied and the quantity demanded is 9.

If supply of cassettes decreases, then the entire supply curve shifts inward to the left, as shown in (b), from S_0 to S_1. At the price of $2.25, the quantity supplied has now decreased to 6 cassettes, but the quantity demanded has remained at 8 cassettes. The excess demand tends to force the price upward. Eventually, an equilibrium is reached at the price of $2.50 and quantity 7 (point C).

As the first dynamic law of supply and demand dictates, the excess demand pushes prices upward in the direction of the small arrows, decreasing the quantity demanded. As it does so, movement takes place along both the supply curve and the demand curve. The first dynamic law of supply and demand tells us that price will be pushed up.

The upward push on price decreases the gap between the quantity supplied and the quantity demanded. As the gap is decreased, the upward pressure decreases, as the second dynamic law requires. But as long as that gap exists at all, price will be pushed upward until the new equilibrium price ($2.50) and new quantity (9) are reached (point B). At point B the third dynamic law of supply and demand takes hold: quantity supplied equals quantity demanded. So the market is in equilibrium. Notice that the adjustment is twofold: The higher price brings about equilibrium by both increasing the quantity supplied (from 8 to 9) and decreasing the quantity demanded (from 10 to 9).

Exhibit 11 (b) begins with the same situation that we started with in Exhibit 11 (a); the initial equilibrium quantity and price are 8 and $2.25 (point A). In this example, however, instead of demand increasing, let's assume supply decreases—say because some suppliers change what they like to do, and decide they will no longer supply this good. That means that the entire supply curve shifts inward to the left (from S_0 to S_1). At the initial equilibrium price of $2.25, the quantity demanded is greater than the quantity supplied. Two more cassettes are demanded than are supplied. (Excess demand = 2.)

HISTORICAL TIME, HISTORESES, AND "TENDENCY TOWARD EQUILIBRIUM" ANALYSIS

A model can be interpreted many different ways, and knowing the various interpretations is as central to understanding the lesson of the model as is knowing the technical aspects of the model. For example, most models we use in economics are equilibrium models; they have a definite equilibrium toward which they move. To use such an equilibrium model to analyze a problem is not to believe that the equilibrium of the model is the one that will be reached in the real world. Other forces may, and often do, prevent that equilibrium from being reached. Moreover, the process of moving toward an equilibrium may change the equilibrium one is aiming at. A model only captures certain aspects of reality. To interpret that model, other aspects must be added in.

When the movement toward equilibrium can affect the equilibrium, there is what is called *historeses* or *path dependency* present. When path dependency exists, as it often does, the supply/demand model is incomplete and the equilibrium of the supply/demand model isn't the equilibrium that one would expect. For example, say the price of a pair of Nike sneakers is $200. These $200 sneakers have lots of snob appeal. Now, say, demand declines, and Nike lowers prices. The falling price causes people to think that Nikes are no longer "in," and *because of the fall in price,* tastes change and the demand falls further. In our supply/demand model, such effects are ruled out by our "other things constant" assumption. The real world need not, and generally does not, follow this assumption.

In the analysis of large changes in the economy or small changes in the aggregate economy, the "other things constant" assumption is inevitably broken because movements along a supply curve cause income to change which causes shifts of the demand curve. To capture these interactive effects we need a different analysis, which is where *macroeconomics* comes in. Macroeconomics goes beyond microeconomic supply and demand and tries to include an analysis of interactive effects. (We write "tries to" because macro hasn't done a great job in understanding these interactive effects.)

Another way in which the "other things constant" assumption is violated is demonstrated in the irreversibility of many actions. For example, say you decide to paint your bike pink in a fit of pink-passion. The cost: $2.98 for the spray can. Now you see the newly-painted bike and decide pink isn't your colour—you want it back to the original colour. You *might* be able to remove the paint at a cost of $75—but probably you can't get the pink paint off. After you've painted the bike, "other things are no longer constant"; you cannot turn back time by pressing a rewind button. Or say you sawed a 10-foot 2x4 to 8′4″. Then, you discover that you really wanted an 8′5″ 2x4. You don't simply run the saw backwards and try again.

The point of these examples is that reality happens in historical time where many actions are irreversible, or are reversible at a much higher cost than was the cost of getting to the situation you'd like to reverse. Supply/demand analysis doesn't capture that dimension of reality, so that dimension must be added back to the analysis in the interpretation.

Economists recognize these problems, but nonetheless they use supply/demand analysis which assumes these problems away to keep the analysis simple. But they keep these limitations in the back of their minds, and add them back, where appropriate, when applying the model to a real-world problem.

As the dynamic laws of supply and demand require, this excess demand exerts upward pressure on price. Price is pushed in the direction of the small arrows. As the price rises, the upward pressure on price is reduced (in accord with the second dynamic law of supply and demand) but will still exist until the new equilibrium price, $2.50, and new quantity, 7, are reached. At $2.50, the quantity supplied equals the quantity demanded. The adjustment has involved a movement along the demand curve and the new supply curve. As price rises, quantity supplied is adjusted upward and quantity demanded is adjusted downward until quantity supplied equals quantity demanded where the new supply curve intersects the demand curve at point *C,* an equilibrium of 7 and $2.50.

We leave a final example as an exercise for you. Demonstrate graphically how the price of computers could have fallen dramatically in the past 10 years, even as demand increased. (Hint: Supply has shifted even more, so even at lower prices, far more computers have been supplied than were being supplied 10 years ago.)

SUPPLY AND DEMAND IN ACTION: OIL PRICE FLUCTUATIONS

Now that we've discussed the basic analysis and its limitations, we can apply the supply/demand model to a real-world situation.

Exhibit 12 (a) shows the changes in the U.S. dollar price of oil from 1973 to 1993. Exhibit 12 (b) demonstrates the supply/demand forces associated with those changes in the period 1973–81, during which the price of oil went up substantially. Prior to the

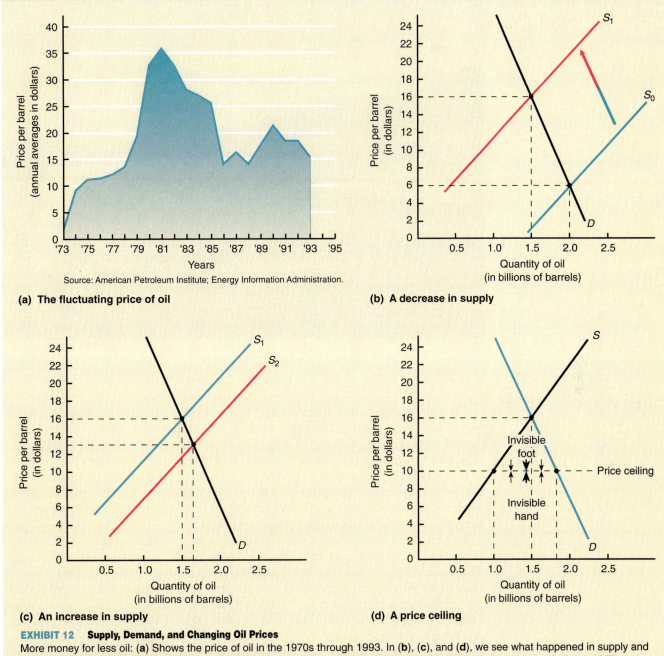

(a) The fluctuating price of oil

Source: American Petroleum Institute; Energy Information Administration.

(b) A decrease in supply

(c) An increase in supply

(d) A price ceiling

EXHIBIT 12   Supply, Demand, and Changing Oil Prices
More money for less oil: (**a**) Shows the price of oil in the 1970s through 1993. In (**b**), (**c**), and (**d**), we see what happened in supply and demand terms in the period from 1973 to 1988. In the early 1970s, OPEC members decided to limit their supply of oil to 1.5 billion barrels, represented by a shift in curve S_1 in (**b**). Initially, supplying 2 billion barrels of oil at $6 per barrel gave them a revenue of $12 billion, but with restricted supply, the price of oil per barrel rose to $16, giving OPEC members a revenue of $24 billion ($1.5 billion x $16). New exploration shifted the supply curve out, lowering price to $13, as in (**c**).

   Graph (**d**) shows the response of a market to a price ceiling such as the one imposed in the 1970s in the United States. In (**d**) the invisible hand is not allowed to operate; quantity demanded exceeds quantity supplied; and the result is shortage. In the 1970s, people lined up to buy limited supplies of gas for their cars.

1970s, its price had been relatively stable. In the early 1970s, at a series of meetings of countries who were members of OPEC (the Organization of Petroleum Exporting Countries), some delegates who had studied economics pointed out how OPEC could get more for less. They argued that if they could somehow all decide to limit oil production (to decrease supply), then even though each of them produced less, actually each would make more money. Exhibit 12 (b) shows why.

The long lines and shortages of the 1974 gas crisis are typical results of a price ceiling.© *George Gardner/The Image Works.*

Initially the quantity supplied was 2 billion barrels and the U.S. dollar price per barrel was $6. Total OPEC revenue was U.S. $12 billion (U.S. $6 × 2 billion). Now say OPEC shifts supply back from S_0 to S_1. The quantity of oil supplied falls to 1.5 billion barrels and the price of oil rises to U.S. $16 per barrel. Now members' revenue is U.S. $24 billion (U.S. $16 × 1.5 billion). In cutting production by 25 percent they double their revenues! Even though each producer is selling less oil, each is earning more income. And that's what OPEC did. The member countries restricted supply, and the price of oil started rising drastically worldwide.

The high price provoked a reaction among a large number of non-OPEC oil suppliers (and from OPEC members who could hide their oil sales from other members). They increased their quantity of oil supplied significantly, causing an upward movement along the original supply curve. At the same time oil exploration boomed, shifting the oil supply curve out to S_2 in Exhibit 12 (c). These new discoveries of oil shifted oil's total supply curve rightward, even as most OPEC countries held their oil back. As supply was responding to higher prices and shortages, so too was quantity demanded. As the price rose, the quantity demanded fell. As people switched to fuel-efficient cars and set the thermostats in their homes lower, there was a resulting movement along the demand curve. By the late 1980s, the invisible hand had effectively broken OPEC's limitation on supply, and price fell to between U.S. $12 and $15 a barrel, as shown in Exhibit 12 (c), approximately where it would have been (after adjustment for inflation) had OPEC never organized to limit supply. (Why not use Canadian dollar figures? Many commodities, including oil, are typically priced in world markets in terms of U.S. dollars.)

Before these adjustments occurred, the sudden jump in oil price caused political reactions both at home and abroad. The invisible foot put downward pressure on the price of oil in North America. It led to **price ceilings** (government-imposed limits on how high a price can be charged). This political pressure prevented the price of oil from rising to the full new supply/demand equilibrium. The result was an oil short-

Price ceiling   A government-imposed limit on how high a price can be charged.

THE SUPPLY AND DEMAND FOR CHILDREN

In Chapter 1, we distinguished between an economic force and a market force. Economic forces are operative in all aspects of our lives; market forces are economic forces that are allowed to be expressed through a market. Our examples in this chapter are of market forces—of goods sold in a market—but supply and demand can also be used to analyze situations in which economic, but not market, forces operate. An economist who is adept at this is Gary Becker of the University of Chicago. He has applied supply and demand analysis to a wide range of issues, even the supply of and demand for children.

Becker doesn't argue that children should be bought and sold. But he does argue that economic considerations play a large role in people's decisions on how many children to have.

In farming communities, children can be productive early in life; by age six or seven, they can work on a farm. In an advanced industrial community, children provide pleasure, but generally don't contribute productively to family income. Even getting them to help around the house can be difficult.

Becker argues that since the price of having children is lower for a farming society than for an industrial society, farming societies will have more children per family. Quantity of children demanded will be larger. And that's what we find. Developing countries that rely primarily on farming often have three, four, or more children per family. Industrial societies average fewer than two children per family.

age—the quantity of oil demanded was greater than the quantity of oil supplied. There were dire predictions that North Americans would freeze to death or wouldn't be allowed to use energy-intensive products. While there were shortages, Canada was better off than the United States, since by the mid-1960s we were able to supply more than half of our domestic needs—a much higher proportion than the United States was able to supply. In fact, in the United States some people were killed at the gas pumps by frustrated motorists vying for position.

Exhibit 12 (d) shows how such a price ceiling will cause such shortages. The price ceiling is U.S. $10, even though the supply/demand equilibrium price is U.S. $16. Quantity supplied is 1 billion barrels, while quantity demanded is 1.8 billion barrels. The difference between quantity supplied and quantity demanded reflects the number of people going without oil. When the invisible foot or invisible handshake prevents price from rising to the equilibrium price, the invisible hand doesn't disappear. It places upward pressure on price while the invisible foot places downward pressure on price. In this case the invisible hand won out, and the price ceilings were eliminated, allowing the price of oil to rise substantially. The rise in price eliminated the shortages.

9 An effective price ceiling will cause Qd > Qs.

It isn't only price ceilings that have predictable effects. **Price floors** (government-imposed limits on how low a price can be charged) also do. A price floor such as the minimum wage or a government-imposed mandatory price for milk creates a situation of excess supply. The quantity supplied exceeds the quantity demanded, and some way must be found to ration the available quantity demanded among the suppliers. We'll deal with these issues in detail later.

Price floor   A government-imposed limit on how low a price may be.

CONCLUSION

Throughout the book, we'll be presenting examples of supply and demand. So we'll end this chapter here because its intended purposes have been served. What were those intended purposes? First, the discussion and examples should have exposed you to enough economic terminology and economic thinking to allow you to proceed to our more complicated examples. Second, the discussion should also have set your mind to work putting the events around you into a supply/demand framework. Doing that will give you new insights into the events that shape all our lives. Finally, this chapter should have made you wary of applying supply/demand analysis to the real world without considering the other invisible forces out there battling the invisible hand.

CHAPTER SUMMARY

- The law of demand (supply): More (less) of a good will be demanded (supplied) the lower its price, other things constant. The demand curve is negatively sloped while the supply curve is positively sloped.

- A market demand (supply) curve is the sum of all individual demand (supply) curves.

- A shift in quantity demanded (supplied) is a movement along the demand (supply) curve. A shift in demand (supply) is a shift of the entire demand (supply) curve.

- The laws of supply and demand refer to relative prices; they hold true because individuals can substitute other goods for the one we're examining.

- When quantity demanded is greater than quantity supplied, there is excess demand and prices tend to rise. When quantity supplied is greater than quantity demanded, there is excess supply and prices tend to fall.

- When quantity supplied equals quantity demanded, prices have no tendency to change. At that price, producers want to sell the same number of units that consumers want to buy.

- When demand shifts right, the equilibrium price rises. When supply shifts right, the equilibrium price falls.

KEY TERMS

demand   *(35)*

demand curve   *(35)*

equilibrium   *(50)*

equilibrium price   *(50)*

excess demand   *(48)*

excess supply   *(48)*

factors of production   *(42)*

firms   *(42)*

first dynamic law of supply and demand   *(48)*

law of demand   *(35)*

law of supply   *(43)*

market demand curve   *(39)*

model   *(51)*

movement along the demand curve   *(41)*

movement along the supply curve   *(47)*

other things constant   *(36)*

partial equilibrium analysis   *(37)*

price ceiling   *(56)*

price floor   *(57)*

quantity demanded   *(35)*

quantity supplied   *(43)*

relative price   *(37)*

second dynamic law of supply and demand   *(49)*

shift factors of demand   *(37)*

shift in demand   *(41)*

shift in supply   *(47)*

supply   *(43)*

third dynamic law of supply and demand   *(49)*

QUESTIONS FOR THOUGHT AND REVIEW

The number after each question represents the estimated degree of critical thinking required. (1 = almost none; 10 = deep thought.)

1. Draw a demand curve from the following demand table. *(1)*

Price	Quantity
37	20
47	15
57	10
67	5

2. Draw a market demand curve from the following demand table. *(1)*

P	D_1	D_2	D_3	Market Demand
37	20	4	8	32
47	15	2	7	24
57	10	0	6	16
67	5	0	5	10

3. It has just been reported that eating meat is bad for your health. Using supply and demand curves, demonstrate the report's likely effect on the price and quantity of steak sold in the market.   *(3)*

4. Toronto has had residential rent control for many years. Using supply/demand analysis, explain what effect eliminating those controls would probably have.   *(4)*

5. Draw a market supply curve from the following supply table.   *(1)*

P	S_1	S_2	S_3	Market Supply
37	0	4	14	18
47	0	8	16	24
57	10	12	18	40
67	10	16	20	46

6. Show, using supply and demand curves, the likely effect of a minimum wage law. If you were a worker, would you support or oppose minimum wage laws? Why?   *(6)*

7. Distinguish the effect of a shift factor of demand from the effect of a change in price on the demand curve.   *(3)*

8. Say Canada were to legalize the sale of certain currently illegal drugs. Using supply/demand analysis, show what effect legalization would have on the price of those drugs and on the quantity bought.   *(7)*

9. Mary has just stated that normally, as price rises, supply will increase. Her teacher grimaces. Why?   *(5)*

10. Supply/demand analysis states that equilibrium occurs where quantity supplied equals quantity demanded, but in Canadian agricultural markets quantity supplied almost always exceeds quantity demanded. How can this be?   *(5)*

PROBLEMS AND EXERCISES

1. You're given the following individual demand tables for comic books.

Price	John	Liz	Alex
$ 2	4	36	24
4	4	32	20
6	0	28	16
8	0	24	12
10	0	20	8
12	0	16	4
14	0	12	0
16	0	8	0

   a. Determine the market demand table.

   b. Graph the individual and market demand curves.

   c. If the current market price is $4, what's total market demand? What happens to total market demand if price rises to $8?

   d. Say that an advertising campaign increases demand by 50 percent. Illustrate graphically what will happen to the individual and market demand curves.

2. Draw hypothetical supply and demand curves for tea. Show how the equilibrium price and quantity will be affected by each of the following occurrences:

   a. Bad weather wreaks havoc with the tea crop.

   b. A medical report implying tea is bad for your health is published.

   c. A technological innovation lowers the cost of producing tea.

   d. Consumers' income falls.

   e. The government imposes a $5 per kilo price ceiling on tea.

   f. The government imposes a $15 per kilo price ceiling on tea.

   g. The government imposes a $15 per kilo price floor on tea.

3. "Scalping" is the name given to the buying of tickets at a low price and reselling them at a high price. Consider the following information: At the beginning of the season:

   a. Tickets sell for $27 and are sold out in pre-season.

   b. Halfway through the season, rival teams have maintained unbeaten records. Resale price of tickets rises to $200.

   c. One week before playing each other, rival teams have remained unbeaten and are ranked 1-2. Ticket price rises to $600.

   d. Three days before the game, price falls to $400.
   Demonstrate, using supply/demand analysis and words, what might have happened to cause these fluctuations in price.

4. In some areas, "scalping" is against the law, although enforcement of these laws is spotty (difficult).

   a. Using supply/demand analysis and words, demonstrate what a weakly enforced anti-scalping law would likely do to the price of tickets in *3b, 3c,* and *3d.*

   b. Using supply/demand analysis and words, demonstrate what a strongly enforced anti-scalping law would likely do to the price of tickets in *3b, 3c,* and *3d.*

5. This is a question concerning what economists call "the identification problem." Say you go out and find figures on the quantity bought of various products. You will find something like the following:

Product	Year	Quantity	Average Price
VCRs	1990	100,000	$210
	1991	110,000	220
	1992	125,000	225
	1993	140,000	215
	1994	135,000	215
	1995	160,000	220

   Plot these figures on a graph.

   a. Have you plotted a supply curve, a demand curve, or what?

   b. If we assume that the market for VCRs is competitive, what information would you have to know to determine whether these are points on a supply curve or on a demand curve?

   c. Say you know that the market is one in which suppliers set the price and allow the quantity to vary. Could you then say anything more about the curve you have plotted?

   d. What information about shift factors would you expect to find to make these points reflect the law of demand?

6. Apartments in Vancouver are often hard to find. You believe one of the reasons is that there are rent controls.

   a. Demonstrate graphically how rent controls could make apartments hard to find.

   b. Often one can get an apartment if one makes a side payment to the current tenant. Can you explain why?

   c. What would be the likely effect of eliminating rent controls?

d. What is the political appeal of rent controls?

7. You're a commodity trader and you've just heard a report that the winter wheat harvest will be 2.09 billion bushels, a 44 percent jump, rather than an expected 35 percent jump to 1.96 billion bushels.

    a. What would you expect would happen to wheat prices?

    b. Demonstrate graphically the effect you suggested in *a.*

8. Mushrooms grow best in carbon-rich soil. The years immediately following a forest fire provide ideal growing conditions for mushrooms. Nowadays wild mushrooms are in demand, which has led to the development of the mushroom-picking profession (individuals travel around to various woods and forests to pick mushrooms).

    Mushroom-pickers often complain that they face a catch-22. Whenever the picking is easy, the prices are low, and whenever the pickings are slim, the prices are high. Can you explain, using supply and demand analysis, why they face this catch-22 situation?

9. Consider the example of ticket scalpers in Montreal presented in the text. Explain why the scalpers didn't lower price until well into the third period (and then what's the point of going to the game?). Use the concept of historical time and path-dependency in your answer.

10. In Canada, gasoline costs much less than it does in Italy. What effect is the price differential likely to have on:

    a. The size of cars in Canada and in Italy?

    b. The use of public transportation in Canada and in Italy?

    c. The fuel efficiency of cars in Canada and in Italy?

3

The Economic Organization of Society

In capitalism man exploits man;
in socialism it's the other way 'round.

~Abba Lerner

After reading this chapter, you should be able to:

1 List three central questions that every economy must answer.

2 Define capitalism and socialism.

3 Explain how capitalist and socialist economies answer the three central economic questions.

4 Give a brief overview of the history of economic systems: how feudalism begat mercantilism which begat capitalism, and how capitalism and socialism continue to evolve.

5 Explain how markets coordinate economic decisions.

6 Explain what is meant by the phrase "Socialism is the longest path from capitalism to capitalism."

The scene is the People's Court in Bucharest, Romania, December 25, 1989. The newly deposed dictator of Romania, Nicolae Ceausescu, and his wife, Elena, are on trial for crimes against the state.

Judge: *What have you done for society?*

Nicolae Ceausescu: *I built hospitals.*

Judge: *What about the food shortage?*

Nicolae Ceausescu: *The people have 440 pounds of corn a year.*

Judge: *You destroyed the Romanian people and their economy.*

Elena Ceausescu: *I gave my entire life for our people.*

Judge: *We condemn the two of you to death.*

On that same day, Elena and Nicolae Ceausescu were executed by a firing squad for economic crimes against the Romanian people.

The political and economic turmoil in the formerly socialist countries have been much in the news in the early 1990s. And with good reason. The Soviet Union is no more; most republics of the former Soviet Union have forsaken socialism and are struggling to introduce a market economy. These events involve some of the most far-reaching changes in the nature of economic systems that the world has seen since the 1930s—changes so major that some social scientists have called the developments "the end of history." Such a sweeping statement is more than a tad too strong, but the developments are certainly important. What's more, they provide us with a good vehicle to introduce some broader issues involving economic systems and the workings of markets.

ECONOMIC SYSTEMS: CAPITALISM AND SOCIALISM

Economic system   The set of economic institutions that determine a country's important economic decisions.

In Chapter 1, we discussed how an **economic system** (the set of economic institutions that determine a country's important economic decisions) works via the interaction of three invisible forces: the invisible hand (economic forces), invisible foot (political forces), and invisible handshake (social forces).

An economic system is closely tied to a political system through which people decide what their society desires. In a democracy, voting procedures determine society's will. In an autocracy, a ruling individual or group of individuals decides what society's desires are. Besides determining what a society wants, an economic system must see that individuals' decisions about what they do are coordinated with what society wants, and with what other individuals do. Coordination is necessary so that the commodities that the market wants match the commodities that are available.

1 Three central questions that economy must answer:
 1. *What* to produce.
 2. *How* to produce it.
 3. *For whom* to produce it.

Before we discuss how the invisible forces operate, we need to consider what people can reasonably expect from an economic system. They can expect it to produce the goods that people want in a reasonably efficient way and to distribute those goods reasonably fairly. Put another way, people can reasonably expect that an economic system will decide:

1. *What* to produce.
2. *How* to produce it.
3. *For whom* to produce it.

These three decisions that an economic system must make are necessarily vague because what people expect is vague. But when people feel that an economic system hasn't given them what they want, the result isn't always so vague—as the Ceausescus found out.

Planning, Politics, and Markets

In making their three decisions, societies have a problem. Usually what individuals, on their own, want to do isn't consistent with what "society" wants them to do. Society would often like people to consider what's good for society, and to fit what's good for themselves into what society wants them to do. For example, say society has garbage, and society determines that your neighbourhood is the best place to set up a garbage dump. Even if you agree a garbage dump is needed, you probably won't want it in your neighbourhood. This **NIMBY** (**N**ot **I**n **M**y **B**ack **Y**ard) attitude has become familiar in the 1990s.

NIMBY   A short way to express "Not In My Back Yard" when a community objects to a proposed development in its neighbourhood.

Another area in which individual goals and social goals come into conflict is in producing and consuming goods. Individuals generally like to consume much more than they like to produce, so society has the problem of scarcity. It must provide incentives for people to produce more and consume less. It's a sure sign that an economic system isn't working when there are important things that need to be done, but many people are sitting around doing nothing because the system doesn't provide individuals with the incentive to do that work.

How hard is it to make the three decisions we've listed? Imagine for a moment the problem of living in a family: the fights, arguments, and questions that come up. "Do I have to do the dishes?" "Why can't I have piano lessons?" "Bobby got a new jacket. How come I didn't?" "Mom likes you best." Now multiply the size of the family by millions. The same fights, the same arguments, the same questions—only for society the problems are millions of times more complicated than for one family.

How do you solve these complicated coordination problems? Do you create an organization to tell people what to do and when to do it? Or do you let people do what they want, subject to a set of rules? The two main economic systems the world has used in the past 50 years—capitalism and socialism—answer these questions differently.

Capitalism

Capitalism is an economic system based upon private property and the market in which, in principle, individuals decide how, what, and for whom to produce. Under capitalism, individuals are encouraged to follow their own self-interest, while market forces of supply and demand are relied upon to coordinate economic activity. Distribution is to each individual according to his or her ability, effort, and inherited property.

2A   Capitalism is an economic system based on private property and the market. It gives private property rights to individuals, and relies on market forces to coordinate economic activity.

Reliance upon market forces doesn't mean that political, social, and historical forces play no role in coordinating economic decisions, because the other forces influence how the market works. For a market to exist, **private property rights** (in which control over an asset or a right is given to a private individual or firm) must be allocated and defended by government. The concept of private ownership must exist and must be accepted by individuals in society. When you say, "This car is mine," it means that it is unlawful for someone else to take it. If someone takes it without your permission, he or she is subject to punishment through the legal system. Private property rights include intellectual property too—when you come up with the design for the proverbial "new and improved mousetrap," that's your intellectual property. When a television entertainer switches networks, that may be a result of a willingness to pay more for her talent—her intellectual property.

Private property rights   Control of an asset or a right given to an individual or a firm.

Markets work through a system of rewards and payments. If you do something, you get paid for doing that something; if you get something, you pay for that something. How much you get is determined by how much you give. This relationship seems fair to most people. But there are instances when it doesn't seem fair. Say someone is unable to work. Should that person not get anything? How about Joe down the street who was given $10 million by his parents? Is it fair that he gets lots of toys like Corvettes and skiing trips to Whistler, and doesn't have to work, while the rest of us have to work 40 hours a week and maybe go to school at night?

We'll consider those questions about fairness in a later chapter. For now, all we want to present is the underlying concept of fairness that capitalism embodies: "Them that works, gets; them that don't, starve."[1] In capitalism, individuals are encouraged to follow their own self-interest.

---

[1]How come the professors get to use rotten grammar but scream when they see rotten grammar in your papers? Well, that's fairness for you. Actually, we should say a bit more about writing style. All writers are expected to know correct grammar; if they don't, they don't deserve to be called writers. Once one knows grammar, one can individualize his or her writing style, breaking the rules of grammar where the metre and flow of the writing require it. Right now you're still proving that you know grammar so, in papers handed in to your teacher, you shouldn't break the rules of grammar until you've proven to the teacher that you know them. We've written a large number of books and journal articles, so our editors give us a bit more leeway than your teachers will give you.

In capitalist economies, individuals are free to do whatever they want as long as it's legal. The market is relied upon to see that what people want to get, and want to do, is consistent with what's available. If there's not enough of something to go around (if there's excess demand), its price goes up; if more of something needs to get done, the price given to individuals willing to do it goes up. If something isn't wanted or doesn't need to be done (if there's excess supply), its price goes down. Under capitalism, fluctuations in prices coordinate individuals' wants.

Chapters 1 and 2 told how the market works. By almost all accounts, capitalism has been an extraordinarily successful economic system. Since much of this book will be devoted to explaining capitalist economies' success, and since capitalism is probably somewhat familiar to you already (to take the course you had to pay a price determined by your institution—your tuition—giving you direct experience with capitalism), let's discuss socialism first.

Socialism in Theory

2B Socialism is an economic system that tries to organize society in the same way as do most families—all people should contribute what they can, and get what they need.

In theory, socialism is an economic system based upon individuals' good will toward others, not their own self-interests.

You can best understand the idea behind theoretical socialism by thinking about how decisions are made in a family. In most families, decisions about who gets what are determined by usually benevolent parents. When Sabin gets a new coat and his sister Sally doesn't, it's because Sabin needs a coat while Sally already has two coats that fit her and are in good condition. Victor may be slow as molasses, but from his family he still gets as much as his superefficient brother Jerry. In fact, Victor may get more than Jerry because he needs extra help.

Markets have little role in most families. In our families, when food is placed on the table we don't bid on what we want, with the highest bidder getting the food. In our families every person can eat all he or she wants, although if one child eats more than a fair share, that child gets a lecture on the importance of sharing—of seeing to it that everyone has already had a fair share before you take or even ask for seconds. "Be thoughtful; be considerate; and think of others first," are among the lessons that many families try to teach.

Socialism Economic system that tries to organize society in such a way that all people contribute what they can and get what they need, adjusting their own wants in accordance with what's available.

In theory, **socialism** is an economic system that tries to organize society in the same way as these families. Socialism tries to see that individuals get what they need. Socialism tries to get individuals to take other people's needs into account and to adjust their own wants in accordance with what's available. A capitalist economy expects people to be selfish; it relies on markets and competition to direct that selfishness to the general good. In socialist economies, individuals are urged to look out for the other person; if individuals' inherent goodness won't make them consider the general good, government will make them.[2]

Socialism in Practice

In practice, socialism became an economic system based on government ownership of the means of production, with economic activity governed by central planning. Because it is based on a system developed in the former Soviet Union, this is often called Soviet-style socialism.

In the 1980s, a number of countries had Soviet-style socialist economies. In the late 1980s and early 1990s, many of those countries were in turmoil. Total output in the economies had fallen significantly, and their economic and political systems were in chaos. Many of the countries undergoing major changes are shown in Exhibit 1. Why did these countries reject the economic system they had followed for almost 50 years (and almost 75 years in the former Soviet Union)? Some economists argue that Soviet-style socialism self-destructed because socialism did not offer acceptable answers to the questions an economic system must address. They claim socialism didn't provide individuals with incentives to produce enough. Soon, they say, the

---

[2]As you probably surmised, the above distinction is too sharp. Even in capitalist societies, one wants people to be selfless, but not too selfless. Children in capitalist societies are generally taught to be selfless, at least in dealing with friends and family. The difficulties parents and societies face is finding a midpoint between the two positions: selfless but not too selfless; selfish but not too selfish.

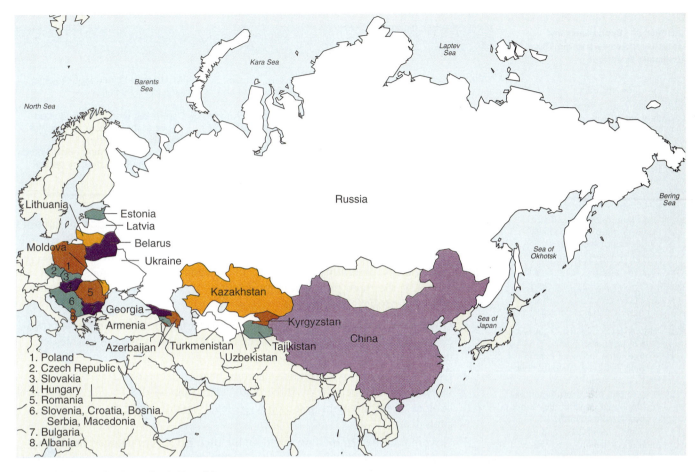

EXHIBIT 1   Socialist Countries in Transition

This map shows the most important formerly traditional socialist economies that are now going through major transitions. China and the former USSR were the largest socialist economies, although there were a number of socialist countries in Eastern Europe, Africa, and Asia.
Source: *CIA World Fact Book.*

world will have only one economic system: capitalism. Other economists argue that the Soviet-style socialism was not socialism at all—that, early on, Soviet-style socialism deviated from the socialistic path. True socialism was not rejected, these economists argue, because true socialism was never tried.

Defining Soviet-style socialism precisely is difficult because it embodies both political and economic features. We will concentrate on the economic features. Specifically, **Soviet-style socialism** uses administrative control or central planning to answer the questions *what, how,* and *for whom.* In a Soviet-style socialist economic system, government planning boards set society's goals and then give individuals directives as to how to achieve those goals.

Let's now discuss how a Soviet-style socialist country and a capitalist country might make different decisions about the what, how, and for whom questions. Let's consider two goods: designer jeans and whole-wheat bread. Compared to their cost in the formerly socialist countries, in most capitalist societies designer jeans are relatively inexpensive while whole-wheat bread is relatively expensive. Why? One reason is that central planners decide that designer jeans are frivolous luxury items, so they produce few or none and charge a high price for what they do produce. Similarly, they decide that whole-wheat bread is good for people, so they produce large quantities and price it exceptionally low. Planners, not supply and demand, determine what, how, and for whom to produce.

To accomplish planners' ends—getting people to do what planners think is best— requires stronger government control than exists in capitalist countries. To maintain

Soviet-style socialism   Economic system that uses central planning and government ownership of the means of production to answer the questions: what, how, and for whom.

Central economic question	Capitalism's answer	Soviet-Style socialism's answer
What to produce?	What firms believe people want and will make the firm a profit.	What central planners believe is socially beneficial.
How to produce?	Businesspeople decide how to produce efficiently, guided by their desire to make a profit.	Central planners decide, guided by what they believe is good for the country (ideally).
For whom to produce?	Distribution according to ability and inherited wealth.	Distribution according to individuals' need (as determined by central planners).

3A   Capitalism's answers to the central economic questions:
1. What to produce: what businesses believe people want, and is profitable.
2. How to produce: businesses decide how to produce efficiently, guided by their desire to make a profit.
3. For whom to produce: distribution according to individuals' ability and/or inherited wealth.

3B   Soviet-style socialism's answers to the three questions:
1. What to produce: what central planners believe is socially beneficial.
2. How to produce: central planners decide, based on what they think is good for the country.
3. For whom to produce: central planners distribute goods based on what they determine are individuals' needs.

that control, government generally owns the means of production, such as factories and machines, and tells people where they will work and how much they will receive. In Soviet-style socialism, individuals' choices are limited and planners' choices, not individuals' choices, determine the answers to the central economic questions.

In summary, the three principal components of a Soviet-style socialist economy compared to a capitalist economy are:

1. Government ownership of the means of production, rather than private ownership as in capitalism. Central planners, rather than owners of businesses, decide what to produce.
2. Directed labour. A government planning board directs where workers will work and how much they will be paid, rather than workers making individual choices of employment based on wage levels in different jobs, as in capitalism.
3. Government-determined prices. Usually, high prices are charged for luxury goods and low prices for necessities, rather than market-determined prices as in capitalism.

There are, of course, markets in Soviet-style socialist economies. Just as in capitalist economies, individuals buy goods by going to the store. The difference between stores in the two kinds of economies is that, in a Soviet-style socialist economy, the government tells the storekeeper what goods will be offered, what price to charge, and how much of a good will be delivered to the store, while in a capitalist society, the store-owner can order as much of any good as he or she wants and can charge any price he or she wants—whatever the market will bear.

Differences between Soviet-Style Socialism and Capitalism

The difference between Soviet-style socialist economies and capitalist economies is not that Soviet-style socialist economies are planned economies and capitalist economies are unplanned. Both economies involve planning. **Planning** simply involves deciding—before the production takes place—what will be produced, how to produce it, and for whom it will be produced. The differences are in who does the planning, what they try to do in planning, and how the plans are coordinated.

In capitalist countries, businesspeople do the planning. Businesspeople decide that they can sell designer jeans, Nintendo games, or economics textbooks. They target their likely customers and decide how much to produce and what price to charge. In Soviet-style socialist countries, government planners decide what people need and should have.

In an idealized capitalist society, businesses design their plans to maximize their profit; the market is relied upon to see that individual self-interest is consistent with society's interest. In an idealized socialist society, the government designs its plans to make society better.

Planning   Deciding, before the production takes place, what will be produced, how to produce it, and for whom to produce it.

In a capitalist economy, coordination of plans is left to the workings of the market. In a Soviet-style socialist economy, coordination is done by government planners.

Exhibit 2 summarizes how capitalism and Soviet-style socialism answer the three central economic questions: how, what, and for whom.

Soviet people happily tear down a statue of Lenin, which they saw as a symbol of Soviet-style socialism. Reuters/Bettmann.

Evolving Economic Systems

Capitalism and socialism have not existed forever. Capitalism came into existence in the mid-1700s; socialism came into existence in the early 1900s.

Both capitalism and socialism have changed over the years, and a look at their evolution will give us a good sense of the struggle among the invisible forces to dominate our lives. In the 1930s, during the Great Depression, capitalist countries integrated a number of what might be called *socialist institutions* with their existing institutions. Distribution was no longer, even in theory, only according to ability; need also played a role. Government's economic role in capitalist societies increased, and some of the how, what, and for whom decisions were transferred from the market to the government. For example, most capitalist nations established a welfare system and a social security system, providing an economic safety net for people whose incomes were inadequate for their needs.

The 1980s saw the reverse process take place, with socialism integrating some capitalist institutions with its existing institutions. Market sectors in socialist countries expanded, government's economic importance decreased, and some how, what, and for whom decisions were transferred from government to the market. Instead of being assigned jobs by the government, workers were often allowed to choose jobs themselves, and some firms were allowed to produce independently of planners' decisions. Even in cases where production decisions weren't transferred, socialist planning boards used market principles more and more in making their decisions.

The result has been a blending of economic systems and a blurring of the distinctions between capitalism and socialism. If the trend toward the use of market mechanisms in socialist countries continues, in the 21st century there may be only one general type of economic structure. It won't be pure socialism and it won't be pure capitalism. It will be a blend of the two.

For students of history, the recent changes in economic systems are not surprising. Economic systems are in a continual state of evolution. To understand recent movements in socialist countries and to put market institutions in perspective, in the next section we briefly consider the history and nature of economic systems.

THE HISTORY OF ECONOMIC SYSTEMS

4A Economic systems evolve because the institutions of the new system offer a better life for at least some—and usually a large majority—of the individuals in a society.

Remember the distinction between market and economic forces: Economic forces have always existed—they operate in all aspects of our lives; but market forces have not always existed. Markets are social creations societies use to coordinate individuals' actions. Markets developed, sometimes spontaneously, sometimes by design, because they offered a better life for at least some—and usually a large majority of—individuals in a society.

To understand why markets developed, it is helpful to look briefly at the history of the economic systems from which our own system descended.

Feudal Society: Rule of the Invisible Handshake

Let's go back in time to the year 1000, when Europe had no nation-states as we now know them. There was no coordinated central government, no unified system of law, no national patriotism, no national defense, although there was a strong religious institution simply called the Church that fulfilled some of these roles. There were few towns; most individuals lived in walled manors or "estates." These manors "belonged to" the "lord of the manor."[3] We say "belonged to" rather than "were owned by" because most of the empires or federations at that time were not formal nation-states that could organize, administer, and regulate ownership. There were no documents or deeds giving ownership of the land to an individual. Instead there was tradition, and in normal times nobody questioned the lord's right to the land. The land "belonged to" the lord because the land "belonged to" him—that's the way it was.

Because there was no central nation-state, the manor served many functions a nation-state would have served had it existed. The lord provided protection, often within a walled area surrounding the manor house or, if the manor was large enough, a castle. He provided administration and decided disputes. He also decided *what* would be done, *how* it would be done, and *who* would get what, but these decisions were limited. In the same way that the land belonged to the lord because that's the way it always had been, what people did and how they did it were determined by what they always had done. Tradition ruled the manor more than the lord did.

The Life of a Serf
Individuals living on the land were called *serfs*. What serfs did was determined by what their fathers had done. If the father was a farmer, the son was a farmer. A woman followed her husband and helped him do what he did. That was the way it always had been and that's the way it was—tradition again.

Most serfs were farmers, and surrounding the manor were fields of about a half acre each. Serfs were tied by tradition to their assigned plots of land; according to tradition, they could not leave those plots and had to turn over a portion of their harvest to the lord every year. How much they had to turn over varied from manor to manor, but payments of half the total harvest were not unheard of. In return, the lord provided defense and organized the life of the manor—boring as it was. Thus, there was a type of trade between the serf and the lord, but it was nonnegotiable and did not take place through a market.

Feudalism Political system divided into small communities in which a few powerful people protect those who are loyal to them.

Problems of a Tradition-Based Society
This system, known as **feudalism,** developed about the 8th and 9th centuries and lasted until about the 15th century, though in isolated countries such as Russia it continued well into the 19th century, and in all European countries its influence lingered for hundreds of years (as late as about 140 years ago in some parts of Germany). Such a long-lived system must have done some things right, and feudalism did: it answered the what, how, and for whom questions in an acceptable way.

But a tradition-based society has problems. In a traditional society, because someone's father was a baker, the son must also be a baker, and because a woman was a homemaker, she wouldn't be allowed to be anything but a homemaker. But what if Joe Blacksmith, Jr., the son of Joe Blacksmith, Sr., is a lousy blacksmith and longs to knead dough, while Joe Baker, Jr., would be a superb blacksmith but hates making pastry? Tough. Tradition dictated who did what. In fact, tradition probably arranged

---

[3]Occasionally the "lord" was a lady, but not often.

ADDED DIMENSION

MILESTONES IN
ECONOMICS

6700 B.C.	First known coins (Iran).
3600 B.C.	First system of taxation (Mesopotamia).
2100 B.C.	First welfare system (Egypt).
2000 B.C.	Coins in general use.
2000 B.C.–500 A.D.	International trade flourishes.
100 B.C.	First corporation (Rome).
105 A.D.	Chinese invent paper (a cheap substance to replace parchment).
301 A.D.	First wage and price controls (Emperor Diocletian of Rome).
700–1400	Development of feudal estates.
1275	Development of tariffs in England.
1400–1800	End of feudal estates and development of private property and wage workers.
1600–1800	Mercantilism and state control of economic activity.
1700s	Development of paper money (France).
1750–1900	Industrial Revolution.
1760–1800	Enclosure movement in England, solidifying private property and market economy.
1776	Publication of Adam Smith's *Wealth of Nations*.
1860–1960	Development of social security and unemployment insurance (Germany).
1867	Publication of Karl Marx's *Das Kapital*.
1935–1970	Integration of socialist institutions into capitalism.
1988 onward	Socialist economies in upheaval adopt markets and capitalist institutions.

things so that we will never know whether Joe Blacksmith, Jr., would have made a superb baker.

As long as a society doesn't change too much, tradition operates reasonably well, although not especially efficiently, in holding the society together. However, when a society must undergo change, tradition does not work. Change means that the things that were done before no longer need to be done, while new things do need to get done. But if no one has traditionally done these new things, then they don't get done. If the change is important but a society can't figure out some way for the new things to get done, the society falls apart. That's what happened to feudal society. It didn't change when change was required.

Some individuals in feudal society just couldn't take life on the manor, and they set off on their own. Because there was no organized police force, they were unlikely to be caught and forced to return to the manor. Going hungry, being killed, or both, however, were frequent fates of an escaped serf. One place to which serfs could safely escape, though, was a town or city—the remains of what in Roman times had been thriving and active cities. These cities, which had been decimated by plagues, plundering bands, and starvation in the preceding centuries, nevertheless remained an escape hatch for runaway serfs because they relied far less on tradition than did manors. City dwellers had to live by their wits; many became merchants who lived predominantly by trading. They were middlemen; they would buy from one group and sell to another.

Trading in towns was an alternative to the traditional feudal order because trading allowed people to have an income independent of the traditional social structure. Markets broke down tradition. Initially merchants traded using barter (exchange of one kind of good for another): silk and spices from the Orient for wheat, flour, and artisan products in Europe. But soon a generalized purchasing power (money) developed as a medium of exchange. Money greatly expanded the possibilities of trading because its use meant that goods no longer needed to be bartered. They could be sold for money, which could then be spent to buy other goods.

In the beginning, land was not one of the goods that could be traded, but soon the feudal lord who just had to have a silk robe but had no money was saying, "Why not?

4B Feudalism evolved into mercantilism because markets and the development of money allowed trade to expand, which undermined the traditional base of feudalism. Tradition that can be bought and sold is no longer tradition—it's just another commodity.

I'll sell you a small piece of land so I can buy a shipment of silk." Once land became tradeable, the traditional base of the feudal society was undermined. Tradition that can be bought and sold is no longer tradition—it's just another commodity.

From Feudalism to Mercantilism

Toward the end of the Middle Ages, markets went from being a sideshow, a fair that spiced up peoples' lives, to being the main event. Over time, some traders and merchants started to amass fortunes that dwarfed those of the feudal lords. Rich traders settled down; existing towns and cities expanded and new towns were formed. As towns grew and as fortunes shifted from feudal lords to merchants, power in society shifted to the towns. And with that shift came a change in society's political and economic structure.

As these traders became stronger politically and economically, they threw their support behind a king (the strongest lord) in the hope that the king would expand their ability to trade. In doing so, they made the king even stronger. Eventually, the king became so powerful that his will prevailed over the will of the other lords and even over the will of the Church. As the king consolidated his power, nation-states as we know them today evolved. *The invisible foot—government—became an active influence on economic decision making.*

Mercantilism   Economic system in which government doles out the rights to undertake economic activities.

As markets grew, feudalism evolved into **mercantilism** (an economic system in which the government determines the what, how, and for whom decisions by doling out the rights to undertake certain economic activities). Political rather than social forces came to control the central economic decisions.

The evolution of feudal systems into mercantilism occurred in somewhat this way: As cities and their markets grew in size and power relative to the feudal manors and the traditional economy, a whole new variety of possible economic activities developed. It was only natural that individuals began to look to a king to establish a new tradition that would determine who would do what. Individuals in particular occupations organized into groups called *guilds,* which were similar to strong labour unions today. These guilds, many of which had financed and supported the king, now expected the king and his government to protect their interests.

As new economic activities, such as trading companies, developed, individuals involved in these activities similarly depended on the king for the right to trade and for help in financing and organizing their activities. For example, in 1492, when Christopher Columbus had the wild idea that by sailing west he could get to the East Indies and trade for their riches, he went to Spain's Queen Isabella and King Ferdinand for financial support.

Since many traders had played and continued to play important roles in financing, establishing, and supporting the king, the king was usually happy to protect their interests. The government doled out the rights to undertake a variety of economic activities. By the late 1400s, Western Europe had evolved from a feudal to a mercantilist economy.

The mercantilist period was marked by the increased role of government, which could be classified in two ways: by the way it encouraged growth, and by the way it limited growth. Government legitimized and financed a variety of activities, thus encouraging growth. But government also limited economic activity in order to protect the monopolies of those it favoured, thus limiting growth. So mercantilism allowed the market to operate, but it kept the market under its control. The market was not allowed to respond freely to the laws of supply and demand.

From Mercantilism to Capitalism

The mercantilist period saw major growth in Western Europe, but mercantilism also unleashed new tensions within society. Like feudalism, mercantilism limited entry into economic activities. It used a different form of limitation—the invisible foot (politics) rather than the invisible handshake (social and cultural tradition)—but individuals who were excluded still felt unfairly treated.

Capitalists   Businesspeople who have acquired large amounts of money and use it to invest in businesses.

The most significant source of tension was the different roles played by craft guilds and owners of new businesses, who were called **capitalists** or industrialists. Craft guild members were artists in their own crafts: pottery, shoemaking, and the like.

TRADITION AND TODAY'S ECONOMY

In a tradition-based society, the invisible handshake (the social and cultural forces embodied in history) gives a society inertia (a tendency to resist change) which predominates over economic and political forces.

"Why did you do it that way?"
"Because that's the way we've always done it."

Tradition-based societies had markets, but those were peripheral, not central, to economic life. In feudal times what was produced, how it was produced, and for whom it was produced were primarily decided by tradition.

In today's economy, the market plays the central role in economic decisions. But that doesn't mean that tradition is dead. As we said in Chapter 1, tradition still plays a significant role in today's society, and, in many aspects of society, tradition still overwhelms the invisible hand. Consider the following:

1. The persistent view that women should be homemakers rather than factory workers, consumers rather than producers.
2. The raised eyebrows when a man is introduced as a nurse, secretary, homemaker, or member of any other profession conventionally identified as *women's work.*
3. Society's unwillingness to permit the sale of individuals or body organs.
4. Parents' willingness to care for their children without financial compensation.

Each of these tendencies reflects tradition's influence in Western society. Some are so deep-rooted that we see them as self-evident. Some of tradition's effects we like; others we don't—but we often take them for granted. Economic forces may work against these traditions, but the fact that they're still around indicates the continued strength of tradition in our market economy.

New business owners destroyed the art of production by devising machines to replace hand production. Machines produced goods cheaper and faster than craftsmen.[4] The result was an increase in supply and a downward pressure on the price, which was set by government. Craftsmen didn't want to be replaced by machines. They argued that machine-manufactured goods didn't have the same quality as hand-crafted goods, and that the new machines would disrupt the economic and social life of the community.

Industrialists were the outsiders with a vested interest in changing the existing system. They wanted the freedom to conduct business as they saw fit. Because of the enormous cost advantage of manufactured goods over crafted goods, a few industrialists overcame government opposition and succeeded within the mercantilist system. They earned their fortunes and became an independent political power.

Once again the economic power base shifted, and two groups competed with each other for power—this time, the guilds and the industrialists. The government had to decide whether to support the industrialists (who wanted government to loosen its power over the country's economic affairs) or the craftsmen and guilds (who argued for strong government limitations and for maintaining traditional values of workmanship). This struggle raged in the 1700s and 1800s. But during this time, governments themselves were changing. This was the Age of Revolutions, and the kings' powers were being limited by democratic reform movements—revolutions supported and financed in large part by the industrialists.

The Need for Coordination in an Economy   One argument craftsmen put forward was that coordination of the economy was necessary, and the government had to be involved. If government wasn't going to coordinate economic activity, who would? To answer that question, a British moral philosopher named Adam Smith developed, in his famous book *The Wealth of Nations* (1776), the concept of the invisible hand, and used it to explain how markets could coordinate the economy without the active involvement of government. Smith wrote:

> Man has almost constant occasion for the help of his brethren, and it is in vain for him to expect it from their benevolence only. He will be more likely to prevail, if he can interest their self-love in his favour, and show them that it is for their own advantage to do for him what he requires of them. Whoever offers to another a bargain of any kind proposes

4C   Mercantilism evolved into capitalism because the Industrial Revolution undermined the craft-guided mercantilist method of production. Machines produced goods cheaper and faster, making industrialists rich. They used their economic power to change the political support for mercantilism.

5   Markets coordinate economic activity by turning self-interest into social good. Competition directs individuals pursuing profit to do what society needs to have done.

---

[4]Throughout this section we use *men* to emphasize that these societies were strongly male-dominated. There were almost no businesswomen. In fact, a woman had to turn over her property to a man upon her marriage, and the marriage contract was written as if she were owned by her husband!

ADDED DIMENSION   THE RISE OF MARKETS IN PERSPECTIVE

B ack in the Middle Ages, markets developed spontaneously. "You have something I want; I have something you want. Let's trade" is a basic human attitude we see in all aspects of life. Even children quickly get into trading: chocolate ice cream for vanilla, two action figures for a ride on a motor scooter. Markets institutionalize such trading by providing a place where people know they can go to trade. New markets are continually coming into existence. Today there are markets for baseball cards, pork bellies (which become bacon and pork chops), rare coins, and so on.

Throughout history, societies have tried to prevent some markets from operating because they feel those markets are ethically wrong or have undesirable side effects. Societies have the power to prevent markets. They make some kinds of markets illegal. In Canada, the addictive drug market, the baby market, and the sex market, to name a few, are illegal. In socialist countries, markets in a much wider range of goods (such as clothes, cars, and soft drinks) and activities (such as private business for individual profit) have been illegal.

But, even if a society prevents the market from operating, it cannot escape the dynamic laws of supply and demand. If there's excess supply, there will be downward pressure on prices; if there's excess demand, there will be upward pressure on prices. To maintain an equilibrium in which the quantity supplied does not equal the quantity demanded, a society needs a force to prevent the invisible hand from working. In the Middle Ages, that strong force was religion. The Church told people that if they got too far into the market mentality—if they followed their self-interest—they'd go to Hell.

Until recently in socialist society, the state has provided the preventive force. In their educational system, socialist countries would emphasize a more communal set of values. They taught students that a member of socialist society does not try to take advantage of other human beings but, rather, lives by the philosophy "From each according to his ability; to each according to his need."

For whatever reason—some say because true socialism wasn't really tried; others say because people's self-interest is too strong—the "from each according to his ability; to each according to his need" approach didn't work in socialist countries. They have switched (some say succumbed) to greater reliance on the market.

---

to do this. Give me that which I want, and you shall have that which you want, is the meaning of every such offer; and it is in this manner that we obtain from one another the far greater part of those good offices which we stand in need of. It is not from the benevolence of the butcher, the brewer, or the baker, that we expect our dinner, but from their regard to their own interest. We address ourselves, not to their humanity but to their self-love, and never talk to them of our own necessities but of their advantages.

Smith argued that the market's invisible hand would guide suppliers' actions toward the general good. No government coordination was necessary.

With the help of economists such as Adam Smith, the industrialists' view won out. Government pulled back from its role in guiding the economy and adopted a **laissez-faire** policy, leaving coordination of the economy to the invisible hand. (*Laissez faire*, a French term, means "Let events take their course; leave things alone.")

Laissez-faire   Economic policy of leaving coordination of individuals' wants to be controlled by the market.

The Industrial Revolution   The invisible hand worked; capitalism thrived. During the **Industrial Revolution,** which began about 1750 and continued through the late 1800s, machine production increased enormously, almost totally replacing hand production. The economy grew faster than ever before. Society was forever transformed. New inventions changed all aspects of life. James Watt's steam engine (1769) made manufacturing and travel easier. Eli Whitney's cotton gin (1793) changed the way cotton was processed. James Kay's flying shuttle (1733),[5] James Hargreaves's spinning jenny (1765), and Richard Arkwright's power loom (1769), combined with the steam engine, changed the way cloth was processed and the clothes people wore.

Industrial Revolution   Period (1750–1900) during which technology and machines rapidly modernized industrial production.

The need to mine vast amounts of coal to provide power to run the machines changed the economic and physical landscapes. The repeating rifle changed the nature of warfare. Modern economic institutions replaced guilds. Stock markets, insurance companies, and corporations all became important. Trading was no longer financed by

---

[5]The invention of the flying shuttle frustrated the textile industry because it enabled workers to weave so much cloth that the spinners of thread from which the cloth was woven couldn't keep up. This challenge to the textile industry was met by offering a prize to anyone who could invent something to increase the thread spinners' productivity. The prize was won when the spinning jenny was invented.

ADDED DIMENSION

THE ROLE OF ECONOMISTS IN ECONOMIC TRANSITIONS

For economics to be relevant, it must have something to say about social policy. Good economists try to be objective and recommend policies that they believe would be good for society in general rather than for any particular group in society.

Deciding what is in society's interest isn't always easy. For economists, it requires interpreting what society wants and comparing different policies, using what economists believe is society's preference. That often means proposing policies that will help some people but hurt others.

Adam Smith's "invisible hand" argument for the free working of the market and against government intervention is a good example. Smith favoured a laissez-faire policy, meaning the government should not interfere with the operation of the economy. In this argument, Smith and other Classical economists found themselves aligned with the industrialists or manufacturers, who wanted the right to enter into markets as they saw fit, and against the guilds and independent artisans, who wanted government to control who did what.

These two groups each had different reasons for supporting laissez-faire policy, however. Industrialists supported the policy because they believed it benefited them. Sometimes they claimed policies that helped them actually benefited society, but they only made this argument because it helped make their case more persuasive. Economists supported the laissez-faire policy because they believed it benefited society.

It's not easy to decide which policies will benefit society when the policies you're looking at will help some people and hurt other people. It's hard to weigh a policy and decide whether the good that it will probably do outweighs the harm that it may cause.

Modern economists have spent a long time struggling with this problem. Some have avoided the problem. They have refused to advocate any policy that might hurt anyone, which pretty much eliminates advocating any policy at all. Good policy-oriented economists make working judgements of what they believe is in society's interest; these working judgements determine which policies they advocate.

In reality, economists' (or anyone's) arguments for the general good of society are unlikely to have much effect on the policies of any government unless their arguments coincide with the interests of one group or another. A policy of less government involvement favoured manufacturers over craftspeople. That the policy favoured manufacturers or industrialists isn't the reason economists favoured it (they argued that less government involvement would be good for society as a whole), but it is the reason industrialists supported laissez-faire, and the industrialists' support of laissez-faire was critical in getting the policy adopted in Britain in the late 1700s.

Once markets were established, the terms of the debate changed. Many economists stopped advocating laissez-faire policies. Good economists recognize the advantages of markets, but they also recognize the problems of markets.

---

government; it was privately financed (although government policies, such as colonial policies giving certain companies monopoly trading rights with a country's colonies, helped in that trading). The Industrial Revolution, democracy, and capitalism all arose in the middle and late 1700s. By the 1800s, they were part of the institutional landscape of Western society. Capitalism had arrived.

Capitalism was marked by significant economic growth in the Western world. But it was also marked by human abuses—18-hour workdays, low wages, children as young as five years old slaving long hours in dirty, dangerous factories and mines—to produce enormous wealth for an elite few. Such conditions and inequalities led to criticism of the capitalist or market economic system.

From Capitalism to ~~Socialism~~
Welfare Capitalism

Marx's Analysis The best-known critic of this system was Karl Marx, a German philosopher, economist, and sociologist who wrote in the 1800s and who developed an analysis of the dynamics of change in economic systems. Marx argued that economic systems are in a constant state of change, and that capitalism would not last. Workers would revolt, and capitalism would be replaced by a socialist economic system.

Marx saw an economy marked by tensions among economic classes. He saw capitalism as an economic system controlled by the capitalist class (businessmen). His class analysis was that capitalist society is divided into capitalist and worker classes. He said constant tension between these economic classes causes changes in the system. The capitalist class made large profits by exploiting the **proletariat** class (working class) and extracting what he called *surplus value* from workers who, according to Marx's labour theory of value, produced all the value inherent in goods. Surplus value was the profit that, according to Marx's normative views, capitalists

Proletariat The working class.

added to the price of goods. What economic analysis sees as recognizing a need that society has and fulfilling it, Marx saw as exploitation.

Marx argued that this exploitation would increase as production facilities became larger and larger and as competition among capitalists decreased. At some point, he believed, exploitation would lead to a revolt by the proletariat, who would overthrow their capitalist exploiters.

By the late 1800s, some of what Marx predicted had occurred, although not in the way that he thought it would. Production moved from small to large factories. Corporations developed, and classes became more distinct from one another. Workers were significantly differentiated from owners. Small firms merged and were organized into monopolies and trusts (large combinations of firms). The trusts developed ways to prevent competition among themselves and ways to limit entry of new competitors into the market. Marx was right in his predictions about these developments, but he was wrong in his prediction about society's response to them.

The Revolution that Did Not Occur   Western society's response to the problems of capitalism was not a revolt by the workers. Whereas Marx said capitalism would fall because of the exploitation of workers by the owners of businesses or capitalists, what actually happened was that the market economy was modified by political forces. Governments stepped in to stop the worst abuses of capitalism. The hard edges of capitalism were softened.

Evolution, not revolution, was capitalism's destiny. The democratic state did not act, as Marx argued it would, as a mere representative of the capitalist class. Competing pressure groups developed; workers gained political power which offset the economic power of businesses.

In the late 1930s and the 1940s, workers dominated the political agenda. During this time, capitalist economies developed an economic safety net which included government-funded programs, such as public welfare and unemployment insurance, and established an extensive set of regulations affecting all aspects of the economy. Today, depressions are met with direct government policy. Anti-combines laws, regulatory agencies, and social programs of government softened the hard edges of capitalism. Laws were passed prohibiting child labour, mandating a certain minimum wage, and limiting the hours of work. Capitalism became what is sometimes called **welfare capitalism**, an economic system in which the market is allowed to operate, but in which government plays key roles in determining distribution and making the *what, how,* and *for whom* decisions.

Welfare capitalism   Economic system in which the market operates but government regulates markets significantly.

Due to these developments, government spending now accounts for nearly half of all spending in Canada, and for more than half in some European countries. Were an economist from the late 1800s to return from the grave, he'd probably say socialism, not capitalism, exists in Western societies. Most modern-day economists wouldn't go that far, but they would agree that our economy today is better described as a welfare capitalist economy than as a capitalist, or even a market, economy. Because of these changes, Canada and Western European economies are a far cry from the competitive "capitalist" economy that Karl Marx criticized. Markets operate, but they are constrained by the government.

The concept *capitalism* developed to denote a market system controlled by one group in society, the capitalists. Looking at Western societies today, we see that domination by one group no longer characterizes Western economies. Although in theory capitalists control corporations through their ownership of shares of stock, in practice corporations are controlled in large part by managers. There remains an elite group who control business, but "capitalist" is not a good term to describe them. Managers, not capitalists, exercise primary control over business, and even their control is limited by laws or the fear of laws being passed by governments.

Governments in turn are controlled by a variety of pressure groups. Sometimes one group is in control; at other times, another. Government policies similarly fluctuate. Sometimes they are proworker, sometimes proindustrialist, sometimes progovernment, and sometimes prosociety.

You probably noticed that we crossed out "Socialism" in the previous section's heading and replaced it with "Welfare Capitalism." That's because capitalism did not evolve to socialism as Karl Marx predicted it would. Instead, Marx's socialist ideas took root in Russia, a society that the Industrial Revolution had in large part bypassed. Arriving at a different place and a different time than Marx predicted it would, socialism, you should not be surprised to read, arrived in a different way than Marx predicted. There was no revolution of the proletariat to establish socialism. Instead, there was World War I, which the Russians were losing, and there was Russia's feudal economy and government, which were crippled by the war effort. A small group of socialists overthrew the czar (Russia's king) and took over the government in 1917. They quickly pulled Russia out of the war, and then set out to organize a socialist society and economy.

From Feudalism to Socialism

Russian socialists tried to adhere to Marx's ideas, but they found that Marx had concentrated on how capitalist economies operate, not on how a socialist economy should be run. Thus, Russian socialists faced a huge task with little guidance. Their most immediate problem was how to increase production so that the economy could emerge from feudalism into the modern industrial world. In Marx's analysis, capitalism was a necessary stage in the evolution toward the ideal state for a very practical reason. The capitalists exploit the workers, but in doing so capitalists extract the necessary surplus—an amount of production in excess of what is consumed. That surplus had to be extracted in order to provide the factories and machinery upon which a socialist economic system would be built. But since there had been no capitalism in Russia, a true socialist state could not be established immediately. Instead, the socialists created an economic system that they called **state socialism.** The state would see to it that people worked for the common good until they could be relied on to do so on their own.

State socialism Economic system in which government sees to it that people work for the common good

Socialists saw state socialism as a transition stage to pure socialism. This transition stage still exploited the workers; when Joseph Stalin took power in Russia in the late 1920s, he took the peasants' and small farmers' land and turned it into collective farms. The government then paid farmers low prices for their produce. When farmers balked at the low prices, millions of them were killed.

Simultaneously, Stalin created central planning agencies which directed individuals on what to produce and how to produce it, and determined for whom things would be produced. During this period, *socialism* became synonymous with *central economic planning,* and Soviet-style socialism became the model of socialism in practice.

Also during this time, Russia took control of a number of neighbouring states and established the Union of Soviet Socialist Republics (USSR), the formal name of the Soviet Union. The Soviet Union also installed Soviet-dominated governments in a number of Eastern European countries. In 1949 most of China, under the rule of Mao Tse-tung, adopted Soviet-style socialist principles.

Since the late 1980s, the Soviet socialist economic and political structure has fallen apart. The Soviet Union as a political state broke up, and its former republics became autonomous. Eastern European countries were released from Soviet control. Now they faced a new problem: transition from socialism to a market economy. Why did the Soviet socialist economy fall apart? Because workers lacked incentives to work; production was inefficient; consumer goods were either unavailable or of poor quality; and high Soviet officials were exploiting their positions, keeping the best jobs for themselves and moving themselves up in the waiting lists for consumer goods. In short, the parents of the socialist family (the Communist party) were no longer acting benevolently; they were taking many of the benefits for themselves.

6 Socialism was an attempt to bring out people's social conscience, rather than their self-interest. Many of the countries that attempted to introduce socialism have recently reverted to capitalism.

Recent political and economic upheavals in Eastern Europe and the Soviet Union suggest that the kind of socialism these societies tried did not work. However, that

ADDED DIMENSION SHAREHOLDERS AND STAKEHOLDERS

orporations (businesses) are technically owned by the owners of capital (shareholders). In theory, at least, they control corporations by electing the officers (the people who make the *what, how,* and *for whom* production decisions). In practice, however, effective control of corporations is generally in the hands of a small group of managing officers.

In the debate about the possible future evolution of capitalism, the question of who controls business decisions is likely to take centre stage. Some reformers argue that the current system is wrong in both theory and practice. They argue that corporations should reflect the need of stakeholders (all the individuals who have a stake in a corporation's activities). Stakeholders include the corporation's shareholders and officers as well as workers, customers, and the community where the corporation operates. An economy in which all stakeholders, not just shareholders, elect the officers who make the *what, how,* and *for whom* decisions would still use the market. It would still be a market economy, but it would no longer be a capitalist economy.

---

failure does not mean that socialist goals are bad; nor does it mean that no type of socialism can ever work. To overthrow socialist-dominated governments it is not necessary to accept capitalism, and many citizens of these countries are looking for an alternative to both systems. Most, however, wanted to establish market economies.

From Socialism to ?

The upheavals in the former Soviet Union and Eastern Europe have left only China as a major power using a socialist economic system. But even in China there have been changes, and the Chinese economy is socialist in name only. Almost uncontrolled markets exist in numerous sectors of the economy. These changes have led some socialists to modify their view that state socialism is the path from capitalism to true socialism, and instead to joke: "Socialism is the longest path from capitalism to capitalism."

ECONOMIC SYSTEMS OF THE FUTURE

Our economic system will probably be different 30 years from now. If the debate between socialism and capitalism disappears, another debate will rise up to take its place. A new topic for debate may be: Who should be the decision makers in a market economy? In the Canadian economy in the late 1980s, a handful of financiers became celebrities by reaping billions of dollars in profits for themselves. Many people came to wonder whether an economic system that so glorified greed was really desirable, and in the 1990s some of those same financiers found themselves near bankruptcy, with the financial institutions they had controlled in ruins. Such widespread reactions may well lead to further evolution of the capitalist system.

Asian tigers Group of Asian countries that have achieved economic growth well above the level of other developing countries.

Also in the early and mid-1990s, the **Asian tigers**—a collection of Asian countries such as Singapore, South Korea, and Hong Kong—are the economic stars. As we will discuss in a later chapter, these countries' economies are similar to Japan's economy, which, in turn, has many similarities to mercantilism. In Japan, government and industrialists work closely together, and government plays a key role in the economy. Given the success of the Asian tigers, a push in North America toward a type of mercantilism similar to theirs exists. And so it's safe to predict that the 1990s will see further evolution of economic systems. With the advent of knowledge-based production, the lesson of history seems to be that change remains the one constant in economic systems.

CHAPTER SUMMARY

- Any economic system must answer three central questions:

  What to produce?

  How to produce it?

  For whom to produce it?

- In capitalism, the what, how, and for whom decisions are made by the market.

- In Soviet-style socialism, the what, how, and for whom decisions are made by government planning boards.

- Political, social, and economic forces are active in both capitalism and socialism.

- Economic systems are in a constant state of evolution.

- In feudalism, tradition rules; in mercantilism, the government rules; in capitalism, the market rules.

- In welfare capitalism, the market, the government, and tradition each rule components of the economy.

- Socialism is currently undergoing a major transition; Soviet-style socialism is almost dead, and the future structure of socialist society is unclear.

KEY TERMS

Asian tigers   *(76)*
capitalism   *(63)*
capitalists   *(70)*
economic system   *(62)*
feudalism   *(68)*
Industrial Revolution   *(72)*

laissez-faire   *(72)*
mercantilism   *(70)*
NIMBY   *(63)*
planning   *(66)*
private property rights   *(63)*
proletariat   *(73)*

socialism   *(64)*
Soviet-style socialism   *(65)*
state socialism   *(75)*
welfare capitalism   *(74)*

QUESTIONS FOR THOUGHT AND REVIEW

The number after each question represents the estimated degree of critical thinking required. (1 = almost none; 10 = deep thought.)

1. Is capitalism or socialism the better economic system? Why?   *(9)*

2. What three questions must any economic system answer?   *(2)*

3. How does Soviet-style socialism answer these three questions?   *(3)*

4. How does capitalism answer these three questions?   *(3)*

5. What arguments can you give for supporting a socialist organization of a family and a capitalist organization of the economy?   *(6)*

6. Why did feudalism evolve into mercantilism? Could feudalism stage a return? Why?   *(6)*

7. Why did mercantilism evolve into capitalism? Could mercantilism stage a return? Why?   *(6)*

8. Some intellectuals have argued "history is ended" because of recent developments in socialist economies. Respond, basing your answer on Marx's analysis.   *(7)*

9. A common joke in socialist countries in the early 1990s was that a person went into a free market store and asked how much a loaf of bread cost. "A dollar," said the clerk. "But that's outrageous. Down the street at the state-run store, it only costs a nickel." "So why don't you buy it there?" said the clerk. "Well," said the customer, "they don't have any." Using supply/demand analysis, show why this situation makes economic sense.   *(4)*

10. The Heisenberg principle states that it's impossible to know the true nature of reality because in analyzing that reality, you change it. How might the Heisenberg principle apply to Marx's economic analysis?   *(6)*

PROBLEMS AND EXERCISES

1. Suppose a Soviet-style socialist government decided to set all prices at the supply/demand equilibrium price.

   a. Show graphically what price they'd set.

   b. How would such an economy differ from a market economy?

   c. Do you think a socialist government could carry out that decision?

   d. Show graphically what would happen if it set the price

   too high and if it set the price too low.

   e. Which of the preceding two situations best describes what the actual situation was in socialist economies?

2. Poland, Bulgaria, and Hungary (all former socialist countries) were in the process of changing to a market economy in the early 1990s.

   a. Go to the library and find the latest information about their transitions.

b. Explain what has happened in those countries, using the invisible hand, invisible handshake, and invisible foot metaphors.

3. Economists Edward Lazear and Robert Michael have calculated that the average family spends two-and-one-half times as much on each adult as they do on each child.
   a. Does this mean that children are deprived and that the distribution is unfair?
   b. Do you think these percentages change with family income? If so, how?
   c. Do you think that the allocation would be different in a family in a Soviet-style socialist country than in a capitalist country? Why?

4. One of the specific problems Soviet-style socialist economies had was keeping up with capitalist countries technologically.
   a. Can you think of any reason inherent to a centrally planned economy that would make innovation difficult?
   b. Can you think of any reason inherent in a capitalist country that would foster innovation?
   c. Joseph Schumpeter, a famous Harvard University economist of the 1930s, predicted that as firms in capitalist societies grew in size, they would innovate less. Can you suggest what his argument might have been?
   d. Schumpeter's prediction did not come true. Modern capitalist economies have had enormous innovations. Can you provide explanations why?

5. Canada's health care system is the envy of the Western world, but it is becoming increasingly expensive to maintain. Can you think of a reason why a capitalist economy like Canada would allow government-run health care? Why doesn't the United States adopt a similar system?

6. "Government restraint has affected the quality of medical care in Canada." Do you agree?

4

Canadian Economic Institutions

The business of government is to keep the government out of business—that is, unless business needs government aid.

~Will Rogers

After reading this chapter, you should be able to:

1 Provide a bird's-eye view of the Canadian economy.

2 Explain the role of consumer sovereignty in the Canadian economy.

3 Go out and learn more about Canadian economic institutions on your own.

4 Summarize briefly the advantages and disadvantages of various types of business.

5 Explain why, even though households have the ultimate power, much of the economic decision making is done by business and government.

6 List two general roles of government and seven specific roles of government.

You saw in Chapter 2 that supply and demand are the driving forces behind the invisible hand. But the invisible hand doesn't operate in an invisible world; it operates in a very real world—a world of institutions that sometimes fight against, sometimes accept, and sometimes strengthen the invisible hand. Thus, to know how the invisible hand works in practice, we need to have some sense of economic institutions and data about the Canadian economy. Let's first look at some data.

A BIRD'S-EYE VIEW OF THE CANADIAN ECONOMY

The Canadian economic machine generates enormous economic activity and provides a high standard of living (compared to most other countries) for almost all its inhabitants. It also provides economic security for its citizens. Starvation is far from most people's minds. Exhibit 1 gives you an idea of what underlies the Canadian economy's strength. For example, in it you can see that Canada is a large country with a temperate climate across the south and taiga (forestland) and polar regions to the north, and a wide range of natural resources. It has excellent transportation facilities and a multicultural population, most of which speaks English and/or French. Its characteristics are, however, changing. Large-scale immigration is increasing the Asian population, especially on the west coast and in large cities such as Vancouver, Toronto, and Montreal.

The Importance of Geographic Economic Information

1 For a bird's-eye view of the Canadian economy see Exhibit 2.

Such geographic economic information is vitally important. To understand an economy you should know: Where are goods produced? Where are natural resources found? What natural resources does it lack? What are normal transportation routes? To keep their analyses simpler, economists often discuss economic problems without discussing geographic dimensions. But no discussion of an economy should forget that geographic dimensions of economic problems are significant. To determine whether to send our students off to the library to learn this information, we give them a quiz. We present them with two lists like those in the box on page 83. The list on the right gives 20 places in Canada. The list on the left gives a particular economic characteristic, such as an industry, product, activity, or natural condition that has been turned to economic advantage. Students are asked to match the numbers with important characteristics of each area.

If you can answer 15 or more of the 20 questions on this quiz correctly, we're impressed with your knowledge of economic geographic facts. If you answer fewer than 15, we strongly suggest learning more geographic facts. The study guide has a number of other projects, information, and examples. An encyclopedia has even more, and your library has a wealth of information. You could spend the entire semester acquiring facts. We're not suggesting that, but we *are* suggesting that you follow the economic news carefully and pay attention to where various *whats* are produced.

The positive attributes of the Canadian economy don't mean that Canada has no problems. Critics point out that crime is on the rise, drugs are omnipresent, economic resources such as oil and minerals are declining, the environment is deteriorating, the distribution of income is skewed toward the rich, and an enormous amount of economic effort goes into economic gamesmanship (real estate deals, stock market deals, deals about deals) which seems simply to reshuffle existing wealth, not to create new wealth. Internationally, the Canadian economy is the seventh largest among the western industrialized countries in terms of our total output of goods and services. While our output per capita is second only to that of the United States, Canada remains plagued by high levels of unemployment and an ever-increasing debt load. In short, the Canadian economy is great, but it's far from perfect.

Diagram of the Canadian Economy

Exhibit 2 diagrams the Canadian economy. Notice it's divided into three groups: business, households, and government. Households supply factors of production to business and are paid by business for doing so. The market where this interaction takes place is called a *factor market*. Business produces goods and services and sells them to households and government. The market where this interaction takes place is called the *goods market*.

EXHIBIT 1 CIA Information Survey on Canada: 1994

GEOGRAPHY

Total area: 9,976,140 km²

Land area: 9,220,970 km²

Comparative area: slightly larger than U.S.

Land boundaries: total 8,893 km, U.S. 8,893 km (includes 2,477 km with Alaska)

Coastline: 243,791 km

Maritime claims: *continental shelf* 200-m depth or to depth of exploitation; *exclusive fishing zone* 200 nm; *territorial sea* 12 nm; *International disputes* maritime boundary disputes with the US; Saint Pierre and Miquelon is focus of maritime boundary dispute between Canada and France

Climate: varies from temperate in south to subarctic and arctic in north

Terrain: mostly plains with mountains in west and lowlands in southeast

Natural resources: nickel, zinc, copper, gold, lead, molybdenum, potash, silver, fish, timber, wildlife, coal, petroleum, natural gas

Land use: arable land 5%; permanent crops 0%; meadows and pastures 3%; forest and woodland 35%; other 57%

Irrigated land: 8,400 km² (1989 est.)

PEOPLE

Population: 28,434,545 (July 1995 est.)

Population growth rate: 1.18% (1994 est.)

Birth rate: 13.74 births/1,000 population (1995 est.)

Death rate: 7.43 deaths/1,000 population (1995 est.)

Net migration rate: 4.55 migrant(s)/1,000 population (1995 est.)

Infant mortality rate: 6.9 deaths/1,000 live births (1994 est.)

Life expectancy at birth: total population 78.29 years; male 74.93 years; female 81.81 years (1995 est.)

Total fertility rate: 1.83 children born/woman (1995 est.)

Nationality: noun: Canadian(s); adjective: Canadian

Ethnic divisions: British Isles origin 40%, French origin 27%, other European 20%, indigenous Indian and Eskimo 1.5%

Religions: Roman Catholic 46%, United Church 16%, Anglican 10%, other 28%

Languages: English (official), French (official)

Literacy: (age 15 and over can read and write (1986)): total population 97%; male NA%; female NA%

Labor force: 13.38 million; *by occupation:* services 75%, manufacturing 14%, agriculture 4%, construction 3%, other 4% (1988)

ECONOMY

Overview: As an affluent, high-tech industrial society, Canada today closely resembles the U.S. in per capita output, market-oriented economic system, and pattern of production. Since World War II, the impressive growth of the manufacturing, mining, and service sectors has transformed the nation from a largely rural economy into one primarily industrial and urban. In the 1980s, Canada registered one of the highest rates of real growth among the OECD nations, averaging about 3.2%. With its great natural resources, skilled labor force, and modern capital plant, Canada has excellent economic prospects, although the country still faces high unemployment and a growing debt. Moreover, the continuing constitutional impasse between English- and French-speaking areas has observers discussing a possible split in the confederation; foreign investors have become edgy.

National product: GDP (purchasing power equivalent) $639.8 billion (1994)

National product real growth rate: 4.5% (1994)

National product per capita: $22,760 (1994)

Inflation rate (consumer prices): 0.2% (1994)

Unemployment rate: 9.6% (December 1994)

Budget: revenues $85 billion (Federal); expenditures $115.3 billion, including capital expenditures of $NA (FY93/94 est.)

Exports: $164.3 billion (f.o.b., 1994); *commodities:* newsprint, wood pulp, timber, crude petroleum, machinery, natural gas, aluminum, motor vehicles and parts, telecommunications equipment; *partners:* U.S., Japan, UK, Germany, South Korea, Netherlands, China

Imports: $151.5 billion (c.i.f., 1994); *commodities:* crude oil, chemicals, motor vehicles and parts, durable consumer goods, electronic computers; telecommunications equipment and parts; *partners:* U.S., Japan, UK, Germany, France, Mexico, Taiwan, South Korea

External debt: $243 billion (1993)

Industrial production: growth rate 4.8% (1993)

Electricity: capacity 108,090,000 kW; production 511 billion kWh consumption per capita 16,133 kWh (1993)

Industries: processed and unprocessed minerals, food products, wood and paper products, transportation equipment, chemicals, fish products, petroleum and natural gas

Agriculture: accounts for about 3% of GDP; one of the world's major producers and exporters of grain (wheat and barley); key source of U.S. agricultural imports; large forest resources cover 35% of total land area; commercial fisheries provide annual catch of 1.5 million metric tons, of which 75% is exported

Illicit drugs: illicit producer of cannabis for the domestic drug market; use of hydroponics technology permits growers to plant large quantities of high-quality marijuana indoors; growing role as a transit point for heroin and cocaine entering the U.S. market

Economic aid: donor; ODA and OOF commitments (1970–89), $7.2 billion

Currency: 1 Canadian dollar (Can$) = 100 cents

Exchange rates: Canadian dollars (Can$) per U.S.$1:   1.4129 (January 1995), 1.3636 (1994), 1.2901 (1993), 1.2087 (1992), 1.1457 (1991), 1.1668 (1990)

Fiscal year: 1 April – 31 March

COMMUNICATIONS

Railroads: 78,148 km total; two major transcontinental freight railway systems—Canadian National (government owned) and Canadian Pacific Railway; passenger service—VIA (government operated); 158 km is electrified

Highways: *total* 849,404 km; *paved* 253,692 km; *unpaved* gravel 595,712 km, earth 171,336 km

Inland waterways: 3,000 km, including Saint Lawrence Seaway

Pipelines: crude and refined oil 23,564 km; natural gas 74,980 km

Ports: Becancour, Churchill, Halifax, Montreal, New Westminster, Prince Rupert, Quebec, Saint John (New Brunswick), Saint John's (Newfoundland), Toronto, Vancouver

Merchant marine: 71 ships (1,000 GRT or over) totaling 617,010 878,819 DWT; bulk 17, cargo 10, chemical tanker 5, container 1, oil tanker 22, passenger 1, passenger-cargo 1, railcar carrier 2, roll-on/roll-off cargo 6, short-sea passenger 3, specialized tanker 2; *note:* does not include ships used exclusively in the Great Lakes

Airports: total 1,386 1,107; with permanent-surface runways 458; with runways over 3,659 m 4; with runways 2,440–3,659 m 29; with runways 1,220–2,439 m 326

Telecommunications: excellent service provided by modern media; 18.0 million telephones; broadcast stations—900 AM, 29 FM, 53 (1,400 repeaters) TV; 5 coaxial submarine cables; over 300 earth stations operating in INTELSAT (including 4 Atlantic Ocean and 1 Pacific Ocean) and domestic systems

Source: *CIA World Factbook,* 1994.

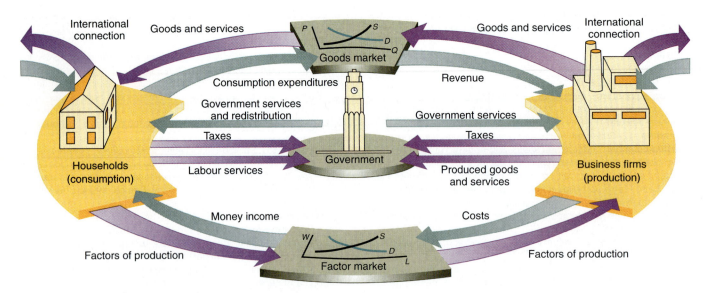

EXHIBIT 2 **Diagrammatic Representation of the Canadian Economy**

Notice also the arrows going out and coming in for both business and households. Those arrows represent the international connection, which we'll discuss in Chapter 5.

Finally, consider the arrows connecting government with households and business. Government taxes business and households. It buys goods and services from business and buys labour services from households. Then, with some of its tax revenue, it provides services to both business and households (roads, education) and gives some of its tax revenue directly back to individuals. In doing so, it redistributes income. But government also serves a second function. It oversees the interaction of business and households in the goods and factor markets. Government, of course, is not independent. Canada is a democracy, so households vote to determine who shall govern.

Exhibit 2 gave you an overview of the institutional organization of the Canadian economy. Let's now consider some specifics. First look at business, second at households, and finally at government.

BUSINESS

Business The private producing unit in our society.

Business is responsible for over 77 percent of Canadian production (government is responsible for the other 23 percent). In fact, any time a household decides to produce something, it becomes a business. **Business** is simply the name given to private producing units in our society.

Businesses in Canada decide *what* to produce, *how* much to produce, and *for whom* to produce it. They make these central economic decisions on the basis of their own feelings, which are influenced by market incentives. Anyone who wants to can start a business, provided he or she can come up with the required cash and meet the necessary regulatory requirements.

Entrepreneurship and Business

Entrepreneurship Labour services that involve high degrees of organizational skills, concern, and creativity.

Don't think of business as something other than people. Businesses are ultimately made up of a group of people organized together to accomplish some end. In terms of numbers, most businesses are one- or two-person operations. Home-based businesses, at least if they're part-time activities, are easy to start. All you have to do is say you're in business, and you are. If that business becomes complex enough and big enough to have employees (especially if it needs its own building), the difficulties begin. Before the business may expand its operations, a large number of licenses, permits, approvals, and forms must be obtained from various government agencies. That's why **entrepreneurship** (the ability to organize and get something done) is an important part of

ECONOMIC GEOGRAPHY OF CANADA

The Quiz

In the first column, we list 20 economic characteristics. In the second and third columns, we list 20 provinces, cities, or areas of the country. Associate the locale with the proper characteristic by printing the letter on the line.

____ 1.	Province hardest hit by fishing moratorium	a. Niagara Falls	k. Alberta
____ 2.	Over half of all manufacturing takes place here	b. Saskatchewan	l. St. Lawrence Seaway
____ 3.	Island economy driven by tourism	c. Winnipeg	m. Northwest Territories
____ 4.	Maritime seaport serving U.S., Europe, and Africa	d. Newfoundland	n. Halifax
____ 5.	Site of large GM plant	e. Hamilton	o. British Columbia
____ 6.	Most of Canada's potash is produced here	f. New Brunswick	p. Toronto
____ 7.	Grain is shipped through this system	g. Ont., Que., NB	q. Victoria
____ 8.	Majority of natural gas is produced here	h. Vancouver	r. Canada
____ 9.	Hollywood producers like this western city	i. Great Lakes	s. Ontario
____ 10.	Major commodity exchange is in this city	j. Oshawa	t. Prince Edward Island
____ 11.	Forestry is this province's largest manufacturing sector		
____ 12.	City where most of Canada's steel is produced		
____ 13.	Major stock exchange in this city		
____ 14.	Only officially bilingual province		
____ 15.	Nuclear energy produced in these provinces		
____ 16.	One of the largest freshwater bodies		
____ 17.	Geographically largest and most rural area		
____ 18.	You might move here to retire		
____ 19.	Major source of hydroelectric power		
____ 20.	World's largest producer of uranium		

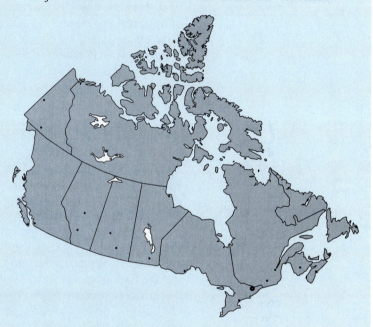

business. To give you a sense of what it's like to run a business, let's consider a real-world example.

In 1982, Jane and Lee Corey wanted to start a business. Jane worked as a registered nurse and Lee worked as a biologist for the civil service. They decided that it would be fun to get into aquaculture, a new and growing industry in Atlantic Canada.

Trials and Tribulations of Starting a Business

They found a site, bought it, and, after getting a building permit, began building. Because it was to be the home of a business, the building had to meet strict fire, electrical, and plumbing codes. They had to establish contacts with suppliers, get insurance, obtain permits from the city to comply with zoning, and satisfy all provincial and federal regulations surrounding their activities. They incorporated the new business as Corey Feed Mills Ltd., bought a machine, and started to produce aquaculture feeds and supplies.

All this costs a lot of money. Jane and Lee had to open a business chequing account with their bank. (They couldn't run all that expense through their personal chequing accounts because sound accounting practice requires people to keep their business cheques separate from their personal cheques.) They had to have some

Answers: 1–d, 2–s, 3–t, 4–n, 5–j, 6–b, 7–l, 8–k, 9–h, 10–c, 11–o, 12–e, 13–p, 14–f, 15–g, 16–i, 17–m, 18–q, 19–a, 20–r.

Corey Feed Mills Ltd. produces a wide range of pet and aquaculture products.

money to put in the business account. They used some of their savings, but they needed more funds. That meant they had to apply for a loan from the bank. The bank required them to present a formal business plan.

The company's first year of sales was less than $100,000—Lee took no salary for the first three years and Jane continued to work outside the business to provide an income to assure the bank that loan payments would be made. Over the next 10 years, all company profits were reinvested. New equipment and additional staff were needed to maintain increasing accounting, legal, and production demands. Employment grew to over 30 people in 1995.

Then, of course, there are taxes. Any business with employees must withhold taxes from their wages and send those taxes periodically to the various taxing authorities. This includes Canada Pension plan contributions, unemployment insurance contributions, federal income taxes, and provincial income taxes. There are also property taxes and sales taxes that the business, not the employees, must pay.

It took several years and hundreds of thousands of dollars to start the business. And this was a small business. Somebody without training and background in handling forms, taxes, and bureaucratic regulations usually doesn't do well in business. To such a person, entry into business isn't free; it isn't even possible. Still, many people try it, and many succeed. Their business was one of the successful ones. Today, Corey Feed products include an expanding line of pet and aquaculture foods which are sold across North America. The company is now turning to export markets worldwide.

Consumer Sovereignty and Business

2 Although businesses decide what to produce, they are guided by consumer sovereignty.

Consumer sovereignty The right of the individual to make choices about what is consumed and produced.

To say that businesses decide what to produce isn't to say that **consumer sovereignty** (the consumer's wishes) doesn't reign in Canada. Businesses decide what to produce based on what they believe will sell. A key question a person in Canada should ask about starting a business is: Can I make a profit from it? **Profit** is what's left over from total revenues after all the appropriate costs have been subtracted. Businesses that guess correctly what the consumer wants generally make a profit. Businesses that guess wrong generally operate at a loss.

People are free to start businesses for whatever purposes they want. No one asks them: "What's the social value of your term paper assistance business, your hair-replacement business, your fur coat business, or your textbook publishing business?" Yet the Canadian economic system is designed to channel individuals' desire to make a profit into the general good of society. That's the invisible hand at work. As long as the business doesn't violate a law and conforms to regulations, people in Canada are free to start whatever business they want, if they can get the money to finance it. That's a key difference between the Canadian market economy and a traditional Soviet-style economy where people weren't free to start a business even if they could get the financing.

Profit A return on entrepreneurial activity and risk taking.

Categories of Business

Exhibit 3 (a) shows a selection of various categories of Canadian businesses with their relative contributions to total output for each category. Output shares aren't necessarily the best indicator of the importance of various types of business to the economy. Exhibit 3 (b) ranks businesses by their relative employment.

Stages of Business

Stage of production Any of the various levels, such as manufacturing, wholesale, or retail, on which businesses are organized.

Businesses in Canada are organized on a variety of levels: manufacturing firms, wholesale firms, and retail firms. For most products, the manufacturer doesn't sell the product to you. Often products are sold five or six times before they reach the consumer. Each of these levels is called a **stage of production.** Thus, most firms *provide a service*—getting you the good when you want it—rather than producing the good. Firms are continually deciding whether to combine these stages of production under one firm, or whether to divide the stages up and allow many firms. Recently, for example, retailing firms such as Wal-Mart have been vertically integrating and combining various stages into their firms. Factory outlets are examples of manufacturing firms undertaking retailing functions.

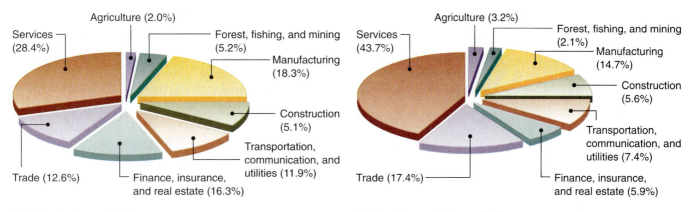

(a) Output shares: 1994

(b) Employment shares: 1994

EXHIBIT 3   Importance and Size of Various Types of Business

The general types of business are listed here: **(a)** shows their relative share of output; **(b)** shows their relative importance by employment. Notice that less than half the population is involved in what most laypeople consider production—manufacturing, construction, mining, and agriculture.

Source: *Statistics Canada, CANSIM Database,* March 1995.

in the mid-1990s, it was only 18 percent. This is reflected in employment figures: manufacturing employment has fallen from about 27 percent in 1950 to about 15 percent in the mid-1990s. The reason is twofold: first, manufacturing has become more productive, so we get more output per worker; and second, we now import many more components of the products we produce. In the 1990s, parts of manufactured goods are produced around the world, and service jobs such as retailing have replaced manufacturing jobs.

The growing importance of the service sector to the economy has led some observers to say that we're in a postindustrial society. In their view, the Canadian economy today is primarily a service economy, not a production economy. So classifying the economy may or may not be helpful, but you should note how important the provision of services and the distribution of goods are to our economy.

From Manufacturer to You   To give you a sense of the path of a good from manufacturer to ultimate buyer, let's consider a hypothetical example of a window. Clearview Window Limited bought the glass, wood, and machines needed to make the window from other companies, perhaps spending a total of $20 per window. Those purchases all fell within what is classified as wholesale trade. Clearview Window then assembled the components (cost of assembly: $60), making Clearview's total cost of the window $80.

One of us needed a window for his house, so he went down to Buildright, a local building supply store, which sells both wholesale to general contractors and retail to plain people who walk in off the street. Wholesale customers get a 20 percent discount from the retail price, which is deducted at the end of the month from the total bill they've run up. These wholesale customers charge their own customers the full retail price. We're plain people, so when one of us ordered a window, Buildright said the cost would be $200. However, it didn't have the right size in stock.

Buildright stacked the order with orders from other customers and called up its Clearview distributor (who has a franchise from Clearview Window in the territory where we live) to place one big order for a number of windows, including the one we ordered. The Clearview distributor charged Buildright $140 for our window. The Clearview distributor keeps a pile of windows in stock which she replenishes from a shipment of newly made windows that come in once a month from the Clearview plant. For our window, she pays about $100 plus freight.

So it costs Clearview $80 to make our window; Clearview sells it to the distributor for $100 plus freight. The distributor needs to cover her costs for storage, handling,

3A   The five largest industries in Canada are:
1. Services
2. Manufacturing
3. Finance, insurance, and real estate
4. Trade
5. Transportation, communication, and utilities.

3B   A useful way to learn about the economy is to trace the path of a product from raw material to final product.

BALANCE SHEET AND INCOME STATEMENT

Accounting for revenues and expenditures is an important part of business. Elaborate methods of keeping track of those revenues and expenses have developed over the years. A firm's balance sheet (a statement of the firm's net worth at a point in time) is shown in (a) below.

Company Name
Balance Sheet
December 31, 1995

Assets*		Liabilities and Shareholders' Equity*	
Current assets	$13,859	Current liabilities	$12,675
Property, plant, and equipment	20,362	Long-term Liabilities	5,843
		Shareholders' equity	15,703
		Total liabilities and	
Total Assets	$34,221	shareholders' equity	$34,221

*Dollars in millions

(a) Balance sheet

As you can see, the balance sheet is divided into assets on the left side and liabilities and shareholders' equity (also called net worth) on the right side. An *asset* is anything of value. An asset need not be a physical item. It might be a right to do something or use something. For example, landing rights are important assets of airline companies. A *liability* is an obligation. When a firm borrows money, it takes on a liability because it has an obligation to pay the money back to the lender. The totals of the two sides must be equal, since *shareholders' equity (net worth)* is defined as the difference between assets and liabilities. That is:

$$\text{Assets} = \text{Liabilities} + \text{Shareholders' equity}$$
or
$$\text{Assets} = \text{Liabilities} + (\text{Assets} - \text{Liabilities})$$
$$\text{Assets} = \text{Assets.}$$

The two sides of the equation are equal by definition. Both assets and liabilities are divided into various subcategories on a balance sheet, but at this stage, all you need to remember is the sheet's general structure.

Company Name
Statement of Income and Expenses*
For the Year Ending December 31, 1995

Sales	$8,710
Cost of goods sold	5,980
Gross profit	2,730
Operating expenses	1,509
Fixed interest payment	165
Income before federal income taxes	1,056
Federal income taxes	509
Net income	$ 547

*Dollars in millions

(b) Statement of income and expenditures

A firm's statement of income and expenses is shown in (b). Whereas a balance sheet measures a stock concept (a firm's position at a point in time), a statement of income and expenses measures a flow concept (the amount of income and expenses passing through a company during a particular period of time). A firm's sales, or total revenue, is given at the top. Then the cost of goods sold is subtracted from total revenue. The resulting number is called *gross profit,* although many income statements don't list gross profits. Next, operating costs and fixed interest payments are subtracted, giving earnings before taxes. Finally, income taxes are subtracted, giving the firm's net income.

IS CANADA A POSTINDUSTRIAL SOCIETY?

Producing physical goods is only one of a society's economic tasks. Another task is to provide services (activities done for others). Services do not involve producing a physical good. When you get your hair cut, you buy a service, not a good. Much of the cost of the physical goods we buy actually is not a cost of producing the good, but is a cost of one of the most important services: distribution (getting the good to where the consumer is). After a good is produced, it has to get to the individuals who are going to consume it at the time they need it. If the distribution system gets botched up, it's as if the good had never been produced.

Let's consider a couple of examples. Take Christmas trees. Say you're sitting on 60,000 cut spruce trees in New Brunswick, but an ice storm prevents you from shipping them until December 26. Guess what? You're now stuck with 60,000 spruce trees and the problem of somehow getting rid of them. Or take hot dogs. How many of us have been irked that a hot dog that cost 25¢ to fix at home costs $2 at a football game? But a hot dog at home isn't the same as a hot dog at a game. Distribution of the good is as important as production; you're paying the extra $1.75 for distribution.

inventory, and billing, and of course she has to make a profit, so she sells the window to Buildright for $140. The owner of Buildright has to cover expenses and make a profit, so he sells us the window for $200 ($160—a 20 percent discount—if he thought we were wholesale customers).

Producing the good is only a small component of the cost. Distribution—getting the good where it is wanted when it is wanted—makes up 60 percent of the total cost of the window in this example. That large percentage is not unusual. The same story holds true for most goods you buy.

Given the importance of distribution, firms are always looking for new ways to make the distribution process more efficient. Recent approaches include just-in-time inventory systems in which computers track a firm's needs—the needed inputs are shipped to the firm just in time and its outputs are similarly shipped to customers just in time. Another new practice is for retail firms to keep instantaneous tabs on what is selling. That is why, when you buy something, the clerk has to type a whole load of numbers into the computerized cash register (or have the scanner read the bar code with a whole load of numbers). This practice lets the store know what's selling and what isn't so it knows what to order. This makes the distribution process more efficient, and thereby reduces the firm's costs, although it sometimes makes checkouts a pain.

Sizes of Business

Another way to classify businesses is by size. Contrary to popular belief, many sectors of Canada contain small (fewer than 100 employees), not large, firms. This is especially true in retail trade and construction industries. The notable exception is manufacturing, which has a group of large producers, such as auto manufacturers.

Exhibit 4 combines activity and size of firms, looking at the largest businesses in various types of activities.

A sector's relative size does not necessarily capture its importance to the economy. Take agriculture, for example. It's small in terms of both payroll and revenue, but if it stopped doing its job of providing our food, its importance would quickly become apparent. Similarly, the financial sector is relatively small, but modern industry couldn't function without a highly developed financial sector. Just as a missing bolt can bring a car to a sudden halt, so too can problems in one sector of the economy bring about a sudden halt to a much larger part of the economy.

Goals of Business

Another way to classify businesses is by their goals. They can be either for-profit businesses or nonprofit businesses. For-profit businesses keep their earnings after they pay expenses (if there are any to keep); **nonprofit businesses** try only to make enough money to cover their expenses with their revenues. If a nonprofit business winds up with a profit, that money goes into "reserves" where it's saved to use in case of later losses.

Nonprofit business Business that does not try to make a profit. It tries only to make enough money to cover its expenses with its revenues.

EXHIBIT 4   The Largest Canadian Businesses

The Top Five	Revenues (thousands)	Assets
General Motors of Canada Ltd.	$ 24,919,421	$ 8,050,837
BCE Inc.	21,670,000	38,092,000
Ford Motor Co. of Canada, Ltd.	20,100,600	5,029,000
Chrysler Canada Ltd.	15,722,000	4,317,800
George Weston Ltd.	13,002,000	4,744,000

Top Five Conglomerates	Revenues	Assets
Imasco Ltd.	$ 8,134,000	$53,482,000
Canadian Pacific Ltd.	7,053,000	16,912,300
Power Corp. of Canada	6,904,240	31,526,382
Noranda Inc.	6,633,000	11,836,000
Brascan Ltd.	6,149,000	4,244,800

Top Five Merchandisers	Revenues	Assets
George Weston Ltd.	$ 13,002,000	$ 4,744,000
Provigo Inc.	6,176,400	1,026,000
The Oshawa Group Ltd.	6,069,800	1,313,700
Hudson's Bay Co.	5,829,243	4,016,626
Canada Safeway Ltd.	4,628,300	1,153,900

Top Five Telecommunications Companies	Revenues	Assets
BCE Inc.	$ 21,670,000	$38,092,000
Anglo-Canadian Telephone Co.	2,550,000	4,965,000
TELUS Corp.	1,360,149	3,483,722
Rogers Cantel Mobile Communications Inc.	750,420	1,219,467
Teleglobe Inc.	643,000	1,934,400

Top Five Financial Institutions	Assets	Revenues
Royal Bank of Canada	$173,079,000	$13,434,000
Canadian Imperial Bank of Commerce	151,032,554	11,214,000
Bank of Montreal	138,175,000	9,108,000
Bank of Nova Scotia	132,928,000	9,376,000
Toronto-Dominion Bank	99,759,000	6,993,000

Source: *The Financial Post 500*, May 1995.

The goal of a nonprofit business is to serve the community or some segment of the community. Nonprofit businesses include all government-run businesses, some hospitals, pension funds, foundations, many fund-raising organizations such as the Canadian Cancer Society, most universities and colleges, and many museums. Working for a nonprofit organization doesn't mean working for free. Salaries are an expense of a business, and are paid by both for-profit and nonprofit firms. In fact, salaries paid to individuals managing nonprofit organizations can be higher than in for-profit organizations, and perks of the job can be fantastic.[1] But perks are classified as "expenses" and aren't included in "profits."

Why discuss the goals of business? Because the goals of business are central to economic theory and economists' insight into how economies function. In a pure capitalist country, all businesses are for-profit businesses. In a pure socialist country, all businesses are nonprofit. As we discussed in Chapter 3, Canada is far from a pure cap-

---

[1] *Perks* is short for *perquisites*. An example of a "fantastic" perk might be the business supplying you with a limousine and driver in Ottawa or Montreal, an unlimited expense account, trips to Europe and the Far East, and a condo in Victoria.

	Sole Proprietor	Partnership	Corporation
Advantages	1. Minimum bureaucratic hassle 2. Direct control by owner	1. Ability to share work and risks 2. Relatively easy to form	1. No personal liability 2. Increasing ability to get funds 3. Ability to shed personal income and gain added expenses
Disadvantages	1. Limited ability to get funds 2. Unlimited personal liability	1. Unlimited personal liability (even for partner's blunder) 2. Limited ability to get funds	1. Legal hassle to organize 2. Possible double taxation of income 3. Monitoring problems

Advantages and Disadvantages of Various Forms of For-Profit Businesses

italist country, and nonprofit businesses play significant roles in the Canadian economy.

The three primary forms of business are sole proprietorships, partnerships, and corporations. Each of the different forms of business has certain advantages and disadvantages. These are summarized in the above table.

Sole proprietorships are the easiest to start and have the fewest bureaucratic hassles. **Partnerships**—businesses with two or more owners—create possibilities for sharing the burden, but they also create unlimited liability for each of the partners. **Corporations**—businesses that are treated as a person, and are legally owned by their stockholders who are not liable for the actions of the corporate "person"—are the largest form of business when measured in terms of receipts. Thus their income is taxed, which leads to charges of double taxation of income.

When a corporation is formed, it issues **stock** (certificates of ownership in a company) which is sold or given to individuals. Proceeds of the sale of that stock make up what is called the *equity capital* of a company. Ownership of stock entitles you to vote in the election of a corporation's directors.

Corporations were developed as institutions to make it easier for company owners to be separated from company management. A corporation provides **limited liability** for the owners. Whereas with the other two forms of business, owners can lose everything they possess even if they have only a small amount invested in the company, in a corporation the owners can lose only what they have invested in that corporation. If you've invested $100, you can lose only $100. In the other kinds of business, even if you've invested only $100, you could lose everything; the business's losses must be covered by the individual owners.

Another advantage of corporations involves taxes. While it is true that corporate income is taxed, corporate expenses can be deducted and thus corporate "perks"—a hunting lodge in James Bay—which is actually a consumption good, can be rented tax free if one has a creative accountant.

A corporation's stocks can be distributed among as few as three persons or among millions of stockholders. Shares can be bought and sold either in an independent transaction between two people (an over-the-counter trade) or through a broker and a *stock exchange*. Appendix A provides a brief introduction to the stock market.

In corporations, there is a separation of ownership and control. Most shareholders have little input into the decisions a corporation makes. Instead, corporations are often controlled by their managers, who often run them for their own benefit as well as for the owners'. The reason is that owners' control of management is limited.

A large percentage of most corporations' shares are not even controlled by the owners; instead, they are controlled by financial institutions such as mutual funds

Forms of Business

Sole proprietorship Business with only one owner.

Partnership Business with two or more owners.

Corporation Business that is treated like a person, legally owned by its stockholders. Its stockholders are not personally liable for the actions of the corporate "person."

4 The advantages and disadvantages of the three forms of business are shown in the table.

Limited liability The liability of a stockholder (owner) in a corporation; it is limited to the amount the stockholder has invested in the company.

(financial institutions that invest individuals' money for them) and by pension funds (financial institutions that hold people's money for them until it is to be paid out to them upon their retirement). Thus, ownership of corporations is another step removed from individuals.

Why is the question of who controls a firm important? Because economic theory assumes a business owners' goal is to maximize profits, which would be true of corporations if shareholders made the decisions. Managers don't have the same incentives to maximize profits that owners do. There's pressure on managers to maximize profits, but that pressure can often be weak or ineffective.

HOUSEHOLDS

Households Groups of individuals living together and making joint decisions.

The second classification we'll consider in this overview of Canadian economic institutions is households. **Households** (groups of individuals living together and making joint decisions) are the most powerful economic institution. They ultimately control government and business, the other two economic institutions. Households' votes in the political arena determine government policy; their decisions about supplying labour and capital determine what businesses will have available to work with; and their spending decisions or expenditures (the "votes" they cast with their dollars) determine what businesses will be able to sell.

While the ultimate power does in principle lie with the people and households, we, the people, have assigned much of that power to representatives. As we discussed above, corporations are only partially responsive to owners of their shares, and much of that ownership is once-removed from individuals. Ownership of 1,000 shares in a company with a total of 2 million shares isn't going to get you any influence over the corporation's activities. As a shareholder, you simply accept what the corporation does.

5 Although, in principle, ultimate power resides with the people and households (consumer sovereignty), in practice the representatives of the people—firms and government—are sometimes removed from the people and, in the short run, are only indirectly monitored by the people.

A major decision that corporations make independently of their shareholders concerns what to produce. True, ultimately we, the people, decide whether we will buy what business produces, but business spends a lot of money telling us what services we want, what products make us "with it," what books we want to read, and the like. Most economists believe that consumer sovereignty reigns—that we are not fooled or controlled by advertising. Still, it is an open question in some economists' minds whether we, the people, control business or the business representatives control people. There's similar debate in the political sphere of our lives. Members of Parliament feel only partially responsible to voters. (They feel slightly more responsible around election time.)

Because of this assignment of power to other institutions, in many spheres of the economy households are not active producers of output but merely passive recipients of income. That's why much of the discussion of the household sector focuses on the distribution of household income. Thus, our consideration of households will be short and will focus on their income and their role as suppliers of labour.

Household Types and Income

The Canadian population of about 30 million is composed of about 7 million households. Exhibit 6 looks at three ways income is divided up among households. Notice the relatively low incomes of female lone-parent households. Of similar interest is the regional distribution of income. With few exceptions, Ontario, Quebec, and British Columbia offer the highest median income. Because income determines how many goods and services a person will get, family structure and geographic location play a big role in the *for whom* department.

low-income cutoff The income level at which families spend at least 20 percent more than the average family on the necessities of life. Used by Statistics Canada to define low-income families.

One political concern about income is whether it is fairly (equitably, as opposed to equally) distributed, and whether all households have sufficient income. That's a tough question to answer. For now, let us simply note that, unlike the United States, in Canada poverty is not defined by a "poverty line" based on a calculation of needs. Statistics Canada uses a **low-income cutoff** which defines low-income families as those who spend proportionately more (at least 20 percent more) than the average family on the necessities of life—food, clothing, and shelter. Using this measure, in

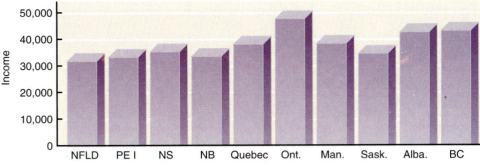

(a) Median income, all families

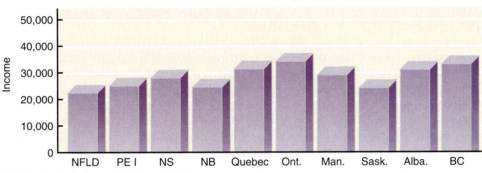

(b) Median income, male-lone parent

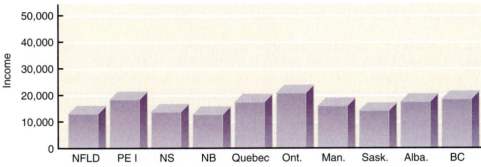

(c) Median income, female-lone parent

EXHIBIT 5   1990 Median Income by Family Structure and Province

These bar charts illustrate that median family income varied considerably by province and family structure in 1990.

Source: *Statistics Canada*, 93–331, 1993.

1993 there were almost 5 million Canadians living in low-income conditions—about one-sixth of the total population! As Exhibit 5 (c) suggests, the highest rate of incidence of low-income families were female lone-parent—almost 62 percent.

The largest source of household income is wages and salaries (the income households get from labour). Households supply the labour with which businesses produce and government governs. In 1994, the total Canadian labour force was 14.8 million, about 10 percent (1.5 million) of whom were unemployed. The average Canadian work week in 1994 was about 42 hours.

Exhibit 6 divides Canadian employment by types of jobs and average salaries. Notice that many are service jobs, since Canada has become largely a service economy. Exhibit 7 shows that this greater emphasis on services rather than goods is continuing. Many of the fastest-growing jobs are in service industries; many of the fastest-declining are in manufacturing and agriculture.

Other divisions of jobs show even more differences. For example, physicians earn about $150,000 per year, lawyers often earn $100,000 per year, and CEOs of large cor-

Households as Suppliers of Labour

Type of Job	Number of Full-Time Workers		Average Earnings per Year	
	Female	Male	Female	Male
Managerial, administrative and related occupations	462,000	882,000	$33,000	$51,000
Medicine and health	267,000	95,000	32,000	62,000
Service	338,000	405,000	17,000	31,000
Farming	47,000	166,000	13,000	21,000
Construction	9,000	349,000	26,000	35,000

Source: *Statistics Canada,* 93–332, 1993.

porations often make $1,000,000 per year or more. A beginning McDonald's employee generally makes less than $10,000.

One of the biggest changes in the labour market in the 1980s was unions' decline in importance. Labour unions are an economic institution closely associated with households. They were initially created to balance businesses' power. By organizing into unions, workers became an economic institution and gained a larger say in the production process. Unions pushed Canadian wages up relative to wages in other countries, and established in Canada some of the best working conditions in the world. But unions also had a negative effect; part of businesses' response to the high Canadian wages has been to move production facilities to countries where workers receive lower wages. That's one reason the Canadian manufacturing sector has declined relative to the service sector, and union membership and influence have fallen substantially. Service workers have far fewer unions, and their jobs are much more difficult to move to other countries.

People Power

An important way households influence government and business is in their cultural and ideological beliefs. Those beliefs determine what is allowable and what isn't. When those beliefs differ from the existing situation, "people power" has the potential to change the existing institutions significantly. For example, in Eastern Europe by the late 1980s, people's beliefs had become so inconsistent with the existing institutions that people demanded and brought about major economic and political reforms even though there was no formal mechanism, such as free elections, by which they could exert their power. People power goes beyond the power people exert in elections. People in an economy have a cultural sensibility, or outlook, which limits actions of both government and business.

Households can exert people power to keep government and business in line. Do people accept the existing situation, or do they feel business or government is wrong? To keep people power on their side, Canadian businesses spend a lot of money on public service and advertisements stating that they, the businesses, are good citizens.

Because of the importance of these cultural and social limitations to business (the invisible handshake), you need some sense of which way the invisible handshake will push. While summarizing the sensibility of a country's people is impossible, it is necessary to make the attempt because it is through those sensibilities—through informal, invisible channels—that households exert much of their power on the economy. Thus, in the next section, we will present our view of the sensibility of the Canadian people.

The Social, Cultural, and Ideological Sensibilities of Canadian People

Although, as we've pointed out, the actual Canadian economy is best described as welfare capitalism or a mixed economy due to a number of government programmes designed to blunt the sharp edge of the market's forces, the Canadian **ideology** (values held so deeply that they are not questioned) is, in word if not in deed, "let the market do it." Like maple syrup and motherhood, competition and freedom to undertake economic activities are seen as sacred. That is not to say that Canadians loathe government intervention. When markets fail to operate in a timely manner, Canadians are quick to call for government action.

Software engineer	New Media packaging and marketing	**EXHIBIT 7** **Fastest-Growing Occupations in the 1990s**
Geriatric-care aide	English-as-a-second-language teacher	
Human-resources facilitator	Derivatives trader	
Financial counsellor	Wastemanagement	
Genetic mapping	Information highway pothole repair	

Source: The *Financial Post*, October 14, 1995, p.15.

Maple syrup and motherhood have changed over the years, and so has competition. In the Great Depression of the 1930s, the Canadian population's unbridled faith in the market was tested. Under Prime Minister R.B. Bennett, and later under Prime Minister Mackenzie King, numerous government programmes were developed to ease the market's harshness. Laws were passed establishing minimum prices at which goods could be sold. Labour was given the right to organize to achieve its ends; a new farm programme limited price fluctuations of agricultural goods; a welfare system, including social security programmes and unemployment insurance, was established. These laws and programmes are generally viewed as good.

With the advent of World War II (1939–45), defense spending zoomed and government spending as a percentage of total Canadian spending increased. After the war, the share of government spending on output declined, but the march of government programmes to regulate the market continued. In the decade following the war, the government sector's role increased further and the economy grew rapidly. The government took responsibility for maintaining high employment, and the safety net (a set of programmes that guaranteed individuals a minimum standard of living) was expanded.

During the postwar period, a number of special interest groups developed—we'll call them **interest groups.** They are involved in encouraging and protecting government spending in certain areas of the economy. For example, we could say there's a social-educational interest group which protects education interests, while a welfare interest group protects social benefits. These interest groups compete for government expenditures.

Interest groups Individuals and others who band together to encourage and protect government spending in certain areas of the economy.

These developments may seem to go against the cultural and ideological support the Canadian public gives the market. Support for the market and tolerance of vested interests seem contradictory, but people's ideological views need not be consistent, and they often aren't. A new and larger role for government in the market has been accepted by most people. They believe these programmes are proper, so now government programmes that restrict the market (for example, the social security system) are seen to be as fundamentally Canadian, as is the market.

Another important aspect of a people's sensibility is their view of morality. Compared to other countries, Canada has a relatively strict standard of economic morals—activities such as direct bribery and payoffs are illegal. (In some countries, these activities aren't illegal. In numerous others, they're illegal but openly tolerated.) The Canadian government bureaucracy, while considered by many to be inefficient, is generally thought to be honest and not corrupt; moreover, by international standards it's actually efficient. Around the fringes of standard morality there's still room for influence peddling, discreet payoffs, and trading favours, but by international standards of corruption they're small potatoes.

There's much more to be said about the cultural sensibilities of the Canadian people, but we'll stop here. Those of you unfamiliar with Canadian cultural and social norms can best find out about them by following the newspapers and by having discussions with friends. Our goal in presenting this material isn't to cover the Canadian people's social and cultural sensibilities completely—that would take a whole book by itself—but simply to remind you how important they are: How an economy functions, what types of policies can be instituted, and what people's perceptions of the economic problems are, are all shaped by its people's social, cultural, and ideological sensibilities. The invisible handshake is an important determinant of economic events.

GOVERNMENT

The third major Canadian economic institution we'll consider is government. Government plays two general roles in the economy. It's both a referee (setting the rules that determine relations between businesses and households) and an actor (collecting money in taxes and spending that money on its own projects, such as defence and education). Let's first consider government's role as an actor.

Government as an Actor

6A Two general roles of government are (1) as a referee and (2) as an actor.

Canada has a federal government system, which means we have various levels of government (federal, provincial, and municipal), each with its own powers. All levels of government combined consume about 48 percent of the country's total output and employ about 2.7 million individuals. The various levels of government also have a number of programmes that redistribute income through taxation or through a variety of social welfare and assistance programmes designed to help specific groups. Many of the programmes are based on a system of **transfer payments**—payments by governments to individuals that are not in payment for goods and services.

Transfer payments Payments by government to individuals that are not in payment for goods or services.

Special purpose transfers Payments from the federal government to provincial and local governments for funding social spending on health care, welfare, and post-secondary education.

Provincial and Local Government Provincial and local governments employ over 1.9 million people and spend almost $230 billion a year. Provincial and local governments get much of their income from taxes: property taxes, consumption taxes, and provincial income taxes. They are also heavily reliant on general and special purpose transfers from the federal government. **Special purpose transfers** are primarily aimed at funding social spending on health care, welfare, and post-secondary education. **General purpose transfers** are equalization payments that are meant to reduce disparities between the "have" and the "have-not" provinces. They are supposed to provide for comparable levels of public service at comparable levels of taxation. They spend their tax revenues on social services, health care, administration, education (education through high school is available free in public schools), and roads. These activities fall within microeconomics, which we'll discuss when we study microeconomics.

General purpose transfers Payments from the federal government to the provincial and local governments meant to reduce disparities between "have" and "have not" provinces.

Federal Government Probably the best way to get an initial feel for the federal government and its size is to look at the various categories of its tax revenues and expenditures in Exhibit 8. Notice that direct taxes from persons make up about 58 percent of the federal government's revenue, while direct taxes from businesses make up about 9 percent. That's more than 65 percent of the federal government's revenues, most of which shows up as a deduction from your paycheque. In Exhibit 9 (b), notice the federal government's two largest categories of spending are, first, transfers to persons, with expenditures on interest payments close behind.

Debt Accumulated deficits minus accumulated surpluses.

Interest payments are important because the Canadian government has a large debt. **Debt** is an amount of money that one owes to others. It is a stock concept, which corresponds to the liability portion of a company's balance sheet. The Canadian government has accumulated a large debt—over $500 billion in the mid-1990s, or over $20,000 per person. Interest must be paid on that debt, which explains why the budget's interest component is so high. The national debt has accumulated because the federal government has run almost continual budget deficits since the 1940s. A deficit is a flow concept that corresponds to the net income portion of a company's income statement. A **government budget deficit** occurs when government expenditures exceed government revenues—that is, when tax revenues fall short of budgeted expenditures and the government borrows to make up the difference. A **government budget surplus** occurs when revenues exceed expenditures.

Government budget deficit Situation when government expenditures exceed government revenues.

Government budget surplus Situation when government revenues exceed expectations.

Individuals like government programmes that assist them, and they pressure politicians to provide these programmes. However, people don't like the taxes they have to pay for those programmes, and they put pressure on politicians to lower taxes. These two pressures have resulted in the federal government's significant deficits since the 1970s.

Government as a Referee

Even if government spending made up only a small proportion of total expenditures, government would still be central to the study of economics. The reason is that, in a

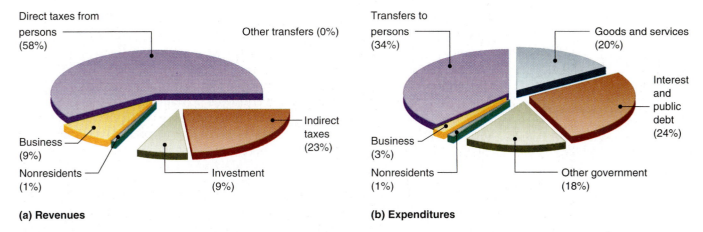

(a) Revenues

(b) Expenditures

EXHIBIT 8   Federal Government Revenues and Expenditures: 1994

(a) Direct taxes from persons and indirect taxes are the largest sources of federal government revenues.

(b) Transfers to persons and interest on the public debt are the largest of federal government expenditures.
Source: *Statistics Canada,* CANSIM Database, March 1995.

market economy, government controls the interaction of business and households. Government sets the rules of interaction and acts as a referee, changing the rules when it sees fit. Government decides whether the invisible hand will be allowed to operate freely.

Government is involved in every interaction between households and business in the form of laws regulating that interaction. For example, in Canada today:

1. Businesses are not free to hire and fire whomever they want. They must comply with employment equity and labour laws. Even closing a plant requires a period of notice for many kinds of firms.
2. Many working conditions are subject to government regulation: safety rules, wage rules, overtime rules, hours-of-work rules, and the like.
3. Businesses cannot meet with other businesses to agree on prices they will charge.
4. Workers in a union cannot require all workers in a firm to join the union before they are hired. In some provinces, they cannot require workers to join the union at all.

Most of these laws evolved over time. Up until the 1930s, household members, in their roles as workers and consumers, had few rights. Businesses were free to hire and fire at will and, if they chose, to deceive and take advantage of consumers.

Over time, laws have changed. New laws to curb business abuses have been passed, and government agencies have been formed to enforce these laws. Now many people think the pendulum has swung too far the other way. They believe businesses are saddled with too many regulatory burdens.

One big question that we'll address throughout this book is: What referee role should the government play in an economy? For example, should government redistribute income from the rich to the poor through taxation? Should it allow a merger between two companies? Should it regulate air traffic? Should it regulate prices?

Since considering government's role will be a central element of the entire book, we'll present a few terms and roles now to establish a framework for the later chapters.

Economic Roles of Government   We first consider the economic roles of government. These roles tend to be somewhat less controversial than its political roles.

Providing a Stable Institutional Framework   A basic economic role of government is to provide a stable institutional framework (the set of rules determining what we can and

6B Seven specific roles of government are:
1. Providing a stable structure within which markets can operate.
2. Promoting workable, effective competition.
3. Correcting for external effects of individuals' decisions.
4. Providing public goods that the market doesn't adequately supply.
5. Ensuring economic stability and growth.
6. Providing acceptably fair distribution of society's production among its individuals.
7. Encouraging merit and discouraging demerit goods or activities.

can't do). Before people conduct business, they need to know the rules of the game and have a reasonable belief about what those rules will be in the future. The modern economy requires contractual arrangements to be made among individuals. These arrangements must be enforced if the economy is to operate effectively. Ultimately, only the government can create a stable environment and enforce contracts through its legal system. Where governments don't provide a stable environment, as often happens in developing countries, economic growth is difficult; usually such economies are stagnant. Liberia in the early 1990s is an example. As two groups there fought for political control, the Liberian economy stagnated.

Almost all economists believe that providing an institutional framework within which the market can operate is an important function of government. However, they differ significantly as to what the rules for such a system should be. Even if the rules are currently perceived as unfair, an argument can be made for keeping them. Individuals have already made decisions based on the existing rules, so it's unfair to them to change the rules in midstream. Stability of rules is a benefit to society.

Recent economic reforms in the former Soviet Union provide a good example of this point. First, the Soviets modified their rules to encourage profits and entrepreneurship. Within a year they changed the rules again, attacking entrepreneurs as profiteers and confiscating their earnings. Then they began to encourage entrepreneurship again, but the second time few entrepreneurs came forward because of fear that the rules would change once again. Then there was a conservative coup; then a reestablishment of the market. Finally the entire political structure fell apart, and the Soviet Union was no more.

When rules are perceived as unfair and changing them is also perceived as unfair, which often happens, the government finds itself in the difficult position of any referee, trying to strike a balance between the two degrees of unfairness.

Promoting Effective and Workable Competition One of the most difficult economic functions of government is its role in protecting and promoting competition. As we discussed above, Canadian ideology sees **monopoly power** as bad. Monopoly power is the ability of individuals or firms currently in business to prevent other individuals or firms from entering the same kind of business; thereby monopoly power can raise existing firms' prices. Similarly, Canadian ideology sees **competition** (individuals' or firms' ability to enter freely into business activities) as good. Government's job is to promote competition and prevent monopoly power from limiting competition.

Monopoly power Ability to prevent others from entering a business field, which enables a firm to raise its price.

Competition Ability of individuals to freely enter into business activities

What makes this a difficult function for government is that most individuals and firms believe that competition is far better for the other guy than it is for themselves, that their monopolies are necessary monopolies, and that competition facing them is unfair competition. For example, farmers support competition, but they also support government farm subsidies and import restrictions, which make it harder for foreign individuals to compete in Canada. Likewise, firms support competition, but they also support tariffs which protect them from foreign competition. Professionals, such as architects and engineers, support competition, but they also support professional licensing, which limits the number of competitors who can enter their field.

Correcting for Externalities When two people freely enter into a trade or agreement, they both believe that they will benefit from that trade. But unless they're required to do so, traders are unlikely to take into account the effect that that agreement or trade may have on others. (An effect of a trade or agreement on a third party that the people who made the trade did not take into account is called an *external effect* or **externality.**) An externality can be positive (in which case society as a whole benefits even more than the two traders) or negative (in which case society as a whole benefits less than the two parties). In either case, externalities provide a potential role for government. If one's goal is to benefit society as much as possible, trades with positive externalities should be encouraged, and trades with negative externalities should be restricted.

Externality A result of a decision that is not taken into account by the decision maker.

An example of a positive externality is education. When someone educates herself or himself, it is not only the person who is helped. All society benefits since better-educated people make better citizens and can often figure out new approaches to solving problems, solutions that benefit everyone.

An example of a negative externality is pollution. For example, when people use air conditioners, they'll probably let loose a small amount of chlorofluorocarbons, which go up into the earth's atmosphere and contribute to the destruction of the ozone layer. The ozone layer protects all living things by filtering some of the sun's ultraviolet light rays, which can contribute to cancer and other harmful or fatal conditions. Neither the firms that produce the air conditioners nor the consumers who buy them pay for the negative effect those chlorofluorocarbons have on society. This means that the destruction of the ozone layer is an externality—the result of an action that is not taken into account by traders.

When externalities exist, government has a potential role: to step in and change the rules so that the actors must take into account the effect of their actions on society as a whole. We emphasize that the role is a *potential* one, because government often has difficulty dealing with externalities in such a way that society gains. For example, even if the Canadian government totally banned chlorofluorocarbons, the problem wouldn't be solved because ozone layer destruction is an international, rather than a national, problem. We also emphasize *potential* because government isn't simply an institution trying to do good. It's an institution that reflects, and is often guided by, politics and vested interests. It's not clear that, given the political realities, government intervention to correct externalities would improve the situation. In later chapters we'll have a lot more to say about government's role in correcting for externalities.

Providing for Public Goods **Public goods** are goods whose consumption by one individual does not prevent their consumption by other individuals. This means that when a supplier supplies a public good to one person, he or she supplies the good to all. In contrast, a **private good** is one that, when consumed by one individual, cannot be consumed by other individuals. An example of a private good is an apple; once that apple is eaten, no one else can consume it.

Public goods Goods whose consumption by one individual does not prevent their consumption by other individuals.

An example of a public good is national defence. National defence must protect all individuals in the country; it cannot protect some people but leave others unprotected. Everyone agrees that national defence is needed. But will everyone, as individuals, supply it, or will everyone rely on someone else doing it? Self-interested people would like to enjoy the benefits of defence, while letting someone else pay for it. Because national defence is a public good, if someone else defends the country you're defended for free; you can be a **free rider.** Everyone has an incentive to be a free rider, but if everyone is a free rider, there won't be any defence. In such cases, government can step in to require that everyone pay part of the cost of national defence to make sure that no one is a free rider.

Private good A good that, when consumed by one individual, cannot be consumed by other individuals.

Free rider Person who participates in something for free because others have paid for it.

Ensuring Economic Stability and Growth In addition to providing general stability, government has the potential role of providing economic stability. If it's possible, most people would agree that government should prevent large fluctuations in the level of economic activity, maintain a relatively constant price level, and provide an economic environment conducive to economic growth. These aims are generally considered macroeconomic goals. They're justified as appropriate aims for government to pursue because they involve **macroeconomic externalities** (externalities that affect the levels of unemployment, inflation, or growth in the economy as a whole).

Macroeconomic externality Externality that affects the levels of unemployment, inflation, or growth in the economy as a whole.

Here's how a macroexternality could occur. When individuals decide how much to spend, they don't take into account the effects of their decisions on others; thus, there may be too much or too little spending. Too little spending often leads to unemployment. But in making their spending decisions, people don't take into account the fact that spending less might create unemployment. So their spending decisions can involve a macroexternality. Similarly, when people raise their price and don't consider its effect on inflation, they too might be creating a macroexternality.

Political Roles of Government The other group of possible roles for government, *political roles,* involves more controversial issues.

Providing for a Fair Distribution of Society's Income The first, and probably most controversial, of these roles concerns income distribution. Many believe the government should see that the economic system is fair, or at least is perceived as fair, by the majority of the people in the society.

But determining what's fair is a difficult philosophical question. Let's simply consider two of the many manifestations of the fairness problem. Should the government use a **progressive tax** (a tax whose rates increase as a person's income increases) to redistribute money from the rich to the poor? (A progressive income tax schedule might tax individuals at a rate of 15 percent for income up to $20,000; at 25 percent for income between $20,000 and $40,000; and at 35 percent for every dollar earned over $40,000.) Or should government impose a **regressive tax** (a tax whose rates decrease as income rises) to redistribute money from the poor to the rich? Or should government impose a flat or **proportional tax** (a tax whose rates are constant at all income levels, say 25 percent on every dollar of income, no matter what your total annual income is) and not redistribute money? Canada has chosen a somewhat progressive income tax.

Another tax question government faces is: Should there be *exemptions* (items of income that aren't taxed at all)? An exemption might be granted for $2,400 of income multiplied by the number of children the taxpayer has. A single mother with five children wouldn't be taxed at all on $12,000 ($2,400 × 5) of her annual income. Or is that a *tax loophole* (a legal but unfair exemption)? Many Canadian economists would argue that a more equitable approach is to give the mother a tax credit rather than an exemption. Economists can tell government the effects of various types of taxes and forms of taxation, but we can't tell government what's fair. That is for *the people,* through the government, to decide. Of course, interest groups place a great deal of pressure on the government, as we've already seen. Members of Parliament sometimes have a difficult time remembering just who *the people* really are.

Consider, for example, spending programmes targeted at historically depressed regions of the country. People in, for example, central Ontario or Alberta may have a hard time understanding why the federal government transfers millions of their tax dollars to firms in Atlantic Canada (through government agencies like the Atlantic Canada Opportunities Agency, known as ACOA) in an attempt to encourage regional economic development. Many might argue that regional development programmes are economically inefficient—and, while that might be true, we need to remember that economic institutions—such as the invisible handshake and the invisible foot—and political considerations colour every decision the government makes.

Determining Demerit and Merit Goods or Activities Another controversial role for government involves deciding what's best for people independently of their desires. The externality justification of government intervention assumes that individuals know what is best for themselves.

But what if people don't know what's best for themselves? What if they do know but don't act on that knowledge? For example, people might know that addictive drugs are bad for them but because of peer pressure, or because they just don't care, they may take addictive drugs anyway. Government action prohibiting such activities through law or high taxes may then be warranted. Goods or activities that are deemed bad for people even though they choose to use the goods or engage in the activities are known as **demerit goods or activities.** The addictive drug is a demerit good; using addictive drugs is a demerit activity.

Progressive tax   Average tax rate increases with income.

Regressive tax   Average tax rate decreases with income.

Proportional tax   Average tax rate is constant with income.

Demerit goods or activities   Things government believes are bad for you, although you may like them.

ADDED DIMENSION

FINDING MORE INFORMATION ABOUT THE ECONOMY

No introductory book is able to provide you with all the information you should have about the economy. You should know about:

- Financial institutions, such as banks, insurance companies, and stock markets.
- The state of the economy: unemployment rates, inflation rates, and growth rates.
- The operations of business, such as advertising and assembly line production.

We'll provide general information on such topics, but you should get up-to-date specifics by following the economic news. Such current information is integral to any economics course. Where should you look? A good beginning is the following:

- Cursory: Business section of your local paper and network news on TV. A slim treatment of the economic issues, but at least it introduces you to the terms.
- One step up from cursory: Time, *Newsweek, MacLean's;* CBC, CTV, CNN on TV.
- Reasonably thorough: *Business Week, Forbes, Fortune, Canadian Business* magazines; "Question Period," "Venture," "Wall Street Week," and "The McNeil-Lehrer Report" on TV.
- Excellent: *The Economist, The Financial Post, The Financial Times, The Globe and Mail, The Wall Street Journal.*

Alternatively, there are some activities that government believes are good for people, even if people may not choose to engage in them. For example, government may believe that going to the opera or contributing to charity is a good activity. But in Canada only a small percentage of the population goes to the opera, and not everyone in Canada contributes to charity. Similarly, government may believe that whole-wheat bread is more nutritious than white bread. But many consumers prefer white bread. Activities and goods that government believes are good for you even though you may not choose to engage in the activities or consume the goods are known as **merit goods or activities,** and government support for them through subsidies or tax benefits may be warranted.

Merit goods or activities Things government believes are good for you, although you may not think so.

The Limits of Government Action

Economic theory doesn't say government should or shouldn't play any particular role in the economy. Those decisions depend on costs and benefits of government action. The public often perceives economic theory and economists as suggesting the best policy is a policy of laissez-faire, or government noninvolvement in the economy. Many economists do suggest a laissez-faire policy, but that suggestion is based on empirical observations of government's role in the past, not on economic theory.

Still, economists as a group generally favour less government involvement than does the general public. We suspect that the reason is that economists are taught to look below the surface at the long-run effect of government actions. They've discovered that the effects of government actions often aren't the intended effects, and that programmes frequently have long-run consequences that make the problems worse, not better. Economists, both liberal and conservative, speak in the voice of reason: "Look at all the costs; look at all the benefits. Then decide whether government should or should not intervene."

Political pressures often force government to act, regardless of what rational examination suggests. A good example is new air safety regulations after a plane crash. The public generally favours these overwhelmingly. Most economists we know say: "Wait. Don't act in haste. Consider the benefits and costs that would result." After careful consideration, advantages and disadvantages aren't always clear; some economists favour more regulation, some economists favour less regulation—but they all make their assessments on the basis of rational examination, not emotion.

CHAPTER SUMMARY

- The invisible hand doesn't operate in an invisible world. Knowing economics requires knowing real-world information.
- Views about government's appropriate role in the economy have changed over time.
- In Canada, businesses make the *what, how much,* and *for whom* decisions.
- Businesses, households, and government can be categorized in a variety of ways.
- Although businesses decide what to produce, they succeed or fail depending on their ability to meet consumers' desires. That's consumer sovereignty.
- The three main forms of business are corporations, sole proprietorships, and partnerships.
- Income is unequally divided among households. Whether that's bad, and whether anything should be done about it, are debatable.

- Governments play two general roles in the economy: (1) as a referee, and (2) as an actor.
- Government has seven possible economic roles in a capitalist society:
  1. Providing a stable institutional and legal structure within which markets can operate.
  2. Promoting workable and effective competition.
  3. Correcting for external effects of individuals' decisions.
  4. Providing public goods that the market doesn't adequately supply.
  5. Ensuring economic stability and growth.
  6. Providing an acceptably fair distribution of society's products among its individuals.
  7. Encouraging merit and discouraging demerit goods or activities.
- In deciding whether government has a role to play, economists look at the costs and benefits of a given role.

KEY TERMS

business *(82)*
competition *(96)*
consumer sovereignty *(84)*
corporation *(89)*
debt *(94)*
demerit goods or activities *(98)*
entrepreneurship *(82)*
externality *(96)*
free rider *(97)*
general purpose transfers *(94)*
government budget deficit *(94)*

government budget surplus *(94)*
households *(90)*
ideology *(92)*
interest groups *(93)*
limited liability *(89)*
low-income cutoff *(90)*
macroeconomic externality *(97)*
merit goods or activities *(99)*
monopoly power *(96)*
nonprofit business *(87)*
partnership *(89)*

private good *(97)*
profit *(84)*
progressive tax *(98)*
proportional tax *(98)*
public good *(97)*
regressive tax *(98)*
sole proprietorship *(89)*
special purpose transfers *(94)*
stage of production *(84)*
stock *(89)*
transfer payments *(94)*

QUESTIONS FOR THOUGHT AND REVIEW

The number after each question represents the estimated degree of critical thinking required. (1 = almost none; 10 = deep thought.)

1. A market system is often said to be based on consumer sovereignty—the consumer determines what's to be produced. Yet business decides what's to be produced. Can these two views be reconciled? How? If not, why? *(5)*

2. Should conservation be left to the free market to determine price and availability of resources, or is there a role for government intervention in the conservation debate? *(8)*

3. Canada is sometimes classified as a postindustrial society. What's meant by this? And, if it's an accurate classification, is it good or bad to be a postindustrial society? *(7)*

4. A nonprofit company will generally charge lower prices than a for-profit company in the same business because the nonprofit company doesn't factor a profit into its prices. True or false? Why? *(6)*

5. You're starting a software company in which you plan to sell software to your fellow students. What form of business organization would you choose? Why? *(5)*

6. The social security system is inconsistent with pure capitalism, but is almost an untouchable right of Canadians. How can this be? *(6)*

7. You've set up the rules for a game and started the game, but now realize that the rules are unfair. Should you change the rules? *(6)*

8. Say the government establishes rights to pollute so that without a pollution permit you aren't allowed to emit pollutants into the air, water, or soil. Firms are allowed to buy and sell these rights. In what way will this correct for an externality? *(9)*

9. What are two general roles of government and seven specific roles? *(3)*

10. According to polls, most economists classify themselves as liberal, but they generally favour less government involvement in the economy than does the general public. Why? *(7)*

PROBLEMS AND EXERCISES

1. Go to a store in your community.
   a. Ask what limitations the owners faced in starting their business.
   b. Were these limitations necessary?
   c. Should there have been more or fewer limitations?
   d. Under what heading of reasons for government intervention would you put each of the limitations?
   e. Ask what taxes the business pays and what benefits it believes it gets for those taxes.
   f. Is it satisfied with the existing situation? Why? What would it change?

2. You've been appointed to a provincial counterterrorist squad. Your assignment is to work up a set of plans to stop a group of 10 terrorists the government believes are going to disrupt the economy as much as possible with explosives.
   a. List their five most likely targets in your province, city, or town.
   b. What counterterrorist action would you take?
   c. How would you advise the economy to adjust to a successful attack on each of the targets?

3. The technology is now developing so that road use can be priced by computer. A computer in the surface of the road picks up a signal from your car and automatically charges you for the use of the road.
   a. How could this technological change contribute to ending bottlenecks and rush hour congestion?
   b. What are some of the problems that might develop with such a system?
   c. How would your transportation habits likely change if you had to pay to use roads?

4. Tom Rollins heads a new venture called Teaching Co. He has taped lectures at the top universities, packaged the lectures on audio- and videocassettes, and sells them for $90 and $150 per eight-hour series.
   a. Discuss whether such an idea could be expanded to include college courses that one could take at home.
   b. What are the technical, social, and economic issues involved?
   c. If it is technically possible and cost-effective, will the new venture be a success?

5. You've just been hired by a government department whose primary responsibility is to monitor the economic activities of foreign countries.
   a. What kind of information are you going to want to examine? Make a list of the ten most important topics. Now go to your library and try to find that information on any country of your choosing.
   b. How readily available was that information?
   c. If you wanted to disrupt that country's economy, on which sectors would you want to focus your energies?
   d. Now repeat this for Canada.

6. Boris Gaussware is a leading expert in the analysis of bankruptcy. He argues that government "red tape" is the primary cause of business failure in the nation. Do you agree? Ask someone who operates a business if they think red tape is what causes bankruptcies. What was their first reaction? Did they have any other explanation for why firms fail?

7. The government uses tax policy to redistribute income. The government also tries to set the rules of business so that firms know what they can and cannot do. Which of the seven roles of government would be applicable to these examples? Why?

A P P E N D I X   A

Trading in Stocks

Small corporations' stock is usually traded *over-the-counter,* which doesn't mean you go in a store and walk up to the counter. *Over-the-counter* is an expression representing the stock exchange on which these stocks are bought and sold. An over-the-counter share has a *bid* price and a higher *ask* price. The bid price is the price someone has offered to pay for shares; the ask price is the price a shareholder has told her brokers she wants to get for her shares. Trades are usually made at some price between the bid and ask figures, with the broker collecting a commission for arranging a trade.

Exhibit A1 shows a typical stock exchange listing.

In order to buy or sell a Toronto Stock Exchange stock, you go to a stockbroker and say you want to buy or sell whatever stock you've decided on—say Ford Motor Company. The commission you're charged for having the broker sell you the stock (or sell it for you) varies. Any purchase of fewer than 100 shares of one corporation is called an *odd lot* and you'll be charged a higher commission than if you buy a 100-share lot or more.

There are a number of stock exchanges. The largest and most familiar is the Toronto Stock Exchange.

To judge how stocks as a whole are doing, a number of indexes have been developed. The one you're most likely to hear about in the news is the TSE 300. American indexes include Standard and Poor's (S&P 500), the Wilshire Index, and the Dow Jones Industrial Average.

When a share of a corporation's existing stock is sold on the stock exchange, corporations get no money from that sale. The sale is simply a transfer of ownership from one individual (or organization) to another. The only time a corporation gets money from the sale of stock is when it first issues the shares.

EXHIBIT A1 Stock Exchange Listings and Explanation

Source: The Globe and Mall, March 3, 1995, p. BB.

B8 Friday March 3, 1995 Globe and Mail Toronto

52-week high	52-week low	Stock	Sym	Div	High	Low	Close	Chg	Vol (100s)	Yield	P/E ratio
		A-B									
6 3/8	1.00	ABL Canada	ABL		1.05	1.00	1.05		1617		
20 1/2	14	AGF nv	AGF.PR.B	0.60	15	15	15		8	4.00	7.7
14 3/8	8	AIT Advanced	AIV		10 1/2	10 1/2	10 1/2		25		15.9
.145	0.10	AJ Perron	AJP		0.11	0.11	0.11	+0.01	350		
12 1/4	6 1/2	AT Plastics	ATP	0.18	11 1/8	11 1/8	11 1/8	−1/8	13	1.62	8.6
19 1/4	4.50	ATI Techs	ATY		7 1/2	7 1/2	7 1/2	+1/8	66		
12 1/8	6 5/8	ATS Automat	ATA		10	10	9 3/4	+1/8	37		15.0
14 5/8	3.95	Aberj	ABZ		8 1/8	8 1/4	8 1/2	−1/4	1570		
20 4/8	15 5/8	Abitibi-Price	A		17 3/8	17 1/4	17 1/2	−1/4	1368		
8 1/8	1.50	Accugraph j	ACU.A		7	6 1/2	6 3/8	+1/8	879		15.9
14 1/8	10 1/2	Acklands	ACK		12	11 3/8	11 5/8	−3/8	13		8.5
34 1/8	20 1/2	Acme Metal	AMK		21 1/2	20 3/4	21		22		6.2
0.48	0.15	Adex Mining	AMG		0.35	.325	.325	−0.15	4220		
5 1/4	2.70	Adrian Res	ADL		3.80	3.60	3.70	−0.15	573		
3.00	1.10	Advancd Grv j	AED		1.60	1.55	1.60	+0.05	186		
0.60	0.42	Advancd Ma	AMR		0.60	0.60	0.60		50		
7	4.50	Adventure El	AVN	0.14	5 1/2	5 1/2	5 1/2	+0.75	2	2.55	9.2
1.16	0.33	Advent	AVN.WT.A		0.45	0.35	0.35	−0.10	606		
19 3/8	11 1/4	Agnico Eagle	AGE	a0.10	13 1/8	13	13 1/4	+1/4	106	1.05	34.9
9 1/4	5 1/8	Agra nv	AGR.B	0.16	6 1/4	6 1/2	6 3/4	+1/4	58	2.37	
9 1/8	5 7/8	Agra Ind	AGR.A	0.14	7	7	7		51	2.00	
12 1/4	3.30	Aim Safety	AIM		9 7/8	9 1/2	9 3/4	−1/8	52		
18 1/8	10 1/4	Ainsworth Lu	ANS		11 1/8	11 1/4	11 1/4	−1/8	34		6.8
8 2/8	5 5/8	Air Canada	AC		7 5/8	7 3/8	7 3/8	−1/4	1385		6.8
3.15	1.75	Air Canad	AC.WT		2.00	1.80	1.80	−0.20	136		
5 1/4	2.30	Akita Dri nv	AKT.A		2.75	2.70	2.75	+0.05	9		4.6
22 1/4	16 1/8	Alberta Ener	AEC	0.40	18 3/4	18 1/2	18 5/8	−1/4	142	2.15	13.7
17 1/8	13 1/4	Alta Nat Gas	ANG	0.68	14 1/2	14 1/4	14 1/4	−1/4	275	4.77	11.5
38 3/8	27 1/8	Alcan	AL	a0.30	33 1/8	33 1/8	33 1/4	+1/8	3625	1.24	71.2
24 1/8	21 1/4	Alcan C	AL.PR.E	1.81	21 1/4	21 5/8	21 3/8		24	8.32	
2.25	0.50	Algo sv	AO.A		0.50	0.50	0.50	−0.09	10		
↑26	14	Algoma Cnti	ALC		26	24 3/4	26	+1	19		14.9
22 1/2	19 3/4	Algoma	AFC.PR.A	1.38	22	22	22	−1/2	497	6.25	
11 1/8	9	Algoma Steel	ALG		9 3/8	9 1/4	9 1/4	−1/8	15		
8 5/8	5 1/8	Allelix	AXB		5 5/8	5 5/8	5 5/8		10		
18 1/4	12 3/8	Alliance Com	AAC		14	13 1/4	14		44		11.0
25	16 1/4	Alliance Fore	ALP		23 1/2	22 1/4	22 3/4	−5/8	401		8.9
14 1/2	7	AlphaNet Tel	FAX		8 1/4	8 1/2	8 1/4	+1/4	32		
2.77	0.50	Altai Res	ATI		0.55	0.55	0.55		68		
6 1/2	2.35	Amer Eco	ECX		2.55	2.55	2.55		30		4.7
25 1/8	9 3/8	Amer Sensor	ASZ		12 1/4	12 3/4	12 1/8	+5/8	2543		

How to read the stock tables

1 2	3	4	5	6	7	8	9	10	11	12
52-week high low	Stock	Sym	Div	High	Low	Close	Chg	Vol (100s)	Yield	P/E ratio

1. Arrow up or down - new 52-week high or low in day's trading
2. 52-week high/low - highest and lowest inter-day price in past 52 weeks
3. Stock - abbreviated company name
4. Sym - Ticker symbol assigned to issue by exchange; .PR is preferred share, .WT is warrant, .UN is unit, .S means stacks are subject to regulation of the SEC Act, .W means when issued.
5. Div - Indicated annual dividend (excluding special dividends)
6. High - Highest inter-day trading price
7. Low - Lowest inter-day trading price
8. Close - Closing price
9. Chg - Change between closing price and previous closing board lot price
10. Vol - Number of shares traded in 100s; z preceding figure indicates sales are reported in full
11. Yield - expressed as percentage, calculated by dividing the dividend by current market price
12. P/E ratio - Price/earnings ratio; current stock price divided by the company's earnings per share from continuing operations for the latest 12 months

Footnotes

a - in U.S. dollars (on Canadian exchanges)
au - in Australian dollars
b - in British pounds or pence
c - in Canadian dollars (on U.S. exchanges)
cl - commercial/industrial stock (on the Vancouver Stock Exchange)
da - dividend in arrears
dc - dividends paid in Canadian dollars, but stock trades in U.S. funds
g - coming capital gains distribution will be paid to the current owner
in - inactive stock (on the VSE)
j - subject to special reporting rules
n - stock is new issue
nl - mutual fund with no front-end load or contingent deferred sales load
nv - non-voting
rc - in bankruptcy or receivership or being reorganized under the Bankruptcy Act, or securities assumed by such companies
rf - redemption fee or contingent deferred sales load may apply
rs - resource stock (VSE)
rv - shareholders' voting is restricted
s - indicates 52-week high-low range has been adjusted to reflect stock split or consolidation
sv - subordinate-voting
x - stock is trading ex-dividend
y - in Japanese yen.
Data supplied by Dow Jones Telerate Canada Inc.

5

An Introduction to the World Economy

As for foreign exchange, it is almost as romantic as young love, and quite as resistant to formulae.

~H. L. Mencken

After reading this chapter, you should be able to:

1 Explain what is meant by *the industrial countries of the world* and *the developing countries of the world.*

2 State where in the world various resources are found and where goods are produced.

3 State two ways international trade differs from domestic trade.

4 Make sense of an exchange rate table in the newspaper.

5 Explain two important determinants of the trade balance.

6 List five important international economic institutions.

7 Give a brief economic history of the European Union and Japan since the 1940s.

International issues have always been at the centre of economic activity and economic policy in Canada. The Canadian economy is integrated with the world economy, and we cannot reasonably discuss Canadian economic issues without discussing the role that international considerations play in these issues. The aim of this chapter is to get you to start thinking about how the international marketplace affects the Canadian economy. Later in the course we'll examine the international dimensions of economic activity in much greater detail—by then you'll be well versed in Canada's dependence on the international economy.

Consider the clothes on your back. Most likely they were made abroad. Similarly with the cars you drive. It's likely that half of you drive a car that was made abroad. Of course, it's often difficult to tell. Just because a car has a Japanese or German name doesn't mean that it was produced abroad. Some Japanese and German companies now have manufacturing plants in Canada, and some Canadian firms have manufacturing plants abroad. When goods are produced by **global corporations** (corporations with substantial operations on both the production and sales sides in more than one country are called global, or multinational, corporations), corporate names don't always tell much about where a good is produced. As global corporations' importance

Global corporations   Corporations with substantial operations on both the production and sales sides in more than one country. Another name for multinational corporations.

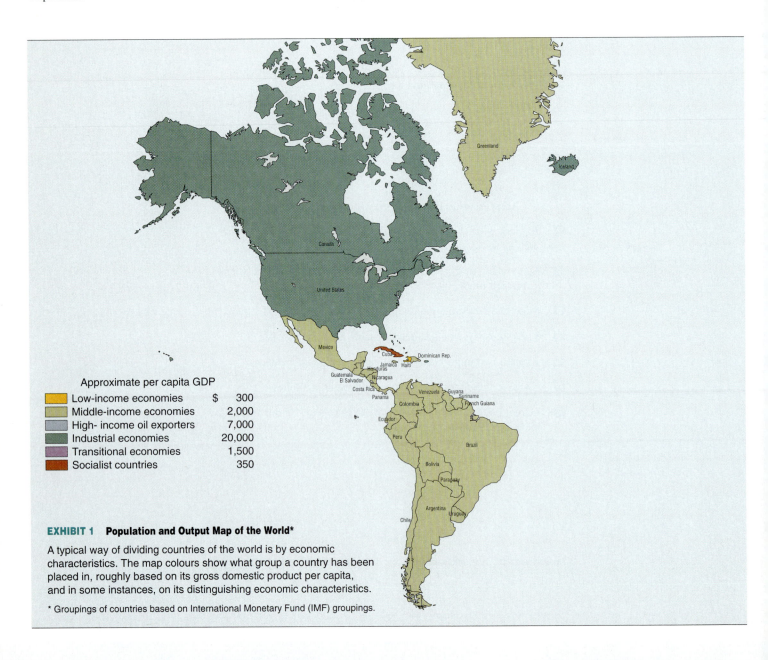

EXHIBIT 1   Population and Output Map of the World*

A typical way of dividing countries of the world is by economic characteristics. The map colours show what group a country has been placed in, roughly based on its gross domestic product per capita, and in some instances, on its distinguishing economic characteristics.

Approximate per capita GDP

Low-income economies	$	300
Middle-income economies		2,000
High- income oil exporters		7,000
Industrial economies		20,000
Transitional economies		1,500
Socialist countries		350

* Groupings of countries based on International Monetary Fund (IMF) groupings.

has grown, most manufacturing decisions are made in reference to the international market, not the domestic Canadian market.

The international connection means international economic problems and the policies of other countries—U.S. and European trade policies, developing countries' debt problems, questions of competitiveness, transfer of technology to China, Japanese microeconomic policy, Organization of Petroleum Exporting Countries (OPEC) pricing policies—all have moved to the centre of the economic stage. This chapter introduces you to such issues.

Exhibit 1's map of the world is divided into categories based on per capita output (output per person, valued in U.S. dollars) and other relevant economic characteristics. *Industrial economies* (such as Canada, the United States, Germany, and Britain) have a large industrial production base. A second group of countries, such as Kuwait and Saudi Arabia, have high incomes, but don't have the industrial base. Since their high income is primarily based on oil exports, those countries are known as high-income *oil exporters.* The next two classifications, *middle-income economies* and *low-income economies* (or, as they are sometimes called, *developing economies*), make up

INTERNATIONAL ECONOMIC STATISTICS: AN OVERVIEW

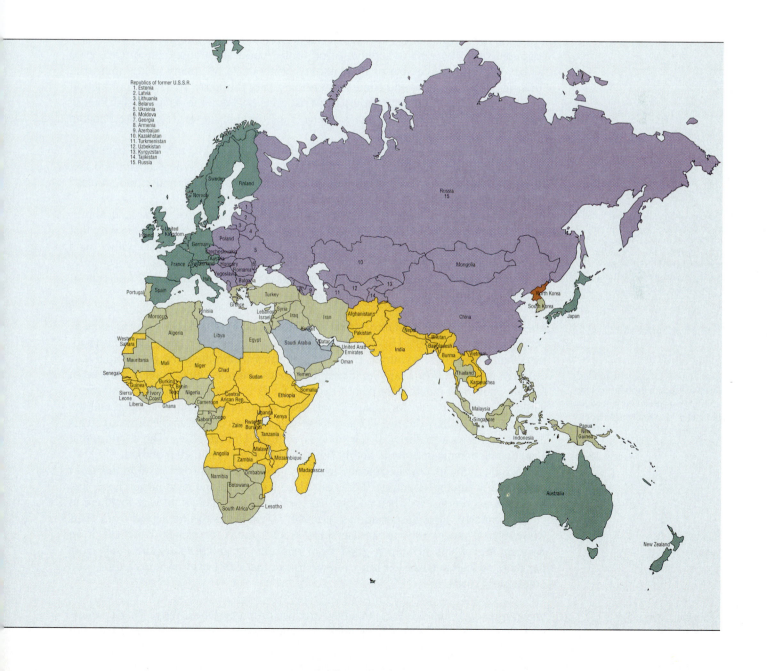

the majority of countries in the world. The *transitional economies* consist of the formerly socialist economies. These economies are in a period of flux and will probably be much in the news in the late 1990s. It is unclear what form of economic organization these transitional economies will take. The final category is *socialist economies;* only North Korea and Cuba still fit in this category.

This isn't the only method of classification. An alternative method is by region: Latin American, African, Middle Eastern, Asian, Western European, North American, and Eastern European countries. Since geographically grouped countries often share a cultural heritage, they also often face similar problems.

None of these classifications is airtight. Each country is different from every other, so no grouping works perfectly. Exhibit 1's classification system, based largely on output per person, is the most commonly used, and should give you a sense of what's meant by such classifications. The next time you hear "the industrial nations of the world" or "the developing countries of the world," you should be able to close your eyes and picture the relevant group of economies on a map or, at least, have a general idea of which countries are meant.

Economic Geography

Most classifications are based on a country's total output or production. Production statistics, however, don't necessarily capture a nation's importance or the strategic role it plays in the world economy. Consider Saudi Arabia. Its total output isn't particularly large, but since it's a major supplier of oil to the world, its strategic importance goes far beyond the relative size of its economy. Without its oil, many of the industrial countries of the world would come to a grinding halt. Similarly, Panama's production is minuscule, but its location on a narrow isthmus between the Atlantic and Pacific Oceans and the fact that the Panama Canal runs through its territory make Panama vital to the world economy.

These examples demonstrate why we need, besides a knowledge of countries' productive capacities, a knowledge of economic geography: Where do the world's natural resources lie? Which countries control them? What are the major trade routes? How are goods shipped from one place to another?

Exhibit 2 locates some of the world's major energy resources and trade routes. Note the major flow of energy resources from the Middle East: You can see why that region is so important to the world economy (oil and the Suez Canal). Other such resource maps would show why many countries treat South Africa with care (gold, many other alloying metals, and diamonds) and why Chile (with about 27 percent of all copper) is important to the world economy.

Differing Economic Problems

The economic problems countries face are determined by a variety of factors such as per capita income levels. High-income countries generally face quite different problems than low-income countries. Even two countries within the same group often face different problems. For example, the United States **imports** (buys goods produced in foreign countries) much more than it **exports** (sells U.S. goods to foreign countries), while the reverse is true for Japan. When trade disputes arise between Japan and the United States, as they did in 1993 and 1994, Canada gets caught in the crossfire. This is because the vast majority of our trade is with the United States. The result is that Canadian economic activity is highly sensitive to events originating abroad.

Although the identical economic insights apply to all countries, institutions differ substantially among countries. For example, many developing countries have few financial institutions, so when people there want to save, there's no way for them to do so. Similarly with transportation systems. If a firm wants to ship a good from Trois Rivières to Thunder Bay, it can use ships, trucks, trains, or planes. However, if an African firm wants to ship a good from one city to another in Zaire—say from Kinshasa to Lubumbashi—it must import trucks that can travel on unpaved or even nonexistent roads.

Comparative Advantage and Trade

One reason economies differ is that they produce different goods. Why? That's a question we'll explore in macroeconomics in a later chapter on international trade. For

1 The industrial countries of the world have a large industrial base and a per capita income of about $20,000 a year; the developing countries of the world include low- and medium-income economies that have a per capita income of between $300 and $2,000 a year.

2 Some major producing areas for some important raw materials are:
Aluminum—Guinea, Australia
Cobalt—Zaire, Zambia, Russia
Copper—Chile, U.S., Poland
Iron—Russia, Brazil, Australia
Zinc—Canada, Australia, Russia

Imports Goods produced in foreign countries but sold in the home country.
Exports Goods produced in the home country but sold to foreign countries.

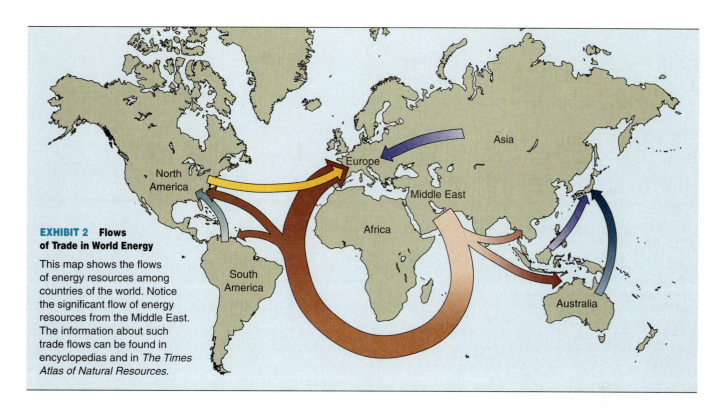

EXHIBIT 2 Flows of Trade in World Energy

This map shows the flows of energy resources among countries of the world. Notice the significant flow of energy resources from the Middle East. The information about such trade flows can be found in encyclopedias and in *The Times Atlas of Natural Resources.*

now, we'll simply introduce you to a key term in international trade which plays a major role in what different countries produce. That term is **comparative advantage.** A country has a comparative advantage in producing a good if it can produce that good at a lower opportunity cost (forgone production of another good) than another country can.

Comparative advantage The ability to produce a good at a lower opportunity cost (forgone production of another good) than another country can.

For example, say Canada can produce widgets at a cost of $4 apiece and wadgets at $4 apiece, while South Korea can produce widgets at a cost of 300 won apiece and wadgets at a cost of 100 won apiece. In Canada, the opportunity cost of one widget is one wadget. (Since each costs $4, Canada must reduce its production of wadgets by one to produce another widget.) In South Korea, the opportunity cost of a widget is three wadgets since it costs three times as much to produce a widget as it does to produce a wadget. Because Canada's opportunity cost of producing widgets is lower than South Korea's, Canada is said to have a comparative advantage in producing widgets. Similarly, South Korea is said to have a comparative advantage in producing wadgets because its opportunity cost of wadgets is one-third of a widget while Canada's opportunity cost of wadgets is one widget.

If one country has a comparative advantage in one good, the other country must necessarily have a comparative advantage in the other good. Notice how comparative advantage hinges on opportunity cost, not total cost. Even if one country can produce all goods cheaper than another country, trade between them is still possible since the opportunity costs of various goods differ.

There's much more to be said about comparative advantage and how changes in a nation's resource base force it to restructure its economy to take advantage of those changes. For now, we want you to remember that different countries produce different goods because opportunity costs vary considerably across countries.

Countries not only produce different goods, they also consume different goods. Exhibit 3 presents per capita consumption of some foods in selected countries. Notice the differences.

Other differences in consumption (and production) are explained by custom, history, and tradition. For example, Japanese traditionally eat rice with meals; Canadians eat bread and potatoes. Drinking alcoholic beverages in Russia is a time-honoured tradition; Muslim countries, such as Saudi Arabia, forbid consumption of

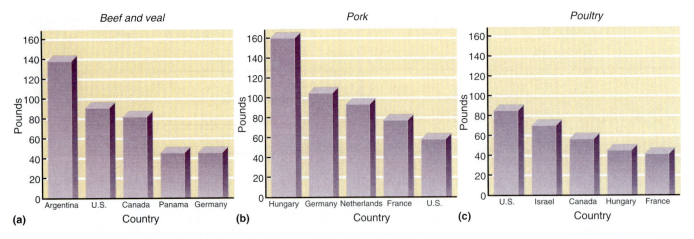

EXHIBIT 3   Per Capita Consumption of Different Commodities, 1990

In Exhibit 3 you can see the per capita consumption of selected goods in various countries. Notice that Canada consumes less beef and veal than does Argentina, and its consumption of poultry is small compared to the United States.

alcoholic beverages. Understanding international economic issues often requires an in-depth understanding of various countries' histories and cultures.

HOW INTERNATIONAL TRADE DIFFERS FROM DOMESTIC TRADE

3 Two ways in which *inter*national trade differs from *intra*national (domestic) trade are:
(1) International trade involves potential barriers to trade; and
(2) International trade involves multiple currencies.

Quotas   Limitations on how much of a good can be shipped into a country.

Tariff tax   A tax governments place on internationally traded goods—generally imports. Tariffs are also called *customs duties*.

Nontariff barriers   Indirect regulatory restrictions on exports and imports.

Foreign exchange market   Market in which one country's currency can be exchanged for another country's.

4 By looking at an exchange rate table, you can determine how much various goods will likely cost in different countries.

*Inter*national trade differs from *intra*national, or domestic trade in two ways. First, international trade involves potential barriers to the flow of inputs and outputs. Before they can be sold in Canada, international goods must be sent through Canada Customs; that is, when they enter Canada they are inspected by Canadian officials and usually charged fees, known as *customs*. A company in Vancouver can produce output to sell in any Canadian province without worrying that its right to sell will be limited; a producer outside the Canada boundary cannot. That is not to say that there aren't barriers to domestic trade: there are. These typically take the form of provincial regulations that attempt to protect local workers and firms from competition from outside the province. (In 1994, the provincial premiers announced their commitment to lessen interprovincial trade barriers and promised to introduce legislation to do so.) At any time, a foreign producer's right to sell in Canada can be limited by government-imposed **quotas** (limitations on how much of a good can be shipped into a country), **tariffs** (taxes on imports), and **nontariff barriers** (indirect regulatory restrictions on imports and exports).

The last category, indirect regulatory restrictions on imports and exports, may be unfamiliar to you, so let's consider an example. U.S. building codes require that plywood have fewer than, say, five flaws per sheet. Canadian building codes require that plywood have fewer than, say, two flaws per sheet. The different building codes are a nontariff barrier, making trade in building materials between the United States and Canada difficult.

The second way international trade differs from domestic trade is countries' use of different currencies. When people in one country sell something to people in another, they must find a way to exchange currencies as well as goods. **Foreign exchange markets** (markets where one currency can be exchanged for another) have developed to provide this service.

How many dollars will a Canadian have to pay to get a given amount of the currency of another country? That depends on the supply of and demand for that currency. To find what you'd have to pay, you look in the newspaper for the exchange rate set out in a foreign exchange table. Exhibit 4 shows such a table.

If you want shekels, you'll have to pay about 47 cents apiece. If you want Punt, one Punt will cost you $ 2.22. (If you're wondering what shekels and Punt are, look at Exhibit 4.)

A WORLD ECONOMIC GEOGRAPHY QUIZ

Economic geography isn't much covered in most economics courses because it requires learning enormous numbers of facts. Universities and colleges are designed to teach you how to interpret and relate facts. Unfortunately, if you don't know facts, much of what you learn in university and college isn't going to do you much good. You'll be relating and interpreting air. The following quiz presents some facts about the world economy. On the left we list characteristics of countries or regions. On the right we list 20 countries or regions. Associate the characteristics with the country or region.

If you answer 15 or more correctly, you have a reasonably good sense of economic geography. If you don't, we strongly suggest learning more facts. The study guide has other projects, information, and examples. An encyclopedia has even more, and your library has a wealth of information. You could spend the entire term acquiring facts. We're not suggesting that; we are suggesting following the economic news carefully, paying attention to where various commodities are produced, and picturing in your mind a map whenever you hear about an economic event.

_____ 1. Former British colony, now small independent island country famous for producing rum.

_____ 2. Large sandy country contains world's largest known oil reserves.

_____ 3. Very large country with few people produces 25 percent of the world's wool.

_____ 4. Temperate country ideal for producing wheat, soybeans, fruits, vegetables, wine, and meat.

_____ 5. Small tropical country produces abundant coffee and bananas.

_____ 6. Has world's largest population and world's largest hydropower potential.

_____ 7. Second-largest country in Europe; famous for wine and romance.

_____ 8. Former Belgian colony has vast copper mines.

_____ 9. European country; exports luxury clothing, footwear, and automobiles.

_____ 10. Large country that has depleted many of its own resources but has enough coal to last its people for hundreds of years.

_____ 11. Long, narrow country of four main islands; most thickly populated country in the world; exports majority of the world's electronic products.

_____ 12. Recently politically reunified country; one important product is steel.

_____ 13. Second-largest country in the world; leading paper exporter.

_____ 14. European country for centuries politically repressed; now becoming industrialized; chemicals are one of its leading exports.

_____ 15. 96 percent of its people live on 4 percent of the land; much of the world's finest cotton comes from here.

_____ 16. African nation has world's largest concentration of gold.

_____ 17. Huge, heavily populated country eats most of what it raises but is a major tea exporter.

_____ 18. Large country that produces oil and gold; has recently undergone major political and economic changes.

_____ 19. Has only about 50 people per square mile but lots of trees; major timber exporter.

_____ 20. Sliver of a country on Europe's Atlantic coast; by far the world's largest exporter of cork.

a. Argentina
b. Australia
c. Barbados
d. Canada
e. China
f. Costa Rica
g. Egypt
h. France
i. Germany
j. India
k. Italy
l. Japan
m. Portugal
n. Russia
o. Saudi Arabia
p. South Africa
q. Spain
r. Sweden
s. United States
t. Zaire

Answers: 1–c, 2–o, 3–b, 4–a, 5–f, 6–e, 7–h, 8–t, 9–k, 10–s, 11–l, 12–i, 13–d, 14–q, 15–g, 16–p, 17–j, 18–n, 19–r, 20–m.

EXHIBIT 4   A Foreign Exchange-Rate Table

From the exchange-rate table, you learn how much a dollar is worth in other currencies. For example, on this day, March 2, 1995, one franc would cost 27.36 cents; one British pound would cost 2.2336 dollars.

Source: The *Globe and Mail,* March 3, 1995.

B16

Foreign Exchange

Cross Rates

	Canadian dollar	U.S. dollar	British pound	German mark	Japanese yen	Swiss franc	French franc	Dutch guilder	Italian lira
Canada dollar	—	1.4036	2.2336	0.9624	0.014650	1.1351	0.2736	0.8592	0.000848
U.S. dollar	0.7125	—	1.5913	0.6857	0.010437	0.8087	0.1949	0.6121	0.000604
British pound	0.4477	0.6284	—	0.4309	0.006559	0.5082	0.1225	0.3847	0.000380
German mark	1.0391	1.4584	2.3209	—	0.015222	1.1794	0.2843	0.8928	0.000861
Japanese yen	68.26	95.81	152.46	65.69		77.48	18.68	58.65	0.057884
Swiss franc	0.8810	1.2365	1.9678	0.8479	0.012906	—	0.2410	0.7569	0.000747
French franc	3.6550	5.1301	8.1637	3.5175	0.053545	4.1488	—	3.1404	0.003099
Dutch guilder	1.1639	1.6336	2.5996	1.1201	0.017051	1.3211	0.3184	—	0.000987
Italian lira	1179.25	1655.19	2633.96	1134.91	17.275943	1338.56	322.64	1013.21	—

Mid-market rates in Toronto at noon, Mar. 2, 1995. Prepared by the Bank of Montreal Treasury Group.

	$1 U.S. in Cdn.$ =	$1 Cdn. in U.S.$ =
U.S./Canada spot	1.4036	0.7125
1 month forward	1.4062	0.7111
2 months forward	1.4087	0.7099
3 months forward	1.4106	0.7089
6 months forward	1.4158	0.7063
12 months forward	1.4220	0.7032
3 years forward	1.4431	0.6930
5 years forward	1.4776	0.6768
7 years forward	1.5356	0.6512
10 years forward	1.6156	0.6190

Canadian dollar in 1995:			
	High	1.3885	0.7202
	Low	1.4267	0.7009
	Average	1.4066	0.7109

Country	Currency	Cdn. $ per unit	U.S. $ per unit
Britain	Pound	2.2336	1.5913
1 month forward		2.2372	1.5909
2 months forward		2.2402	1.5902
3 months forward		2.2422	1.5895
6 months forward		2.2459	1.5863
12 months forward		2.2430	1.5773
Germany	Mark	0.9624	0.6857
1 month forward		0.9650	0.6863
3 months forward		0.9699	0.6876
6 months forward		0.9761	0.6894
12 months forward		0.9849	0.6926
Japan	Yen	0.014650	0.010437
1 month forward		0.014725	0.010471
3 months forward		0.014871	0.010542
6 months forward		0.015088	0.010657
12 months forward		0.015490	0.010893
Algeria	Dinar	0.0332	0.0236
Antigua, Grenada and St. Lucia	E.C.Dollar	0.5208	0.3711
Argentina	Peso	1.40360	1.00000
Australia	Dollar	1.0340	0.7367
Austria	Schilling	0.13674	0.09742
Bahamas	Dollar	1.4036	1.0000
Barbados	Dollar	0.7053	0.5025
Belgium	Franc	0.04679	0.03333
Bermuda	Dollar	1.4036	1.0000
Brazil	Real	1.653239	1.177856
Bulgaria	Lev	0.0215	0.0153
Chile	Peso	0.003424	0.002440
China	Renminbi	0.1665	0.1186
Cyprus	Pound	3.0680	2.1858
Czech Rep	Koruna	0.0525	0.0374
Denmark	Krone	0.2426	0.1728
Egypt	Pound	0.4125	0.2939

Country	Currency	Cdn. $ per unit	U.S. $ per unit
Fiji	Dollar	0.9853	0.7020
Finland	Markka	0.3144	0.2240
France	Franc	0.2736	0.1949
Greece	Drachma	0.00604	0.00431
Hong Kong	Dollar	0.1815	0.1293
Hungary	Forint	0.01258	0.00896
Iceland	Krona	0.02136	0.01522
India	Rupee	0.04473	0.03187
Indonesia	Rupiah	0.000634	0.000452
Ireland	Punt	2.2219	1.5830
Israel	N Shekel	0.4701	0.3349
Italy	Lira	0.000848	0.000604
Jamaica	Dollar	0.04373	0.03115
Jordan	Dinar	2.0225	1.4409
Lebanon	Pound	0.000856	0.000610
Luxembourg	Franc	0.04679	0.03333
Malaysia	Ringgit	0.5501	0.3919
Mexico	N Peso	0.2377	0.1693
Netherlands	Guilder	0.8592	0.6121
New Zealand	Dollar	0.8913	0.6350
Norway	Krone	0.2179	0.1552
Pakistan	Rupee	0.04557	0.03247
Philippines	Peso	0.05396	0.03845
Poland	Zloty	0.5795450	0.4128990
Portugal	Escudo	0.00927	0.00660
Romania	Leu	0.0008	0.0006
Russia	Ruble	0.000310	0.000221
Saudi Arabia	Riyal	0.3743	0.2667
Singapore	Dollar	0.9700	0.6911
Slovakia	Koruna	0.0461	0.0329
South Africa	Rand	0.3892	0.2773
South Korea	Won	0.001781	0.001269
Spain	Peseta	0.01093	0.00779
Sudan	Dinar	0.0366	0.0261
Sweden	Krona	0.1918	0.1366
Switzerland	Franc	1.1351	0.8087
Taiwan	Dollar	0.0537	0.0382
Thailand	Baht	0.0565	0.0403
Trinidad, Tobago	Dollar	0.2469	0.1759
Turkey	Lira	0.0000338	0.0000241
Venezuela	Bolivar	0.00827	0.00589
Zambia	Kwacha	0.001755	0.001250

	Cdn. $	U.S. $
European Currency Unit	1.7910	1.2760
Special Drawing Right	2.1002	1.4963

The U.S. dollar closed at $1.4034 in terms of Canadian funds, up $0.0057 from Wednesday. The pound sterling closed at $2.2644, up $0.0469.

In New York, the Canadian dollar closed down $0.0029 at $0.7126 in terms of U.S. funds. The pound sterling was up $0.0270 to $1.6135.

Unless you collect currencies, the reason you want the currency of another country is that you want to buy something that country produces or an existing asset of that country. Say you want to buy a car which costs 9,684,000 South Korean won. Looking at the table you see that the exchange rate is $1 for 562 won. Dividing 562 into 9,684,000 won tells you that you need $17,231 to buy the car. So before you can buy the car, somebody must go to a foreign exchange market with $17,231 and exchange those dollars for 9,684,000 won. Only then can the car be bought in Canada.

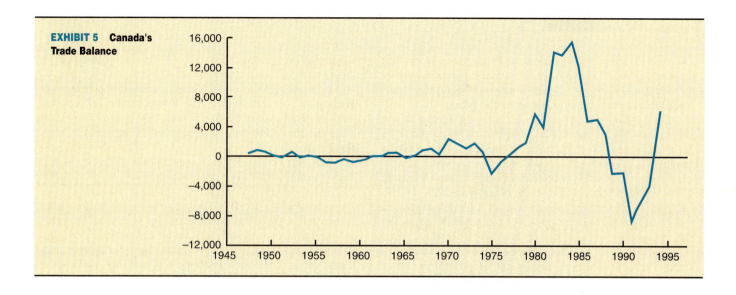

EXHIBIT 5   Canada's Trade Balance

Most final buyers don't do this; the importer does it for them. But whenever a foreign good is bought, someone must trade currencies.

One reason a Canadian economics course must consider international issues early on is the Canadian **balance of trade** (the difference between the value of the goods and services Canada exports and the value of the goods and services it imports). When imports exceed exports, a country is running a **balance of trade deficit;** when exports exceed imports, a country is running a **balance of trade surplus.**[1]

Exhibit 5 shows that Canada ran a trade surplus from 1978 to 1988. In 1984, when the trade surplus was at its peak, Canadian exports of goods and services were about 28.5 percent of gross domestic product (GDP); imports of goods and services were about 25 percent. The 3.5 percent difference meant Canada exported about $15.5 billion worth of goods and services more than it imported. In 1994 Canada ran a trade surplus, partly as a result of the increased world demand for Canadian goods that came from a lower value of the dollar.

We have to be careful about the terminology we use when we look at Canada's international position, since the balance of trade contains two components. The first is the **merchandise trade balance**—it measures the difference between our exports and our imports of goods. The second component is the **services balance**—it captures trade in services. If we took a close look at Canada's trade in merchandise, we'd see that Canada has been a net exporter of goods since at least 1973. The deficit in the balance of trade that we see in Exhibit 5 is due to the fact that Canada has been a net importer of services. It may sound funny, but when your cousin Fred vacations in Florida during spring break, he's really importing the services that the Florida vacation provides. While we export more goods to the rest of the world than we import from the rest of the world, it isn't enough to compensate for the deficit in the services account. That's why the balance of trade is negative even though you might hear on the news or read in the newspaper that Canada just ran a record merchandise trade surplus.

Running a trade deficit isn't necessarily bad, nor is running a trade surplus. In fact, while you're running a trade deficit, it's rather nice. If you were a country, you probably would be running a trade deficit now since, most likely, you're consuming

THE CANADIAN INTERNATIONAL TRADE BALANCE

Balance of trade   The difference between the value of goods a nation exports and the value of goods it imports.

Balance of trade deficit   When a nation imports more than it exports.

Balance of trade surplus   When a nation exports more than it imports.

Merchandise trade balance   The difference between the goods a nation exports and the goods a nation imports.

Services balance   The difference between the services a nation exports and the services a nation imports.

Debtor and Creditor Nations

---

[1] We're only interested in the balance of trade right now. There's much more to be said about Canada's international trade position, and we'll come back to this in much greater detail in macroeconomics in a later chapter—as if you haven't had enough already!

F oreign exchange markets are a good example of supply and demand forces at work. Whenever there's excess supply or demand for something, there's incentive for suppliers and demanders to get together to eliminate the excess.

Let's consider the issue in relation to the former Soviet Union. In 1989, at the official price of 0.64 rubles per U.S. dollar, the quantity of U.S. dollars demanded far exceeded the quantity of U.S. dollars supplied. In the former Soviet Union, adventurous individuals (who weren't worried about the wrath of the invisible foot—that is, about being prosecuted for violating foreign exchange laws) traded in a black market at a higher price, which in the early 1990s reached 30 rubles per U.S. dollar.

A black market, which involves trades of a good that can't legally be traded, is a natural result of government price restrictions. Often the government knows that such trading goes on and chooses, for political reasons, not to enforce its own laws strictly. (There are situations like this in Canada. Here the speed limit is 100 kilometres per hour on many roads,

but almost everyone drives at 110 kilometres per hour, which some police tend to accept as a fact of life.)

An unofficially condoned black market is a *grey market*. Trading on it is more open, risk of prosecution and upward pressure on price from the invisible foot are less, and prices on it are usually closer to the supply/demand equilibrium than black market prices.

The Soviet foreign exchange market became a grey market in late 1989. (The grey market price of a U.S. dollar was between 5 and 15 rubles rather than the .64 rubles you'd get at the official rate.) If you went to the former Soviet Union at that time, individuals would come up to you on the street and offer to trade rubles for U.S. dollars at something near the grey market price. In 1991 the Soviet Union broke apart and Russia began to let the ruble be freely tradable. Because of political and economic problems, the ruble's value fell enormously and it took thousands of rubles to get one U.S. dollar.

(importing) more than you're producing (exporting). How can you do that? By living off past savings, getting support from your parents or a spouse, or borrowing.

Countries have the same options. They can live off foreign aid, past savings, or loans. For example, the American economy is currently running a trade deficit, and the United States is financing the trade deficit by selling off assets—financial assets such as shares and bonds, or real assets such as real estate and corporations. Since the assets of the United States total many billions of dollars, it can continue to run trade deficits for decades to come.

Canada hasn't always had a balance of trade deficit. We've had periods of deficits, surpluses, and fairly consistent cyclical patterns around zero, as shown in Exhibit 5. The problem with running a prolonged trade deficit is that a country ends up borrowing more from abroad than it lends abroad. This means it becomes a large debtor nation—and it ends up paying interest on its borrowed money every year without getting anything for it.

Determinants of the Trade Balance

5   Two important determinants of the trade balance are:
(1) A country's competitiveness; and
(2) The relative state of a country's economy.

Competitiveness   A country's ability to produce goods and services more cheaply than other countries.

In determining the size of the trade balance, two factors are important:

1. Canadian competitiveness and the value of the Canadian dollar.
2. The state of the Canadian economy compared to that of other countries.

Let's look at each factor.

Canadian Competitiveness   Probably the single most important issue in determining whether a country runs a trade deficit or a trade surplus is its **competitiveness** (the ability to produce goods more cheaply than other countries). Competitiveness depends upon productivity—a country's output per worker and its technological innovativeness (its ability to develop new and different products).

In the 1950s and early 1960s, Canada was highly competitive. Even though Canadian workers were paid substantially more than foreign workers, Canadian goods were cheaper, better, and more desired than foreign goods. In the 1950s, the label MADE IN JAPAN was a sign of low-quality, cheap goods. That has changed since the late 1970s. While Canada lost its competitive edge, Japan gained one. Today MADE IN JAPAN is a sign of quality.

Japan's rise from a defeated country after World War II, with few natural resources, little land, and a devastated economy, to an international economic power that outcompetes Canada in almost every aspect of economics, was an important economic story of the 1980s. One reason for Japan's rise was cultural. Another reason was the relative values of the Japanese yen and Canadian dollar. Throughout much of the 1960s, 1970s, and 1980s, the yen's relative value was low. A major determinant of a country's competitiveness is the value of its currency. A currency that is low in value relative to other currencies encourages the country's exports by lowering their prices and discourages its imports by raising their prices. (In 1965, $1 bought about 300 yen; in the mid-1990s, $1 bought less than 60 yen. Conversely, the dollar's relatively high value during the 1960s undermined Canadian competitiveness.)

In the late 1980s, the dollar's value relative to the yen fell substantially, making Canadian goods more competitive. That didn't immediately reduce the Canadian balance of trade deficit, and it became apparent that the problems of Canada in international competitiveness had additional causes. But it did eventually help improve Canadian competitiveness. By 1993, the rise in value of the yen had pushed Japanese car prices up sufficiently so that Canadian cars seemed like bargains, causing a recovery of the Canadian automobile industry in 1994. However, the fall in the dollar's value has a downside: It means that Canadian assets are cheaper for foreigners. They can buy not only the products, but also the firms that make those products, the buildings within which those products are made, and the land upon which those buildings stand. In the 1990s, we'll likely hear much about foreigners "buying up Canada."

Talk of foreign control over Canadian resources isn't new. In 1974, the federal government established the Foreign Investment Review Agency (FIRA) to oversee foreign investment and foreign takeovers of large Canadian firms. There was concern that foreigners were gaining too much power over *what* and *how* Canada produced. Foreign investment has been an important source of Canadian economic growth, and FIRA was directly opposed to overseas investment. In 1985, the federal government replaced FIRA with Investment Canada. Its mandate was to encourage investment without primary concern over the source of funds, since by then it was felt that both foreign and domestic capital were needed to restore growth in the Canadian economy. Today, foreign direct investment in Canada totals over $140 billion. Nevertheless, domestic concerns over foreign control remain, so we shouldn't be surprised to hear about it in the news.

The State of the Canadian Economy   A second factor in determining the trade balance is the state of the economy. The level of Canadian income affects the trade balance, and the trade balance affects the level of Canadian income. The reason for the first effect is simple. Say Canada is running a balance of trade deficit. When Canadian income rises, Canada imports more goods and services (you can finally afford that trip to France), so the balance of trade deficit increases.

The second effect—the trade balance's effect on Canadian income—isn't so simple. Say Canada has a balance of trade deficit. When Canada imports more (or exports less), the trade deficit worsens and the rise in imports means Canadian production falls, which means Canadian citizens have less income; they spend less and Canadian income falls even more. So an increase in the trade deficit lowers income. It also works the opposite way: When Canada exports more (imports less), Canadian production rises; as Canadian production rises, Canadian citizens have more income; they spend more and Canadian income rises even more. This effect of exports on domestic income is what economists mean when they say a country has "export-led growth." A country with export-led growth has a balance of trade surplus which stimulates growth in income.

Large trade deficits often inspire politicians to call for trade restrictions prohibiting imports. Most economists, liberal and conservative alike, generally oppose such restrictions. The reason is that even though trade restrictions directly decrease the trade deficit, they also have negative effects on the economy that work in the opposite direction.

One negative effect is that trade restrictions reduce domestic competition. When

Economists' View of Trade Restrictions

a group of Canadian producers can't compete with foreign producers—either in price or in quality—that group often pushes for trade restrictions to prevent what they call "unfair" foreign competition. Canadian producers benefit from the trade restrictions, but consumers are hurt. Prices rise and the quality of the goods falls.

A second negative effect is that trade restrictions bring retaliation. If one country limits imports, the other country responds; the first country responds to that . . . The result is called a *trade war,* and a trade war hurts everyone.

Such a trade war occurred in the 1930s and significantly contributed to the Great Depression of that period. To prevent trade wars, countries have entered into a variety of international agreements. The most important is the **World Trade Organization (WTO),** the successor agency to the **General Agreement on Tariffs and Trade (GATT).** Under GATT, countries agreed not to impose new tariffs or other trade restrictions except under certain limited conditions. These agreements are continued under WTO.

World Trade Organization (WTO)
World body charged with reducing impediments to trade; it replaced GATT in 1995.

INTERNATIONAL ECONOMIC POLICY AND INSTITUTIONS

Just as international trade differs from domestic trade, so does international economic policy differ from domestic economic policy. When economists talk about Canadian economic policy, they generally refer to what the Canadian federal government can do to achieve certain goals. In theory, at least, the Canadian federal government has both the power and the legal right of compulsion to make Canadian citizens do what it says. It can tax, it can redistribute income, it can regulate, and it can enforce property rights.

There is no international counterpart to a nation's federal government. Any meeting of a group of countries to discuss trade policies is voluntary. No international government has powers of compulsion. Hence, dealing with international problems must be done through negotiation, consensus, bullying, and concessions.

Governmental International Institutions

6 Five important international economies institutions are:
1. The UN;
2. The WTO;
3. The World Bank;
4. The IMF; and
5. The EU.

World Bank A multinational, international financial institution that works with developing countries to secure low-interest loans.

International Monetary Fund (IMF) A multinational, international financial institution concerned primarily with monetary issues.

Group of Five Group that meets to promote negotiations and coordinate economic relations among countries. The Five are Japan, Germany, Britain, France, and the United States.

Group of Seven Group that meets to promote negotiations and coordinate economic relations among countries. The Seven are Japan, Germany, Britain, France, Canada, Italy, and the United States.

To discourage bullying and to encourage negotiation and consensus, governments have developed a variety of international institutions and agreements to promote negotiations and coordinate economic relations among countries. These include the United Nations (UN), World Trade Organization (WTO), World Bank, World Court, International Monetary Fund (IMF), and regional organizations such as the Organization of Petroleum Exporting Countries (OPEC), European Union (EU), and North American Free Trade Agreement (NAFTA).

These organizations have a variety of goals. For example, the **World Bank** works closely with developing countries, channelling low-interest loans to them to foster economic growth. The **IMF** is concerned with international financial arrangements. When developing countries encountered financial problems in the 1970s and had large international debts that they could not pay, the IMF helped work on repayment plans.

In addition to these formal institutions, there are informal meetings of various countries. These include **Group of Five** meetings of Japan, Germany, Britain, France, and the United States; and **Group of Seven** meetings with Japan, Germany, Britain, France, Canada, Italy, and the United States.

Since governmental membership in international organizations is voluntary, their power is limited. When Canada doesn't like a World Court ruling, it simply states that it isn't going to follow the ruling. When Canada is unhappy with what the United Nations is doing, it can withhold some of its dues. Other countries do the same from time to time. Other member countries complain, but can do little to force compliance. It doesn't work that way domestically. If you decide you don't like Canadian policy and refuse to pay your taxes, you'll wind up in jail.

What keeps nations somewhat in line when it comes to international rules is a moral tradition: Countries want to (or at least want to look as if they want to) do what's "right." Countries will sometimes follow international rules to keep international opinion favourable to them. But national self-interest often overrides scruples.

Global Corporations

Chapter 4 introduced you to Canadian corporations and listed the largest corporations in Canada. More and more of these and other corporations are transcending national

INTERNATIONAL ECONOMIC INSTITUTIONS

A REMINDER

The *United Nations* was founded in 1945, after World War II, in the hope of providing a place where international problems could be resolved through discussion and negotiation rather than through war.

The *World Bank* is a multilateral, international financial institution established in 1944. One of its main objectives is to provide funding to developing countries.

The *International Monetary Fund* (IMF), another international financial institution founded in 1944, lends money to developing countries in the form of "aid" packages which require recipient countries to try to reach certain economic goals.

The *Organization of Petroleum Exporting Countries* (OPEC) consists of 13 major oil-exporting countries in the Middle East, Far East, Africa, and South America. Formed in 1960, the organization promotes its member countries' joint national interests, such as preventing reductions in the price of oil.

The *Organization of Economic Cooperation and Development* (OECD) was set up in 1961 to promote economic cooperation among individual countries. Its 24 members include all major industrial countries and most Western European countries. The OECD is the best source of comparative statistics for Western economies.

---

boundaries. They have branches on both the production and sales sides throughout the world. As they do, they become global, or multinational, corporations rather than national corporations.

Global corporations offer enormous benefits for countries. They create jobs; they bring new ideas and new technologies to a country, and they provide competition for domestic companies, keeping them on their toes. But global corporations also pose a number of problems for governments. One is their implications for domestic and international policy. A domestic corporation exists within a country and can be dealt with using policy measures within that country. A global corporation exists within many countries and there is no global government to regulate or control it. If it doesn't like the policies in one country—say taxes are too high or regulations too tight—it can shift its operations to other countries.

Countries often compete for these global corporations by changing their regulations to encourage companies to use them as their home base. For instance, firms might register their oil tankers in Liberia to avoid paying Canadian wages, and put their funds in Bahamian banks to avoid Canadian financial disclosure laws.

At times it seems that global corporations are governments unto themselves, especially in relation to poorer countries. Consider Exhibit 6 (a)'s list of some large global corporations and their sales. Then compare it with Exhibit 6 (b)'s list of some small and middle-size economies and their output. In terms of sales, a number of global corporations are larger than the economies of middle-size countries. This comparison is not quite accurate, since sales do not necessarily reflect power; but when a company's decisions can significantly affect what happens in a country's economy, that company has significant economic power.

When global corporations have such power, it is not surprising that they can sometimes dominate a country. The corporation can use its expertise and experience to direct a small country to do its bidding rather than the other way around.

Another problem global corporations present for governments involves multiple jurisdiction. Global corporations can distance themselves from questionable economic activities by setting up *dummy corporations*. A dummy corporation exists only on paper, and is actually controlled by another corporation. Sometimes when a corporation really wants to separate itself from the consequences of certain actions, it creates dummy corporations, in which one paper corporation controls another paper corporation, which in turn controls another paper corporation. Each corporation is incorporated in a different nation, which makes it difficult, if not impossible, to trace who is actually doing what and who can be held accountable.

Before you condemn globals, remember: Globals don't have it so easy either.

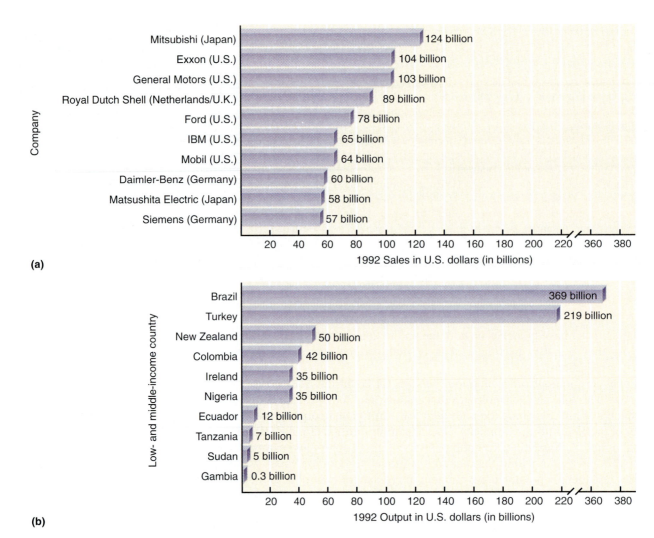

(a)

(b)

EXHIBIT 6   Global Corporations

As you can see in the charts, a number of global corporations are larger than the economies of some countries in terms of sales. This is important to a small country whose economy can be affected by a decision a global corporation might make.

Source: *CIA World Fact Book,* 1993 and *World Almanac,* 1994.

Customs and laws differ among countries. Trying to meet the differing laws and ambiguous limits of acceptable action in various countries is often impossible. For example, in many countries bribery is an acceptable part of doing business. If you want to get permission to sell a good, you must pay the appropriate officials *baksheesh* (as it's called in Egypt) or *la mordita* (as it's called in Mexico). In Canada, such payments are illegal bribes. Given these differing laws, the only way a Canadian company can do business in some foreign countries is to break Canadian laws.

Moreover, global corporations often work to maintain close ties among countries and to reduce international tension. If part of your company is in an Eastern European country and part in Canada, you want the two countries to be friends. So beware of making judgements about whether global corporations are good or bad. They're both simultaneously.

WHO ARE OUR INTERNATIONAL COMPETITORS?

So far we've given you a brief introduction to the international economic problems Canada faces and to some of the international institutions that exist to coordinate international economic activity. In this section we introduce three of our rivals, the United States, the European Union, and Japan, giving you a brief background of their histories and economic institutions. We also briefly discuss a fourth competitor—the devel-

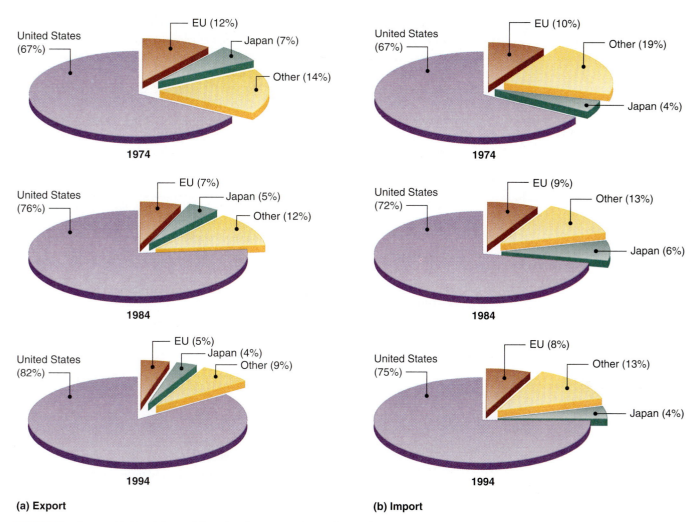

(a) Export   **(b) Import**

EXHIBIT 7   **Geographic Breakdown of Canada's Import and Export Shares for 1974, 1984, 1994**

You can see that Canada's share of exports to the United States and imports from the United States have grown substantually over the last 20 years. Trade with the EU (formerly the EEC) has fallen off during this period.
Sources: *Statistics Canada, CANSIM Database,* March 1995.

oping world—and explain why, with the new North American Free Trade Agreement (NAFTA), questions of our economic and political relations with Mexico and the United States are likely to be much in the news in the 1990s.

The United States is by far our most important trading partner. In 1994, Canada exported over $44 billion worth of merchandise to the United States while we imported only $38 billion from the United States. In 1994, trade with the United States represented 82 percent of exports and 75 percent of imports. Exhibit 7 shows how Canada's trade shares have changed over the last 20 years.

The geographic and cultural ties linking Canada and the United States are strong and resilient to changes in the political landscape in both countries. The economies are highly integrated in both trade and financial markets. They are similarly endowed, with Canada relatively resource rich as compared to the industrial machine that drives the United States economy.

That is not to say that trade relations have always been rosy. Disputes over government subsidies and unfair trading practices have been common since Confederation. These were perhaps most apparent during the recession in 1982–83. It saw the United States adopt **protectionist policies**—policies that favour domestic

Protectionist policies   Policies that favour domestic products over foreign-produced products.

products over foreign-produced products—in an attempt to shelter domestic firms and workers from foreign competition through the introduction of tariffs, import licenses, and other nontariff barriers (like quality controls over imported agricultural goods) that were to the detriment of Canada. Public debate in Canada led to the view that we might be best served by entering into an agreement with the United States to reduce impediments to the free flow of goods and services across the Canada–U.S. border. Negotiations led to an historic agreement—The Canada–U.S. **Free Trade Agreement** (FTA) came into effect on January 1, 1989. It set into place a schedule for reducing trade barriers and the elimination of many nontariff barriers. Its primary objectives were outlined in the Preamble to the agreement:

Free Trade Agreement (FTA) Trade deal signed by Canada and the United States aimed at reducing barriers to trade. It took effect on January 1, 1989.

PREAMBLE

The Government of Canada and the Government of the United States of America, resolved:

TO STRENGTHEN the unique and enduring friendship between their two nations;

TO PROMOTE productivity, full employment, and a steady improvement of living standards in their respective countries;

TO CREATE an expanded and secure market for the goods and services produced in their territories;

TO ADOPT clear and mutually advantageous rules governing their trade;

TO ENSURE a predictable commercial environment for business planning and investment;

TO STRENGTHEN the competitiveness of the United States and Canadian firms in global markets;

TO REDUCE government-created trade distortions while preserving the Parties' flexibility to safeguard the public welfare;

TO BUILD on their mutual rights and obligations under the *General Agreement on Tariffs and Trade* and other multilateral and bilateral instruments of cooperation; and

TO CONTRIBUTE to the harmonious development and expansion of world trade and to provide a catalyst to broader international cooperation;

HAVE AGREED as follows: . . .

While few would argue against the objectives outlined in the Preamble, labour groups in Canada were vehemently opposed to the deal. They saw it as an attempt by Canadian firms to break the unions by threatening to move production to low-wage areas of the United States if the Canadian unions didn't make wage and benefit concessions. Business argued that these concessions were necessary if Canadian firms were to compete in the global marketplace and that rationalization would be necessary to increase the efficiency of Canadian industry. Proponents of the FTA argued that only through a process of cooperation would Canada hope to maintain its standard of living during the process of **globalization**—the cross-border spread of goods and services, factors of production, firms, and markets. The FTA was seen as a critical step in revitalizing the Canadian economy.

Globalization The cross-border spread of goods and services, factors of production, firms, and markets.

Have the objectives outlined in the Preamble been accomplished? Is Canada better off as a result of the FTA? It's difficult to say, since the recession of 1990–91 hastened changes to the structure of the Canadian economy, as did the process of globalization that encompassed the United States and Canada. It's fairly safe to say that the agreement provided better Canadian access to United States markets than we would have had in the absence of a trade deal, especially given the recession of the early 1990s and the ensuing wave of United States protectionism. The effects that United States protectionism might have had during this period were minimized. We'll look at our trade relations with the United States later in this chapter and in more detail in the macroeconomic chapters on international trade and finance.

The European Union

In 1957, several governments of Europe formed the European Economic Community. This organization, now called the **European Union (EU),** has undergone many changes since its founding—changes that have strengthened the economic and politi-

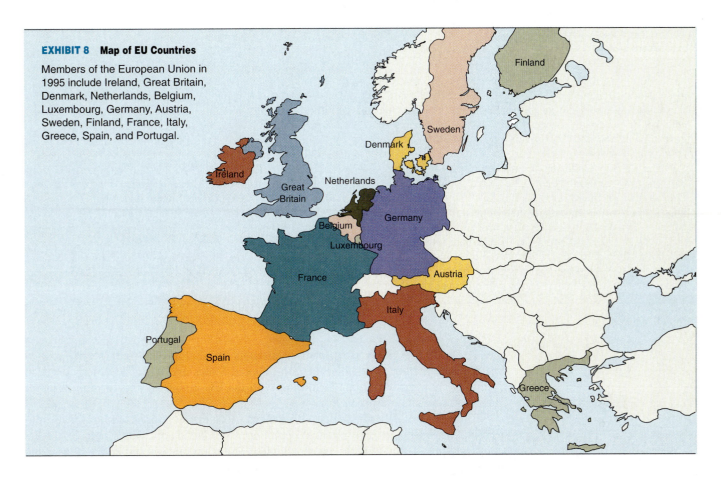

EXHIBIT 8   Map of EU Countries

Members of the European Union in 1995 include Ireland, Great Britain, Denmark, Netherlands, Belgium, Luxembourg, Germany, Austria, Sweden, Finland, France, Italy, Greece, Spain, and Portugal.

cal ties among the countries. In the EU, as in any economic union, members allow free trade among themselves to help their economies by providing a larger marketplace and more competition for their own companies. Over time, the EU has expanded from 6 countries to the 15 shown in Exhibit 8's map. In 1995, Austria, Sweden, Norway, and Finland are scheduled to join.

The EU's initial goals were:

1. To remove barriers to trade among member nations;
2. To establish a single commercial policy toward nonmember countries;
3. To better coordinate member countries' economic policies; and
4. To promote competitiveness with other countries.

Meeting those goals hasn't been easy, but the EU has made significant progress.

Why did the countries of the EU combine? Two primary reasons were to establish better markets for European companies and to compete better against Canadian and United States goods. In the 1950s and 1960s, when Canada and the United States were highly competitive with other countries and had a trade surplus, they could look beneficently at, and even encourage, such developments. In the 1990s, however, United States and Canadian goods are far less competitive and there are large trade deficits, so the United States and Canada find it much harder to encourage a potential competitor. The EU's gains likely will come at the expense of the United States and Canada.

These fears have increased as cooperation among EU countries has grown. In 1992, most trade barriers among member nations were removed, and the EU adopted a single commercial policy toward outside nations. The movement toward economic integration has not gone easily, and attempts at further unification have been fraught with political difficulties and confusion. Specifically, the movement toward a common currency—the ECU (European Currency Unit)—and a single monetary policy broke down in the 1990s and now likely won't take place until the 21st century, if at all.

7A   The European Union (EU) is an economic and political union of European countries that allow free trade among countries. It was created to provide larger marketplace for member countries.

European Union (EU)   An economic and political union of European countries that allow free trade among countries.

THE NORTH AMERICAN FREE TRADE AGREEMENT

The North American Free Trade Agreement (NAFTA) came into effect on January 1, 1994. It created the world's largest free-trade area—360 million consumers in Mexico, Canada, and the United States. Since Mexico is one of the fastest-growing markets in the world, this gives Canada an excellent opportunity to expand to Mexico.

The NAFTA eliminates a number of tariff and nontariff barriers to trade between the three countries. The Canada–United States Free Trade Agreement has already improved Canadian access to United States markets, and the gains to Canada from NAFTA arise primarily from access to the Mexican market. Until now, Mexico has followed very restrictive trade practices, with import licenses and tariffs all but pricing Canadian goods and services out of the market. Under the new agreement, Mexico will eliminate or substan-

tially lessen trade barriers in agriculture and automobiles. Canada also stands to gain from exporting services in the form of information and communications expertise as well as financial services.

Critics of NAFTA argue that low Mexican wages will attract firms that would otherwise have located in Canada. While it is true that industries that are labour-intensive will gravitate towards Mexico, Mexican wages will increase as productivity in Mexico rises toward United States and Canadian levels. Along the way, income in all three nations should rise, but there may be significant short-run implications for Canadian industry and labour, with competitive pressures forcing firms and workers to become more efficient. The agreement should be much in the news in the 1990s.

The early 1990s saw significant discussions on what the EU's commercial policy will be and whether it will be fair to the United States and Canada. Other European countries are also talking about uniting with the EU countries and forming a larger European trading community.

Regardless of what happens with further European economic and political integration, the EU makes a formidable competitor for Canada and the United States. Its combined production slightly exceeds United States production but is much less than that of Canada and the United States combined. The EU has a strong international economic position, since many member countries enjoy trade surpluses while Canada and the United States have trade deficits.

Developments in the EU have been made even more important by recent events in Eastern Europe. Eastern European countries have changed from socialist to more market-oriented economic systems and are attempting to establish closer economic and political ties with the West. East and West Germany are reunified. These developments will open up new markets for which Canada, the United States, and the EU will all compete. In that competition, the EU has both cultural and geographic advantages over the United States and Canada.

In response to the EU's increasing strength, Canada has entered into a free-trade agreement with the United States and Mexico (with Chile set to join in the late 1990s) called the **North American Free Trade Agreement (NAFTA).** Once the agreement is in place (it is to be phased in over 15 years), Canadian firms will be able to produce in Mexico—or vice versa—subject to Mexican regulations and at Mexican wage rates, and ship directly into the United States without international legal hurdles. NAFTA raises significant questions about the short-run effects of free trade, such as: Should goods sold in Canada all be subject to the same regulations regardless of where they are produced? Will free trade with Mexico and the United States increase jobs or decrease jobs in Canada?

The agreement should be much in the news in the 1990s, particularly since the Mexican peso underwent a significant depreciation in late 1994 and 1995. Even though the Canadian and American governments intervened in an attempt to lessen the decline in the value of the peso, serious concerns were raised by international investors who feared Mexican firms and the Mexican government might default on their external obligations. In an attempt to assuage their fears, the Mexican minister of finance went on a whirlwind tour of the world's financial markets in early 1995 to explain how Mexico was going to deal with the depreciation. Given that the Canadian dollar had been steadily losing value against the U.S. dollar in late 1994 and early 1995, the gains to Canada from international trade agreements were no longer as pre-

North American Free Trade Agreement (NAFTA) Trade deal signed by Canada, Mexico, and the United States aimed at reducing barriers to North American trade; went into effect January 1, 1994.

Japan has become a major player in the world economy.
Reuters/Bettman.

dictable as was once thought. We'll come back to this in a later chapter in macroeconomics on international trade.

Besides entering into NAFTA, Canada and the United States also argued strongly against high EU protective barriers on imports from foreign countries. Since there are no international organizations specifically designed to coordinate and facilitate international trade among trading areas, a new policy problem of the 1990s may be trade wars among "free trading" areas.

Japan is a little country with a lot of people—about 125 million, over four times as many people as Canada—but it fits them into 146,000 square miles, less than 4 percent of the area of Canada. Almost two-thirds of Japan is covered with forest, and much of the rest of the land has poor soil. It has almost no oil; its coal is very low grade; it must import nearly 100 percent of its petroleum and all of its iron ore (used to make steel) and bauxite (used to make aluminum). It has some copper and other minerals such as zinc, but not enough. Even with heavy forestation, it doesn't have enough lumber for domestic use and must import lumber.

"Japan, Inc."

Besides being small, crowded, and poorly endowed, Japan is a chain of islands and has a language that is extremely difficult to learn. These facts have tended, until very recently, to isolate it from the rest of the world. Japan broke its isolation by entering World War II, which it lost, leaving its economy in ruins.

7B Japan is a small, crowded, poorly endowed chain of islands which has been enormously successful economically.

By almost all objective analyses, then, one would expect Japan to be a poor, underdeveloped country. It isn't. Instead, it is one of the most successful and developed economies in the world. In the 1980s, its economic strength earned it the nickname *Japan, Inc.* In the 1990s, while still successful, Japan has had its problems. Its stock market crashed in the early 1990s, and the government has spent considerable resources propping up its financial sector. Moreover, with the rise in the value of the yen in the early 1990s and the subsequent rise in price of its exports, Japanese exports declined and the Japanese economy fell into a recession; unemployment rose because exports fell due to limited demand. With these events, Japan has lost its "supereconomy" status, and has joined the ranks of the other industrialized economies. It is successful, but it is not without its problems.

Cultural Reasons for Japan's Success One reason is cultural. Japan has a social and cultural commitment to hard work. A second cultural trait that has helped Japan's economy is its strong tradition of saving money. These cultural traits are reinforced by social and economic institutions. Japan's educational system is much more demanding than that of Canada. Students go to school longer and are required to work harder than most

The largest European Union economy is Germany. Germany has been on the losing end of two world wars and, nonetheless, has emerged as one of the leading economies of the world. One reason is cultural: German culture reinforces hard work and makes saving a virtue. Also, the country's coal and iron resources helped it establish a strong industrial base as long ago as the early 1900s.

After losing World War II in 1945, Germany was divided into East and West Germany. East Germany, which had a large part of the manufacturing base of prewar Germany, was controlled by a Communist government. West Germany was controlled by the victorious Allied forces, who encouraged it to set up a democratic market economy. The Allies limited West German military spending, while the United States, through the Marshall Plan (an assistance plan for Europe which the United States ran after World War II), pumped in large amounts of money to help the West German economy recover from the war. And recover it did. In the 1960s and 1970s, the West German economy grew so fast that it was called an *economic miracle*.

West Germany's economic story contrasted significantly with East Germany's. East Germany grew more than any of the other Eastern bloc Communist economies, but its growth didn't match West Germany's. To prevent East Germans from emigrating to West Germany, East Germany closed its borders with West Germany in 1961 and built a wall between the two countries. Economic and political changes in East Germany at the end of the 1980s led to the introduction of a market economy in East Germany, an opening of the border, and physical destruction of the wall. In 1990, East and West Germany were reunified.

The problems of economic and political reunification were immense. They placed enormous strains on the German political and economic system. To fund the reunification, the German government borrowed (it ran deficits) and raised taxes. Interest rates rose in Germany, placing significant strains on the European Union. In the 1990s, the German economy remained relatively strong, but it was no longer the economic miracle. It found itself with many of the same difficulties as Canada.

Canadian students. This imposes on children a discipline and a habit of hard work that persists in later life. Many Japanese enjoy work. Their work is their hobby as well as their job. Only in Japan will you find government-sponsored classes teaching people how not to work so hard.

The Japanese savings tradition is also encouraged by government policies that keep prices of consumer goods high, make borrowing for consumer goods comparatively expensive, and maintain a skimpy government pension system. One of the reasons the Japanese save a much higher percentage of their incomes than most other people do is that they worry about supporting themselves in their old age.

Neomercantilist   Market economy guided by government.

Japan as a Neomercantilist Country   Another reason that some economists cite for Japanese development is its government's strong role in stimulating export-led growth. These economists argue that Japan's economic growth is not an example of the power of the invisible hand, but of the three invisible forces working together to direct an economy toward growth. In many economists' view, the Japanese economic system is as closely related to mercantilism as to capitalism. Some have called it a **neomercantilist** economic system.

The power of Japan's neomercantilist approach is striking. In the late 1940s, with few resources and raw materials and devastated by World War II, Japanese firms, under government direction, borrowed in order to finance the purchase of raw materials from abroad. The Japanese government directed firms to allocate a large portion of output for export. They started with small products, paid workers low wages, saved their profits, and learned about international markets. Then they ploughed back those savings into more raw materials, more manufacturing, and more exports. They continued this process, each time manufacturing more sophisticated products than before.

Japan put off making improvements in housing, transportation, highways, parks, cultural institutions, and public health while it directed its efforts to rebuilding and developing technology. Government policy encouraged and sheltered business.

MITI   Japanese agency, the Ministry of International Trade and Industry, that guides the Japanese economy.

The Japanese government developed an aggressive trading policy under the control of its **Ministry of International Trade and Industry (MITI).** It encouraged businesses to cooperate, not compete, with one another in order to be more efficient. The government instituted strong tariffs that are still in force. It prohibits altogether

ECONOMIES THAT DON'T WORK SO WELL

For every economy that works well, there are many more economies that aren't achieving their goals. Considering one of them helps us keep our perspective. Take Pakistan, a country of about 120,000,000 people. Pakistan is poor; the average per capita income is about $400. In Canada the equivalent figure is about $22,000. Its political structure is, in theory, democratic, but the army plays a major role in determining who will rule. Coups d'état (overthrows of the government) and unexplained deaths of high leaders are common. The resulting political instability keeps out most foreign investments.

Pakistan is an Islamic republic which has had significant fights with India ever since the two nations were created out of the former single British commonwealth country. The British commonwealth "India" was divided into "India" and "Pakistan" in 1947 after World War II. In 1971, Pakistan's internal strife led to half the country declaring its independence and forming a separate country, Bangladesh.

Pakistan's economy is primarily agricultural, although it also manufactures textiles and chemicals. One out of every 60 people has a TV; one out of every 165 has a car. In North America the equivalent figures are one TV for every 1.3 people, and one car for every 1.8 people. Housing is poor for the majority of the people, and many barely get enough to eat. Income distribution is highly unequal, with a small group being very rich and a great majority being extremely poor.

Most industry has heavy government involvement and is highly inefficient. Without large tariff barriers, it could not compete. Such dependency on the government's prevention of competition breeds corruption. Most Pakistanis have little faith that their government bureaucracy will work for the benefit of society.

---

the import of some articles that might compete with Japanese manufacturers. In short, Japan does not follow a laissez-faire policy in either the domestic or the international economy, and it is successful.

Not all economists agree that the government's role in Japanese economic development has been positive. Some economists argue that hard work and high savings led to growth that was partially offset by the government's involvement. They point out that MITI often backed the losing, not the winning, industries. The companies and technologies *it didn't back,* not the ones it did back, were the growth sectors of the Japanese economy. They argue that Japanese growth occurred in spite of, not because of, government involvement.

The Japanese Cooperative Spirit Japan's labour market is remarkably different from that in Canada. Large companies have what are called *permanent employees.* By tradition, a man, once hired, stays with the same company for his entire working life. Women are unlikely to be permanent employees and are expected to resign their jobs when they get married. The relationship between the company and the worker is close—workers are members of the corporate family and their social life revolves around the company. The nature of the Japanese labour market is now changing. Some women can be permanent employees and some employees move to other companies, and downsizing employment has begun to enter corporate strategy, but the traditional system still predominates.

Labour unions exist in Japan, but are organized according to industry. In Canada, unions are more likely to be organized by type of skill. Organization by industry allows Japanese workers to do many different jobs within a firm. Until recently, Canadian organized workers would not work outside their specialty.

Japan's pay structure is also different from that in Canada. Japanese workers know that their bonuses, gifts, and special allowances depend on how well their company is doing. Until recently, most Canadian workers received only a wage or salary and no bonus. Another Japanese characteristic contributing to its economic success is the tradition of cooperation between unions and business; in Canada, labour and management are frequently in conflict.

Another difference is that Japan has few lawyers and is a far less litigious society than Canada. Some cynics have suggested the small number of lawyers is a major reason for Japan's great success. Businesses don't get bogged down by legal maneuvering and litigious behaviour. Less-cynical people downplay this issue, but they agree Japanese people's cooperative spirit contributes to Japan's success.

Inefficient Japanese Traditions   Not all Japanese institutions promote efficiency. Some Japanese institutions hinder economic progress. Take its agricultural system. Before the war, most farmland in Japan that was not owned by the government was owned by a few individuals who rented it out in small parcels to others. After the war, the big farmland holdings were broken up by the government and sold off to former tenants at low prices. The result was thousands of small farms, averaging an acre in size. Few are larger than three acres. These small farms are highly inefficient, but are kept in business by large government subsidies and tariffs on foreign agricultural products. Because of the structure of Japanese political institutions, these subsidies are almost untouchable, despite Canadian farmers' complaints about trade restrictions.

In the 1990s, a second inefficient Japanese tradition was being seen more and more. That tradition was political corruption in which Japanese politicians received large payoffs from Japanese businesses for government support. In 1993, this corruption brought down the ruling party, and led to its replacement by a series of coalitions of reformist parties. Whether these changes will improve the system, or whether such corruption is inherent in any neomercantilist system, remains to be seen.

Japan, Inc., versus Canada

Both the Japanese and Canadian economies are successful, but they differ significantly from each other. There is less competition among firms in Japan than in Canada. Japanese firms work closely with government in planning their industrial strategy. Canadian firms often see government as an opponent, not a partner. Similarly with labour and business: In Japan they generally cooperate; in Canada they generally are opponents.

The Japanese Ministry of International Trade and Industry plays a key role in determining what will be produced and who will produce it. MITI's goal has been to establish strong export-led growth, and that goal has been accomplished, although whether it was because of MITI, or in spite of MITI, is debatable. MITI also has an economic planning board that oversees many parts of the Japanese economy. Japan is no laissez-faire economy.

Don't Overestimate the Differences

The differences between the Canadian and Japanese economies are large, but should not be overestimated. Both economies rely on markets. In both, profit incentives motivate production.

As global corporations bridge the gap between these two economies, the differences (once very large) are shrinking. Canadian labour unions and firms are cooperating more, while Japanese firms and labour unions are cooperating less. The Japanese system of permanent employment in large firms is breaking down.

With both systems successful, it is difficult to say that one set of institutions is better than the other. They are merely distinct from each other. The differences reflect social, cultural, and geographic conditions in the two countries. Some people have suggested that Canada should adopt a neomercantilist system like Japan's. Maybe it should, but it is not at all clear that Japanese institutions could be transferred to Canada. What works in one country can bomb in another.

The argument that policies that work in one country cannot necessarily be translated into policies that work in another country doesn't mean Japan's experience is of no relevance to Canada. In itself, the fact that a policy works in one country means that policy deserves consideration by other countries. That's tough for economists with a strong distrust of government to say, but it must be said. An open mind is a necessary attribute of a good economist.

The Developing Countries of the World as Competitors

Japan and the EU have developed industrial economies similar to Canada's economy. There is, however, a much larger group of countries out there that are at various lower levels of industrial development. Many of them are anxious for industrial development and will likely provide significant competition for the Canadian economy. If Japan and the EU can't out-compete Canada, these other countries, with low wage rates and governments eager to give global corporations whatever they want, often can. If Canadian firms don't take advantage of this low-cost labour, Japanese and European firms will, and will export the output to Canada.

Of these developing countries, Mexico is of special interest to Canada. The reason is NAFTA, which will allow easy access into the Canadian market for firms producing in Mexico. As NAFTA brings in freer trade, Canadian companies are likely to experience significant Mexican competition. In return, of course, Canadian companies will have a new open market to sell to—Mexico. As inevitably happens with competition, some people will be helped, and some will be hurt.

Knowing about other countries' economies helps us keep our own economy in perspective. We don't have the space here (an example of scarcity) to look at other countries' tax structures, public finances, support of education, labour markets . . . the list is endless. But as you wonder about any of the economic policies that are discussed throughout this book, take a few minutes to ask somebody from a foreign country about its economy, and go to the library and look up another country's way of handling its economy (even if you look no further than an encyclopedia). See how that country compares to Canada. Then try to explain what does or doesn't work in that country and whether it would or would not work in Canada. Doing so will make the course more meaningful and your understanding of economics stronger.

CONCLUSION

CHAPTER SUMMARY

- To understand the Canadian economy, one must understand its role in the world economy.
- Knowledge of the facts about the world economy is necessary to understand the world economy.
- Countries can be classified in many ways, including industrial, middle-income, and low-income economies.
- International trade differs from domestic trade because (1) there are potential barriers to trade and (2) countries use different currencies.
- The relative value of a currency can be found in an exchange rate table.
- The Canadian trade deficit is large. It is financed by selling Canadian assets to foreign owners.

- Canadian competitiveness and the state of the Canadian economy compared to other countries are important in determining the trade deficit's size.
- International policy coordination must be achieved through consensus among nations.
- Global corporations are corporations with significant operations in more than one country.
- Two important international competitors to Canada are the EU and Japan. In Japan and in many EU nations, government plays a larger role in directing the economy than in Canada.

KEY TERMS

balance of trade *(111)*
balance of trade deficit *(111)*
balance of trade surplus *(111)*
comparative advantage *(107)*
competitiveness *(112)*
European Union (EU) *(119)*
exports *(106)*
foreign exchange market *(108)*
Free Trade Agreement (FTA) *(118)*
General Agreement on Tariffs and
   Trade (GATT) *(114)*

global corporations *(104)*
globalization *(118)*
Group of Five *(114)*
Group of Seven *(114)*
imports *(106)*
International Monetary Fund
   (IMF) *(114)*
merchandise trade balance *(111)*
Ministry of International Trade and
   Industry (MITI) *(123)*
neomercantilist *(122)*

nontariff barriers *(108)*
North American Free Trade Agreement
   (NAFTA) *(120)*
protectionist policy *(118)*
quotas *(108)*
services balance *(111)*
tariffs *(108)*
World Bank *(114)*
World Trade Organization
   (WTO) *(114)*

QUESTIONS FOR THOUGHT AND REVIEW

The number after each question represents the estimated degree of critical thinking required. (1 = almost none; 10 = deep thought.)

1. A good measure of a country's importance to the world economy is its area and population. True or false? Why? *(5)*

2. Canada exports wheat while Japan exports cars. Why? *(5)*

3. What are the two ways in which international trade differs from domestic trade? *(3)*

4. Find the exchange rate for Swedish krone in Exhibit 4 and also the most current rate from your newspaper. *(3)*

5. If one Canadian dollar will buy .67 Swiss francs, how many Canadian dollars will one Swiss franc buy? *(5)*

6. The Canadian economy is falling apart because Canada is one of the biggest debtor nations in the world. Discuss. *(7)*

7. What is likely to happen to the Canadian trade deficit if the Canadian economy grows rapidly? Why? *(5)*

8. Why do most economists oppose trade restrictions? *(5)*

9. What effect has the establishment of the EU had on the economy? Why? *(9)*

10. Japan's successful economy is an example of the power of the invisible hand. True or false? Why? *(6)*

PROBLEMS AND EXERCISES

1. This is a library research question.
   a. What are the primary exports of Brazil, Honduras, Italy, Pakistan, and Nigeria?
   b. Which countries produce most of the world's tin, rubber, potatoes, wheat, marble, and refrigerators?

2. This is an entrepreneurial research question. You'd be amazed about the information that's out there if you use a bit of initiative.
   a. Does the largest company in your relevant geographic area (town, city, whatever) have an export division? Why or why not?
   b. If you were an advisor to the company, would you suggest expanding or contracting its export division? Why or why not?
   c. Go to a store and look at 10 products at random. How many were made in Canada? Give a probable explanation why they were produced where they were produced.

3. Assume Canada can produce Toyotas at the cost of $8,000 per car and Chevrolets at $6,000 per car. In Japan, Toyotas can be produced at 1,000,000 yen and Chevrolets at 500,000 yen.
   a. In terms of Chevrolets, what is the opportunity cost of producing Toyotas in each country?
   b. Who has the comparative advantage in producing Chevrolets?
   c. Assume Canadians purchase 500,000 Chevrolets and 300,000 Toyotas each year. The Japanese purchase far fewer of each. Using productive efficiency as the guide, who should most likely produce Chevrolets and who should produce Toyotas, assuming one is going to

   be produced in one country and one in the other?

4. From 1984 to 1994, the share of Canadian exports to Western Europe fell from 7 percent to 5 percent, while the share going to the United States rose from 76 percent to 82 percent.
   a. What are likely reasons why this change occurred?
   b. What would you predict would happen to these percentages if the Western European economy boomed?
   c. Why would Prime Minister Jean Chretien urge the Western Europeans to stimulate their economy?

5. In one of the boxes, a grey market in Russian rubles is discussed.
   a. Draw the supply and demand curves for rubles in terms of dollars and show where the quantity supplied or demanded would be at an official price of .05 rubles per dollar, which is significantly below the equilibrium price.
   b. In the graph in *a,* show what the grey market price of dollars would be.
   c. In that same graph, show what the black market price of rubles would have likely been if the Russian government had enforced the exchange laws.

6. From your knowledge of current events, are Canada and the United States currently embroiled in a trade dispute? Over what commodity are they arguing? Which country feels it is being harmed? How do trade agreements affect the dispute?

7. What is the current exchange rate of the Canadian dollar against: the Italian lire? the Iranian rial? the Australian dollar? the Jamaican dollar? Why isn't a Canadian dollar equal in value to a Jamaican dollar? A U.S. dollar?

2

MACROECONOMIC

Part I   Macroeconomic Problems

Chapter 6   Economic Growth, Business Cycles,
Unemployment, and Inflation

Chapter 7   National Income Accounting

Part II   Macroeconomics: The Basics

Chapter 8   The Macroeconomic Debate

Chapter 9   The Keynesian Aggregate Production/Aggregate
Expenditures Model

Chapter 10   Fiscal Policy and the Debate about Activist
Macroeconomic Policy

Part III   Monetary and Financial Institutions

Chapter 11   Financial Institutions

Chapter 12   Money and Banking

Chapter 13   Central Banks, the Bank of Canada, and
Monetary Policy

Chapter 14   Money, Inflation, and Macroeconomic Policy

Part IV   International Dimensions of Economic Problems

Chapter 15   International Trade

Chapter 16   International Economics: The Basics

Chapter 17   International Dimensions of Monetary and Fiscal
Policies

Part V   Macroeconomic Policy Debates

Chapter 18   Deficits and Debt

Chapter 19   The Art of Macro Policy

Chapter 20   Growth and the Macroeconomics of Developing
and Transitional Economies

In the early 1990s, unemployment in Western Europe hit 11 percent, and its economic growth rate fell to zero. In Canada, the situation wasn't much better and there was serious concern about the level of unemployment and economic growth. People turned to macroeconomists for suggestions about what to do. This section of the book explains the ideas of competing groups of macroeconomists about such issues. It tells you how the ideas developed, and what relevance they have for policy in the 1990s.

The specific focus of macroeconomics is the study of unemployment, business cycles (fluctuations in the economy), growth, and inflation. While the macroeconomic theories studied have changed considerably over the past 60 years, macroeconomics' focus on those problems has remained. Thus, we'll define **macroeconomics** as *the study of the economy in the aggregate with specific focus on unemployment, inflation, business cycles, and growth.*

In the following chapters, we provide you with the background necessary to discuss the modern debate about these issues. Let's begin with a little history.

Macroeconomics emerged as a separate subject within economics in the 1930s when the Canadian, United States, and United Kingdom economies fell into a Great Depression. Businesses collapsed and unemployment rose until almost 20 percent of the workforce in Canada—millions of people—were out of work.

The depression changed the way economics was taught and the way in which economic problems were conceived. Before the 1930s, economics was microeconomics (the study of partial-equilibrium supply and demand). After the 1930s, the study of the core of economic thinking was broken into two discrete areas: microeconomics, as before, and macroeconomics (the study of the economy in the aggregate).

Macroeconomic policy debates have centred on a struggle between two groups: *Keynesian* (pronounced KAIN-sian) economists and Classical economists. Should the government run a budget deficit or a surplus? Should the government increase the money supply when a recession threatens? Should it decrease the money supply when inflation threatens? Can government prevent recessions? Keynesians generally answer one way; Classicals, another.

Each group has many variants. On the Classical side are neo-Classicals, New Classicals, and monetarists. On the Keynesian side are neo-Keynesians, New Keynesians, and post-Keynesians, just to name a few. At the introductory level we needn't concern ourselves with these various subdivisions. We'll focus on Keynesians and Classicals.

While there are many differences between Keynesians and Classicals, the fundamental policy difference is the following: Classical economists generally oppose government intervention in the economy; they favour a *laissez-faire policy.*[1] Keynesians are more likely to favour government intervention in the economy. They feel a laissez-faire policy can sometimes lead to disaster. Both views represent reasonable economic positions. The differences between them are often subtle and result from their taking slightly different views of what government can do and slightly different perspectives on the economy.

Part I, Macroeconomic Problems (Chapters 6 and 7), introduces you to the macroeconomic problems, terminology, and statistics used in tracking the economy's macroeconomic performance.

Part II, Macroeconomic Theory: The Basics (Chapters 8–10), provides the background you need to understand macroeconomic theory sufficiently so that you can understand the policy debates that have been going on for the last 50 years and continue unabated. In these chapters, the terms of the debate between Keynesians and Classicals will become clear.

Part III, Monetary and Financial Institutions (Chapters 11–14), discusses the financial sector and shows you how that sector fits into the macroeconomic landscape. It gives you a sense of the nuts and bolts of macroeconomic policy, the financial institutions in the economy, and how those institutions influence inflation.

Part IV, International Dimensions of Monetary and Fiscal Policies (Chapters 15–17), zero in on the international dimensions of macroeconomic policy. It shows how the additional complications that the international sector brings to macroeconomics can be added to the models and ideas discussed in earlier chapters. Since Canada relies to a great extent on international trade, these issues are central to our study of macroeconomics in Canada.

Part V, Macroeconomic Policy Debates (Chapters 18–20), discusses the art of macroeconomic policy. It applies the terminology, theory, and knowledge of institutions that you'll have gained from earlier chapters.

---

[1]"Laissez-faire" (introduced to you in Chapter 3) is a French expression meaning "leave things alone; let them go on without interference."

6

Economic Growth, Business Cycles, Unemployment, and Inflation

Remember that there is nothing stable in human affairs; therefore avoid undue elation in prosperity, or undue depression in adversity.

~ Socrates

After reading this chapter, you should be able to:

1 Summarize some relevant statistics about growth, business cycles, unemployment, and inflation.

2 Name four ingredients of growth.

3 List four phases of the business cycle.

4 Relate the target rate of unemployment to potential income.

5 Explain how unemployment is measured and state some microeconomic categories of unemployment.

6 State three important costs of unemployment.

7 Define inflation and distinguish a real concept from a nominal concept.

8 Explain how index numbers are used to describe the price level.

9 Differentiate between cost-push and demand-pull inflation and expected and unexpected inflation.

10 State two important costs of inflation.

Like people, the economy has moods. Sometimes it's in wonderful shape—it's expansive; at other times, it's depressed. Like people whose moods are often associated with specific problems (headaches, sore back, bad relationships), the economy's moods are associated with various problems.

Macroeconomics is the study of the aggregate moods of the economy, with specific focus on problems associated with those moods—the problems of growth, business cycles, unemployment, and inflation. These four problems are the central concern of macroeconomics. The macroeconomic theory we'll consider is designed to explain how supply and demand forces in the aggregate interact to create these problems. The macroeconomic policy controversies we'll consider concern these four problems. So it's only appropriate that in this first macroeconomics chapter we consider an overview of these problems, their causes, their consequences, and the debate about what to do about them. It introduces you to some of the terms we'll be using and gives you a sense of the interrelationship of these problems. Just how are business cycles and growth related to inflation and unemployment? The chapter won't answer all your questions (if it did, we wouldn't need the other chapters), but it will provide you with a framework for the remaining chapters.

We'll start with the problems of growth.

GROWTH

1A   Canadian economic output has grown at an annual 3 to 3.5 percent rate.

Generally the Canadian economy is growing or expanding. Economic activity—the production of goods and services (output)—is increasing. When people produce and sell their goods, they earn income, so when an economy is growing, both total output and total income are increasing. Such growth gives most people more this year than they had last year. Since most of us prefer more to less, growth is easy to take.

Statistics Canada traced Canadian economic growth and found that, in recent decades, output of goods and services grew at about 3 percent per year. This 3 percent growth rate is sometimes called the *secular trend rate of growth*. The rate at which actual output grows in any one year fluctuates, but on average the Canadian economy has been growing at that long-run trend. This growth trend can be divided into two components, one reflecting the change in population, and one consisting of changes in productivity (output per input). Since population has also been growing, per capita economic growth (growth per person) has been less than 3 percent. When economists talk about economic growth, they generally mean this long-term growth trend of output of about 3 percent per year.

The Benefits and Costs of Growth

Economic growth (per capita) allows everyone in society, on average, to have more. Thus, it isn't surprising that most governments are generally searching for policies that will allow their economies to grow. Indeed, one reason market economies have been so successful is that they have consistently channelled individual efforts toward production and growth. Individuals feel a sense of accomplishment in making things grow and, if sufficient economic incentives and resources exist, individuals' actions can lead to a continually growing economy.

Politically, growth, or predictions of growth, allows governments to avoid hard distributional questions of who should get what part of our existing output. With growth there is more to go around for everyone. A growing economy generates jobs, so politicians who want to claim that their policies will create jobs generally predict those policies will create growth. For example, in the mid-1990s, Jean Chretien estimated his policies would maintain over 3 percent growth and, because of that growth, thousands of new jobs.

Of course, there are also costs to material growth—pollution, resource exhaustion, and destruction of natural habitat. These costs lead some people to believe that we would be better off in a non-material-growth society that de-emphasized material growth. (That doesn't mean we shouldn't grow emotionally, spiritually, and intellectually; it simply means we should grow out of our material good fetish.) Many people believe these costs are important, and the result is often an environmental/economic growth stalemate.

To reconcile the two goals, some have argued that spending on the environment can create growth and jobs, so the two need not be incompatible. Unfortunately, there's a problem with this argument. It confuses growth and jobs with increased material consumption—what most people are worried about. As more material goods made available by growth are used for antipollution equipment, less is available for the growth of an average individual's personal consumption, since the added material goods created by growth have already been used. What society gets, at best, from these expenditures is a better physical environment, not more of everything. Getting more of everything would violate the TANSTAAFL law.

Economists have thought a lot about growth, and have many ideas about it. But they have no magic recipe of policies that can be directly related to growth. They have, however, specified some of the ingredients of that recipe. Four of the most important causes of growth are the following.

1. Institutions with incentives compatible with growth;
2. Technological development;
3. Available resources; and
4. Capital accumulation—investment in productive capacity, including *human capital.*

Let's consider each in turn.

Institutions with Incentives Compatible with Growth

Throughout this book we have emphasized the importance of economic institutions. Those institutions are vitally necessary for growth. **Growth-compatible institutions**—institutions that foster growth—must have *incentives* built into them that lead people to put out effort—to work hard—and must discourage people from activities that inhibit growth, such as spending a lot of their time in leisure pursuits or in gaining income for themselves by creating impediments for others. Let's consider some examples of each.

When individuals get much of the gains of growth themselves, they have incentives to work harder. That's why private ownership of property plays an important role in growth. It is the institution that *supply-side* economists focus on. In the former Soviet Union, individuals didn't get much of the gain of their own initiative, and hence often spent their time in pursuits other than activities fostering growth. Another example of a growth-compatible institution is the corporation, a legal fiction that gives owners limited liability, thereby encouraging large enterprises because people are more willing to invest their savings when they have limited liability than they would be if they did not.

Many developing countries follow a type of mercantilist policy in which government approval is necessary before any economic activity is allowed. Government officials' income often comes from bribes offered to them by individuals who want to be able to undertake economic activity. Such policies inhibit economic growth. Many regulations, even reasonable ones, also tend to inhibit economic growth because they inhibit entrepreneurial activities. But we should mention that to ensure that the growth is of a socially desirable type, some regulation is necessary. The policy problem is in deciding between necessary and unnecessary regulation.

Technological Development

Growth is sometimes thought of as the same things getting bigger, or getting more of the same things. That's an incorrect view of growth. While growth in some ways involves more of the same, a much larger aspect of growth involves changes in technology—*changes* in the goods we buy, and *changes* in the way we make goods. Think of what this generation spends its income on—CDs, cars, computers, fast food—and compare that to what the preceding generation spent money on—LP records, cars that would now be considered obsolete, and tube and

The Causes of Growth

2   Four important ingredients of growth are:
1. Institutions with incentives compatible with growth;
2. Technological development;
3. Available resources; and
4. Capital accumulation—investment in productive capacity, including human capital

Growth-compatible institutions
Institutions that foster growth.

per capita growth rate of 1 percent per year means, on average, people will be able to consume 1 percent more per year. Most of you, we suspect, are hoping to do better than that, and most of you will do better, both because you're in college or university studying economics (so you'll do better than average) and because most individuals in their working years can expect to consume slightly more each year than they did the previous year. Since income also tends to increase with age up to retirement, and ends completely at death, a specific individual's income, and hence his or her consumption, will generally increase by more than the per capita growth in income.

So, if the future is like the past, the average (living) person can look forward to a rate of increase in consumption significantly above average. The average dead person will have a rather significant decrease.

transistor radios. (When one of us was 11, he saved $30—the equivalent of over $100 now—so he could afford a six-transistor Motorola radio; computers didn't exist.)

Contrast this with the goods the next generation might spend its income on: video brain implants (little gadgets in your head to receive sound and full-vision broadcasts—you simply close your eyes and tune in whatever you want, if you've paid your cellular fee for that month), electric cars (gas cars will be considered so quaint, but so polluting), and instant food (little pills that fulfil all your nutritional needs, letting your brain implant gadget supply all the ambiance)—just imagine! You probably can get the picture even without a video brain implant.

How does society get people to work on these new developments to change the very nature of what we do and how we think? One way is through economic incentives; another is with institutions that foster creativity and bold thinking—like this book; a third is through institutions that foster hard work. There are, of course, trade-offs. Institutions that foster hard work and require discipline—such as the Japanese educational system—don't do as good a job at fostering creativity as the Canadian educational system, and vice versa: the Canadian educational system isn't great at fostering hard work. Thus, many of the new technologies of the 1980s have been thought up in Canada, but have been translated into workable products in Japan.

Available Resources   If an economy is to grow it will need resources. Thus England grew in the late 1700s because it had iron and coal; and Canada grew in the 20th century because it had a major supply of many resources, and it imported people, who can also be thought of as a resource (the Canadian-born population has only recently "taken off").

Of course, you have to be careful in thinking about what is a resource. A resource in one time period may not be a resource in another—what is a resource depends on the technology being used (think of writing a book of this size using a typewriter rather than a computer!). So creativity can replace resources, and if you develop new technology fast enough, you can overcome any lack of existing resources. Even if a country doesn't have the physical resources it needs, if it can import them, it can grow—as did Japan following World War II.

Investment and Accumulated Physical and Human Capital   At one point, capital accumulation (where capital was thought of as buildings and machines—what we'll call physical capital) and investment were seen as forming the key element in growth. While buildings and machines are still considered a key element in growth, it is now generally recognized that the growth recipe is far more complicated. One of the reasons for this recognition is the empirical evidence; for instance, the former Soviet Union invested a lot and accumulated lots of physical capital goods, but their economy didn't grow much because that capital was often internationally obsolete. Another

When we first went to college, we thought that there were facts and there were theories, and that theories were tested by comparing them to the facts. Alas, our professors delighted in twisting any neat divisions we made, and our neat distinction between fact and theory is one of the things that bit the dust.

INTERPRETING EMPIRICAL EVIDENCE

The difficulty is that facts are simply empirical observations. What is a fact depends on who is doing the observing. Economic facts (data) must often be collected through more complicated methods than simple observation. Numbers must be collected (presenting first the collector and then the viewer with possible errors). Numbers must be combined, and often subsets of numbers must be chosen (opening up the possibility of more errors). Finally, numbers must be interpreted.

Much of the debate in economics is conducted in the statistical trenches: looking at the data and attempting to pull out "facts" from that data. The "fact" that business cycles' peaks and troughs were reduced after World War II was pretty much accepted as a fact until economists started looking at the data more closely and came up with a different conclusion: no postwar change in business cycles has occurred. Many economists disagreed with this finding, but whether they are right or wrong is not the important point. The important point is that after economists presented their new interpretation, the "fact" was in dispute, and no longer a fact. The moral: Beware of "facts."

reason for this de-emphasis on capital accumulation is a recognition that products change, and useful buildings and machines in one time period may be useless in another. The value of the capital stock depends on the future, and there is no real way of measuring the value of capital independently of its future expectation of earnings. Capital's role in growth is extraordinarily difficult to accurately measure empirically.

A third reason for this de-emphasis on capital accumulation is that it became clear that capital was far more than machines. People's knowledge is a type of capital, called **human capital,** and the habitual way of doing things that guides people in how they approach production is **social capital.** For example, the existence of money and a well developed financial market makes many investment projects possible that otherwise wouldn't be possible, and hence such institutions are a type of social capital. In a way, anything that contributes to growth can be called a type of capital, and anything that slows growth can be called a destruction of capital. With the concept of capital including such a wide range of things, it is difficult to say what is *not* capital, which makes the concept of capital less useful. However, there's general agreement among economists that economic growth and prosperity depend critically on the right mix of physical, human, and social capital. Part of government policy is to encourage the market to provide that magic capital mix.

Human capital   People's knowledge.

Social capital   The habitual way of doing things that guides people in how they approach production.

Turning the Causes of Growth into Growth   The four causes of growth cannot be taken as given. Even if each of these four ingredients exists, they may not exist in the right proportions. For example, economic growth depends upon people saving and investing rather than consuming their income. Investing now helps create machines that can be used in the future to produce more output with less effort. Growth also depends upon technological change—finding new, better ways to do things. For instance, in the 19th century when Nicolas Appert discovered canning (the ability to cook and store food in a sealed container so it wouldn't spoil), the economic possibilities of society expanded enormously. But if, when technological changes occur, the savings aren't there to finance the investment, the result will not be growth. It is the *combination* of investing in machines and technological change that plays a central role in the growth of any economy.

There are, of course, many other causes of growth. Nonetheless, this brief introduction should identify some growth issues to keep in the back of your mind as we consider other goals, because policies that sometimes seem to help alleviate other problems, like unemployment or inflation, can have negative effects on growth.

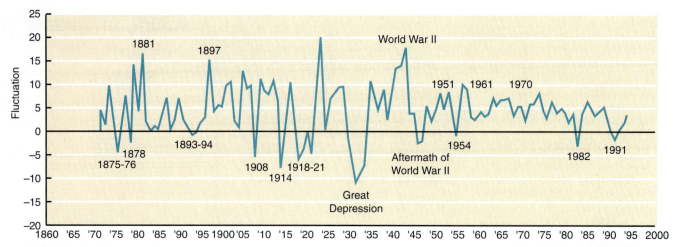

(a) Canadian business cycles

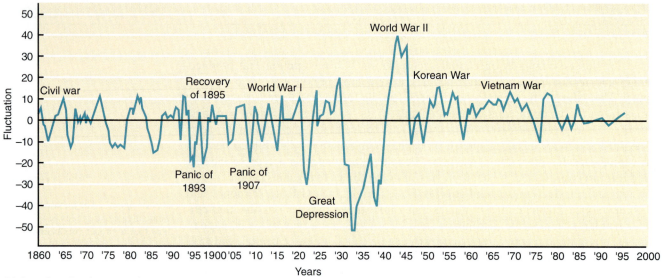

(b) American business cycles

EXHIBIT 1   Canadian and U.S. Business Cycles

Business cycles in Canada are directly related to American business cycles.

BUSINESS CYCLES

Business cycle   The upward or downward movement of economic activity that occurs around the growth trend.

While the secular, or long-term, trend is about a 3 percent increase in total output, there are numerous fluctuations around that trend. Sometimes total output is above the trend; at other times total output is below the trend. Such a short-term fluctuation of output around the long-term trend is called a **business cycle.** Thus, a business cycle is the upward or downward movement of economic activity that occurs around the growth trend. Exhibit 1 graphs the fluctuations in the Canadian and United States economies since 1871. It's clear that Canadian business cycles are highly related to cycles in U.S. economic activity. That's because of our strong economic ties to each other.

Until the late 1930s, economists took such cycles as facts of life. They had no convincing theory to explain why business cycles occurred, nor did they have policy suggestions to smooth them out. In fact, they felt that any attempt to smooth them through government intervention would make the situation worse.

Since the 1940s, however, many economists have not taken business cycles as facts of life. They have hotly debated the nature and causes of business cycles and of the underlying growth. Classical economists argue that fluctuations are to be expected in a market economy. Indeed, it would be strange if fluctuations did not occur when

	Pre-World War II (1879–39)	Post-World War II (1945–95)	
Number	15	8	**EXHIBIT 2** **Duration of Business Cycles in Canada (number of months)**
Average duration (trough to trough)	47	72	
Length of longest cycle	103 (1924–33)	170 (1961–75)	
Length of shortest cycle	29 (1919–21)	29 (1980–82)	
Average length of expansion	29	52	
Length of longest expansion	56 (1924–29)	159 (1961–74)	
Length of shortest expansion	14 (1919–20)	11 (1980–81)	
Average length of recession	23	11	
Length of longest recession	66 (1879–82)	17 (1990–91)	
Length of shortest recession	8 (1891–93)	4 (1980–80)	

Note: As of September 1995, Statistics Canada had yet to date the recession in the early 1990s. We'll assume it began in April 1990 and lasted through September 1991.

individuals are free to decide what they want to do. We should simply accept these fluctuations as we do the seasons of the year. If you have no policy to deal with some occurrence, you might as well accept that occurrence. Keynesian economists argue that fluctuations can and should be controlled. They argue that *expansions* (the part of the business cycle above the long-term trend) and *contractions* (the part of the cycle below the long-term trend) are symptoms of underlying problems of the economy, which should be dealt with. Which of these two views is correct is still a matter of debate.

If prolonged contractions (recessions) are a type of cold the economy catches, the Great Depression of the 1930s was double pneumonia. The Great Depression led to changes in the structure of the Canadian economy. The new structure included a more active role for government in reducing the severity of cyclical fluctuations. Look at Exhibit 1 and compare the periods before and after World War II. (World War II began in 1939 (1941 in the United States) and ended in 1945.) Notice that the downturns and panics since 1945 have generally been less severe than before.

This change in the nature of business cycles can be better seen in Exhibit 2, which is based on Statistics Canada data. Notice that since 1945 business cycles' duration has increased, but, more important, the average length of expansions has increased while the average length of contractions has decreased.

How to interpret these statistics is the subject of much controversy. As is the case with much economic evidence, the data are subject to different interpretations. Some economists argue the reduction in fluctuations' severity is an illusion.

If the severity of the fluctuations has been reduced (which most economists believe has happened), one reason is that changes in institutional structure were made as a result of the Great Depression. Both the financial structure and the government taxing and spending structure were changed, giving the government a more important role in stabilizing the economy. Consideration of that stronger government role is a key element of macroeconomics.

Much research has gone into measuring business cycles and setting official reference dates for the beginnings and ends of contractions and expansions. As a result of this research, business cycles have been divided into phases, and an explicit terminology has been developed. Statistics Canada announces the government's official dates of contractions and expansions. In the postwar era (since mid-1945), the average business expansion has lasted about 52 months. A major expansion occurred from 1982 until 1990, when the economy fell into a recession, where it remained through late 1991. Then it slowly came out, but slow growth remained.

Business cycles have varying durations and intensities, but economists have developed a terminology to describe all business cycles and just about any position we

The Phases of the Business Cycle

1B   Since 1945 the average expansion has lasted about 52 months.

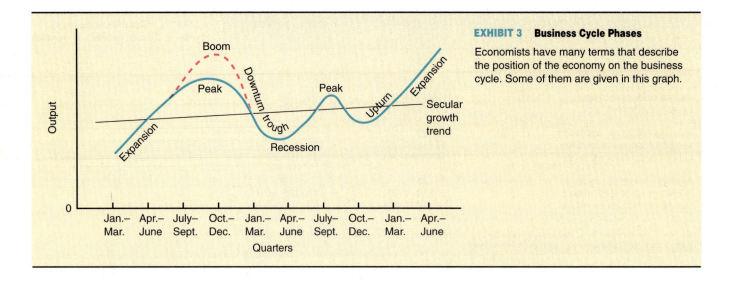

EXHIBIT 3   Business Cycle Phases

Economists have many terms that describe the position of the economy on the business cycle. Some of them are given in this graph.

3 The four phases of the business cycle are: the peak, the downturn, the trough, and the upturn.

Boom   In the business cycle, a very high peak representing a big jump in output.

Downturn   Segment of the business cycle characterized by the economy starting to fall from the top of the cycle.

Recession   A downturn that persists for more than two consecutive quarters of a year.

Depression   A large recession.

Expansion   Upturn that lasts for more than two consecutive quarters of a year.

Diffusion index   An average that captures changes across a variety of sectors over time. Used to illustrate how the business cycle affects different industries.

might find ourselves in on the business cycle. Since this terminology is often used by the press it is helpful to go over it. We do so in reference to Exhibit 3 which gives you a visual picture of a business cycle.

Let's start at the top. The top of a cycle is called the *peak*. A very high peak, representing a big jump in output, is called a **boom.** (That's when the economy is doing great. Most everyone who wants a job has one and everyone is happy.) Eventually an expansion peaks. (At least, in the past, they always have.) When the economy starts to fall from that peak, there's a **downturn** in business activity. If that downturn persists for more than two consecutive quarters of the year, that downturn becomes a **recession.** (In a recession the economy isn't doing so great; many people are unemployed and a number of people are depressed.)

A large recession is called a **depression.** There is no formal line indicating when a recession becomes a depression. In general, a depression is much longer and more severe than a recession. This ambiguity allows some economists to joke, "When your neighbour is unemployed, it's a recession; when you're unemployed, it's a depression." If pushed for something more specific, we'd say that if unemployment exceeds 14 percent for more than a year, the economy is in a depression.

The bottom of a recession or depression is called the *trough*. When the economy comes out of the trough, economists say it's in an *upturn*. If an upturn lasts two consecutive quarters of the year, it's called an **expansion,** which leads us back up to the peak. And so it goes.

The process of dating business cycles and determining the dates of expansion and recession is actually quite difficult. That's because economists are concerned with both the level of economic activity and how changes in production are distributed across industries. To deal with these issues economists look at **diffusion indices—** they tell us something about how changes in production are distributed across the economy. Generally, we need to look at the data for a long time before we can conclusively state that the economy was in a contractionary or an expansionary stage.

This terminology is important because if you're going to talk about the state of the economy, you need the terminology to do it. Why are businesses so interested in the state of the economy? They want to be able to predict whether it's going into a contraction or an expansion. Making the right prediction can determine whether the business will be profitable or not. That's why a large amount of economists' activity goes into trying to predict the future course of the economy.

Leading and Coincidental Indicators

Two measures that economists use to determine where the economy is on the business cycle are the **unemployment rate** (the percentage of people in the labour force—the number of people in the economy willing and able to work—who can't find a job) and the **capacity utilization rate** (the rate at which factories and machines are operating compared to the rate at which they could be used). Generally, economists feel that 7–9 percent unemployment and 80–85 percent capacity utilization are about as much as we should expect from the economy. Therefore, they use them as targets. Thus the **target rate of unemployment** is defined as the lowest sustainable rate of unemployment economists believe is possible under existing conditions. To push the economy beyond that would be like driving your car 200 kilometres an hour. True, the marks on your speedometer might go up to 200, but 150 is a more realistic top speed. Beyond 200 (assuming that's where your car is red-lined), the engine is likely to blow up (unless you have a Maserati).

Economists translate the target unemployment rate and target capacity utilization rate into the level of output with which those rates will be associated. That level of output is called **potential output** (or *potential income,* because, as we mentioned, output creates income). Potential output is the output that would materialize at the target rate of unemployment and the target level of capacity utilization. Potential output grows at the secular (long-term) trend rate of about 3 percent per year. When the economy is in a downturn or recession, actual output is below potential output. When the economy is in a boom, actual output is above potential output.

Economists have developed a set of leading and **coincidental indicators** that, as their labels suggest, give us a good idea of when a recession is about to occur and when the economy is in one. **Leading indicators** tell us what's likely to happen several months from now, much as a barometer gives us a clue about tomorrow's weather. They include:

1. Furniture and appliance sales.
2. Sales of other durable goods.
3. Housing starts.
4. New orders for durable goods.
5. Ratio of shipments to stocks.
6. Average manufacturing workweek.
7. Personal and business services employment.
8. U.S. leading index.
9. TSE 300 index.
10. Money supply.

Coincidental indicators tell us what phase of the business cycle the economy is currently in, much as a thermometer tells us the current temperature. Coincidental indicators include:

1. Number of employees on nonagricultural payrolls.
2. Personal income minus transfer payments (like welfare, unemployment insurance, veterans' benefits, etc.).
3. Industrial production.
4. Manufacturing and trade sales volume.

Economists use leading indicators in making forecasts about the economy. Leading indicators are called *indicators,* not *predictors,* because they're only rough approximations of what's likely to happen in the future. For example, before you can build a house, a building permit must be applied for. Usually this occurs several months before the actual start of construction. By looking at the number of building permits that have been issued, you can predict how much building is likely to begin in six months or so. But the prediction might be wrong, since getting a building permit does not require someone to actually build. Business economists spend much of their time and effort delving deeper into these indicators, trying to see what they are really telling us, as opposed to what they seem to be telling us. Business economists joke that the leading indicators have predicted six of the past two recessions.

Unemployment rate   The percentage of people in the labor force who can't find a job.

Capacity utilization rate   Rate at which factories and machines are operating compared to the maximum rate at which they could be used.

Target rate of unemployment   Lowest sustainable rate of unemployment economists believe is possible under existing conditions.

4   Potential income is defined as the output that will be achieved at the target rate of unemployment and at the target level of capacity utilization.

Potential output   Output that would materialize at the target rate of unemployment and the target level of capacity utilization.

Coincidental indicators   Indicators that tell us what phase of the business cycle the economy is currently in.

Leading indicators   Indicators that tell us what's likely to happen 12 to 15 months from now.

BUSINESS CYCLES AND THE STOCK MARKET

You might think that there is a strong association between the state of the economy and the stock market—and you'd be half-right. Sometimes changes in stock prices lead changes in output, but there's no stable link that we can rely on to predict the onset of recession and expansion. If we look at an index of the prices of stocks traded in Toronto and the Canadian business cycle, we might see some evidence that the end of the depression in the 1930s was preceded by a rise in the stock price index, but that doesn't mean that when stock prices rise times will be good, and when stock prices fall, times will be bad. We only need to look at recent history to show that the links between stock prices and the state of the economy are weak and unreliable. In 1987 the Toronto stock price index fell over 25 percent, but the figure below clearly demonstrates that Canada was growing. The economic downturn didn't come until 1990 (proponents of the link between stock prices and economic activity might suggest that the signal just came early—maybe they're right). Note that the stock price index did fall in advance of the 1990–91 recession.

Why is the link between stock prices and the state of the economy so unstable? It has to do with expectations. As we'll see in later chapters, stock prices are largely determined by expectations about the future state of the economy and government policy. When there appears to be a strong link between changes in stock prices and economic activity, that might just signal the fact that expectations about the future course of events were fulfilled. When the link breaks down, perhaps as it did with the 1987 crash, that just might reflect expectations that weren't consistent with the underlying economic fundamentals. We'll return to this in later chapters on monetary policy and try to draw some definite conclusions about the links between stock prices and the economy.

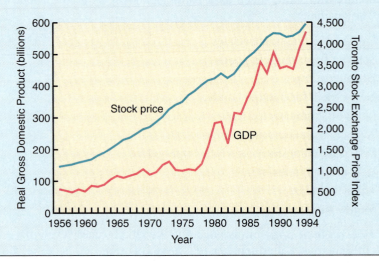

Sifting through the data to find clues in new statistical series is drudgery detective work, but it's the backbone of business economists' work. Just as TV detectives' antics don't reflect what most detectives do, economists' brief appearances on the TV news don't reflect what economists do.

UNEMPLOYMENT

Business cycles and growth are directly related to unemployment in the Canadian economy. When an economy is growing and is in an expansion, unemployment is usually falling; when an economy is in a downturn, unemployment is usually rising. That's why the unemployment rate is an indicator of the business cycle.

The relationship between the business cycle and unemployment is obvious to most people, but often the seemingly obvious hides important insights. Just why are business cycles and growth related to unemployment? True, aggregate income must fall in a recession, but, logically, unemployment need not result. A different result could be that everyone's income falls. Looking at the problem historically, we see unemployment has not always been a problem associated with business cycles.

Unemployment became a problem about the time of the Industrial Revolution. In pre-industrial farming societies, unemployment wasn't much of a problem; there was always work to be done and most people had their assigned tasks. The reason is that

Using "the fear of hunger" to see that people work may sound rather mean, but looked at from a societal view it can be "kind." For example, consider the socialist countries that wiped out the fear of unemployment. All people were guaranteed a job. (In fact, all people were required by law to have one.) By law, unemployment was eliminated. But this created other problems. People would show up at work but not really work. After all, they couldn't be fired. The results were shoddy products, shortages, and general dissatisfaction. As one cynical citizen said, "We pretend to work and they pretend to pay us." These negative consequences of eliminating unemployment were a significant reason why people pushed for the elimination or modification of socialism. They said, "If this is the result of eliminating unemployment, bring back unemployment." And the formerly socialist countries have done that with a vengeance in the early 1990s.

We use the term *fear of hunger* rather than *fear of unemployment* to emphasize that if people can expect a good income even if they lose their jobs, the fear of unemployment loses some of its bite. For example, in European countries like The Netherlands people were guaranteed almost as much income if they had no job as they would have earned if they did have a job. The result: the unemployment rate rose and the Dutch economy stagnated. The effect of such high support payments to people who didn't work acquired a name: *the Dutch disease*.

No one argues that unemployment or the fear of hunger is good. But many do argue that going too far in eliminating it has such negative effects on growth that unemployment is the better of two bads.

pre-industrial farmers didn't receive wages—they received net revenue (the income left after all costs had been paid). That means the average amount they netted per hour (the equivalent of a wage) was flexible. In good years they had a high income per hour; in bad years they had a low income per hour.

The flexibility in people's net income per hour meant that when there were fluctuations in economic activity, people's income rose or fell, but they kept on working. Low income was a problem, but, since people didn't become unemployed, **cyclical unemployment** (unemployment resulting from fluctuations in economic activity) was not a problem.

Cyclical unemployment
Unemployment resulting from fluctuations in economic activity.

While cyclical unemployment did not exist in preindustrial society, **structural unemployment** (unemployment resulting from changes in the economy itself) did. For example, say demand for a product falls because of technological change. Some unemployment would likely result; that unemployment would be called *structural unemployment*. But structural unemployment wasn't much of a problem for government, or at least people did not consider it government's problem. The reason is that unemployment of family members was dealt with internally, by the family. If someone in the family had income, that person would share it with unemployed family members.

Structural unemployment
Unemployment resulting from changes in the economy itself.

The Industrial Revolution changed the nature of work and introduced unemployment as a problem for society. This is because the Industrial Revolution was accompanied by a shift to wage labour and to a division of responsibilities. Some individuals (capitalists) took on ownership of the means of production and *hired* others to work for them, paying them a wage per hour. This change in the nature of production marked a significant change in the nature of the unemployment problem.

First, it created the possibility of cyclical unemployment. With wages set at a certain level, when economic activity fell, workers' income per hour did not fall. Instead, when slack periods occurred, factories would lay off or fire some workers. That isn't what happened on the farm; when a slack period occurred on the farm, the income per hour of all workers fell and few were laid off.

Second, the Industrial Revolution was accompanied by a change in how families dealt with unemployment. Whereas in pre-industrial farm economies individuals or families took responsibility for their own slack periods, in a capitalist industrial society factory owners didn't take responsibility for their workers in slack periods. The pink slip (a common name for the notice workers get telling them they are laid off) and the problem of unemployment were born in the Industrial Revolution.

Without wage income, unemployed workers were in a pickle. They couldn't pay their rent, they couldn't eat, they couldn't put clothes on their backs. So what was previously a family problem became a social problem. Not surprisingly, it was at that time—the late 1700s—that economists began paying more attention to the problem of unemployment.

Initially, economists and society still did not view unemployment as a societal problem. It was the individual's problem. If people were unemployed, it was their own fault; hunger, or at least the fear of hunger, and people's desire to maintain their lifestyle would drive them to find other jobs relatively quickly. Thus, early capitalism didn't have an unemployment problem; it had an unemployment solution: the fear of hunger.

As capitalism evolved into welfare capitalism, the hunger solution decreased in importance. Capitalist societies no longer saw the fear of hunger as an acceptable answer to unemployment. Social welfare programs such as unemployment insurance and assistance to the poor were developed to help deal with unemployment.

During the Depression, in an attempt to assuage the fears of rioting unemployed workers, Prime Minister Bennett introduced the Federal Employment and Social Insurance Act. It was to provide for sweeping changes to the labour market and included minimum wage legislation, unemployment insurance, and social insurance programs. It was passed in 1935 but later found to be unconstitutional. The Federal Unemployment Insurance Act of 1940 replaced the 1935 Act. It assigned government the responsibility for providing assistance to the unemployed. The government had already committed itself to creating an economic climate in which just about everyone who wanted a job could have one—a situation that economists defined as **full employment.** It was government's responsibility to offset cyclical fluctuations and thereby prevent cyclical unemployment and to somehow deal with structural unemployment.

Initially, government regarded low rates of about 3 percent unemployment as a condition of full employment. This was made up of **frictional unemployment** (unemployment caused by people quitting a job just long enough to look for and find another one) and of a few "unemployables," such as alcoholics and drug addicts, along with a certain amount of necessary structural unemployment resulting when the structure of the economy changed. Thus, any unemployment higher than about 3 percent was considered either unnecessary structural or cyclical unemployment and was now government's responsibility; frictional and necessary structural unemployment were still the individual's problem.

Macroeconomics developed as a separate field and focused on how to combat cyclical unemployment. As you will see in coming chapters, government believed it could offset cyclical unemployment and achieve full employment by seeing to it that there was sufficient aggregate demand.

By the 1950s, government had given up its view that very low rates of unemployment were consistent with full employment. Since then the government has continually raised its target rate of unemployment. In the late 1980s and early 1990s the appropriate target rate of unemployment is a matter of debate, but most economists place it at somewhere between 7 percent and 9 percent unemployment.

Why these changing definitions of *full employment?* One reason is that, in the 1970s and early 1980s, a low inflation rate, which also was a government goal, seemed to be incompatible with a low unemployment rate. We'll talk about this incompatibility later when we discuss "stagflation". A second reason is demographics: Different age groups have different unemployment rates, and as the population's age structure changes, so does the target unemployment rate. Thirdly, there are regional differences in unemployment rates across the country. As regions grow at different rates, the target rate of unemployment for the nation changes.

A fourth reason is our economy's changing social and institutional structure. These social and institutional changes affected the nature of the unemployment problem. For example, in the post-World War II period, family wealth increased substantially and borrowing became easier than before, giving many unemployed indi-

---

Full employment   An economic climate in which almost everyone who wants a job has one.

Frictional unemployment
Unemployment caused by new entrants to the job market and people who have left their jobs to look for and find other jobs.

1C   In the 1980s and 1990s, the target rate of unemployment has been between 7 and 9 percent.

viduals a bit more leeway before they were forced to find a job. For instance, more family wealth meant that upon graduation from high school or college, children who couldn't find the job they wanted could live at home and be supported by their parents for a year or two.

Another example of how changing institutions changed the unemployment problem is women's expanding role in the economy. In the 1950s, the traditional view that "woman's place is in the home" remained strong. Usually only one family member—the man—had a job. If he lost his job, no money came in. In the 1970s to 1990s, more and more women entered the workforce so that today over two-thirds of women with children under six are in the labour force. In a two-earner family, if one person loses a job, the family doesn't face immediate starvation. The other person's income carries the family over.

Yet another example involves the changing structures of the economy. In the 1990s the Canadian economy, and much of the European economy, went through major **structural readjustments**—modifications of the types of goods produced and the methods of production. Firms laid off high-wage workers even as they were increasing output. The result was that structural unemployment increased as cyclical unemployment decreased. At times this led to the unemployment rate and the level of output moving in opposite directions.

Structural readjustment
Phenomenon of economy trying to change from what it had been doing to doing something new instead of repeating what it had done in the past.

Government institutions also changed. Programs like unemployment insurance and public welfare were created to reduce suffering associated with unemployment. But in doing so, these programs changed the way people responded to unemployment. People in the 1990s are more picky about what jobs they take than they were in the 1920s and 1930s. People don't want just any job, they want a *fulfilling* job with a decent wage. As people have become choosier about jobs, a debate has raged over the extent of government's responsibility for unemployment. We'll look at recent proposals for the reform of unemployment insurance in chapter 19.

Differing views of individuals' responsibility and society's responsibility affect people's views on whether somebody is actually unemployed. In this book we distinguish two groups of macroeconomists: **Keynesians** (who generally favour activist government policies) and **Classicals** (who generally favour laissez-faire or non-activist policies).

Whose Responsibility Is Unemployment?

Keynesians Economists who generally favour government intervention in the aggregate economy.

The Classical View of Unemployment
Classical economists take the position that, generally, individuals should be responsible for finding jobs. They emphasize that an individual can always find *some* job at *some* wage rate, even if it's only selling apples on the street for 40¢ apiece. Given this view of individual responsibility, unemployment is impossible. If a person isn't working, that's his or her choice; the person simply isn't looking hard enough for a job. For an economist with this view, almost all unemployment is actually frictional unemployment.

Classical Economists who generally oppose government intervention.

The Keynesian View of Unemployment
Keynesian economists tend to say society owes a person a job commensurate with the individual's training or past job experience. They further argue that the job should be close enough to home so a person doesn't have to move. Given this view, frictional unemployment is only a small part of total unemployment. Structural and cyclical unemployment are far more common.

Shifts in the View of Unemployment
Which of these two views—Classical or Keynesian—most people hold depends partly on the general state of the economy. The more people are unemployed, the more tempting it is to see unemployment as a structural or cyclical problem. To see it in either of those ways puts more of the blame on society and less on unemployed individuals. In the Great Depression of the 1930s, with almost 20 percent of the population unemployed, views about unemployment changed. Most people came to see it as society's and not the individual's problem.

Keynesian economics was born in the Great Depression. In the 1950s and 1960s, as Keynesian economics expanded to include a majority of macroeconomists, the

CATEGORIES OF UNEMPLOYMENT

A good sense of the differing types of unemployment and the differing social views that unemployment embodies can be conveyed through three examples of unemployed individuals. As you read the following stories, ask yourself which category of unemployment each individual falls into.

Example 1: Joe is listed as unemployed and collects unemployment insurance. He's had various jobs in the past and was laid off from his last one. He spent a few weeks on household projects, believing he would be called back by his most recent employer—but he wasn't. He's grown to like being on his own schedule. He's living on his unemployment insurance (while it lasts, which usually isn't more than six months), his savings, and money he picks up by being paid cash under the table working a few hours now and then at construction sites.

The Unemployment Insurance office requires him to make at least an attempt to find work, and he's turned up a few prospects. However, some were backbreaking labouring jobs and one would have required him to move to a distant city, so he's avoided accepting regular work. Joe knows the unemployment payments won't last forever. When they're used up, he plans to increase his under-the-table activity. Then, when he gets good and ready, he'll really look for a job.

Example 2: Flo is a middle-aged, small-town housewife. She worked before her marriage, but when she and her husband started their family she quit her job to be a full-time housewife and mother. She never questioned her family values of hard work, independence, belief in free enterprise, and scorn of government handouts. When her youngest child left the nest, she decided to finish the college education she'd only just started when she married.

After getting her degree, she looked for a job, but found the market for middle-aged women with no recent experience was depressed—and depressing. The provincial employment office where she sought listings recognized her abilities and gave her a temporary job in that very office. Because she was a "temp", however, she was the first to be laid off when the provincial legislature cut the local office budget—but she'd worked long enough to be eligible for unemployment insurance.

She hesitated about applying, since handouts were against her principles. On the other hand, while working there she'd seen plenty of people, including her friends, applying for benefits after work histories even slimmer than hers. She decided to take the benefits. While they lasted, she found family finances on almost as sound a footing as when she was working. Although she was bringing in less money, net family income didn't suffer much since she didn't have as many deductions from her paycheque nor did she have the commuting and clothing expenses of going to a daily job.

Example 3: Tom had a good job at a manufacturing plant where he'd worked up to a wage of $450 a week. Occasionally he was laid off, but only a few weeks, and then he'd be called back. In 1989 the plant was bought by an out-of-province corporation which laid off half the workforce and put in automated equipment. Tom, an older worker with comparatively high wages, was one of the first to go, and he wasn't called back.

Tom had a wife, three children, a car payment, and a mortgage. He looked for other work but couldn't find anything paying close to what he'd been getting. Tom used up his unemployment insurance and his savings. He sold the house and moved his family into a trailer. Finally he heard that there were a lot of jobs in New Brunswick, 800 kilometres away. He moved there, found a job, and began sending money home every week. Then the New Brunswick economy faltered. Tom was laid off again, and his unemployment insurance ran out again. Relying on his $100,000 life insurance policy, he figured he was worth more to his family dead than alive . . .

As these three examples suggest, unemployment encompasses a wide range of cases. Unemployment is anything but a one-dimensional problem, so it's not surprising that people's views of how to deal with it differ.

Keynesian view of unemployment also became the view of the majority of the population.

But in the 1970s and 1980s that view started to change. In Britain, for example, Prime Minister Margaret Thatcher stated specifically that unemployment was not a societal problem; it was an individual problem. Similar views were expressed in the United States. By 1990 an increasing number of people followed the Classical view and saw unemployment as an individual responsibility. In 1991 the pendulum swung back; as the economy fell into recession, the Keynesian view was once again gaining. When Bill Clinton took office in 1993, he made government creation of jobs a key part of his program. The view may change again in the political climate of the mid-1990s.

The story in Canada is similar. Jean Chretien is undertaking a radical reform of all social programs, including the Unemployment Insurance Program. The reforms are shifting the focus to the individual. (In 1994 New Brunswick introduced legislation to reduce welfare payments to those able-bodied recipients who refused to search for work.) Emphasis is placed on how the unemployed can upgrade their skills and education to be ready for the 21st century. Government creation of jobs remains a key part

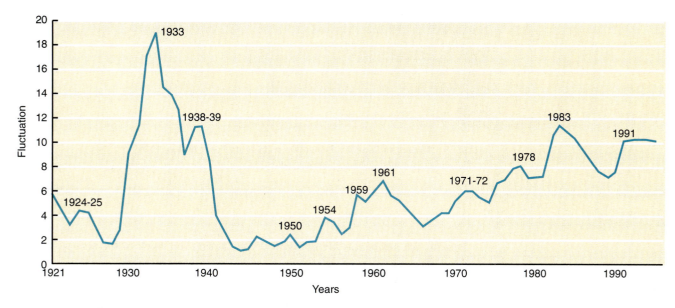

EXHIBIT 4   Canadian Unemployment Rate, 1921-1994

of his program through billions spent on infrastructure programs, but the trend is definitely towards making unemployment less of a societal problem.

When there's debate about what the unemployment problem is, it isn't surprising that there's also a debate about how to measure it. When talking about unemployment, economists usually refer to the "unemployment rate" published by Statistics Canada. Fluctuations in the official unemployment rate since 1921 appear in Exhibit 4. In it you can see that during World War II (1939–45), unemployment fell from the high rates of the 1930s Depression to an extremely low rate, less than 2 percent. You can also see that while the rate started back up in the 1950s, reaching almost 8 percent, it fell to under 4 percent until the mid-1960s, when the rate began gradually to rise again. After peaking in the early 1980s it began to descend again. In early 1990 it was about 8 percent; then in mid-1990 the economy fell into recession and the unemployment rate rose to over 11 percent in 1992 and 1993. By early 1995 it was below 10 percent.

How Is Unemployment Measured?

Calculating the Unemployment Rate   The Canadian unemployment rate is determined by dividing the number of unemployed individuals by the number of people in the civilian labour force and multiplying by 100. For example, in 1994 the total number of persons unemployed stood at 1.54 million—the labour force was 14.83 million—so the 1994 unemployment rate was (after rounding) 10.4 percent:

5A   The unemployment rate is measured by dividing the number of unemployed individuals by the number of people in the civilian labour force.

$$\frac{1.54 \text{ million}}{14.83 \text{ million}} = .1038 \times 100 = 10.4 \text{ percent}$$

To determine the civilian labour force, start with the total population and subtract from that all persons incapable of working, such as inmates of institutions. Then subtract persons living on Indian reserves, full-time members of the armed forces, people under 15 years of age, and residents of the Yukon and Northwest Territories. From that figure another subtraction is made—the number of people not in the labour force, including homemakers, students, retirees, the voluntarily idle, and the disabled. The result is the civilian labour force. Today the civilian labor force is about 15 million, as you can see in Exhibit 5.

The civilian labour force can be divided into employed and unemployed persons. Summary measures of employment are based on the **Labour Force Survey** in which 58,000 representative households are interviewed each month. From the survey data, Statistics Canada is able to provide information on employment and unemployment for Canada and the Provinces.

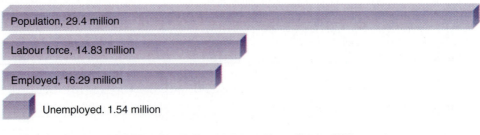

EXHIBIT 5   **Figures on Canada's Population and Labour Force Status, 1994**
Source: *Statistics Canada,* CANSIM Database, March 1995.

Persons are defined as being employed if, during the week of the survey, they:

1. Performed work for pay or profit, including unpaid work in a family owned business; or
2. Had a job but were not at work because of illness or disability, personal or family responsibilities, bad weather, labour disputes, vacation, or other reasons.

Unemployed persons are those who, during the survey week, were:

1. Without work but had actually looked for work in the last four weeks;
2. Were on layoff and available for work; or
3. Were available to work but had already been hired for a new job to begin within the next four weeks.

When we divide the number of persons employed by the total civilian labour force we obtain an employment rate; the unemployment rate is the number of persons unemployed divided by the total civilian labour force.

How Accurate Is the Official Unemployment Rate? Statistics Canada measures unemployment using a number of assumptions that have been the source of debate. For example, people may be staying at home and not looking for a job because they feel they don't have a chance to find one. These workers are called **discouraged workers.** Some Keynesian economists believe these individuals should be considered unemployed. Moreover, they question whether part-time workers should be classified as employed.

Discouraged workers   People who do not look for a job because they feel they don't have a chance of finding one.

The Keynesian argument is that there is a lack of decent jobs and of affordable transportation to get to the jobs that do exist, resulting in a high degree of discouragement so that many people have simply stopped trying. Because Statistics Canada statisticians define these people as voluntarily idle and do not count them as unemployed, Keynesians argue that Statistics Canada undercounts unemployment significantly. Some studies suggest that if discouraged workers were included, the official unemployment rate would rise by about 2 percent.

The Classical argument about unemployment is that being without a job often is voluntary. People say they are looking for a job, but they're not really looking. Many are working "off the books"; others are simply vacationing. Some Classicals contend that the way Statistics Canada measures unemployment exaggerates the number of those who are truly unemployed. A person is defined as unemployed if he or she is not employed and is actively seeking work.

So is the official unemployment rate too high or too low? The definition of *unemployment* involves value judgements. Both the Keynesian and the Classical arguments are defensible. But both sides agree the unemployment measure is imperfect, missing many people who should be included and including many people who should not be counted. This means that official unemployment figures must be carefully interpreted and modified in the light of other information, such as the number of people employed, part-time employment, and your own perspective on the problem. In short, measuring and interpreting the unemployment rate (like measuring and interpreting most economic statistics) is an art, not a science.

Despite problems, the unemployment rate statistic still gives us useful information about changes in the economy. Measurement problems themselves are little changed from year to year, so in comparing one year to another, those problems are not an issue. Keynesian and Classical economists agree that a changing unemployment rate generally tells us something about the economy, especially if interpreted in the light of other statistics. That's why the unemployment rate is used as a measure of the state of the economy.

Right after World War II, economists talked about achieving full employment so that everyone who wanted a job could have one. But, over time, economists increased their perceptions of the level of unemployment consistent with full employment. As this happened, the concept *full employment* no longer seemed an appropriate description of the lowest achievable rate of unemployment. So economists replaced it with other concepts that were more consistent with economic reality. The concept we'll use in this book is the *target rate of unemployment,* which is defined as the lowest sustainable rate of unemployment economists believe possible under existing conditions.

As we've said, the target rate of unemployment changes over time. In the early 1990s, most economists believe that somewhere between 7 and 9 percent is a reasonable target rate. If the economy were to have lower unemployment, they believe the result would be accelerating inflation—too much demand compared to available supply. With more unemployment, economists see the economy going into a downturn or a recession—too much supply compared to available demand. That's why in 1991 and 1992, when the economy had over 10 percent unemployment, most economists believed that the economy was in recession. When the economy is in neither boom nor bust, economists expect between 7 and 9 percent unemployment (the target rate).

Full Employment and the Target Rate of Unemployment

The target unemployment rate is used as a reference point for the economy. It establishes potential income (the income in the economy at the target rate of unemployment and target level of capacity utilization). To determine what effect changes in the unemployment rate will have on income, we use **Okun's rule of thumb,** which states that a 1 percent change in the unemployment rate will cause income to change in the opposite direction by 2.5 percent. For example, if unemployment rises from 5 percent to 6 percent, total output of $800 billion will fall by 2.5 percent, or $20 billion, to $780 billion. This suggests that if the unemployment rate were to fall from 11 percent to 10 percent, total output would rise by about $20 billion more than it otherwise would have.

These figures are rough, but they give you a sense of the implications of a change. Notice we said "will be $20 billion higher than it otherwise would have" rather than simply saying will increase "by about $20 billion." As we discussed in the growth section, generally the economy is growing as a result of increases in productivity or increases in the number of people choosing to work. Changes in either of these can cause income and employment to grow, even if there's no change in the unemployment rate. We must point this out because in the 1980s the number of people choosing to work increased substantially, significantly increasing the labour participation rate to about 67 percent. Then, starting in 1993, as many large firms structurally adjusted their production methods to increase their productivity, unemployment sometimes rose, and employment fell, even as output rose. Thus, when the labour participation rate and productivity change, an increase in unemployment doesn't necessarily mean a decrease in employment or a decrease in income.

Unemployment and Potential Income

Okun's rule of thumb   Another name for Okun's Law: A one-percent change in the unemployment rate will cause income in the economy to change in the opposite direction by 2.5 percent.

In the post-World War II period, unemployment was seen primarily as cyclical unemployment, and the focus of macroeconomic policy was on how to eliminate that unemployment through a specific set of macroeconomic policies—monetary and fiscal policies, which we'll discuss in Parts 2 and 3.

Microeconomic Categories of Unemployment

ADDED DIMENSION

FROM FULL EMPLOYMENT TO THE TARGET RATE OF UNEMPLOYMENT

As we emphasized in Chapter 1, good economists attempt to remain neutral and objective. It isn't always easy, especially when the language we use is often biased. (Think back to the puzzle about the doctor in Chapter 1. Have you solved it yet?)

This problem has proved to be a difficult one for economists in their attempt to find an alternative to the concept, *full employment*. An early contender was the *natural rate of unemployment*. Economists have often used the term *natural* to describe economic concepts. For example, they've talked about "natural" rights and a "natural" rate of interest. The problem with this usage is that what's natural to one person isn't necessarily natural to another. The term *natural* often conveys a sense of "that's the way it should be." However, in describing as "natural" the rate of unemployment that an economy can achieve, economists weren't making any value judgements about whether 5.5 percent unemployment is what should, or should not, be. They simply were saying that, given the institutions in the economy, that was what was achievable. So a number of economists objected to the use of the term *natural*.

As an alternative, a number of economists started to use the term *nonaccelerating inflation rate of unemployment (NAIRU)*, but even users of this term agreed it was a horrendous term. And so most avoided its use and shifted to the relatively neutral term, *target rate of unemployment*.

The target rate of unemployment is the rate that one believes is attainable without causing accelerating inflation. It is not determined theoretically; it is determined empirically. Economists look at what seems to be achievable and is historically normal, adjust that for structural and demographic changes they believe are occurring, and come up with the target rate of unemployment.

5B Two microeconomic categories of unemployment are demographic unemployment, and duration of unemployment.

Understanding monetary and fiscal policies is important, but in the 1990s it's not enough. Unemployment has many dimensions, so different types of unemployment are susceptible to different types of policies. Today's view is that you don't use a sledge hammer to pound in finishing nails, and you don't use macro policies to deal with certain types of unemployment; instead you use micro policies. To determine where microeconomic policies are appropriate as a supplement to macroeconomic policies, economists break unemployment down into a number of categories and analyze each category separately. These categories include demographic characteristics and the duration of unemployment. (See Exhibit 6.)

While Canada's unemployment rate moves in tandem with the business cycle, we have seen a gradual upward trend in the average unemployment rate over the last 30 years. We've also seen an increase in the average duration of unemployment—it was just 15.1 weeks in 1981, but in 1994 it was over 25 weeks. As Canada emerges from the recession of the early 1990s, we want to look at these figures carefully when discussing changes to unemployment insurance policies.

Regional Patterns of Unemployment The regional distribution of unemployment has always been a concern in Canada. The Atlantic provinces have historically been subject to higher rates of unemployment than the rest of the country, primarily because they are more reliant on resource-based industries (fishing, forestry, and mining) than the rest of the country. Combined with the fact that most of Canada's industrial activity takes place in Ontario, Quebec, Alberta, and British Columbia, we can begin to understand why regional issues are at the heart of most policy debates. When the industrially oriented provinces experience a cyclical downturn, the other provinces usually suffer proportionately greater effects. With declines in traditional resource activities like fishing, it's not surprising to find that Prince Edward Island and Newfoundland had unemployment rates around 20 percent in 1994. Exhibit 7 shows the regional distribution of unemployment in 1975 and 1994.

The Costs of Unemployment Economists worry about unemployment because it has serious implications for economic growth. Not only are there the direct losses of

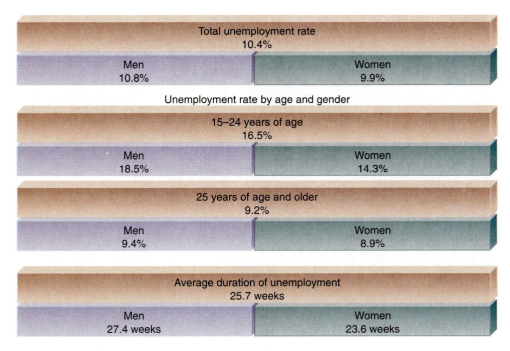

EXHIBIT 6   Unemployment Rate by Subcategories, 1994

Unemployment isn't all the same. This exhibit gives you a sense of some of the categories of unemployment.

Source: *Statistics Canada,* CANSIM Database, March 1995.

EXHIBIT 7   Regional Unemployment in Canada, 1975 and 1994

	1975	1994
Canada	6.9%	10.4%
Newfoundland	14.0	20.4
Prince Edward Island	8.0	17.0
Nova Scotia	7.7	13.3
New Brunswick	9.8	12.5
Quebec	8.1	12.2
Ontario	6.3	9.6
Manitoba	4.5	9.2
Saskatchewan	2.9	7.0
Alberta	4.1	8.6
British Columbia	8.5	9.4

Source: *Statistics Canada, CANSIM* Database, March 1995.

output and income from those who want to work, but there are also other costs to unemployment. Perhaps the most obvious cost is the decline in human capital (acquired knowledge and education). As new production processes and innovations occur, the job skills that once served the unemployed worker become obsolete (hence the focus on government retraining programs). Given the rate at which technological change is taking place, it doesn't take long for the unemployed to lose all of their job skills. This makes them much less attractive to potential employers.

Other costs to unemployment are less tangible but equally important. The social costs of unemployment are high—increasing rates of crime and the breakdown of the family, just to mention two. We've all heard stories about unemployed heads of families who commit suicide in the mistaken belief that their families would be better off with the insurance. The loss of self-respect and dignity can lead to destructive behaviour, further taxing society. That's why governments worry so much about unemployment. We'll come back to a lot of these issues in later chapters.

6   Three important costs of unemployment are lost output, a decline in human capital, and a frayed social fabric.

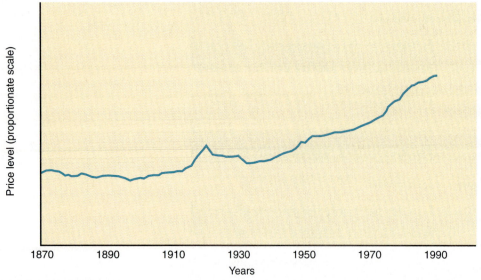

EXHIBIT 8

(a) This figure shows the GDP deflator on a proportionate scale for the period 1870–1994. The GNP deflator is used from 1870–1925.
(b) This figure shows the annual rate of change of the GDP deflator.
Source: *Statistics Canada*, CANSIM Database, March 1995.

(a) Price Level, 1870–94

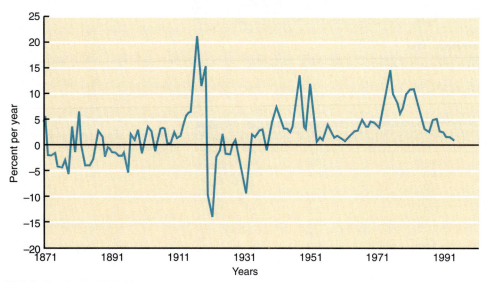

(b) Inflation Rate, 1871–94

INFLATION

7A Inflation is a continual rise in the price level.

Inflation A continual rise in the price level.

1D Since World War II, the Canadian inflation rate has almost always remained positive.

Inflation is a continual rise in the price level. The price level is an index of all prices in the economy. Even when inflation isn't roaring and inflation itself isn't a problem, the fear of inflation guides macroeconomic policy. Fear of inflation prevents governments from expanding the economy and reducing unemployment. It prevents governments from using macroeconomic policies to lower interest rates. It gets some political parties booted out of office.

A one-time rise in the price level is not inflation. Unfortunately, it's often hard to tell if a one-time rise in the price level is going to stop, so the distinction blurs in practice, but we must understand the distinction. If the price level goes up 10 percent in a month, but then remains constant, the economy doesn't have an inflation problem. Inflation is an *ongoing rise* in the price level.

From 1871 until World War II, the Canadian inflation rate fluctuated, as we see in Exhibit 8 (a), which shows historical movements of the price level. Since World War II the price level has continually risen, which means the inflation rate (the measure of the change in prices over time) has been positive, as can be seen in Exhibit 8 (b). (One exception—in early 1995 the price level actually fell, making the inflation rate negative.) The rate at which the price level rises fluctuates, but the movement has been consistently upward.

EXHIBIT 9   Consumer Price Index:
Expenditure Weights

Item	1986=100	1982=100
Food	18.05	20.02
Housing	36.32	38.14
Clothing	8.69	8.37
Transportation	18.29	15.75
Health and personal care	4.20	4.02
Recreation, reading, and education	8.84	8.25
Tobacco products and alcoholic beverages	5.60	5.45

Source: *Statistics Canada*, 62–010.

Measurement of Inflation

Since inflation is a sustained rise in the general price level, one must first determine what the general price level was at a given time and then decide how much it has changed. Because there are a number of different ways of doing this, there are a number of different measures of the price level. The most often used are the Industrial Products Price Index, the GDP deflator, and the Consumer Price Index. Each has certain advantages and disadvantages.

Published monthly, the **Consumer Price Index (CPI)** is the index of inflation most often used in news reports about the economy. As opposed to measuring the prices of all goods, it measures the prices of a fixed "basket" of goods that consumers buy, weighting each component of the basket according to its share of an average consumer's expenditures. Exhibit 9 shows the relative percentages. As you can see, housing, transportation, and food make up the largest percentages of the CPI. To illustrate the concepts behind the construction of the CPI, let's think about how you would construct a consumer price index for a hypothetical economy.

Consumer Price Index (CPI)   Index of inflation measuring prices of a fixed "basket" of consumer goods, weighted according to each component's share of an average consumer's expenditures.

Suppose it's 1996 and you've just been named Chief Economist for the Republic of Wombatia. One of your first assignments from the Prime Minister is to construct a consumer price index. You must first decide what a "representative household" looks like—say you decide that household includes two adults, four kids, two dogs, eight pigs, and a mule. Now you need to determine from survey data the proportion of that representative household's expenditures spent on things like food, shelter, clothing, and entertainment (just to name a few). Say you take a survey and find :

Item	Share in Household Expenditures, 1996
Food	25%
Clothing	15
Shelter	50
Entertainment	10

Now you have the expenditure shares. All you need to do next is find out what the prices of the different items are, and you're home free. But there are many, many stores in the Republic, and you cannot visit each one to find out what they charge for each item in the consumer's basket, so you take another survey and sample prices from a number of stores, and construct an average price for each item. Let's say you find:

Item	Average Price, 1996
Food	$ 1,000.00
Clothing	300.00
Shelter	10,000.00
Entertainment	200.00

To construct the consumer price index for the representative household in the Republic, you need to weight each average price by the expenditure share, and then add up the figures:

$$\text{Consumer prices} = \text{Share of food} \times \text{average food price}$$
$$+ \text{Share of clothing} \times \text{average clothing price}$$
$$+ \text{Share of shelter} \times \text{average shelter price}$$
$$+ \text{Share of entertainment} \times \text{average entertainment price}$$

or, using our numbers,

$$\text{Consumer prices} = (0.25 \times \$1,000.00) + (0.15 \times \$300.00) + (0.50 \times \$10,000)$$
$$+ (0.10 \times \$200)$$

$$\text{Consumer prices} = \$250.00 + \$45.00 + \$5,000.00 + \$20 = \$5,315$$

8 An index number is an average that captures change over time, usually in relation to a base year figure of 100. It is used to construct price indexes like the consumer price index.

Index number An average that captures change over time, usually in relation to a base year figure of 100. Used to construct price indexes like the consumer price index.

Base year The year against which all comparisons are made.

But wait—we're not done yet. What we have now is the price of a basket of consumer goods in 1996. We need to convert this to an **index number**—that's a number that allows us to easily compare the prices of a basket of consumer goods over time. Typically we construct an index number so that it takes on the value of 100 in what we call the **base year**—the year against which we compare all subsequent prices. So, if we continue with our previous example and assume we want 1996 to be the base year, we could divide the price of the consumer basket by $5,315 and multiply by 100 to put consumer prices in terms of that index number concept. We'd have a value of 100 for 1996:

$$\text{CPI} = 100 \times \left(\frac{\$5,315}{\$5,315}\right) = 100$$

Why do we want an index number rather than a dollar figure? Say next year the Queen wanted to know what happened to consumer prices over the year—did they go up or down? Assuming the expenditure shares didn't change during the year, you would run another survey to find out what the 1997 prices of the goods were. Let's suppose you found that all prices had doubled:

Item	Average Price, 1997
Food	$ 2,000.00
Clothing	600.00
Shelter	20,000.00
Entertainment	400.00

Constructing the price of the consumer basket as we did before, you'd get:

$$\text{Consumer prices} = (0.25 \times \$2,000.00) + (0.15 \times \$600.00) + (0.50 \times \$20,000)$$
$$+ (0.10 \times \$400)$$

$$\text{Consumer prices} = \$500.00 + \$90.00 + \$10,000.00 + \$40 = \$10,630$$

Dividing by the value of consumer prices in 1996 (since 1996 is the base year), we'd obtain a CPI of 200. This index number is interpreted as "consumer prices in 1997 were twice as high as they were in 1996". If we went through the whole exercise again in 1998 and calculated the CPI to be 234, we would interpret this as saying that a bundle of consumer goods in 1998 cost 2.34 times as much as an identical bundle cost in 1996.

Periodically, Statistics Canada revises the expenditure weights used to construct the Canadian Consumer Price Index, since the introduction of new products and changes in tastes for certain goods alter the way that we spend our income. We need to take those factors into account when we construct an index of consumer prices (think of constructing the CPI back in the 1960s when households bought more furs and fewer computers relative to today—if you kept 1960s expenditures shares when constructing your CPI today, your estimate of the cost of a basket of consumer goods would be way off).

GDP deflator Index of the price level of aggregate output or the average price of the components in GDP relative to a base year.

The total output deflator, or **GDP deflator** (gross domestic product deflator), is an index of the price level of aggregate output or the average price of the components in total output (known as GDP), relative to a base year.[1] It's the inflation index econ-

---

[1] We'll discuss why total output is called GDP in the next chapter.

INDEX NUMBERS AND THE CONSUMER PRICE INDEX

We said the price level is an index of all prices in an economy. Let's look at the Consumer Price Index (CPI) as an example of an index number.

Statistics Canada periodically surveys households to get an idea of the proportion of total expenditures made on things like transportation, shelter, food, and other components of spending. This information is used when Statistics Canada constructs summary measures of what it costs the representative household to buy their usual "bundle" of goods every month. They take the prices of the goods in the bundle, weigh them by their share of total household spending, and when this is done for all goods in the household's basket, they arrive at an index of consumer prices.

There are several things we need to note about this process. The first is that when we price the goods in the basket, we are using prices as of a particular date. This gives us a reference point for use in measuring how the price of the basket of consumer goods is changing over time. For example, if we base prices as of January 1996, and if we don't change the expenditure shares in the index, any changes in the cost of the basket will be due solely to changes in prices.

The second point we need to remember is that the bundle of consumer goods that makes up the CPI basket really doesn't reflect your family's consumption bundle (unless yours is the representative household). That means when you look at the inflation rate based on changes in the CPI, you can't really say that the cost of your bundle of goods is changing at the same rate. Any one household's basket of goods can be changing at a rate that's either above or below the change in the CPI.

Why does this matter? Well, during the 1970s when inflation was high and variable, workers and firms decided to index wages to changes in the CPI. These cost-of-living adjustments (COLA) usually allowed wages to rise once a year, based on the most recent 12-month change in the CPI. In theory, this should protect a household from inflation, since its income is rising at the same rate as consumer prices. For example, if the bundle of goods costs $100 in 1996, and between 1996 and 1997 there had been 10 percent inflation based on the change in the CPI, a 10 percent increase in income should allow it to buy the same bundle, now priced at $110.

As we'll see in later chapters, there are a number of reasons to suspect that wage indexation will not lead to perfect protection from inflation. For now, we'll just point out one obvious problem. If the cost of your household's bundle rises at a slower rate than the representative household's, COLA clauses make you better off, since your income rises proportionately more than the price of your bundle of goods. On the other hand, if the cost of your bundle of goods rises faster than that of the representative household, you're worse off, since the COLA didn't adjust your salary enough to allow you to buy your original bundle.

The final point we want to make is based on the fact that new products evolve quickly, and if the CPI bundle of goods doesn't keep up, it won't be reflective of the representative household's expenditure patterns. Think of VCRs, microwaves, CD players, and computers. All of these goods were once very expensive, but now prices are so low that at least one is in almost every household. If the weights used to construct the CPI don't change as the representative household changes its expenditure patterns, the CPI won't be a useful measure of the cost of a bundle of consumer goods. As well, the CPI can't adequately account for the evolving quality of goods and services. Similar arguments can be made with respect to the Industrial Products Price Index.

---

omists generally favour because it includes the widest number of goods. Unfortunately, since it's difficult to compute, it's published only quarterly and with a fairly substantial lag. (That is, by the time the figures come out, the period the figures measure has been over for quite a while.)

The **Industrial Products Price Index (PPI)** is an index or ratio of a composite of prices of a number of important raw materials and semi-finished goods relative to a composite of the prices of those raw materials and goods in a base year. It does not correctly measure actual inflation, but it does give an early indication of which way inflation will likely head since many of its components are the prices of raw materials used as inputs in the production of other goods.

Measuring changes in prices over time is difficult. One of the most vexing price indexing problems is how to include quality changes. For example, say 1996 cars have a new style and, unlike 1995 models, provide airbags as a standard feature. They cost 15 percent more. Has the price of cars really gone up 15 percent, or is the 15 percent simply the cost of improving cars' design and equipment? There are ways to answer these questions, but none are totally satisfactory. With significant changes in goods' quality occurring every year, most economists don't worry about small amounts of inflation (1 or 2 percent), because it's not even certain such small changes actually represent inflation.

Industrial Products Price Index (PPI)
An index or ratio of a composite of prices of a number of important raw materials and semi-finished goods.

EXHIBIT 10   A Simple Example of Real GDP, Nominal GDP, and the GDP Deflator

Commodity	1996 Price	Quantity	1997 Price	Quantity
Ladders	$10.00 ea.	10	$10.50	11
Bananas	1.00/kg	250 kg	1.07/kg	268 kg
Radios	2.50 ea.	20	3.61 ea.	16

1996
Nominal GDP ($10 × 10) + ($1 × 250) + ($2.50 × 20) = $400
Real GDP ($10 × 10) + ($1 × 250) + ($2.50 × 20) = $400

1997
Nominal GDP ($10.50 × 11) + ($1.07 × 268) + ($3.61 × 16) = $460
Real GDP ($10 × 11) + ($1 × 268) + ($2.50 × 16) = $418

$$\text{GDP deflator} = 100 \times \frac{\text{Nominal GDP}}{\text{Real GDP}} = 100 \times \frac{\$460}{\$418} = 110.04$$

Real and Nominal Concepts

Real output The total amount of goods and services produced, adjusted for price level changes.

Nominal output Output as measured, without any adjustments.

One important way in which inflation indices are used is to separate changes in real output from changes in nominal output. **Real output** is the total amount of goods and services produced, adjusted for changes in the price level. It is the measure of output that would exist if we valued today's physical production at prices in some base period. **Nominal output** values today's physical production at current prices. To move between nominal and real measures of GDP we use the GDP deflator. Let's look at a couple of examples, and, to make things easy, let's first assume that total output consists of only three goods: ladders, bananas, and radios.

Exhibit 10 provides information on production and prices in our hypothetical economy. We have data for 1996 and 1997, and we want to determine what real and nominal output were in each year. To do this we first need to choose a base period at which to price physical production; let's pick 1996. Nominal output in 1996 is just the sum of the products of the price of a ladder and the number of ladders produced, the price of bananas and the number of bananas produced, and the price of radios and the number of radios produced. That is, we are valuing 1996 production at 1996 prices. (Note that since 1996 is the base year for calculating real output, nominal output and real output are the same. This is necessarily true only in the base year.) In 1997 nominal output is much higher than real output, since the prices of all goods rose. Physical production of ladders and bananas went up in 1997, but radio output fell from 20 to 16. How much of the increase in nominal output was due to changes in physical production? Looking at real output will tell us, since it "controls" for changes in prices. When we value 1997 production at 1996 prices (the base year), we find that real output has risen. The ratio of nominal output to real output times 100 gives us the GDP deflator—it's how we deflate nominal output to arrive at real output. In this example the GDP deflator has gone from 100 to 110.04. This means output is 10.04 percent more expensive in 1997 relative to 1996. This example shows us that real and nominal GDP are the same in the base year 1996. In 1997 nominal output rose by $60, but only $18 of that $60 was due to a change in physical production. The other $42 resulted from higher prices.

Let's look at another example. Say total output rises in one year from $400 billion to $500 billion. Nominal output has risen by

$$\frac{\$500 \text{ billion} - \$400 \text{ billion}}{\$400 \text{ billion}} = \frac{\$100 \text{ billion}}{\$400 \text{ billion}} = 25\%.$$

Let's say, however, the price level has risen 20 percent, from 100 to 120. Because the price level has increased, real output (nominal output adjusted for inflation) hasn't risen by 25 percent; it has risen by less than nominal output has increased. To determine how much less, we use our formula to adjust the nominal figures to account for inflation. This is called *deflating* the nominal figures. To deflate we divide the most recent nominal figure, $500 billion, by 1.20 (prices are 20 percent higher):

$$\text{Real output} = \frac{\text{Nominal output}}{1.20} = \frac{\$500 \text{ billion}}{1.2} = \$416.7 \text{ billion.}$$

That $416.7 billion is the measure of output that would have existed if the price level had not changed. What output would have been if the price level had remained constant is the definition of real output, so $416.7 billion is the measure of real output. Real output has increased from $400 billion to $416.7 billion, or by $16.7 billion.

When you consider price indexes, you mustn't lose sight of the forest for the trees. Keep in mind the general distinction between real and nominal GDP. The concepts *real* and *nominal* and the process of adjusting from nominal to real by dividing the nominal amount by a price index will come up again and again. So whenever you see the word *real,* remember:

The "real" amount is the nominal amount divided by the price index. It is the nominal amount adjusted for inflation.

7B   The "real" amount is the nominal amount divided by the price index. It is the nominal amount adjusted for inflation.

Why Does Inflation Occur?

Inflation results when more people on average raise their nominal prices than lower their nominal prices. Thus, to explain why inflation occurs we must explain why people raise their nominal prices. The logical answer is that they believe that in doing so they can get a larger slice of the total output pie for themselves. But shares of the pie are determined by relative, not nominal, prices. To see the difference, say you raise your nominal price by 10 percent, but everyone else does, too. So the prices of the goods you sell go up by 10 percent and the prices of the goods you buy go up by 10 percent. Your nominal price has gone up, but your relative price has not, and you're no better off.

Our economy has nominal wage- and price-setting institutions in which people set their relative prices by setting a nominal price. This means that if we are careful, we can gain insight into inflation by considering a representative market and distinguishing two reasons for individuals wanting to raise their relative price (which, given our price-setting institutions, they do by raising their nominal price).

To see this distinction, think back to Chapter 2's discussion of the dynamic laws of supply and demand. There we saw that a gap between the quantity demanded and the quantity supplied leads to upward pressure on price. Exhibit 11 (a) demonstrates this for an individual market. If price is initially P_0 and demand rises from D_0 to D_1, there will be upward pressure on the good's price. When the majority of markets in the economy experience increases in demand, we say there's demand-pull pressure, and the inflation that results is called **demand-pull inflation.** Where does this increase in demand come from? It can come from numerous sources, but many economists focus on government's demands and increases in the money supply as important causes of increases in demand in markets on average.

Demand-pull inflation   Inflation resulting from the pressure exerted when the majority of markets in the economy experience increases in demand.

When demand is high, from an independent perspective, a price increase enlarges a person's share. But if overall demand is high, and everyone raises their nominal price, that nominal price increase does not increase a person's share. Overall nominal prices rise, and hence the price level rises, but relative prices are little affected.

Demand-pull inflations are generally characterized by shortages of goods and shortages of workers. Because there's excess demand, firms know that if they raise their prices, they'll still be able to sell their goods, and workers know if they raise their wages, they will still get hired.

Demand-pull pressure can be a catalyst for starting inflation; it is not a cause of continued inflation. If aggregate demand-pull pressure continues unabated even as prices rise, the inflation will quickly blow up into an ever-increasing inflation as expectations of rising price levels cause people to raise their nominal price even more in order to have a desired relative price increase. Remember, Exhibit 11 is a graph of one individual market; it refers to a relative price. If all people are trying to raise their relative prices by raising their nominal prices, everyone will expect the price level to rise, and will raise their prices even more. The demand-pull pressure will quickly generate an accelerating expectational inflation. Societies don't want that to happen, so

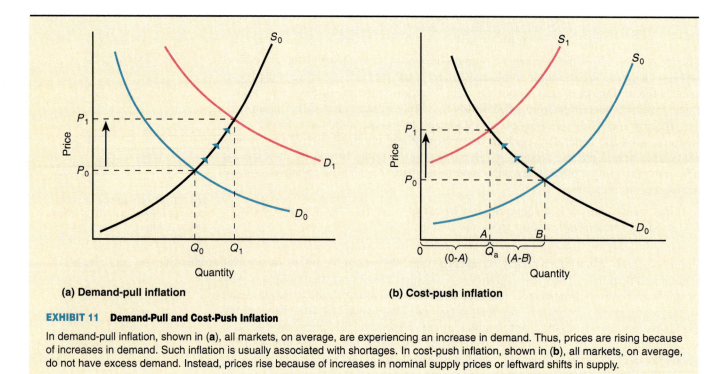

EXHIBIT 11   Demand-Pull and Cost-Push Inflation

In demand-pull inflation, shown in (**a**), all markets, on average, are experiencing an increase in demand. Thus, prices are rising because of increases in demand. Such inflation is usually associated with shortages. In cost-push inflation, shown in (**b**), all markets, on average, do not have excess demand. Instead, prices rise because of increases in nominal supply prices or leftward shifts in supply.

9A   Cost-push inflation involves a rise in the price level resulting from restrictions on supply due to some sort of legal or social pressure. When excess demand causes the price level to rise, it is referred to as demand-pull inflation.

Cost-push inflation   Inflation resulting from the pressure exerted when a significant proportion of markets (or one very important market) experiences restrictions on supply.

while excess demand may be an explanation of the start of inflation, it is not an explanation of ongoing inflation.

Exhibit 11 (b) shows a second possible explanation why people might raise their price in an individual market. Say one group of individuals (0–A) figured out a way to limit the quantity supplied to Q_a. To do so, they must keep suppliers A–B out of the market through some type of legal or social pressure. If they succeed, price rises from P_0 to P_1 as supply shifts to the left. When a significant proportion of markets (or one very important market, such as the labour market or the oil market) experience restrictions on supply, we say that there is cost-push pressure. The resulting inflation is called **cost-push inflation.**

In cost-push inflation, because there is no excess demand (there may actually be excess supply), firms are not sure there will be sufficient demand to sell off their goods, and all workers are not sure that, after raising their wage, they will all be hired, but the ones who actually do the pushing are fairly sure they won't be the ones who can't sell off their goods or the ones fired. A classic cost-push example occurred in the 1970s when OPEC raised its price on oil, triggering cost-push inflation.

The demand-pull/cost-push distinction is helpful as long as one remembers that it must be used with care. The price level is always determined by both demand pressures and cost pressures. In all inflations, both demand-pull and cost-push pressures play a role. As Alfred Marshall (the 19th-century English economist who originated supply and demand analysis) said, it is impossible to separate the roles of supply and demand in influencing price, just as it is impossible to separate which blade of the scissors is cutting a sheet of paper. Both sides always play a role.

To see the difficulty, let's consider the OPEC oil price rise. What would have happened if all prices rose but total quantity demanded did not rise? The result would have been unemployment, a fall in production, and a decrease in the demand for oil. Prices, on average, wouldn't have continued to rise as demand fell. But prices on average *did* continue to rise because total demand did not stay constant—it rose significantly for reasons that we'll discuss in later chapters. So some economists called it demand-pull inflation rather than cost-push inflation. Since inflation is an ongoing rise in prices and, in any ongoing rise, both demand and supply play a role, the cost-push/demand-pull distinction must be used carefully.

A second helpful distinction is between expected and unexpected inflation. **Expected inflation** is inflation people expect to occur. **Unexpected inflation** surprises people.

To see why this expected/unexpected distinction is important, remember when an individual sets a price (for goods or labour) he or she is actually setting a relative price—relative to some price level that they expect to exist out there. The dynamic laws of supply and demand affect relative prices, not nominal prices. Now let's say everyone suddenly expects the price level to rise 10 percent. Let's also say that all individual sellers want a 1/2 percent raise in their relative price. They're not greedy; they just want a little bit more than what they're currently getting.

The reason expectations of inflation are important is the relative price increase people want must be tacked onto the inflation they expect. When people expect a 10 percent inflation, in order to have a 1/2 of 1 percent rise in their relative price, they have to raise their money price by 10-1/2 percent—10 percent to keep up and 1/2 percent to get ahead. Ten percent of the inflation is caused by expectations of inflation; 1/2 percent of the inflation is caused by cost-push pressures. The cost-push/demand-pull distinction concerns what causes the 1/2 percent pressure. The expected/unexpected distinction refers to the cause of that 10 percent inflation. Thus, whether or not inflation is expected makes a big difference in individuals' behaviour. If people expect inflation, they'll raise their prices to get ahead or to keep up. They won't do that for unexpected inflation, because of course they don't know unexpected inflation is coming.

Since prices and wages are often set for periods of two months to three years ahead, whether inflation is expected can play an important role in the inflation process. In the early 1970s people didn't expect the high inflation rates that did occur. When inflation hit, people just tried to keep up with it. By the end of the 1970s, people expected more inflation than actually occurred and raised their prices—and, in doing so, caused the inflation rate to increase.

Expectations of inflation play an important role in any ongoing inflation. They can snowball a small inflationary pressure into an accelerating large inflation. Individuals keep raising their prices because they expect inflation, and inflation keeps on growing because individuals keep raising their prices. That's why expectations of inflation are of central concern to economic policy makers.

Inflation has costs, but not the costs that noneconomists often associate with it. Specifically, inflation doesn't make the nation poorer. True, whenever prices go up somebody (the person paying the higher price) is worse off, but the person to whom the higher price is paid is better off. The two offset each other. So inflation does not make the society on average any poorer. Inflation does, however, redistribute income from people who cannot or do not raise their prices to people who can and do raise their prices. This often creates feelings of injustice about the economic system. Thus, inflation can have significant distributional or equity effects.

This is easy to see if you think about lending money to your brother-in-law. If you expect inflation to be about 5 percent over the period of the loan, you'll want your brother-in-law to pay you back what he has borrowed *plus 5 percent*. That extra 5 percent will allow you to buy your original bundle of goods—you went without that bundle so your brother-in-law could borrow your money. Now you want to buy your bundle and it costs 5 percent more, so it's only fair that your brother-in-law compensates you for expected inflation. The problem is that you set the interest rate on the loan *when he borrows the money*—not when he pays it back. That means that if you both thought inflation would be 5 percent but it actually turns out to be 10 percent, your brother-in-law isn't providing you full compensation for inflation. He's only paying you 5 percent, when he should be paying 10 percent. You can't buy your original bundle—he's better off (since he got away with paying less than full inflation protection), and you're worse off. His gain is your loss (but then, he did marry your sister!). There's been a redistribution of wealth as a result of unexpected inflation. Economists summarize this by saying that *unexpected inflation benefits debtors.*

A second cost of inflation is its effect on the information content of prices.

Expected and Unexpected Inflation

9B   Expected inflation is the amount of inflation that people expect. Unexpected inflation is a surprise to them.

Expected inflation   Inflation people expect to occur.

Unexpected inflation   Inflation that surprises people.

Costs of Inflation

A REMINDER ✔

THE COSTS OF INFLATION

Inflation is a problem, but we need to differentiate between the costs of expected and unexpected inflation. When inflation is unexpected, workers and firms end up making decisions that they later regret. That's because they didn't factor into their plans the change in the price level.

In addition, when inflation becomes high and variable, people attempt to predict the inflation rate, and they'll enter into contracts based on their expectations. If those expectations aren't realized, another round of bad decisions will have been made. That's the cost of imperfectly anticipated inflation. Even when inflation is expected, if it is relatively high it can lead to hyperinflation; money breaks down as a medium of exchange, since no one will be willing to be paid in a currency that doesn't keep its value between the factory floor and the supermarket.

Finally, think of how inflation affects people on fixed incomes. Say your grandparents retired in the early 1970s when inflation was relatively low. They decided to take their pension in the form of a stream of fixed payments that they thought would be enough to satisfy their needs, even in the face of a small rate of inflation (say, less than 2 percent). Then inflation skyrocketed beyond anyone's wildest dreams—and what looked good as a retirement income 25 years ago won't even pay this month's rent. People on fixed incomes—generally the elderly—end up losing from inflation.

---

10 While inflation may not make the nation poorer, it does cause income to be redistributed, and it can reduce the amount of information that prices are supposed to convey.

Consider an individual who laments the high cost of housing, pointing out that it has doubled in 10 years! But if inflation averaged 7 percent a year over the past 10 years, a doubling of housing prices should be expected. In fact, with 7 percent inflation, on average *all* prices double every 10 years. That means the individual's wages have probably also doubled, so he or she is no better off and no worse off than 10 years ago. The price of housing relative to other goods, which is the relevant price for making decisions, hasn't changed. When there's inflation it's hard for people to know what is and what isn't a relative price. People's minds aren't computers, so inflation reduces the amount of information that prices can convey and causes people to make choices that do not reflect relative prices.

Despite these costs, inflation is usually accepted by governments as long as it stays at a low rate. What scares economists are inflationary pressures above and beyond expectations of inflation (for example, if the money supply is increasing at a fast rate). In that case, expectations of higher inflation can cause inflation to build up and compound itself. A 3 percent inflation becomes a 6 percent inflation, which in turn becomes a 12 percent inflation. Once inflation hits 5 percent or 6 percent, it's definitely no longer a little thing. Inflation of 10 percent or more is significant. While there is no precise definition, once inflation hits triple digits—100 percent or more—it is reasonable to say that it has become a **hyperinflation.**

Hyperinflation Inflation that hits triple digits (100 percent) or more.

Canada has been either relatively lucky or wise because it has not experienced hyperinflation (the United States experienced it during their Civil War—1861–1865). Other countries, such as Brazil, Israel, and Argentina, have not been so lucky. These countries have frequently had hyperinflations. But even with inflations at these levels, economies have continued to operate and, in many cases, continued to do well.

In a hyperinflation people try to spend their money quickly, but they still use the money. Let's say the Canadian price level is increasing 1 percent a day, which is a yearly inflation rate of about 4,000 percent.[2] Is an expected decrease in value of 1 percent per day going to cause you to stop using dollars? Probably not, unless you have a good alternative. You will, however, avoid putting your money into a savings account unless that savings account somehow compensates you for the expected inflation (the expected fall in the value of the dollar), and you will try to ensure your wage

---

[2]Why about 4,000 percent and not 365 percent? Because of compounding. In the second day the increase is on the initial price level *and* the 1 percent rise in price level that occurred the first day. When you carry out this compounding for all 365 days, you get almost 4,000 percent.

is adjusted for inflation. In a hyperinflation, wages, the prices firms receive, and individual savings are all in some way adjusted for inflation. Hyperinflations lead to economic institutions with built-in expectations of inflation. For example, usually in a hyperinflation the government issues indexed bonds whose value keeps pace with inflation.

Once these adjustments have been made, substantial inflations will not destroy an economy, but they certainly are not good for it. Such inflations tend to break down confidence in the monetary system, the economy, and the government.

THE INTERRELATIONSHIP OF GROWTH, INFLATION, AND UNEMPLOYMENT

In this chapter, we've talked about growth, inflation, and unemployment. Before we move on, let's briefly address their interrelationship. That interrelationship centres on trade-off between inflation on the one hand and growth and unemployment on the other. If the government could attack inflation without worrying about unemployment or growth, it probably would have solved the problem of inflation by now. Unfortunately, solving inflation often worsens unemployment and slows growth. When the government tries to stop inflation, it often causes a recession—increasing unemployment and slowing growth. Similarly, reducing unemployment by stimulating growth tends to increase inflation. To the degree that inflation and unemployment are opposite sides of the coin, the opportunity cost of reducing unemployment is inflation. The government must make a trade-off between low unemployment and slow growth on the one hand and inflation on the other.

CHAPTER SUMMARY

- The secular trend growth rate of the economy is about 3 percent. Fluctuations around the secular trend growth rate are called *business cycles.*
- Two important causes of growth are appropriate economic incentives and people.
- Phases of the business cycle include peak, trough, upturn, and downturn.
- The target rate of unemployment is the lowest sustainable rate of unemployment possible under existing institutions. It's associated with an economy's potential income. The lower the target rate of unemployment, the higher an economy's potential income.
- The microeconomic approach to unemployment subdivides

unemployment into categories and looks at those individual components.
- A real concept is a nominal concept adjusted for inflation.
- Inflation is a continual rise in the price level. Both cost-push and demand-pull pressures play a role in any inflation.
- Expectations of inflation can provide pressure for an inflation to continue even when other causes don't exist.
- For inflation to continue, it must be accompanied by an increase in the money supply.
- Two important costs of inflation are an equity cost and an information cost.

KEY TERMS

base year *(152)*
boom *(138)*
business cycle *(136)*
capacity utilization rate *(139)*
Classicals *(143)*
coincidental indicators *(139)*
Consumer Price Index (CPI) *(151)*
cost-push inflation *(156)*
cyclical unemployment *(141)*
demand-pull inflation *(155)*
depression *(138)*
diffusion index *(138)*
discouraged workers *(146)*
downturn *(138)*

expansion *(138)*
expected inflation *(157)*
frictional unemployment *(142)*
full employment *(142)*
GDP deflator *(152)*
growth-compatible institutions *(133)*
human capital *(135)*
hyperinflation *(158)*
index number *(152)*
Industrial Products Price Index (PPI) *(153)*
inflation *(150)*
Keynesians *(143)*
Labour Force Survey *(145)*

leading indicators *(139)*
nominal output *(154)*
Okun's rule of thumb *(147)*
potential output *(139)*
real output *(154)*
recession *(138)*
social capital *(135)*
structural readjustments *(143)*
structural unemployment *(141)*
target rate of unemployment *(139)*
unemployment rate *(138)*
unexpected inflation *(157)*

QUESTIONS FOR THOUGHT AND REVIEW

The number after each question represents the estimated degree of critical thinking required (1 = almost none; 10 = deep thought).

1. An economist has just made an argument that rules should be followed because they're rules. Which kind of economist is this person: Keynesian or Classical? Why? *(This question uses material from the section introduction.)* *(7)*

2. If unemployment fell to 1.2 percent in World War II, why can't it be reduced to 1.2 percent in the 1990s? *(8)*

3. The index of leading indicators has predicted all past recessions. Nonetheless it's not especially useful for predicting recessions. Explain. *(7)*

4. Distinguish between structural unemployment and cyclical unemployment. *(3)*

5. Does the unemployment rate underestimate or overestimate the unemployment problem? Explain. *(5)*

6. If unemployment rises 2 percent, what will likely happen to income in Canada? *(7)*

7. Why are expectations central to understanding inflation? *(5)*

8. Inflation, on average, makes people neither richer nor poorer. Therefore it has no cost. True or false? Explain. *(7)*

9. Who would be more likely to see a psychiatrist: a Keynesian economist or a Classical economist? Why? *(This question uses material from the section introduction.)* *(8)*

10. Would you expect that inflation would generally be associated with low unemployment? Why? *(7)*

PROBLEMS AND EXERCISES

1. The following questions require library research.
   a. What are the current unemployment rate, capacity utilization rate, and rate of inflation? What do you predict they will be next year?
   b. Find some predictions for each of these figures for next year.
   c. Are these predictions consistent with your predictions? Why?
   d. In what position on the business cycle does the economy currently find itself?

2. The following questions concern statistics and economic institutions.
   a. Go to the local unemployment office and ask to see the form people fill out to collect unemployment insurance. What are the eligibility criteria?
   b. A friend shows you a newspaper article saying unemployment increased but output also increased. He says that this doesn't make sense and it must be a mistake. What do you tell your friend?
   c. Inflation rose 5 percent; real output rose 2 percent. What would you expect to happen to nominal output?
   d. Real output rose 3 percent and nominal output rose 7 percent. What happened to inflation?

3. Congratulations! You've just been named chief economist in Wombatia. The queen would like you to construct an index of consumer prices for use in adjusting wages throughout the land. There are only three consumer goods (with no prospects for new products on the horizon): hot dogs, cheese, and paper towels (they're messy eaters). The queen's statistician provides you with the following table:

Year	Prices		
	Cheese	Hot Dogs	Paper Towels
1996	$2/kg	$4/kg	$1/roll
1997	3/kg	3/kg	2/roll
1998	4/kg	5/kg	3/roll

She also tells you that cheese makes up 40 percent of total household expenditures while hot dogs make up 50 percent of total spending. The statistician also tells you that her method of guessing what's been happening to consumer prices is flawless, and that the general price level actually fell between 1996 and 1997. Is she right?

4. In H.G. Wells's *Time Machine,* a late Victorian time traveller arrives in England in A.D. 802700 to find a new race of people, the Eloi, in their idleness. Their idleness is, however, supported by another race, the Morlocks, who are underground slaves and who produce the output. If technology were such that the Elois' lifestyle could be sustained by machines, not slaves, is it a lifestyle that would be desirable? What implications does the above discussion have for unemployment?

5. Suppose Japanese workers' average tenure with a firm is 10.9 years, whereas in Canada the average tenure of workers is 6.7 years.
   a. What are two possible explanations for these differences?
   b. Which system is better?
   c. In the mid-1990s Japan has experienced a recession while the Canadian economy has been growing. What effect will this likely have on these ratios?

6. One quarter prior to the peak in a business cycle, what is most likely happening to the following indicators (up or down)?
   a. Average workweek
   b. Employees on nonagricultural payrolls
   c. Industrial production
   d. Net change in inventories on hand
   e. New business formation
   f. Personal income minus transfer payments

National Income Accounting

The government is very keen on amassing statistics . . . They collect them, add them, raise them to the nth power, take the cube root, and prepare wonderful diagrams. But you must never forget that every one of these figures comes in the first instance from the village watchman, who just puts down what he damn pleases.

~ Sir Josiah Stamp
(head of Britain's revenue department in the late 19th

After reading this chapter, you should be able to:

1 State why national income accounting is important.

2 Define GDP, GNP, NDP, NDI, and NNI.

3 Calculate GDP in a simple example, avoiding double counting.

4 Explain why GDP = C + I + G + (X − M).

5 Distinguish between real and nominal values.

6 State some limitations of national income accounting.

Before you can talk about macroeconomics in depth, you need to be introduced to some terminology used in macroeconomics. That terminology can be divided into two parts. The first part deals with national income accounting, which was specifically developed to handle macroeconomic aggregate concepts (concepts embodying a number of components). Examples include total consumption, total income, and the price level.

Real concepts Concepts adjusted for inflation.

The second part distinguishes between real and nominal (or money) concepts. As we discussed in an earlier chapter, **real concepts** are concepts adjusted for inflation; **nominal concepts** are concepts specified in monetary terms with no adjustment for inflation. Real and nominal concepts are used to differentiate and compare goods and actions over time.

Nominal concepts Economic concepts specified in monetary terms (current dollars) with no adjustment for inflation.

In the 1930s, it was impossible for macroeconomics to exist in the form we know it today because many aggregate concepts of macroeconomics we now take for granted either had not yet been formulated or were so poorly formulated that it was useless to talk rigorously about them. This lack of aggregate terminology was consistent with the Classical economists' lack of interest in the aggregate approach in the 1930s; they preferred to focus on microeconomics.

NATIONAL INCOME ACCOUNTING

1   National income accounting enables us to measure and analyze how much the nation is producing and consuming.

With the advent of Keynesian macroeconomics in the mid-1930s, development of a terminology to describe macroeconomic aggregates became crucial. Measurement is a necessary step towards rigor. A group of Keynesian economists set out to develop an aggregate terminology and to measure the aggregate concepts they defined, so that people would have concrete terms to use when talking about macroeconomic problems. Their work (for which two of them, Simon Kuznets and Richard Stone, received the Nobel prize) is called **national income accounting** (a set of rules and definitions to use in measuring activity in the aggregate economy—that is, in the economy as a whole). To talk about the aggregate economy without knowing the concepts of national income accounting is equivalent to talking about cricket without knowing what a wicket is, or to talk about rock music without knowing U2.

National income accounting A set of rules and definitions for measuring economic activity in the aggregate economy.

National income accounting provides a way of measuring total, or aggregate, economic production. In national income accounting, aggregate economic production is broken down into subaggregates (such as consumption, investment, and personal income); national income accounting defines the relationship among these subaggregates. In short, national income accounting enables us to measure and analyze how much the nation is producing and consuming.

Learning national income accounting is necessary. Before you play Chopin, you must learn to play scales, and before you fiddle with the aggregate economy, you must learn national income accounting.

Measuring Total Economic Output of Goods and Services

2A   *Gross domestic product (GDP)* Aggregate final output of residents and businesses in an economy in a one-year period.

A firm generally measures how busy it is by how much it produces. To talk about how well the aggregate economy is doing, national income accounting uses a corresponding concept, aggregate output, which goes under the name **gross domestic product (GDP).**

GDP is the total market value of all final goods and services produced in an economy in a one-year period. It's probably the single most-used economic measure. When economists, journalists, and other analysts talk about the economy, they continually discuss GDP—how much it has increased or decreased, and what it's likely to do. In deciding whether a change in GDP means a growth in real output, we must take account of inflation (the rise in prices of goods on average). If we don't, we won't know whether output has really risen.

2B   *Gross national product (GNP)* Aggregate final output of citizens and businesses of an economy in a one-year period.

Gross National Product and Gross Domestic Product   Whereas *gross domestic product* measures the economic activity that occurs *within a country,* **gross national product (GNP)** measures the economic activity of the citizens and businesses *of a country.* So the economic activity of Canadian citizens working abroad is counted in Canadian GNP but isn't counted in Canadian GDP. Similarly for the foreign economic activity of Canadian companies. However, the income of a Mexican or German person or

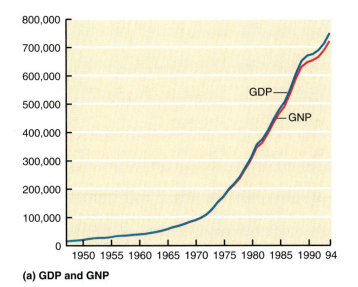

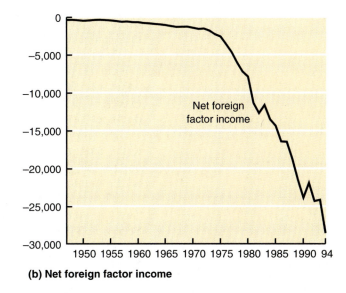

(a) GDP and GNP

(b) Net foreign factor income

EXHIBIT 1   Canadian GDP, GNP, and Net Foreign Factor Income

In (**a**) we see that nominal GDP in Canada has exceeded nominal GNP for some time. This is consistent with what we see in (**b**)—net foreign factor income has been consistently negative.

business working in Canada isn't counted in Canadian GNP but is counted in Canadian GDP. Thus, GDP describes the economic output within the physical borders of a country while GNP describes the economic output produced by the citizens of a country. To move from GDP to GNP one must add **net foreign factor income** to GDP. Net foreign factor income is defined to be the difference between the income Canadians earn from the foreign use of their factors of production, and the income that foreigners earn from the use of their factors in the production of goods and services in Canada. Put another way, one must add the foreign income of one's citizens and subtract the income of residents who are not citizens.

Net foreign factor income   Income from foreign domestic factor sources minus foreign factor incomes earned domestically.

For many countries there's a significant difference between GNP and GDP. For example, consider Kuwait. Its citizens have significant foreign income—income that far exceeds the income of the foreigners in Kuwait. This means that Kuwait's GNP (the income of its citizens) far exceeds its GDP (the income of its residents). For the United States, foreign output of U.S. businesses and people for the most part offsets the output of foreign businesses and people within the United States. And in Canada, nominal GDP in 1994 was $749 billion while nominal GNP was $720 billion As Exhibit 1 (a) demonstrates, Canadian GDP is much higher than its GNP. Net foreign income in Canada has been negative for some time, as illustrated by Exhibit 1 (b).

Aggregate final output (GDP) consists of millions of different services and products: apples, oranges, computers, haircuts, financial advice. . . . To arrive at total output, somehow we've got to add them all together into a composite measure. Say we produced 7 oranges plus 6 apples plus 12 computers. We have not produced 25 comapplorgs. You can't add apples and oranges and computers. You can only add like things (things that are measured in the same units). For example, 2 apples + 4 apples = 6 apples. If we want to add unlike things, we must convert them into like things. We do that by multiplying each good by its *price*. Economists call this *weighting* the importance of each good by its price. For example, if you have 4 pigs and 4 horses and you price pigs at $200 each and horses at $400 each, the horses are weighted as being twice as important as pigs.

Calculating GDP

Multiplying the quantity of each good by its market price changes the terms in which we discuss each good from a quantity of a specific product to a *value* measure of that good. For example, when we multiply 6 apples by their price, 25¢ each, we get

$1.50; $1.50 is a value measure. Once all goods are expressed in that value measure, they can be added together.

Take the example of seven oranges and six apples. (For simplicity let's forget the computers, haircuts, and financial advice.) If the oranges cost 50¢ each, their total value is $3.50; if the apples cost 25¢ each, their total value is $1.50. Their values are expressed in identical measures, so we can add them together. When we do so, we don't get 13 orples; we get $5 worth of apples and oranges.

If we follow that same procedure with all the final goods and services produced in the economy in the entire year, multiplying the quantity produced by the price per unit, we have all the economy's outputs expressed in units of value. If we then add up all these units of value, we have that year's gross domestic product.

There are two important aspects to remember about GDP. First, GDP represents a flow (an amount per year), not a stock (an amount at a particular moment of time). Second, GDP refers to the market value of *final* output. Let's consider these statements separately.

GDP Is a Flow Concept   In economics it's important to distinguish between flows and stock. Say a student just out of college tells you she earns $8,000. You'd probably think, "Wow! She's got a low-paying job!" That's because you implicitly assume she means $8,000 per year. If you later learned that she earns $8,000 per week, you'd quickly change your mind. The confusion occurred because how much you earn is a *flow* concept; it has meaning only when a time period is associated with it—so much per week, per month, per year. A *stock* concept is the amount of something at a given point in time. No time interval is associated with it. Your weight is a stock concept. You weigh 150 pounds; you don't weigh 150 pounds per week.

GDP is a flow concept, the amount of total final output a country produces per year. The *per year* is often left unstated, but it is important to keep in your mind that it's essential. GDP is usually reported quarterly or every three months, but it is reported on an *annualized basis,* meaning that Statistics Canada, which compiles GDP figures, uses quarterly figures to estimate total output for the whole year.

The stock equivalent to the national income accounts would be the national balance sheet accounts—a balance sheet of an economy's stock of assets and liabilities. These provide a measure of the national wealth, including residential and non-residential structures, inventories, machinery and equipment, and durable goods and land. Statistics Canada publishes information on national wealth every year.

GDP Measures Final Output   As students in our first economics class, we were asked to tell how to calculate GDP. We said, "Add up the value of the goods and services produced by all the companies in Canada to arrive at GDP." We were wrong (which is why we remember it). Many goods produced by one firm are sold to other firms, which use those goods to make something else. GDP doesn't measure total transactions in an economy; it measures *final output.* When one firm sells products to another firm for use in production of yet another good, the first firm's products aren't considered final output. They're **intermediate products** (products used as inputs in the production of some other product). To count intermediate goods as well as final goods as part of GDP would be to double count them. An example of an intermediate good would be wheat sold to a cereal company. If we counted both the wheat (the intermediate good) and the cereal (the final good) made from that wheat, the wheat would be double counted. Double counting would significantly overestimate final output.

If we did not eliminate intermediate goods, a change in organization would look like a change in output. Say one firm that produced steel merged with a firm that produced cars. Both together then produce exactly what each did separately before the merger. Final output hasn't changed, nor has intermediate output. The only difference is that the intermediate output of steel is now internal to the firm. Using only each firm's sales of goods to final consumers (and not sales to other firms) in one's measure of GDP prevents mere changes in organization from affecting the measure of output.

Intermediate products   Products of one firm used in some other firm's production of another firm's product.

Participants	Cost of Materials	Value of Sales	Value Added	Row
Farmer	$ 0	$ 100	$100	1
Cone factory and ice cream maker	100	250	150	2
Middleperson (final sales)	250	400	150	3
Vendor	400	500	100	4
Totals		$1,250	$500	5

EXHIBIT 2   Value Added Approach Eliminates Double Counting

Two Ways of Eliminating Intermediate Goods   There are two ways to eliminate intermediate goods from the measure of GDP. One is to calculate only final output (goods sold to consumers). To do so, firms would have to separate goods they sold to consumers from intermediate goods used to produce other goods. For example, each firm would report how much of its product it sold to consumers and how much it sold to other producers for use that year in production of other goods; one would eliminate the latter to exclude double counting.

A second way to eliminate double counting is to follow the **value added** approach. Value added is the increase in value that a firm contributes to a product or service. It is calculated by subtracting from the value of its sales the cost of materials that a firm uses to produce a good or service. For instance, if a firm buys $100 worth of thread and $10,000 worth of cloth and uses them in making 1,000 pairs of jeans which are sold for $20,000, the firm's value added is not $20,000; it is $9,900 ($20,000 in sales minus the $10,100 in intermediate goods that the firm bought). Exhibit 2 provides another example.

Say we want to measure the contribution to GDP made by a vendor who sells 200 ice cream cones at $2.50 each (they're good cones) for total sales of $500. The vendor bought his cones and ice cream from a middleperson at a cost of $400, who in turn paid the cone factory and ice cream maker a total of $250. The farmer who sold the cream to the factory got $100. Adding up all these transactions, we get $1,250, but that includes intermediate goods. Either by counting only the final value of the vendor's sales, $500, or by adding the value added at each stage of production (column 3), we eliminate intermediate sales and arrive at the street vendor's contribution to GDP of $500.

Value added is calculated by subtracting the cost of materials from the value of sales, leaving only the value added at each stage of production. The aggregate value added at each stage of production is, by definition, precisely equal to the value of final sales, since it excludes all intermediate products. In Exhibit 2, the equality of the value added approach and the final-sales approach can be seen by comparing the vendor's final sales of $500 (row 4, column 2) with the $500 value added (row 5, column 3).

Calculating GDP: Some Examples   To make sure you understand what value added is and what makes up GDP, let's consider some sample transactions and determine what value they add and whether they should be included in GDP. Let's first consider second-hand sales: When you sell your two-year-old car, how much value has been added? The answer is none. The sale involves no current output, so there's no value added. If, however, you sold the car to a used-car dealer for $2,000 and he resold it for $2,500, $500 of value has been added—the used-car dealer's efforts transferred the car from someone who didn't want it to someone who did. We point this out to remind you that GDP is not only a measure of the production of goods; it is a measure of the production of goods *and services.*

Now let's consider a financial transaction. Say you sell a bond (with a face value of $1,000) that you bought last year. You sell it for $1,200 and pay $100 commission to the dealer through whom you sell it. What value is added to final output? You might be tempted to say that $200 of value has been added, since the value of the bond has increased by $200. GDP, however, refers only to value that is added as the result of

Value added   The contribution that each stage of production makes to the final value of a good.

3   To avoid double counting, you must eliminate intermediate goods, either by calculating only final output (expenditures approach), or by calculating only final income (income approach) by using the value added approach.

production, not to changes in the values of financial assets. Therefore the price at which you buy or sell the bond is irrelevant to the question at hand. The only value that is added by the sale is the transfer of that bond from someone who doesn't want it to someone who does. Thus, the only value added as a result of economic activity is the dealer's commission, $100. The remaining $1,100 (the $1,200 you got for the bond minus the $100 commission you paid) is a transfer of an asset from one individual to another, but such transfers do not enter into GDP calculations. Only production of goods and services enters into GDP.

Let's consider a different type of financial transaction: The government pays an individual pension benefits. What value is added? Clearly no production has taken place, but money has been transferred. As in the case of the bond, only the cost of transferring it—not the amount that gets transferred—is included in GDP. This is accomplished by including in GDP government expenditures on goods and services, but not the value of government transfers. Thus, government pension payments, welfare payments, and veterans' benefits do not enter into calculations of GDP.

Now let's consider the work of a house-spouse. How much value does it add to economic activity in a year? Clearly if the house-spouse is any good at what he or she does, a lot of value is added. Taking care of the house and children is hard work. Estimates of the yearly value of a house-spouse's services are often in the $35,000 to $45,000 range. Even though much value is added and hence, in principle, house-spouse services should be part of GDP, by convention a house-spouse contributes nothing to GDP. GDP measures only *market activities;* since house-spouses are not paid, their value added is not included in GDP. This leads to some problems in measurement. For example, suppose a woman divorces her house-spouse and then hires him to continue cleaning her house for $20,000 per year. Then he will be contributing $20,000 value added. That, since it is a market transaction, is included in GDP.

There are other activities that aren't included in our national accounts. The underground economy consists of economic activities that are unreported. When you pay your friend to fix your car, the chances are she won't report it as income. When your cousin Fred finishes your basement, he may not claim the money you pay him in return. Some estimates of the size of the underground economy in Canada put it between 3 and 15 percent of GDP! Statistics Canada's numbers don't include these activities.

Illegal activities like gambling and trade in illicit drugs are also excluded from the official statistics. So are measurements of positive and negative externalities—for instance, environmental damage, and the value of additional leisure time.

These examples show that the GDP measure has some problems. There are other areas in which it also has problems, but since this is an economics text, not an accounting text, we won't go into those problems. What's important for an introductory economics student to remember is that numerous decisions about how to handle various types of transactions had to be made to get a workable measure. Some of those decisions could have gone the other way, but, overall, the terminology of national income accounting is a model of consistency. It focuses on measuring final market output for the entire economy.

TWO METHODS OF CALCULATING GDP

The National Income Accounting Identity

GDP can be calculated in two ways: the expenditures method and the income method. This is because of the *national income accounting identity.*

National income accounting is a form of accounting to which you were introduced in Chapter 4. Accounting is a way of keeping track of things. It is based on certain identities; for a firm, its cost plus profit equals revenues because they are identical to revenues. National income accounting is no different. It too is based on an identity. By definition, whenever a good or service (output) is produced, somebody receives an income for producing it. This relationship between output and income, the **national**

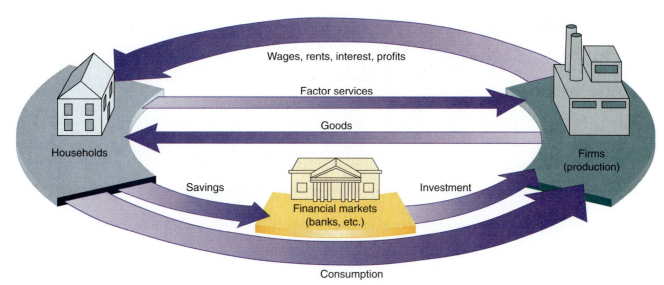

EXHIBIT 3   The Circular Flow

One of the most important insights about the aggregate economy is that it is a circular flow in which output and input are interrelated. Households' expenditures (consumption and savings) are firms' income; firms' expenditures (wages, rent, etc.) are households' income.

income accounting identity, can be seen in Exhibit 3, which illustrates the circular flow of income in an economy.[1]

In Exhibit 3 we see that as firms produce goods, they create income in the form of wages, rents, interest, and profits (the top flow). Consumers either spend or save their income. Their spending comes back to the firms in the form of consumption (consumers buy firms' output) or, if they save their income, in the form of investment (firms borrow the savings and buy other firms' output), assuming financial markets can translate those savings into investment.

The value of the wages, rents, interest, and profits (the flow along the top in Exhibit 3) equals the value of goods bought (the flow along the bottom). How are these values kept exactly equal? That's the secret of double-entry bookkeeping: output must always equal income.

Profit is defined as what remains after all other income (wages, rent, and interest) is paid out. For example, say a firm has a total output of $800 and that it paid $400 in wages, $200 in rent, and $100 in interest. The firm's profit is determined by subtracting that income paid out from the value of total output. Profit equals $800 − $700 = $100. That profit is the income of the owners of the firm. All income (determined by adding profits to wages, rent, and interest) equals $800, which, not surprisingly, equals the value of the output.

The accounting identity even works if a firm incurs a loss. Say that instead of paying $400 in wages, the firm paid $700, along with its other payments of $200 in rent and $100 in interest. Total output is still $800, but total income, excluding profits, is now $1,000. *Profits* are still defined as total output minus income paid out in wages, rent, and interest. Profits in this example are negative: $800 − $1,000 = (−$200). There's a *loss* of $200. Adding that loss to other income ($1,000 + (−$200)) gives total income of $800—which is identical to the firm's total output of $800.

The national income accounting identity (total output = total income) allows us to calculate GDP either by adding up all values of final outputs (the *expenditures approach*) or by adding up the values of all earnings or income (the *income approach*).

National income accounting identity
The relationship between output and income: Whenever a good or service is produced, somebody receives an income for producing it.

---

[1] An *identity* is a statement of equality that's "true by definition." In algebra, an identity is sometimes written as a triple equal sign ≡.

ADDED DIMENSION

NATIONAL INCOME ACCOUNTING AND DOUBLE-ENTRY BOOKKEEPING

The key to all accounting, including national income accounting, is double-entry book-keeping, a system of financial record keeping invented in Italy and attributed to Luigi Pacioli (1494). Double-entry bookkeeping is based on redundancy. It requires that account-ing terms be defined in such a way that the cost side of the ledger is kept exactly equal to the income side. Since they're exactly equal, in theory one need calculate only one of the two sides, but in practice both sides are calculated, so the accountant can check his or her work. If both sides independently add up to the same figure, it's likely that no mistake was made.

In the national income accounts kept by Statistics Canada, the two sides of the ledger are the expenditure accounts and the income accounts. Every entry on one side of the accounts has an offsetting entry on the other side. Whenever production (an increase in output) takes place on the expenditure side, there is a simultaneous increase in income entered on the income side.

As discussed in Chapter 4, in balance sheet accounting (accounting measuring the assets and liabilities of an individual, firm, or country), assets equal liabilities plus net worth. Net worth plays the swing role in balance sheet accounting that profits play in income accounting. *Net worth* is defined as the amount that remains when liabilities are subtracted from assets:

$$\text{Net worth} = \text{Assets} - \text{Liabilities.}$$

Net worth is recorded on the liabilities side of the ledger. Adding liabilities and net worth, we have

$$\text{Assets} = \text{Liabilities} + \text{Net worth.}$$

Substituting in for net worth, we have

$$\text{Assets} = \text{Liabilities} + (\text{Assets} - \text{Liabilities})$$

or

$$\text{Assets} = \text{Assets.}$$

Since by substituting we can get the same term on both sides of the equation, the statement "Assets = Liabilities + Net worth" is true by definition.

In national income accounting, profit plays the swing role. Profits are what is left after all other forms of income are accounted for. *Profits* are defined as the difference between total output and other income and are counted as income. So we have

$$\text{Output} = \text{Other income} + \text{Profits}$$

$$\text{Profits} = \text{Output} - \text{Other income.}$$

Substituting in for profits gives

$$\text{Output} = \text{Other income} + \text{Output} - \text{Other income.}$$

Therefore,

$$\text{Output} = \text{Output.}$$

This 17th-century engraving by Rembrandt, "The Money Lender", shows that careful bookkeeping and accounting have been around for a long time. *Bleichroeder Print Collection, Baker Library, Harvard Business School.*

As with most issues in accounting, there are certain conceptual difficulties in applying seemingly reasonable definitions. In this instance, the difficulty is what to do when two economies are interrelated with individuals and businesses of one country producing in another country so that a distinction must be made between GDP and GNP. Although, by definition, expenditures must equal income, there's a question of whose income whose expenditures must equal. As we've already discussed, in Canada the difference between GDP and GNP is significant. It's important to keep the dis-tinction in mind so that with either the expenditures approach or the income approach one arrives at the same result.

Let's consider these two approaches in detail.

The Expenditures Approach

Exhibit 4 gives the categories of expenditures normally used in the expenditures approach to calculating Canadian GDP: personal consumption expenditures, gross

Nominal GDP	Expenditures (billions)	Percent of GDP
Personal consumption	$453	61%
Government purchases of goods and services	159	23
Investment	122	16
Exports	249	33
Imports	−244	−33
Total	$749	100%

EXHIBIT 4   Nominal GDP via the Expenditures Approach, 1994

Source: *Statistics Canada*, CANSIM Database, March 1995.

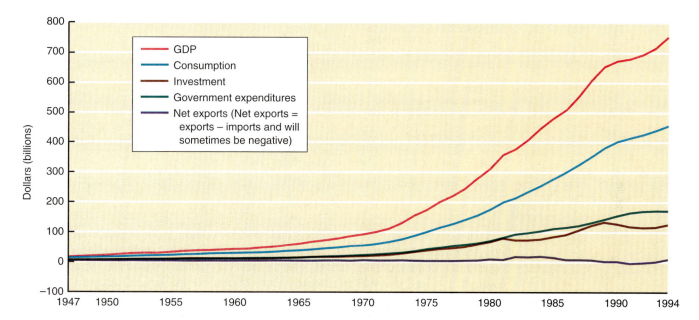

EXHIBIT 5   Movements of Canadian GDP since 1947

This exhibit demonstrates the approximate movement of GDP and its components since 1947. As you can see, GDP tends to rise overall each year.

private investment, government purchases, and net exports. All expenditures fall into one or another of these four divisions, so by adding up these four categories, we get total expenditures on Canadian goods and services minus Canadian residents' expenditures on foreign goods. By definition, in national income accounting those expenditures on Canadian goods and services equal the total amount of production of goods and services (GDP).

Gross domestic product is equal to the sum of these four categories of expenditures:

$$GDP = C + I + G + (X - M)$$

where

C = Consumption
I = Investment
G = Government expenditures
$(X - M)$ = Net exports.

Exhibit 5 demonstrates movements in nominal Canadian GDP and its component parts since 1947. As you can see, the individual parts fluctuate in relative importance. Of the components, investment fluctuates most; personal consumption expenditures fluctuate least. Let's consider each component in turn.

4 $GDP = C + I + G + (X - M)$ is an accounting identity because it is defined as being true.

EXHIBIT 6   **Breakdown of Nominal Consumer Expenditures, 1994**

	Dollars (billions)	Percent of Expenditures
Durable goods,	$ 61	14%
of which:		
Motor vehicles	31	
Furniture and		
appliances	12	
Semi-durable goods,	41	9
of which:		
Clothing and footwear	24	
Nondurable goods,	115	25
of which:		
Food	46	
Motor fuel and lubricants	13	
Electricity and other fuels	17	
Services,	236	52
of which:		
Gross rent	91	
Restaurants and hotels	29	
Net expenditures abroad	3	
Total consumption	$453	100%

Source: *Statistics Canada,* CANSIM database, March 1995.

Consumption Expenditure (C)   All goods and services bought by households are lumped together under "consumption." This huge category includes such purchases as your visit to the dentist, college tuition, and the new car you buy, as well as all actual and estimated "rents" for existing homes. Consumption is the largest category in GDP, accounting for about 60 percent of the total.

Being so large, consumption is normally broken down into subcategories: durable consumer goods, nondurable consumer goods, and services. **Durable goods** are defined as goods expected to last more than one year. (Why one year? Because one year, although arbitrary, is a reasonable cutoff point.) Durables include cars and household appliances. **Nondurable goods** are goods that last less than one year. The food you eat and the movie tickets you buy fall under this heading. **Semi-durable goods** include things like clothing and footwear—they last, but not as long as you'd sometimes like. **Services** are activities done for another person (cutting hair, teaching, and mowing a lawn). They are a form of economic activity, but they do not involve production or sale of goods. Exhibit 6 breaks down these subcategories of consumer expenditures into subsubcategories.

Durable goods   Goods expected to last more than one year.

Nondurable goods   Goods that last less than one year.

Semi-durable goods   Goods expected to last up to about a year.

Services   Activities done for other people not involving the production or sale of goods. Examples include cutting hair, teaching, and lawn-mowing.

Gross and Net Private Investment (I)   Investment is expenditures by firms or households on goods, often called *capital goods,* that are used over and over to make products or provide services. Housing, tractors, steel mills, and wine barrels are examples. Thus, when economists speak of investment they don't mean the kind of activity taking place when individuals buy stocks or bonds—economists consider that saving, not investing. Gross private investment, the third-largest category, makes up about 16 percent of GDP. Exhibit 7 breaks down investment into two subcategories: fixed investment and change in business inventory. Fixed investment is, by far, the larger component. It includes investments in residential and nonresidential buildings and in equipment.

Change in business inventory ("inventory investment" for short) is a different form of investment. It's the increase or decrease in the value of the stocks of inventory that businesses have on hand. Notice we said "increases in the *value* of inventory." Say a car dealership normally keeps 50 cars in stock. Its inventory is 50 cars. In

	Dollars (billions)	Percent of Investment
Construction:		
Residential	$ 45	37%
Nonresidential	33	27
Machinery and equipment	44	36
Total	$122	100%
Inventory investment	3	
Total including inventory change	$125	

Source: *Statistics Canada,* CANSIM database, March 1995.

EXHIBIT 7   Nominal Investment, 1994

1996 it increases its stock of cars to 55. Its inventory investment for 1996 is 5 cars times their value. If inventory remains constant from one year to the next, there's no inventory investment. If inventories fall, inventory investment is negative.

Inventory investment is highly volatile. Drawing implications from an increase in inventory investment is difficult, because a change in inventory investment can mean two different things. When firms expect to sell a lot, they usually produce significant amounts for inventory, so an increase in inventory investment may signal expected high sales. But inventory can also increase because goods the firm produces aren't selling. In that case, an increase in inventory investment signals unexpected low sales. Those five extra cars are just sitting on the dealer's lot. Thus, economists keep a close eye on inventory investment as well as on why inventory investment has changed.

Sooner or later, assets such as plants and equipment wear out or become technologically obsolete. Economists call this wearing out process **depreciation** (the decrease in an asset's value). Depreciation is part of the cost of producing a good; it is the amount by which plants and equipment decrease in value as they grow older. Much of each year's private investment involves expenditures to replace assets that have worn out. For example, as you drive your car, it wears out. A car with 80,000 kilometres on it is worth less than the same type of car with only 1,000 kilometres on it. The difference in value is attributed to depreciation.

Depreciation Decrease in an asset's value.

To differentiate between total or gross investment and the new investment that's above and beyond replacement investment, economists use the term **net private investment** (gross investment minus depreciation). Economists pay close attention to net private investment because it gives an estimate of the increase in the country's productive capacity.

Net private investment Gross investment minus depreciation.

Government Purchases (G) Government purchases are divided into federal expenditures and provincial and municipal expenditures. In macroeconomics, the main focus is on the federal government because only the federal government is directly concerned with the aggregate economy. This doesn't mean provincial and local government expenditures don't affect the economy; they do, as do any expenditures. It simply means that provincial and local governments generally don't take that effect into account since each is relatively small compared to the total economy.

Government uses its tax revenue to build bridges, buy copying machines, print application forms, pay the Prime Minister, and meet innumerable other expenses. Many of these government goods and services are paid for from general tax revenue and are provided free to consumers of the goods or services. As a result, they have no price at which to value them. By convention, economists value these goods and services at cost. Thus, if the federal government spends $300 billion on defence, government spending on defence is valued at $300 billion.

Total government purchases account for about 23 percent of GDP. Exhibit 8 breaks down purchases by various levels of government.

EXHIBIT 8   Breakdown of Nominal Government Expenditures, 1994

	Dollars (billions)	Percent of Category
Federal	$169	
Goods and services	32	19
Transfers	97	57
Interest on public debt	40	24
Provincial	166	
Goods and services	49	30
Transfers	93	56
Interest on public debt	24	14
Local	57	
Goods and services	47	82
Transfers	5	9
Interest on public debt	5	9
Hospitals	24	
Goods and services	23	96
Transfers	0.5	2
Interest on public debt	0.5	2

Source: *Statistics Canada*, CANSIM Database, March 1995.

Transfer payments Payments by government to individuals that are not in payment for goods or services.

General-purpose transfers Payments from the federal government to provincial and local governments meant to reduce disparities between "have" and "have not" provinces.

Special-purpose transfers Payments from the federal government to provincial and local governments for funding social spending on health care, welfare, and post-secondary education.

Notice that provincial and local governments make more purchases than does the federal government, and federal government expenditures total $169 billion. Each year the federal government budget is much larger than these federal government purchases that enter into GDP. The reason is that the remaining part of the federal government budget involves **transfer payments** (payments made to individuals that *aren't* payment for a good or service). Since they're simply a transfer, not a purchase of a good or service, they don't contribute to GDP. The largest of these transfers is for social security programs.

Fiscal relations between the provinces and the federal government are set by formal agreements and acts of Parliament. Many of these agreements involve tax collection and federal-provincial transfers. In the 1995 Federal Budget, the Government of Canada announced its intention to change its funding arrangements with the provinces, beginning in 1996. At that time, provinces will receive a block of funds out of which to pay for the programs they provide, rather than receive grants based on the existing system of transfer agreements. In 1995 the block funding arrangements were still being negotiated between the different levels of government, so it's hard to say what the final system will look like. Let's briefly touch on the transfer programs that were in effect as of early 1995.

General-purpose transfers attempt to provide for an equal distribution of income across the country. Equalization payments are aimed at providing comparable levels of government service in every province. Payments are based on a formula that is revised every five years. Provinces whose revenues are below the representative average, on a per capita basis, receive additional funding from the federal government. In 1993, Newfoundland, Prince Edward Island, Nova Scotia, New Brunswick, Quebec, Manitoba, and Saskatchewan received equalization payments. **Special-purpose transfers** are intended to fund social program spending, health care, social welfare, and post-secondary education. Since transfer payments are an important component of government spending, we will look at these programs in greater detail in the chapter devoted to deficits and debt. For now, you should remember that transfer payments are not included in our measures of GDP.

Net Exports (X − M) Some goods and services produced in Canada (such as wheat, computers, and vacations) are bought by people in foreign countries. Other goods and services (such as French champagne and taxi rides in London) are bought from foreign

EXHIBIT 9   Breakdown of GDP for Selected Countries

Country	Nominal GDP 1992 (U.S. $ in billions)	Personal consumption (% of GDP)	Gross private investment (% of GDP)	Government expenditures (% of GDP)	Exports (% of GDP)	Imports (% of GDP)	(−% of GDP)
Brazil	$ 369	61%	22%	12%	9%	− 5%	
Germany	1,389	55	19	18	37	−29	
Japan	2,468	57	24	17	10	− 8	
Pakistan	48	74	19	12	14	−19	
Tunisia	14	79	24	15	26	−44	
Tanzania	7	85	19	10	6	−20	

countries by Canadian residents. If these exports and imports are equal, they net out and make no contribution to GDP. If the value of what Canada sells to foreign countries is greater than what it buys from foreign countries, Canada is producing more than it is spending. In this case net exports (exports minus imports) are positive, and the difference between exports and imports must be added to GDP, since the increase represents net foreign expenditure on Canadian-produced goods. It's Canadian production bought by foreigners, but Canadian production nonetheless.

If Canada buys more from foreign countries than it sells to them, imports exceed exports, so net exports are negative. In this case, Canadian spending is more than Canadian production. Since GDP measures production, not spending, the excess of imports over exports must be subtracted from Canadian GDP. If it weren't subtracted, we couldn't measure production by measuring expenditures. To some degree, imports and exports offset each other. However, as we said in Chapter 5, if we include both goods and services, imports have significantly exceeded exports in Canada for some time. In 1994 Canada exported $249 billion while imports were $244 billion, leading to net exports of $5 billion.

Summing Up the Components   Now that we've gone through the components, let's put them all together. Exhibit 9 shows rough estimates of the relative sizes of the components for six countries.

GDP and NDP   In the discussion of investment, we differentiated gross investment from net investment. Gross investment minus depreciation equals net investment. Economists have created another aggregate term, **net domestic product (NDP),** to reflect the adjustment to investment because of depreciation. NDP is the sum of consumption expenditures, government expenditures, net exports, and net investment (gross investment − depreciation). Thus,

$$GDP = C + I + G + (X - M)$$
$$NDP = C + (\text{net } I) + G + (X - M).$$

NDP takes depreciation into account, and depreciation is a cost of producing goods; so NDP is actually preferable to GDP as the expression of a country's domestic output. However, measuring true depreciation (the actual decrease in an asset's value) is difficult because asset values fluctuate. In fact, it's so difficult that in the real world accountants don't try to measure true depreciation, but instead use a number of conventional rules of thumb that yield an accepted figure. In recognition of this reality, economists call the adjustment made to GDP to arrive at NDP the **capital consumption allowance** rather than depreciation. Since estimating depreciation is difficult, GDP rather than NDP is generally used in discussions.

As we stated in the last chapter, to separate increases in GDP caused by inflation from increases in GDP that represent real increases in production and income, economists distinguish between **nominal GDP** (GDP calculated at existing prices) and **real GDP** (nominal GDP adjusted for inflation). This distinction is sufficiently important to warrant repetition in this chapter. To adjust nominal output for inflation we create a

2C NDP equals GDP minus depreciation.

Net domestic product (NDP)   GDP adjusted to take account of depreciation.

Capital consumption allowance   Also known as depreciation, the amount by which the capital stock is estimated to have fallen in a year.

5 A real concept is a nominal concept adjusted for inflation.

Real and Nominal GDP

Nominal GDP   GDP calculated at existing prices.
Real GDP   Nominal GDP adjusted for inflation.

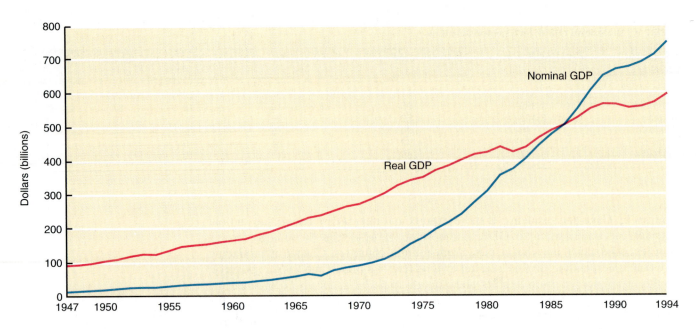

EXHIBIT 10   Real and Nominal GDP in Canada

Nominal GDP values production at current prices whereas real GDP values production at base period prices. Nominal GDP equals real GDP in the base year (1986).

Source: *Statistics Canada,* CANSIM Database, March 1995.

price index (a measure of how much the price level has risen from one year to the next) and divide nominal GDP by that price index.[2]

For example, say the price level rises 10 percent (from a price index of 1 to a price index of 1.1) and nominal GDP rises from $400 billion to $460 billion. Ten percent of that rise in nominal GDP represents the 10 percent rise in the price level. If you divide nominal GDP, $460 billion, by the new price level index, 1.1, you get $418 billion (the amount GDP would have been if the price level had not risen). That $418 billion is called real GDP. To decide whether production has increased or decreased over time, we simply compare real income. In this example, real income has risen from $400 billion to $418 billion, so we can conclude that the real economy has grown by 18/400, or 4.5 percent.

Exhibit 10 shows the relationship between real GDP and nominal GDP in Canada since 1947. As you'll recall from Chapter 6, a price index (like the GDP deflator) has a base year against which all other values are compared. In 1995, real GDP used 1986 prices as this reference point.[3] When physical production is valued at 1986 prices, we get real GDP. When physical production is valued at current prices, we get nominal GDP. That's why the lines cross in 1986—the base year (a fact that escaped one of our graduate students once—much to his dismay).

Real GDP is what is important to a society because it measures what is really produced. Considering nominal GDP instead of real GDP can distort what's really happening. Let's say the Canadian price level doubled tomorrow. Nominal GDP would also double, but would Canada be better off? No.

We'll use the distinction between real and nominal continually in this course, so to firm up the concepts in your mind, let's go through another example. Consider Somalia in 1987 and 1988, when nominal GDP rose from 159 billion to 268 billion (measured in their local currency units) while the GDP deflator rose from 100 percent to 173.5 percent. Dividing nominal GDP in 1988 by the GDP deflator, we see *real*

---

[2]Now you know why the total output deflator is called the *GDP deflator.* It is an index of the rise in prices of the goods and services that make up GDP.

[3]As of late 1995, *Statistics Canada* plans to rebase to 1992 prices, in 1997.

	Dollars (billions)	Percent of Net Domestic Income Nominal at Factor Cost
Labour income	$413	73%
Corporate profits before taxes	56	10
Interest and investment income	57	10
Accrued net farm income	2	0
Unincorporated business income	39	7
Inventory valuation adjustment	−5	0
		100%
Net domestic income at factor cost	$572	

Source: *Statistics Canada*, CANSIM Database, March 1995.

EXHIBIT 11   Components of Nominal Net Domestic Income, 1994

GDP fell by over 2 percent. So not only did Somalia's economy not grow, it actually shrank.

The Income Approach

The alternative way of calculating GDP is the factor incomes approach. It measures nominal GDP by adding up the payments that firms make to households for the use of their labour and nonlabour services. Valuation at factor cost is meant to capture the producer's expenses rather than the purchaser's costs. Thus, estimates based at factor cost do not include indirect taxes (sales taxes), customs duties, or property taxes.

The factor incomes approach provides us with a measure of nominal **net domestic income (NDI) at factor cost.** If we add to this the capital consumption allowance, we arrive at nominal GDP at factor cost. When we add indirect taxes less subsidies, we have nominal GDP at market prices.

There are a number of other measures that are interesting. Working from NDI, if we add investment income received from nonresidents and subtract investment income paid to nonresidents, we arrive at **net national income (NNI) at factor cost.** If we add indirect taxes less subsidies and depreciation, we obtain nominal GNP at market prices.

All of this can be bewildering, so let's look at this in more detail. Net domestic income at factor cost (NDI) is the sum of the components shown in Exhibit 11:

Net Domestic Income at Factor Cost (NDI)   An income measure we arrive at using the factor incomes approach to national income accounting.

2D   NDI at factor cost is obtained under the factor incomes approach to measuring economic activity.

Net National Income (NNI)   A measure of a nation's output that excludes depreciation but includes net foreign income. The total income earned by citizens and businesses of a country, less depreciation.

Wages, Salaries, and Supplementary Labour Income

Exhibit 11 tells us that the total payment by firms to households for their labour services is the largest component of net domestic income. These payments include all wages and salaries and all fringe benefits (such as pension contributions) that firms pay to workers.

Corporate Profits before Taxes

Corporate profits before taxes are paid out to shareholders—households—as a dividend, or they are plowed back into the firm in the form of retained earnings.

Interest and Miscellaneous Investment Income

Exhibit 11 shows that interest and investment income has historically been the second-largest component of net domestic income. It measures the difference between total interest payments that households receive (on loans they have made) and the total interest payments that households make (on funds they have borrowed).

Farm and Nonincorporated Nonfarm Income

These components measure income from activities where the operator is actually the owner of the factors employed in the business. Trying to separate out payments on a detailed basis would be too difficult,

A REMINDER

A REVIEW OF THE EXPENDITURES AND FACTOR INCOME APPROACHES

We've covered a lot of definitions quickly, so a review is in order. GDP (the total output of the residents of a society) can be measured two ways: the expenditures approach and the factor incomes approach.

Under the expenditures approach,

$$GDP = C + I + G + (X - M)$$

Since much investment is replacement investment meant to cover depreciation, net domestic product is,

$$NDP = GDP - Depreciation$$

Under the factor incomes approach, net domestic income at factor cost is the sum of several components:

$$NDI = \text{wages and salaries plus supplementary labour income}$$
$$+ \text{ corporate profits before taxes}$$
$$+ \text{ interest and miscellaneous investment income}$$
$$+ \text{ farm and nonincorporated nonfarm income}$$
$$+ \text{ inventory adjustment}$$

GDP is obtained by adding indirect taxes less subsidies, and depreciation;

$$GDP \text{ at market prices} = NDI + \text{indirect taxes less subsidies} + \text{depreciation}$$

Net national income takes net domestic product at factor cost and adjusts for the difference between investment income from and to nonresidents. GNP at market prices adds indirect taxes (less subsidies) and depreciation to NNI. Personal income (PI) adjusts net national income for earned and unearned components of income. Personal disposable income subtracts personal taxes and property taxes.

Nominal GDP: 1994

Expenditures Approach		Income Approach	
Personal consumption expenditures	$453	Labour income	$413
Government expenditures	169	Corporate profits before taxes	56
Gross investment	122	Interest and investment income	57
Exports	249	Net farm income	2
Imports	244	Unincorporated business income	39
Nominal GDP	$749	Inventory adjustment	−5
		Net domestic income at factor cost	562
		Indirect taxes (less subsidies)	93
		Capital consumption allowance	94
		Nominal GDP	$749

so we simply add them together to measure incomes accruing to owner-operators. Rental income is included in this category.

Inventory Valuation Adjustment Gains and losses from holding inventories are included in corporate profits before taxes—when prices change, changes in the inventory book value and the value of the physical changes in inventories won't be equal. These effects need to be removed to measure current production.

How Do We Get Nominal GDP from Nominal Net Domestic Income at Factor Cost?

Net domestic income doesn't include the effects of indirect taxes (like sales taxes) on income, nor does it account for subsidies the government provides to certain producers (like those paid to dairy farmers). When we add the capital consumption allowance, we arrive at nominal GDP at factor cost.

$$\text{Nominal GDP at factor cost} = NDI + \text{Capital consumption allowance}$$

To arrive at GDP at market prices, we add indirect taxes less subsidies.

Three other often-used concepts deserving mention are net national income, personal income, and disposable personal income.

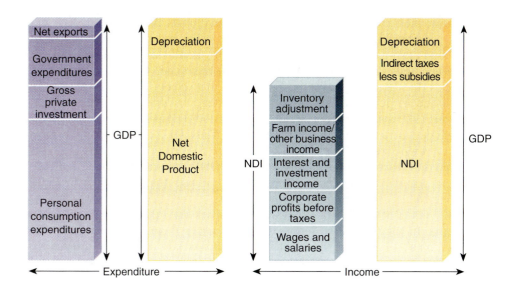

EXHIBIT 12   Two Methods for Calculating GDP

This exhibit demonstrates that both the expenditures approach and the income approach can be used to measure GDP.

Net national income (NNI) measures the total income earned by citizens and businesses of a country. We can obtain this by taking net domestic income at factor cost and accounting for the difference between investment income from and to nonresidents. This provides an estimate of NNI:

$$NNI = NDI + \text{Investment income from nonresidents}$$
$$- \text{Investment income to nonresidents}$$

GNP at market prices is obtained by adjusting NNI for indirect taxes less subsidies, and the capital consumption allowance;

$$GNP = NNI + \text{Indirect taxes less subsidies} + \text{Capital consumption allowance}$$

Net national product would be obtained by subtracting depreciation from GNP.

Personal income (PI) differs from national income because some income that is earned is not received (like pension and unemployment contributions), and some income that is received is not earned (like transfer payments). To obtain personal income we need to adjust national income for these effects. If we subtract personal income taxes, we arrive at **disposable personal income.** Since disposable personal income is what people have readily available to spend, economists follow it carefully.

Now that we have worked our way through two methods of calculating GDP, let's consider what GDP is used for and what it tells us. The most important way GDP figures are used is to make comparisons of one country's production with another country's and one year's production with another year's.

Most countries use somewhat similar measures to calculate GDP. Thus, we can compare various countries' GDP levels and get a sense of their economic size and power.

Per capita GDP is another measure often used to compare various nations' income. To arrive at per capita GDP, we divide GDP by the country's total population. Doing so gives you a sense of the relative standards of living of the people in various countries.

If you look up some of these measures, some of the comparisons should give you cause to wonder. For example, Bangladesh has per capita GDP of only about $300, compared to Canadian per capita GDP of about $20,000. How do people in Bangladesh live? In answering that question, remember GDP measures market transactions. In poor countries, individuals often grow their own food (subsistence

2E   NNI measures the total income earned by businesses and citizens of a country

Personal income (PI)   National income plus net transfer payments from government minus amounts attributed but not received.

Disposable personal income   Personal income minus personal income taxes and payroll taxes.

USING GDP FIGURES

Comparing GDP among Countries

farming), build their own shelter, and make their own clothes. None of those activities are market activities, and while they're sometimes estimated and included in GDP, they often aren't estimated accurately. They certainly aren't estimated at the value of what these activities would cost in Canada. Also, remember GDP is an aggregate measure that values activities at the market price in that society. The relative prices of the products and services a consumer buys often differ substantially among countries. In Vancouver, $900 a month gets you only a small studio apartment. In Haiti, $900 a month might get you a mansion with four servants. Thus, GDP can be a poor measure of the relative living standards in various countries.

To avoid this problem in comparing per capita GDP, economists often calculate a different concept, *purchasing power parity,* which adjusts for the different relative prices among countries before making comparisons.

Just how much of a difference the two approaches can make can be seen in the case of China. In May 1992, the International Monetary Fund (IMF) changed from calculating China's GDP using the exchange rate approach to calculating it using the purchasing power parity approach. Upon doing so, the IMF calculated that China's GDP grew over 400 percent in one year. Per capita income rose from about $400 to well over $1,300. When methods of calculation can make that much difference, one must use statistics very carefully.

Economic Welfare over Time

A second way in which the GDP concept is used is to compare one year with another. Last chapter, when we talked about growth in the economy, we were really talking about growth in total output or GDP. Similarly, when we talked about contractions and expansions, it was in reference to GDP.

Using GDP figures to compare the economy's performance over time is much better than relying merely on our perceptions. Most of us have heard the phrase, *the good old days.* Generally we hear it from our parents or grandparents, who are lamenting the state of the nation or economy. In comparing today to yesterday, they always seem to picture the past with greener grass, an easier life, and happier times. Compared to the good old days, today always comes out a poor second.

Our parents and grandparents may be right when they look back at particular events in their own lives, but if society were to follow such reasoning, it would conclude that all of history has been just one long downhill slide, worsening every year. In actuality, perceptions of the good old days are likely to be biased. It's easy to remember the nice things of yesterday while forgetting its harsh realities. Relying on past perception is not an especially helpful way of making accurate comparisons.

A preferable way is to rely on data that are not changed by emotion or anything else. Looking at GDP over time provides a way of using data to make comparisons over time. For example, say we compare nominal Canadian GDP in 1950 ($19 billion) to nominal GDP in 1994 ($749 billion). Would it be correct to conclude the economy had grown 39 times larger? No. As we discussed in the last chapter, GDP figures aren't affected by emotions, but they are affected by inflation. To make comparisons over time, we can't confine ourselves to a simple look at what has happened to GDP.

In our earlier discussion of supply and demand, we spent quite a bit of space distinguishing between a rise in the price level and a change in relative prices. That's because the distinction is important. A similar important distinction economists make is in comparing output levels over time. Suppose prices of all goods and hence the price level (remember, the price level includes wages) goes up 25 percent in one year, but outputs of all goods remain constant. GDP will have risen 25 percent, but will society be any better off? No. To compare GDP over time, you must distinguish between increases in GDP due to inflation and increases in GDP that represent real increases in production and income.

SOME LIMITATIONS OF NATIONAL INCOME ACCOUNTING

The quotation at this chapter's start pointed out that statistics can be misleading. We want to reiterate that here. Before you can work with statistics, you need to know how they are collected and the problems they have. If you don't, the results can be disastrous. Here's a possible scenario:

ADDED DIMENSION

THE HAPPINESS INDEX

The only way economists can determine how happy people are is to ask them if they're happy and then develop a happiness index. We've done so in some classes by giving students a numerical measure for degrees of happiness:

Ecstatic	5
Very happy	4
Happy	3
Somewhat unhappy	2
Depressed	1

Each student writes down the number that most closely represents his or her average state of happiness for the past year. The average of those calculations forms the "happiness index" for the class—usually between 3 and 3.2. Students are essentially reasonably happy.

In fact, when other economists have taken a type of happiness poll elsewhere, results have been fairly consistent—even in poor countries. Except in times of crisis, people on average are reasonably happy, regardless of their income level, their wealth, or the state of the economy where they live.* We interpret this as meaning there's some level of income below which we'll be unhappy because we're starving, but above that level more output for a society doesn't mean more happiness for a society.

Now this stability of happiness could mean that economics, economic progress, and growth don't matter, that they're irrelevant to happiness. But we economists are naturally loath to give it such an interpretation. Instead, economists slide over such problems and poll people as to how many prefer a higher income to a lower income. We've also conducted these polls and have yet to find an individual who says he or she prefers less income to more income. (If we found one, of course, we'd volunteer to relieve that person of some income, which would make us all happier.)

The fact that everyone, or almost everyone, prefers more output, but that more output or an increase in income doesn't make everyone happier, is not really a contradiction. We know from watching *Star Trek* (and from reading Lord Tennyson) that it's in striving that human beings acquire happiness. Without striving, the human being is but an empty shell. But enough; if this discussion continues, it will, heaven forbid, turn from economics to philosophy.

---

* The test has been given to students in Fredericton, Vermont, New York, and Great Britain, and each time the results have been similar. However, when the test was given to students in Florida at the University of Miami and to students in Bulgaria, the results were different. In Miami they came up consistently higher for each category. Four students actually checked "ecstatic." We're not precisely sure what this Florida factor signifies. In Bulgaria, the results were lower (a 2.8 average). Bulgaria was undergoing a wrenching economic change and many incomes had been cut by two-thirds, so this low result was explainable.

A student who isn't careful looks at the data and discovers an almost perfect relationship between imports and investment occurring in a Latin American country. Whenever capital goods imports go up, investment in capital goods goes up by an equal proportion. The student develops a thesis based on that insight, only to learn after submitting the thesis that no data on investments are available for that country. Instead of gathering actual data, the foreign country's statisticians estimate investment by assuming it to be a constant percentage of imports. Since many investment goods are imported, this is reasonable, but the estimate is not a reasonable basis for an economic policy. It would be back to the drawing board for the student, whose thesis would be useless because the student didn't know how the country's statistics had been collected.

If you ever work in business as an economist, statistics will be your life's blood. Much of what economists do is based on knowing, interpreting, and drawing inferences from statistics. Statistics must be treated carefully. They don't always measure what they seem to measure. Though Canadian national income accounting statistics are among the most accurate in the world, they still have serious limitations.

6A Measurement problems are a limitation of national income accounting

THE UNDERGROUND ECONOMY

The Canadian government has issued billions of dollars worth of cash. Ask yourself how much cash you're carrying on you. Add to that the amounts banks and businesses keep, and divide that by the number of people in Canada. The number economists get when they do that calculation is way below the total amount of cash Canada has issued. So what happens to the extra cash?

Let's switch for a minute to a Montreal safehouse being raided by drug enforcement officers. They find $50 million in cash. That's what most economists believe happens to much of the extra cash: It goes underground. An underground economy lurks below the real economy.

The underground economy consists of two components: (1) the production and distribution of illegal goods and services; and (2) the nonreporting of legal economic activity.

Illegal activity, such as selling illegal drugs and prostitution, generates huge amounts of cash. (Most people who buy an illegal good or service would prefer not to have the transaction appear on their monthly credit card statements.) This presents a problem for a big-time illegal business. It must explain to Revenue Canada where all that money came from. That's where money laundering comes in. Money laundering is simply making illegally gained income look as if it came from a legal business. Any business through which lots of cash moves is a good front for money laundering. Laundromats move lots of cash, which is where the term *money laundering* came from. The mob bought Laundromats and claimed a much higher income from the laundromats than it actually received. The mob thus "laundered" the excess money. Today money laundering is much more sophisticated. It involves billions of dollars and international transactions in three or four different countries, but the purpose is the same: making illegally earned money look legal.

The second part of the illegal economy involves deliberately failing to report income in order to escape paying taxes on it. When people work "off the books," when restaurants don't ring up cash sales, when waiters forget to declare tips on their tax returns, they reduce their tax payments and make it look as if they have less income and as if the economy has less production than it actually does.

How important is the underground economy? That's tough to say; it is, after all, underground. A 1994 Statistics Canada study estimated it at about 3 percent of total Canadian GDP. Other estimates have been much higher—estimates of 20 percent of GDP are common (and one economist suggested it could be anywhere from 33 percent to as much as 100 percent!). Even at 3 percent of nominal GDP, that would be about $21 billion dollars. Figures like this suggest that the government is losing substantial tax revenues. We'll hear much of this in the news in the 1990s.

GDP Measures Market Activity, Not Welfare

6B GDP measures national activity, not welfare

The first, and most important, limitation to remember is that GDP does not measure happiness nor does it measure economic welfare. GDP measures economic (market) activity. Real GDP could rise and economic welfare could fall. For example, say some Martians came down and let loose a million Martian burglars in Canada just to see what would happen. GDP would be likely to rise as individuals bought guns and locks and spent millions of dollars on protecting their property and replacing stolen items. At the same time, however, welfare would fall.

Welfare is a complicated concept. The economy's goal should not be to increase output for the sake of increasing output, but to make people better off or at least happier. But a pure happiness measure is impossible. Economists have struggled with the concept of welfare and have decided that the best they can do is to concentrate their analysis on economic activity, leaving others to consider how economic activity relates to happiness. We should warn you, however, that there is no neat correlation between increases in GDP and increases in happiness. You can see that in the box describing "The Happiness Index."

Measurement Errors

We've already seen that GDP figures don't capture illegal activity, but there are several other problems with the data. Measurement errors occur in adjusting GDP figures for inflation. Measurement of inflation involves numerous arbitrary decisions about changes in quality of goods. For example, if the price of a Toyota goes up 5 percent from 1996 ($20,000) to 1997 ($21,000), that's certainly a 5 percent rise in price. But what if the Toyota has a "new improved" 16-valve engine? Can you say that the price of cars has risen 5 percent, or should you adjust for the improvement in quality? And if you adjust, how do you adjust? The people who keep track of the price indices used to measure inflation will be the first to tell you there's no one right answer. How that question, and a million other similar questions involved in measuring inflation, is answered can lead to significant differences in estimates of inflation and hence in estimates of real GDP growth.

One recent study for Canada argued inflation could be either 5.4 or 15 percent, depending on how the inflation index was calculated! Which inflation figure one chose would make a big difference in one's estimate of how the economy was doing.

A third limitation of national income accounting concerns possible misinterpretation of the components. In setting up the accounts, a large number of arbitrary decisions had to be made: What to include in "investment"? What to include in "consumption"? How to treat government expenditures? The decisions that were made were, for the most part, reasonable, but they weren't the only ones that could have been made. Once made, however, they influence our interpretations of events. For example, when we see that investment rises, we normally think that our future productive capacity is rising, but remember that investment includes housing investment, which does not increase our future productive capacity. In fact, some types of consumption (say, purchases of personal computers by people who will become computer-literate and use their knowledge and skills to be more productive than they were before they owned computers) increase our productive capacity more than some types of "investment."

Misinterpretation of Subcategories

6B Subcategories of national income accounting are often interdependent

By pointing out these problems, economists are not suggesting that national income accounting statistics should be thrown out. Far from it; measurement is necessary, and the GDP measurements and categories have made it possible to think and talk about the aggregate economy. We wouldn't have devoted an entire chapter of this book to national income accounting if we didn't believe it was important. We are simply arguing that national income accounting concepts should be used with sophistication, with an awareness of their weaknesses as well as their strengths.

GDP Is Worth Using Despite Its Limitations

Used with that awareness, national income accounting is a powerful tool; one wouldn't want to be an economist without it. For those of you who aren't planning to be economists, it's still a good idea for you to understand the concepts of national income accounting. If you do, the business section of the newspaper will no longer seem like Greek to you. You'll be a more informed citizen and will be better able to make up your own mind about macroeconomic debates.

CHAPTER SUMMARY

- National income accounting is the terminology used to talk about the aggregate economy.
- GDP measures aggregate final output of an economy. It's a flow, not a stock, measure of market activity.
- Intermediate goods can be eliminated from GDP in two ways:
    1. By measuring only final sales.
    2. By measuring only value added.
- National income is directly related to national output. Whenever there's output, there's income.
- GDP is divided up into four types of expenditures:
    $$GDP = C + I + G + (X - M).$$

NDI = wages and salaries plus supplementary labour income
    + corporate profits before taxes
    + interest and miscellaneous investment income

    + farm and nonincorporated nonfarm income
    + inventory adjustment

GDP at factor cost = NDI + capital consumption allowance

GDP at market prices = GDP at factor cost + indirect taxes less subsidies

NNI = NDI + investment income from nonresidents
    − investment income to nonresidents

GNP at market prices = NNI + indirect taxes less subsidies

- To compare income over time, we must adjust for price-level changes. After adjusting for inflation, nominal measures are changed to "real" measures. The real amount is the nominal amount divided by the price index.
- National income accounting concepts are powerful tools for understanding macroeconomics, but we must recognize their limitations.

KEY TERMS

capital consumption allowance *(173)*	identity *(167)*	nominal GDP *(173)*
depreciation *(171)*	net domestic income (NDI) at factor	nondurable goods *(170)*
disposable personal income *(177)*	cost *(175)*	personal income (PI) *(177)*
durable goods *(170)*	net domestic product (NDP) *(173)*	real concepts *(162)*
general-purpose transfers *(172)*	net foreign factor income *(163)*	real GDP *(173)*
gross domestic product (GDP) *(162)*	net national income (NNI) *(177)*	semi-durable goods *(170)*
gross national product (GNP) *(162)*	net national income (NNI) at factor	services *(170)*
intermediate products *(164)*	cost *(175)*	special-purpose transfers *(172)*
national income accounting *(162)*	net private investment *(171)*	transfer payments *(172)*
national income accounting	nominal concepts *(162)*	value added *(165)*

QUESTIONS FOR THOUGHT AND REVIEW

The number after each question represents the estimated degree of critical thinking required (1 = almost none; 10 = deep thought.)

1. What's the relationship between a stock concept and a flow concept? Give an example that hasn't already been given in this chapter. *(5)*

2. A company sells 1,000 desks for $400 each. Of these, it sells 750 to other companies and 250 to individuals. What is that company's contribution to GDP? *(4)*

3. The kingdom of Wombatia is considering introducing a value added tax. What tax rate on value added is needed to get the same increase in revenue as is gotten from an income tax with a rate of 15 percent? Why? *(8)*

4. If Canada introduces universal child care, what will likely happen to GDP? What are the welfare implications of that rise? *(5)*

5. You've been given the following data:

Wages, salaries and supplementary income	$50
Corporate profits before taxes	70
Interest and miscellaneous investment income	32
Farm and nonincorporated nonfarm income	18
Inventory adjustment	−10
Capital consumption allowance	13
Indirect taxes less subsidies	3
Investment income from nonresidents	6
Investment income to nonresidents	10

   On the basis of the data, calculate GDP at factor cost and at market prices, GNP, NNI, and NDP. *(5)*

6. Consumption is $100, investment is $85, government spending is $3, exports are $12, imports are $17, and the capital consumption allowance is $8. What is NDP? *(5)*

7. Economists normally talk about GDP even though they know NDP is a better measure of economic activity. Why? *(3)*

8. How does personal income differ from national income? *(3)*

9. What is the difference between national personal income and domestic personal income? *(4)*

10. If society's goal is to make society happier, and higher GDP isn't closely associated with society being happier, why do economists even talk about GDP? *(9)*

PROBLEMS AND EXERCISES

1. Given the following data about the economy:

Consumption	$20
Investment	10
Corporate profits before tax	10
Government expenditure	15
Net exports	25
Indirect taxes less subsidies	10
Net foreign factor income	0
Wages, salaries, and supplementary labour income	20
Interest and miscellaneous investment income	10
Inventory Adjustment	5
Capital Consumption Allowance	5

   a. Calculate GDP at market prices using the expenditure approach.

   b. If GDP at market prices is identical under the expenditure and factor income approaches, what must farm and nonincorporated nonfarm income be? Why?

   c. Calculate NDI and NNI.

2. There are three firms in an economy: A, B, and C. Firm A buys $250 worth of goods from firm B and $200 worth of goods from firm C, and produces 200 units of output which it sells at $5 per unit. Firm B buys $100 worth of goods from firm A and $150 worth of goods from firm C, and produces 300 units of output which it sells at $7 per unit. Firm C buys $50 worth of goods from firm A and nothing from firm B. It produces output worth $1,000. All other products are sold to consumers.

a. Calculate GDP.

b. If a value added tax (a tax on the total value added of each firm) of 10 percent is introduced, how much revenue will the government get?

c. How much would government get if it introduced a 10 percent income tax?

d. How much would government get if it introduced a 10 percent sales tax on final output?

3. Below are nominal GDP and GDP deflators for four years.

Year	Nominal GDP (billions)	GDP Deflator (1986 = 100)
1995	$780	124
1996	796	126
1997	815	130
1998	836	132

a. Calculate real GDP in each year.

b. Did the percent change in nominal GDP exceed the percent change in real GDP in any of the last three years?

c. In which year did society's welfare increase the most?

4. You've been called in by your boss with some questions.

a. First, she tells you that she has been told that net private investment was negative and gross private investment was positive this year. She says that is impossible. What do you tell her?

b. Next, she wants you to tell her if you should enter the United States market. Your decision will be based on the level of national income in the United States in 1990. She gives you the following data: 1990 GDP was $5,546.1 billion, net foreign factor income was $21.7 billion, capital depreciated by $607.7 billion, and indirect business taxes stood at $444.0 billion. What was U.S. national income?

c. Finally, she tells you that GDP fell 32 percent in her country last year, and that she must make a "state of the economy" speech next week. She wants to know how she can portray this fall in the best possible light. What do you tell her?

8

The Macroeconomic Debate

The Theory of Economics . . . is a method rather than a doctrine, an apparatus of the mind, a technique of thinking which helps its possessor to draw correct conclusions.

~J. M. Keynes

After reading this chapter, you should be able to:

1 Discuss the historical development of modern macroeconomics.

2 Outline the reasoning behind Say's law.

3 Discuss the emergence of Keynesian economics.

4 Distinguish between an aggregate demand curve and an aggregate equilibrium demand curve.

5 Draw a price-level flexibility curve and specify its three ranges.

6 Distinguish a price-level flexibility curve from an aggregate supply curve.

7 Draw an aggregate equilibrium demand curve and explain the effect of shift factors on it.

8 Discuss the macro economy using the macro policy model.

9 List several reasons why macro policy is more complicated than the model makes it look.

When running for her first elected term as prime minister, Kim Campbell promised the Canadian public thousands of new jobs if she were elected. She didn't convince people; she was replaced by Jean Chretien. Chretien, in turn, promised prosperity and thousands of new jobs in his term of office. Having been elected on these promises, Chretien turned to his economic advisers to tell him how to fulfill them.

The honest answer he would have received from those advisers is that understanding the macro economy is tough and that a simple statement of what he must do to create jobs and prosperity doesn't exist. There are some major policies he could try that would most likely increase jobs, but politically, these major policies would be dangerous; moreover, they would also potentially be highly inflationary. There are also some minor policy initiatives he could try that would probably push the economy in the right direction; alone, these minor policies couldn't be counted on to achieve the promised result, but at least they would give voters the sense that he was dealing with the problem. The mainstream economic view was that his best political bet, and probably his best economic bet, would be to try these minor macro policy initiatives and hope for some luck. If he was lucky, the economy would pick up on its own, income and jobs would increase, and he could credit his policies.

To argue that you need luck for the economy to achieve macroeconomic prosperity is not to argue that the policies he might have tried were wrong or irrelevant; it is only to say that any policy strong enough to deliver lots of jobs and sustained prosperity would also probably push the economy perilously close to increasing inflation. In that case, Chretien could find himself "Trudeaued"—voted out of office because of too much inflation—instead of being "Campbelled"—voted out of office because of too much unemployment.

The economists Chretien turned to for answers were generally considered **activist economists.** They believed that the government could come up with some policy proposals that could positively impact the economy. Activist economists are often called Keynesian economists because they follow in the activist tradition of John Maynard Keynes, an economist who played a major role in convincing some economists that activist policy made sense.

Campbell's advisors were generally **laissez-faire economists.** Laissez-faire economists believe that most government policies would probably make things worse, so the best policy was (relative) government disinvolvement with the economy—lowering taxes and keeping the government out of the market economy as much as possible. Laissez-faire economists are often called Classical economists because they are following in a Classical economic tradition and because they were called that by Keynes when he was contrasting his activist policies with the then-predominant laissez-faire policies.

In this chapter we introduce you to the reasoning behind both the Keynesian activist and Classical laissez-faire economic views in two ways. In the first part of the chapter we present a brief historical discussion of the ideas. Somehow, knowing where the ideas come from makes them a bit more real. Then, in the second part, we present a simple policy model that provides a framework within which you can think about the macro issues.

Our story of modern macroeconomics begins with the Great Depression of the 1930s. The depression marked a significant change in Canadian economic institutions and ideology. It was a defining event for a whole generation. In the depression, not only the deadbeat up the street was unemployed, so were your brother, your mother, your uncle—the hardworking backbone of Canada. These people wanted to work, and if the market wasn't creating jobs for them, the market system was at fault.

During the depression, the popular view of government's proper role in the economy changed considerably. Before, the predominant ideology was laissez-faire: keep the government out of the economy. After the depression, most people believed that government must have a role in regulating the economy.

The Great Depression also led economists to develop theoretical models that allowed for unemployment and left room for government intervention into the market.

Activist economists   Economists who believe that the government can come up with some policy proposals that will positively impact the economy.

Laissez-faire economists   Economists who believe that most government policies would probably make things worse, and favour (relative) government disinvolvement in the economy.

THE HISTORICAL DEVELOPMENT OF MODERN MACROECONOMICS

1   Laissez-faire economists oppose government intervention. Activist economists generally favour government intervention.

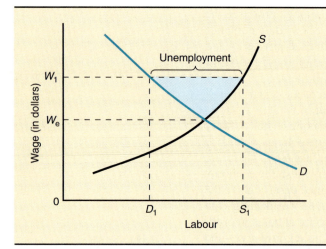

EXHIBIT 1   Unemployment in the Classical Model

If social or political forces hold the wage above the equilibrium wage (at W_1 rather than W_e), the result will be unemployment of $S_1 - D_1$. To eliminate that unemployment, the wage must fall.

Classical economists   Economists who generally oppose government intervention.

Keynesian economists   Economists who generally favour government intervention in the aggregate economy.

The Emergence of Classical Economics

Laissez-faire   Economic policy of leaving coordination of individuals' wants to be controlled by the market.

Real wage   The ratio of the wage rate to the price level.

Adam Smith, a moral philosopher whose book, *The Wealth of Nations*, is seen as the beginning of modern economics. *The Bettmann Archives.*

It was during the depression that it became usual to classify laissez-faire economists—those who generally oppose government intervention—as **Classical economists,** and activist economists—those who generally favour government intervention in the aggregate economy—as **Keynesian economists.**[1]

Classical economics actually began in the late 1700s and early 1800s as economists developed the ideas in Adam Smith's seminal work, *An Inquiry into the Nature and Causes of the Wealth of Nations*. The essence of Classical economics' approach to problems was to use a **laissez-faire** (leave the market policy alone) approach. This policy was based on the view that the market, left to its own devices, was self-adjusting. Wages and prices would adjust to eliminate unemployment. Classicals recognized that in the short run there might be temporary problems, but their analysis focused on the long run.

When the Great Depression hit and unemployment became a problem, most Classical economists avoided the issue (as economists, and most people, tend to do when they don't have a good answer). When pushed by curious students to explain how, if the market's invisible hand was so wonderful, the invisible hand could have allowed the depression and its 20 percent unemployment, Classical economists drew supply-and-demand-for-labour curves like those in Exhibit 1.

They explained, "Unemployment results when the **real wage**—the wage level relative to the price level—is too high. Workers hold their wage above the equilibrium level—that is, they won't take the lower wages offered. Other forces (government policies and economic institutions such as labour unions) can operate to prevent the invisible hand from working its magic." For example, in Exhibit 1, the equilibrium wage is W_e. If the wage is held at W_1 for some reason, quantity of labour supplied is S_1 and quantity of labour demanded is D_1. The difference between the two ($S_1 - D_1$) is unemployment.

Their laissez-faire policy prescription followed from their analysis: The solution to unemployment was to eliminate labour unions and government policies that held wages too high. If these things happened, the wage rate would fall, and unemployment would be eliminated.

Laymen weren't pleased with this argument. (Remember, economists don't try to present pleasing arguments—only arguments they believe are correct.) But laymen couldn't point to anything wrong with it. It made sense, but it wasn't satisfying. People thought, "Gee, Uncle Maurice, who's unemployed, would take a job at half the

---

[1]In this book when describing economists, we use the terms *Keynesian* and *activist,* and the terms *Classical* and *laissez-faire,* interchangeably. This usage hides some subtle differences in meaning, but those differences can be dealt with in higher-level courses. We use both terms, rather than just one, because you will likely see both in the popular press.

going wage. But he can't find one—there just aren't enough jobs to go around at any wage."

Most lay people had a different explanation. The popular lay explanation of the depression was that there was an oversupply of goods which had glutted the market. All that was needed to eliminate unemployment was for government to hire the unemployed, even if it were only to dig ditches and fill them back up. The people who got the new jobs would spend their money, creating even more jobs. Pretty soon, Canada would be out of the depression.

Classical economists argued against this lay view. They argued that money to hire people would have to come from somewhere. It would have to be borrowed. Such borrowing would use money that would have financed private economic activity and jobs; hence, such borrowing would reduce private economic activity. The net effect would mean no increase in the total number of jobs. In short, the Classicals were saying an oversupply of goods was impossible.

This Classical argument that an oversupply of goods was impossible was first made in the 1800s by a French businessman, Jean Baptiste Say, although it was a British stockbroker, David Ricardo, who made it famous. Say's argument went as follows: People work and supply goods to the market because they want other goods. Thus, the very fact that they supply goods means they have income to demand goods of equal value. This idea is normally stated as follows:

Say's law: *Supply creates its own demand.*

Say's law is central to the Classical vision of the economy. It says that there can never be a general glut of goods on the market; demand for goods and services as a whole will always be sufficient to buy what is supplied. (Think back to the circular flow diagram.) This demand for goods and services as a whole is usually called *aggregate demand,* and the supply of goods and services as a whole is usually called *aggregate supply,* so Say's law is equivalent to saying that aggregate supply always equals aggregate demand.

Not all Classical economists initially accepted Say's law. The most spirited argument against it was put forward by Thomas Malthus, a preacher.[2] Malthus argued that when people saved, part of their income would be lost to the economy and there wouldn't be as much demand for total goods and services out there as supply. According to Malthus, Say's law did not necessarily hold true.

Say and Ricardo rejected Malthus's argument. They argued that people's savings were not lost to the economy. When people saved, they did it by lending their savings to other individuals. The people who borrowed the savings would spend what they borrowed on investments. Classical economists argued that the interest rate would fluctuate to equate savings and investment. They argued that if people's desire to save increased, the interest rate would fall and the quantity of investment would increase. So any savings seemingly lost to the system would be actually translated into investment, making aggregate demand (total buying power in the economy) equal to aggregate supply (total production) through either a direct route (consumption) or an indirect route (investment by way of savings). Aggregate demand (investment plus consumption) always equalled aggregate supply.

The direct route and indirect route appear in Exhibit 2, the familiar circular flow diagram. Say's law states that total expenditures (consumption plus investment, depicted by flows *b* and *c*), would just equal production or income (depicted by flow *a*). The financial sector would translate all savings into investment to maintain a continual equilibrium between supply and demand.

Say's law became a tenet of Classical economics. It didn't say that unemployment could never exist—there could be lots of little pockets of unemployment in various

Say's Law

2 Say's Law—supply creates its own demand.

---
[2]Thomas Malthus is most famous for the Malthusian doctrine which stated that population grows much faster than food production so the future of mankind is starvation. It was the Malthusian doctrine that earned economics the name of the dismal science.

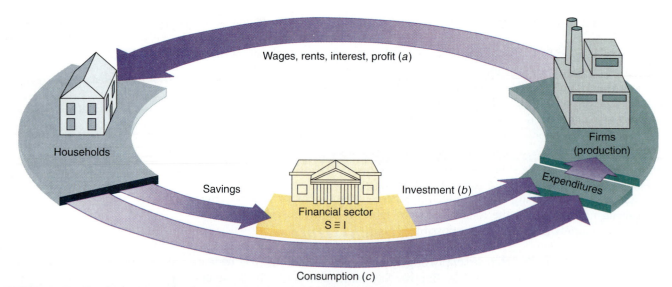

EXHIBIT 2   The Equality of Production (Aggregate Supply) and Expenditures (Aggregate Demand)

According to Say's law, aggregate production always was at the full employment level. Any funds that escaped from the circular flow into the financial sector (savings) would be brought back into the circular flow by the financial sector in the form of investment. Thus, the financial sector was assumed to keep savings always equal to investment.

industries if wages didn't adjust. It did say that whatever unemployment existed was a microeconomic, relative wage-price problem and, if wages and prices were allowed to adjust, unemployment would go away on its own. In terms of the discussion of unemployment in an earlier chapter, Classical economists agreed that *frictional* and *structural unemployment* could exist, but they did not agree that *cyclical unemployment* could be caused by a shortage of aggregate demand.

The Quantity Theory of Money

Money   A highly liquid financial asset that's generally accepted in exchange for other goods and is used as a reference in valuing other goods.

Quantity theory of money   The price level varies in response to changes in the quantity of money.

Classical economists buttressed their Say's law analysis of the aggregate economy with the quantity theory of money. We will discuss money and the Classical quantity theory in much more detail in later chapters. For now all you need have is a general sense of what **money** is: It is a medium of exchange (such as a looney) that individuals use to buy goods. Thus, the quantity of money is the amount of the medium of exchange in the economy. In its simplest terms, the **quantity theory of money** says that the price level varies in response to changes in the quantity of money. In other words, changes in the price level are caused by changes in the money supply. If the money supply goes up 20 percent, prices go up 20 percent. If money supply goes down 5 percent, prices go down 5 percent. Thus, money is only a veil, and the analysis of the real economy (of real output) should concentrate on real economic forces.

Classicals' View of the Great Depression

Classical economists recognized that, in the real world, the price and wage levels weren't going to fall to anywhere near the level necessary to bring about equilibrium in the short run. But their interest was primarily in the long run. Then in the 1930s the long run kept getting longer and longer, politicians were becoming more and more dissatisfied with the policy prescriptions they were getting from Classical economists. More and more Classical economists, despite their laissez-faire leanings, started to come up with alternative policy proposals and to develop a theory that explained short-run temporary fluctuations, which is what they believed the depression was.

But they came to these alternative policy prescriptions reluctantly, as a last resort, because they did not see them as getting at the heart of the problem that their model focused on: wage level rigidities. It was these wage level rigidities that were causing

ADDED DIMENSION

THE TREASURY VIEW, LLOYD
GEORGE, AND KEYNES

The Great Depression descended on Britain in the 1920s, before it hit North America. Therefore many debates about what to do about it occurred first in Britain. British Chancellor of the Exchequer Winston Churchill (a Conservative Party member who later became prime minister) followed the advice of his Treasury Department, which was composed of Classical economists. They advised him that Britain should go back on the gold standard (a monetary system that fixes a currency's price relative to gold and other currencies). All countries that use gold to value their currency have *fixed currency exchange rates*. For example, if 1 British pound = 1 ounce of gold, and 1 Canadian dollar = 1/2 ounce of gold, then 1 British pound = 2 Canadian dollars = 1 ounce of gold.

Churchill followed the Classical economists' advice and returned the pound to the gold standard from which Britain, and all other countries, had departed during World War I. He set a high value on the pound relative to other currencies. As a result, British wages and prices were high relative to those in other countries. Foreign imports were cheap, which was good. British exports were expensive and uncompetitive abroad, which was not good. Unemployment in Britain was high, which was bad. The British Treasury Department's advice on how to eliminate unemployment boiled down to "Keep a stiff upper lip. British wages and prices will eventually fall, or foreign wages and prices will rise."

Regardless of the argument's economic merits, its political merits were dubious. Lloyd George (leader of the opposition Liberal Party) advocated a massive government hiring program to eliminate unemployment. Keynes (a prominent advisor to the Liberal Party, who had, before Lloyd George's proposals, been seen as a Classical economist) modified his economic analysis in part to justify that shift. That was the beginning of the Keynesian approach to macroeconomics.

Needless to say, many of the Classicals were not very pleased with Keynes's shift, and they saw his economic analysis as opportunism. His shifting position led to a well-known joke about economists: If you ask five economists a question, you will get five different answers; if you ask Keynes a question you will get six different answers.

However, stiff upper lips can carry politicians only so far, and soon thereafter the British Conservative Party was also advocating public works programs to help end the depression. Politics often plays a key role in directing economic thinking.

Source: This account is based on Peter Clarke's book, *The Keynesian Revolution in the Making 1924–1936* (Oxford, England: Oxford University Press, 1988).

---

unemployment, and Classical economists would have favoured any policy to rid the economy of them—i.e., create legislation that would undermine unions.

In the Classical view, the depression of the 1930s was lasting so long because social and political forces prevented market forces from operating. Thus, their favoured solution to the depression was the laissez-faire solution: stop the measures governments were passing to hold up wages and prices; break up labour unions; and let market forces operate—let wages and prices adjust to their equilibrium levels.

The Emergence of Keynesian Economics

By the late 1930s, many Classical economists were giving up their laissez-faire policy prescriptions. Politicians weren't listening to them; Classical economists sensed it was not the time to push their ideas. For example, in Britain by the 1930s all three of the country's political parties (the Liberal Party, the Labour Party, and the Conservative Party) had abandoned support of a laissez-faire policy. Each party was offering a competing government-organized program to fight unemployment.

Many students weren't listening to them, either: Students wanted to discuss policies to end the depression. They didn't want to hear about the long run. For example, when Canadian exchange student Robert Bryce came back to Harvard after studying at Britain's Cambridge University where Keynes was a professor, his fellow students asked him to organize seminars to discuss the ideas he'd heard Keynes propound. (It was through Bryce's Harvard seminars that Keynes's ideas were transmitted to the

United States and Canada.) When students organize their own seminars, you know they're interested.[3]

One more reason why Classical economists were giving up their policy prescriptions is that economists are people too. Despite their training, economists are often compassionate people. Their gut feelings were the same as the general population's: There must be a better way. Thus, during the Depression, some Classical economists advocated a variety of policies that didn't follow from their theory.

While there were many dimensions to Keynes's ideas, their essence was that as wages and the price level adjusted to shocks (such as an unexpected decrease in investment demand) the economy could get stuck in a rut. Given the institutional realities of a relatively fixed price level, if, for some reason, people stopped buying—decreased their demand in the aggregate—firms would decrease production, causing people to be laid off; these people would, in turn, buy less—causing other firms to further decrease production, which would cause more workers to be laid off, which would: . . . The cumulative circle of declining production would end with the economy stuck at a low level of income.

Potential income Income level achieved at some previous point plus a normal growth factor.

Short-run potential income The level of income toward which the economy gravitates in the short-run because of cumulative circles of declining production.

Long-run potential income The level of income which the economy is capable of producing if it does not experience cumulative circles of declining production.

The key idea is that, in the short run, **potential income** is not fixed; it fluctuates. Thus, for Keynes, there were two concepts of potential income. The first is **short-run potential income**—the level of income toward which the economy gravitates in the short run because of these cumulative circles of declining production. The second is **long-run potential income**—the level of income that the economy is capable of producing if it does not experience these cumulative circles of declining production. Keynes focused on short-run potential income because he felt that if the economy reached that short-run potential income, the forces pushing it to its long-run potential income would be weak. Long before the long-run equilibrium would be reached, another cumulative circle would push it to another short-run potential income. In Keynes's view, macro analysis should focus on the forces pushing the economy to its short-run potential income.

Market forces that are supposed to bring the economy back to long-run equilibrium don't work fast, and, at times, will not be strong enough to get the economy out of a recession; the economy would be stuck in a low-income rut. Thus, Keynes argued, the Classicals' use of the economy's potential income in the long run as a reference point from which to discuss temporary deviations of output was flawed. As the economy adjusted to deviations of supply and demand in the aggregate, output would shift and the equilibrium income toward which the economy would gravitate would change. An alternative way of putting the argument is that *short run aggregate supply decisions and aggregate demand are interdependent*—if producers expected low aggregate demand, they would decrease their output (supply). And as they decreased their output, people's income would fall, which would further lower aggregate demand. In response, producers' expectations of demand would fall still further. As that happened they would decrease their output even more, causing yet another round of adjustment.

Let's consider an example. Say that a large portion of the people in the Canadian economy suddenly decide to save more and consume less. Consumption demand would decrease and savings would increase. If those savings were not immediately transferred into investment (as the Classicals assumed they would be), investment demand would not increase by enough to offset the fall in consumption demand, and aggregate demand would fall. There would be excess supply. Faced with this excess supply, firms would likely cut back production, which would decrease income. People would be laid off. As people's incomes fell, their desire to consume and their desire to save would decrease. (When you're laid off you don't save.) Eventually income would

---

[3]The basis for much of this discussion about Keynesian economics is a set of interviews with early Keynesians including Canadians Robert Bryce and Lorrie Tarshis. See David Colander and Harry Landreth, *The Coming of Keynesianism to America* (Aldershot, England, and Brookfield, VT: Edward Elgar, 1996).

IN THE LONG RUN, WE'RE ALL DEAD

When Keynes, said, "In the long run, we're all dead," he didn't mean that we can forget the long run. What he meant was that if the long run is sufficiently long so that short-run forces do not let it come about, then for all practical purposes there is no long run. In that case, the short-run problem must be focused on.

Keynes's view of the political and social forces of the time was that voters would not be satisfied waiting for market forces to bring about full employment. Keynes felt that if something were not done in the short run to alleviate unemployment, voters would opt for fascism (as had the Germans) or communism (as had the Russians). He saw both alternatives as undesirable. For him, what would happen in the long run was academic.

Classicals, on the other hand, argued that the short-run problems were not as bad as Keynes made them out to be, so short-run problems should not be focused on to the exclusion of long-run problems. Modern-day Classicals argue that today we are living in Keynes's long run, so that his long-run problems are our short-run problems.

J. M. Keynes. *Bettmann Newsphotos.*

fall far enough so that once again savings and investment would be in equilibrium, but that equilibrium could be at a lower income level at a point below full employment.

In short, what Keynes argued was that the aggregate economy could get stuck in a rut. Once the economy got stuck in a rut with a glut, it had no way out. The government had to do something to pull the economy out of the rut.

It wasn't only Keynes who was making such arguments. It was also top Classical economists, especially Dennis Robertson and Frederick Hayek in England, and Allyn Young and Lauchlin Currie in the United States. These Classical economists were working on explanations of how an economy could end up at an undesirable equilibrium because of expectational and informational problems of prices transmitting appropriate information to decision makers.

Let's consider the work of Dennis Robertson a bit more carefully. Robertson, a close friend of Keynes, was developing an analysis of a sequence economy which could progress to an undesirable equilibrium if certain conditions held. Robertson's analysis led to many of the same results as those of the Keynesian model, but it was far more sophisticated in its treatment of the dynamic problems an economy can experience. But therein lay the problem: not only was it sophisticated, it was also complicated—so complicated that Robertson's book and work were almost indecipherable to all but a few top economists. Thus, most students were taught the simpler Classical model that we outlined above.

Ironically, one of the reasons Keynes's analysis was so contagious for students was that it could be reduced to a very simple model that, on the surface, seemed to make sense. Students are especially susceptible to simple intuitive models, and thus Keynesian ideas spread like wildfire among the younger economists. Older economists, such as Robertson or Frank Knight, kept saying, no, no, it's more complicated than that; but in the marketplace for ideas, complications don't sell well. The result was that Keynesian economics became macroeconomics.

By the 1950s, Keynesian economics became accepted by most of the profession. It was taught everywhere in the United States and Canada. A terminology developed: national income accounting, which was closely tied to Keynesian concepts. As the ter-

3 Keynesian economics provided an explanation as to why the economy could find itself caught in a rut with a glut—and it offered a way to get the economy moving again through the use of government spending policies.

minology became generally used, Keynesian economics became as deeply embedded—and as little thought about—as Say's law had been earlier. That thoughtless acceptance is one of the main reasons why Keynesian economics is not the end of the story and why in this book we emphasize a modern interpretation of the Keynesian model. We should point out, however, that the modern interpretation of the Keynesian model could also be described as Robertsonian Classical rather than Keynesian. As you will see, there has been a merging of Keynesian and Classical analysis in the 1990s and that merging reflects many of the insights of early sophisticated Classical economists. Thus, in the 1990s it is much more difficult to distinguish between Keynesian and Classical thought than it was in the recent past.

THE MACRO POLICY MODEL AND ITS AGGREGATE SUPPLY/AGGREGATE DEMAND FOUNDATIONS

Supply/demand models   Microeconomic models in which the shapes of supply and demand curves are based on the principle of substitution and opportunity cost.

Relative price   The price of a good relative to the price level.

Aggregate supply/aggregate demand macro models   Macroeconomic models in which the shapes of the curves depend on macro relationships, not substitution, and which have the price level, not relative price, on the vertical axis.

The debate between activist and laissez-faire economists can be presented in formal models of the aggregate economy. It would be nice for students if these models were the same as the **supply/demand models**—microeconomic models in which the shapes of supply and demand curves are based on the principle of substitution and opportunity costs. (Supply/demand models are the models you learned in Chapter 2.) In that supply/demand model, **relative price**—the price of a good relative to other goods—goes on the vertical axis. Unfortunately, the aggregate formal models are not the same as the microeconomic models; the aggregate economy, and the debates about it, are too complicated to fit into microeconomic supply/demand models. If we stretch, and are really careful, we can create **aggregate supply/aggregate demand (AS/AD) macro models**—macroeconomic models in which the shapes of the curves depend on macro relationships, not substitution, and which have the **price level,**—the price of goods as a whole—not relative price, on the vertical axis. While the resulting aggregate supply/aggregate demand model may resemble the micro supply/demand models, they aren't the same because aggregate supply and demand are interrelated; and that interrelationship must be taken into account. Taking that into account leads to some messy and complicated graphs.

To avoid these messy graphs, in this chapter we develop a *macro policy model* (called the Aggregate Equilibrium Demand/Price-Level Flexibility (AED/PLF) model). While this model is based on an aggregate supply/aggregate demand model, it seems simpler because it combines shifts of curves with movements along curves. The difference between the AS/AD model and the macro policy model is that the analytic aggregate supply/aggregate demand model goes through the intermediate steps leading to the new equilibrium, and thus is messy and complicated. The macro policy model avoids all the intermediate steps and shows the end result of the shifts under

Macro policy model   A model which combines intermediate adjustments with initial shifts, and shows what the final result will be without explaining each step along the way. It provides a simplified presentation of macro policy issues.

certain assumptions without making those assumptions specific. The **macro policy model** is thus a model which combines intermediate adjustments with initial shifts, and shows what the final result will be without explaining each step along the way of how you get there. They both come to the same results, and hence are fully consistent with one another.

The reason we use this macro policy model is to provide a simplified presentation of macro policy issues—which is our primary interest. Using it, we have a model that can incorporate both Keynesian and Classical views of the economy, and thus can highlight the difference between activist policy views and laissez faire policy views.

The Rudiments of the AS/AD Model

Since the macro policy model is based on the aggregate supply/aggregate demand (AS/AD) model, we begin our discussion of the macro policy model by presenting those rudiments of the AS/AD model that are necessary to understand the macro policy model. (In the appendix we develop the AS/AD model more fully, and show its relation to the macro policy model.)

The Graphical Framework

The first thing to note is both the AS/AD model and the macro policy model have the price level on the vertical axis and the aggregate level of output on the horizontal axis. Those are our axes because when we're talking about the aggregate domestic economy, we are not talking about a particular good—we're talking about a composite of all goods, GDP. That means that we're talking about the

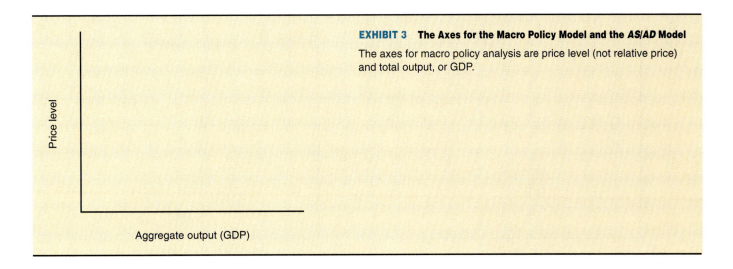

EXHIBIT 3   The Axes for the Macro Policy Model and the *AS/AD* Model

The axes for macro policy analysis are price level (not relative price) and total output, or GDP.

price level—the price of a composite good. The axes for aggregate supply and aggregate equilibrium demand are shown in Exhibit 3.

It is important to recognize that this is a fundamentally different framework than the partial equilibrium framework which has the quantity of a single good on the horizontal axis and a relative price (nominal price of the good relative to the price level) on the vertical axis. If we had relative price on the vertical axis, the aggregate supply/demand framework wouldn't make sense. The price of all goods (price level) relative to the price of all goods is always one.

The Components of the AS/AD Model

Let's consider these underlying components of the AS/AD model: the aggregate supply (AS) and aggregate demand (AD) curves. The **aggregate supply curve** is a *curve that relates the amount individuals as a whole want to supply and the price level, other things constant.* The **aggregate demand curve** is a *curve that relates the amount individuals as a whole want to consume and the price level, other things constant.* These curves are the macro equivalents to micro supply and demand curves and are derived analytically in the same way—through logical deduction from basic initial premises.

Aggregate supply curve (AS) A schedule graphically represented by a curve, which shows how a change in the price level will change the quantity of output supplied, other things (including expectations and aggregate demand) constant.

Now that we've defined the AS and AD curves, let us consider their shapes. The AD curve is generally considered downward sloping as in Exhibit 4 (a). The reason is that as the price level falls, all other things equal, individuals are richer, so they increase their spending.[4] That means that as the price level falls, more will be demanded.

Aggregate demand curve (AD) A schedule, graphically represented by a curve, that shows how a change in the price level will change output demanded, other things (including supply) held constant.

The AS curve is generally considered either perfectly vertical or upward sloping. For our purposes, we shall make the easiest assumption that the AS curve is vertical—that a rise in the price level will not cause output to increase. Thus, the AS curve looks like the one shown in Exhibit 4 (a). When the economy is at its long-run potential income, that assumption makes a lot of sense—there are no more workers or capital to hire so there are no inputs available with which to increase production. When the economy is at less than full employment—at less than its long-run potential income—whether that assumption makes sense depends on whether when prices rise, wages and the price of machines also rise so that firms have no reason to increase production because there is no change in the wage/price ratio. To keep the presentation easy here, we shall assume that the wage level and price level move together, so the AS curve is perfectly vertical. (In the Appendix we discuss other possibilities.)

The Problem of Possible Interdependence of the AS and AD Curves

In micro supply/demand analysis we can stop the analysis there, but in macro there is a problem. In macro we

---

[4]For additional reasons why the aggregate demand curve slopes downward, see the Appendix to this chapter.

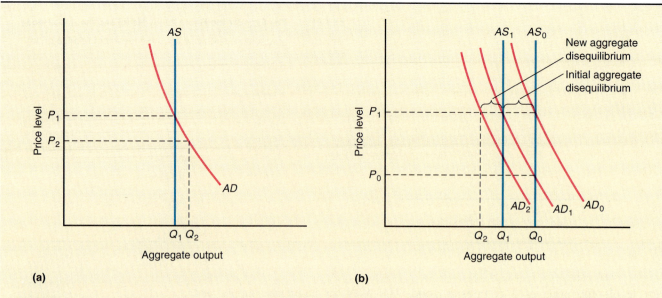

(a)   **(b)**

EXHIBIT 4

The *AD* curve shown in (**a**) tells us how much additional quantity will be forthcoming if there is a fall in the price level, other things, including the supply of output, constant. It tells us that if the price level fell from P_1 to P_2 the quantity of output demanded would increase from Q_0 to Q_1. The *AS* curve shown in (**a**) is a curve that tells us how much less quantity will be supplied if there is a fall in the price level. It is generally considered to be either upward sloping (if nominal wages are fixed) or perfectly vertical (if nominal wages change proportionately with prices). Throughout the chapter, we assume wages change proportionately with prices, which is why we draw the *AS* curve perfectly vertical.

In (**b**) we show the reasoning why the *AS/AD* analysis involving interdependencies between aggregate supply and aggregate demand is more complicated than micro supply and demand analysis. When the *AD* curve shifts (say from AD_0 to AD_1) unless there is instantaneous price level adjustment, the *AS* curve will shift in response to a shift in the *AD* curve (say, from AS_0 to AS_1). But, when the *AS* curve shifts, there will be further shift in the *AD* curve (say, from AD_1 to AD_2). After both of these shifts there is still a disequilibrium of Q_2 to Q_1. The existence of this interdependence means that the shapes of the curves alone do not determine the new equilibrium. The nature of these interdependent shifts—the dynamic interdependencies—must be specified before one can decide where the new equilibrium will be.

Fallacy of composition The false assumption that what is true for a part will also be true for the whole.

cannot reasonably assume other things remain constant. Specifically, it is intuitive that the aggregate supply and aggregate demand curves are interdependent. (Remember Say's Law—supply creates its own demand.) To see the intuitive argument of why they are interdependent, think back to the circular flow diagram presented in Exhibit 2. Whenever firms in the aggregate produce (whenever they supply), they create income (demand for their goods), and most likely additional expenditures. This difference between microeconomic analysis and macroeconomic analysis is often discussed under the name **fallacy of composition** (the potentially false assumption that what is true for a part will also be true for the whole).

This interdependency means that when, for example, the quantity supplied changes, we cannot necessarily assume that aggregate demand remains constant. When one curve moves, so does the other. Thus, to fully specify the AS/AD model we must specify the nature of the interrelationship between the two as well as the shapes of the curve. Keynes's contribution to macroeconomics was in highlighting this interdependence, and explaining how this interdependence can cause the AS curve to shift back in response to a shift back in aggregate demand, causing short-run potential income to be below long-run potential income. The final position of the short-run AS curve, and hence of short-run potential income, is dependent on the adjustment process that occurs if there is a gap between aggregate supply and aggregate demand.

To see this problem in terms of the model, let's assume that we are initially in equilibrium but that suddenly the *AD* curve shifts back from AD_0 to AD_1. We show this in Exhibit 4 (b). We are now in aggregate disequilibrium (Q_0 to Q_1) with the quantity of aggregate supply greater than the quantity of aggregate demand. If the price level adjusts instantaneously (from P_0 to P_1), so firms never experience disequilibrium, output remains constant. But say it doesn't—and realistically everyone agrees it doesn't. Then firms are not going to be able to sell all their goods, and will likely decrease their output—aggregate supply will decrease; it will shift back, say to AS_1. But as all firms decrease their output income will fall. As income falls, the demand for aggregate output will likely fall—there will be a shift of the demand curve back, say to AD_2. (Remember, the AD curve is drawn on the assumption that aggregate supply is constant.) But then there's still a disequilibrium (of Q_1–Q_2) and the whole process will start over again. To have a full analysis of AS/AD, you must carefully spell out the nature of the interdependent shifts of the AS and AD curves. Doing that gets messy, so we banish it to the Appendix, and instead combine the two together into the curves of the macro policy model. These curves take into account both the initial effects of a change in the price level on the curves and the interdependent shifts of the curves that occur in response to the initial shift. The resulting curves give us the final equilibrium, without spelling out the interdependencies.

Now that we've been through the rudiments of AS/AD analysis, let's move on to the main show: the macro policy model. We first consider the two components of the macro policy model: the aggregate equilibrium demand curve and the price-level flexibility curve. The basic macro model consists of two curves: the *aggregate equilibrium demand (AED) curve*—a curve which reflects the net effect of the forces of aggregate demand in an AS/AD model of the economy—and the *price-level flexibility (PLF) curve*—a curve which reflects the net effect of the forces of aggregate supply in an AS/AD model of the economy.

Underlying the AED and PLF curves are two sets of forces: (1) the forces captured by the slopes of the aggregate supply curves and the aggregate demand curve and (2) the disequilibrium adjustment forces that result from any interaction that takes place between these two curves when there is a disequilibrium—when they don't intersect. The AED curve and the PLF curve combine movements along the AD and AS curves with interdependent shifts of the curves, giving us a much neater graphical analysis because it doesn't show all the intermediate shifting. (In the Appendix we go through analytic foundations of the AS and AD curves, and in the next chapter we go through the Keynesian story of the interrelationship of these curves.) Let's now consider the two curves more carefully.

The Aggregate Equilibrium Demand Curve

The **aggregate equilibrium demand curve** is a schedule, graphically represented by a curve, that shows how a change in the price level will change equilibrium output after all interactive effects between aggregate supply and aggregate demand are taken into account. It is called an aggregate equilibrium demand because it tells us where the new equilibrium will be after aggregate supply responses to aggregate demand shifts are taken into account. It differs from the aggregate demand curve because it takes into account any assumed interaction between aggregate supply and demand.

The aggregate demand and the aggregate equilibrium demand curves are related, and in fact have the same general shape; they are both generally considered downward sloping. To see this, let's review the reason why the AD curve was downward sloping. The reason is that, as the price level fell, all other things equal, individuals are richer, so they increase their spending, increasing quantity demanded. This gave us the downward-sloping AD curve presented in Exhibit 4 (a).

Now let's consider likely interactive effects such as discussed above and how they will modify the AD curve. When people increase their spending and the price level does not rise immediately, if there are workers to be hired, firms will likely increase output (shift out the AS curve) which will increase income and cause individuals to buy more, causing the AD curve to shift out. (This induced effect was discussed above in Exhibit 4 (b).) The AED curve includes these induced effects on aggregate supply in its slope. Thus, it is a line which connects a set of points along a shifting AD curve. So the induced effects (often called multiplier effects), if there are any, reinforce the initial effect of a falling price level, making the aggregate equilibrium demand curve

The Macro Policy Model

Aggregate equilibrium demand curve (AED)   A curve which reflects the net effect of the forces of aggregate demand in an AS/AD model of the economy.

4   The AED curve takes into account interactive effects between aggregate supply and aggregate demand.

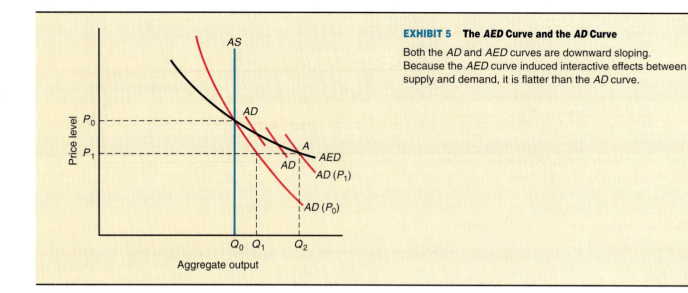

EXHIBIT 5   The *AED* Curve and the *AD* Curve

Both the *AD* and *AED* curves are downward sloping. Because the *AED* curve induced interactive effects between supply and demand, it is flatter than the *AD* curve.

(AED) less downward sloping (flatter) than the AD curve. We draw the *AED* curve and show its relation to the AD curve in Exhibit 5.

As you can see, the dynamic interdependencies of aggregate supply and aggregate demand multiply any effect that the fall in the price level has on the aggregate quantity demanded and make the *AED* curve flatter than the *AD* curve. So, as the price-level decrease causes aggregate supply to increase, the *AD* curve shifts out. The *AED* curve combines these induced shifts with the initial change captured by the *AD* curve. In this example, the initial price-level fall caused quantity demanded to increase from Q_0 to Q_1, and the induced effects caused both aggregate supply and aggregate demand to increase from Q_1 to Q_2. So point A (P_1, Q_2) is a point on the *AED* curve. It includes both the initial and the induced quantity effects of a fall in the price level. If there are no secondary induced effects of a fall in the price level, the *AED* curve and the *AD* curve are identical. (This relationship is considered in more detail in the Appendix.)

Price level flexibility curve (PLF) A curve which reflects the net effect of the forces of aggregate supply in an AS/AD model of the economy.

The Price Level Flexibility Curve   Let's now move on to the second building block of our macro policy model: the price-level flexibility (PLF) curve. The **price-level flexibility curve** is *a curve that tells us how much the price level will rise if there is an increase in demand. It tells us the degree of price-level flexibility in the economy as output changes due to fluctuations in aggregate demand.* If the price level adjusts instantaneously along the AS curve, the PLF curve becomes identical to the AS curve. If it does not, then the PLF curve traces the path of the price level as output changes. Thus it is a curve that tells us how much a shift in the AED curve will be reflected in increases in real output, and how much will be reflected in shifts in the price level. For example, say the AED curve shifts out and the price-level flexibility curve is flat; then all the change will take place in quantity—real output.

The price-level flexibility curve relates to the aggregate supply curve in the same way that the aggregate equilibrium demand curve relates to the aggregate demand curve. Specifically, it combines movements along the aggregate supply curve that occur because of higher price levels with shifts of the aggregate supply curve that are caused by any interconnection between aggregate supply and aggregate demand. If price adjustment is instantaneous, and no interactive effects cause the AS curve to shift, then the price-level flexibility curve will have the same shape as the AS curve. (Given our above assumption that the AS curve is vertical, if price-level adjustment is instantaneous, the PLF curve will be perfectly vertical.) If, however, price-level flexibility is less than instantaneous and the AS curve shifts because of induced effects of a change in AD, then the price-level flexibility curve will be flatter than the AS curve. The price-level flexibility curve is shown in Exhibit 6.

5   The price level flexibility curve tells us the degree of price-level flexibility as output changes due to fluctuations in aggregate demand.

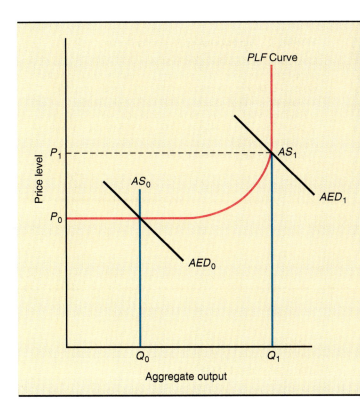

EXHIBIT 6   The *PLF* Curve and the *AS* Curve

The *PLF* curve traces out the price level adjustment path along a shifting *AS* curve. Given our assumption of a perfectly vertical *AS* curve, the slope of the curve depends on the degree of price level adjustment.

In it we show the responses of the price level and aggregate output to shifts in aggregate equilibrium demand. The shape of the PLF curve is institutionally determined by the degree of price-level flexibility that would occur if the AED curve shifts out by various amounts. For example, suppose the AED curve shifts out from AED_0 to AED_1. Say that, in response, the price level rises to P_1 and output increases to Q_1. This means that the point P_1, Q_1 will be a point on the PLF curve. The PLF curve is determined by going through all possible shifts of the AED curve, and determining the relevant price-level/output points. Remember that the AED curve shifting involves interdependent shifts of the AS and AD curves. This means that at the new equilibrium output, Q_1, the relevant AS curve, AS_1, is still vertical.

As the *AS* curve shifts out from AS_0 to AS_1, the price level rises from P_0 to P_1. So even though the *AS* curve is vertical, the price-level flexibility curve is not. To determine whether a real-world change in the price level reflects a movement along an AS curve (which it could if our assumption of a vertical AS curve did not hold true) or a shift of the AS curve is complicated. The advantage of the price-level flexibility curve is that we don't need to do so. The price-level flexibility curve shows the combined net result. (In the Appendix we discuss these issues in more detail.)

6 The price-level flexibility curve combines movements along the aggregate supply curve that occur because of higher price levels with shifts of the aggregate supply curve that are caused by interconnection between aggregate supply and aggregate demand.

The Three Ranges of the Price-Level Flexibility Curve   From empirical observation, economists have come to the conclusion that the price-level flexibility curve has three ranges:

1. A fixed price-level range (a flat PLF curve): When the economy is significantly below its long-run potential output, the price level seems to have a floor—downward shifts in aggregate equilibrium demand do not result in significant falls in the price level, and outward shifts of the AED curve do not seem to cause significant rises in the price level.

2. A partially flexible price level range (an upward-sloping PLF curve): As the economy approaches, but has not yet reached, its long-run potential output, an increase in aggregate equilibrium demand tends to be split into an increase in price level and an increase in aggregate real output. As the economy approaches long-run potential output, a larger percentage of that

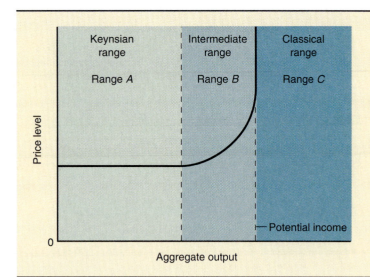

EXHIBIT 7   The Price-Level Flexibility Curve

Most economists believe the economy has three ranges of price-level flexibility. Range *A*, the fixed-price range, is often called the Keynesian range, since in the range, only the income adjustment mechanism is operative. Range *C*, which is reached when the economy reaches its potential income, is often called the Classical range, since only the price-level adjustment mechanism is operative. Range *B* is an intermediate range between the two.

aggregate equilibrium demand increase goes into price increases, and a smaller percentage goes into real output increases.

3. An upwardly flexible price-level range (a vertical PLF curve): Once the economy reaches its potential output, an excess in aggregate equilibrium demand will result in price-level changes, or in shortages, not increases, in real output. The range is generally defined by the economy's potential income—the highest level of output achievable without experiencing runaway inflation.

A price-level flexibility curve exhibiting these three ranges is shown in Exhibit 7. At low levels of output relative to long-run potential output (Range *A*), the price level is fixed; as output changes, the price level doesn't seem to change much. Thus, in the mid-1990s as the Canadian economy picked up and the price level didn't change, we were in that range. This range is also relevant for downward adjustments since the price level seems to cause a ratchet; it seldom falls. This means that the historically determined price level places a floor on the price level, and any adjustment takes place in real output changes, not in price level changes (probably through interdependent shifts of the supply and demand curves). In intermediate levels of output (Range *B*), the economy's expansion leaves a trail of a rising price level and a rising real output (probably through a combination of shifts and movements along the curves). At high levels of output relative to potential output (Range *C*), the price level changes quickly in response to changes in aggregate equilibrium demand. What range of the *PLF* curve the economy is in is important because that range determines how much real output can be expected to change in response to a shift in aggregate equilibrium demand. Committed Keynesians tend to see the economy in Range *A*—where the *PLF* curve is flat. Committed Classicals tend to see the economy in Range *C*—where the *PLF* curve is vertical. Most economists today are somewhere in-between committed Keynesians and committed Classicals; they see the economy in the intermediate range—Range *B*, where real output changes some, and the price level changes some as the *AED* curve shifts.

Important Shift Factors of Aggregate Demand and Aggregate Equilibrium Demand   Because shifts in the AED curve have been seen as the cause of recessions and inflation, the causes of these shifts are central to macro policy discussions. Five important shift factors of aggregate equilibrium demand are world income, expectations, exchange rate fluctuations, the distribution of income, and government policies. These shift factors cause aggregate demand to shift which, in turn, causes the AED curve to shift by more than that amount, the amount more depending on the induced effects of that initial shift.

World Income   A country is not an island unto itself, and Canada knows that more than most countries. How well Canada does is closely tied to how well its major world trading partners do. When the United States goes into a recession, its demand for Canadian goods will fall, causing the Canadian AED curve to shift in. Similarly, a rise in foreign income leads to an increase in Canada's exports and an outward shift of its aggregate equilibrium demand curve. These international interdependencies can become quite complicated. An example of this shift occurred in 1993 when Japan's economy fell into a recession. Japanese income fell, and hence Japan's demand for both United States and Canadian exports fell; as it did, both the U.S. and the Canadian AED curves shifted to the left. But that wasn't the end of it. As U.S. demand for Canadian exports fell, the Canadian AED shifted further to the left.

Expectations   Another important shift factor of aggregate equilibrium demand is expectations. Many different types of expectations can affect the AED curve. To give you an idea of the role of expectations, let's consider two expectational shift factors.

Expectations about Future Income: When businesspeople expect demand to be high in the future, they will want to increase their output capacity; their investment demand, a component of aggregate equilibrium demand, will increase. Thus positive expectations about future demand will shift the AED curve to the right.

Similarly, when consumers expect the economy to do well, they will be less worried about saving for the future, and they will spend more now—AED will shift to the right. Alternatively, if consumers expect the future to be gloomy, they will likely try to save for the future, and will decrease the consumption demand. The AED curve will shift to the left.

Expectations of Future Prices: Another type of expectation that shifts the AED curve concerns expectations of future prices. If the current price level falls relative to the future expected price level, people adjust their current quantity demanded (movement along the AED curve). In this case the price level remains constant, but expectations of future prices rise. If one expects the prices of goods to rise in the future, it pays to buy goods now that you might want in the future—before their prices rise. The current price level hasn't changed, but quantity demanded at that price level has increased, indicating an outward shift in the AED curve. So an increase in expectations of inflation—an expected rise in the price level—will have a tendency to shift the AED curve out.

This expectation of future price level-effect is seen most clearly in a hyperinflation. In most hyperinflations, people rush out to spend their money quickly—to buy whatever they can to beat the price push. So in hyperinflation, even though prices are rising, aggregate equilibrium demand stays high because the rise in price creates an expectation of even higher prices, and thus the current high price is seen as a "low price" relative to the future. We say "have a tendency" rather than "definitely shift the AED curve out" because those expectations of inflation are interrelated with a variety of other expectations. For example, an expectation of a rise in the price of goods you buy could be accompanied by an expectation of a fall in income, and that fall in income would work in the opposite direction, decreasing aggregate equilibrium demand.

This interrelatedness of various types of expectations makes it very difficult to specify precisely what effect certain types of expectation have on the AED curve. But it does not negate the importance of expectations as shift factors. It simply means that we often aren't sure what the net effect on aggregate equilibrium demand of a change in expectations will be.

7 Five important shift factors of the AED curve are:
1. Changes in world income.
2. Changes in expectations.
3. Changes in exchange rates.
4. Changes in the distribution of income.
5. Changes in government aggregate demand policy.

Exchange Rates   Another shift factor of aggregate equilibrium demand is the exchange rate. When a country's currency loses value, the foreign demand for its goods increases and its demand for foreign goods decreases as individuals do their spending at home. Both these effects mean that the AED curve shifts right. By the same reasoning, when a country's currency gains value the AED curve shifts in the opposite direction. You can see these effects on the U.S.–Canadian border. When in the early 1990s the Canadian dollar had a high value relative to the U.S. dollar, many Canadians near the border were making buying trips to the United States. Then in the mid-1990s, when the Canadian dollar fell in value, those buying trips decreased and the Canadian AED curve shifted right.

Distribution of Income   Some people save more than others and everyone's spending habits differ. Thus, as income distribution shifts, so too will aggregate equilibrium demand. One of the most important of these distributional effects concerns the distribution of income between wages and profits. Workers receive wage income and are more likely to spend the income they receive; firms' profits are distributed to richer people or are retained, and a higher portion of income received as profits will likely be saved. Thus, as the real wage—the ratio of the wage rate to the price level—decreases but total income remains constant, it is likely that aggregate equilibrium demand will shift back. Similarly, as the real wage increases, it is likely that aggregate equilibrium demand will shift out.

Government Aggregate Demand Policies   One of the most important reasons why the aggregate equilibrium demand curve has been so important in macro policy analysis is that activist macro policy makers think that they can control it, at least to some degree. For example, if the government goes out and spends lots of money without increases in taxes, it shifts the AED curve out; if the government raises taxes significantly holding spending constant, the AED curve shifts in. Similarly when the Central Bank of Canada expands the money supply it can often lower interest rates and thereby shift the AED curve out. This deliberate shifting of the AED curve to influence the level of income in the economy is what most policy makers mean by the term macro policy. Expansionary macro policy shifts out the AED curve; contractionary macro policy shifts it in.

Shift Factors of the PLF Curve   The PLF curve traces the response of the price level to shifts in aggregate equilibrium demand. If the price level shifts for some reason other than a shift in aggregate equilibrium demand, the PLF curve will shift. For example, say that there is an increase in the nominal price of an important natural resource. That would cause the PLF curve to shift up. It is also possible (but not likely) that the PLF curve can shift down. Say that suddenly, institutions changed, and all firms lowered their nominal wages and prices by 20%. The result would be a fall in the PLF curve.

USING THE MACRO POLICY MODEL

Now that we've been through both the AED curve and the price-level flexibility curve, and factors that can cause them to shift, let us put them together and see what happens to price level and output as the curves shift. Since these curves already include the effects of interdependent shifts, these shifts are due to some other cause than interdependencies. For example, a sudden rise in the nominal price level would shift the PLF curve up. Similarly a sudden increase in a country's exports would shift the AED curve out. (But, remember, because of induced effects, the shift in AED would be by more than the initial increase in exports.)

Equilibrium occurs when the *AED* curve intersects the *PLF* curve. Say we begin with AED_0 and *PLF* in Exhibit 8 (a). The equilibrium price level will be P_e and equilibrium aggregate output will be Q_e. Now say the *AED* curve shifts in, to AED_1. Since the *PLF* curve is flat in this range, the price level will remain constant at P_e and output will fall to Q_1. Alternatively, say that the *AED* curve shifts out to AED_2. Since the *PLF* curve is upward sloping in this range, the price level rises to P_2 and output rises to Q_2.

As a review of the foundation of the AED curve, let's try a specific number. Say

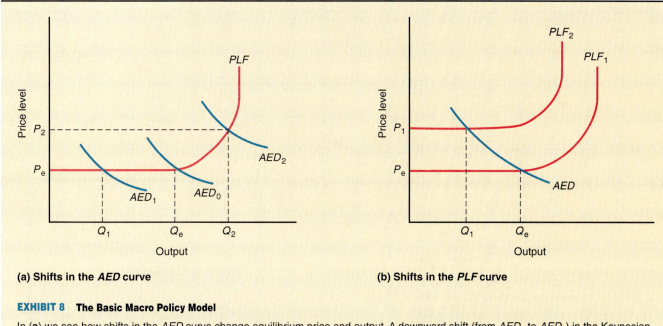

(a) Shifts in the *AED* curve

(b) Shifts in the *PLF* curve

EXHIBIT 8   The Basic Macro Policy Model

In (a) we see how shifts in the *AED* curve change equilibrium price and output. A downward shift (from AED_0 to AED_1) in the Keynesian range decreases output from Q_e to Q_1, price level remaining constant. An outward shift (from AED_0 to AED_2) in the intermediate range increases the price level from P_e to P_2 and output from Q_e to Q_2. In (b) we see how a shift in the *PLF* curve changes equilibrium. A shift upward of the *PLF* curve from PLF_1 to PLF_2 causes output to fall from Q_e to Q_1 and price level to rise from P_e to P_1. This basic policy model will be used throughout our study of macroeconomics to examine unemployment, growth, and inflation.

that, other things equal, something increases *aggregate demand* for Canadian products by 20. How much does the AED curve shift out? If you answered 20, a review is in order. Remember the AED curve considers not only the initial increase in aggregate demand, but the interactive effects that are caused by that initial shift. Thus the AD curve would shift out by 20 but the AED curve could shift out by a multiple of that amount—say two or three times that much. In the next chapter we will look at a model that tells us the relationship between a shift in the AD curve and a shift in the AED curve under specific assumptions. For now, just remember that the AED curve will likely shift out by more than the AD curve.

In Exhibit 8 (b) we show the effect of a shift up in the price level flexibility curve. How might such a shift up occur? One way is for the nominal price of a basic commodity such as oil to increase and for no other nominal price to decrease. That occurred in the 1970s. When that happens, other things constant, output decreases from Q_e to Q_1 and the price level rises from P_e to P_1.

The price-level flexibility curve can shift in either direction. In the first half of the 1990s the effect of oil prices has been in the opposite direction; they have fallen (shifting the price-level flexibility curve down), and, as they have, they have had a tendency to make world economic income higher than it otherwise would have been.

Let us now discuss some policy initiatives and other events that often occur in the economy and show why the shape of the PLF curve is central to policy debates. We do so in Exhibit 9 (a), (b), and (c).

In Exhibit 9 (a), the initial equilibrium of the economy is in Range *A* of the *PLF* curve where the price level remains relatively constant. The economy is way below its long-run potential income. In this range, a policy of increasing aggregate equilibrium demand from AED_0 to AED_1 will expand output and create the jobs Campbell and Chretien promised.

In Exhibit 9 (b), the equilibrium of the economy is in Range *B* in which an increase in aggregate equilibrium demand will cause the price level to rise some, and real output to rise some. The rise in the price level would mean that, for an equal

Macro Policy in the Macro Policy Model

8   The macro policy model lets us interpret events that often occur in the economy.

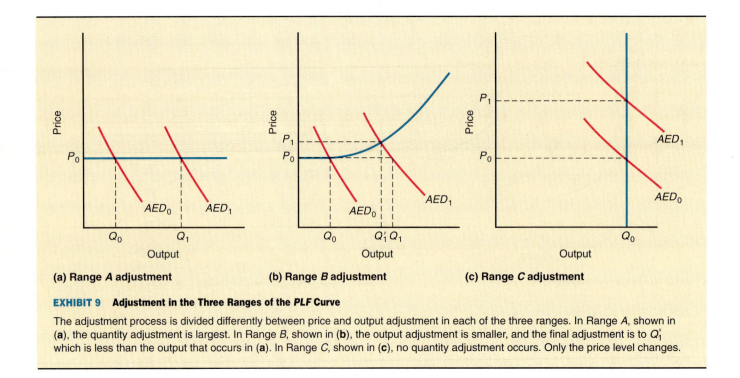

(a) Range A adjustment   **(b) Range B adjustment**   **(c) Range C adjustment**

EXHIBIT 9   Adjustment in the Three Ranges of the PLF Curve

The adjustment process is divided differently between price and output adjustment in each of the three ranges. In Range A, shown in (a), the quantity adjustment is largest. In Range B, shown in (b), the output adjustment is smaller, and the final adjustment is to Q_1' which is less than the output that occurs in (a). In Range C, shown in (c), no quantity adjustment occurs. Only the price level changes.

increase in AED to that assumed in 9 (a) (from AED_0 to AED_1), real output would increase less, and the price level would rise. Economies are often thought to be in this in-between range and that is one of the reasons conducting macro policy is so difficult. To achieve one desired goal—higher output—you have to move further away from another—price-level stability.

In Exhibit 9 (c), the equilibrium of the economy is at its potential income, and the price-level flexibility curve is vertical. An increase in aggregate equilibrium demand may still generate an increase in income, but it will be an increase in nominal, not real, income. The increase in aggregate equilibrium demand will not bring about any increase in real output or additional jobs at all; it will simply cause the price level to rise. When the economy is in this range, there is little debate among economists as to what the appropriate AED policy is—it is contractionary policy.

Some Practice Using the Macro Policy Model

Just to be sure that you have the analysis down, let's make you a policy advisor and give you a potential exam question. The economy initially has 12 percent unemployment and no inflation. Based on past history you believe that the economy is in the fixed price level range. Now a shock hits the economy and, other things constant, aggregate demand increases by 30. What do you predict will happen to the economy? Demonstrate graphically.

The answer is that aggregate output will increase by some multiple of 30 (because we must take into account interactive effects), and the price level may initially stay constant, but may begin to rise depending on how close to the intermediate range (partial price level flexibility) the economy was. Exhibit 10 (a) demonstrates this prediction. Notice the AED curve shifts out by more than 30 (we have arbitrarily chosen 90), equilibrium output increases, and the price level may rise slightly.

Alternatively, say that politicians suddenly cut the government budget deficit to zero, and even achieve a large surplus. What effect will you expect that action to have on the economy in the short run? (The answer is that, assuming we aren't in the flexible price range, the AED curve shifts back by a multiple of the cut, and the economy goes into a recession.)

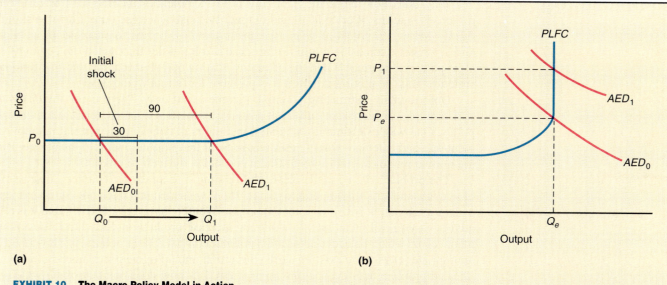

EXHIBIT 10   The Macro Policy Model in Action

When the price level is fixed, a positive shock to demand leads to a large change in output. In **(a)** you can see how the initial shock is multiplied by induced spending. In **(b)** we show how the same demand shock affects the economy when output is at potential. Output remains fixed and the price level rises to P_1.

Now let's try a different prediction. The economy initially has 7 percent unemployment and it is believed that 7 percent is the target rate of unemployment—the rate consistent with potential income. Now that same expansionary demand shock hits the economy. What do you predict will be the result? Demonstrate graphically.

The answer is that the *AED* curve will shift by a multiple of the initial shift as before, but, because the economy is at its potential income, the effect of that shift will be inflation, not an increase in real output. We demonstrate that prediction in Exhibit 10 (b). The initial price level was P_e and the initial output was Q_e. After the shock, the price level rises to P_1 and real output remains at Q_e.

As a final check on your understanding, let's say that you are the government's policy advisor. What policy would you suggest the government should follow in the previous example? If you answered, "Try to cut government spending or raise taxes so that the AED curve shifts in and the economy avoids the inflation," you've got the analysis down pat.

The above macro policy model makes the analysis of the aggregate economy look easy. All you have to do is determine which part of the price-level flexibility curve the economy is in, and, based on that, choose the appropriate AED policy. The problem is that we have no way of precisely determining for sure what range the economy is in, or precisely where potential income is. Much of the debate about macro policy concerns what range of the price-level flexibility curve the economy is in, and not what to do within a range.

To determine what range the economy is in, economists try to estimate potential income since that fixes the highest range. Once they have an estimate of potential income, they can make an estimate of what the other ranges are. The closer the economy is to its potential income, the more we would expect changes in the price level when there is an increase in AED. If potential income is significantly above actual income, the economy is probably in the fixed price-level range. If it is close to potential income, the economy is in the intermediate range. If it is at potential income, then we are in the flexible price-level range.

WHY MACRO POLICY IS
MORE COMPLICATED THAN
THIS MODEL MAKES IT LOOK

9   Knowing where potential income is and dealing with structural change are just two reasons why macro policy is more complicated than the model makes it look.

Why does how close the economy is to its potential income lead to different responses in terms of price level and output? Because when the output level is significantly below its potential level, the institutional structure to increase production already exists. Increasing output in this case is a lot easier than when the economy is at its potential income. When the economy is at its potential income, the institutional structure must be modified before it is possible for output to increase.

Unfortunately, estimating potential income is not easy. There is no obvious way to determine it, which is an important reason why there is so much debate about macro policy. One way of estimating potential income is to consider the normal unemployment rate and calculate what output would be at that normal unemployment rate. But the normal rate of unemployment fluctuates and is difficult to predict.

The problem can be made clearer by relating it to an earlier chapter's discussion of cyclical and structural unemployment. There we stated that cyclical unemployment occurs when output is below potential output. Workers have been laid off, and it is relatively easy to call them back to work and increase production. Structural unemployment occurs when the economy is at its potential output. The problem isn't layoffs; it's appropriate jobs for the existing skills. Structural unemployment is a much more complicated problem than cyclical unemployment. But how does one determine which is which? One cannot always simply look to past output level and assume that potential income can reach that level plus a normal growth rate. In some cases, the economy can be undergoing significant **structural readjustment** in which it is trying to change from what it has been doing to something new, not to repeat what it did in the past. If that is true, the economy can find itself in the Classical range at less than the previously attained output. Unemployment may look like cyclical unemployment, but may actually be structural unemployment.

For example, in 1992 to 1995 the Canadian economy expanded slowly, but that expansion was accompanied by major structural changes. This meant that firms expanded and increased output, but that they often laid off workers simultaneously. Before these workers could be reemployed, they had to structurally change their professions rather than simply be hired back by their former companies. That takes a lot longer—first to realize that one must redefine one's profession, and then to actually do it.

In Canada in the mid-1990s, the unemployment rate was about 9 percent. This was high by normal standards, but as we discussed above many economists felt that what was normal had changed. They lowered their estimates of potential income accordingly and were strongly opposed to any policies to shift the AED curve out. Others felt the normal unemployment rate was lower, so the economy was significantly below its potential income. They were more likely to favour shifting the AED curve out.

Let's consider another example: Europe 1994. Unemployment was over 10 percent, so it would seem the economy was in the *A* range. We didn't have to worry about inflation. But wait—there was major economic restructuring going on in Europe, and social welfare programs significantly reduced people's incentive to work. Thus some economists felt that Europe 1994 was at the outer edge of the intermediate range, and the "no expansionary demand" policy was called for. Others disagreed, and called for significant tax cuts to stimulate the economy. What range was Europe 1994 actually in? Economic theory doesn't tell us.

The problem of structural change is even more real for the formerly socialist economies. Even though their output has fallen by 40 to 50 percent, they still find themselves in the Classical range—they don't want to produce what, or how, they did before. They are trying to develop whole new institutional structures, which means that neither their previous income nor their unemployment rates are especially relevant in determining their potential income. When there is major structural change, normal is no longer normal.

Another way to determine potential income is to take the economy's previous income level, and add the normal growth factor of 3 percent. This gives us a very

Structural readjustment
Phenomenon of economy trying to change from what it had been doing to doing something new instead of repeating what it had done in the past.

rough estimate which needs to be adjusted for such things as regulatory changes: If the government has just passed numerous regulations, most economists would adjust potential income down since those regulations would probably reduce supply. On the other hand, if the value of a country's currency fell, most economists would adjust potential income up, since the depreciation would probably improve the international competitiveness of the country's goods. Similarly, if technology is growing significantly, then potential output is probably increasing faster than normal. Another change involves the labour markets and labour force participation rates: if individuals are increasing labour force participation rates, potential output is adjusted up.

Making all these adjustments is complicated, and the estimates of potential income that come from them leave much room for debate. There's usually a composite estimate, but actual potential income could be higher, or lower, than that composite, leaving room for much debate about what potential income is, and hence about what the appropriate macro policy is.

The problems of estimating potential income have led some economists to argue that the best estimate of potential income that we have is the actual income in the economy. These economists believe the fluctuations in the economy are not caused primarily by fluctuations in aggregate demand, but are instead caused primarily by fluctuations in potential income. In terms of our macro policy model, they see the range *C* as fluctuating in and out as technological changes occur, and desires to work change. Their Classical supply-side explanation is called a **real business cycle** theory because they see all changes in the economy as real shifts—shifts in potential income—which reflect real causes such as technological changes or shifting tastes. Expressed in terms of our macro policy model, a real business cycle is a fluctuation that is caused by supply-side shifting of range *C* on the price flexibility curve. For a real business cycle economist, the economy is always in the flexible price-level range, and the result of macro policy shifting out of the AED would be a rise in the price level, with no effect on real output. Thus it should not be a surprise when we tell you that real business cycle economists are Classical economists.

Real business cycle theory   Real business cycle theories see economic cycles that result from real shifts in the economy. Shocks to technology and tastes? affect the supply side, leading to business cycles.

CONCLUSION AND A LOOK AHEAD

We will stop the analysis there. We hope it wasn't too much exercising of the mind, but enough to make the mind a little sore. But we recognize that it was hard enough to make a very brief summary of the main points useful. So, here goes. First, there is a difference between Classical and Keynesian economists; Classicals favour laissez-faire policy. Keynesians tend to favour activist policy. These policy issues are often discussed in terms of the macro policy model, and the distinction between Keynesians and Classicals can be shown in that model. Essentially, Classicals see the PLF curve as vertical—they believe there is significant price-level flexibility in the economy. Keynesians see the PLF curve as flat as long as the economy is below its long-run potential income. Because it is, flat shifts in aggregate demand will have induced effects on aggregate supply, which will in turn have induced effects on aggregate demand—causing larger-than-desired business cycles. The Keynesian and Classical positions on the PLF curve give us the extremes. Most economists today are neither purely Classical nor purely Keynesian. They are a combination of the two; they see the economy in the intermediate range in which the PLF curve is upward sloping. Thus, the AED/PLF model provides us with a model that most economists today can accept. Understanding its foundations lets us understand the Keynesian and Classical positions from which the modern view developed.

Much of the discussion of macro policy has concerned the Keynesian view of the macro model and the nature of those induced shifts. So, in the next chapter we develop that Keynesian view more fully, showing how one can arrive at specific numerical determinations of what the induced effects will be. Then, in Chapter 10 we discuss policy in reference to that Keynesian model, and conclude our discussion of macro theory with a discussion of policy in reference to both the Keynesian and Classical models. Later chapters further develop this distinction.

CHAPTER SUMMARY

- The evolution of macroeconomic thinking has involved an evolving debate between Keynesian and Classical economists.
- The macro policy model consists of two curves—the AED curve and the PLF curve.
- The AED curve is downward sloping; the price level flexibility curve has three segments: a fixed price-level range, a partially flexible price-level range, and an upwardly flexible price-level range.
- The AED curve is based on the AD curve and the induced effects that any change in AD has. Whereas the AD curve assumes aggregate supply constant, the AED curve does not.

- The PLF curve is based on the AS curve and the dynamic path that adjustment follows when aggregate demand changes; it traces the path that the price level will follow during adjustment. It can involve both movements along and shifts of an AS curve.
- In macroeconomic analysis, one must be careful to avoid the fallacy of composition.
- Macro policy is much more complicated than the macro policy model presents because we have no definitive way of deciding what range the economy is in.

KEY TERMS

activist economists *(185)*
aggregate demand (AD) curve *(193)*
aggregate equilibrium demand (AED) curve *(195)*
aggregate supply (AS) curve *(193)*
aggregate supply/aggregate demand (AS/AD) macro models *(192)*
Classical economists *(186)*
fallacy of composition *(194)*
Keynesian economists *(186)*

laissez-faire *(186)*
laissez-faire economists *(185)*
law of aggregate demand *(208)*
long-run potential income *(190)*
macro policy model *(192)*
money *(188)*
potential income *(190)*
price level *(192)*
price-level flexibility (PLF) curve *(196)*

quantity theory of money *(188)*
real business cycle *(205)*
real wage *(186)*
relative price *(192)*
Say's law *(187)*
short-run potential income *(190)*
structural readjustment *(204)*
supply/demand models *(192)*

QUESTIONS FOR THOUGHT AND REVIEW

The number after each question represents the estimated degree of critical thinking required (1 = almost none; 10 = deep thought).

1. Distinguish between a laissez-faire and an activist economist. *(3)*

2. In the 1930s, Dennis Robertson and John Maynard Keynes's friendship came to a sudden halt. Can you explain a likely reason why? *(6)*

3. What is the difference between a price level and a relative price? *(2)*

4. What is the relationship between the AED curve and the AD curve? *(6)*

5. Under what condition will the AD curve be identical to the AED curve? *(7)*

6. How could a Classical economist accept that there is an interaction between aggregate supply and demand but still believe that laissez-faire is the best policy? *(10)*

7. What are five factors that cause the AED curve to shift? *(8)*

8. What are two factors that cause the price-level flexibility curve to shift? *(7)*

9. What range do you think the Canadian economy is in now? How does your answer to that determine what policy you would suggest the government should follow? *(8)*

10. How might "positive thinking" cause an economy to expand? *(5)*

PROBLEMS AND EXERCISES

1. The opening quotation of the chapter refers to Keynes's view of theory.

   a. What do you think he meant by it?

   b. How does it relate to the emphasis on the "other things constant" assumption?

   c. Do you think Keynes's interest was mainly in positive economics, the art of economics, or normative economics? Why?

2. State why you believe micro supply/demand analysis, used without additions, is or is not useful in determining the following:

   a. The wage of carpenters.

   b. The average wage rate in the economy.

   c. The price of eggs.

   d. The price level.

   e. The level of income in the economy.

3. In the library:

   a. Find Canada's price level and the level of output (GDP) over the last 10 years. Then:

   b. Graph the data with price level on the vertical axis and the level of GDP on the horizontal axis.

   c. Is the curve you have drawn a supply curve, a demand curve, or neither? Why?

4. Explain what will likely happen to the shape or position of the AED curve in the following circumstances.

   a. The exchange rate changes from fixed to flexible.

   b. A fall in the price level doesn't make people feel richer.

   c. A fall in the price level creates expectations of a further-falling price level.

   d. Income is redistributed from rich to poor people.

   e. Autonomous exports increase by 20.

   f. Government spending decreases by 10.

5. Explain what will happen to the slope or position of the price-level flexibility curve in the following circumstances:

   a. Available inputs increase.

   b. A civil war occurs.

   c. The relative price of oil quadruples.

   d. Wages that were fixed become flexible.

   e. The exchange rate changes from fixed to flexible.

6. Congratulations! You have been appointed an economic policy advisor to Textland. You are told that the economy is significantly below its potential income, and that the following shocks will hit the economy next year: World income will fall significantly; and the price of oil will rise significantly. (Your country is an oil importer.)

   a. Demonstrate graphically, using the macro policy model, your predictions.

   b. What policy might you suggest to the government?

   c. How would a real business cycle economist likely criticize the policy you suggest?

7. Write a short essay explaining why macro policy is more difficult than the simple model suggests. Choose a recent macroeconomic event to illustrate your point.

The Analytic Macro Model

In the chapter we carefully distinguished the AED and PLF curves of the macro policy model from aggregate supply and aggregate demand curves and showed briefly the relationship between the two. In this appendix, we show more precisely how those curves relate to appropriately defined aggregate supply and aggregate demand curves.

The Aggregate Demand Curve

We begin with the aggregate demand curve. The aggregate demand curve is a schedule, graphically represented by a curve, that shows how a change in the price level will change output demanded, other things (including supply) held constant.[1]

Generally, economists consider this aggregate demand curve to be downward sloping, as in Exhibit A1, which means that a fall in the price level, *other things constant,* will cause the quantity of aggregate demand to increase. This downward-sloping relationship between the price level and the quantity of aggregate demand is called the **law of aggregate demand**—as the price level falls the quantity of aggregate demand will increase, holding everything else constant.

The aggregate demand (AD) curve is generally considered to be downward sloping because as the price level falls, several effects cause real output to increase. Similarly, changes in a number of factors cause the AD curve to shift left and right. Understanding the shape and location of the AD curve is so important that we want to examine this in detail.

Determinants of the Slope of the Aggregate Demand Curve

There are four effects that have been put forward as explanations of why a fall in the price level will have an

effect on the quantity demanded, causing the aggregate demand curve to be downward sloping. These four effects are the *wealth effect, the price level interest rate effect, the intertemporal price level effect, and the international effect.* Each of these effects makes the aggregate demand curve downward sloping and thereby provides a mechanism through which the price level affects the total quantity demanded.

The Wealth Effect The **wealth effect** (sometimes called the Pigou effect, for A. C. Pigou, one of the first economists to point it out) explains the law of aggregate demand as follows: Say the price level falls. That fall will increase the value of money, since each dollar will buy more than it would have at a higher price level. Therefore you could say that the real money supply (the money supply divided by the price level) has increased. As the real money supply rises, the quantity of aggregate goods demanded increases until it has increased enough to equal aggregate supply.

To see how this occurs, let's consider an example. Assume the economy experiences a recession—there is an excess supply of workers and goods. The wage and price levels begin to fall. That fall in the price level increases the value of the dollars in people's pockets, making them richer. Because they're richer, they spend more—the quantity demanded increases. With this adjustment mechanism, the Classicals had an answer to how an aggregate disequilibrium could, in theory, be eliminated through a fall in the price level.

The Price-Level Interest Rate Effect Another explanation of the law of aggregate demand (quantity of aggregate demand increases as price level falls) is called the price-level interest rate effect. According to the **price-level interest rate effect,** a decrease in the price level will increase the real money supply, as in the wealth effect. But the path of the interest rate does not depend on making holders of cash balances richer. Instead, the price-level interest rate effect focuses on the effect of the increase in real money supply on interest rates: It will

---

[1]This definition of AD, while standard in most introductory books, is different than the aggregate equilibrium demand (AED) curve presented in the chapter. The AED curve includes multiplier effects—induced spending resulting from the initial change in price. That AED curve derived from the Keynesian model is a locus of points tracing a shifting AD curve; it does not distinguish *shifts in* and *movements along* the AD curve. For further development of the problem, see David Colander, "The Stories We Tell: A Reconsideration of AS/AD Analysis," *Journal of Economic Perspectives,* Summer 1995.

EXHIBIT A1   The Aggregate Demand Curve

lower interest rates, which in turn will increase investment. Why? Because at lower interest rates, businesses will find it cheaper to borrow and hence will undertake more investment projects.[2] Since investment is one component of aggregate demand, the quantity of aggregate demand will increase when the price level falls. Instead of relying on the effect that a lower price level has on cash balances (wealth effect), it concentrates on its effect on interest rates. The price-level interest rate effect is another reason why the aggregate demand curve slopes downward to the right.

The Intertemporal Price-Level Effect A third effect is the **intertemporal price-level effect.** Say the price level falls and is expected to rise in the next period. People will decide to purchase some goods now that they would have purchased in the future. As they rearrange their intertemporal demand, they will increase their quantity demanded now and decrease their quantity demanded in the future. Thus, as long as the change in the current price level doesn't affect expectations of the future price level, this intertemporal shift in quantity demanded provides another explanation of the law of aggregate demand.

The International Effect The price-level interest rate effect, the wealth effect, and the intertemporal price-level effect hold for a closed economy—an economy without international trade. As soon as we allow for international trade, there's another reason why the aggregate demand curve slopes downward: the **international effect.** It works as follows: Given a fixed exchange rate (which most developed countries had in the early 1900s, since

they were on the gold standard which uses fixed exchange rates), when the price level in a country goes down, the price of its exports decreases relative to the price of foreign goods, so a country's exports increase. Similarly for imports: When the price level in a country falls, the relative price of its imports rises, so a country's imports decrease.

For example, say the price level (including wages) in Canada falls by 50 percent. That means that a hamburger that previously cost $2 now will cost $1. Of course, people's incomes also fall, so a person who before had earned $400 per week now earns only $200 per week. However, a fall in the Canadian price level does not affect the price of imports. That means French perfume that previously cost $80 an ounce will still cost $80 an ounce. Since you're now earning only $200 a week, the relative price of French perfume to you will have doubled, and by the law of demand you'll consume less French perfume. You'll substitute Canadian perfume. As the Canadian price level falls, Canadian residents substitute Canadian goods for foreign goods, increasing the quantity of Canadian goods demanded.

The effect is the opposite with exports. Consider a reduction in the Canadian price of wheat. Foreigners' income won't have fallen, but the price of Canadian wheat will have declined. So, by the law of demand, foreigners will buy more Canadian wheat than before. As the Canadian price level falls, foreign residents substitute Canadian goods for their own goods, increasing the quantity of Canadian goods demanded. Both of these effects increase aggregate quantity demanded for Canadian goods. Thus, the international effect of a price change is a fourth reason why the aggregate demand curve slopes downward.

The importance of the international effect depends on the importance of international trade to a country. If

---

[2]The price-level interest rate effect can't be fully developed here because it depends on issues that themselves won't be fully developed until later chapters. We present it here for completeness, because it is one of the explanations of the downward-sloping aggregate demand curve.

IN DEFENCE OF THOSE PROFESSORS WHO ASSIGN THE APPENDIX

There are two reasons why students will read this appendix: because of their great desire to understand the deep structure of the macro model, and because their teacher tells them to—and tests them on it. We are under no illusion which of the two reasons will predominate. And, we suspect, those students who are assigned the appendix will complain—our students certainly do. So let us offer a brief defence of "tough-teach" teachers who put students through the analytic hoops of the formal models.

The main reason why a professor requires a student to jump through analytic hoops is the same reason that we require our children to do extra homework. (Yes, they complain about it, too.) It's because he or she believes that working through those analytic hoops will exercise the student's mind—giving her or him practice in understanding interrelationships of economic variables. The justification for doing so can be made clear by an analogy, again to high school sports. In just about any competitive sport, coaches don't let you compete unless you do calisthenics and exercises in preparation. Generally, the better you do the calisthenics, the better you play the sport. The same is true of economics. Formal models are economics' calisthenics of the mind.

Students need such calisthenics. Quite frankly, most students' minds are about as flabby as our bodies, and each of us is a middle-aged male physical mess because we spend all our time exercising our minds (writing this book!!!), and too little time exercising our bodies. Physical exercises would be good for us; we know it, and we keep promising ourselves that tomorrow we'll do some. But you know how it goes: we find this neat article, or argument, and we're off to our computers, sitting on our backsides. Most students have the same problem with their minds that we have with our bodies; they know they should exercise their minds, but they put off doing it.

There is no doubt that people can talk about economic policy even though they have no training in theory and without going through the formal models. It happens all the time. But such talk is the equivalent of sandlot baseball or singing in the shower. In a policy discussion with someone trained to deal with formal economic models, the untrained are annihilated. The point is, no matter what you are doing, you can't immediately just do it (despite what Nike commercials tell you). Instead, you must prepare yourself to do it right. You do exercises—work with abstract formal models. So if your teacher is like us and assigns the appendix, recognize that he or she is doing it for your benefit.

Having made our pitch for the usefulness of formal models, we will now say that we're also realists and not sadists; almost none of you are going on to become professional economists, and very few of you will major in economics. For most of you, this is the end of the road in the study of formal economics. So even the formal models that we present in the Appendix are highly watered-down versions of a far more complex model.

---

the country trades very little, the international effect will be small. If, like Canada, the country trades a large amount, the international effect will be large.

If you reflect upon the international effect, you'll see a relationship between it and the reasoning underlying the partial-equilibrium downward-sloping demand curve. Internationally, a country's price level is a relative price. If economists open the analysis to include goods from other countries, a country's overall price level can be equated to the price for a single good—just the opposite of the case of a country's economy examined by itself. In an international context, the aggregate demand curve of a country is the equivalent of a partial-equilibrium demand curve for a single good within a country. So it isn't surprising that the international effect contributes to a downward-sloping aggregate demand curve.

The importance of the international effect depends on there being fixed exchange rates. If there are flexible exchange rates, a change in a country's price level will

likely be accompanied by an offsetting change in the country's exchange rate. For example, say the price level in a country rises by 10 percent but the value of the country's currency falls by 10 percent. For foreigners, the two effects will be offsetting, and the price they face for Canadian goods will be unchanged. Thus, with flexible exchange rates, the international effect may be inoperative.

These four effects—the wealth effect, the price-level interest rate effect, the intertemporal price-level effect, and the international effect—explain why the AD curve is downward sloping.

Shifts in the AD Curve and Shifts in the AED Curve

The AD curve shifts for the same reason that the AED curve shifts. Thus the discussion in the text is just as relevant for the AD curve as it is for the AED curve. The difference between the two is the amount of shifting that will take place in response to an autonomous shift. *The*

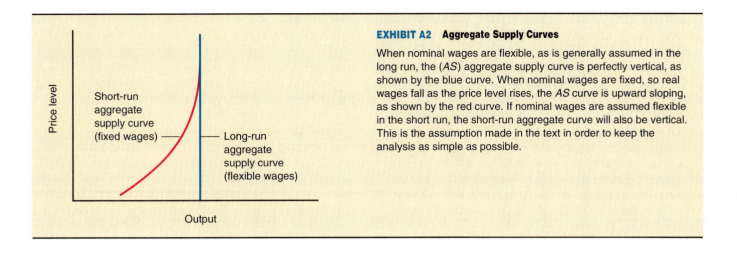

EXHIBIT A2   Aggregate Supply Curves

When nominal wages are flexible, as is generally assumed in the long run, the (*AS*) aggregate supply curve is perfectly vertical, as shown by the blue curve. When nominal wages are fixed, so real wages fall as the price level rises, the *AS* curve is upward sloping, as shown by the red curve. If nominal wages are assumed flexible in the short run, the short-run aggregate curve will also be vertical. This is the assumption made in the text in order to keep the analysis as simple as possible.

AD curve shifts only by the amount of the autonomous shift; the AED curve shifts by the amount of the autonomous shift plus an amount that reflects the dynamic interaction that that shift causes. For example, say aggregate demand shifted out by 10. The AD curve would shift out by 10. But that shift might cause a supply response which would feed back on demand, etc. The AED curve would shift out by an amount that includes all the dynamic interactions. Thus it will not shift out by only 10. To say how much it will shift out one must specify what dynamic interactions one believes will occur in response to that autonomous shift. We consider that issue in the next chapter.

The AS Curve

Economists usually distinguish two AS curves—a short-run *AS* curve and a long-run vertical *AS* curve. These two curves are drawn in Exhibit A2. The reasoning for the difference between the shapes of the two curves is that, in the short run, input prices, mainly wages, are assumed constant, so as output prices rise relative to input prices, profits increase and firms have an incentive to increase output. This leads to the short-run upward-sloping curve. As long as workers are willing to supply more labour even though their real wage has decreased, this reasoning makes sense.

In the long run, input prices and output prices are assumed to move in tandem. Thus, the reasoning for an upward-sloping AS curve does not apply and, in the long run (or in the short run if input prices adjust as fast as output prices), the AS curve is perfectly vertical. A vertical curve means that a change in the price level, other things equal, will not cause the quantity of aggregate supply to change.

It is important for us to understand what shifts the AS curve and what determines its shape.

Determining the Shape of the Aggregate Supply Curve

As was the case with the AD curve, specifying precisely what remains constant as we draw these curves is difficult. We will follow the standard practice by ruling out many of the fine points, and focus on constant input prices as the basis for the slope of the short-run AS curve. For the long-run AS curve, we define the price level in such a way that it includes input prices so that relative input/output price-level changes cannot occur.

For both cases, we rule out the international effect on the quantity of aggregate supply either because the exchange rate is flexible, or because the country has no international trade. We also assume that the intertemporal price-level effect on supply is inoperative. (These assumptions can be eliminated, and one could have an upward-sloping aggregate supply curve even without fixed input prices. But since the debate about aggregate supply and demand which we will be discussing at length in this and the next few chapters has focused on the law of aggregate demand, we follow standard practice and assume these additional effects away; doing so does not substantially change the nature of the debate.)

The Slope of the Short-Run Aggregate Supply Curve The standard argument for an upward-sloping short-run AS curve is the following: If input prices are constant, an increase in demand will cause firms' profits to increase, which will lead firms to want to raise output. Thus if output prices rise relative to input price, the quantity of aggregate supply can be expected to increase as the price level rises, given an upward-sloping short-run AS curve.

The difficulty with this argument is in determining where the additional workers are going to come from. If the labour market was initially in equilibrium, then the rise in output price will mean a fall in the real wage— what workers can buy with their pay—which would cause them to work less, not more. So the upward-sloping short-run AS curve is based on the assumption that there is excess supply in the labour market. But why should there generally be excess supply in the labour market?

Unless one specifies why, the standard argument for an upward-sloping short-run AS curve is suspect.

The Slope of the Long-Run AS Curve Questions about the justification for assuming excess supply in the labour market led economists to move away from using the short-run supply curve, and to focus more on the long-run supply curve in which input prices and output prices move together. When input and output prices rise in tandem, the standard explanation of the upward-sloping AS curve no longer holds. The assumption of input and output prices rising in tandem, combined with the other above-mentioned assumptions, leads to a vertical long-run AS curve.

To see this, ask yourself the following question: What effect on suppliers would there be if the supplier's price went up 100 percent, but all his or her costs also went up one hundred percent? The common-sense answer to this question is: There would be no effect on the quantity supplied; it's simply a change in the measuring rod. This common-sense view means that the AS curve is vertical—the aggregate quantity people want to supply is unaffected by a change in the price level.

Short-Run Shift Factors of Aggregate Supply The macroeconomic debate about business cycles that is the focus of much of the next few chapters has not centred around long-run shift factors of supply. All macroeconomists agree that these long-run shift factors of supply are important causes of growth, although precisely how they each contribute to growth is subject to significant debate. Instead, the macroeconomic debate about business cycles has centred around short-run shift factors of supply, specifically expectations.

Once one allows for short-run shift factors, the long-run supply curve—potential output—provides an upper limit beyond which output cannot go. But it can go lower if the short-run shift factors shift the short-run supply curve back—causing a recession. Thus, an understanding of short-run shift factors is essential to understanding recessions, and what policies might pull an economy out of a recession. Let's now consider how shifting expectations can lead to fluctuations in output.

Expectations As was the case with aggregate demand, one of the most important shift factors of short-run aggregate supply is expectations. Expectations can affect aggregate supply in many ways, but one of the most important, and the one that is the focus of much of the debate in macroeconomics, is *expectations of aggregate demand.*

Say suppliers expect aggregate demand to be low, and hence expect that demand for the product they produce will be low. They will likely decide to reduce supply, shifting the aggregate supply curve left. Alternatively, say expectations of aggregate demand are high, so that suppliers think that demand for their product will be high. Aggregate supply will increase. So, our general conclusion is that *expectations of an increase in aggregate demand will cause the short-run AS curve to shift right, and expectations of a decrease in aggregate demand will cause the short-run AS curve to shift left.* These shifts in expectations play a central role in leading the economy to an aggregate equilibrium.

Just how important expectations of aggregate demand are can be seen by the amount of time and effort firms spend trying to measure what future demand will be. There are large numbers of consumer sentiment surveys, polls, and market research surveys which firms use to decide how much to produce—what their supply will be. Recognizing the importance of expectations of demand to supply decisions is easy for businesspeople who are trying to predict demand, and for students trying to understand the economy.

It was somewhat more difficult for Classical economists who were trained to think about the economy as one in which firms had no short-run price-setting role, one in which firms produced and sold whatever they could at whatever price they could receive. In a perfectly flexible price world, the quantity demanded would always equal the quantity supplied, so expectations of aggregate demand should not play a role. In any other world—with less than perfectly flexible prices, such as the world we live in—expectations of aggregate demand are a central shift factor.

Other Shift Factors of Short-Run Supply There are many other shift factors of short-run supply. For example, bad weather will decrease aggregate supply, and a war in a country can destroy its productive capacity. Alternatively, a major strike by producers could decrease supply so that even if potential output is high, little output is forthcoming as suppliers refuse to work.

Classical and Keynesian Aggregate Adjustment

Now that we've presented the analysis of the underlying shapes of the curves and the reasons they shift, let's use them to discuss aggregate dynamic adjustment in both the Classical and the Keynesian cases. In Exhibit A3 we can see the Classical dynamic adjustment to a shift in aggregate demand.

For reasons discussed above, the AD curve is downward sloping and the AS curve is vertical at long-run potential output. A demand shock hits, shifting the AD curve down to AD_1. Because the supply curve is upward sloping, and fixed in the short run at its initial output, in the Classical case aggregate output never decreases by assumption—either because there is instantaneous price-level adjustment or because suppliers do not change output even though there is a shortfall of demand. There is only one adjustment mechanism possible. In the Classical adjustment, the price level (including the wage level) falls to P_1 keeping the aggregate economy in equilibrium. This assumption means that not only is the aggregate supply curve vertical, so too is the price-level

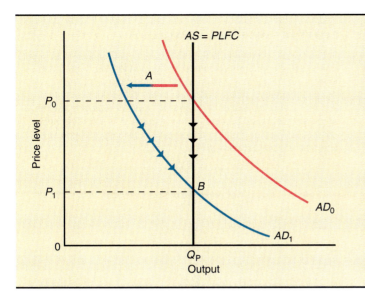

If aggregate supply and aggregate demand are independent of each other and nominal wages and the price level are flexible, a decrease in aggregate demand will lead to an adjustment process in which output remains constant and the price level falls. Many other adjustment processes are possible, depending on assumptions.

flexibility curve. You are always in range C of the price-level flexibility curve.

Keynes thought this Classical model of aggregate disequilibrium adjustment was too simple (as did many Classical economists such as Dennis Robertson). To see why, let's consider his argument against it. As before, let's say that the economy finds itself in aggregate disequilibrium at the existing price level, so the quantity of aggregate supply is greater than the quantity of aggregate demand. This disequilibrium may create a tendency for wages and prices to fall, but Keynes argued that a fall in the price level will not be instantaneous. He argued that, in the interim, a second adjustment force—one of the shift factors discussed above—enters the picture.[3]

Specifically, in the short run, firms' expectations about demand cannot be assumed constant. When firms can't sell all their goods, they will cut production—decrease aggregate supply. So unlike the Classical case where aggregate supply was fixed, in Keynes's view the short-run aggregate supply curve would shift in response to a shortage in aggregate demand. The aggregate supply curve might be perfectly vertical, but the price-level flexibility curve was not. We show this Keynesian adjustment in Exhibit A4. In response to a shift in AD, the AS curve shifts back. To understand aggregate equilibrium, Keynes argued, you had to understand the nature of these interdependent shift factors. *The interactions of these shift factors determined the income level at which the economy would equilibrate.*

So in Keynes's model, *aggregate supply depends on expected aggregate demand.* If demand isn't there to buy all that is supplied, the supply will shift back to meet the demand. But, Keynes argued, that shift back in aggregate supply would not bring about equilibrium. As aggregate supply shifts back, society's income will fall. Therefore the shift back in aggregate supply will cause the aggregate demand curve to shift back again. What Keynes called effective demand would fall because, in Keynes's model, not only is aggregate supply dependent on expected aggregate demand, aggregate demand is also dependent on aggregate supply. **Effective demand** is the aggregate demand that exists after suppliers cut production in response to aggregate supply exceeding aggregate demand. Comparing the two shifts in Exhibit A4, we see that the initial difference (Q_0–Q_1) between the AS_0 and AD_1 curves is more than the difference (Q_1–Q_2) between the AS_1 and AD_2 curves. So as we have drawn it, the AD curve shifts back by less than the AS curve shifts, which means with each shift the two curves move closer together; the shifting is an equilibrating force.

Where will the new equilibrium be in the Keynesian case? If the price level remains constant, short-run aggregate supply could shift back from AS_0 to AS_1 before the price level falls. Thus it might seem to you that the new equilibrium will be at the same price level P_0 and a lower output level Q_1 (point A). It won't be there. Why? Because of the interdependency between shifting aggregate supply and shift factors in demand. Specifically, say aggregate supply shifts back to AS_1. As output falls, income falls, and income is a shift factor of demand. So as the AS curve shifts back, that very shift can cause a shift in aggregate demand from AD_1 to AD_2. But it's even more complicated—expected demand is a shift factor of supply, so the mere expectation of the shift in demand can bring about a further shift in supply.

Keynes's conclusion from the above reasoning was that one cannot understand aggregate equilibrium without understanding the interrelation between aggre-

---

[3]Keynes did not explore what would happen if nominal prices and wages did not move in tandem. He ruled that possibility out by a wage unit assumption that assumed wages and prices move in tandem. He argued, however, that (1) his conclusions were not based on this assumption, and (2) for the large movement in price level necessary for the Classical price-level adjustment mechanism to work, wages and prices would move roughly equally.

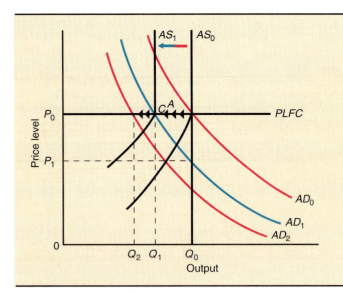

EXHIBIT A4   Shift of the Curves Adjustment

In the Keynesian adjustment analysis, aggregate supply and aggregate demand are assumed interdependent, and the price level flexibility curve is assumed flat. In this case a shift in demand causes a shift in supply, and the shift in supply causes a shift in demand. Since the price level is assumed constant the adjustment path will be along arrow *A* in A4. With interdependent shifts, one must go through an interactive process to determine what the final equilibrium will be.

gate supply and demand, and the effect that has on the short-run equilibrium that the economy arrives at. For Keynes, this interrelationship between aggregate supply and demand is a fundamentally important insight because it undermines the logical underpinnings of a belief that, in the short run, a market economy will automatically gravitate toward its potential income. The interdependency of aggregate supply and demand can prevent the economy from arriving at its long-run potential income.

At this point in the analysis, we are not interested in determining where the aggregate equilibrium will be. The models in the next chapter will consider that in both the classical and the Keynesian case. What we want to accomplish in this appendix is to impress upon you the complicated nature of aggregate disequilibrium adjustment analysis when all other things are not—as they cannot be in the real world—assumed constant. There are many, many logical possibilities, and the process is mindboggling. Such mind-boggling processes make theoretical economists' mouths water, and students' eyes gloss over. We won't be discussing them here.

The problem many economists have with what has become known as Keynesian theory and policy is not that it is too complicated; it is that it is too simple. It may well focus on only one of 100 interrelationships and in doing so make it look like we understand something that we do not. When one really looks into the interdependent shifting of the AS and AD curves, the analysis of aggregate equilibrium quickly becomes very complicated and it is not clear that formal AS/AD models are going to shed much light on the process. In making that adjustment, the Canadian economy has developed a variety of private institutions that adjust. The Canadian economy is not perfectly competitive; these private institutions can help

prevent the instability described by the model. So the policy implications of the model are unclear.

The AS/AD Model and the Macro Policy Model in the Text
Now that we've worked our way through the AS/AD model, we're ready to compare it to the AED/PLF macro policy model presented in the text. As you will see, the central difference between them is that the AS/AD model carefully separates out dynamic adjustment forces from static forces, making it necessary to specify what dynamic adjustment interrelationship we are assuming as well as what we are assuming about the shapes of the curves.

In the macro policy model we combine the two and only have an analysis of final equilibrium points. This is both a strength and a weakness of the model. The strength is that it simplifies the analysis enormously; the weakness is that the AED curve and the PLF curves are hybrid curves which combine dynamics and statics and leave much of the reasoning implicit. Because they do, they can seriously mislead. If one correctly specifies the curves, and carefully spells out the assumptions upon which they are based, one arrives at the same equilibrium point from both analyses.

To see that you do understand the difference, let's consider the Keynesian and Classical adjustments described above in terms of our macro policy model. The difference concerns the assumed shape of the PLF curve. The Keynesian view is that it is relatively flat—adjustment takes place through shifts in income. The Classical view is that the PLF curve is vertical—adjustment takes place through shifts in the price level.

At this point you might be asking: If the simple macro policy model arrives at the same results, why bother with the more complicated AS/AD model? The answer is that the AS/AD model makes the dynamic adjustment process by which one gets there clearer.

The AD Curve and the AED Curve

The central difference between the AD curve and the AED curve is that the AED curve includes any adjustment which occurs in regard to an initial demand shock, whereas the AD curve includes only the initial effect of a price-level shift on aggregate output. Both Keynesians and Classicals accepted the same reasoning about the shape of the AD curve, so these do not differ. However, Classicals were unclear about the existence of the income adjustment mechanism; sophisticated Classical models allowed for it, but the simple Classical model did not. When it was not allowed for, the AED curve became identical to the AD curve, and the curves didn't explain why expectations of supply would lead the economy back to its potential income.

The essence of the Keynesian revolution was to point out that the assumption that the AD curve and the AED curve were identical was problematic—that expectations could get discoordinated when there was aggregate disequilibrium, short-run aggregate supply could fall due to a fall in expectations, and an undesirable equilibrium of aggregate supply and demand could be reached. That aspect of the Keynesian revolution would have been acceptable to sophisticated Classicals. Where Keynes parted company from sophisticated Classicals was in the model he proposed to distinguish between the AED curve and the AD curve. It was a very mechanistic relationship, and sophisticated Classicals disagreed that, in most circumstances, changes in expectations of demand would cause the short-run supply curve to shift in such a mechanistic manner.

The Price-Level Flexibility Curve and the Short-Run AS Curve

The institutional structure of the Canadian and most Western economies is not perfectly competitive. It's highly competitive all right, but it is not perfectly competitive in the sense that firms offer goods on the market and accept whatever price they receive. Instead, the firm both makes the product and makes the market within which that product is sold. What this means is that for most goods, and hence for GDP (a composite of all goods), it doesn't make sense to assume that firms offer their goods on the market and accept whatever price the market chooses the pay them. Instead, firms either negotiate price, or set it in relation to expected competition from other sellers. In setting their price they take into account demand conditions, so the price they set reflects both supply and demand conditions; but they set it—the market does not set it. For the market to set the price, the suppliers would have to offer all they have to the market in a type of auction and accept whatever price the market determined. That does not happen in most goods.

The price-level flexibility curve accepts this institutional reality and simply is based on historical observation of how the price level has tended to fluctuate with fluctuations in aggregate demand. It has no high theory behind it, but a fair amount of institutional reality. Thus, it is compatible with the institutional structure that we have; it is simply a curve that reflects these institutional realities.

The short-run aggregate supply curve is something quite different; it is a deduced curve—which reflects deductive reasoning—and is subject to all the assumptions upon which that deductive reasoning is based. Thus, it must be modified to fit the institutional realities if it is to be used to shed light on macroeconomic problems. Given the nature of the Canadian institutional structure, assuming perfectly competitive markets with aggregate supply independent of aggregate demand won't do because it doesn't allow a reasonable disequilibrium adjustment that reflects institutional realities.

Perfectly competitive markets would require the price level to fluctuate to whatever level was necessary to achieve aggregate equilibrium. But for individual price setters, there is no incentive to set their nominal price at a level that will bring about aggregate equilibrium. They are only interested in setting their relative price at a level that will achieve the desired profits. Given that no individual is directly concerned with the price level, it is highly unlikely that the price level fluctuates instantaneously to maintain aggregate equilibrium at the desired level of output. If that adjustment occurs, and the initial equilibrium output is maintained, then the adjustment most likely occurs through other mechanisms.

It is important to point out that the argument—that a fluctuating price level is relatively unimportant as an aggregate dynamic adjustment process—is not an argument that *relative price adjustment* is not important to adjustment among markets. Relative price adjustment in individual markets is a quite different phenomenon than aggregate price-level adjustment. Firms have an enormous incentive to see that they get their relative price set correctly, and they spend a lot of time and effort (1) choosing their nominal price and (2) predicting the price level, so the ratio of the two—their relative price—will be where they want it. They don't change their nominal prices instantaneously because there are costs of doing so, but they change it sufficiently frequently so that it does not make sense to assume relative prices are institutionally determined. But the price level is a quite different matter. Each firm's contribution to the price level is minuscule, and no firm has an incentive to see that the price level comes out right. Thus, the price level is the result of the aggregation of individuals; it is not a choice variable of decision makers in the economy. That's why aggregate analysis must be considered separately from individual analysis.

With the above discussion, we can relate the AS curve to the PLF curve. The short-run AS curve reflects only static equilibrium forces. The PLF curve reflects both those static equilibrium forces and dynamic adjustment forces. It traces the price-level, quantity adjustment path of shifting short-run AS curves in response to a shift in the AED curve. When the economy is far from its potential output, that path is relatively flat—the price level doesn't change much. When the economy is at its potential output, the PLF curve is vertical—it becomes the equivalent to the long-run AS curve.

A Final Comment

The issues that we have discussed in the appendix are complicated. That's why they are in the appendix. They likely will push your reasoning powers to their limit. That's what so appealing about the policy model presented in the chapter. The aggregate equilibrium demand curve and the PLF curve are curves that incorporate all the disequilibrium adjustment into their shapes, so you don't have to worry about it. As long as the direction of adjustment is unchanged by the dynamic adjustment, the analysis gets the qualitative movements right.

But the cost of that simplicity is losing quantitative measures of how much the adjustment will be. Thus, the price-level flexibility curve could be perfectly flat, and autonomous demand shifts out by 10 so that the AD curve shifts out by 10. But since the AED curve incorporates the interdependent shifts of the AS and AD, the AED curve will shift out by something more than that, say by 20, with the amount that it shifts dependent on the dynamic adjustment process assumed. So care must be taken when using these curves to discuss quantitative movements. In Chapter 9 we explore the Keynesian model which provides one way of quantifying the shifts in the AED curve, given a shift in the AD curve.

KEY TERMS

effective demand   *(213)*
international effect   *(209)*

intertemporal price-level effect   *(209)*
Law of aggregate demand   *(208)*

price-level interest rate effect   *(208)*
wealth effect   *(208)*

9

The Keynesian Aggregate Production/Aggregate Expenditures Model

Keynes stirred the stale economic frog pond to its depth.
~Gottfried Haberler

After reading this chapter, you should be able to:

1 Explain the difference between induced and autonomous consumption.

2 Show how the level of income is graphically determined in the Keynesian aggregate production/aggregate expenditures model.

3 Use the Keynesian equation to determine equilibrium income.

4 Explain the multiplier process.

5 Show how shifts in autonomous expenditures change equilibrium income.

6 Relate the Keynesian aggregate production/aggregate expenditure model to the macro policy model.

7 Distinguish between mechanistic and interpretative Keynesian and Classical models.

Policy fights in economics occur on many levels. Keynes fought on most of them. But it wasn't Keynes who got Canadian policy makers to accept his ideas. Instead it was a small group of powerful civil servants, including R.B. Bryce (a former student of Keynes), W. Clifford Clark (a deputy minister of finance), and W.A. MacKintosh (the director general of economic research in the Department of Reconstruction and Supply). MacKintosh wrote a policy paper that adapted the salient features of Keynesian economics to the Canadian environment—strong-willed federal and provincial governments in a small open economy. The Liberal government of the day used the paper in its 1945 election campaign, but it soon became apparent that the policies would be difficult to implement. They required a significant redistribution of powers between the federal and provincial governments, and the provinces were unwilling to hand over control to the federal authorities.

What made these mandarins switch to Keynesian economics? It was the Depression; the Keynesian story explained it much better than did the Classical real-wage story of the Depression.

At the same time that Canadian policy was being pushed towards Keynesian theories, influential American economists were advising the U.S. government to adopt similar economic policies. These economists, along with Canadian economist Laurie Tarshis, developed what is now called the textbook model of Keynesian economics. That model gave the Keynesian ideas a structure embodied in the specific models that policy makers demanded. While all of this was taking place, Dutch and Norwegian economists developed an empirically determined macro model that policy makers could use. For their contributions, many in this group won Nobel prizes.

THE TEXTBOOK KEYNESIAN MODEL

In the last chapter we developed the macro policy model. In that model we carefully differentiated between a shift in aggregate demand (other things equal) and a shift in aggregate equilibrium demand, after all induced effects of an initial shift are taken into account. We stated that the AED curve would shift by a multiple of the initial shift but we did not say how much of a multiple.

Such ambiguity was unacceptable to early Keynesians who wanted to have input into policy. They wanted their model to have direct policy relevance. To have direct policy relevance they needed to be able to discuss not only the *qualitative* direction of a shift in the AED curve, as we did in the last chapter, but also the *quantitative* amount of change. To do that they needed to make explicit the induced effects that would occur when there was an autonomous (outside the system) shock to aggregate demand. Once they specified what the induced effects would be, they could give quantitative recommendations about policy—for example, if government wanted to increase income by 20, it must increase government spending by, say, 8.

Aggregate Production/Aggregate Expenditures (AP/AE) Model
Keynesian model giving *aggregate supply* the name *aggregate production* and focusing on total production changes, not on changes in output caused by price-level changes. Emphasizes the difference between the Keynesian focus and the Classical focus on quantity of aggregate supply and demand changes resulting from changes in the price level.

The Keynesian model they developed to do this is called the **Aggregate Production/Aggregate Expenditures (AP/AE) Model.** It is called that to separate it from the model presented in the last chapter. This Keynesian *AP/AE* model assumes the price level flexibility curve is flat—that the price level remains constant—and then explores the question: when aggregate expenditures expand by, say, 20, how much will aggregate equilibrium income expand by? In terms of the macro policy model, the question it explores is shown by Exhibit 1: when the *AD* curve shifts by, say, 20 (from AD_0 to AD_1), how much will the *AED* curve shift out if we are in the flat range of the price-level flexibility curve? The Keynesian *AP/AE* model is designed to fill in the question mark in Exhibit 1.

Income adjustment mechanism
Chase between aggregate supply and aggregate demand.

Whereas the macro policy model gives us insight into the general qualitative effects of shifts, hiding the induced effects, the Keynesian *AP/AE* model focuses on the induced effects. It looks specifically at the relationship between aggregate production and aggregate expenditures and concentrates on the **income adjustment mechanism** (interrelated chase between aggregate supply and demand). That income adjustment mechanism is the reason the Keynesian *AED* curve differs from the *AD* curve, and why it shifts by a different amount than any initial shift. That mechanism will be set in motion any time there is aggregate disequilibrium—any time that individuals' planned expenditures differ from firms' planned production. Thus, the

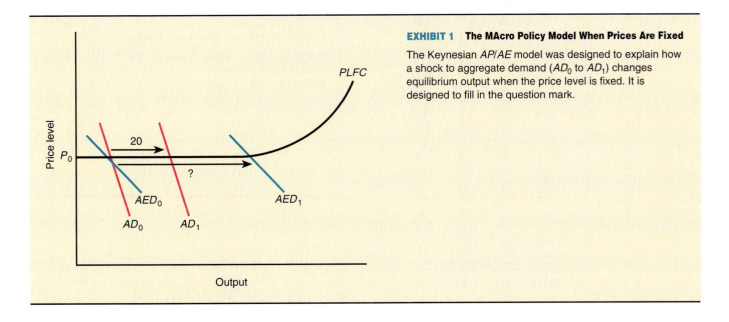

EXHIBIT 1   **The MAcro Policy Model When Prices Are Fixed**

The Keynesian AP/AE model was designed to explain how a shock to aggregate demand (AD_0 to AD_1) changes equilibrium output when the price level is fixed. It is designed to fill in the question mark.

Keynesian model fills in a gap in the macro policy model by specifying the interactive effects between aggregate supply and demand. It is, however, important to remember that this Keynesian AP/AE model is not a different model; it is totally consistent with the macro policy model and if you truly understand both of them you can move from one to the other, as long as you keep the assumptions of each model straight.

To see Keynes's exposition of the model, we'll start, as Keynes did, by looking separately at production decisions and expenditures decisions.

Aggregate Production in the Keynesian Model

Aggregate production is the total amount of production of all goods and services in every industry in an economy. It is the equivalent to the concept of aggregate supply we introduced to you in the last chapter. It is at the centre of the Keynesian model. Production creates an equal amount of income, so income and production are always equal; the terms can be used interchangeably.

While aggregate production creates an amount of income equal to that production, it does not necessarily create expenditures equal to that production. Expenditures can be higher or lower than production. Moreover, aggregate production depends on expectations of expenditures which is the equivalent to the concept of aggregate demand we introduced to you in the last chapter. If businesspeople expect high expenditures, they produce a lot; if they expect low expenditures, they produce a little. Keynes's model showed that these expectations of businesspeople can become partially self-fulfilling. Thus, expectations play a central role in the Keynesian model: Production will be driven by expected expenditures. Stated another way, Keynes's model is a model in which aggregate supply depends upon aggregate demand.

Graphically, aggregate production in the Keynesian model is represented by a 45° line on a graph, with real income in dollars measured on the horizontal axis and real production measured in dollars on the vertical axis, as in Exhibit 2. Given the definition of the axis, connecting all the points at which production equals income produces a 45° line through the origin. Since, by definition, production creates an amount of income equal to the amount of production or output, this 45° line is the **aggregate production curve,** or alternatively the **aggregate income curve.** At all points on the aggregate production curve, income equals production. For example, consider point A in Exhibit 2, where income (measured on the horizontal axis) is \$4,000 and production (measured on the vertical axis) is also \$4,000. That identity between production and income is true only on the 45° line. Output and income, however, cannot expand without limit. The model is relevant only when output is below its potential. Once pro-

Aggregate production curve   In the Keynesian model, the 45-degree line on a graph with real income measured on the horizontal axis and real production on the vertical axis. Alternatively called the *aggregate income curve.*

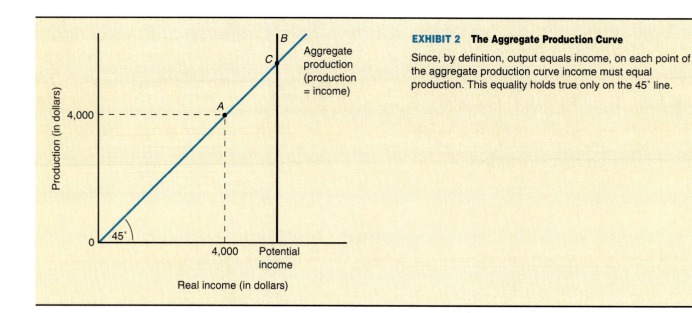

EXHIBIT 2   The Aggregate Production Curve

Since, by definition, output equals income, on each point of the aggregate production curve income must equal production. This equality holds true only on the 45° line.

duction expands to the capacity constraint of the existing institutional structure—to potential income (line *B*)—no more output expansion is possible. At that point we are no longer in the Keynesian range of the economy.

In the simple Classical model the economy was always in equilibrium because of Say's Law: supply created its own demand. Keynes's analysis differs from the Classical analysis because he said that planned aggregate expenditures (demand), while they were related to income (which equals production—supply), need not be precisely equal to income, and if they were not, aggregate supply and aggregate demand would start chasing each other; that chase would lead the economy to an undesirable equilibrium. In the equilibrium supply and demand are equal, but the level of supply is determined by demand, causing some to called Keynes's model a demand-based model in which Say's Law is replaced by **Keynes's Law:** Demand creates its own supply. In Keynes's model production brings about equal income, but does not necessarily bring about equal expenditures. Thus, to understand Keynes's argument, one must analyze aggregate expenditures separately from aggregate production.

Keynes's Law   Demand creates its own supply.

Aggregate Expenditures in the Keynesian Model

Aggregate expenditures   The summation of all four components of expenditures: aggregate of consumption (spending by consumers), investment (spending by business), spending by government, and net foreign spending on Canadian goods (the difference between Canadian exports and Canadian imports). It is expressed by the equation $AE = C + I + G + (X - M)$.

Disposable income   Income remaining after paying taxes.

Aggregate expenditures consist of consumption (spending by consumers), investment (spending by business), spending by government, and net foreign spending on Canadian goods (the difference between Canadian exports and Canadian imports). These four components were presented in our earlier discussion of national income accounting, which isn't surprising since the national income accounts were designed around the Keynesian model. We now consider each of those components more carefully.

Consumption   The largest component of expenditures is consumption. While various things affect the level of consumption expenditures, it is most affected by disposable income. **Disposable income** is that part of income left after paying taxes which, in a simple Keynesian model, are assumed to be constant.

The assumed relationship between consumption and disposable income is reasonable: Most of us look at our disposable income, and then determine how much of it we will spend. Thus in the Keynesian model the central relationship is between consumer spending and disposable income.

Let's consider the consumption decisions of an individual who earned $12,000 and paid $2,000 in taxes last year. That leaves $10,000 in disposable income. Assume $9,000 goes to consumption and $1,000 goes to savings. If next year this person's dis-

Disposable Income (Y_d)	Changes in Disposable Income (ΔY_d)	Consumption (C)	Change of Consumption (ΔC)	Row
$ 0	—	$1,000	—	A
1,000	$1,000	1,800	$800	B
2,000	1,000	2,600	800	C
3,000	1,000	3,400	800	D
4,000	1,000	4,200	800	E
5,000	1,000	5,000	800	F
6,000	1,000	5,800	800	G
7,000	1,000	6,600	800	H
8,000	1,000	7,400	800	I
9,000	1,000	8,200	800	J
10,000	1,000	9,000	800	K
11,000	1,000	9,800	800	L
12,000	1,000	10,600	800	M
13,000	1,000	11,400	800	N
14,000	1,000	12,200	800	O
15,000	1,000	13,000	800	P

EXHIBIT 3   Consumption Related to Disposable Income

posable income rises to $12,000, we would expect consumption also to increase to, say, $10,600. If disposable income fell to $8,000, consumption would fall to $7,400.

Exhibit 3 shows a consumer's entire hypothesized relationship between possible disposable income and consumption levels. Notice that when disposable income is zero, we still assume the person consumes. How? By borrowing or dipping into previous savings. Consumption that would exist at a zero level of disposable income is called **autonomous consumption** (consumption that's unaffected by changes in disposable income). It includes those expenditures a person would make even if he or she were unemployed.

Notice that as disposable income rises, consumption also rises, but not by as much as disposable income. The relationship between changes in disposable income and changes in consumption is shown in columns 2 and 4. The numbers in these columns can be derived from columns 1 and 3. Each entry in column 2 represents the difference between the corresponding entry in column 1 and the entry in the previous row of column 1. Similarly, each entry in column 4 is the difference between the corresponding entry in column 3 and the entry in the previous row of column 3. For example, as disposable income rises from $10,000 to $ 11,000 the change in disposable income is $1,000. Similarly, as consumption rises from $9,000 to $9,800, the change in consumption is $800.

Since much of Keynes's analysis focuses on changes in expenditures that occur in response to changes in income, it is important to distinguish that portion of consumption that changes in response to changes in income from that portion that does not. As previously stated, that portion of consumption that does not change when income changes is called *autonomous consumption*. **Induced consumption** is consumption that changes as disposable income changes.

The relationship between consumption and disposable income (as in the table in our example) can be expressed more concisely as a **consumption function** (a representation of the relationship between consumption and disposable income as a mathematical function):

$$C = C_0 + mpc\ Y_d$$

where: C = consumption expenditures
C_0 = autonomous consumption
mpc = marginal propensity to consume
Y_d = disposable income = $Y - T$
T = taxes

The consumption function corresponding to the table in Exhibit 3 is

$$C = \$1,000 + .8Y_d$$

Autonomous consumption
Consumption that is unaffected by changes in disposable income.

1   Autonomous consumption is unrelated to income; induced consumption is directly related to income.

Induced consumption   Consumption that changes as disposable income changes.
Consumption function
Representation of the relationship between consumption and disposable income as a mathematical function ($C = C_0 + mpcY_d$, where C = consumption expenditures, C_0 = autonomous consumption, mpc = marginal propensity to consume, and Y_d = disposable income).

Notice that if you substitute the data from any row in the table in Exhibit 3, both sides of the consumption function are equal. For example, in row C of Exhibit 3, we see that consumption (C) equals \$2,600. So \$2,600 = \$1,000 + .8Y_d. Since disposable income (Y_d) = \$2,000, we can calculate (.8)(\$2,000) = \$1,600 and add it to \$1,000, giving us \$2,600. So the two sides are equal.

The Marginal Propensity to Consume   There is one part of the consumption function we haven't talked about yet: the letters *mpc* (.8 in the numerical example). The letters *mpc* are the marginal propensity to consume. Keynes was interested in what would happen to consumption spending as disposable income changed. He argued that when disposable income fell by, say \$1,000, consumption would fall by somewhat less than that amount (\$800 in the example). He defined the **marginal propensity to consume (*mpc*)** as the relationship between a change in consumption, ΔC, that resulted from a *change* in disposable income, ΔY_d. (The Greek letter Δ, or delta, which corresponds to the letter D in our alphabet, is commonly used to designate *change in.*) The *mpc* is the fraction consumed from an additional dollar of disposable income.

$$mpc = \frac{\text{Change in consumption}}{\text{Change in disposable income}} = \frac{\Delta C}{\Delta Y_d}$$

Using the data in Exhibit 3, let's determine the level of the *mpc* by dividing a change in consumption by a corresponding change in disposable income:

$$mpc = \frac{\Delta C}{\Delta Y_d} = \frac{\$800}{\$1000} = .8$$

Based on figures for consumption and disposable income for Britain at the time, Keynes estimated that the *mpc* was between .8 and .9. That estimate is not central to his argument, as long as the *mpc* remains between zero and one.

Graphing the Consumption Function   Now that we're familiar with the components and terminology used with the consumption function, let's see how to graph it. Exhibit 4 graphs the particular consumption function given by

$$C = \$1,000 + .8Y_d$$

Notice that at zero disposable income, consumption is \$1,000. This is the autonomous portion of consumption.

The consumption function's slope tells us how much consumption changes with a particular change in disposable income. In other words, the slope of a consumption function graphically represents the marginal propensity to consume for a total particular consumption function.

The *apc* and the *mpc*   Besides the marginal propensity to consume, there's one other term you need to know, both because we'll use it in the future and because it will help cement your understanding of *mpc*. That term is the **average propensity to consume (*apc*),** *defined as consumption divided by disposable income:*

$$apc = \frac{\text{Consumption}}{\text{Disposable income}} = \frac{C}{Y_d}$$

For example, if disposable income is \$400, and consumption is \$370, apc = \$370/\$400 = .925. Alternatively, if disposable income is \$500 and consumption is \$450, apc = .9.

Notice that the *apc* changes as income changes. That makes it different from *mpc*. (By assumption, *mpc* is constant at all levels of income.) The reason is the constant term, C_0, in the consumption function. (The subscript $_0$ is used throughout the book to indicate what a term such as C will equal when the variable it depends on—in this case, Y_d—is zero.) The relationship between *apc* and *mpc* is given by

$$apc = \frac{C_0}{Y_d} + mpc$$

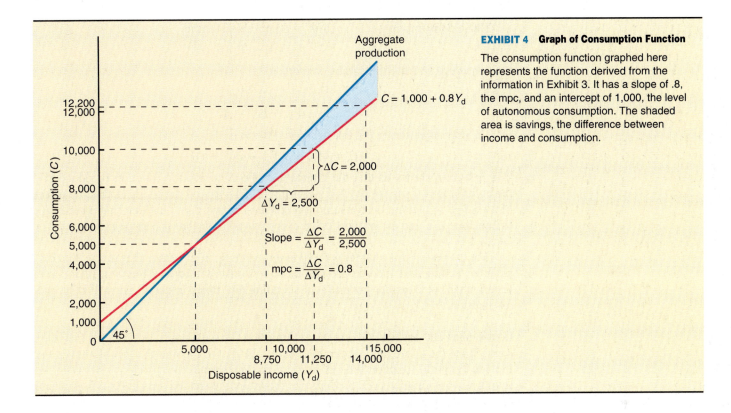

As long as autonomous consumption, C_0, is positive, *apc* is greater than *mpc*. Only when $C_0 = 0$ are *mpc* and *apc* equal.

The Aggregate Consumption Function Thus far we've been looking at the consumption function for an individual. Now let's examine aggregate consumption. The **aggregate consumption function** is the sum of all the consumption functions of all individuals in society. Instead of dealing with thousands of dollars, we're now dealing with billions.

Aggregate consumption function
The sum of all consumption functions of all individuals in society.

In the aggregate, many individual fluctuations in consumption offset each other. For example, the Smith family may have an emergency that causes them to increase their consumption above their normal spending level, while the Levesque family might find that they can save more than planned. Offsetting events such as these occur all the time; they make the aggregate consumption function much more stable than the individual consumption functions.

Disposable Income, Income, and Taxes It's customary to present the consumption function in terms of disposable (after-tax) income. But the aggregate production curve relates total income and total production, so to make the two fit we must modify the consumption relationship.

The tax function tells us that total taxes are partly autonomous and partly a function of income:

$$T = T_0 + tY$$

where: T = total taxes
T_0 = autonomous taxes
t = tax rate, $0 \leq t \leq 1$.

The tax rate tells us how a change in income affects total tax payments. It lies between zero and one, since the government can, at the extreme, tax all or none of every extra dollar earned.

Since consumption is a function of disposable income

$$Y_d = Y - T$$

the consumption function can be written as

$$C = C_0 + bY_d$$
$$C = C_0 + b(Y - T)$$

which, after substituting the tax function, becomes

$$C = (C_0 - b\,T_0) + b(1 - t)Y$$

The first term shows us that the intercept of the consumption function is reduced by the autonomous taxes we pay the government. The second term tells us that the effect of a change in income on consumption consists of two parts: the marginal propensity to consume (b), and the proportion of every extra dollar that is earned and not paid in taxes ($1 - t$).

For the rest of this chapter we will assume that taxes are zero. This means that disposable income and income are identical, so consumption is a function of income. Later, when we consider government spending and taxes in detail, we will relax this assumption.

Consumption and Savings Given our assumptions, what people don't consume, they save. Since the aggregate production curve tells us the income that people have, and the consumption function tells us how much they spend, the difference between the two is how much they save. Savings are shown by the shaded area in Exhibit 4. There are no savings at income level $5,000, where expenditures equal income (where the consumption function crosses the aggregate production curve). At lower levels of income, savings are negative; at higher levels of income, savings are positive.

Savings, the *mps*, and the *aps* You know from the circular flow diagram that when all individuals spend all their income (which they derive from production), the aggregate economy is in equilibrium. *Injections* into the system will equal *withdrawals* from the system. In this simple Keynesian model, savings represent withdrawals; autonomous expenditures represent injections.

The circular flow diagram expresses the national income identity: aggregate income equals aggregate output. Keynes asked: (1) does aggregate expenditure always equal aggregate production? and (2) if not, what will happen in the economy to bring them into equilibrium? Since individuals save some of their income, expenditures and income need not be equal. The question is: Are the savings translated back into expenditures? If they aren't, injections will not equal withdrawals and income will have to change. Thus, in the hypothesized relationship, and in the economy, savings play an important role. What people don't consume, they save. Specifically,

$$\text{Savings} = \text{Disposable income} - \text{Consumption}$$

If savings are translated back into expenditures, no adjustment is necessary. If savings are not translated back into expenditures, the aggregate economy will not be in equilibrium.

As with consumption, we can use a savings table and savings function to show the relationship between savings and income. Exhibit 5 presents the savings table and graph of the savings function corresponding to the relationships for consumption in Exhibits 3 and 4.

You can see that the amount saved increases as income increases—the higher the level of income, the higher the level of savings. For example, as income goes up from $10,000 to $11,000 (rows K and L of column 1), savings rises from $1,000 to $1,200 (rows K and L of column 3).

Column 2 shows the change in disposable income, and column 4 shows the change in savings that occurs as income increases from one row to another. In

EXHIBIT 5 Savings Table, Savings Function, and Consumption Function

The information in the table (a) can be translated into a graph. That is done in (b). In the bottom half of (b) you can see the relationship between the savings curve and the difference between the consumption function and the aggregate production curve.

(1) Disposable income (Y_d)	(2) Change in disposable income (ΔY_d)	(3) Savings (S)	(4) Change in savings (ΔS)	Row
0	–	–1,000	–	A
1,000	1,000	–800	200	B
2,000	1,000	–600	200	C
3,000	1,000	–400	200	D
4,000	1,000	–200	200	E
5,000	1,000	0	200	F
6,000	1,000	200	200	G
7,000	1,000	400	200	H
8,000	1,000	600	200	I
9,000	1,000	800	200	J
10,000	1,000	1,000	200	K
11,000	1,000	1,200	200	L
12,000	1,000	1,400	200	M
13,000	1,000	1,600	200	N
14,000	1,000	1,800	200	O
15,000	1,000	2,000	200	P

(a) Savings table

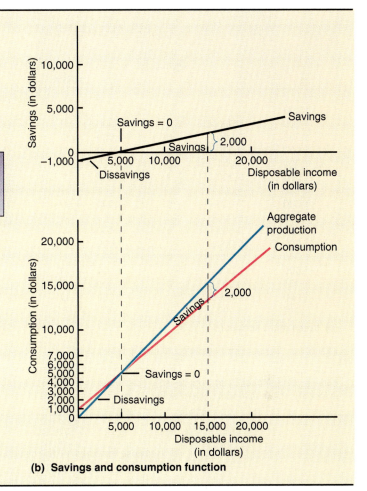

(b) Savings and consumption function

the example, the change in disposable income was $1,000 and the change in savings was $200.

Just as we defined *mpc* and *apc* with the consumption function, so too can we define **marginal propensity to save (*mps*)** and **average propensity to save (*aps*).**

The *mps* is the percentage saved from an additional dollar of disposable income:

$$mps = \frac{\text{Change in savings}}{\text{Change in disposable income}} = \frac{\Delta S}{\Delta Y_d}$$

The *aps* is savings divided by disposable income:

$$aps = \frac{\text{Savings}}{\text{Disposable income}} = \frac{S}{Y_d}$$

The *aps* changes with disposable income. If disposable income is $10,000, the *aps* = 1,000/10,000 = .1. If disposable income is $15,000, savings is $2,000, so *aps* = 2,000/15,000 = 0.133.

The top half of Exhibit 5 (b) graphs the savings function. Notice that it is an upward-sloping function whose slope equals the *mps* and whose intercept (the point where it crosses the vertical axis) is negative. In this example it is −$1,000.

The consumption function and the savings function are related. The bottom half of Exhibit 5 (b) shows the consumption function presented earlier. By extending the income levels between the two graphs you can see that the distance between the consumption function and the production curve equals the distance between the horizontal axis and the savings function. Each function provides us with the same information

Marginal propensity to save (mps)
Percentage saved from an additional dollar of disposable income.

Average propensity to save (aps)
Savings divided by disposable income.

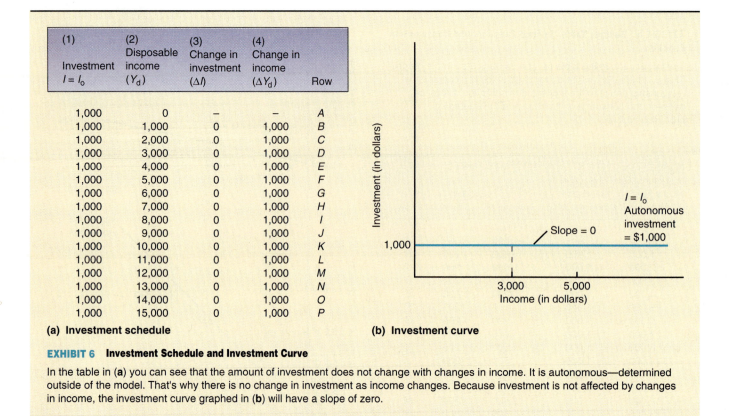

(1) Investment $I = I_o$	(2) Disposable income (Y_d)	(3) Change in investment (ΔI)	(4) Change in income (ΔY_d)	Row
1,000	0	—	—	A
1,000	1,000	0	1,000	B
1,000	2,000	0	1,000	C
1,000	3,000	0	1,000	D
1,000	4,000	0	1,000	E
1,000	5,000	0	1,000	F
1,000	6,000	0	1,000	G
1,000	7,000	0	1,000	H
1,000	8,000	0	1,000	I
1,000	9,000	0	1,000	J
1,000	10,000	0	1,000	K
1,000	11,000	0	1,000	L
1,000	12,000	0	1,000	M
1,000	13,000	0	1,000	N
1,000	14,000	0	1,000	O
1,000	15,000	0	1,000	P

(a) Investment schedule   **(b)** Investment curve

EXHIBIT 6   Investment Schedule and Investment Curve

In the table in **(a)** you can see that the amount of investment does not change with changes in income. It is autonomous—determined outside of the model. That's why there is no change in investment as income changes. Because investment is not affected by changes in income, the investment curve graphed in **(b)** will have a slope of zero.

because savings is the mirror image of consumption. What isn't consumed is saved.

When we add up the marginal propensity to consume and the marginal propensity to save, we arrive at 1:

$$mpc + mps = 1$$

In our example, this works. Since $mpc = .8$ and $mps = .2$, the sum equals 1. The same holds true for the apc and aps:

$$aps + apc = 1$$

Investment Expenditures by business on plants and equipment.

Investment The second component of aggregate expenditures is **investment** (expenditures by businesses on plants and equipment). To keep his model simple, Keynes assumed investment depends on the "animal spirits of investors." In other words, investment is *autonomous;* it's independent of the level of disposable income and is determined outside the model.

The most important determinant of autonomous investment is expectations of the future. If businesspeople think the future will be good, they will invest; if they get depressed about the future, they will not invest. For example, the U.S. and Canadian editions of this text and ancillaries cost the publisher over $1,000,000 to develop and bring to market. Ultimately the decision whether to proceed or not fell on the CEO's shoulders, and the CEO's (chief executive officer's) expectations about the future played a key role in the decision to go ahead with the investment.
Investment is represented by

$$I = I_0$$

Exhibit 6 (a) relates society's income and investment. It represents the amount all firms invest at each level of income. As you can see, the amount of investment doesn't change in response to income changes. Exhibit 6 (b) graphs the relationship between investment and income. The relationship is simply the function $I = \$1,000$. Notice that the investment function is a perfectly horizontal line. That means the investment function's slope is zero. When income is \$0, investment is \$1,000; when income is \$5,000, investment is still \$1,000. That's because in order to keep the model simple, investment is assumed to be independent of income; that's the meaning of a graphical zero slope.

Just as autonomous consumption can change, so can autonomous investment. Keynes believed investment could shift around a lot, just as he believed the consumption function was capable of shifting. As we'll see shortly, it was precisely those sudden, unexpected shifts in investment spending that Keynes saw as the cause of booms as well as recessions. He also believed investment would be influenced by other variables such as the interest rate, but he didn't include these other influences in the simple model.

Government Expenditures   To keep this first look at the Keynesian model simple, let's also assume government spending is autonomous. That is, it does not change as income changes. Therefore the general equation for government spending on goods and services would be

$$G = G_0$$

which is represented graphically as a horizontal line, just like the investment function. We will assume $G_0 = \$1,000$.

Net Exports   When people in Canada spend their income on foreign imports (M), the expenditures are lost to the Canadian economy. However, when foreigners spend their income on Canadian exports (X), that spending adds to Canadian expenditures. The common convention is to subtract imports from exports and to talk about **net exports** ($X - M$). When net exports are positive, exports exceed imports; when net exports are negative, imports exceed exports.

Net exports   A country's exports minus its imports.

Exports tend not to change much as income changes so they are generally assumed constant. Imports, however, change substantially with changes in income: when a country's income increases, imports increase; when a country's income decreases, its imports decrease. To capture this relationship, imports (M) are usually written as follows:

$$M = M_0 + m\,Y$$

where M_0 denotes autonomous imports and mY represents induced imports. So, for example, if m = .1 and income rises by \$100, induced imports will rise by \$10, as will total imports.

Combining the two together we have the net export function:

$$X - M = X_0 - M_0 - m\,Y$$

Again, to keep the algebra of the Keynesian model simple at this point, we assume induced imports equal zero (m = 0) which means that net exports are autonomous—net exports do not change as income changes. The equation for net exports becomes:

$$X - M = X_0 - M_0$$

Since they are autonomous, net exports are graphically represented by a horizontal line, just like the graphs of investment and government spending. To keep the analysis simple, we will assume that net exports are also constant at \$1,000.

Aggregate Expenditures   *Aggregate expenditures (AE)* is the summation of all four components of expenditures:

$$AE = C + I + G + (X - M)$$

Exhibit 7 (a) lists the values of each expenditure at a different level of income, or production, as discussed in the preceding several sections. The summation of expenditures—aggregate expenditures—is in column 5. Notice that, by assumption in our example, the only endogenous expenditure that changes as income changes is consumption.

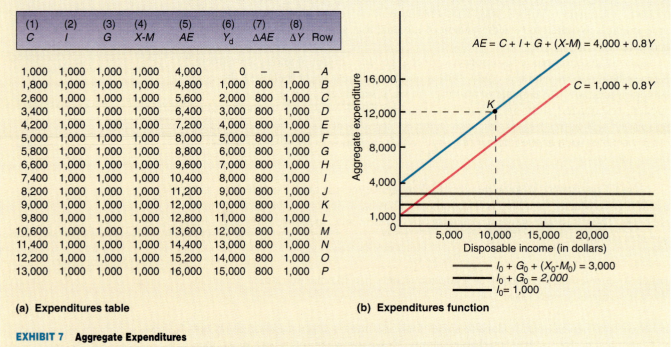

(1) C	(2) I	(3) G	(4) X-M	(5) AE	(6) Y_d	(7) ΔAE	(8) ΔY	Row
1,000	1,000	1,000	1,000	4,000	0	–	–	A
1,800	1,000	1,000	1,000	4,800	1,000	800	1,000	B
2,600	1,000	1,000	1,000	5,600	2,000	800	1,000	C
3,400	1,000	1,000	1,000	6,400	3,000	800	1,000	D
4,200	1,000	1,000	1,000	7,200	4,000	800	1,000	E
5,000	1,000	1,000	1,000	8,000	5,000	800	1,000	F
5,800	1,000	1,000	1,000	8,800	6,000	800	1,000	G
6,600	1,000	1,000	1,000	9,600	7,000	800	1,000	H
7,400	1,000	1,000	1,000	10,400	8,000	800	1,000	I
8,200	1,000	1,000	1,000	11,200	9,000	800	1,000	J
9,000	1,000	1,000	1,000	12,000	10,000	800	1,000	K
9,800	1,000	1,000	1,000	12,800	11,000	800	1,000	L
10,600	1,000	1,000	1,000	13,600	12,000	800	1,000	M
11,400	1,000	1,000	1,000	14,400	13,000	800	1,000	N
12,200	1,000	1,000	1,000	15,200	14,000	800	1,000	O
13,000	1,000	1,000	1,000	16,000	15,000	800	1,000	P

(a) Expenditures table

(b) Expenditures function

EXHIBIT 7   Aggregate Expenditures

Aggregate expenditures are the sum of all the components of expenditures. These can be added numerically in the table, as they are in (a), or graphically, as they are in (b). Notice that the table and the graph correspond. For example, in row K of the table, aggregate expenditures are $12,000, just as they are at point K, which graphs expenditures at income $10,000.

As you can see in Exhibit 7 (b), the aggregate expenditures curve is the graphical sum of all four expenditures curves, and it has the same slope, $mpc = 0.8$, as the consumption function. Notice that the aggregate expenditures curve crosses the vertical axis at a point that's the sum of all four autonomous expenditures: $C_d + I_0 + G_0 + (X_0 - M_0) = \$4,000$. A good exercise to help you visualize the relationships involved here is to compare the data in the columns in the table with points on the graphs to see how they correspond.

DETERMINING THE LEVEL OF AGGREGATE INCOME

Now that we've developed the graphical framework (the aggregate production/aggregate expenditure, or *AP/AE*, framework), we can put the two together and see how the level of aggregate income is determined in the Keynesian model. We begin by representing a different aggregate expenditures curve and the aggregate production curve on the same graph, as in Exhibit 8.

The aggregate production curve is the 45° line. It tells you the level of aggregate production and also the level of aggregate income since, by definition, income equals production. Expenditures, which do not necessarily equal production or income, are represented by the aggregate expenditures curve. Let's now take a closer look at the relationship between the *AE* and *AP* curves.

Let's first say that income is $12,000. As you can see, at an income of $12,000, expenditures are $11,400. Aggregate income exceeds aggregate expenditures. This is true for any income level above $10,000. Similarly at all income levels below $10,000, aggregate production is less than aggregate expenditures. For example, at a production level of $8,000, aggregate expenditures are $8,600.

The only income level at which aggregate production equals aggregate expenditures is $10,000. Since we know that, in equilibrium, aggregate expenditures must equal aggregate production, $10,000 is the equilibrium level of income in the economy. It is the level of income at which neither producers nor consumers have any

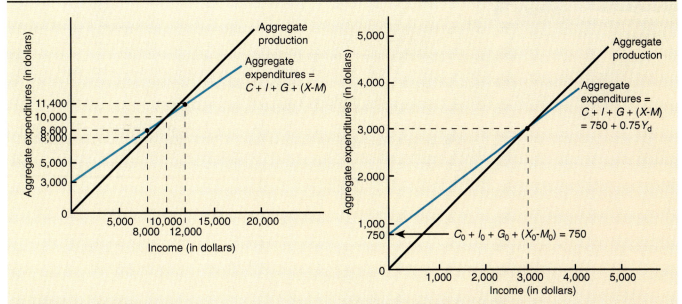

EXHIBIT 8   **Comparing AE to AP**

The aggregate expenditures curve intersects the aggregate production curve at $10,000; therefore, this is the equilibrium level of income in the economy. Above $10,000, aggregate production exceeds aggregate expenditures. Below $10,000, aggregate expenditures exceed aggregate production. For the aggregate production curve, the Y-axis is production in dollars. For the aggregate expenditures curve, it is expenditures in dollars.

EXHIBIT 9   **Solving for Equilibrium Graphically**

The aggregate expenditures curve combines consumption, government spending, investment, and net exports. Equilibrium occurs where the aggregate expenditures curve intersects the aggregate production curve.

reason to change what they are doing. At any other level of income, since there is either a shortage or a surplus of goods, there will be incentive to change. Thus, you can use the aggregate production curve and the aggregate expenditures curve to determine the level of income at which the economy will be in equilibrium.

Let's go through another example. Say the consumption function is

$$C = \$400 + .75Y$$

Government spending is $200. Investment is $100 and net exports are $50. What is the equilibrium level of income in this economy? Exhibit 9 shows the aggregate expenditures curve and the aggregate production curve that go with these numbers. In it you can see that the equilibrium income is $3,000. This is the only income level where aggregate expenditures equal aggregate production.

Another way to determine the level of income in the Keynesian model (a way that's useful to know) is through the **Keynesian equation,**

$$Y = [1/(1 - b)] \, [C_0 + I_0 + G_0 + (X_0 - M_0)]$$

which shows the relationship between autonomous expenditures and the equilibrium level of income. The Keynesian equation does not come out of thin air. It comes from combining the set of equations underlying the graphical presentation of the Keynesian model into the two brackets. Let's consider how it is done.

We start by writing the equations presented in the text algebraically to arrive at the equation for income. Rewriting the expenditures relationships, and letting $b =$ the mpc, we have:

Solving for Equilibrium Graphically

2   To determine income graphically in the Keynesian AP/AE model, you find the income level at which aggregate expenditures equal aggregate production.

Determining the Level of Aggregate Income with the Keynesian Equation

Keynesian equation   Equation that tells us that income equals the multiplier times autonomous expenditures ($Y = $ (Multiplier)(Autonomous Expenditures).

3   To determine income using the Keynesian equation, you determine the multiplier and multiply it by the level of autonomous expenditures.

In the text we calculated the multiplier using the simplifying assumptions we made—that autonomous taxes (T_0) were zero, that the marginal tax rate, t, equals zero, and that the marginal propensity to import, m, equals zero. For those of you mathematically inclined, it is a useful exercise to redo the math and derive the Keynesian multiplier when those are not equal to zero. If you do it, the answer you should get for equilibrium income is:

$$Y = [1/(1 - b(1 - t) + m)] [C_0 + I_0 + G_0 + (X_0 - M_0) - bT_0]$$

The multiplier becomes more complicated, but the general form of the argument remains the same (the actual derivation is done for you in the appendix to the next chapter).

$$C = C_0 + bY$$

$$I = I_0$$

$$G = G_0$$

$$(X - M) = (X_0 - M_0)$$

Aggregate production, by definition, equals aggregate income (Y) and, in equilibrium, aggregate income must equal the four components of aggregate expenditures. Beginning with the national income accounting identity, we have

$$Y = C + I + G + (X - M)$$

Substituting the terms from the first four equations, we have

$$Y = C_0 + bY + I_0 + G_0 + (X_0 - M_0)$$

Subtracting bY from both sides,

$$Y - bY = C_0 + I_0 + G_0 + (X_0 - M_0)$$

To arrive at the Keynesian equation we factor out Y:

$$Y(1 - b) = C_0 + I_0 + G_0 + (X_0 - M_0)$$

Now solve for Y by dividing both sides by $(1 - b)$:

multiplier × autonomous expenditure

$$Y = [1/(1 - b)] [C_0 + I_0 + G_0 + (X_0 - M_0)]$$

This is the Keynesian equation. It embodies all the equations that went into the Keynesian model. When we combine a group of related equations into a single equation, as we did here, that single equation is called a *reduced-form equation.*

The Multiplier

Multiplier Key aspect of the Keynesian model that differentiates it from the Classical model. It is a number that tells us how much income will change in response to a change in autonomous expenditures.

The multiplier captures the key aspect of the Keynesian model that differentiates it from the Classical model. Specifically, the **multiplier** tells us how much income will change in response to a change in autonomous expenditures.

To calculate the multiplier, you divide one by the marginal propensity to save (one minus the marginal propensity to consume). Thus:

$$\text{Multiplier} = 1/mps = 1/(1 - mpc)$$

Once you know the value of the marginal propensity to consume, you can calculate the multiplier by reducing $[1/(1 - mpc)]$ to a simple number. For example, if $mpc = .8$, the multiplier is

$$1/(1 - .8) = 1/.2 = 5$$

4 The multiplier process works because when expenditures don't equal production, businesspeople change production, which changes income, which changes expenditures, which . . . .

The multiplier provided precisely the relationship policy makers needed. It gave them something specific. It gave them an intuitive story of why the Depression occurred and, as we will see in the next chapter, it gave them a story of how certain policies can change it. The story went as follows: When the stock market crashed, businesspeople and consumers got scared and cut their investment (remember, investment is spending) and consumption. Aggregate expenditures decreased. That decrease sent the multiplier into action. It induced businesses to further decrease production (shift supply back), which lowered income and induced a further decrease in aggregate expenditures. This cumulative downward spiral of expenditures was the multiplier process. The multiplier story made sense to policy makers and, hence, played a big role in the acceptance of Keynesian economics into policy.

Since the multiplier tells you the relationship between autonomous expenditures and income, once you know the multiplier, calculating the equilibrium level of income is easy. All you do is multiply autonomous expenditures by the multiplier. For example, if autonomous expenditures are $4,000 and the multiplier is 5, equilibrium income in the economy will be $20,000.

Let's see how the equation works by considering our previous example. In it the *mpc* was .75. Subtracting .75 from 1 gives .25. Dividing 1 by .25 gives 4. (Remember, dividing 1 by 0.25 is asking how many 1/4ths there are in 1.) So our first term is 4. In that example, autonomous consumption (C_0) was $400; investment ($I_0$) was $100; government spending (G_0) was $200; and net exports ($X_0 - M_0$) were $50. Adding these up gives $750. The Keynesian equation tells us to multiply this total autonomous expenditures, $750, by 4. Doing so gives $4 \times \$750 = \$3,000$, the same answer we got graphically.

The Keynesian equation gives you a simple way to determine equilibrium income in the Keynesian model. You determine the multiplier [$1/(1 - mpc)$] and multiply it by the sum of all autonomous expenditures.

Five different marginal propensities to consume and the multiplier associated with each are shown in the following table.

Notice as *mpc* increases, the multiplier increases. Knowing the multiplier associated with each marginal propensity to consume gives you an easy way to determine equilibrium income in the economy.

Total Marginal Propensities to Consume and Multipliers

mpc	multiplier = $1/(1 - mpc)$
.50	2
.75	4
.80	5
.90	10
.95	20

Let's look at one more example of the multiplier. Say that the *mpc* is .8 but that autonomous expenditures are $4,500 instead of $4,000. What is the level of income? Multiplying the sum of autonomous expenditures, $4,500, by 5 tells us that income is $22,500. With a multiplier of 5, income rises by $2,500 because of the $500 increase in autonomous expenditures.

The multiplier gives us what we need to quantify the macro policy model. It tells us that when autonomous expenditures shift out by x (*AD* shifts out, by x) that *AED* will shift out by ($1/(1 - mpc$) times x. Thus, once we know the multiplier we know what the induced effects of a shift of autonomous expenditures are.

The preceding discussion provides a technical method of determining equilibrium income in the Keynesian model. But it doesn't help us understand what the model means for the economy and what forces are operating to ensure that the income level we determined is the equilibrium income level. For it to be the equilibrium level of income, there must be adjustment forces that push the economy toward that equilibrium whenever the economy is not in equilibrium. Let's now discuss those forces.

A Closer Look at the Income Adjustment Mechanism

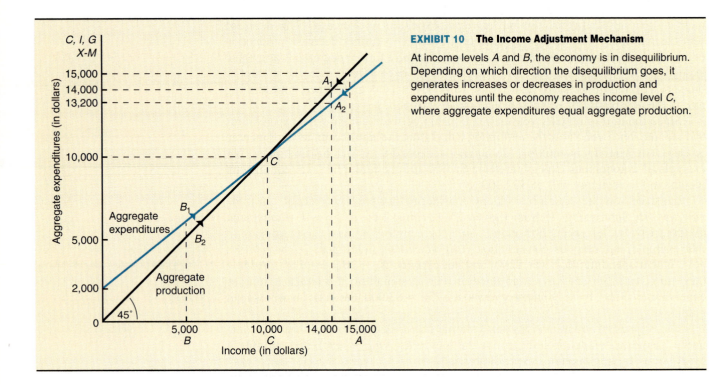

EXHIBIT 10   The Income Adjustment Mechanism

At income levels *A* and *B*, the economy is in disequilibrium. Depending on which direction the disequilibrium goes, it generates increases or decreases in production and expenditures until the economy reaches income level *C*, where aggregate expenditures equal aggregate production.

Let's ask what happens when the macro economy is in disequilibrium—when aggregate production does not equal aggregate expenditures. Exhibit 10 shows us.

Let's first consider the economy at income level *A* where aggregate production equals $15,000 and aggregate expenditure equals $14,000. Since production exceeds expenditures by $1,000 at income level *A,* firms can't sell all they produce; inventories pile up. In response, firms make an adjustment. They decrease aggregate production and hence income. As businesses slow production, the economy moves inward along the aggregate production curve as shown by arrow A_1. As income falls, the gap between aggregate production and aggregate expenditures decreases. For example, say businesses decrease aggregate production to $14,000. Aggregate income also falls to $14,000, which causes aggregate expenditures to fall, as indicated by arrow A_2, to $13,200. There's still a gap, but it's been reduced by $200, from $1,000 to $800.

Since a gap still remains, income keeps falling. A good exercise is to go through two more steps. With each step, the economy moves closer to equilibrium.

Now let's consider the economy at income level *B* ($5,000). Here production is less than expenditures. Firms find their inventory is running down. (Their investment in inventory is far less than they'd planned.) In response, they increase aggregate production and hence income. The economy starts to expand as aggregate production moves along arrow B_2 and aggregate expenditures move along arrow B_1. As individuals' income increases, their expenditures also increase, but by less than the increase in income, so the gap between aggregate expenditures and aggregate production decreases. But as long as expenditures and income exceed production, production and hence income keep rising.

Finally, let's consider the economy at income level *C,* $10,000. At point *C,* income is $10,000 and expenditures are $10,000. Firms are selling all they produce, so they have no reason to change their production levels. The aggregate economy is in equilibrium.

The equilibrium income level is what we determined earlier by multiplying autonomous expenditures by the multiplier. This discussion should give you insight into what's behind the arithmetic of those earlier models.

Determining the equilibrium level of income using the multiplier is an important first step in understanding Keynes's analysis. The second step is to modify that analysis to answer a question that interested Keynes more: How much would a change in autonomous expenditures change the equilibrium level of income? This second step is important since it was precisely those sudden changes in autonomous expenditures Keynes said caused the aggregate disequilibrium, and it was these sudden changes he said the Classical model couldn't handle.

Because Keynes felt autonomous expenditures are subject to sudden shifts, we were careful to point out *autonomous* meant "determined outside the model and not affected by income." Autonomous expenditures can, and do, shift for a variety of other reasons. When they do, the adjustment process is continually being called into play. We discussed the nature of those shifts in the last chapter when we discussed shift factors of the AED curve, which combined the initial shifts with the induced shifts caused by the multiplier effect. Let's review some of the important shift factors.

SHIFTS IN AUTONOMOUS EXPENDITURES

5   Changes in autonomous spending shift the AE curve up and down, leading to changes in equilibrium income.

Shifts in Autonomous Consumption

Autonomous consumption can shift because of natural disasters such as the California earthquake in 1994 or the Japanese earthquake in 1995 (which cause people on average to consume more), but the most important reason it shifts is due to changes in people's expectations about the future. When consumers are confident, the consumption function shifts up. When consumers are scared about the future (as happened in late 1991, early 1992, and early 1995), the consumption function shifts down. When consumers feel good about the future (as happened in late 1993 and early 1994), the consumption function shifts up. The aggregate expenditures curve shifts up or down accordingly.

Because autonomous consumption shifts around so much, economists measure consumer confidence carefully. These measurements play a large role in economists' estimates of what is likely to happen in the economy.

Shifts in the Investment Function

Another expenditure Keynes believed was continually shifting is the investment function. Reasons the investment function shifts include:

1. Changes in interest rates.
2. Changes in expectations.
3. Technological developments.

Changes in Interest Rates   If the interest rate falls, firms will want to invest more; assuming savings are, or will become available for them to do so, a fall in the interest rate will cause investment to increase.

Changes in Expectations   Keynes saw expectations of future sales and profits as the most important determinant of investment demand. When businesspeople expect sales to be good, they invest a lot; when they expect sales to be poor, they cut back on investment.

Keynes believed these expectations could be highly unstable. They were based on rumours, beliefs about future tax policy, and world events. To convey a sense of unpredictability to the expectations, he called them *animal spirits*.

For Keynes, unpredictability was not irrationality. Some things in life, he argued, are unpredictable. Future demand for your product was one of these things. Thus, basing your decision on rumours and guesses was the best you could do; it wasn't irrational.

Technological Development   A third major cause of shifts in the investment function is technological development. When a new technology develops, it makes the old technology obsolete. Firms using that old technology find they can't compete; to keep up they must invest in the new technology. Some economists define periods in economic history by technological development and the investment resulting from that technological development. For example, the 1880s was the railroad period.

A recent major technological advance is the computer revolution beginning in the 1960s. In the 1990s, the biotechnological revolution could dwarf the effects of the computer revolution. These technological advances open up new opportunities and generate large amounts of investment by making past investment obsolete. As investment increases, aggregate expenditures and aggregate income increase.

Shifts in Government Expenditures

In the same way that private expenditures can shift, so too can government expenditures. During a war, government expenditures can increase significantly. In peacetime, government defense expenditures can fall. As we'll see in the next chapter, government's desire to affect the level of income is another reason government expenditures can change.

Shifts in Autonomous Imports and Exports

Even if expenditures within a country are stable, outside expenditures often are not. A war or a shift in political alignments can totally change flows of exports and imports. For example, World Wars I and II brought Canadian trade with Germany to a halt, but significantly increased Canadian exports to other countries. The Canadian economy boomed. The depression in Europe in the middle and late 1920s cut back on European imports from Canada, significantly decreasing Canadian exports and further pushing the Canadian economy into a recession. In the 1990s, the events in the former Soviet Union lowered Canadian exports and lowered Eastern European countries' exports even more. We already know from history that exchange rates and tariff policies impact both imports and exports. All these changes show up as shifts in the autonomous expenditures curve.

Shifts in Autonomous Expenditures and Keynes's Model

To give you a sense of how Keynes saw his model working, let's say that for some reason there is a shock to the economy, decreasing aggregate expenditures so that aggregate production is greater than aggregate expenditures. Suppliers can't sell all they produce. Their reaction, Keynes argued, would be to lay off workers and decrease output. That response would solve the problem if only one firm was in disequilibrium, but wouldn't solve the problem if all firms were in disequilibrium. When all producers respond in this fashion, aggregate income, and hence aggregate expenditures, will also fall. The suppliers' cutback will simply start a vicious cycle, which is multiplied. As the laid-off workers cut their expenditures, producers will cut back production, laying off more workers. The economy will enter into a downward spiral with aggregate production and expenditures chasing each other. The result will be an economic depression.

Will the downward spiral ever end? Keynes argued that eventually it would; fired individuals will dip into savings and not cut their expenditures by the full amount of their decrease in income. Because they do, as income falls, aggregate production and aggregate expenditures will get closer and closer together, and at some level of income aggregate production will equal aggregate expenditures. The algebraic and geometric models we considered in this chapter tell us how much income must fall to bring the economy to aggregate equilibrium.

The Income Adjustment Process: An Example   The income adjustment process is directly related to the multiplier. The reason is that any initial shock (a change in autonomous aggregate expenditures) is *multiplied* in the adjustment process. Let's see how this works in Exhibit 11's example, which will also serve as a review of the Keynesian model. In this example, let's say trade negotiations between Canada and other countries have fallen apart and Canadian exports decrease by $20. This is shown in the AE curve's downward shift from AE_0 to AE_1.

How far must income fall until equilibrium is reached? To answer that question, we need to know the initial shock, $\Delta X = -\$20$, and the size of the multiplier, $[1/(1 - mpc)]$. In this example, $mpc = .8$, so the multiplier is 5. That means the final decrease in income that brings about equilibrium is $100 (five times as large as the initial shock of $20).

Exhibit 11 (b), a blowup of the circled area in Exhibit 11 (a), shows the detailed

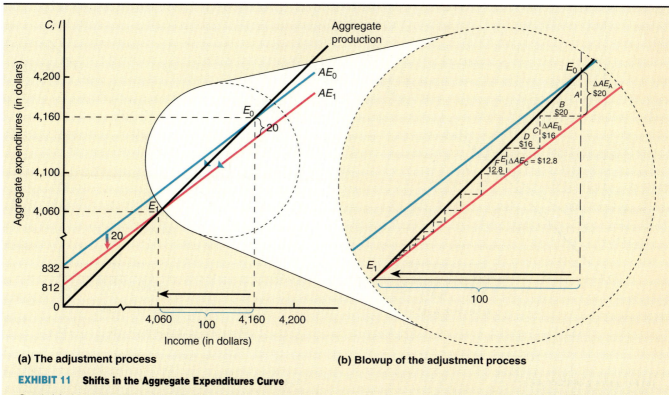

(a) The adjustment process   **(b) Blowup of the adjustment process**

EXHIBIT 11   Shifts in the Aggregate Expenditures Curve

Graph **(a)** shows the effect of a shift of the aggregate expenditures curve. When exports decrease by $20, the aggregate expenditures curve shifts downward from AE_0 to AE_1. In response, income falls by a multiple of the shift, in this case by $100.

Graph **(b)** shows the multiplier process under a microscope. In it the adjustment process is broken into discrete steps. For example, when income falls by 20 (shift *B*), expenditure falls by (16) (shift *C*). In response to that fall of expenditures, producers reduce output by 16, which decreases income by 16 (shift *D*). The lower income causes expenditures to fall further (shift *E*) and the process continues.

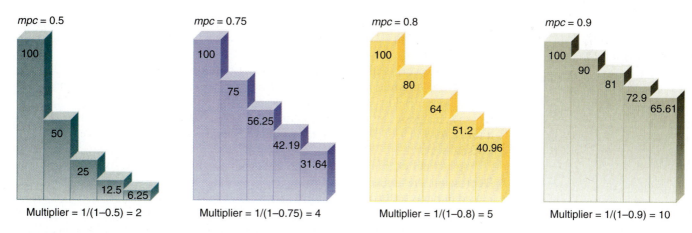

EXHIBIT 12   The First Five Steps of Four Multipliers

The larger the marginal propensity to consume, the more steps are required before the shifts become small.

steps of the adjustment process so you can see how it works. Initially, autonomous expenditures fell by $20 (shift *A*), causing firms to decrease production by $20 (shift *B*). But that decrease in income caused expenditures to decrease by another $16 (0.8 × $20) (shift *C*). Again firms respond by cutting production, this time by $16 (shift *D*). Again income falls (shift *E*) causing production to fall (shift *F*). The process continues again and again (the remaining steps) until equilibrium income falls by $100, five times the amount of the initial shock. The *mpc* tells how much closer at each step

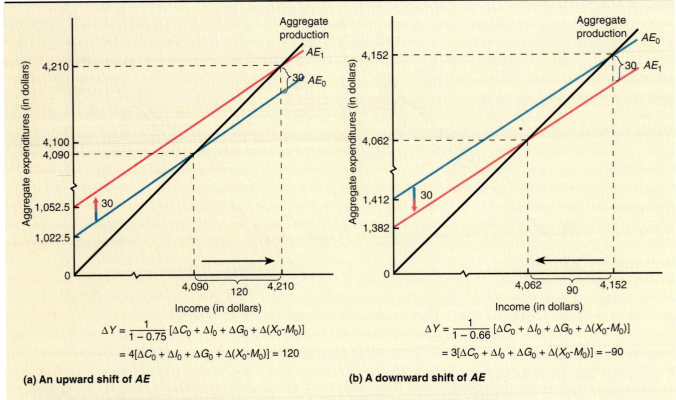

$$\Delta Y = \frac{1}{1 - 0.75} [\Delta C_0 + \Delta I_0 + \Delta G_0 + \Delta(X_0\text{-}M_0)]$$

$$= 4[\Delta C_0 + \Delta I_0 + \Delta G_0 + \Delta(X_0\text{-}M_0)] = 120$$

(a) An upward shift of AE

$$\Delta Y = \frac{1}{1 - 0.66} [\Delta C_0 + \Delta I_0 + \Delta G_0 + \Delta(X_0\text{-}M_0)]$$

$$= 3[\Delta C_0 + \Delta I_0 + \Delta G_0 + \Delta(X_0\text{-}M_0)] = -90$$

(b) A downward shift of AE

EXHIBIT 13   Two Different Expenditure Functions and Two Different Shifts in Autonomous Expenditures

The steeper the slope of the AE curve, the greater the effect on equilibrium income. In **(a)** the slope of the AE curve is .75 and a shift of $30 causes a shift in income of $120. In **(b)**, the slope of the AE curve is .66 and a shift of $30 causes a shift in income of $90.

aggregate expenditures will be to aggregate production. You can see this adjustment process in Exhibit 12, which shows the first steps with multipliers of various sizes.

FURTHER EXAMPLES OF THE KEYNESIAN MODEL

Learning to work with the Keynesian model requires practice, so in Exhibit 13 we present two different expenditures functions and two different shifts in autonomous expenditures. Below each model is the equation representing how much aggregate income changes in terms of the multiplier and the components of autonomous expenditures. As you see, this equation calculates the shift, while the graph determines it in a visual way.

As a final example, let's see how Keynes used his model to explain the 1930s Depression. He argued the following: In 1929 there was a financial crash which continued into the 1930s. Financial markets were a mess. Businesspeople became scared, so they decreased investment; consumers became scared, so they decreased autonomous consumption and increased savings. The result was a sudden large shift downward in the aggregate expenditures curve.

Businesspeople responded by decreasing output, which decreased income and started a downward spiral. This downward spiral confirmed business's fears. The decreased output further decreased income and expenditures. The process continued until eventually the economy settled at a low-income equilibrium, far below the potential, or full-employment, level of income.

Paradox of thrift   Individuals attempting to save more cause income to decrease; thereby, they end up saving less.

The process that Keynes argued played an important role in bringing about the Depression is sometimes called the **paradox of thrift.** Individuals attempted to save more, but in doing so caused income to decrease, and they ended up saving less.

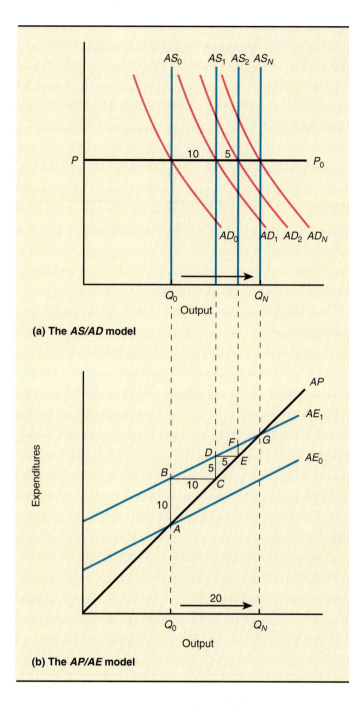

EXHIBIT 14   The Relation of the *AS/AD* to the *AP/AE* Model

In (**a**) we show the interactive effects of an initial shift in expenditures of 10. That initial shift causes the *AE* curve to shift up and the *AD* curve to shift up. That initial shift causes induced shifts in *AS* and *AD* curves, which are shown by the *AP* curve and *AE* curves, respectively. The new equilibrium occurs at point *G* at output Q_N. At that output, the *AE* and *AP* curves intersect, and the *AS* and *AD* curves also intersect—because they have stopped shifting.

(a) The *AS/AD* model

(b) The *AP/AE* model

Let us now consider the relationship between the *AP/AE* model and the macro policy model in the last chapter.

Since the macro policy model is based on the *AS/AD* model, let us briefly show the relationship between these two models. (In Appendix A we give a more complete exposition.) The *AS/AD* model has a vertical aggregate supply curve and a downward sloping *AD* curve as in Exhibit 14 (a).

The equilibrium where *AS* and *AD* intersect is at output *d*. This same equilibrium is shown in Exhibit 14(b) in the Keynesian model. It occurs at point *A* where AE_0 intersects *AP*.

THE RELATIONSHIP BETWEEN THE *AP/AE* MODEL AND LAST CHAPTER'S MACRO POLICY MODEL

The *AS/AD* Model and the *AP/AE* Model

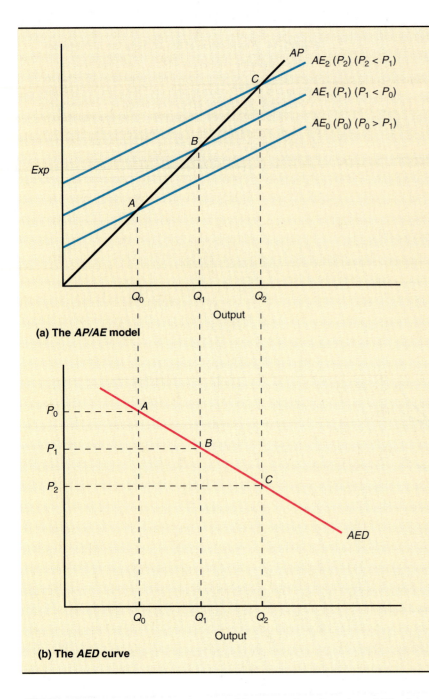

EXHIBIT 15   Deriving the *AED* Curve
The *AED* curve is derived from the *AP/AE* model by asking what effect a fall in the price level has on equilibrium output. As we discussed in the last chapter, that fall in the price level increases equilibrium output, as shown in (a). In (b) we combine the price level with the equilibrium output it is associated with, (points *A*, *B*, and *C*). Those points give us the *AED* curve.

(a) The *AP/AE* model

(b) The *AED* curve

6 The multiplier process depends on whether the price level is fixed or flexible. When prices are relatively stable the macro policy model suggests that changes in aggregate expenditures change output while the price level remains unchanged. If the economy is operating in the upward-sloping region of the price level flexibility curve, both the level of output and the level of prices change in response to a change in aggregate expenditures.

Now, say that there is a shift of autonomous expenditures (aggregate demand) by 10. This shift is shown by a shift of the *AD* curve from AD_0 to AD_1 and a shift up of the *AE* curve from AE_0 to AE_1 (from point *A* to *B*). This initial shift causes the *AS* curve to shift out along the P_0 line to AS_1, which is the equivalent of a movement along the *AP* curve from point *A* to point *C*. But that increase in supply causes the *AD* curve to shift out by the *mpc* times the initial shift—in this case by 5, since the *mpc* is assumed to be .5. The second shift is shown by the shift of *AD* from AD_1 to AD_2, and by a movement along the *AE* curve from point *B* to point *D*. (Remember: a shift of the *AD* curve is the equivalent of a movement along the *AE* curve.) So we still have a disequilibrium in both models with $AD > AS$ and $AE > AP$.

This disequilibrium causes an induced shift of the *AS* curve to AS_2, and a further movement along the *AP* curve to point *E*. These shifts occur because supplier's expectations of demand change; as those expectations of demand increase the *AS* curve shifts out and there is a movement along the *AP* curve. These increases in supply cause a further induced shift in AD to AD_2 and a further movement along the AE curve from point D to point F. The movements and shifts continue until point G at output Q_N. At that point the AE and the AP curves intersect, and the interactive shifts between AS and AD have become so small as to be negligible.

Now let's move on to a consideration of the relation between the macro policy model and the AP/AE model. Let's first derive the AED curve. We do so in Exhibit 15.

The *AP/AE* Model and the Macro Policy Model

In Exhibit 15 (a) we draw three AE curves—one for each of price levels P_0, P_1, and P_2. where $P_0 > P_1 > P_2$. The initial equilibrium is at point A. Notice that as the price level falls aggregate expenditures rise due to the effects we described above when we discussed the reasons the AED curve slopes downward. These initial increases cause induced expenditures and production shifts as discussed above increasing output further at P_1. The new equilibrium output is Q_1 (point B) and at P_2, the new equilibrium output is Q_2 (point C).

In Exhibit 15 (b) we show the equilibrium price levels and outputs on a graph, with price level on the vertical axis and output on the horizontal axis. That gives us points A, B, and C, which correspond to points A, B, and C in Exhibit 15 (a). Drawing a line through these points gives us the aggregate equilibrium demand curve: a curve which shows how a change in the price level will affect equilibrium output.

The first thing to note when considering the two models is that the AP/AE model assumes the price level constant, so it assumes that the price level flexibility curve is flat. This means that the AP/AE model tells us precisely how much the AED curve will shift when the AD curve shifts by a specified amount. The difference between the shift in the AD curve and the AED curve shift is due to the multiplier.

The relationship between a shift in autonomous expenditures in the macro policy model and the AP/AE model can be seen in Exhibit 16. It considers a fall in autonomous exports of $20 when the multiplier is 2. In Exhibit 16 (a) you can see that, in the AP/AE model, a fall in exports of $20 will cause income to fall by $40, from $4,052 to $4,012.

Exhibit 16 (b) shows that same adjustment in the macro policy model. The fall in exports is the equivalent to a fall in aggregate demand of 20, but the AED curve shifts back not by 20, but by 40—the initial shift multiplied by the multiplier. That's because the AED curves take into account the interdependent shifts between supply and demand that are set in motion by the initial shift. Thus we need the Keynesian model, or some alternative model of induced effects, before we can draw an AED curve. (We make the qualification—or some other model—to emphasize that the interdependent shifts assumed in the Keynesian model are not the only interdependent shifts that could occur. Had we assumed a different dynamic adjustment process, we would have had a different AED curve.)

One final point. Notice we haven't shown the AS curve in Exhibit 16 (b). That doesn't mean supply isn't changing. Any movement along the PLF curve corresponds to a shift of the aggregate supply curve.

Exhibits 16 (c) and (d) show what happens when the economy is in the partially flexible price-level range. Here the AE curve shifts down by 20, and the AED curve shifts in by 40. But the reduction in the AED curve causes the price level to fall which causes income to rise somewhat so that the AE curve shifts up (from $AE_1(P_0)$ to $AE_1(P_1)$). The final decrease in income is now not 40, but is instead 36 in this example.

A good test of your understanding here is to ask yourself what happens if there is perfect price-level flexibility. (In that case, the rise in aggregate equilibrium demand is fully offset by a rise in the price level, and the AE curve shifts right back where it started.)

Much of the modern debate in macro concerns the nature of those interdependent shifts. We won't go into that debate here since it quickly becomes very complicated, but we do want to point out to you that the Keynesian adjustment model is not the end of the analysis; it is simply the beginning—the simplest case of interdependence.

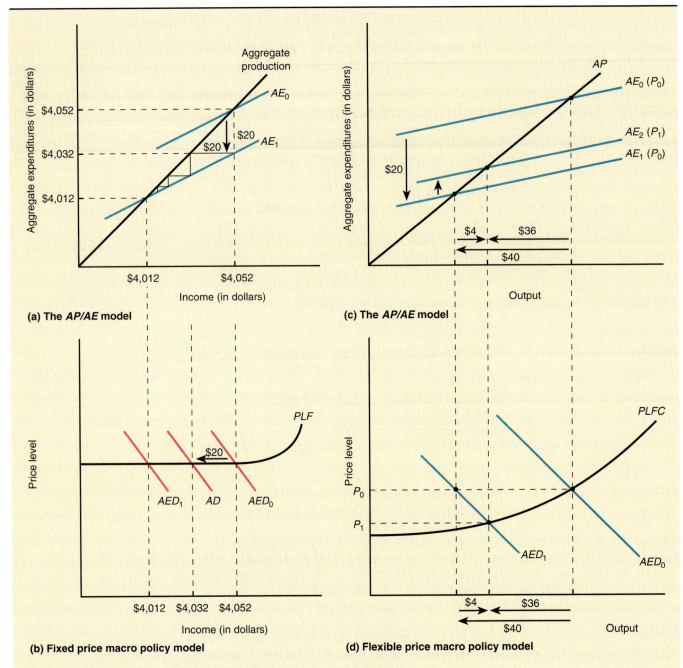

EXHIBIT 16 **Relationship between the Macro Policy Model and the *AP/AE* Model**

In **(a)** and **(b)** exhibits you can see the equivalency of the macro policy dynamics and the *AP/AE* dynamics where there is a fixed price level. Where *AE* equals *AP*, as it does at $4,012, we see how far the *AED* curve shifts back. Thus the *AD* curve shifts back by 20, the same as the *AE* curve shifts down. The *AED* curve shifts back by 40.

When the price level is flexible, as in **(d)** a reduction in aggregate demand reduces prices, leading to less of a change in output relative to the fixed-price model. The fall of the price level (from P_0 to P_1 in **(d)**) causes the *AE* curve to partially shift back up (from AE_1 to AE_2 in **(c)**), leading to a new equilibrium shift of only $36 rather than $40.

The Keynesian Model as an Historical "Model in Time"

The preceding discussion provides a technical method of determining equilibrium income in the Keynesian model, and hence in the macro policy model. But in reality the model doesn't do what it purports to do—determine equilibrium income from scratch. Why? Because it doesn't tell us where those autonomous expenditures come from, or how we would go about measuring them.

At best, what we can measure, or at least estimate, are directions and rough sizes of autonomous demand or supply shocks, and determine the direction and possible over-adjustment the economy might make in response to those shocks. If you think back to our initial discussion of the Keynesian model, this is how we introduced it—as an explanation of forces affecting the adjustment process, not as a determinant of the final equilibrium independent of where the economy started.

The central Keynesian idea is that the economy will overreact to shocks—shifts in aggregate supply and demand—leading income in the economy to fluctuate more than individuals desire. Without some additional information about where the economy started from, or what is the desired level of output, the Keynesian theory is not a complete theory. Put another way, *the Keynesian model is a historical model in time*. Each equilibrium that the economy arrives at is dependent on the past; the equilibrium that the economy arrives at is a **path-dependent equilibrium**—an equilibrium that is influenced by the adjustment process to that equilibrium. All history determines current reality and all models must reflect that historical connection. Models that reflect history are called historical models. In any model that involves hysteresis, you can't understand the current situation separately from the entire past. The future is unfolding in ways that can be understood only as part of historical time.

There are a number of heavy philosophical points in the last paragraph which have wild mathematical counterpart formulations. Path-dependent equilibria and hysteresis are all the rage in graduate economics schools today. Luckily, we don't have to get into any of that—the basic ideas are simple for introductory students to understand.

All that introductory students need understand are the different visions of the circular flow of income that follow from the Keynesian and Classical models. Those different visions can be seen by remembering the circular flow analysis.

The circular flow diagram expresses the national income identity: aggregate income equals aggregate output. The Classical school saw forces outside of economics determining the size of the circular flow. It was a circular flow. Keynes did not; he saw the adjustment process to equilibrium changing the size of the income flow and hence changing the equilibrium. Any real shock to the economy would tend to be exaggerated, causing larger-than-desired fluctuations in income. Thus in a Keynesian model it isn't quite correct to see the aggregate economy as a timeless circular flow; instead it should be seen as a pulsating spiral expanding and contracting in response to unexpected shocks.

Understanding the pulsating income (business cycles) could not be accomplished by considering equilibrium separately from disequilibrium adjustment. Keynes's model offered one simple way of considering both simultaneously and arriving at a specific solution. Keynes asked: (1) Does aggregate expenditure always equal aggregate production? and (2) If not, what will happen in the economy to bring them into equilibrium?

The "in time" interpretation was not always the interpretation of Keynesian economics that students were taught. In the 1960s, the interpretation of the Keynesian model that was taught was mechanistic. The **mechanistic Keynesian model** pictured the economy as representable by a mechanistic, timeless model with a determinant equilibrium. It involved little or no discussion of the fleetingness of that equilibrium, or of the limitations of that equilibrium with respect to the starting position.

At that time, the Keynesian model was presented as definitive; all economists had to do was to go out and collect the measurements they needed and they could control the level of income in the economy, independent of where the level had been or of what people wanted. Reality proved that interpretation wrong; mechanistic Keynesian economics doesn't work, any more than mechanistic Classical economics does. Modern economists have come to the conclusion that *there is no simple way to understand the aggregate economy*. You can't separate dynamics from the equilibrium analysis; you can't study the economy in a historical vacuum, and any mechanistic interpretation of an aggregate model is doomed to failure.

Mechanistic Keynesianism is not the Keynesian economics presented in this book. The model outlined in this chapter is what we call the **interpretative Keynesian**

Path-dependent equilibrium
Equilibrium that is influenced by the adjustment process to that equilibrium.

Mechanistic and Interpretative Keynesians
Mechanistic Keynesian model
Model picturing the economy as representable by a mechanistic, timeless model with a determinant equilibrium.

7 A mechanistic Keynesian model sees the model as a direct guide for policy; it tells you what policy to follow. An interpretative Keynesian model sees the model as a guide to one's common sense; highlighting important dynamic interdependencies. Before applying the model, other interdependencies must be considered.

Interpretative Keynesian model
Keynesian model that is an aid in understanding complicated disequilibrium dynamics.

model—it views the Keynesian model as an aid in understanding complicated disequilibrium dynamics. The specific results of the Keynesian model are a guide to one's common sense, letting one emphasize a particular important dynamic interdependency while keeping others in the back of one's head. With that addendum—that the Keynesian model is not meant to be taken literally, but only as an aid to our intuition—the simple Keynesian model of the 1950s and 1960s is extraordinarily modern and up to date, dealing with the issues with which the highest-level macro theorists of the 1990s are struggling.

Mechanistic and Interpretative Classicals

We concentrate on the Keynesian model not because we believe it is the best description of the aggregate adjustment process in the economy, but because it is a good introduction into the complexities of that aggregate adjustment process. In many ways we find ourselves more convinced by the Robersonian classical description of the adjustment process, but we could not think of any simple way of presenting it. It was too complicated to be "sold" in the 1930s and it is too complicated now.

But we should not leave this discussion without mentioning that just as the mechanistic Keynesian model should not be seen as the model modern Keynesians believe, so too is it the case that the mechanistic Classical model should not be seen as the model modern Classicals believe. Most modern Classicals are quite willing to accept that there are induced effects of autonomous shifts, but they are not willing to accept that these induced effects follow the simple pattern that the simple Keynesian model ascribes to them.

Put another way, modern Classicals do not see the consumption function as stable. They believe spending decisions are far more complicated than can be described by a simple rule about saving a constant proportion of current income. They see wealth or permanent income as playing a much more important role, stabilizing expenditure changes that result from short-run fluctuations in current income. Hence, the induced effects of shifts in aggregate expenditures cannot be determined until you understand the complicated spending decisions. That's why there are debates about macro policy. Both modern Keynesians and modern Classicals recognize that the real policy issues involve aggregate dynamics, and that these aggregate dynamics become very complicated very quickly.

A Final Word

In the preface of this book, we stated that an important goal of this text was teaching economic sensibility. We stated that we wanted to give students a feel for the way the real economy works. After reading this chapter, you probably have a sense that the macro economy is very complicated and that there is no simple model which will tell you "here's how it works." That, we know, is a bit frustrating, but an important part of learning economic sensibility is recognizing how complicated the macro economy is.

The macro economy is complicated, and if we were to tell you that in the two weeks that you'll probably devote to these chapters you will understand it, we'd be lying (and any book that tells you that is also lying). Macroeconomic issues are complicated, and there is no simple model that can capture all the complexities. What a macro model can do is to help guide your common sense; it cannot replace your common sense with a mechanistic understanding of the macro economy.

CHAPTER SUMMARY

- The Keynesian multiplier model tells us that the *AED* curve will shift by an amount $(1/(1 - mpc))$ times the shift in the *AD* curve.
- The Keynesian model is made up of the aggregate production and aggregate expenditure curves. In equilibrium, planned aggregate production must equal planned aggregate expenditures.
- Aggregate expenditures (*AE*) are made up of consumption, investment, government spending, and net exports:

$$AE = C + I + G + (X - M)$$

- Consumption depends upon the level of income; the *mpc* tells us the change in consumption that occurs with a change in income.
- Savings are the mirror image of consumption. When planned aggregate production equals planned aggregate expenditures, planned savings equals planned investment.
- Investment doesn't depend upon the level of income.

- Shifts in investment or shifts in autonomous consumption can be the initial shock that begins the multiplier process.
- Keynes believed a business cycle is caused by (1) a shock creating a small disequilibrium and (2) the multiplier, which expands that initial shock to a much larger decrease or increase in production and income. The multiplier $(1/(1 - mpc))$ is the income adjustment mechanism.
- The Keynesian equation is

$$Y = (1/(1 - b)) [C_0 + I_0 + G_0 + (X_0 - M_0)].$$

- The multiplier tells us how much a change in autonomous expenditures will change income.
- The Keynesian model comes to the same results as does the macro policy model when the price-level flexibility curve is flat.
- The Keynesian model cannot be applied mechanistically; it is only a guide to common sense.

KEY TERMS

aggregate consumption
  function *(223)*
aggregate expenditures *(220)*
aggregate income curve *(219)*
Aggregate Production/Aggregate
  Expenditures (AP/AE)
  Model *(218)*
aggregate production curve *(219)*
autonomous consumption *(221)*
average propensity to consume
  (apc) *(222)*

average propensity to save
  (aps) *(225)*
consumption function *(221)*
disposable income *(220)*
income adjustment mechanism *(218)*
induced consumption *(221)*
interpretative Keynesian
  model *(241)*
investment *(226)*
Keynesian equation *(229)*
Keynes's Law *(220)*

marginal propensity to consume
  (mpc) *(222)*
marginal propensity to save
  (mps) *(225)*
mechanistic Keynesian model *(241)*
multiplier *(230)*
net exports *(227)*
paradox of thrift *(236)*
path dependent equilibrium *(241)*

QUESTIONS FOR THOUGHT AND REVIEW

The number after each question represents the estimated degree of critical thinking required. (1 = almost none; 10 = deep thought.)

1. If nominal income, rather than real income, were measured on the vertical axis, what would the *AP* curve look like in each of the three ranges of the economy discussed in the last chapter? *(9)*

2. If savings were instantaneously translated into investment, what would be the multiplier's size? What would be the level of autonomous expenditures? *(7)*

3. Name some forces that might cause shocks to aggregate expenditures. *(2)*

4. Mr. Whammo has just invented a magic pill. Take it and it transports you anywhere. Explain his invention's effects on the economy. *(10)*

5. The marginal propensity to consume is .8. Autonomous expenditures are $4,200. What is the level of income in

the economy? Demonstrate graphically. *(3)*

6. The marginal propensity to save is .33 and autonomous expenditures have just fallen by $20. What will likely happen to income? *(5)*

7. The marginal propensity to save is .5 and autonomous expenditures have just risen $200. The economy is at its potential level of income. What will likely happen to income? Why? *(6)*

8. Demonstrate graphically the effect of an increase in autonomous expenditures of $20 in the Keynesian model if the *mpc* = .66. *(3)*

9. Why is the circular flow diagram of the economy an only partially correct conception of Keynesian economics? *(7)*

10. How does a mechanistic Keynesian differ from an interpretative Keynesian? *(3)*

PROBLEMS AND EXERCISES

1. Congratulations! You've been appointed economic advisor to Happyland. Your research assistant says the country's *mpc* is .8 and autonomous investment has just risen by $20.

   a. What will happen to income?

   b. Your research assistant comes in and says he's sorry but the *mpc* wasn't .8; it was .5. How does your answer change?

   c. He runs in again and says exports have fallen by $10 and investment has risen by $10. How does your answer change?

   d. You now have to present your analysis to the Prime Minister, who wants to see it all graphically. Naturally you oblige.

2. Congratulations again. You've just been appointed economic advisor to Examland. The *mpc* is .6; investment is $1,000; government spending is $8,000; autonomous consumption is $10,000; and net exports are $1,000.

   a. What is the level of income in the country?

   b. Net exports increase by $2,000. What will happen to income?

   c. What will happen to unemployment? (Remember Okun's law.)

   d. You've just learned the *mps* changed from .4 to .5. How will this information change your answers in *a, b,* and *c?*

3. In 1993, as Prime Minister Campbell was running (unsuccessfully) for election, the economy slowed down; then in late 1993, after Prime Minister Chretien's election, the economy picked up steam.

   a. Demonstrate graphically with the *AP/AE* model a shift in the *AE* curve that would have caused the slowdown. Which component of aggregate expenditures was the likely culprit?

   b. Demonstrate graphically with the *AP/AE* model a shift in the *AE* curve that would have caused the improvement. Which component of aggregate expenditures was likely responsible?

   c. What policies do you think Prime Minister Campbell could have used to stop the slowdown?

   d. What policies do you think Prime Minister Chretien used to try to speed up the economy?

4. Demonstrate graphically the effect of an increase in autonomous expenditures when the *mpc* = .5 and the price level is fixed:

   a. In the *AP/AE* model.

   b. In the macro policy model.

   c. Do the same thing as in *a* and *b,* only this time assume prices are somewhat flexible. (Appendix B may help in answering this part.)

5. State how the following information changes the shape of the *AED* curve discussed in the previous chapter.

   a. The effect of price-level changes on autonomous expenditures is reduced.

   b. The size of the multiplier increases.

   c. Autonomous expenditures increase by $20.

   d. Falls in the price level disrupt financial markets which offsets the normally assumed effects of a change in the price level.

The Macro Policy Model, the AS/AD Model, and the AP/AE Model

In Chapter 8, Appendix A to Chapter 8, and Chapter 9 we have developed three models—the macro policy model, the *AS/AD* model and the *AP/AE* model. If you have understood the models you will understand that these were not three distinct models at all, but in fact, were slightly different expositions of the same macro model. The macro policy model is the most general of the three; the other two give one insight into what lies underneath that model. Specifically, the *AS/AD* model gives you a sense of the price-level adjustment that is an alternative path to equilibrium, and the *AP/AE* model gives you a quantitative specification of how much the *AED* curve shifts when the *AD* curve shifts by a specified amount. (It shifts by the multiplier times the initial shift.)

In this chapter we briefly considered the relationship between the *AP/AE* model and the macro policy model. As we discussed in Appendix A to Chapter 8, the macro policy model was the end result of the dynamic adjustment process of the *AS/AD* model we presented in the appendix. In this appendix we relate that *AS/AD* model to the AP/AE model, completing the unification of the three models.

The Relation between the AS/AD Curve from the AP/AE Model

Let us first derive the aggregate demand curve from the *AP/AE* model. To do so we must remember that a change in the price level will be seen in the *AP/AE* model as a change in autonomous expenditures. The amount of the change will depend on the size of the direct responsiveness of aggregate output to changes in the price level (i.e., the initial effect, not the indirect effect caused by the multiplier).

We show this relationship in Exhibit A1. Say that when the price level falls from P_0 to P_1, the direct response will be for expenditures (aggregate quantity demanded) to increase by 10. Similarly when the price level falls from P_1 to P_2, the direct response is for expenditures to increase by 12. This means that we have three different expenditures functions—one for each price

level. We draw those three expenditures functions in Exhibit A1 (a).

Since this diagram contains the information about the effect of a change in the price level on the quantity of aggregate demand, we can derive an *AD* curve from it. To do so, let's start at equilibrium (point A) at price level P_0 and output level Q_0 in Exhibit $A1$ (b). Since at A aggregate demand is Q_0 and the price level is P_0, we can determine one point on the aggregate demand curve. We do so by extending a vertical line down from point A in (a) to price level P_0 in (b). Now say that the price level falls from P_0 to P_1. This causes the AE curve to shift up by 10, from $AE_0(P_0)$ to $AE_1(P_1)$. Initially, expenditures increase from point A to point B. We can show that increase in expenditures of 10 horizontally by drawing a line over from point B to point C on the aggregate production line. That increase of 10 is the initial effect of the change in the price level from P_0 to P_1 on aggregate expenditures. It is the total shift in output that would take place if there were no multiplier effect. Extending a vertical line down from point C to price level P_1 in (b), we have a second point on the aggregate demand curve (point C).

Now say that instead of the price level falling to P_1, it fell to P_2. That would cause the AE curve to shift further from $AE_1(P_1)$ to $AE_2(P_2)$, for a total increase in expenditures of 22 (from point A to point D). That increase of 22 can be shown on the horizontal axis by drawing a horizontal line from point D to point E for a total increase of 22. Extending a vertical line down from point E to price level P_2 in (b), we have a third point on the aggregate demand curve (point E). If we connect the points $A, C,$ and $E,$ we have part of the aggregate demand curve, and if we continue the thought experiment, we can derive the entire aggregate demand curve.

Notice that when deriving the aggregate demand curve, we specifically did not include the multiplier in determining the slope of the *AD* curve. Those multiplier effects are dependent on interactive shifts in the aggre-

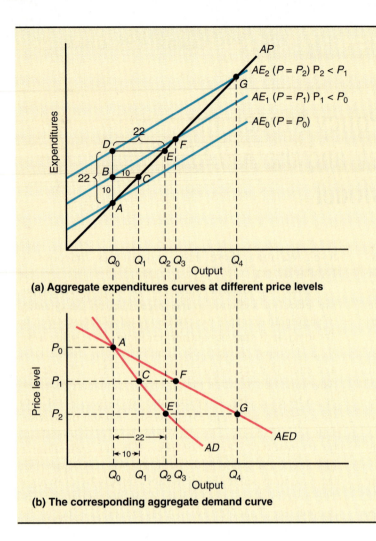

(a) Aggregate expenditures curves at different price levels

(b) The corresponding aggregate demand curve

EXHIBIT A1 (a and b)

The *AD* curve can be derived from the *AP/AE* curves by asking what effect a price level change has on aggregate expenditures (other things constant). In **(a)** three *AE* curves are drawn, each for a different price level—the lower the price level, the higher the expenditures. Since these three curves give us information about what expenditures will be at different price levels, we can relate these *AE* curves to an aggregate demand curve. We do that in **(b)**. For example, point *A* in **(a)** represents a price level of P_0 and an output level of Q_0. If the price level falls to P_1, the expenditures function shifts up by the 10, which means that the quantity of aggregate demand increases by 10. Tracing over 10 from point *B*, we arrive at point *C*. (Notice that we did not move along the *AE* curve; that includes induced effects—shifts of the demand curve—and they should not be included in the derivation of the slope of the aggregate demand curve). So at the lower price P_1, there is a higher output Q_1. That point can be found by extending a vertical line from *C* in **(a)** to price level P_1 (point *C*) in **(b)**. Doing the same thing for point *E*, and connecting the three points, gives us the aggregate demand curve.

The *AED* curve is derived in the same manner. For the *AED* curve, however, we include the induced effects of that price level change—the multiplier effect. Including these induced effects, a shift of 10 causes aggregate equilibrium output to increase to Q_3, not Q_1, and a shift of 22 causes aggregate equilibrium output to increase to Q_4, not Q_2. Graphing point *F* and *G* in **(b)** gives us the *AED* curve.

gate supply and demand curves, and including them would have mixed up shifts of the demand curve caused by induced effects, and movements along the aggregate demand curve caused by changes in the price level. In the *AED* curve in the text where we are being less precise, we mix those up. Thus, the *AED* curve can be derived directly from the Keynesian model; we do so in Exhibit A1 (a) and (b) using the points *F* and *G*. These points include the induced effects of the price-level change and cause the *AED* curve to be flatter than the *AD* curve. Only if the multiplier is zero will the two curves be the same.

Now, let us consider the relationship between the two models if the price level isn't fixed—when the economy is in the other two ranges of price-level flexibility: The partially flexible price-level range and the perfectly flexible price-level range. Keep in mind that when we talk about changes in aggregate production and aggregate expenditures, we are talking about shifts of the aggregate supply and aggregate demand curves, not movements along these curves. (Remember: a movement along the aggregate production and aggregate expenditure curves is a shift in the aggregate supply and aggregate demand curves.) Exhibit A2 (a) and (b) shows how a fall in

exports of $20 when the multiplier is 2 is seen in both the *AP/AE* model and the *AS/AD* model. As you can see, the net effect of that fall in exports of $20 will cause income to fall $40, from $4,052 to $4,012. This was the case we considered in the text.

Each shift back of the *AS* curve in Exhibit A2 (b) is equivalent to a movement along the aggregate production curve in (a). Similarly, each shift back of the *AD* curve is equivalent to a movement along the aggregate expenditures curve. When the *AE* and *AP* curves intersect, so do the *AS* and *AD* curves.

In Exhibit A2 (c) we consider that same shift, only this time we assume the economy is in the intermediate range where the price level is partially flexible. Again for simplicity we assume wages and prices equally flexible, so the *AS* curve is vertical. As opposed to moving along a fixed price line, we move along a sloping line, shown by the *A* arrow in Exhibit A2 (d). This is the price-level flexibility curve. It shows the relative speeds of dynamic adjustment of price level relative to real output.

As you can see, the multiplier effect is muted by the fall in the price level. As output decreases, the price level falls, and as the price level falls, the *AE* curve shifts left

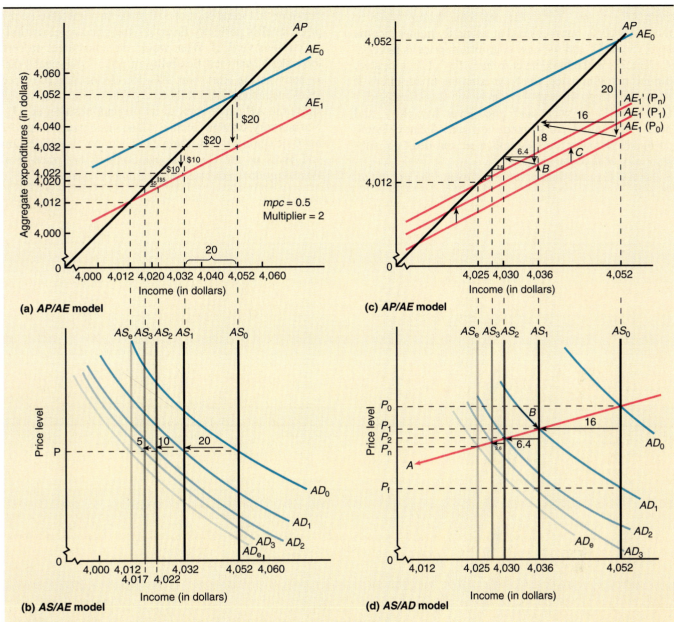

(a) *AP/AE* model

(b) *AS/AE* model

(c) *AP/AE* model

(d) *AS/AD* model

EXHIBIT A2   The Relationship between the *AS/AD* Model and the *AE/AP* Model

In (**a**) and (**b**) you can see the equivalency of the *AS/AD* dynamics and the *AP/AE* dynamics where there is a fixed price level. In this case the *PLF* curve would be flat. Notice that a movement along the *AE* curve corresponds to a shift of the *AD* curve, and a movement along the *AP* curve corresponds to a shift of the *AS* curve. When *AE* equals *AP*, as it does at $4,012, the *AS* and *AD* curves will stop shifting. In (**c**) and (**d**) We consider the equivalency of the two adjustment processes when there is a partially flexible wage and price level. The fall in the wage and price level (shown by arrow *A*) reduces the size of the multiplier at each step. For example, as aggregate demand fell by 20, aggregate supply does not shift by 20, but instead shifts by 16 since the fall in the price level causes the *AE* curve to shift up (arrow *B* in (**c**)) and movement along the *AD* curve (arrow *B* in (**d**)). This fall in the price level means that output only falls 16 rather than 20.

A similar type modification occurs for each step of the adjustment process, which makes the final decrease only to $4,025, not to $4,012 as occurred in the fixed price level case. The larger the degree of price level flexibility, the smaller the multiplier. In the limit, with instantaneous price level adjustment, demand shocks are instantaneously offset, the *AE* curve shifts back to its original position, and no output adjustment is required. This, of course, assumes that all other things remain constant and that an equilibrium exists—two highly unlikely assumptions.

from AE_1 to $AE_1'(P_1)$. The new equilibrium is not at income \$4,012, but is instead at a slightly higher income level (\$4,025), and the new equilibrium price is lower at P_1. The fall in the price level from P_0 to P_n has mitigated, but has not eliminated, the Keynesian multiplier effect. It is possible to go through the same analysis assuming different levels of wage and price-level flexibility, and hence with an upward-sloping short-run AS curve. Doing so makes it much more complicated, but does not substantially change the analysis.

Finally, to see that you are following the argument, consider that same shift of \$20, only this time assume the price level is perfectly flexible—the price-level flexibility curve is vertical. What would the adjustment process look like? That total flexibility of price level means that as soon as the shift from AE_0 to AE_1 occurs, the price level instantaneously falls to P_2 (shown in (d)), which shifts the AE curve back to its original position at AE_0. No quantity change occurs. Thus, instantaneous price-level flexibility means there can never be disequilibrium and gives us the Classical position—if that price-level flexibility does not cause other things to change.

Wage and Price-Level Flexibility
and Macroeconomic Theory

We ended Appendix A with a statement that with instantaneous price-level flexibility the aggregate economy would follow the Classical view—it would always remain at the desired level of output. The issue of price-level flexibility and aggregate output has been at the heart of many debates in theoretical macroeconomics: Will wage and price-level flexibility solve the problem and eliminate the possibility of the economy falling into a recession? When Keynes challenged the simple Classical view of the macro economy, the Classicals responded to that challenge with a formalistic argument of how price-level flexibility could, in theory, eventually lead the economy back to its potential income. It was formalistic because it had to be. The entire discussion in last chapter's appendix on the shape of the *AD* curve was based on that discussion. We put it in an appendix because it is academic for most policy situations. Almost no one really believed then, and almost no one really believes now that the price and wage level was going to fall as much as it would have to, or that we'd still have an economy left if the price level fell that much. Keynes and many sophisticated Classicals said "hogwash" to it. That isn't the way equilibrium comes about.

Keynes's primary argument against that Classical story did not concern the shape of the *AS* or *AD* curves (although he did argue that the *AD* curve would be almost vertical so that enormous price-level flexibility would be needed); it concerned the disequilibrium dynamics. Keynes argued that *all other things could not, and would not, remain equal.* Long before any price-level adjustment would take place to the degree needed to bring about significant increases in the quantity of aggregate demand, Keynes argued, an alternative adjustment mechanism—the income adjustment mechanism—would cause the *AS* and *AD* curves to shift, leading the economy to a new short-run equilibrium from which it could not escape on its own.

Keynes believed that the **income adjustment mechanism**—the chase between aggregate supply and aggregate demand reflected in the multiplier—is the mechanism by which the aggregate economy arrives at equilibrium through interdependent *shifts* of aggregate supply and aggregate demand, rather than through movements along the aggregate demand curve. Thus for Keynes, equilibrium in the macro economy was similar to a dog chasing its tail, and it wasn't clear where the final equilibrium would end up. For Classicals, aggregate equilibrium was set by individuals, and it reflected their desires.

Keynes focused on the income adjustment mechanism, as opposed to the Classical price-level adjustment mechanism, for two reasons. The first is that he felt the price-level adjustment mechanism was, from a practical standpoint, impossible. If it worked at all, it worked too slowly for political and social forces to accept. In response to the Classical argument that the price-level adjustment mechanism would work in the long run, he quipped, "In the long run we're all dead."

Yes, he agreed, there were some theoretical issues raised by the price-level adjustment mechanism, but he argued that those issues weren't especially important during the Depression. Social pressures (the invisible handshake) wouldn't let prices and wages fall fast enough for the Classical price-level adjustment mechanism to work. And even if the social pressures were overcome, political pressures (the invisible foot) would stop the fall in the price level, if it started.

Keynes argued that Classical economists failed to see the importance of the income adjustment mechanism because they were too caught up in Say's law and the quantity theory of money. Classicals assumed that unless the money supply changed, aggregate demand would not change, without any logical or empirical justification for that assumption. Keynes argued that the same quantity of

ADDED DIMENSION WORMHOLES AND THE CLASSICAL ADJUSTMENT STORY

Keynes did not spend much time discussing the effect on output of changes in the price level, but later economists have. What they have found is an asymmetry in the effects of price-level changes: upward movements in the price level are far less disruptive to the economy than are the equivalent downward movements of the price level. The reason is that the financial system in our economy is built on credit secured by assets. When the price level unexpectedly falls, it undermines the financial system because it transfers wealth away from borrowers, and borrowers are generally the entrepreneurs, the people responsible for supply. When the price level falls significantly, there is a financial panic and chaos. Firms go bankrupt and the institutional foundation of the economy is undermined. This effect might be called the *wormhole effect*.

For those of you who aren't astrophysicists or Trekie IIs, wormholes are disruptions in space. You enter a wormhole and you find yourself in a place somewhere completely different than the one where you started: For example, if you start in a house in Toronto and take just one step, you find yourself on the planet Pluto. That is about what happens when a financial panic is caused by a falling price level. The fall in the price level undermines existing institutions, and both aggregate demand and aggregate supply shift back. The economy finds itself in a depression—because the price level fell!

When the wormhole effect is taken into account, the real income equilibrium at which the economy arrives by letting the price level fall may well be at a lower level of output than it began with! Instead of increasing real income, a flexible price which pulls the economy into a wormhole will decrease it. That's why societies seldom let the price level fall significantly.

When the price level rises, the process is different—the wealth transfer is initially in the opposite direction; wealth is transferred from lenders to borrowers. Since these lenders are generally not the entrepreneurs, the same institutional disruption does not occur, at least initially. In fact, as money flows to entrepreneurs the economy often experiences a boom as more and more people try to become entrepreneurs. But to the degree this boom is based on unexpected wealth transfers, the boom is only temporary, and soon the price level increase becomes expected, and inflation becomes built into the economy. The institutional costs of inflation occur over longer periods of time; we'll discuss those costs in the chapter on inflation.

There are a number of complicated institutional issues upon which the above argument depends, such as whether the economy can develop financial institutions that are less fragile in respect to the price level than are our existing financial institutions (i.e., new institutions that avoid the wormhole effect), but that will be as conducive to production as are existing institutions. When, and if, such less-fragile institutions develop, money will be obsolete and we'll all carry our little financial Credit-Debit Wizard with us to pay all our bills. Perhaps, because it's a pain to carry, we will have the Wizard implanted under our skin and directly connected to our brain so that all we have to do is to think "payment" and the Wizard will arrange payment, or think "financing" and the Wizard will arrange financing for us. That is still a few years away, but, hey, it's possible. Don't underestimate those Wizards. (Some economists at the California Institute of Technology are currently designing moneyless computer-payment systems.)

---

money could support different levels of nominal income. Since both Keynes and the Classical economists agreed the price level did not decrease quickly, Keynes argued that aggregate demand for real output could fluctuate around, even if the money supply remained constant.

The second reason Keynes objected to the Classical disequilibrium dynamics was that he believed that Classical dynamic analysis was theoretically flawed. He believed a falling price level would set in motion other dynamic adjustment forces that would more than offset the equilibrating tendencies of the Classical price-level adjustment mechanism. Specifically, a falling price level would disrupt financial markets and create bearish (negative) expectations in businesspeople, which would cause aggregate supply to decrease. As aggregate supply decreased, aggregate demand would also decrease, and a downward spiral of output would result.

Keynes believed that such alternative dynamic effects of a falling price level would swamp any increase in the quantity of aggregate output caused by a lower price level as the economy moved along the demand curve. To say that theoretically, *other things constant,* an

adjustment force exists is one thing; Keynes agreed the price level could be made to fall (if the government wasn't worried about not being reelected), but if it did, that fall in the price level would cause shifts in the *AS* and *AD* curves. To say a falling price level is strong enough to achieve aggregate equilibrium at an economy's potential output when other things aren't held equal is another thing. It was not only a statement about the existence of the force; it was a statement of its strength and the absence of other forces. Keynes said the Classical adjustment mechanism was too weak to bring about an aggregate equilibrium, and that it would, by necessity, violate the "other things equal" assumption.

For much of Keynes's book, *The General Theory of Employment, Interest, and Money,* in which he developed the Keynesian model, he never got into such issues. Instead, he put aside that second, academic reason because the first reason (the real-world reason) was a sufficient reason not to consider wage and price-level flexibility. Thus, in the simple Keynesian model that we discussed in this chapter, wage and price levels are assumed to be institutionally fixed, leaving the model free to concentrate on what Keynes considered to be the most important dynamic adjustment force: the income adjustment force.

This assumption of fixed wages and prices without a full theoretical explanation of why it is a necessary and justifiable, not an ad hoc (arbitrary), assumption would later come back to haunt Keynesian economists. The reason why is that while wages and prices are slow to adjust downward, they are not so slow to adjust upward when the economy starts approaching its level of potential output. In the 1970s, the wage and price levels rose continuously, and inflation became the economy's biggest problem. Many Classical economists blamed this inflation on Keynesian policies that were based on a model that assumed the wage and price level fixed. This led to a resurgence of Classical analysis in the 1980s.

In response to that resurgence, Keynesian economists considered the issue of price-level flexibility, and argued that, as long as the economy is below potential income, removing that assumption does not change the basic argument; it only modifies it slightly. Moreover, they argued that Keynesian economists had never said that the Keynesian model was applicable once the economy has reached its potential output. They refined the interpretation of the Keynesian model so that it was not dependent on fixed nominal wages or prices. Rather, it concerned the adjustment dynamics—shifts of the curves, not movements along the curves. It is that refined Keynesian interpretation of the Keynesian model that we present in this chapter. So while the model you see in the text is the traditional Keynesian model, the interpretation is the modern interpretation of 1990s Keynesians.

Similarly with Classicals; the modern Classical interpretation accepts that short-run adjustment can occur through dynamic shifting of the *AS* and *AD* curves, but Classicals see the shifting to be far less predictable than modern Keynesians see it. But if the adjustment is unpredictable, much of the policy importance of the Keynesian model is lost. In the policy sections of the book, it is that modern Classical interpretation that we will emphasize.

10

Fiscal Policy and the Debate about Activist Macroeconomic Policy

An economist's lag may be a politician's catastrophe.
~George Schultze

After reading this chapter, you should be able to:

1 Explain expansionary and contractionary fiscal policies.

2 Demonstrate fiscal policy using words and graphs.

3 List three alternatives to fiscal policy.

4 Distinguish a structural deficit from a passive deficit.

5 List six problems with fiscal policy and explain how those problems limit its use.

6 Define crowding out and explain how it can undermine the Keynesian view of fiscal policy.

7 Describe how automatic stabilizers work.

The discussion in the previous chapter highlighted the Keynesian story of (1) how aggregate income is determined, and (2) how small shifts in aggregate expenditure could be multiplied into larger fluctuations in aggregate production and aggregate income. Together these two stories form the Keynesian explanation of why there can be equilibrium at an income level below the full-employment income level and why income in the economy fluctuates.

The Keynesian model was not designed only to understand why fluctuations (booms and busts) occur in the economy; it was also designed to suggest *policies* to deal with the depression, policies that would get the economy out of its under-full-employment equilibrium. Keynes offered an alternative to the Classical laissez-faire policy.

Keynes's initial policy proposals were for public works (for the government to spend more without collecting more taxes to pay for the spending or, in other words, to run a deficit by spending more). Keynesians soon broadened that policy to include: (1) another way to stimulate the economy—by reducing taxes, (2) a way to slow down the economy when it was called for—by decreasing government spending or increasing taxes, (3) policies to change the money supply as a way of controlling the economy, and (4) general policies to influence the four specific components of autonomous expenditures.

We'll see Keynesian policy affecting money in later chapters. In this chapter, we consider government policies that change the level of government spending and taxes as a way of affecting the economy.

Policy aimed at changing the level of income in the economy by a combination of a change in autonomous expenditures and the multiplied induced expenditures resulting from that change is called **aggregate demand (expenditure) management policy.** One of the most well-known of these aggregate demand management policies is **fiscal policy**—the deliberate change in either government spending or taxes to stimulate or slow down the economy. If aggregate income is too low (actual income is below target income), the appropriate fiscal policy is *expansionary fiscal policy:* decrease taxes or increase government spending. If aggregate income is too high (actual income is above target income), the appropriate fiscal policy is *contractionary fiscal policy:* increase taxes or decrease government spending.

Keynesians considered fiscal policy the steering wheel for the aggregate economy. They said Classical economists with their laissez-faire policy were trying to drive an economy without any steering wheel. If that were the case, is it any wonder the economy crashed?

In the 1930s everyone agreed that income was too low and that, if fiscal policy worked, the appropriate fiscal policy was expansionary. Keynesians advocated that governments run deficits. That advocacy made Keynesian economics the centre of political debate at the time. Keynesians were accused of being communists, of looking for a way to destroy the Canadian economy, because they advocated running a deficit. In the late 1940s and early 1950s, textbooks that included the Keynesian model were subject to vehement attack; university presidents and trustees were pressured to fire any professor who used a "Keynesian" text. Much has changed since then. By the 1960s and 1970s, fiscal policy was a well-established tool of most governments, and Keynesian economics had become mainstream economics. Such was the influence of the Keynesian model.

Let's start this discussion with the story of fiscal policy for an economy in a depression. What caused that depression? As we saw in the last two chapters, when people got scared and cut back their spending, the multiplier took over and expanded that small negative shock into a full-blown depression. In a depression, aggregate production and aggregate expenditures are equal, but at a level of income and production far below the potential level of income—below full employment of all productive resources.

FISCAL POLICY AND AGGREGATE DEMAND MANAGEMENT

Aggregate demand (expenditure) management policy Policy aimed at changing the level of income in the economy by a combination of a change in autonomous expenditures and the multiplied induced expenditures resulting from that change.

Fiscal policy Deliberate change in either government spending or taxes to stimulate or slow down the economy.

1 Expansionary fiscal policy involves decreasing taxes or increasing government spending. Contractionary fiscal policy involves increasing taxes or decreasing government spending.

The Story of Keynesian Fiscal Policy

THE ECONOMIC STEERING WHEEL

Our economic system is frequently put to shame in being displayed before an imaginary visitor from a strange planet. It is time to reverse the procedure.

Imagine yourself instead in a Buck Rogers interplanetary adventure, looking at a highway in a City of Tomorrow. The highway is wide and straight, and its edges are turned up so that it is almost impossible for a car to run off the road. What appears to be a runaway car is speeding along the road and veering off to one side. As it approaches the rising edge of the highway, its front wheels are turned so that it gets back onto the road and goes off at an angle, making for the other side, where the wheels are turned again. This happens many times, the car zigzagging but keeping on the highway until it is out of sight. You are wondering how long it will take for it to crash, when another car appears which behaves in the same fashion. When it comes near you it stops with a jerk. A door is opened, and an occupant asks whether you would like a lift. You look into the car and before you can control yourself you cry out, "Why, there's no steering wheel."

"Of course we have no steering wheel," says one of the occupants rather crossly. "Just think how it would cramp the front seat. It's worse than an old-fashioned gear-shift lever and it's dangerous. Suppose we have a steering wheel and somebody held on to it when we reached a curb. He would prevent the automatic turning of the wheel, and the car would surely be overturned. And besides, we believe in democracy and cannot give anyone the extreme authority of life and death over all the occupants of the car. That would be dictatorship."

"Down with dictatorship," chorus the other occupants of the car.

"If you are worried about the way the car goes from side to side," continues the first speaker, "forget it. We have wonderful brakes so that collisions are prevented nine times out of ten. On our better roads the curb is so effective that one can travel hundreds of miles without going off the road once. We have a very efficient system of carrying survivors of wrecks to nearby hospitals and for rapidly sweeping the remnants from the road to deposit them on nearby fields as a reminder to man of the inevitability of death."

You look around to see the piles of wrecks and burned-out automobiles as the man in the car continues. "Impressive, isn't it? But things are going to improve. See those men marking and photographing the tracks of the car that preceded us? They are going to take those pictures into their laboratories and pictures of our tracks, too, to analyze the cyclical characteristics of the curves, their degree of regularity, the average distance from turn to turn, the amplitude of the swings, and so on. When they have come to an agreement on their true nature we may know whether something can be done about it. At present they are disputing whether this cyclical movement is due to the type of road surface or to its shape or whether it is due to the length of the car or the kind of rubber in the tires or to the weather. Some of them think that it will be impossible to avoid having cycles unless we go back to the horse and buggy, but we can't do that because we believe in Progress. Well, want a ride?"

The dilemma between saving your skin and humoring the lunatics is resolved by your awakening from the nightmare, and you feel glad that the inhabitants of your own planet are a little more reasonable. But are they as reasonable about other things as they are about the desirability of steering their automobiles? Do they not behave exactly like the men in the nightmare when it comes to operating their economic system? Do they not allow their economic automobile to bounce from depression to inflation in wide and uncontrolled arcs? Through their failure to steer away from unemployment and idle factories are they not just as guilty of public injury and insecurity as the mad motorists of Mars?

Source: Abba Lerner, "The Economic Steering Wheel," first published in *The University Review*, vol. 7, no. 4 (June 1941), pp. 257–65 (now *NEW LETTERS*). Used by permission.

Seeing this low level of income and understanding the Keynesian model of the previous chapter, you should be led to the following insight: If somehow you can generate a countershock (a jolt in the opposite direction of the shift in autonomous expenditure that started the depression), you can get the multiplier working in reverse, expanding the economy in the same way the initial shock and multiplier had contracted it. You need a countershock to motivate people to spend, and as they increase their spending, society will be better off. But each individual, acting in her own interest, has no incentive to spend more. Each individual would reason: If I spend more, I'll be worse off. Theoretically, my additional spending might help society, but the positive effect would be so diluted that, in terms of my own situation, I don't see how my increased spending is going to benefit me.

For example, if a grocery store clerk increased her shopping expenditures by $100, only about $25 of that expenditure would go into food, so if her store is one of five stores selling various articles in the area where she shops, only $5 would go to her store. If she were one of 20 employees, her $5 represents only an additional 25¢ spending per employee at the store. If she were about to lose her job, her $100 spend-

ADDED DIMENSION

KEYNES AND KEYNESIAN POLICY

One of the subthemes of this book is that economic thought and policy are more complicated than an introductory book must necessarily make it seem. "Keynesian policy" is a good case in point. In the early 1930s, before Keynes wrote *The General Theory,* he was advocating public works programs and deficits as a way to get the British economy out of the Depression. He came upon what we now call the *Keynesian theory* as he tried to explain to Classical economists why he supported deficits. After arriving at his new theory, however, he spent little time advocating fiscal policy and, in fact, never mentions fiscal policy in *The General Theory,* the book that presents his theory. The book's primary policy recommendation is the need to socialize investments—for the government to take over the investment decisions from private individuals. When one of his followers, Abba Lerner, advocated expansionary fiscal policy at a seminar Keynes attended, Keynes strongly objected, leading Evsey Domar, another Keynesian follower, to whisper to a friend, "Keynes should read *The General Theory.*"

What's going on here? There are many interpretations, but the one we find most convincing is the one presented by historian Peter Clarke. He argues that, while working on *The General Theory,* Keynes turned his interest from a policy revolution to a theoretical revolution. He believed he had found a serious flaw in Classical economic theory. The Classicals assumed full employment, but did not show how the economy could move to that equilibrium from a disequilibrium. That's when Keynes's interest changed from a policy to a theoretical revolution.

His followers, such as Lerner, carried out the policy implications of his theory. Why did Keynes sometimes oppose these policy implications? Because he was also a student of politics and he recognized that economic theory can often lead to politically unacceptable policies. In a letter to a friend he later said Lerner was right in his logic, but he hoped the opposition didn't discover what Lerner was saying. Keynes was more than an economist; he was a politician as well.

ing wouldn't save it. However, if all individuals, or a large proportion of all individuals, increased their spending by $100 each, spending at her store would rise considerably and her job would likely be saved.

How do you simultaneously get all or most individuals to spend more than they want to? In the 1930s, government found it wasn't easy. Social unrest and the growth of left-leaning political parties made Prime Minister Bennett nervous. In an attempt to calm people's fears, Bennett went on radio promising a legislative agenda that would deal with the "grave defects and abuses of the capitalist system." Strong words from a Conservative Prime Minister.

With fiscal policy, government could provide the needed increased spending by decreasing taxes, increasing government spending, or both. Fiscal policy would provide the initial expansionary spending, increasing individuals' incomes. As individuals' incomes increased, they would spend more. As they spent more, the multiplier process would take over and expand the effect of the initial spending.

> **2A**   Expansionary fiscal policy stimulates autonomous expenditures, which increases people's income, which increases people's spending even more.

Keynesians argued that fiscal policy—the policy of government changing its spending and taxing to influence production and income levels in the economy—was the missing steering wheel of the economy.

Thus, cutting taxes and increasing government expenditures are both expansionary fiscal policy. The government provides the initial expansionary shock, and then the multiplier takes hold and expands the economy.

There is nothing special about government's ability to stimulate the economy with additional spending. If a group of individuals wanted to—and had spending power large enough to make a difference—they could do so, but private individuals don't have the incentive to do so. Their spending helps mainly other people and has only a small feedback on themselves. Unless they're altruistic, they don't take into account the effect of their spending on the aggregate spending stream and hence on aggregate income.

Aggregate Demand Management

The significantly different effects when everyone does something rather than when only one person does it play an important role in economics. This difference has a number of names: the public goods problem, the tragedy of the commons, the fallacy of composition, and the multiperson dilemma.

The problem is neatly seen by reconsidering a football game analogy. If everyone is standing, and you sit down, you can't see. Everyone is better off standing. No one has an incentive to sit down. However, if somehow all individuals could be enticed to sit down, all individuals would be even better off. Sitting down is a public good—a good that benefits others—but one that nobody on his or her own will do. Keynes argued that, in times of depression, spending is a public good because it benefits everyone, so government should spend or find ways of inducing private individuals to spend. This difference between individual and economy-wide reactions to spending decisions creates a possibility for government to exercise control over aggregate demand and thereby over aggregate output and aggregate income. As we stated above, government's attempt to control the aggregate level of spending in the economy is called aggregate demand management. It involves changing the level of autonomous expenditures through the government's influence of a shift factor of aggregate demand, and then relying on the multiplier effect to multiply that initial effect into a larger effect on income.

The Tax/Transfer Multiplier and the Government Spending Multiplier

Transfer payments   Payments by government to individuals that are not in payment for goods or services.

The precise size of the multiplier depends on the way in which government changes its spending or its taxes. If it increases spending on goods and services, the full multiplier effect takes place since that initial government spending counts as part of GDP. So the government spending multiplier is $1/(1 - mpc)$. That's the multiplier we discussed in the last chapter. In that chapter, we also mentioned that taxes directly influenced consumption. Taxes shift consumption spending down, making expenditures lower than they would have been had there been no taxes. But, to keep the presentation simple, we didn't explore the issue there. If we had, we would have also mentioned that **transfer payments**—payments by government to individuals that are not in payment for goods or services—work in the opposite direction than taxes; transfer payments shift the consumption function up, making expenditures higher than they would have been.

Unfortunately, when discussing fiscal policy that specifically involves changing taxes and government expenditures, we cannot avoid discussing these issues in a bit more detail. The reason is that the way in which the expenditures enter the income stream makes a difference to the size of the multiplier. Specifically, if the government decreases taxes or increases transfer payments, the multiplier is smaller since that initial injection is not counted in GDP. Thus the multiplier starts not with the initial injection, but with the resulting increase in individuals' spending. Say government decreases taxes by x. Expenditures will rise by a fraction of x—specifically $mpc\, x$. The multiplier then operates on that increased spending. So, since people spend only a portion of their additional income—the mpc times the added income—the tax and transfer multiplier is $mpc\,[1/(1 - mpc)] = mpc/(1 - mpc)$.

Let's consider an example: say the marginal propensity to consume is 0.67. The spending multiplier is $1/(1 - 0.67) = 3$, so if government increases spending by $100, income will rise by $300. Now, say that government cuts taxes by $100, or raises transfer payments by $100. Because this fiscal policy is being implemented by a tax cut or a transfer payment, only a fraction of the $100 tax cut translates into increased spending ($0.67 \times \$100$). This increase $[0.67 \times \$100]$ is then multiplied by the spending multiplier $[1/(1 - 0.67)]$ to arrive at increased income of $200. In this case, the tax/transfer is $[.67/(1 - 0.67)] = 2$, less than the spending multiplier of 3.

You should try a couple of other examples to be sure you've got it. Here's one: government spending goes up by $30 and transfer payments are lowered by $20. The $mpc = .5$. How much will income change? Your answer should be: Income goes up by $40. If that wasn't your answer, work through a few more examples.

In practice, the difference between the tax/transfer multiplier and the spending multiplier is not very important. As we emphasized throughout the last chapter, the Keynesian model is about tendencies only—it is about dynamic processes that might push the economy off course, not about final equilibrium. The Keynesian theory simply tells us that fiscal policy can modify the direction of income movement of the economy, not that it can precisely control the level of income. The Keynesian *AP/AE* model gives us a concrete example of how the control of income might work, but it does not directly describe reality, which is far more complicated than this model allows.

As we will discuss below, the actual practice of fiscal policy is a very rough practice indeed; no Keynesian we know of now believes that we can fine tune the equilibrium income of the economy with fiscal policy, and an increasing number of Keynesians wonder whether, given the politics of today, we can even significantly affect it. Still, as an exercise in logical thinking and modelling, it is helpful to make the distinction between the differential effects of a tax cut and a spending cut on income. As long as you remember not to take the actual solution of the Keynesian model too literally, it is a useful calisthenic for the mind.

Exhibit 1 shows the way fiscal policy works in graphs. An increase in government expenditures (or a decrease in taxes) shifts the aggregate expenditures curve up and the *AED* curve out, as in Exhibit 1 (a) and (c); a decrease in government expenditures (or an increase in taxes) shifts the aggregate expenditures curve down and the *AED* curve in, as in Exhibit 1 (b) and (d). In both cases, notice that income changes by a multiple of the change in government expenditure. That's the multiplier in action. Notice also that to determine how far to shift out the *AED* curve, given a change in government spending, ΔG, you must use the multiplier relationship which is shown directly in the *AP/AE* model. The reason for this is that the *AED* curve incorporates both supply/demand interactive effects and initial effects in its slope.

Fiscal Policy in Graphs

2B Expansionary fiscal policy shifts up the aggregate expenditure curve and increases income by a multiple of that shift.

Controlling the Level of Income with Fiscal Policy

Having determined how an increase in government spending can shift the aggregate expenditures curve, let's now consider how, in this model, government can control the level of aggregate income in the economy with fiscal policy.

Fighting Recession: Expansionary Fiscal Policy

Let's first consider the case where the economy is in a recession (Exhibit 2). Initially the economy is at equilibrium at income level $1,000, which is below potential income ($1,180). When equilibrium income is below potential income, this difference is called a **recessionary gap.** If everything goes as it should in the Keynesian story, this is what happens: The government recognizes this recessionary gap in aggregate income of, say, $180, and responds by increasing government expenditures by $60. This shifts the *AE* curve from AE_0 upward to AE_1, increasing aggregate income to the full-potential aggregate income level. Such government action is called *expansionary fiscal policy.*

Recessionary gap The difference between equilibrium income and potential income when potential income exceeds equilibrium income.

Businesses that receive government contracts hire the workers who have been laid off by other firms and open new plants; income increases by $60. But the process doesn't stop there. At this point, the multiplier process sets in. As the newly employed workers spend more, other businesses find that their demand increases. They hire more workers, who spend an additional $40 (since their *mpc* = .67). This increases income further. The same process occurs again and again. By the time the process has ended, income has risen by $180 and is up to $1,180, the potential level of income.

How did the government economists know to increase spending by $60? They knew by backward induction. They empirically estimated that the *mpc*—the slope of the aggregate expenditures curve—was .67, which meant that the multiplier was $1/(1 - .67) = 1/.33 = 3$. They divided the multiplier, 3, into the recessionary gap, $180, and determined that if they increased spending by $60, income would increase by $180. A good exercise is to show this same policy using the macro policy model. (Make sure when you do so you make the *AED* curve shift by 180, not 60.)

Fighting Inflation: Contractionary Fiscal Policy

Keynes devised and developed his model around a depression. However, in principle there's no reason why fiscal policy can't work in reverse (decreasing expenditures that are too high), given the assumptions of

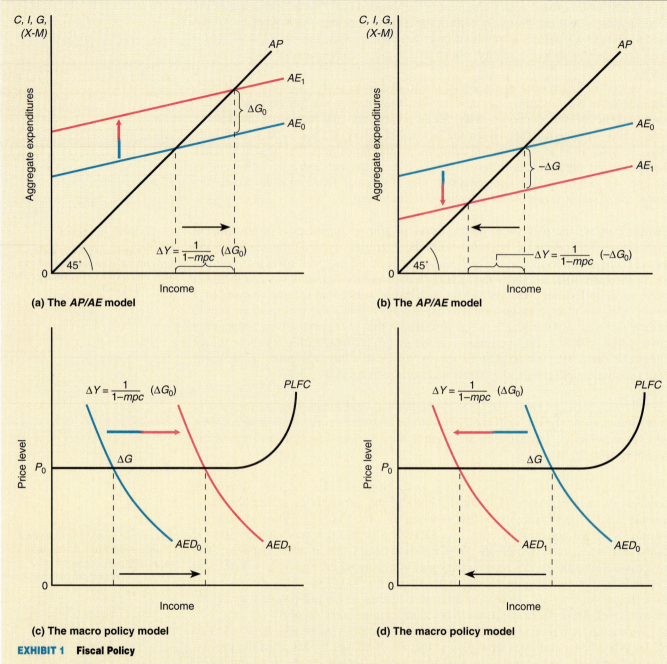

(a) The *AP/AE* model

(b) The *AP/AE* model

(c) The macro policy model

(d) The macro policy model

EXHIBIT 1   Fiscal Policy

The government can use fiscal policy as a tool to shift the *AE* and *AED* curves. An increase in government spending (or a decrease in taxes) **(a)** shifts the *AE* curve upward by ΔG_0 ($-mpc\ \Delta T_0$). A decrease in government spending (or an increase in taxes) **(b)** shifts the *AE* curve down by $-\Delta G_0$ ($mpc\ \Delta T_0$). Income changes by a multiple of the change in taxes or spending. The AED curves shift right and left by the amount of the total change in income—that is, by the mutiplier effect of the initial change ΔG.

the model. You might think that it's impossible for income to be too high, and that, instead, at higher incomes everyone is better off. This is not always the case. Expenditures are "too high" when the economy is in the vertical range of the price-level flexibility curve. In this range, instead of causing real income to increase, additional expenditures cause inflationary pressure. If there's inflationary pressure, people on average want to raise their prices, which either causes shortages if wages and prices are fixed (can't be raised) or inflation if wages and prices are not fixed.

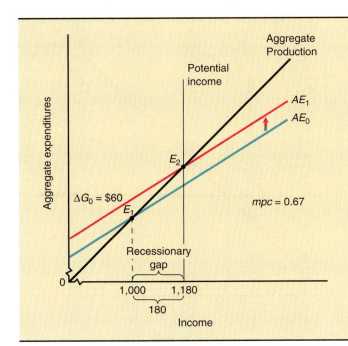

EXHIBIT 2   Fighting a Recession

If the economy is below its potential income level, the government can increase its expenditures to stimulate the economy. The multiplier process takes over and expands the initial shock of the additional spending until actual income equals potential income.

When this is the case, the price-level flexibility curve is vertical so there is excess demand and demand-pull inflation, as Exhibit 3 (a) shows.

Remember the Keynesian *AP/AE* model is a *fixed price* model that tells a story about a chase between aggregate supply and demand when the economy is in Range A. For that chase to occur, aggregate supply must be below potential output. Once the quantity of aggregate demand shifts up beyond potential output, the fixed price assumption is no longer relevant and inflation occurs. Whenever equilibrium income exceeds potential income, there's said to be an **inflationary gap.** When there's an inflationary gap, expenditures are too high. To prevent inflation, Keynesians believe that the government should exercise contractionary fiscal policy (cutting government spending or raising taxes).

Exhibit 3 (b) shows a numerical example of contractionary fiscal policy at work. Potential income is $4,000, $mpc = .8$, but the equilibrium level of income is $5,000. Thus, there is an inflationary gap of $1,000, which causes upward pressure on wages and prices with no additional output resulting.

An inflationary gap calls for contractionary fiscal policy. The government increases taxes by $250, shifting the *AE* curve from AE_0 to AE_1, which decreases the equilibrium level of income by $1,000, back to $4,000, the potential level of income. The government has offset the expansionary shock with contractionary fiscal policy.

How did the government know to increase taxes by $250? Again, by backward induction. The spending multiplier, $[1/(1 - mpc)]$, is 5, but the government knows that not all the tax increase will decrease expenditures since people will reduce their savings in order to hold their expenditures up. Expenditures will initially fall by the *mpc* multiplied by the increased taxes, or $(.8 \times \$250) = \$200$, rather than $250. The tax/transfer multiplier $mpc/(1 - mpc) = .8/.2 = 4$ takes that into account, so they use the tax multiplier of 4 rather than the spending multiplier of 5. So the total decrease in income is $4 \times \$250 = \$1,000$. As you can see, once the government knows the multiplier and the inflationary or recessionary gap, it can determine what fiscal policy it should use to achieve the potential level of income.

Inflationary gap   The difference between equilibrium income and potential income when equilibrium income exceeds potential income.

There are two ways to think about the effectiveness of fiscal policy—in the model, and in reality.

Applying the Models and the Questionable Effectiveness of Fiscal Policy

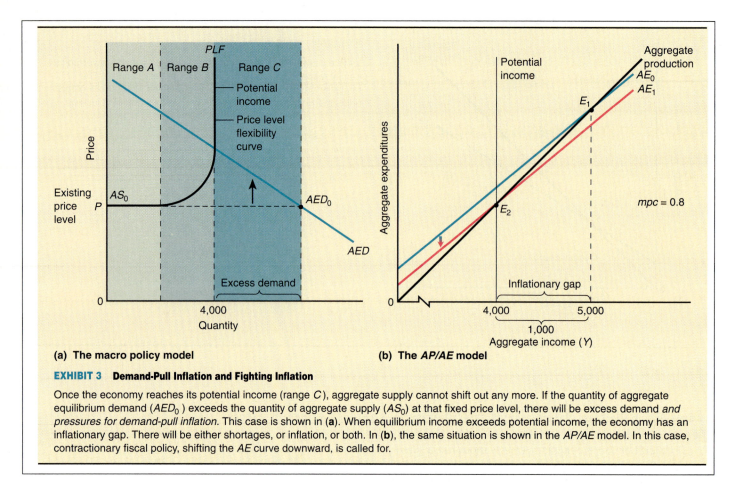

(a) The macro policy model

(b) The *AP/AE* model

EXHIBIT 3   Demand-Pull Inflation and Fighting Inflation

Once the economy reaches its potential income (range *C*), aggregate supply cannot shift out any more. If the quantity of aggregate equilibrium demand (*AED*₀) exceeds the quantity of aggregate supply (*AS*₀) at that fixed price level, there will be excess demand *and pressures for demand-pull inflation*. This case is shown in (**a**). When equilibrium income exceeds potential income, the economy has an inflationary gap. There will be either shortages, or inflation, or both. In (**b**), the same situation is shown in the *AP/AE* model. In this case, contractionary fiscal policy, shifting the *AE* curve downward, is called for.

Effectiveness of Fiscal Policy in the Model How effective fiscal policy is in the model depends on the size of the multiplier which, as we saw in the last chapter, depends on the size of the marginal propensity to consume. That model was a highly simplified model that focused on induced consumption spending—spending dependent on income. That is why the multiplier depended on the size of the marginal propensity to consume.

In reality, consumption is not the only component of income with an induced component. Other expenditures also have induced elements and hence provide leakages from the circular flow. We can include the induced component of these other expenditures by discussing the **marginal propensity to expend (*mpe*)**—the additional spending that will be translated into the income stream when all induced expenditures are included. The marginal propensity to expend is the generalized equivalent of the marginal propensity to consume. As with the *mpc*, a high marginal propensity to expend means a large multiplier; a low marginal propensity to expend means a low multiplier. Thus, in a generalized model, the multiplier is:

generalized expenditures multiplier = $1/(1 - mpe)$

The size of the marginal propensity to expend depends in turn on the size of the induced expenditures and leakages from the circular flow, the three most important of which are the marginal propensity of individuals to save, the marginal propensity to import, and the marginal tax rate. The larger these three are, the smaller is the multiplier. Why? Because each of these draws income from the circular flow and reduces the degree to which expenditure is connected to income. (In Appendix A, we go through explicitly the relationship between these three variables and the multiplier.)

When one includes all induced expenditures for Canada, one comes up with a marginal propensity to expend of about .4 or .5, which means that 40 to 50 percent of all spending escapes the circular flow and does not induce new spending. Thus,

Marginal propensity to expend (mpe)
The additional spending that will be translated into the income stream when all induced expenditures are included.

for Canada, a realistic multiplier is about $1/(1 - .4)$ or $1/(1 - .5)$, or between 1.67 and 2.0.

Expanding the model to include all induced expenditures gives us a way of thinking about relative sizes of multipliers for various countries. For example, would you say that small countries will likely have higher or lower multipliers than Canada? They probably will have smaller multipliers than Canada since they will have higher marginal propensities to import. This means that expansionary policy in small countries is in large part exported abroad.

Effectiveness of Fiscal Policy in Reality Models are great, and simple models, like the one we've presented in this book that you can understand intuitively, are even greater. You put in the numbers, and out comes the answer. Questions based on such models make great exam questions. But don't think that policies that work in a model will work in the real world.

The effectiveness of fiscal policy in reality depends on the government's ability to perceive a problem, and to react appropriately to it. The essence of fiscal policy is government changing its taxes and its spending to offset any deviation that would occur in other autonomous expenditures, thereby keeping the economy at its potential level of income. If the model is a correct description of the economy, and if the government can act fast enough and change its taxes and spending in a *countercyclical* way, depressions can be prevented. A fiscal policy in which the government offsets any shock that would create a business cycle is called **countercyclical fiscal policy.** Such countercyclical policy designed to keep the economy always at its target or potential level of income is called **fine tuning.**

As we will discuss below, almost all economists, whether Keynesian or Classical, agree the government is not up to fine tuning the economy. The debate in the 1990s is whether it is up to any tuning of the economy at all.

At one time, some Keynesians thought the economy followed a simple adjustment process such as described by this model, and that it could be modeled simply, and controlled. No more. Why? Because this, or any, simple model captures only one aspect of the dynamic adjustment process.

All economists now recognize that the dynamic adjustment in the economy is extraordinarily complicated, and that once you take into account reasonable expectations of future policy, the formal model becomes hopelessly complex. Graduate students in economics get Ph.D.s for worrying about such hopeless complexities. At the introductory level, all we require is that you (1) know this simple Keynesian model, and (2) remember that, in the real world, it cannot be used in a mechanistic manner; it must be used with judgement.

As questions about the effectiveness of fiscal policy have developed, policy discussions have moved toward alternatives to fiscal policy. To understand how these alternatives work, you must simply remember that any change in autonomous expenditures, ΔE—not just changes in the government deficit—will affect the level of income. You can see the alternatives to fiscal policy by thinking of the Keynesian equation:

$$\Delta Y = \text{multiplier} \times [\Delta \text{ autonomous consumption}$$
$$+ \Delta \text{ autonomous investment}$$
$$+ \Delta \text{ autonomous government spending}$$
$$+ \Delta \text{ autonomous net exports}]$$

Any policy that affects any of these four components of autonomous expenditures—autonomous consumption, autonomous investment, autonomous government spending, and autonomous net exports—can achieve the same results as fiscal policy. So three alternatives to fiscal policy are directed investment policies, trade policies, and autonomous consumption policies. The above requires one addendum: any policy that can influence *autonomous* expenditures *without having offsetting effects on other*

Countercyclical fiscal policy   Fiscal policy in which the government offsets any shock that would create a business cycle.

Fine tuning   Countercyclical fiscal policy designed to keep the economy always at its target or potential level of income.

ALTERNATIVES TO FISCAL POLICY

3   Three alternatives to fiscal policy are directed investment policies, trade policies, and autonomous consumption policies.

expenditures can be used to influence the direction and movement of the aggregate income. That addendum in italics is important because, in the Classical view, no expenditure is autonomous. If you push on one type of expenditure, you simply pull on another, and the net effect is a wash. But in the Keynesian view there is an autonomous component of each of those expenditures that in principle can be affected by policy. We have already considered government spending policy when we talked about fiscal policy. Let us briefly consider some of the other policies that could be used to influence income. We discuss investment first, then net exports, and, finally, consumption.

Directed Investment Policies: Policy Affecting Expectations

Let's first consider investment. Remember our discussion in an earlier chapter in which we explained that Keynes thought that the Depression was caused by some type of collective psychological fear on the part of investors who, because they predicted that the economy was going into a recession, decided not to invest. As a result, the economy went into a recession, and then eventually a depression, as the fear built upon itself. If somehow government could have supported investment, it could have avoided the Depression.

A Numerical Example

To give you some practice with the model, let's consider a numerical example. Say that income is $400 less than desired and that the marginal propensity to expend is .5. How much will government policy have to increase autonomous investment in order to achieve the desired level of income? Working backwards, we see that the multiplier is 2, so autonomous investment must be increased by $200.

Rosy Scenario: Talking the Economy Well

Numerical examples like the one above are a bit far-fetched since it is difficult to relate a specific policy to a specific numerical result or investment. But the relationship is there, and you can see examples of government trying to exploit it every day. For example, listen to government officials on the radio or television. Almost inevitably you will hear rosy scenarios from them—the **Rosy Scenario policy.** You almost never hear a policy-level government economist telling the newspapers how bad the economy is going to be. Why? Because a gloomy prediction could affect expectations and decrease investment and consumption spending. If you're a high-level government policy economist and you have a gloomy forecast, you're told to keep quiet or quit. In the Great Depression, U. S. President Roosevelt, in a famous radio address, told the nation not to fear—that the only thing it had to fear was fear itself. Jean Chretien's upbeat talk about the economy is another example: if he can get people to think the economy in the 1990s will be in good shape, it will be in good shape because people expect it to be.

Another way to influence investment is to protect the financial system by government guarantees or promises of guarantees. Nothing can decrease business confidence quite like a large number of bank and financial institution failures. Precisely that type of financial institution failure changed a recession in the 1930s to the Great Depression. As we will see in later chapters, to prevent such failures in the future the government instituted a number of guarantee-type policies after the Depression.

Let's consider how such investment-expectations policies work in practice. Say the economy is in a slight recession, and because of that, banks are in financial trouble. The government recognizes that if the public decides that banks are in trouble, they will try to get their money out of the banks, in which case banks will have to close. As banks close, loans will dry up, investment will decrease, and the economy will fall into a deep recession. To prevent that, the government comes along and tells everyone that it will bail out the banks so that people's money is safe. If the government is believed, everything stays fine and the recession doesn't happen (and, hopefully, the banks get themselves out of their financial trouble).

Japan used such a "save the financial institutions" policy in the 1990s. When the

Rosy Scenario policy   Government policy of making optimistic predictions and never making gloomy predictions.

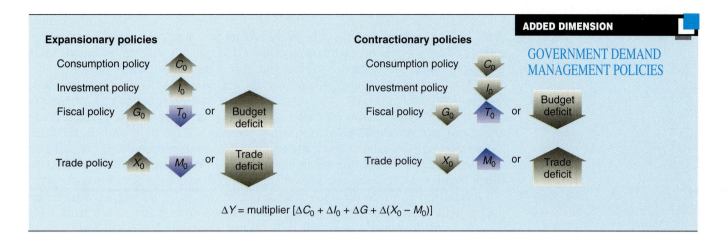

$$\Delta Y = \text{multiplier} \, [\Delta C_0 + \Delta I_0 + \Delta G + \Delta(X_0 - M_0)]$$

Japanese stock and real estate markets collapsed in the early 1990s, the Japanese government loosened bank accounting rules in order to prevent banks from failing. Similarly, in the early 1990s, when the U. S. banking system was seriously in trouble due to loan losses, the U.S. government modified institutional rules to increase banking profitability. It worked, and by the mid-1990s the U.S. banking system had recovered.

Another way in which the government can influence investment is through influencing the interest rate. We will discuss this policy in detail in a later chapter when we discuss monetary policy.

The answer to the question, "When do such policies affecting expectations make sense?" doesn't follow from the models; it is a matter of judgement. In the 1930s, Keynes didn't see any of these policies affecting investment as being sufficient; in his book, *The General Theory,* he advocated the government taking over the investment decisions—nationalizing investment. That policy didn't receive high marks in Canada. Instead, Keynesian policy quickly came to mean fiscal policy. Why? Because politically, Keynesians quickly saw that fiscal policy could be sold to the public, whereas the more radical Keynesian nationalizing investment policies couldn't be.

Trade Policy and Export-Led Growth

Any policy that increases autonomous exports or decreases autonomous imports (and thereby increases autonomous expenditures) will also have multiplied effects on income. Examples of such policies abound. The Canadian federal government has entire subdepartments assisting firms to develop their export markets. Similarly, Canadian trade delegations frequent other nations, pushing to get the other nations' trade restrictions on Canadian goods lowered. The idea is to stimulate Canadian exports and increase aggregate expenditures on Canadian goods, and hence to have a multiplied effect on Canadian income. Such policies are part of a set of policies that generally go under the name **export-led growth policies.**

Export-led growth policy   Any policy that increases autonomous exports or decreases autonomous imports, thereby increasing autonomous expenditures.

Notice that it is the trade balance (exports minus imports) that affects aggregate expenditures, so any policy that will reduce imports, such as tariffs, will have the same expansionary effect on income. That's why you hear so much about trade restrictions from Ottawa. They're a way of protecting jobs and of stimulating the economy.

A Numerical Example   Let's start with a numerical example of a small country with a large percentage of imports. Say one country's income is $300 million too low and its marginal propensity to expend is .33. How must it affect net exports to achieve its desired income? Since the *mpe* is low, the multiplier is small (1.5), which means that net exports must be increased by approximately $200 million (either by decreasing imports or increasing exports by that amount).

Exchange rate policy   Deliberately affecting a country's exchange rate in order to affect its trade balance.

Interdependencies in the Global Economy   We'll discuss these trade policies in much more detail in later chapters, but for now, let us remind you that one country's exports are another country's imports, so that every time Canada is out pushing its exports in an attempt to follow an export-led growth policy, it is the equivalent to getting another country to follow an *import-led decline* for its economy. Similarly, every trade restriction on foreign goods has an offsetting effect on another country's economy, an effect that will often lead to retaliation. So a policy of trying to restrict imports can often end up simultaneously restricting exports as other countries retaliate. Expectation of such retaliation is one of the reasons many economists support free trade agreements, such as the North American Free Trade Agreement (NAFTA), in which member countries agree not to engage in restrictive trade policies on imports.

A final way in which the trade balance can be affected is through **exchange rate policy,** deliberately affecting a country's exchange rate in order to affect its trade balance. In the long run, a low value of a country's currency relative to currencies of other countries encourages exports and discourages imports; a high value of a country's currency relative to other countries discourages exports and encourages imports.

The effect of such exchange rates can be seen in the automobile industry. In the 1970s and 1980s, Japanese exports of cars were increasing enormously. An important reason for that was the relative value of the Japanese yen (somewhere around 250 to the dollar). In the 1990s, the value of the dollar fell relative to the yen, so that in 1995 it was less than one third the value (about 70 to the dollar) of what it was in the 1970s. With this change, Japanese cars no longer seemed the good buy that they were before, and the Canadian automobile industry made a comeback. Again, we'll discuss such policies in more detail in a later chapter.

Autonomous Consumption Policy

The third alternative to fiscal policy is consumption policy. Any policy designed to encourage autonomous consumption can hold autonomous expenditures up and have the same effect as fiscal policy. Increasing consumer credit availability to individuals by making the institutional environment conducive to credit is one way of achieving this.

The growth of the Canadian economy from the 1950s through the 1980s was marked by significant institutional changes that made credit available to a larger and larger group of people. This increased consumer credit allowed significant expansion in income of the Canadian economy. In the 1990s, there was some cutback by consumers as they tried to consolidate their financial obligations, and that has played a major role in the slow growth of the Canadian economy in the early 1990s. Similarly, the resolution of those problems played a major role in the rise in growth in the mid-1990s.

As a final review, to be sure you have the model down pat, calculate how much autonomous expenditure should change to decrease income by $60 if the *mpe* = 2/3.[1]

Structural versus Passive Government Budget and Trade Deficits

The above discussion of exogenous expenditure policy made it look as if there were a one-way flow from exogenous expenditure to income. Thus one could talk about fiscal policy, and the size of the deficit, or trade policy, and the size of the trade balance as policies to control the level of income. But when one is thinking about such policies, it is important to remember that not all of these expenditures are autonomous. Most consumption is induced, and separating out an autonomous component is difficult. Imports are also partially dependent on income, so some portion of them is induced. When income in a country goes up, the country's imports go up.

Similarly with taxes: when income goes up, so do taxes, so taxes have an induced effect as well. Each of these induced elements affects the marginal propensity to expend, and thereby affects the size of the multiplier. (How these effects are mathematically related to the size of the multiplier is shown in Appendix A.) Higher tax rates

---

[1] If you came up with any answer but "Decrease C_0 by $20," a review is in order.

REGIONAL MULTIPLIERS

The macro policies discussed in the book are national policies. A parallel policy discussion goes on in just about every community when regional planning units consider the effect of the closure of a military base, or the relocation of a new company into a community. All such policies to affect such decisions are based on the assumption that regional multipliers exist—that the impact of an expenditure will have a multiplied effect on the income of the community.

We can fit such policies into our Keynesian model by thinking of a community as having imports and exports. While there are no measured exports and imports, there are unmeasured imports and exports. For example, colleges and universities are an export of a regional area (why?), and their maintenance can be seen as a regional export-led growth policy. Building expensive stadiums for professional sports teams is usually similarly justified by such multiplier-effect reasoning.

Looking in your local paper, you will most likely see evidence of such policies; most regional areas give tax benefits and other concessions to firms that locate there. (Ironically, many of these initiatives are supported by businesspeople who, on a national level, reject Keynesian policies.)

When thinking about these regional policies, it is important to remember that all the same problems that exist with Keynesian policy on the national level also exist on the local level: retaliation, inability to decide what to affect, and inability to decide what is the "appropriate" target level of income. In the Classical view, in the aggregate, all these regional policies are simply offsetting each other, and the net effect of such policies on the aggregate economy is more waste in government. But even if one is persuaded by this Classical argument, one might still support regional policies based on multiplier analysis. The reason is that unless such regional incentives are prohibited for all communities, once one area introduces them, the others must follow or lose out.

and higher marginal propensities to import decrease the size of the multiplier; lower tax rates and lower marginal propensities to import increase the size of the multiplier.

The induced elements of taxes and imports mean that when we are discussing export-led growth policies or fiscal policy, we must remember that while *the budget deficit and the trade balance will affect aggregate income, simultaneously aggregate income will affect the deficit and trade balance.* So if we're using the deficit or the trade balance as policy tools, they themselves will change as income changes, and the ending trade balance and ending budget deficit might be quite different than the initial trade balance or initial budget deficit.

For example, say the multiplier is two and the government is running expansionary policy. It increases government spending by $100, which causes income to rise by $200. If the tax rate is 20 percent, tax revenues will increase by $40 and the final deficit will be $60, not $100. Alternatively, consider a successful export-led growth policy. Say the multiplier is again 2, the marginal propensity to import is .3, and the government wants to eliminate a $40 billion trade deficit. The government introduces policies that expand exports by $40 billion and income by $80 billion. That $80 billion increase in income causes imports to increase by $24 billion, so the $40 billion trade deficit will not be eliminated. It will instead be reduced by $16 billion.

To differentiate between a budget deficit being used as a policy instrument to affect the economy, and a budget deficit that is the result of income being below its potential, economists use a reference income level at which to judge fiscal policy. That reference income level is their estimate of the economy's potential level of income. They then ask: Would the economy have a budget deficit if it were at its potential level of income? The portion of the budget deficit that would exist even if the economy were at its potential level of income is called a **structural deficit.** If an economy is operating below its potential, the actual deficit will be larger than the structural deficit. The portion of the deficit that exists because the economy is operating below its potential level of output is called a **passive deficit.** Economists believe that an economy can eliminate a passive budget deficit through growth in income, whereas it can't grow out of a structural deficit. Because the economy can't grow out of structural budget deficits, they are of more concern to policy makers than are passive budget deficits.

Let's give an example. If potential income is $700 billion and actual income is $680 billion, there's a shortfall of $ 20 billion. Say the marginal tax rate is 25 percent

4 A structural deficit is a deficit that would exist at potential income. A passive deficit is the deficit that exists because income is below potential income.

Structural deficit Portion of the budget deficit that would exist even if the economy were at its potential level of income.

Passive deficit Portion of the deficit that exists because the economy is operating below its potential level of output.

ADDED DIMENSION   SHIFTING TERMS OF THE KEYNESIAN/CLASSICAL TRUCE

Until the 1980s, most Keynesian economists were primarily interested in policy, and theoretical revolution in Keynes's work was not expanded upon. A truce was arrived at between Keynesians and Classicals. The truce stated that (1) Classical theory was theoretically correct, but the assumptions it made were inapplicable to many real-world situations, and (2) Keynesian theory was, theoretically, a special case of Classical theory, but it was a special case that just happened to be relevant to the real world. This gave Keynesians the policy applicability they were interested in, and Classicals the theoretical laurels.

In the 1980s, Keynesian policy came under fire and the truce broke down on the real-world policy side. More and more economists came to believe that Keynesian policy wasn't so relevant after all. As that happened, modern Keynesians returned to Keynes's work and argued against the other part of the truce that gave the theoretical laurels to the Classicals. These modern Keynesians argued that Keynes's theory was the more general theory since it allowed for the aggregate economy to have multiple equilibria, which modern theoretical work concluded it would likely have unless one assumed them away with ad hoc assumptions.

Thus in the 1990s, a new truce is developing. While modern macro theorists agree that the mechanistic multiplier models of Keynesian economics are far too simple, they are more and more accepting that, in its general approach, Keynesian economics (the interpretive, not the mechanistic brand) is capable of explaining much more than was once thought, because it includes the effects of dynamic disequilibrium feedback on the equilibrium—what in mathematics is called path dependency. Almost all modern theoretical work—both Keynesian and Classical—is being directed at such dynamic issues, making the Keynesian/Classical distinction almost irrelevant when talking about theoretical work. What this development means is that in theory, what in this book we call Keynesian economics has been accepted as more general than what in this book we call Classical economics (although many modern Classical economists would argue that it is they, not the Keynesians, who led the modern theoretical change into path dependency).

In the real world, however, many Keynesian economists now also agree that the dynamic interactions are so complicated that, in most circumstances—except for serious recession—Classical economics, with its focus on establishing a system of rules within an institutional environment, is the most relevant. So the new truce is precisely the reverse of the old truce. In the new truce, Keynesians have the theoretical laurels and Classicals have the policy relevance.

and the actual federal government deficit is $50 billion. Let's also assume that if the economy were at its potential income, the deficit would be $45 billion. That $45 billion is the structural deficit. The $5 billion (25 percent multiplied by the $20 billion shortfall) is the passive deficit.

In reality there is significant debate about what an economy's potential income level is, and hence there is disagreement about what percentage of a deficit is structural and what percentage is passive. Nonetheless, the distinction is often used and is important to remember.

Some Real-World Examples

So much for our discussion of the theoretical issues surrounding Keynesian economics and policies. Let's now turn to how they work in practice. To give you an idea of how fiscal and other expenditures policies work in the real world, we'll look at a couple of examples. Let's first consider what happened in World War II.

Fiscal Policy in World War II   The Depression in Canada continued through the 1930s. However, by the beginning of the 1940s it was no longer the focus of Canadian policy as the war in Europe and in the Pacific became more and more the central issue.

Fighting a war costs money, so economists' attention turned to how to raise that money. Taxes went up enormously, but government expenditures rose far more. The result can be seen in Exhibit 4 (a), which tabulates GNP, the deficit, and unemployment data for 1937–46. As you can see, the deficit increased greatly and income rose by more than the deficit. Exhibit 4 (b) shows the Keynesian multiplier model which describes those effects. As predicted, the Canadian economy expanded enormously in response to the expansionary fiscal policy that accompanied the war. (The wartime expansion was accompanied by wage and price controls and a large increase in the money supply, so we must be careful about drawing too strong an inference from this expansion.)

EXHIBIT 4   War Finance in Canada: Expansionary Fiscal Policy

During wars, government budget deficits have risen significantly. As they have, unemployment has fallen and GNP has risen enormously. You can see the effect in the table in (a), which presents the Canadian government budget deficit and unemployment rate during World War II. The graph in (b) shows that this is what would be predicted by the Keynesian model.

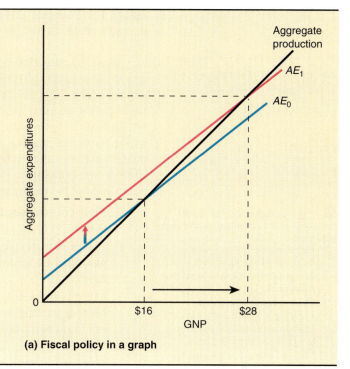

Year	GNP (billions of 1971 dollars)	Deficit (millions of dollars)	Unemployment rate (percent)
1937	16	16	9.1
1938	17	17	11.4
1939	18	51	11.4
1940	20	119	9.2
1941	23	378	4.4
1942	27	396	2.9
1943	29	2,137	1.7
1944	30	2,557	1.4
1945	29	2,559	1.6
1946	28	2,123	2.6

(a) Fiscal policy in a table

(a) Fiscal policy in a graph

It might seem from the example of World War II, when the Canadian economy expanded sharply, that wars are good for the economy. They certainly do bring about expansionary policy, increase GNP, and decrease unemployment. But remember, GNP is *not* welfare and a decrease in unemployment is not necessarily good. In World War II people went without basic necessities; production of guns and bombs increased but production of butter decreased. Many people were killed or permanently disabled, which decreases unemployment but can hardly be called a good way to expand the economy and lower unemployment.

Fiscal Policy in the 1990s   Now let's talk about more recent examples: The mid-1990s and Prime Minister Jean Chretien's policy proposal to get the economy going—to increase income. Chretien is a Liberal, and has generally Keynesian advisers. So what kind of policy do you think he advocated? If you said, "Increase the budget deficit to stimulate the economy," you've learned the model we discussed above, but you haven't been reading the paper. Instead, from reading the newspaper you should know that he proposed a policy of *decreasing the deficit* to stimulate the economy! (The path by which a decrease in the deficit was to stimulate the economy was through the deficit's effect on the long-term interest rate and investment. A smaller deficit means less government borrowing which, as we will discuss later, means lower interest rates, which means higher investment.)

Actually, his policy was more complicated than that; he did propose to initially increase the budget deficit slightly to stimulate the economy, through spending on infrastructure. Moreover, like much in politics, a lot of his talk about deficit reduction was aimed at influencing expectations. If markets think the situation is getting better, the outlook will be more positive (and investment will be higher) than if the news is all "doom and gloom." But the lesson of this case is clear: Applying the simple Keynesian model discussed above is not going to give you an understanding of policy discussions today.

But that does not mean you don't have to know the above models. It means you must know them better than did earlier students. As we've emphasized continually—to understand a model you must understand the limitations of the model and the assumptions that make it work, and determine whether those assumptions fit the reality. It's clear that the assumptions of the simple model discussed above don't fit the facts of the 1990s. In the following pages we consider some reasons why.

PROBLEMS WITH FISCAL AND OTHER ACTIVIST KEYNESIAN POLICY

Keynesian fiscal policy, and activist government policy in general, sounds so easy—and in the model it is. If there's a contraction in the economy, the government runs an expansionary fiscal policy; if there's inflation, the government runs a contractionary fiscal policy, keeping the economy at the desired level of income.

In reality, that's not the way it is. A number of important problems arise, which makes the actual practice of fiscal policy difficult. These problems don't mean that the model is wrong; they simply mean that for fiscal policy to work, the policy conclusions drawn from the model must be modified to reflect the real-world problems. Let's consider how the reality might not fit the model. The model assumes:

5 Six assumptions of the model that could lead to problems with fiscal policy are:
1. Financing the deficit doesn't have any offsetting effects.
2. The government knows what the situation is.
3. The government knows the economy's potential income.
4. The government has flexibility in terms of spending and taxes.
5. The size of the government debt doesn't matter.
6. Fiscal policy doesn't negatively affect other government goals.

1. Financing the deficit doesn't have any offsetting effect. In reality, it often does.
2. The government knows what the situation is (for instance, the size of the *mpc* and other exogenous variables). In reality, the government must estimate them.
3. The government knows the economy's potential income level (the highest level of income that doesn't cause inflation). In reality, the government may not know what this level is.
4. The government has flexibility in changing spending and taxes. In reality, government cannot change them quickly.
5. The size of the government debt doesn't matter. In reality, the size of the government debt often does matter.
6. Fiscal policy doesn't negatively affect other government goals. In reality, it often does.

Let's consider each a bit further.

Financing the Deficit Doesn't Have Offsetting Effects

One of the most important limitations of the Keynesian model is that it assumes that financing the deficit has no offsetting effects on income. Classicals argue that is not the case—that fiscal policy will have significant offsetting effects, and that the government financing of a deficit will offset the deficit's expansionary effect.

Classical economists say that the Keynesian model assumes savings and investment are unequal, and that the government can increase its expenditures without at the same time causing a decrease in private expenditures. Classical economists object to that assumption. They believe the interest rate equilibrates savings and investment. They argue that when the government sells bonds to finance the deficit, that sale of bonds will crowd out private investment.

Crowding out The offsetting effect on private expenditures caused by the government's sale of bonds to finance expansionary fiscal policy.

Crowding out occurs as follows: When the government runs a deficit, it must sell bonds to finance that deficit. To get people to buy and hold the bonds, the government must make them attractive. That means the interest rate the bonds pay must be higher than it otherwise would have been. This tends to push up the interest rate, which makes it more expensive for private businesses to borrow, so they reduce their borrowing and their investment. That private investment is crowded out by expansionary fiscal policy. Hence the name "crowding out." Increased government spending crowds out private spending.

Exhibit 5 (a) shows the interconnection. The top arrows represent the direct effect of increased spending. The bottom arrows represent the effects of financing that increased spending. Each set of arrows works in the opposite direction from the other set. Crowding out is shown graphically in the Keynesian model in Exhibit 5 (b). Income in the economy is Y_0 and government has decided to expand that income to Y_1 by increasing its spending by ΔG.

6 Crowding out is the offsetting effect on private expenditures caused by the government's sale of bonds to finance expansionary fiscal policy.

If financing were not an issue, expansionary fiscal policy would shift up aggregate expenditures from AE_0 to AE_1, increasing income from Y_0 to Y_1. Financing the deficit, however, increases interest rates and decreases investment by ΔI, which shifts

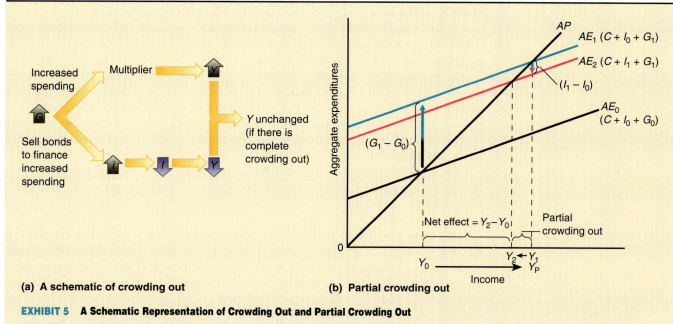

EXHIBIT 5   A Schematic Representation of Crowding Out and Partial Crowding Out

An increase in government spending will expand income through the multiplier as in the top portion in (**a**). However it will also cause interest rates to rise and thereby cause investment to decrease, which will tend to decrease income, as shown in the bottom portion of (**a**). This is called *crowding out*. The net effect of fiscal policy depends on the degree of crowding out that takes place. When there is complete crowding out, the effect of fiscal policy will be totally offset. Where there is partial crowding out, as in (**b**), an increase in government spending will still have an expansionary effect, but the effect will be smaller than it otherwise would have been.

the AE curve back to AE_2. Income falls back to Y_2. Because of crowding out, the net expansionary effect of fiscal policy is much smaller than it otherwise would have been. Some Classicals argue that crowding out could totally offset the expansionary effect of fiscal policy, so the net effect is zero, or even negative, since they consider private spending more productive than government spending.

The crowding out effect also works in reverse on contractionary fiscal policy. Say the government runs a surplus. That surplus will slow the economy via the multiplier effect. But it also means the government can buy back some of its outstanding bonds, which will have a tendency to push bond prices up and interest rates down. Lower interest rates will stimulate investment which, in turn, will have an offsetting expansionary effect on the economy. So when we include financing the deficit in our consideration of fiscal policy, the net multiplier effect is reduced.

How large this financing offset to fiscal policy will be is a matter of debate. Classicals see the crowding out effect as relatively large, in many cases almost completely negating the effect of expansionary fiscal policy. Keynesians see it as relatively small, as long as the economy is in a recession or operating below its potential income level. Some Keynesians even argue that often the crowding out will be offset by **crowding in**—positive effects of government spending on other components of spending. Where there is crowding in, the increased government spending will cause investment to increase as businesses prepare to meet the government's demand for goods.

Crowding in   Positive effects of government spending on other components of spending.

The empirical evidence is mixed and has not resolved the debate. Both sides see some crowding out occurring as the debt is financed by selling bonds. The closer to the potential income level the economy is, the more crowding out is likely to occur.

All our examples used numbers that were chosen arbitrarily. In reality, the numbers used in the model must be estimated since data upon which estimates can be made aren't always available. Most economic data are published quarterly, and it usually takes six to nine months of data to indicate, with any degree of confidence, the state

Knowing What the Situation Is

of the economy and which way it is heading. Thus, we could be halfway into a recession before we even knew it was happening. (Data are already three months old when published; then we need two or three quarters of such data before they compose a useful body of information to work with.)

In an attempt to deal with this problem, the government relies on large macroeconomic models and leading indicators to predict what the economy will be like six months or a year from now. As part of the input to these complex models, the government must predict economic factors that determine the size of the multiplier. These predictions are imprecise so the forecasts are imprecise. Economic forecasting is still an art, not a science.

Economists' data problems limit the use of fiscal policy for fine tuning. There's little sense in recommending expansionary or contractionary policy until you know what policy is called for.

Knowing the Level of Potential Income

This problem of not knowing the level of potential income is related to the problem we just discussed. The target level of employment and the potential level of income are not easy concepts to define. At one time it was thought 6 percent unemployment meant full employment. Some time later it was generally thought 8 percent unemployment meant full employment. About that time economists stopped calling the potential level of income the *full-employment* level of income.

Any variation in potential income can make an enormous difference in the policy prescription that could be recommended. To see how big a difference, let's translate a 1 percent change in unemployment into a change in income. According to **Okun's law,** the general rule of thumb economists use to translate changes in the unemployment rate into changes in income is that a 1 percent fall in the unemployment rate equals a 2.5 percent increase in income. Thus, if in 1995 income is about $800 billion, a 1 percent fall in the unemployment rate would have increased income $20 billion.

Okun's law   Rule of thumb economists use to translate the unemployment rate into changes in income: "A one percent fall in the unemployment rate equals a 2.5 percent increase in income."

Now let's say one economist believes 6 percent is the long-run achievable target unemployment level, while another believes it's 4.5 percent. That's a 1.5 percent difference. Since a 1 percent decrease in the unemployment rate means an increase of about $20 billion in national income, their views of the income level we should target differ by over $30 billion (1.5 × $20 = $30). Yet both views are reasonable. Looking at the same economy (the same data), one economist may call for expansionary fiscal policy while the other may call for contractionary fiscal policy.

In practice, differences in estimates of potential income often lead to different policy recommendations. Empirical estimates suggest that the size of the multiplier is between 2 and 2.5. Let's say it's 2.5. That means autonomous expenditures must be predicted to shift either up or down by more than $12 billion before an economist who believes the target unemployment rate is 4.5 percent would agree in policy recommendation with an economist who believes the rate is 6 percent. Since almost all fluctuations in autonomous investment and autonomous consumption are less than this amount, there's no generally agreed-upon policy prescription for most fluctuations. Some economists will call for expansionary policy; some will call for contractionary policy; and the government decision makers won't have any clear-cut policy to follow.

You might wonder why the range of potential income estimates is so large. Why not simply see whether the economy has inflation at the existing unemployment and income levels? Would that it were so easy. Inflation is a complicated process. Seeds of inflation are often sown years before inflation results. The main problem is that establishing a close link between the level of economic activity and inflation is a complicated statistical challenge to economists, one that has not yet been satisfactorily met. That leads to enormous debate as to what the causes are.

Economists believe that outside some range (perhaps 7 percent unemployment on the low side and 11 percent on the high side), too much spending causes inflation and too little spending causes a recession. That 7 to 11 percent range is so large that in most cases the Canadian economy is in an ambiguous state where some economists are calling for expansionary policy and others are calling for contractionary policy.

Once the economy reaches the edge of the range or falls outside it, the economists' policy prescription becomes clearer. For example, in 1933, when this Keynesian model was developed, unemployment was nearly 20 percent—well outside the range. Should the economy ever go into such a depression again, economists' policy prescriptions will be clear. The call will be for expansionary fiscal policy. Most times the economy is within the ambiguous range so there are disagreements among economists.

For argument's sake, let's say economists agree that contractionary policy is needed and that's what they advise the government. Will the government implement it? And, if so, will it implement contractionary fiscal policy at the right time? The answer to both questions is: probably not. There are also problems with implementing economists' calls for expansionary fiscal policy. Even if economists are unanimous in calling for expansionary fiscal policy, putting fiscal policy in place takes time and has serious implementation problems.

The Government's Flexibility in Changing Taxes and Spending

Numerous political and institutional realities in Canada today make the task of implementing fiscal policy difficult. Government spending and taxes cannot be changed instantaneously. New taxes and new spending must be legislated. It takes time for the government to pass a bill. Politicians face intense political pressures; their other goals may conflict with the goals of fiscal policy. For example, few members of Parliament who hope to be reelected would vote to raise taxes in an election year. Similarly few members would vote to slash military spending when military bases are a major source of employment in their ridings, even when there's little to defend against. By the time the fiscal policy is implemented, what may have once been the right fiscal policy may have ceased to be right, and some other policy may have become right.

Imagine trying to steer a car at 100 kilometres an hour when there's a five-second delay between the time you turn the steering wheel and the time the car's wheels turn. Imagining that situation will give you a good sense of how fiscal policy works in the real world.

There is no inherent reason why the adoption of Keynesian policies should have caused the government to run deficits year after year and hence to incur ever-increasing debt. Keynesian policy is consistent with running deficits some years and surpluses other years. In practice, the introduction of Keynesian policy has been accompanied by many deficits and few surpluses, and by a large increase in government debt. If that increase in government debt hurts the economy, one can oppose Keynesian policy, even if one believes that policy might otherwise be beneficial.

Size of the Government Debt Doesn't Matter

There are two reasons why Keynesian policy has led to an increase in government debt. First, early Keynesian economists favoured large increases in government spending as well as favouring the government's using fiscal policy. These early Keynesians employed the Keynesian economic model to justify increasing spending without increasing taxes. A second reason is political. Politically it's much easier for government to increase spending and decrease taxes than to decrease spending and increase taxes. Due to political pressure, expansionary fiscal policy has predominated over contractionary fiscal policy.

Whether debt is a problem is an important and complicated issue as we'll see in a later chapter devoted entirely to the question. For now, all you need remember is that if one believes that the debt is harmful, then there might be a reason not to conduct expansionary fiscal policy, even when the model calls for it.

An economy has many goals; achieving potential income is only one of those goals. So it's not surprising that those goals often conflict. In an earlier example in this chapter, we saw those conflicts. When the government ran expansionary fiscal policy, the balance-of-trade deficit grew. As the economy expands and income rises, exports remain constant but imports rise. If a nation's international considerations do not

Fiscal Policy Doesn't Negatively Affect Other Government Goals

allow a balance-of-trade deficit to become larger, as is true in many countries, those governments cannot run expansionary fiscal policies—unless they can somehow prevent this balance-of-trade deficit from becoming larger.

Fiscal Policy in Practice: Summary of the Problems

So where do these six problems leave fiscal policy? While they don't eliminate it, they restrict its usefulness. Fiscal policy is a sledgehammer, not an instrument for fine tuning. When the economy goes into a depression, the appropriate fiscal policy is clear. Similarly when the economy has a hyperinflation, the appropriate policy is clear. But in less extreme cases, there will be debate on what the appropriate fiscal policy is—a debate economic theory can't answer conclusively.

Building Keynesian Policies into Institutions

Automatic stabilizer   Any government program or policy that will counteract the business cycle without any new government action.

Economists quickly recognized the political problems with instituting direct counter-cyclical fiscal policy. To avoid these problems they suggested policies that built fiscal policy into Canadian institutions so that it would be put into effect without any political decisions being necessary. They called a built-in fiscal policy an **automatic stabilizer,** which is any government program or policy that will counteract the business cycle without any new government action. Automatic stabilizers include welfare payments, unemployment insurance, and the income tax system.

To see how automatic stabilizers work, consider the unemployment insurance system. When the economy is slowing down or is in a recession, the unemployment rate will rise. When people lose their jobs, they will reduce their consumption, starting the multiplier process, which decreases income. Unemployment insurance immediately helps offset the decrease in individuals' incomes as the government pays benefits to the unemployed. Thus, the budget deficit increases, and part of the fall in income is stopped without any explicit act by the government. Automatic stabilizers also work in reverse. When income increases, they decrease the size of the deficit.

Another automatic stabilizer is our income tax system. Earlier in this chapter we said that tax revenue fluctuates as income fluctuates and that this makes the deficit hard to predict. When the economy expands unexpectedly, the budget deficit is lower than originally expected; when the economy contracts unexpectedly, the budget deficit is higher than expected. Let's go through the reasoning why. When the economy is strong, people have more income and thus pay higher taxes. This increase in tax revenue reduces expenditures from what they would have been, and moderates the economy's growth. When the economy goes into a recession, the opposite occurs.

7   An automatic stabilizer is any government program or policy that will counteract the business cycle without any new government action.

Automatic stabilizers may seem like the solution to the economic woes we have discussed, but they, too, have their shortcomings. One problem is that when the economy is first starting to climb out of a recession, automatic stabilizers will slow the process, rather than help it along, for the same reason they slow the contractionary process. As income increases, automatic stabilizers increase government taxes and decrease government spending, and as they do, the discretionary policy's expansionary effects are decreased.

Despite these problems, most Keynesians believe automatic stabilizers have played an important role in reducing fluctuations in our economy. They point to the kind of data we see in Exhibit 6, which they say show a significant decrease in fluctuations in the economy. Other economists aren't so sure; they argue the apparent decrease in fluctuations is an optical illusion. As usual, economic data are sufficiently ambiguous to give both sides strong arguments. The verdict is still out.

Fiscal Policy in Perspective

By now you should be able to think in terms of the Keynesian model and see how disequilibria between aggregate production and aggregate expenditures can be resolved by adjustments in aggregate income. But beware. The Keynesian model is only a model. It's a tool, a crutch, to help you see certain relationships. It does so by obscuring others, including interest rate adjustment, price level adjustment, and supply incentive effects.

Consideration of these aspects led to significant changes in macroeconomic think-

EXHIBIT 6   Decrease in Fluctuations in the Economy

One of the arguments in favour of Keynesian economics is that since it was introduced into the Canadian economy, fluctuations in the economy have decreased.

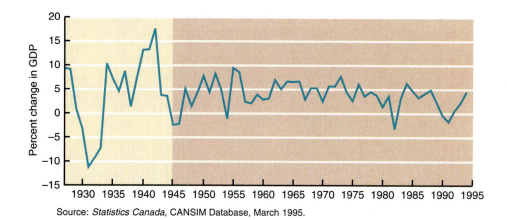

Source: *Statistics Canada*, CANSIM Database, March 1995.

ing over the years. In the 1970s, Classical economics rose like a phoenix from the ashes and reemerged. Modern Classical economists challenged the way Keynesian economists thought about expansionary effects of fiscal policy. They won many converts and modified the presentation of Keynesian economics so that it focuses on dynamic adjustment and is no longer presented mechanistically.

The modern Classical economists argue that expectations of policy can change the dynamic adjustment process, and that any simple dynamic adjustment models are unlikely to describe the aggregate economy. But while they are working on alternative aggregate dynamic adjustment models, they haven't come up with any that have been accepted as a way of describing the adjustment process of the aggregate economy. In the absence of an alternative model, the Keynesian model is the model used by most macro policy economists. Therefore, it is useful to know this model, as long as you keep in mind that it is only a first approximation to analyzing what happens in the economy.

Earlier, we went through the Keynesian model so carefully for two reasons. (1) It describes tendencies that affect economies and highlights important dynamic interrelationships among aggregates. The equilibrium it describes doesn't matter much; it is never reached, but the tendencies the model highlights for the economy to move in certain directions do matter. (2) It is the model that is in the back of most macro policy economists' minds when they discuss macro policy. This means that to understand how most policy economists talk about the macro economy, you must understand the tendencies given in the Keynesian model.

Not only did we carefully go through the model, we also carefully went through limitations of the model. The reason we did so is that Canada has gotten about as much as it can out of Keynesian demand management policy. To see this it is helpful to think back to the discussion of the three ranges of the economy presented in earlier chapters—the Keynesian range, the Intermediate range, and the Classical range, shown in Exhibit 7.

Demand management policies are useful in keeping the economy out of range *A* and range *C*. And they are used that way. But that means that the economy is almost always in the Intermediate range—where there is significant debate about whether an expansionary demand management policy is going to be inflationary, or will lead to higher output.

The dilemma of macro policy is that we have no way of specifying precisely where these ranges are. There is no signpost on the economy saying, "This is the economy's potential income, and this is the appropriate target unemployment." The majority of the profession, however, see the economy in the mid-1990s as being in the Intermediate range (range *B*). In this intermediate range the science of economics does not present a policy guide, and we enter the art of economics which involves choos-

THE KEYNESIAN MODEL AND THE PRACTICE OF FISCAL POLICY IN THE 1990s

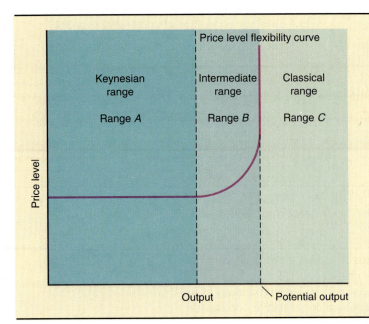

EXHIBIT 7   The Three Ranges of Output

When discussing macro policy, it is important to keep in mind the three ranges of output. Demand management policies are useful in keeping the economy out of ranges *A* and *C*, which means the economy is generally in range *B* where the appropriate policy is debatable.

ing between conflicting goals when one is not sure of the results. We'll discuss the art of macroeconomics in later chapters.

CHAPTER SUMMARY

- Aggregate demand management policy attempts to influence the level of output in the economy by influencing aggregate demand and relying on the multiplier to expand any policy-induced change in aggregate demand.
- Fiscal policy—the change in government spending or taxes—works by providing a deliberate countershock to offset unexpected shocks to the economy.
- Expansionary fiscal policy is represented graphically as an upward shift of the aggregate expenditures curve.
- Contractionary fiscal policy is represented graphically as a downward shift of the aggregate expenditures curve.
- The effect of fiscal policy can be determined by using the Keynesian model.
- The size of the deficit or surplus influences the level of income in the economy, but is also influenced by it.

- The size of the trade balance (net exports) influences the level of income in the economy but is also influenced by it.
- Fiscal policy is affected by the following problems, among others:
  1. Lack of knowledge of what policy is called for.
  2. Government's inability to respond quickly enough.
  3. Government debt.
  4. Crowding out.
- Keynesian fiscal policy is now built into Canadian economic institutions through automatic stabilizers.
- Aggregate demand management policies are most effective in the Keynesian range of the economy—when the economy is significantly below its potential income.

KEY TERMS

aggregate demand (expenditure)
  management policy *(253)*
automatic stabilizer *(272)*
countercyclical fiscal policy *(261)*
crowding in *(269)*
crowding out *(268)*

exchange rate policy *(264)*
export-led growth policies *(263)*
fine tuning *(261)*
fiscal policy *(253)*
inflationary gap *(259)*
marginal propensity to expend (*mpe*) *(260)*

Okun's law *(270)*
passive deficit *(265)*
recessionary gap *(257)*
Rosy Scenario policy *(262)*
structural deficit *(265)*
transfer payment *(256)*

QUESTIONS FOR THOUGHT AND REVIEW

The number after each question represents the estimated degree of critical thinking required. (1 = almost none; 10 = deep thought.)

1. Congratulations! You've just been appointed chairman of the Council of Economic Advisers in Textland. The *mpc* is .8; all nonconsumption expenditures and taxes are exogenous. There is a recessionary gap of $400, which the government wants to eliminate by changing taxes. What policy would you suggest? *(4)*

2. Your research assistant comes running in and tells you that instead of changing taxes, the government wants to achieve the same result by increasing expenditures. What policy would you recommend now? *(4)*

3. Your research assistant has a worried look on her face. "What's the problem?" you ask. "I goofed," she confesses. "I thought taxes were exogenous when actually there's a marginal tax rate of .1." Before she can utter another word, you say, "No problem. I'll simply recalculate my answers to Question 1 and change them before I send them in." What are your corrected answers? (Requires reading Appendix A.) *(5)*

4. She still has a pained expression. "What's wrong?" you ask. "You didn't let me finish," she says. "Not only was there a marginal tax rate of .1; there's also a marginal propensity to import of .2." Again you interrupt to make sure she doesn't feel guilty. Again you say, "No problem," and recalculate your answers to Question 3 to account for the new information. What are your new answers? (Requires reading Appendix A.) *(5)*

5. That pained look is still there, but this time you don't interrupt. You let her finish. She says, "And they want to see the answers graphically." You do the right thing. *(4)*

6. Two economists are debating whether the normal rate of unemployment is 4 or 6 percent. Mr. A believes it's 4 percent; Ms. B believes it's 6 percent. One says the structural deficit is $40 billion; the other says it is $20 billion. Which one says which? Why? *(5)*

7. What is the current state of Canadian fiscal policy? Would you advise Canada to change its fiscal policy? Why? *(7)*

8. If interest rates have no effect on investment, what percentage of crowding out will there be? *(5)*

9. A country has a balance-of-trade deficit and a recessionary gap. Advise it how to eliminate both. *(9)*

PROBLEMS AND EXERCISES

1. Congratulations! You've just been appointed economic adviser to Easyland. You go to your first board meeting and are asked the following questions. What are the answers you would give?

   a. Why does cutting taxes by $100 have a smaller effect on GDP than increasing income by the same amount?

   b. If they cut taxes and want a neutral fiscal policy, what should they do with their trade policy?

   c. Why does the trade deficit generally increase as the economy improves?

   d. How does your answer to *c* change if all world economies are moving together?

2. Congratulations! You've just been appointed economic advisor to Dreamland. The Prime Minister wants your advice on how to reduce unemployment from 8 to 6 percent. Income is $40,000, and the *mpe* is .4.

   a. Advise her.

   b. She wants to know what would happen to her formerly balanced budget if she follows your advice. You naturally tell her.

   c. Now she wants to know what will happen to her formerly zero trade deficit. You tell her.

   d. Hearing your answers, she tells you that your policy is unacceptable. She wants to reduce unemployment and keep both the trade and the government budget in balance. How do you respond?

3. Condolences. You've been fired from your job in Dreamland, but you found another job in neighbouring Fantasyland. Its economy is almost the same as Dreamland's but you must rely on your research assistant for the specific numbers. He says income is $50,000, *mpe* is .75, and the premier wants to lower unemployment from 8 to 6 percent.

   a. Advise him.

   b. Your research assistant comes in and says "Sorry, I meant that the *mpe* is .66." You redo your calculations.

   c. You're just about to see the premier when your research assistant comes running, saying "Sorry, sorry, I meant that the *mpe* is .5." Redo your calculations.

4. Prime Minister Chretien's policy in 1995 was designed to reduce the deficit but increase employment.

   a. Why would such a policy not fit well in the Keynesian model presented in this chapter?

   b. Explain in words how such a policy might achieve the desired effect.

   c. Graphically demonstrate your answer in *b*.

   d. What data would you look at to see if your explanations in *b* and *c* are appropriate?

5. Explain the following observations in terms of the Keynesian model.

   a. In the early 1990s, Canada was pushing Japan to increase its budget deficit.

   b. In the early 1990s, Canada was pushing Japan to decrease its trade deficit.

   c. In the early 1990s, unemployment in Europe exceeded 10 percent but few economists were pushing for an increase in European governments' budget deficits.

   d. When running for reelection, most prime ministers increase government spending programs.

   e. A maxim in politics is that if you are going to increase taxes, the time to do it is right after your election, when reelection is far off.

The Algebraic Keynesian Model

In this chapter we used a multiplier based on the marginal propensity to consume and briefly introduced the marginal propensity to expend. This kept the math to a minimum, but obscured some of the ways in which the components of expenditures affected income, and in turn how those components of income are affected by income. In this appendix we briefly outline a fuller presentation and show the relationship between the marginal propensity to expend (*mpe*), specified as *e* in the equations, and the marginal propensities to consume (*mpc*), specified as *b* in the equation, the marginal propensity to import (*mpm*), specified as *m* in the equations, and the marginal tax rate, specified as *t* in the equations.

The basic Keynesian model consists of the following equations:

(1) $C = C_0 + bY_d$

(2) $Y_d = Y - T + R$

(3) $I = I_0$

(4) $G = G_0$

(5) $R = R_0$

(6) $T = T_0 + tY$

(7) $X = X_0$

(8) $M = M_0 + mY$

(9) $C + I + G + (X - M) = Y$

Equation (1) is the consumption function. C_0 is autonomous consumption; bY_d is the *mpc* multiplied by disposable income.

Equation (2) defines disposable income as a function of real income minus taxes plus transfers (*R*).

Equation (3) is the investment function. I_0 is autonomous investment.

Equation (4) is the government expenditures function. G_0 is autonomous spending.

Equation (5) is the government transfer function. R_0 is autonomous transfer payments.

Equation (6) is the tax function. Taxes are composed of two parts. The autonomous component, T_0, is unaffected by income. The induced portion of taxes is tY. The tax rate is represented by *t*.

Equation (7) is the exogenous export function.

Equation (8) is the import function. Imports are composed of two parts. M_0 is the autonomous portion. The induced portion is mY. The marginal propensity to import is represented by *m*.

Equation (9) is the national income accounting identity: Total expenditures = income.

To use this model meaningfully, we must combine all these equations into a single equation, called a *reduced-form equation*, which will neatly show the effect of various shifts on the equilibrium level of income. To do so we first substitute Equation (6) into Equation (2), and then Equation (2) into Equation (1):

(1a) $C = C_0 + b(Y - T + R_0)$

We then substitute (1a), (3), (4), (5), (6), (7), and (8) into Equation (9), giving:

$$C_0 + b[Y - (T_0 + tY) + R_0] + I_0 + G_0 + (X_0 - (M_0 + mY)) = Y$$

Removing the parentheses:

$$C_0 + bY - bT_0 - btY + bR_0 + I_0 + G_0 + X_0 - M_0 - mY = Y$$

Moving all of the Y terms to the right side:

$$C_0 - bT_0 + bR_0 + I_0 + G_0 + X_0 - M_0 = Y - bY + btY + mY$$

Factoring out Y on the right side:

$$C_0 - bT_0 + bR_0 + I_0 + G_0 + X_0 - M_0 = Y(1 - b + bt + m)$$

Dividing by $(1 - b + bt + m)$ gives:

$$(C_0 - bT_0 + bR_0 + I_0 + G_0 + X_0 - M_0)[1/(1 - b + bt + m)] = Y$$

$1/(1 - b + bt + m)$ is the multiplier for a simple Keynesian model with endogenous taxes and endogenous imports.

The marginal propensity to expend, *mpe,* discussed in the text would equal $b - bt - m$. The additional terms adjust by the *mpc,* for the other induced expenditures that the simple model did not consider. Notice that they both make the multiplier smaller. For example, if the *mpc* is .8, $t = .25$, and $m = .1$, the multiplier using only the *mpc* would be $1/(1 - .8) = 5$. Taking into account other induced expenditures, we can calculate the *mpe.* It equals $.9 - .8(.25) - .1 = .6$. Substituting .6 into our generalized multiplier formula, $1/(1 - .6)$, we see that the multiplier becomes $(1/.4) = 2.5$. This is the approximate multiplier for Canada.

Thus, the general structure of the reduced form equation is:

$$Y = (\text{multiplier})(\text{autonomous expenditures})$$

When we discuss changes in autonomous expenditures, the general form is:

$$\Delta Y = (\text{multiplier}) (\Delta \text{ autonomous expenditures})$$

To see whether you follow the argument, let's try another numerical example. Say you want to increase income (Y) by 100. Assume $b = .8$, $t = .2$, and $m = .04$. Substituting in these numbers, you find that $e = .8 - .8(.2) - .04 = .6$. Thus, in this example we also get a multiplier of 2.5.

We can now determine how much to change autonomous expenditure to affect income. For example, to increase income by 100, we must increase autonomous expenditure, by $(100/2.5) = 40$.

The Circular Spiral, Real Business Cycles, and Dynamic Externalities

It is important, when thinking about Keynesian policies, you remember that *it is only autonomous expenditures that have no offsetting effects on other expenditures* that cause a multiplied effect on income. When the expenditures we make aren't autonomous, the expansion won't necessarily take place. For example, when we increase consumption, we might be decreasing saving which might lead to decreased investment, and hence to a direct offsetting effect. That's precisely what Classicals contend happens in general—when the government pushes on one of these supposedly autonomous expenditures, it simply pulls down on another and the net effect is a wash. *Classicals see everything as induced—dependent on everything else—so forget activist government policy and rely on a laissez faire-policy.*

The Keynesian Spiral

When you think of the circular flow diagram, the Classical conception of a flow in which everything depends on everything else seems to make sense in the aggregate: Something can't come out of nothing. Thus a reasonable question for you to ask is: "Where do Keynesians see this autonomous expenditure coming from; isn't any expenditure going to have to come from somewhere?"

For Keynesians the answer to this question is: Not necessarily. They don't see financial markets as operating smoothly in translating savings into investment. More generally, they don't see the economy operating efficiently in translating all leakages from the circular flow into injections into the circular flow. What that means is that, for Keynesians, the circular flow is not a flow at all, but is, instead, a spiral that shrinks or expands in response to the dynamic disequilibrium adjustment forces in the economy. If people save too much, the spiral will shrink and aggregate income will fall, causing people to save less; people will end up sitting around doing nothing—unemployed, not saving, and not earning income. If people save too little, the spiral will expand beyond what

the current institutions can handle and an accelerating inflation will result.

Keynesians see policies directed at autonomous expenditures as preventing that from happening, or at least preventing the income from shrinking or expanding too much. Expansionary autonomous policies generate income, and as they do, they generate saving, which prevents the offsetting effect on other autonomous investment. Contractionary policies decrease income and, as they do, they decrease spending.

Real Business Cycles, Keynesian Business Cycles, and Macro Policy

Recent developments in modern Classical economics have also accepted a version of this circular spiral notion of the economy. It is called the *real business cycle theory*. It says that business cycles occur because of technological and other "natural" shocks.

The difference between the Classical real business cycle theory and the Keynesian business cycle theory is that, in the Classical view, the spiralling nature of income in the economy simply reflects individuals' desires, while in the Keynesian view, the initial fluctuations may begin from individuals' desires, or from some other cause, but those fluctuations are multiplied into larger-than-desired fluctuations. In that sense, the Keynesian economic theory of business cycles presented in this book can be interpreted as a modification of the Classical real business cycle theory—one that allows for deviations from the desired dynamic equilibrium path. It follows that in their policies Keynesians should not be trying to prevent all the fluctuations in income—only larger-than-individually-desired fluctuations.

Another way of expressing this dynamic interpretation of Keynesian economics is to say that Keynesians see the aggregate income level as fluctuating more than individuals' desires due to **dynamic externalities**—effects of adjustment decisions that are not taken into account by the decision maker. Keynesians' policies are designed to offset these dynamic externalities. Some Classicals see the aggregate income reflecting the desires of individuals, and hence see the Keynesian policies designed to affect aggregate income as inappropriate. Other Classicals agree that, in principle, dynamic externalities can exist; they argue, however, that generally the dynamic interrelationships are so complicated that the government is not going to be able to react to them in a reasonable manner. So even though they accept the Keynesian intuitive model of the aggregate economy, they still reject the use of Keynesian policies and come to Classical policy conclusions.

11

Financial Institutions

Finance is a means of assuring the flow of capital. Historically it has also been a means for guiding that flow. In the first case, it is a mechanism in aid of the industrial system as we know it. In the second, it is a power controlling it.

~Adolf A. Berle, Jr.

After reading this chapter, you should be able to:

1   Explain how financial assets can be created by an agreement between two people.

2   List three types of financial institutions.

3   Distinguish a primary financial market from a secondary financial market.

4   List four money market assets and two capital market assets.

5   Explain why, when interest rates fall, bond prices rise—and vice versa.

6   Roughly determine the present value of an amount of money at a future date.

7   Differentiate the Classical and Keynesian views of the financial sector.

Markets make specialization and trade possible and thereby make the economy far more efficient than it otherwise would be. But the efficient use of markets requires a financial sector that facilitates and lubricates those trades.

In thinking about the economy, students often focus on the *real* economy: producing real goods or services such as shoes, operas, automobiles, and textbooks. That's an incomplete view of the economy. The financial sector plays a central role in organizing and coordinating our economy; it makes modern economic society possible. A car won't run without oil; a modern economy won't operate without a financial sector.

In thinking about the financial sector's role, remember the following insight. *For every real transaction there is a financial transaction that mirrors it.* For example, when you buy an apple, the person selling the apple is buying 35¢ from you by spending his apple. The financial transaction is the transfer of 35¢; the real transaction is the transfer of the apple.

For larger items, the financial transaction behind the real transaction can be somewhat complicated. When you buy a house, you'll probably pay for part of that house with a mortgage, which requires that you borrow money from a bank. The bank, in turn, borrows from individuals the money it lends to you. There's a similar financial transaction when you buy a car, or even a book, on credit.

There's a financial transaction reflecting every real transaction. The financial sector is important for the real sector. If the financial sector doesn't work, the real sector doesn't work. All trade involves both the real sector and the financial sector. Thus in this book we don't have a separate section on the steel sector or even the computer sector of the economy, but we do have a separate section on the financial sector of the economy.

To understand the financial sector and its relation to the real sector, you must understand: (1) what financial assets are, (2) how financial institutions work, (3) what financial markets are, and (4) how financial markets work.

An *asset* is something that provides its owner with expected future benefits. There are two types of assets: real assets and financial assets. Real assets are assets such as houses or machinery whose services provide direct benefits to their owners, either now or in the future. A house is a real asset—you can live in it. A machine is a real asset—you can produce goods with it.

Financial assets are assets, such as stocks or bonds, whose benefit to the owner depends on the issuer of the asset meeting certain obligations. These obligations are called **financial liabilities.** *Every financial asset has a corresponding financial liability;* it's that financial liability that gives the financial asset its value. In the case of bonds, for example, a company's agreement to pay interest and repay the principal gives bonds their value. If the company goes bankrupt and reneges on its liability to pay interest and repay the principal, the asset becomes worthless. The corresponding liability gives the financial asset its value.

The financial liability created by a financial asset can be either an *equity instrument* or a *debt instrument.* An example of an equity instrument is a share of stock that a firm issues. It is a liability of the firm; it gives the holder ownership rights which are spelled out in the financial asset. An equity instrument such as a stock usually conveys a general right to dividends, but only if the company's board of directors decides to pay them.

A debt instrument conveys no ownership right. It's a type of loan. An example of a debt instrument is a bond that a firm issues. The bond is a liability of the firm but an asset of the individual who holds the bond. A debt instrument such as a bond usually conveys legal rights to interest payments and repayment of principal.

Real assets are created by real economic activity. For example, a house or a machine must be built. Financial assets are created whenever somebody takes on a financial liability. For example, say we promise to pay you $1,000,000,000 in the future. You now have a financial asset and we have a financial liability. Understanding

FINANCIAL ASSETS AND FINANCIAL LIABILITIES

1 Every financial asset has a corresponding financial liability.

Financial assets   Assets, such as stocks or bonds, whose benefit to the owner depends on the issuer of the asset meeting certain obligations called *financial liabilities.*

Financial liabilities   Liability incurred by the issuer of a financial asset to stand behind the issued asset.

that financial assets can be created by a simple agreement of two parties is fundamentally important to understanding how the financial sector works.

FINANCIAL INSTITUTIONS

Financial institution   A business whose primary activity is buying, selling, or holding financial assets.

Depository institutions   Financial institution whose primary financial liability is deposits in chequing or savings accounts.

Contractural intermediaries   Financial institution that holds and stores individuals' financial assets.

2   Financial institutions buy, sell, or hold financial assets. They include depository, contractual, and investment intermediaries.

Depository Institutions

A **financial institution** is a business whose primary activity is buying, selling, or holding financial assets. For example, some financial institutions (depository institutions and investment intermediaries) sell promises to pay in the future. These promises can be their own promises or someone else's promises. When you open a savings account at a bank, the bank is selling you its own promise that you can withdraw your money, plus interest, at some unspecified time in the future. Such financial institutions are called **depository institutions.** When you buy a government bond or security from a securities firm, it's also selling you a promise to pay in the future. But in this case, it's a third party's promise. So a securities firm is a financial institution that sells third parties' promises to pay. It's a type of investment intermediary.

As financial institutions sell financial assets, they channel savings from savers (individuals who give other people money now in return for promises to pay it back with interest later) to borrowers (investors or consumers who get the money now in return for their promise to pay it and the interest later).

As economists use the term, *to save* is to buy a financial asset. *To invest* (in economic terminology) is to buy real, not financial, assets that you hope will yield a return in the future.[1] How do you get funds to invest if you don't already have them? You borrow them. That means you create a financial asset which you sell to someone else who saves.

Some financial institutions also hold and store individuals' financial assets. Such financial institutions are called **contractual intermediaries** because they intermediate (serve as a go-between) between savers and investors. For example, a pension fund is a financial institution that holds individuals' savings and pays back those savings plus interest after the individuals retire. It uses individuals' savings to buy financial assets from people and firms who want to borrow. Similarly, a bank is a financial institution that holds an individual's cash in the form of chequing deposits; it distributes that cash to others when that individual tells it to. A chequing deposit is a financial asset of an individual and a financial liability of the bank.

Exhibit 1 lists three types of financial institutions and shows the percentage of total Canadian financial assets each holds, along with the sources and uses of funds for each. These percentages give you an idea of the institution's importance, but an institutions' importance can come in other ways. For example, investment dealers hold less than one percent of total financial assets, yet they're important because they facilitate buying and selling such assets. Let's consider each grouping separately.

Depository institutions, by far the largest category, are financial institutions whose primary financial liability is deposits in chequing accounts. They hold approximately 57 percent of all the financial assets in Canada. This category includes chartered banks, trust and mortgage loan companies, and credit unions and caisses populaires. In Canada banks are referred to as *chartered banks* because the financial institution must obtain a charter from the government to call itself a bank. Trust companies engage in some depository functions, but they are primarily involved in administering trusted pension funds (pension plans where a trustee is responsible for managing and investing the funds).

You might well wonder why there are so many different types of depository institutions. Why not just have banks? The reason has to do with the evolution of the Canadian financial system. At one time, trust companies flourished because there were legal restrictions that precluded chartered banks from acting as trustees. Similarly with respect to mortgage loan companies—they initially sprang from restrictions on the ability of a chartered bank to offer mortgages on residential property. Credit unions

[1]This terminology isn't the terminology most lay people use. When a person buys a stock, in economic terms that person is saving, though most lay people call that *investing*.

	Percent of Total Financial Assets	Primary Assets (uses of funds)	Primary Liabilities (sources of funds)	
Depository Institutions				**EXHIBIT 1 List of Financial Institutions**
Chartered banks	39.5%	Bank loans, mortgages, and consumer credit	Currency and bank deposits	
Trust and mortgage loan companies	10.5	Mortgages, consumer credit	Deposits	
Credit unions and caisses populaires	7	Mortgages, consumer credit	Deposits	
Contractual Intermediaries				
Insurance companies	15.75	Mortgages, bonds, and shares	Life insurance, pensions, shares	
Pensions	19	Bonds, short-term paper	Life insurance, pensions	
Investment Intermediaries				
Investment dealers	.5	Short-term paper	Loans	
Mutual funds	5.75	Short-term paper, shares, and foreign investment	Shares	
Finance companies	2	Consumer credit, loans	Short-term paper, bonds	

Source: National Balance Sheet Account, 13–214 (February 1994).

and caisses populaires popped up around the country because small investors had limited access to financial institutions—you had to have a lot of money to put into the bank before it would be interested in your account. Locally owned and operated intermediaries such as credit unions and caisses populaires developed as community-level financial institutions.

As you can see in Exhibit 1, chartered banks hold the greatest proportion of financial assets among the depository institutions. The primary financial liability of each is deposits. For example, the amount in your chequing account or savings account is a financial asset for you and a financial liability for the bank holding your deposit.

Banks make money by lending your deposits (primarily in the form of business and commercial loans), charging the borrower a higher interest rate than they pay the depositor. Those loans from banks to borrowers are financial assets of the bank and financial liabilities of the borrower.

Over the years there have been significant changes to federal and provincial laws governing financial institutions. When the first Canadian banks came on the scene in the early 19th century, some provinces wouldn't allow a bank to have more than one branch. That's in stark contrast to the current system of multibranch banking. Other arcane regulations include the restriction that cheques had to be written in blue fountain pen ink. Now you can use passion pink pencils, if that's your fancy.

These restrictions were usually aimed at constraining the behaviour of chartered banks, who were able to use their size to exert control over to whom funds were channelled. Regulations affect the activities that financial institutions undertake, and they allow us to make sharp, clear distinctions among financial institutions.

Changes in the laws have eliminated many of these restrictions, blurring the distinction between the various types of financial intermediaries. In Canada, the main

Financial assets are neat. You can call them into existence simply by getting someone to accept your IOU. *Remember, every financial asset has a corresponding financial liability equal to it.* So when you say a country has $1 trillion of financial assets, you're also saying that the country has $1 trillion of financial liabilities. An optimist would say a country is rich. A pessimist would say it's poor. An economist would say that financial assets and financial liabilities are simply opposite sides of the ledger and don't indicate whether a country is rich or poor.

To find out whether a country is rich or poor, you must look at its *real assets.* If financial assets increase the economy's efficiency and thereby increase the amount of real assets, they make society better off. This is most economists' view of financial assets. If, however, they decrease the efficiency of the economy (as some economists have suggested some financial assets do because they focus productive effort on financial gamesmanship), financial assets make society worse off.

The same correspondence between a financial asset and its liability exists when a financial asset's value changes. Say stock prices fall significantly. Is society poorer? Clearly the people who own the stock are poorer, but the people who might want to buy stock in the future are richer since the price of assets has fallen. So in a pure accounting sense, society is neither richer nor poorer when the prices of stocks rise or fall.

But there are ways in which changes in the value of financial assets might signify that society is richer or poorer. For example, the changes in the values of financial assets might *reflect* (rather than cause) real changes. If suddenly a company finds a cure for cancer, its stock price will rise and society will be richer. But the rise in the price of the stock doesn't cause society to be richer. It reflects the discovery that made society richer. Society would be richer because of the discovery even if the stock's price didn't rise.

There's significant debate about how well the stock market reflects real changes in the economy. Classical economists believe it closely reflects real changes; Keynesian economists believe it doesn't. But both sides agree that the changes in the real economy, not the changes in the price of financial assets, underlie what makes an economy richer or poorer.

banking legislation is revised, on average, about every 10 years. The Bank Act essentially sets the rules that chartered banks have to follow. The most recent changes to the act were aimed at establishing safeguards to reduce the potential for bank failures and at eliminating the legal differences between chartered banks and other financial institutions. For example, trust companies can now offer commercial loans—something they were not permitted until mid-1992. Also, chartered banks can now own trust and insurance companies, and they are allowed to offer life insurance. Some economists argue that banks should be excluded from offering life insurance. Why? Let's say you have a medical condition that will raise the likelihood of your death at an early age. If your bank has that information as part of the medical history it requires for your life insurance policy, there's a chance you'll never be able to secure a mortgage, even if conventional medical wisdom changes and your life expectancy returns to normal.

Some differences remain that reflect their history. Chartered banks' primary assets are loans, and their loans include business loans, mortgages, and consumer loans. Trust and mortgage loan companies' primary assets are the same kind as those of commercial banks, but their loans are primarily mortgage loans.

Contractual Intermediaries

The most important contractual intermediaries are insurance companies and pension funds. These institutions promise, for a fee, to pay an individual a certain amount of money in the future, either when some event happens (a fire or death) or, in the case of pension funds and some kinds of life insurance, when the individual reaches a certain age or dies. Insurance policies and pensions are a form of individual savings. Contractual intermediaries manage those savings. As the average age of the Canadian population increases, as it will throughout the 1990s, the share of assets held by these contractual intermediaries will increase.

Throughout the next few chapters we'll be discussing financial institutions and how money affects the economy. Here's a brief review of the different types of financial institutions:

Chartered banks	Engage in depository activities that fund loans—must obtain a federal charter to be called a bank.
Trust and mortgage loan companies	Engage in depository activities that primarily fund mortgages; also administer trusteed pension funds.
Credit unions and caisses populaires	Engage in depository activities—grew from small community-based institutions; make mortgages and loans.
Insurance companies	Offer bonds, shares, and mortgages; pay out contingent claims (fire, accident, death).
Pension funds	Manage pension funds.
Mutual funds	Pooled funds that reduce risk—offer shares whose value fluctuates with the market.
Investment dealers	Agents who assist in buying and selling financial instruments.
Finance companies	Engage in commercial and personal loans—issue short-term paper and bonds.

Investment Intermediaries

Investment intermediaries provide a mechanism through which small savers pool funds to invest in a variety of financial assets rather than in just one or two. An example of how pooling works can be seen by considering a mutual fund company, which is one type of investment intermediary.

A mutual fund enables a small saver to diversify (spread out) his or her savings (for a fee, of course). Savers buy shares in the mutual fund which, in turn, holds stocks or bonds of many different companies. When a fund holds many different companies' shares or bonds, it spreads the risk so a saver won't lose everything if one company goes broke. Such spreading of risks by holding many different types of financial assets is called **diversification.**

A finance company is another type of investment intermediary. Finance companies make loans to individuals and businesses, as do banks, but instead of holding deposits, as banks do, finance companies borrow the money they lend. They borrow from individuals by selling them bonds and commercial paper. **Bonds** are promissory notes specifying that a certain amount of money plus interest will be paid back in the future. **Commercial paper** is a short-term promissory note that a certain amount of money plus interest will be paid back on demand.

Finance companies charge borrowers higher interest than banks do, in part because their cost of funds (the interest rate they pay to depositors) is higher than banks' cost of funds. (The interest rate banks pay on savings and chequing accounts is the cost of their funds.) As was the case with depository institutions, a finance company's profit reflects the difference between the interest rate it charges on its loans and the interest rate it pays for the funds it borrows.

Why do people go to finance companies if finance companies charge higher interest than banks? Because of convenience and because finance companies' loan qualifications are easier to meet than banks'.

The final investment intermediary is the investment dealer. These dealers assist companies in selling financial assets such as stocks and bonds. They provide advice, expertise, and the sales force to sell the stocks or bonds. They handle such things as *mergers* and *takeovers* of companies. A merger is the joining of two or more companies to form one new company. A takeover occurs when one company buys out another company.

Diversification   Spreading of risks by holding many different types of financial assets.

Bond   Promissory note that a certain amount of money plus interest will be paid back in the future.

Commercial paper   Short-term IOU of a large corporation.

The market for financial instruments is sometimes rather hectic, as suggested by this famous painting. © *New York Historical Society*.

Secondary financial market Market in which previously issued financial assets can be bought and sold.

Many investment dealers are closely associated with brokerage houses. They assist individuals in selling previously issued financial assets. Brokerage houses create a secondary market in financial assets, as we'll see shortly. A **secondary financial market** is a market in which previously issued financial assets can be bought and sold.

FINANCIAL MARKETS

A financial market is a market where financial assets and financial liabilities are bought and sold. The stock market, the bond market, and bank activities are all examples of financial markets.

Financial institutions buy and sell financial assets in financial markets. Sometimes these markets are actual places, like the Toronto Stock Exchange, but generally a market simply exists in the form of a broker's Rolodex files, computer networks, telephone lines, and lists of people who sometimes want to buy and sell. When individuals want to sell, they call their broker and their broker calls potential buyers; when individuals want to buy, the broker calls potential sellers. A market is an institution that brings buyers and sellers together; a **financial market** is an institution (the Rolodex cards and the telephone) that brings buyers and sellers of financial assets together.

Financial market Institution that brings buyers and sellers of financial assets together.

Primary and Secondary Financial Markets

3 Primary financial markets sell newly issued financial assets. Secondary financial markets transfer existing financial assets from one individual to another.

There are various types of financial markets. A **primary financial market** is a market in which newly issued financial assets are sold. These markets transfer savings to borrowers who want to invest (buy real assets). Sellers in this market include *venture capital firms* (which sell part ownerships in new companies) and *investment dealers* (which sell new stock and new bonds for existing companies). Whereas investment dealers only assist firms in selling their stock, venture capital firms often are partnerships that invest their own money in return for part ownership of a new firm.

Primary financial market Market in which newly issued financial assets are sold.

Many new businesses will turn to venture capital firms for financing because only established firms can sell stock through an investment dealer. Risks are enormous for venture capital firms since most new businesses fail. But potential gains are huge. A company that's already established will most likely use an investment dealer to get additional funds. Investment dealers know people and institutions who buy stocks; with a new stock offering they use those contacts. They telephone these leads to try to *place* (sell) the new issue.

Generally, new offerings are too large for one investment bank to sell. So it contracts with other investment banks and brokerage houses to sell portions of the new stock or bond issue. Exhibit 2 shows an advertisement announcing the initial public offering and the secondary offering of a stock. Notice there are 10 different institutions involved in the offering.

There are many different types of buyers for newly issued financial assets. They

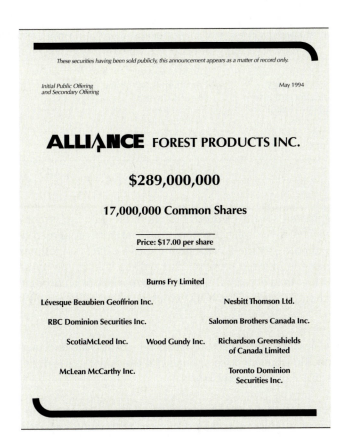

These securities having been sold publicly, this announcement appears as a matter of record only.

Initial Public Offering
and Secondary Offering   May 1994

ALLI∧NCE FOREST PRODUCTS INC.

$289,000,000

17,000,000 Common Shares

Price: $17.00 per share

Burns Fry Limited

Lévesque Beaubien Geoffrion Inc.   Nesbitt Thomson Ltd.

RBC Dominion Securities Inc.   Salomon Brothers Canada Inc.

ScotiaMcLeod Inc.   Wood Gundy Inc.   Richardson Greenshields
of Canada Limited

McLean McCarthy Inc.   Toronto Dominion
Securities Inc.

EXHIBIT 2   Stock Offering Announcement

Source: *Globe and Mail*, Toronto, May 17, 1994, p. B14.

include rich individuals and financial institutions, such as life insurance companies, pension funds, and mutual funds.

A secondary financial market transfers existing financial assets from one saver to another. (Remember, in economics, when an individual buys a financial asset such as a stock or bond, he or she is a saver. In economics, investment occurs only when savings are used to buy items such as machines or a factory.) A transfer on a secondary market does not represent any new savings; it is savings for one person and dissavings for another. One cancels out the other. The Toronto Stock Exchange is probably the best-known secondary financial market. It transfers stocks from one stockholder to another.

The secondary market does, however, have an important role to play in new savings. The existence of a secondary market lets the individual buyer of a financial asset know that she can resell it, transferring the asset back into cash at whatever price the secondary market sets. This ability to turn an asset into cash quickly is called **liquidity.** Secondary markets provide liquidity for financial asset holders and thereby encourage them to hold financial assets. If no secondary market existed, most people would hesitate to buy a stock or a 30-year bond. What if they needed their money in, say, 10 years? Or 10 weeks?

Besides the organized secondary financial markets we often hear about—the Toronto Stock Exchange, the Vancouver Stock Exchange—there are informal *over-the-counter* markets. Over-the-counter markets work like the primary financial markets: Brokers know of other individuals interested in buying what's for sale. Buying and selling takes place over the phone, with the broker acting as an intermediary.

Financial markets can also be divided into two other categories: **money markets** (in which financial assets having a maturity of less than three years are bought and sold) and **capital markets** (in which financial assets having a maturity of more than three

Secondary financial market Market in which previously issued financial assets can be bought and sold.

Liquidity Ability to turn an asset into cash quickly.

Money market Financial market in which financial assets having a maturity of less than three years are bought and sold.

Capital market Financial market in which financial assets having a maturity of more than three years are bought and sold.

Money Markets and Capital Markets

EXHIBIT 3   Principal Money Market Instruments

Instruments	Maturity
Canada treasury bills	90–365 days
Short-term Canada bonds	Less than three years
Provincial and municipal bonds	90–365 days
Bank of Canada advances	Several days
Bankers acceptances	10–365 days
Day-to-day loans	Callable any time
Commercial paper	30–365 days

years are bought and sold).[2] (*Maturity* refers to the date the issuer must pay back the money that was borrowed plus any remaining interest, as agreed when the asset was issued.) For example, say the government issues an IOU (sometimes called a *Treasury bill*) that comes due in three months. This will be sold in the money market because its maturity is less than a year. Or say the government or a corporation issues an IOU that comes due in 20 years. This IOU, which is called a *bond,* will be sold in a capital market.

TYPES OF FINANCIAL ASSETS

Now that you've been introduced to financial institutions and markets, we can consider some specific financial assets. Financial assets are generally divided into money market assets and capital market assets.

Money Market Assets

Money market assets are financial assets that mature in less than three years. They usually pay lower interest rates than do longer-term capital assets because they offer the buyer more liquidity. A general rule of thumb is: The more liquid the asset, the lower the return. As in the over-the-counter market, money market and capital market transactions are made over the phone lines using computers. Newly issued money market assets are sold through an investment dealer. Exhibit 3 lists some of the most important money market assets and their maturities. Let us briefly discuss each of these.

4 Financial assets with a maturity of less than three years (such as treasury bills, commercial paper, day loans, and some provincial bonds) are sold in money markets. Financial assets with a maturity of over three years (such as bonds and mortgages) are sold on capital markets. They usually pay a higher rate of return than money market assets because they are less liquid.

Canada Treasury Bills   These are Canadian government IOUs that mature in less than a year. Since it's unlikely the Canadian government will go broke, IOUs of the Canadian government are very secure, so Canada treasury bills pay a relatively low rate of interest.

Where do the IOUs come from? Think back to the discussion of fiscal policy in which the government spent more than it took in in revenues. That deficit must be financed by borrowing. Selling Canada treasury bills is one way the Canadian government borrows money.

Short-Term Canada Bonds   Canadian government bonds with maturities of less than three years are almost as liquid as treasury bills. These bonds usually carry fixed interest rates, but have fallen in relative importance since the early 1970s.

Provincial and Municipal Bonds   Canadian provincial and municipal governments also issue bonds to finance large expenditures on things such as hydro-electric plants, waste treatment, and other areas of spending that cannot be financed out of current revenues. They fund these large projects by borrowing from domestic and international markets, usually by issuing bonds denominated in Canadian dollars. Sometimes these bonds are issued in foreign currencies to entice foreigners to invest in Canada. The only problem with this is that if the Canadian dollar loses a lot of value against that foreign currency, in 20 or 30 years when it is time to repay the principal,

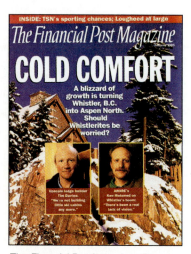

The *Financial Post* is must reading material for businesspeople.

---

[2]While we use the three-year term as the dividing point between the money market and the capital markets, most money market transactions have a maturity of less than a year.

Instruments	Maturity
Government of Canada bonds	From 3 years and up
Provincial and municipal bonds	From 3 years and up
Corporate bonds	From 3 years and up
Debentures	From 3 to 20 years
Stocks	Variable

EXHIBIT 4   Principal Capital Market Instruments

a foreign currency loan may turn out to be more expensive than anyone had ever imagined. This happened in Nova Scotia when funds to build a large bridge were borrowed in Swiss francs. The total cost of the loan was much more than expected, leading to ever-increasing tolls on the bridge.

Commercial Paper   Why borrow from a bank if you can borrow directly from the public? Why not cut out the middleman? Large corporations often do precisely that. The borrowings are called commercial paper. Commercial paper is a short-term IOU of a large corporation. It pays higher rates of interest than Canada treasury bills, but a lower interest rate than banks would charge the corporation. The same reasoning holds for a person who buys commercial paper. Commercial paper generally pays a higher interest rate than a term deposit, which is why people are willing to lend directly to the firm. Since the bank is an intermediary between the lender of funds and the borrower, the process of lending directly and not going through a financial intermediary is called **disintermediation.**

Disintermediation   Borrowing directly from an individual without going through an intermediary bank.

Differences among Money Market Assets   Money market assets differ slightly from each other. For example, treasury bills are safer than commercial paper (usually there's more chance of a firm defaulting than a government) and pay slightly lower interest. For the most part, however, they are interchangeable, and the interest rates paid on them tend to increase or decrease together.

Capital market assets have a maturity of over one year. Exhibit 4 shows several important capital market instruments and their maturities. Let's briefly discuss stocks and bonds.

Capital Market Assets

Stocks   A **stock** is a partial ownership right to a company. The stock owner usually has the right to vote on company policy, although generally, for smaller shareholders, this right doesn't convey much power. Stock shares can be common or preferred. Common stock carries voting rights, whereas preferred stock pays a higher dividend in return for an absence of voting rights. There are other fundamental differences between common and preferred shares that are outside the scope of this course. A shareholder can, however, attend the firm's shareholder meeting and ask questions of the firm's officers. Exhibit 5 shows a stock certificate certifying that the holder (who's named on the certificate's face) owns a specified number of shares in the firm—in this case, 120 shares of Cyprus Minerals. This is a valuable certificate, printed on special paper, which will last indefinitely without turning yellow or crumbling away. If the stock certificate is lost or stolen, the owner's investment will still be safe because no one can sell a stock certificate unless the owner has endorsed it on the back (somewhat like a cheque), which she should not do until the moment she's ready to sell it or confer it as a gift. If a stock certificate is lost or destroyed, the owner can get another one from the company because the company keeps a list of its owners (the people who own stock) and their addresses, but the owner must pay a fee.

Stock   A partial ownership right to a company.

The owner of a stock can sell it at any time she pleases, provided someone wants to buy it. She will get whatever the going price is at the moment her sale is closed, minus a commission to the broker. Or she can keep it, hoping that its price will go up and it will be worth more. If the company is paying dividends (periodic payments to

EXHIBIT 5   A Stock Certificate
Stock certificates generally look impressive to make holders think they have something valuable. Recently there has been a move to replace certificates with computer entries, but somehow a computer entry doesn't give one a feeling of real value. Most people care about such things; large companies, that hold much of the stock on the exchange, don't. They prefer computer entries.

The floor of a stock exchange is often a hectic place. *Canapress Photo Service.*

owners of its stock), every three months she gets a cheque for those dividends. She doesn't have to do anything to get these cheques—the company mails them automatically to "the shareholder of record."

Stocks have no maturity date. The money you paid for them never has to be paid back to you. Stocks require no periodic payments to you every year. So it's possible

THE TSE 300

Of all the current economic institutions, perhaps the one you hear most about is Bay Street. Bay Street is a real street in Toronto, but the term *Bay Street* is often used to refer to the entire financial sector. Probably the most important institution on Bay Street is the Toronto Stock Exchange, where ownership rights in corporations are traded. These ownership rights are called *stocks*. Stocks are also called *shares,* because they represent the share of a business the stockholder owns. While individuals who own stocks are chiefly interested in the price of shares they own, they also want to know the general movement of prices in the market as a whole.

A measure indicating this is the TSE 300 Index. It is an average of the prices of 300 different stocks traded on the Toronto Stock Exchange. Investors watch the TSE 300 for signs of boom and bust.

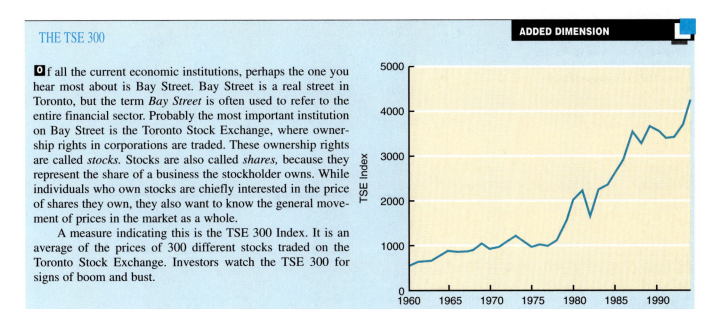

to buy a stock and get nothing for it. So why would anyone buy a stock? Because with it come ownership rights—all the company's income that isn't paid out to factors of production belongs to the stockholders. For example, say you own one share of the million shares Cyprus Minerals has issued, and after paying all costs and debts due, Cyprus Minerals has $6 million in after-tax profits. Your percentage of that $6 million is $6. This $6 can be paid out to stockholders in dividends. Or the company can retain the $6 (which would then be called *retained earnings*), in which case the stock's value will likely increase because the firm can invest the retained earnings and earn more profit. (An increase in the value of a stock is called a *capital gain.*) The company's board of directors decides which option the company will follow.

Notice that a share of stock gives you the right to a percentage of the company's profits this year and all future years. Because it does, the price of a stock depends upon investors' opinions of a company's prospects. A company with excellent prospects sells for a high price; a company whose prospects are dim sells for a low price. What's high? What's low? That depends. A rough rule of thumb is to take a multiple of the company's earnings (its *earnings per share*) to determine the price a person would be willing to pay for a share. For instance, "15 times earnings" means a share is selling for 15 times the company's annual earnings divided by the number of shares outstanding. If Cyprus Minerals in our previous example was expected to continue earning $6 a share, and stock buyers applied the 15-times-earnings rule of thumb, the stock would sell for $90 a share.

An average company stock sells for somewhere around 10 times earnings. (This average price/earnings ratio fluctuates somewhat over time.) A company with excellent future prospects might sell for 30 or 40 times earnings. A company with poor prospects might sell for a mere 2 or 3 times earnings. The price/earnings ratio for a company is reported in the newspaper stock tables.

Bonds   A bond is a promise of the bond-issuer to pay interest of a certain amount at specified intervals (usually annually) to the bondholder and to pay the bond's face value when the bond matures. Bonds are different from stocks. They generally have a maturity date when borrowers pay back the money.

A bond's value depends on a bond's face value and its coupon rate (the interest rate stated on the bond). For example, a bond could have a face value of $5,000 and a

The divergent interests of debtors and creditors are nicely captured in this late 19th-century drawing by W. W. Chenery. *Bleichroeder Print Collection, Baker Library, Harvard Business School.*

coupon rate of 12.75 percent per year. That means that the bondholder would receive $637.50 each year in interest payments. When the bond matures, the bondholder would receive $5,000.

Also printed on every bond is the *maturity date*—for the sake of argument, let's suppose it's October 1, 2002. There's no sense hanging onto that bond after October 1, 2002, because after that its interest is all used up.

If you need the money from the bond before the maturity date, you'll enter into the secondary bond market. Call your bond broker and ask what your bond is selling for. What price you will get depends in large part on the interest rate.

Generally when bonds are issued, their coupon rate is close to the market interest rate prevailing in the economy for bonds of similar risk. These bonds sell *at par* (at their face value). If market interest rates rise, the future stream of income becomes worth less and the bond sells at a discount (at less than its face value). If the market interest rate falls, the future stream of income becomes worth more and the bond sells at a premium (at more than its face value).

Exhibit 6 shows a bond table. Let's see what it tells us. Government of Canada bonds, the first bond issue on the list, pay a coupon rate of 4.75 percent annual interest and come due on March 15, 1996. On Wednesday, April 20, 1994, they sold for $95.865 for every $100 of their par value (the value stated on the bond), which means that their yield (the net interest rate you get if you buy the bond at the closing price) was 7.115 percent. Every year you would get $6.82 from the bond that cost you $95.865. Dividing $6.82 by $95.865 gives 7.115 percent.

At the time the bond table in Exhibit 6 appeared, 7.115 percent was lower than the interest rate on corporate bonds in Canada. This reflects the view that there's little chance the Canadian government will go bankrupt and that there is some small positive chance that some corporations might default on their bonds. Notice some other bonds in the table are selling at premiums. They were issued with a face value of $100, but their current prices are over $100. If you sell a BC Telephone bond for $105.375 but paid only $100 for it, you make a gain of $5.375 on the sale price, but the new owner's yield or net annual interest per dollar is lower than the 9.65 percent stated coupon rate on these bonds. That's because 9.65 percent of $100 is $9.65, but $9.65 as a percentage of $105.375 is only 9.15 percent. This 9.15 percent is the bond's yield (note that's not the 9.115 yield that was reported, since in the exhibit yields are calculated to full maturity).

Capital gains and losses aren't limited to stock. They can occur with any asset—financial or real. A capital gain or loss is simply the change in the value of an asset.

Noneconomists often call capital gains and losses *paper gains and losses* because no money changes hands as the gain or loss occurs. Often you'll hear, "Oh, it's only a paper loss," as if somehow a capital loss wasn't quite as bad as a loss that has to be paid for in money. It's the same for a "paper gain," which they feel isn't as good as a gain that puts money in your pocket.

Economists don't use the "paper" terminology. They emphasize the opportunity cost concept. When you have a capital gain, you have the option of realizing that gain by selling the asset for the increased price. The opportunity cost of not selling that asset is the price of that asset including the capital gain. Say the price of a share of Cyprus Minerals goes from $21 to $30. If you sell the share, you get $9 (minus transaction costs) in your pocket. If you don't sell the share, the cost of not selling the share is $30. If you didn't sell the share at $21, the cost of not selling it was only $21. Thus, using the opportunity cost framework, a capital gain or loss is as real as any other gain or loss.

EXHIBIT 6   A Bond Table

Source: The *Globe and Mail*, Thursday, April 21, 1994.

CANADIAN BONDS

Selected quotations, with changes since the previous day, on actively traded bond issues, provided by RBC Dominion Securities. Yields are calculated to full maturity, unless marked C to indicate callable date. Price is the midpoint between final bid and ask quotations April 20, 1994.

Issuer	Coupon	Maturity	Price	Yield	$ Chg
GOVERNMENT OF CANADA					
CANADA	4.75	15 MAR 96	95.885	7.115	+0.090
CANADA	6.50	1 AUG 96	98.425	7.255	+0.050
CANADA	7.50	1 JUL 97	99.950	7.512	+0.050
CANADA	6.25	1 FEB 96	95.450	7.659	+0.100
CANADA	6.50	1 SEP 96	95.650	7.693	+0.150
CANADA	5.75	1 MAR 99	92.100	7.733	+0.150
CANADA	9.25	1 DEC 99	106.175	7.862	+0.200
CANADA	11.50	1 SEP 00	117.175	7.992	+0.300
CANADA	9.75	1 JUN 01	109.050	8.048	+0.300
CANADA	9.50	1 OCT 01	107.875	8.066	+0.350
CANADA	9.75	1 DEC 01	109.350	8.077	+0.350
CANADA	8.50	1 APR 02	102.200	8.117	+0.300
CANADA	10.00	1 MAY 02	110.725	8.150	+0.350
CANADA	11.75	1 FEB 03	121.175	8.219	+0.400
CANADA	7.25	1 JUN 03	94.200	8.164	+0.350
CANADA	7.50	1 DEC 03	96.550	8.176	+0.360
CANADA	10.25	1 FEB 04	113.150	8.187	+0.400
CANADA	6.50	1 JUN 04	86.550	8.187	+0.400
CANADA	10.00	1 JUN 08	112.600	8.452	+0.550
CANADA	9.50	1 JUN 10	108.550	8.513	+0.550
CANADA	9.00	1 MAR 11	104.100	8.534	+0.550
CANADA	10.25	15 MAR 14	115.900	8.569	+0.950
CANADA	9.75	1 JUN 21	112.050	8.595	+0.800
CANADA	8.00	1 JUN 23	94.300	8.532	+0.700
CMHC	6.00	1 DEC 96	92.850	7.882	+0.150
REAL RETURNS	4.25	1 DEC 21	100.750	4.204	NC
PROVINCIAL					
ALBERTA	7.00	20 AUG 97	98.075	7.663	+0.050
ALBERTA	7.75	4 FEB 98	99.600	7.869	+0.100
ALBERTA	7.75	5 MAY 03	95.486	8.475	+0.350
BC	7.00	2 MAR 98	97.150	7.868	+0.100
BC	9.00	9 JAN 02	103.075	8.445	+0.250
BC	7.75	16 JUN 03	95.350	8.469	+0.350
BC	8.50	23 AUG 13	96.250	8.906	+0.700
BC	8.75	19 AUG 22	97.525	8.990	+0.450
HYDRO QUEBEC	9.25	2 DEC 96	103.575	7.700	+0.50
HYDRO QUEBEC	10.88	25 JUL 01	110.875	8.807	+0.350
HYDRO QUEBEC	11.00	15 AUG 26	114.075	9.529	+0.700
HYDRO QUEBEC	9.63	15 JUL 22	100.625	9.558	+0.650
MANITOBA	6.75	24 AUG 95	99.475	7.161	NC
MANITOBA	9.25	21 MAY 97	104.050	7.737	+0.050
MANITOBA	7.86	7 APR 03	95.575	8.593	+0.350
MANITOBA	10.50	5 MAR 31	114.950	9.066	+0.800
NEW BRUNSWIC	7.00	17 MAR 96	96.900	7.939	+0.100
NEW BRUNSWIC	8.36	25 AUG 02	96.550	8.619	+0.250
NEW BRUNSWIC	8.50	26 JUN 13	95.225	9.026	+0.700
NEWFOUNDLAND	10.13	22 NOV 14	105.425	9.518	+0.560
NOVA SCOTIA	9.60	30 JAN 22	101.775	9.416	+0.650
ONTARIO HYD	10.88	8 JAN 96	105.450	7.366	+0.120
ONTARIO HYD	7.25	31 MAR 96	97.325	8.056	+0.100
ONTARIO HYD	9.63	3 AUG 99	105.950	8.206	+0.150
ONTARIO HYD	8.63	6 FEB 02	99.575	8.697	+0.250

Issuer	Coupon	Maturity	Price	Yield	$ Chg
GOVERNMENT OF CANADA					
ONTARIO HYD	9.00	24 JUN 02	101.525	8.731	+0.250
ONTARIO HYD	8.90	16 AUG 22	96.725	9.225	+0.750
ONTARIO	8.75	16 APR 97	102.515	7.783	+0.040
ONTARIO	8.00	11 MAR 03	95.325	8.765	+0.350
ONTARIO	9.50	13 JUL 22	102.625	9.234	+0.700
P E I	9.75	30 APR 02	104.425	8.964	+0.250
P E I	11.00	19 SEP 11	113.800	9.374	+0.750
QUEBEC	8.00	30 MAR 96	99.475	8.156	+0.150
QUEBEC	10.25	7 APR 96	106.775	8.202	+0.150
QUEBEC	10.25	15 OCT 01	107.600	8.837	+0.350
QUEBEC	9.38	16 JAN 23	98.175	9.560	+0.600
SAKATCHEWAN	8.13	4 FEB 97	100.750	7.811	+0.050
SAKATCHEWAN	9.60	4 FEB 22	101.900	9.403	+0.650
TORONTO -MET	10.38	4 SEP 01	108.950	8.698	-0.300
CORPORATE					
ALTA ENERGY	8.15	31 JUL 03	95.375	8.890	+0.250
BELL CANADA	9.50	15 JUN 02	104.425	8.726	+0.250
BELL CANADA	9.70	15 DEC 32	105.125	9.211	+0.750
BELL CDA ENT	7.13	1 MAY 98	96.875	8.052	+0.125
BC GAS	8.15	26 JUL 03	95.375	8.890	+0.250
BC TELEPHONE	9.65	8 APR 22	105.375	9.115	+0.750
BANK OF N S	8.10	24 MAR 03	96.500	8.670	+0.375
CDN IMP BANK	7.10	10 MAR 04	89.625	8.664	+0.375
CDN UTIL	9.40	1 MAY 23	102.875	9.116	+0.625
IMASCO LTD	8.38	23 JUN 03	97.00	8.857	+0.250
INTERPRV PIP	8.20	15 FEB 24	90.00	9.184	+0.625
MOLSON BREW	8.20	11 MAR 03	96.500	8.773	+0.375
MOLSON BREW	8.40	7 DEC 18	91.575	9.274	+0.625
NATIONAL BNK	7.50	30 DEC 03	90.500	9.987	+0.375
NVA SCOT PWR	6.50	15 DEC 98	93.875	9.108	+0.250
NVA SCOT PWR	7.70	15 OCT 03	93.125	8.874	+0.375
NRTH TELECOM	7.45	10 MAR 96	97.750	8.135	+0.125
NOVA CORP	8.30	15 JUL 03	96.250	8.901	+0.375
ROYAL BANK	10.50	1 MAR 02	110.125	8.689	+0.250
SUNCOR INC	7.40	23 FEB 04	90.625	8.845	+0.500
TRANSALTA UT	7.25	15 DEC 03	91.075	8.631	+0.375
TELEGLOBE	8.35	20 JUN 03	96.750	8.873	+0.375
THOMSON CORP	7.70	15 DEC 03	92.875	8.810	+0.375
TRANSCDA PIP	9.45	20 MAR 18	101.750	9.265	+0.625
UNION GAS	8.75	3 AUG 18	94.125	9.364	+0.625
WSRCOAST TRN	8.30	30 DEC 13	91.625	9.228	+0.625

BENCHMARK INTERNATIONAL BONDS

Issuer	Coupon	Maturity	Price	Yield	$ Chg
U.S. Treasury	6¼	Aug/23	87 4/32	7.32+	17/32
British gilt	9	Oct/08	108 16/32	7.94	-29/32
German	6¼	Sep/04	97.16	6.65	-0.62
Japan # 157	4.5	2003	103.20	4.02	+0.04

Name of bond

Coupon rate

Maturity date

Current price

Change in closing price of previous day

Yield calculated to maturity

ADDED DIMENSION

WHAT WILL A BOND SELL FOR?

To determine what a bond will sell for, first remember a bond is a flow of payments over time. Its selling price depends on how much those payments are worth. If it's unlikely those payments will continue (for example, if the company issuing the bond is close to bankruptcy), the bond isn't worth much. This *risk* plays an important role in determining the bond's price.

A second factor in determining a bond's price is the current interest rate in the economy. If the interest rate today (for bonds of similar riskiness) is higher than the bond's coupon rate (which generally represents the interest rate that existed when the bond was originally issued), a bond will sell for less than its face value on the secondary market. Why? Because if it sold at its face value, it would make more sense for people to buy newly issued bonds paying higher interest rates. When a bond sells for less than its face value, its yield (the rate of return you receive per dollar of purchase price per year from a bond) increases. For example, say there's a one-year 5 percent coupon bond with $100 face value, and this bond is selling for $50. For $50 you'll get a $5 payment (5 percent of $100). That comes out to a 10 percent yield.

If the interest rate is lower than the coupon rate, bonds will sell for more than their face value. Why? Because at its face value, the bond is much more desirable than newly issued bonds. The market value of the bond will rise until the yield on the bond equals the interest rate on similar newly issued bonds. Only then will the buyer be indifferent between the old and new bonds.

Because of this relationship between interest rates and bond prices, generally whenever market interest rates rise, bond prices fall; whenever market interest rates fall, bond prices rise. Thus, the interest rate in the economy plays an important role in determining a bond's price on the secondary market.

THE VALUE OF A FINANCIAL ASSET

5   When the interest rate falls, the present value of a dollar to be received in the future rises, so you are willing to pay more for the promise to receive that future dollar (a bond). When the interest rate rises, the present value of that future dollar falls, so you are willing to pay less for the promise to receive that future dollar (a bond).

Present Value and Interest Rate

Present value   Method of translating a flow of future income or savings into its current worth.

To understand financial assets, you must understand how financial asset prices are determined. Why does an average share of stock sell for about 15 times earnings? Why do bond prices rise as market interest rates fall, and fall as market interest rates rise? In answering such questions, the first point to recognize is that $1 today is not equal to $1 next year. Why? Because if we have $1 today we can invest it and earn interest (say 10 percent per year), and next year we will have $1.10, not $1. So if the annual interest rate is 10 percent, $1.10 next year is worth $1 today or, alternatively, $1 next year is worth roughly 91 cents today. A dollar two years in the future is worth even less today, and dollars 30 years in the future are worth very little today.

How much less $1 in the future is worth today depends on the interest rate. If the interest rate is close to zero, $1 is worth only a little bit less; if the interest rate is 5 percent, $1 is worth quite a bit less. The higher the interest rate, the less a dollar is worth in the future. How do we know? Because we pulled out our handy business calculators and pressed in the numbers to calculate the **present value** (the value now of income payments in the future).

Exhibit 7 graphically displays, for three different annual interest rates, how much a given amount of money at various lengths of time in the future is worth now. Notice that: (1) the higher the interest rate, the less a given amount of money in the future is worth now; and (2) the present value falls quickly at higher annual interest rates. At 15 percent interest, $100 thirty years from now is currently worth $1.50, as shown in Exhibit 7(c).

The present value reasoning also works in reverse. You can determine the future value of a given amount of money today. Say you have $100 now. If you earn 8 percent annual interest on it, it will be $215.89 in 10 years and $466.10 in 20 years. The higher the interest rate and the longer the time frame, the greater the future value will be.

Most of you, we suspect, don't have business calculators. For people who don't,

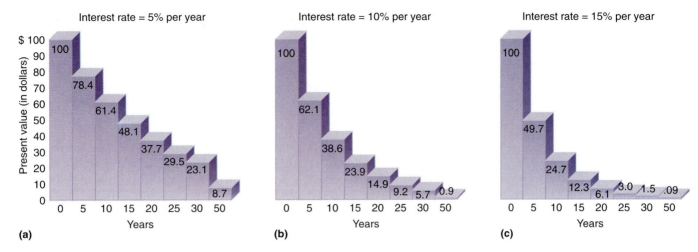

EXHIBIT 7   Present Value of $100 to Be Received a Certain Number of Years in the Future

The present value of money in the future declines as the interest rate increases. Notice how once the interest rate hits 10% or more as in (**b**) and (**c**), the present value of money to be received 50 years in the future is close to worthless.

there are bond tables to tell you present values of future dollars. A table or a calculator is extremely helpful in determining the price a bond should sell for. That's because a bond consists of a stream of income payments over a number of years and the repayment of the face value of the bond. Each year's interest payment and the eventual repayment of the face value must be calculated separately and then the results added together.

All financial assets can be broken down into promises to pay certain amounts at certain times in the future, or, if the financial asset is a share of stock, not a promise but an expectation of such payment. So all financial assets (stocks or bonds) can be valued. You simply calculate the present value of all expected future payments. For example, say a share of stock is earning $1 per share and is expected to do so long into the future. If the interest rate is 6.5 percent, the present value of that future stream of expected earnings is about $15. With this knowledge, let's return to our question, "Why do stocks generally sell for 15 times earnings?" We now have an answer. It's because that's roughly what the present value formula says they should sell for.

There is, however, a proviso to the preceding reasoning. If promises to pay aren't trustworthy, you don't put the amount that's promised into your calculation; you put in the amount you expect. That's why when a company or a country looks as if it's going to default on loans or stop paying dividends, the value of its bonds and stock will fall considerably. For example, in the late 1980s many people thought Brazil would default on its bonds. That expectation caused the price of Brazilian bonds to fall to about 40¢ on the dollar. Then in the 1990s, when people believed total default was less likely, the value rose.

6 Present value is the current value of a future amount of money. As the interest rate rises, the present value of a future amount of money falls.

This chapter isn't meant to cover the intricacies of valuation over time. That's done in a finance course. The point of this chapter is to help you understand the relationship between interest rates and asset prices. Increases in interest rates (because they make future flows of income coming from an asset worth less now) make financial asset prices fall. Decreases in interest rates (because they make the future flow of income coming from an asset worth more now) make financial asset prices rise.

Since a slight change in interest rates can lead to a large change in asset prices, many individuals speculate on what's going to happen to interest rates and switch their investments from one type of financial asset to another, causing potential problems for

Asset Prices, Interest Rates, and the Economy

the macroeconomy. So understanding how assets are valued is fundamental to understanding the macroeconomic debate.

We've covered a lot of material quickly, so the institutions discussed may be a bit of a blur in your mind. To get a better idea of how these financial markets work, let's follow two transactions you'll likely make in your lifetime and see how they work their way through the financial system.

LEADING YOU THROUGH TWO FINANCIAL TRANSACTIONS

Insuring Your Car

You want to drive. The law requires you to have insurance, so you go to two or three insurance companies, get quotes of their rates, and choose the one offering the lowest rate. Say it costs you $800 for the year. You write a cheque for $800 and hand the cheque to the insurance agent who keeps a commission (let's say $80) and then sends her cheque for $720 to the insurance company. The insurance company has $720 more sitting in the bank than it had before you paid your insurance premium.

The insurance company earns income in two ways: (1) in the difference between the money it receives in payments and the claims it pays out, and (2) in the interest it makes on its financial assets. What does the company use to buy these financial assets? It has payments from its customers (your $720, for example) available because payments come in long before claims are paid out.

Because earnings on financial assets are an important source of an insurance company's income, your $720 doesn't stay in the insurance company's bank for long. The insurance company has a financial assets division which chooses financial assets it believes have the highest returns for the risk the assets involve. Bond salesmen telephone the financial assets division offering to sell bonds. Similarly, developers who want to build shopping malls or ski resorts go to the financial assets division, offering an opportunity to participate (really asking to borrow money).

The financial assets division might decide to lend your $720 (along with $10 million more) to a mall developer who builds in suburban locations. The division transfers the $720 to the mall developer and receives a four-year, 12 percent promissory note (a promise to pay the $720 back in four years along with $86.40 per year in interest payments). The promissory note is a financial asset of the insurance company and a financial liability of the developer. When the developer spends the money, the $720 leaves the financial sector and reenters the spending stream in the real economy. At that point it becomes investment in the economic sense.

Buying a House

Mortgage A special name for a secured loan on real estate.

Most people, when they buy a house, don't go out and pay the thousands of dollars it costs in cash. Instead they go to a bank or similar financial institution and borrow a large portion of the sales price, taking out a mortgage on the house. A **mortgage** is simply a special name for a secured loan on real estate. By mortgaging her house, a person is creating a financial liability for herself and a financial asset for someone else. This financial asset is secured by the house. If the person defaults on the loan, the mortgage holder can foreclose on the mortgage and take title to the house.

The funds available in banks come primarily from depositors who keep their savings in the bank in the form of savings accounts or chequing accounts. Balances in these accounts are often small, but with lots of depositors they add up and provide banks with money to lend out. If you're planning to buy a house, you'll most likely go to a bank.

The bank's loan officer will have you fill in a lengthy form, and the bank will send an appraiser out to the house to assess its value. The appraiser asks questions about the house: Does it meet the electrical code? What kind of pipes does it have? What kind of windows does it have? Information about you and the house is transferred onto a master form that the loan officer uses to decide whether to make the loan. (Contrary to what many lay people believe, in normal times a loan officer wants to make the loan. Remember, a bank's profits are the difference between what it pays in interest and what it receives in interest; it needs to make loans to make profits. So he or she often looks at hazy answers on the form and puts an interpretation on them that's favourable to making the loan.)

In a week or so, depending on how busy the bank is, you hear back that the loan is approved for, say, $80,000 at 9 percent interest. The bank credits your account with $80,000, which allows you to write a cheque to the seller of the house at a meeting called the *closing*.

We could go through other transactions, but these two should give you a sense of how real-world financial transactions work their way through financial institutions. Financial institutions make money by the fees and commissions they charge, and on the difference between the interest they pay to get the money and the interest they receive when they lend the money out.

Now that you have a sense of the financial sector, let's briefly consider how it fits into the macroeconomic models and debates discussed in earlier chapters. The debate was between Classicals who believed government should follow a laissez-faire policy and Keynesians who believed government should take an activist role in controlling the aggregate economy with policies such as fiscal policy.

Classical economists see the financial sector operating relatively smoothly. It is like a mirror that reflects the real sector, and as long as government doesn't disturb that mirror the financial sector won't be a problem. That's why Classical economists said that savings will be translated into investment relatively smoothly and that the Keynesian problem of insufficient demand wouldn't arise. Say's law is based on a smoothly working financial sector.

Exhibit 8 (a) shows the Classical view of the financial market. The supply of savings is upward sloping, and the demand for investment is downward sloping. The interest rate adjusts to maintain savings equal to investment at the full-employment level of income.

Because Classicals see the financial sector working smoothly, they generally oppose any meddling with the financial system (last-ditch loans to companies about to go out of business, credit controls, limitation on interest rates, and other government involvement in financial markets).

Keynesian economists see the financial sector differently. While they also see the financial sector as a mirror, often it's more like a reflecting pond with waves. These waves in the financial sector can have serious repercussions in the real sector. Specifically, Keynesians do not believe that the financial market efficiently translates savings into investment. Sometimes, because the financial sector isn't working correctly, there's too much savings; sometimes there's too little savings. When the financial sector fails to translate savings back into investment, the quantity of aggregate supply differs from the quantity of aggregate demand. When this occurs, the multiplier process starts, causing unwanted business cycles. Put simply, Keynesians believe the financial sector can get messed up, and when it gets messed up it messes up the real economy too.

The Keynesian view of financial markets can best be seen in Exhibit 8 (b). In it you can see that the supply of savings is relatively vertical—the interest rate doesn't have much effect on it. Similarly with the demand for investment. Keynes argued that investment was not a simple decision based on interest rates but was a difficult decision based on expectations of the future and gut feelings. Why are the shapes of these curves important? Because those shapes tell us how much the interest rate must change to bring the financial market back into equilibrium. If the curves are relatively vertical (as Keynesians believe) and there's a shift in demand for investment from I_0 to I_1, the interest rate must change enormously (from i_0 to i_1) to bring the economy back into equilibrium. Such large interest rate fluctuations would cause serious problems in the financial sector.

If a change in the interest rate doesn't bring about equilibrium in the savings/investment market, what does? Changes in income. Since saving often doesn't equal investment, the result is income fluctuations in the real economy. Those fluctu-

Summary

WHY FINANCIAL INSTITUTIONS ARE IMPORTANT FOR MACROECONOMICS

The Classical View of the Financial Sector

The Keynesian View of the Financial Sector

7 Classicals believe the financial market works efficiently; Keynesians believe it often gets messed up.

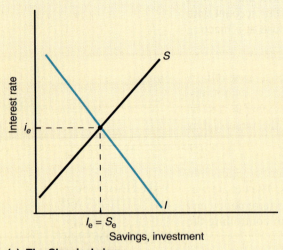

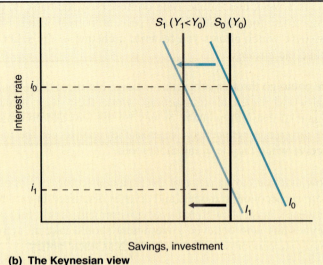

(a) The Classical view

(b) The Keynesian view

EXHIBIT 8   The Classical View of the Financial Sector and the Keynesian View of the Financial Sector

Classical economists see the financial market working smoothly so that savings and investment would always be equal. If they weren't, the interest rate would change so they were equal. Since savings always equal investment, there can be no Keynesian-type multiplier process.

Keynesians see financial markets working in fits and starts and often staying in disequilibrium for long periods of time. If the interest rate adjusts, it does so slowly. Before the interest rate adjusts to bring savings and investment into equilibrium, the multiplier process would be set in motion, causing income to shift and the savings curve to shift. Shifts in the savings curve, not changes in the interest rate, bring about equilibrium in the Keynesian model.

ations change income and hence savings. Equilibrium between savings and investment is brought about by the savings curve shifting (shown in Exhibit 8 (b) as the shift from S_0 to S_1) as income falls from Y_0 to Y_1.

If the interest rate isn't determined in the savings/investment market in the Keynesian model, where is it determined? Keynesians believe it's determined in the money market, by people's demand for highly liquid assets and the supply of those liquid assets, specifically money. This means that a change in the money supply could affect interest rates and could play a role in equilibrating savings and investment.

We'll discuss these questions more in later chapters. Before we do, we'll take a much closer look at how one particular financial institution—banks—and one particular financial asset—money—fit into the macroeconomic landscape.

CHAPTER SUMMARY

- Every financial asset has a corresponding financial liability.
- Financial institutions buy, sell, or hold financial assets.
- Primary financial markets sell newly issued financial assets. Secondary financial markets transfer existing financial assets from one individual to another.
- Financial assets with a maturity of less than three years (such as treasury bills and commercial paper) are sold in money markets. Financial assets with a maturity of over three years (such as bonds and mortgages) are sold on capital markets. They usually pay a higher rate of return

than money market assets because they are less liquid.
- Bonds pay a fixed interest on an investment each year until maturity, at which point the face value is paid.
- Stocks have no maturity date, pay no interest, and do not return your original investment, but they give you ownership rights to a company and, thus, its profits.
- Present value is the current value of a future amount of money. As the interest rate rises, the present value of a future amount of money falls.
- Classicals believe the financial market works efficiently; Keynesians believe it often gets messed up.

KEY TERMS

bonds *(285)*
capital market *(287)*
commercial paper *(285)*
contractual intermediary *(282)*
depository institution *(282)*
disintermediation *(289)*

diversification *(285)*
financial asset *(281)*
financial institution *(282)*
financial liability *(281)*
financial market *(286)*
liquidity *(287)*

money market *(287)*
mortgage *(296)*
present value *(294)*
primary financial market *(286)*
secondary financial market *(286)*
stock *(289)*

QUESTIONS FOR THOUGHT AND REVIEW

The number after each question represents the estimated degree of critical thinking required. (1 = almost none; 10 = deep thought.)

1. Is the cash in your pocketbook or wallet a real or a financial asset? Why? *(3)*

2. If financial institutions don't produce any tangible real assets, why are they considered a vital part of the economy? *(4)*

3. Which market, the primary or secondary, contributes more to the production of tangible real assets? Explain why. *(4)*

4. Why do money market assets generally yield lower interest payments than capital assets? *(3)*

5. Suppose that in 1990 you bought a newly issued bond with a $10,000 face value, a coupon rate of 9 percent, and a maturity date of 2020. How much interest would it pay each year? If the interest rate in the economy is 8 percent, would the bond be likely to sell for more or less than $10,000? *(4)*

6. Consider a company whose stock sells for $24 a share, has about $2 million in annual earnings, and has a million shares outstanding. What's that firm's price/earnings ratio? *(3)*

7. If a bond with a $5,000 face value and a 7.5 percent coupon rate is selling on the secondary bond market for $4,000, what can you say about the interest rate in the economy? *(2)*

8. A candidate for prime minister favours little government intervention in the economy. Would Classicals or Keynesians be more likely to support her candidacy? Why? *(3)*

9. How might a Keynesian economist explain a stock market crash? *(5)*

10. How might a Classical economist explain a stock market crash? *(9)*

PROBLEMS AND EXERCISES

1. A bond has a face value of $10,000 and a coupon rate of 10 percent. It is issued in 1991 and matures in 2001.
   a. How much does the bond pay annually?
   b. If the bond is currently selling for $9,000, what is its yield?
   c. If the interest rate in the economy rises, what will happen to the bond's price? Why?

2. Go to a local bank.
   a. Ask for a loan application. Inquire if you will be eligible for a loan.
   b. Ask why or why not.
   c. Find out how many different types of accounts they have and how these accounts differ.
   d. Ask if they will cash a $1,000 out-of-province cheque. If so, how long will it take for them to do so?

3. For the following financial instruments, state for whom it

is a liability and for whom it is an asset. Also state whether the transaction occurred on the capital or money markets.
   a. Lamar opens a $100 chequing account at his credit union.
   b. First Bank grants a mortgage to Sandra.
   c. Sean purchases a $100 jacket using his credit card with First Bank.
   d. The city of Calgary issues $1 billion in municipal bonds, most of which were purchased by Calgary residents, to build a community centre.
   e. Investment broker sells 100 shares of existing stock to Lanier.
   f. Investment broker sells 1,000 shares of new-issue stock to Lanier.

4. Your employer offers you a choice of two bonus packages: $1,400 today or $2,000 five years from now. Assuming a

5 percent rate of interest, which is the better value? Assuming an interest rate of 10 percent, which is the better value?

5. State whether you agree or disagree with the following statements and explain why:

  a. If stock market prices go up, the economy is richer.

  b. A real asset worth $1,000,000 is more valuable to an individual than a financial asset worth $1,000,000.

  c. Financial assets have no value to society since each such asset has a corresponding liability.

  d. Canada has much more land than does Japan. Therefore, the value of all Canadian land should significantly exceed the value of land in Japan.

  e. United States GDP exceeds Canada's GDP; therefore, the stock market valuation of U.S.-based companies should exceed that of Canadian-based companies.

12

Money and Banking

The process by which banks create money is so simple that the mind is repelled.

~John Kenneth Galbraith

After reading this chapter, you should be able to:

1 Explain what money is.

2 Enumerate the three functions of money.

3 State the alternative definitions of money and their primary components.

4 Explain how banks create money.

5 Calculate both the simple and the approximate real-world money multipliers.

6 Explain how a financial panic can occur and the potential problem with government guarantees to prevent such panics.

The financial institutions and assets discussed in the previous chapter are many and complicated. Each has its own peculiarities and interrelationships with the economy. Absorbing as our overview of them was, we suspect you've had enough, and if we tried to present in its entirety the debate between Keynesians and Classicals about the financial sector that was introduced at the end of the last chapter, we would soon send you into a mental institution or at least into psychology or sociology.

So instead, to simplify, we will follow the usual practice and focus on one of a group of the most important financial assets, which collectively are called *money,* and on a single financial institution, banks, which directly affect money.

THE DEFINITION AND FUNCTIONS OF MONEY

1 Money is a financial asset that makes the real economy function smoothly by serving as a medium of exchange, a unit of account, a standard of deferred payment, and a store of wealth.

Money   A highly liquid financial asset that's generally accepted in exchange for other goods and is used as a reference in valuing other goods.

Bank of Canada   Canada's central bank, its liabilities serve as cash in Canada.

At this point you're probably saying, "I know what money is; it's cash—the loonies and dollar bills I carry around." In one sense you're right; cash is money. But in another sense you're wrong. Money is much more than cash. In fact, a number of short-term financial assets are included as money. To see why, let's consider the definition and uses of money and then see which financial assets meet that definition.

The definition is as follows: **Money** is a highly liquid financial asset that's generally accepted in exchange for other goods and is used as a reference in valuing other goods. Consider a five-dollar bill that you know is money. Look at it; it states on it that it is issued by the Bank of Canada, which means that it is an IOU (a liability) of the **Bank of Canada,** which is the Canadian central bank. (We'll discuss the Bank of Canada in depth in the next chapter, but at this point all you need know is that the Bank of Canada's liabilities serve as cash in Canada.)

Functions of Money

2 The three functions of money are:
1. Medium of exchange;
2. Unit of account; a standard of deferred payment; and
3. Store of wealth.

From the previous chapter we know what a liquid financial asset is. It's an asset that can be quickly exchanged for another good. But the definition of money also requires that these financial assets are generally accepted in exchange for other goods and are used as a reference in valuing other goods. This definition says money serves three functions:

1. It serves as a medium of exchange.
2. It serves as a unit of account and a standard of deferred payment.
3. It serves as a store of wealth.

To get a better understanding of what money is, let's consider each in turn.

Money as a Medium of Exchange
The easiest way to understand money's medium-of-exchange use is to imagine what an economy would be like without money. Say you want something to eat at a restaurant. Without money you'd have to barter with the restaurant owner for your meal. *Barter* is a direct exchange of goods and/or services. You might suggest bartering one of your papers or the shirt in the sack that you'd be forced to carry with you to trade for things you want. Not liking to carry big sacks around, you'd probably decide to fix your own meal and forego eating out. Bartering is simply too difficult.

The use of money as a medium of exchange makes it possible to trade real goods and services without bartering. It facilitates exchange by reducing the cost of trading. Instead of carrying around a sack full of goods, all you need to carry around is a billfold full of money. You go into the restaurant and pay for your meal with money; the restaurant owner can spend (trade) that money for anything she wants.

Money doesn't have to have any inherent value to function as a medium of exchange. All that's necessary is that everyone believes that other people will accept it in exchange for their goods. This neat social convention makes the economy more efficient.

That social convention depends on there not being too much or too little money. If there's too much money compared to the goods and services offered at existing prices, the goods and services will sell out, and money won't buy you anything. The social convention will break down, or prices will rise. If there's too little money com-

Dies used to create a looney. *Canapress Photo Service.*

pared to the goods and services offered at the existing prices, there will be a shortage of money and people will have to resort to barter, or prices will fall.

In order to maintain money's usefulness and to prevent large fluctuations in the price level, the money issuer, which in Canada is the Bank of Canada, must issue neither too much nor too little money. (As we stated previously, the Bank of Canada is the central bank of Canada; its liabilities serve as money for the Canadian economy.) People accept money in payment and agree to hold money because they believe the Bank of Canada will issue neither too little nor too much money. This explains why the Bank of Canada doesn't freely issue large amounts of money. To issue money without restraint would destroy the social convention that gives money its value.

Money as a Unit of Account and a Standard of Deferred Payment   A second use of money is as a unit of account. As we'll see shortly, this includes the role money plays as a standard of deferred payment. Throughout the book we've emphasized that money prices are actually relative prices. A nominal price, say 25¢, for a pencil conveys the information of a relative price: 1 pencil = 1/4 of 1 dollar or 1/6 of a hamburger because money is both our unit of account and our medium of exchange. When you think of 25¢, you think of 1/4 of a dollar and of what a dollar will buy. The 25¢ a pencil costs only has meaning relative to the information you've stored in your mind about what it can buy. If a hamburger costs $1.50, you can compare hamburgers and pencils (1 pencil = 1/6 of a hamburger) without making the relative price calculations explicitly.

Having a unit of account makes life much easier. For example, say we had no unit of account and you had to remember the relative prices of all goods. For instance, with

CHARACTERISTICS OF A GOOD MONEY

The characteristics of a good money are that its supply be relatively constant, that it be limited in supply (sand wouldn't make good money), that it be difficult to counterfeit, that it be divisible (have you ever tried to spend half a horse?), that it be durable (raspberries wouldn't make good money), and that it be relatively small and light compared to its value (watermelon wouldn't make good money either). All these characteristics were reasonably (but not perfectly) embodied in gold. Many other goods have served as units of account (shells, wampum, rocks, cattle, horses, silver), but gold historically became the most important money, and in the 17th and 18th centuries gold was synonymous with money.

But gold has flaws as money. It's relatively heavy, easy to counterfeit with coins made only partly of gold, and, when new gold fields are discovered, subject to fluctuations in supply. These flaws led to gold's replacement by paper currency backed only by trust that the government would keep its commitment to limit its supply.

Paper money can be a good money if somehow people can trust the government to limit its supply and guarantee that its supply will be limited in the future. That trust has not always been well placed.

three goods you'd have to memorize that an airplane ticket to Kingston, Ontario, costs 6 lobster dinners or 4 pairs of running shoes in Halifax, which makes a pair of shoes worth 1-1/2 lobster dinners in Halifax.

Memorizing even a few relationships is hard enough, so it isn't surprising that societies began using a single unit of account. If you don't have a single unit of account, to know the relative prices of all combinations of just 21 goods you need to remember over a million relative prices. If you have a single unit of account, you need know only 21 prices. A single unit of account saves our limited memories and helps us make reasonable decisions based on relative costs.

Money is a useful unit of account only as long as its value relative to other prices doesn't change too quickly. That's because it's not only used as a unit of account at a point in time, it's also a unit of account *over time*. Money is a standard of deferred payment. The value of payments that will be made in the future (such as the university loan payments many of you will be making in the future) is determined by the future value of money. A hyperinflation would significantly reduce the value of what you have to pay back. So a hyperinflation would help you, right? Actually, probably not—because a hyperinflation would also rapidly destroy money's usefulness as a unit of account and thereby destroy the Canadian economy.

In a hyperinflation, all prices rise so much that our frame of reference is lost. Is 25¢ for a pencil high or low? If the price level changed 33,000 percent (as it did in 1988 in Nicaragua) or over 100,000 percent (as it did in 1993 in Serbia), 25¢ for a pencil would definitely be low, but would $100 be low? Without a lot of calculations we can't answer that question. A relatively stable unit of account makes it easy to answer.

The unit-of-account usefulness of a money also requires that prices don't change too quickly. If the government printed money to pay all its expenses, money's relative price would fall quickly (an increase in supply lowers price), which is another way of saying that the price level would explode and the unit-of-account function of money would be seriously undermined. Maintaining the unit-of-account usefulness of money is a second reason government doesn't pay all its bills by printing money.

Given the advantages to society of having a unit of account, it's not surprising that a monetary unit of account develops even in societies with no government. For example, in a prisoner of war camp during World War II, prisoners had no money, so they used cigarettes as their unit of account. Everything traded was given a price in cigarettes. The exchange rates on December 1, 1944, were:

1 bar of soap: 2 cigarettes

1 candy bar: 4 cigarettes

1 razor blade: 6 cigarettes

1 can of fruit: 8 cigarettes

1 can of cookies: 20 cigarettes

As you can see, all prices were in cigarettes. If candy bars rose to 6 cigarettes and the normal price was 4 cigarettes, you'd know the price of candy bars was high.

Money as a Store of Wealth   In an earlier chapter, we saw that financial assets serve as a store of wealth. Whenever you save, you forgo consumption now so that you can consume in the future. To bridge the gap between now and the future, you must acquire a financial asset. This is true even if you squirrel away cash under the mattress. In that case, the financial asset you've acquired is simply the cash itself. Money is a financial asset. So a third use of money is as a store of wealth. As long as money is serving as a medium of exchange, it automatically also serves as a store of wealth. The restaurant owner can accept your money and hold it for as long as she wants before she spends it. (But had you paid her in fish, she'd be wise not to hold it more than a few hours.)

Money's usefulness as a store of wealth also depends upon how well it maintains its value. If prices are going up 100,000 percent per year, the value of a stated amount of money is shrinking fast. People want to spend their money as quickly as possible before prices rise any more. Thus, once again, money's usefulness as a social convention depends upon the government not issuing too much money.

Even if prices aren't rising, you might wonder why people would hold money which pays no interest, rather than holding a government bond which does pay interest. The reason is that money is more easily translated into other goods than are bonds. Since money is also the medium of exchange, it can be spent instantaneously (as long as there's a shop open nearby). Our ability to spend money for goods makes money worthwhile to hold even if it doesn't pay interest.

According to the definition of *money,* what people believe is money is a determining factor in deciding whether a financial asset is money. What is money depends on what people will accept as money; consequently it's difficult to define *money* unambiguously. A number of different financial assets serve some of the functions of money and thus have claims to being called *money.* To handle this ambiguity, economists have defined different concepts of money and have called them M1, M2, M2+, and M3. Each is a reasonable concept of money. Let's consider their components.

Alternative Definitions of Money

M1   **M1** consists of currency in the hands of the public and chequing account balances at the chartered banks. Clearly, currency in the hands of the public (the bills and coins you carry around with you) is money, but how about your chequing account deposits? The reason they're included in this definition of money is that just about anything you can do with cash, you can do with a cheque. You can store your wealth in your chequing account; you can use a cheque as a medium of exchange (indeed, for some transactions you have no choice but to use a cheque), and your chequing account balance is denominated in the same unit of account (dollars) as is cash. If it looks like money, acts like money, and functions as money, it's a good bet it's money. Indeed, chequing account deposits are included in all definitions of money.

Currency and chequing account deposits make up the components of M1, the narrowest definition of money. Exhibit 1 (a) presents the relative sizes of M1's components.

M1   Component of the money supply that consists of cash in the hands of the public and chequing account balances.

3A   M1 is the component of the money supply that consists of currency in the hands of the public plus chequing accounts at chartered banks.

M2   **M2** is made up of M1 plus personal savings deposits and nonpersonal notice deposits (deposits that can be withdrawn only after prior notice) at the chartered banks. The relative sizes of the components of M2 are given in Exhibit 1 (b). The money in savings accounts (savings deposits) is counted as money because it is readily

M2   Component of the money supply that consists of M1 plus personal savings deposits and nonpersonal notice deposits at the chartered banks.

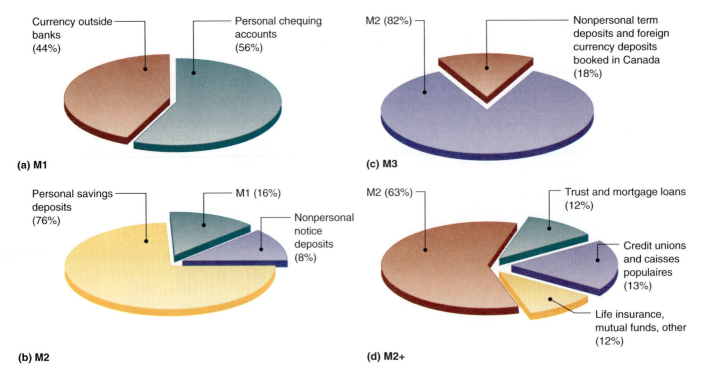

EXHIBIT 1   Components of M1, M2, M3, and M2+ : 1994

The two most-used definitions of money are M1 and M2+. The primary components of M1 are currency and chequing deposits at the chartered banks. M2+ includes M2 and adds savings and notice deposits at the chartered banks and other financial institutions, mutual funds, and life insurance annuities.

3B M2 is the component of the money supply that consists of M1 plus other relatively liquid assets at chartered banks.

M3 The broadest definition of money in terms of deposits held by Canadian chartered banks.

3C M2+ is the definition of money most closely linked to prices and economic activity. It includes deposits held at near banks.

Near banks Deposit taking institutions such as trust and mortgage loan companies, credit unions, and caisses populaires.

spendable—all you need do is go to the bank and draw it out or transfer it to your chequing account. Notice that M2 captures both the medium of exchange role of money and the store of wealth role of money—many people let their funds build up in a savings account rather than take on the risk that a corporate bond might offer, even though the bond pays a higher interest rate than a savings account.

M2's components include more financial assets than M1, some of which don't quite meet all the requirements of being called money (in the narrowest sense). But all the components are highly liquid and play an important role in providing reserves for chartered banks.

M3 The broadest definition of money in Canada, **M3,** adds chartered bank nonpersonal term deposits and foreign currency deposits of residents booked in Canada to M2. The latter deposit is denominated in a foreign currency and is held by a resident in a chartered bank in Canada. It includes, for instance, the U.S. dollar chequing account you use for cross-border shopping trips to Maine. Exhibit 1 (c) shows that nonpersonal term deposits and foreign currency deposits in chartered banks are larger than M1.

M2+ You'll note that so far our definitions of money have included only deposits at chartered banks. We know that a chequing account held at a trust company, credit union, or caisse populaire can be used in the same way as a cheque drawn on a chartered bank, so M1 and M2 don't really provide us with an accurate measure of what is used as money. To compensate for these deficiencies, economists define **M2+** to be M2 plus deposits at trust and mortgage loan companies, credit unions, caisses populaires, and other financial institutions. Economists refer to these intermediaries as **near banks**. Exhibit 1 (d) shows the relative sizes of the components of M2+. What makes the M2+ definition important is that economic research has shown that it is the definition of money that is most closely correlated with the price level and economic activity.

Distinguishing between Money and Credit   You might have thought that credit cards would be included in one of the definitions of *money*. But we didn't include them. In fact, credit cards are nowhere to be seen in a list of financial assets. Credit cards aren't a financial liability of the bank that issues them. Instead, credit cards create a liability for their holders (money owed to the company or bank that issued the card) and the banks have a financial asset as a result.

Let's consider how a credit card works. You go into a store and buy something with your credit card. You have a real asset—the item you bought. The store has a financial asset—an account receivable. The store sells that financial asset to the bank (the store owes the bank a fee, of course) and gets cash in return. Either the bank collects cash when you pay off your financial liability or, if you don't pay it off, the bank earns interest on its financial asset (usually at a high rate, about 18 percent per year).

This distinction between credit and money should be kept in mind. Money is a financial asset of individuals and a financial liability of banks. Credit is savings made available to be borrowed. Credit is not an asset. Sometimes economists refer to credit cards as **money substitutes,** since they allow you to transact (capturing the medium of exchange role of money), and allow you to defer payment (one of us knew a student who paid his tuition using his credit card—hoping he would find a part-time job to finance the monthly payments!), but they do not provide the store of wealth role that money offers. Hence the name, money substitutes.

Money substitute   Medium of exchange other than money, including credit cards.

Credit cards and credit impact the amount of money people hold. When credit is instantly available (as it is with a credit card), there's less need to hold money. (If you didn't have a credit card, you'd carry a lot more cash.) If you have a credit card in your wallet, you don't need to worry about your liquidity—you can always use your credit card (as long as it's accepted). So credit and credit cards do make a difference in how much money people hold, but because they are not financial assets, they are not money.

The same holds true with respect to debit cards—we've all seen the little machines next to the cash register at a store. After the cashier rings up your bill, you insert your debit card (which probably also serves as your interbranch banking card), key in your personal identification code, and presto—you've paid for your items: no cash, no cheques. The debit card acts just like a cheque, since the amount of your bill is automatically transferred out of your bank account and into the bank account belonging to the store. If we could come up with a dollar figure for the amount of goods and services paid for using debit cards, we wouldn't want to add that to our measure of the money supply, since that would double-count the chequing account balances that the debit card accessed. If we're going to include chequing accounts, we cannot also include the value of items paid for by using debit cards.

With the introduction of new technology comes change, so we shouldn't be surprised by claims that the cashless society is coming. The introduction of debit cards and credit cards is one step in that direction. Both tend to reduce the amount of cash you have to hold in your pocket.

Near Money   Just as you thought you understood the difference between money and money substitutes, we've got one more wrinkle to throw at you—near money. **Near money** is defined to include financial assets that can be easily converted into money— very liquid interest-earning assets such as Canada Savings Bonds and certain types of notice deposits (some of these near monies are included in the definitions of M2 and M3). Since people can transfer their near money into money with relative ease, any one measure of the Canadian money supply (M1, M2+, etc.) could jump around quite a bit as people shift between money and near money assets. That's one reason why

Near money   Financial assets that can be easily converted into money— very liquid interest-earning assets such as Canada Savings Bonds.

economists look at several definitions of money when they want to know what's happening to the Canadian money supply.

Now that we've considered what money is, both in theory and in practice, let's consider the banking system's role in creating money.

BANKS AND THE CREATION OF MONEY

Asset management   How a bank handles its loans and other assets.

Liability management   How a bank attracts deposits and what it pays for them.

Banks are financial institutions that borrow from people (take in deposits) and use the money they borrow to make loans to other individuals. Banks make a profit by charging a higher interest on the money they lend out than they pay for the money they borrow. They also charge service fees.

Banking is generally analyzed from the perspective of **asset management** (how a bank handles its loans and other assets) and **liability management** (how a bank attracts deposits and what it pays for them). When banks offer people "free chequing" accounts and other "special accounts" paying high rates of interest, they do so after carefully considering the costs of those liabilities to them.

To think of banks as borrowers as well as lenders may seem a bit unusual, but borrowing is what they do. When you keep money in a savings account or a chequing account, the bank is borrowing from you, paying you a zero (or low) interest rate and lending your money to other people at a high interest rate. Much of banks' borrowing is short-term borrowing, meaning banks must pay the money back to the lender either on demand (as in the case of chequing accounts or savings accounts) or within a specific period of time (as in the case of term deposits).

In Canada, banks operate in a regulated environment. They have limits on what kinds of loans they can make and what types of borrowing they're allowed to do. The primary regulator of the money supply in Canada is the Bank of Canada, which we'll consider in detail in the next chapter.

How Banks Create Money

4   Banks "create" money because a bank's liabilities are defined as money. So when a bank incurs liabilities it creates money.

How do banks create money? As John Kenneth Galbraith's epigram at the start of this chapter suggested, the process is simple—so simple it seems almost mystical to many.

The key to understanding how banks create money is to remember the nature of financial assets: Financial assets can be created from nothing as long as an offsetting financial liability is simultaneously created. Since money is any financial asset that serves the function of money, money can be created rather easily. Seeing how paper money, called bills for short, is created is the easiest way to begin examining the process. Bills are IOUs of the Bank of Canada that serve the three functions of money. So whenever the Bank of Canada issues an IOU, it creates money.[1] Similarly, other banks can create money by creating financial assets that serve the functions of money. As we saw when we considered the definition of *money*, bank chequing accounts serve those functions, so they are money, just as cash is. When a bank places the proceeds of a loan it makes to you in your chequing account, it is creating money. You have a financial asset that did not previously exist.

The First Step in the Creation of Money
To see how banks create money, let's consider what would happen if you were given a freshly printed $100 bill. Remember, the Bank of Canada created that $100 bill simply by printing it. The $100 bill is a $100 financial asset of yours and a financial liability of the Bank of Canada, which issued it.

If the process of creating money stopped there, it wouldn't be particularly mysterious. But it doesn't stop there. Let's consider what happens next as you use that money.

The Second Step in the Creation of Money
Say you decide to put the $100 bill in your chequing account. To make the analysis easier, let's assume that your bank is a branch of the country's only bank, Big Bank. All money deposited in branch banks goes into Big Bank. After you make your deposit, Big Bank is holding $100 cash for you, and you have $100 more in your chequing account. You can spend it whenever you want

---

[1]As we'll see in the next chapter, these bills aren't the Bank of Canada's only IOUs.

simply by writing a cheque. So Big Bank is performing a service for you (holding your money and keeping track of your expenditures) for free. Neat, huh? Big Bank must be run by a bunch of nice people.

But wait. You and we know that bankers, while they may be nice, aren't as nice as all that. There's no such thing as a free lunch. Let's see why the bank is being so nice.

Banking and Goldsmiths   To see why banks are so nice, let's go way back in history to when banks first developed.[2] At that time, gold was used for money and people carried around gold to make their payments. But gold is rather heavy, so if they had to make a big purchase, it was difficult to pay for the purchase. Moreover, carrying around a lot of gold left them vulnerable to being robbed by the likes of Robin Hood. So they looked for a place to store their gold until they needed some of it.

From Gold to Gold Receipts   The natural place to store gold was the goldsmith shop, which already had a vault. For a small fee, the goldsmith shop would hold your gold, giving you a receipt for it. Whenever you needed your gold, you'd go to the goldsmith and exchange the receipt for gold.

Pretty soon most people kept their gold at the goldsmith's, and they began to wonder: Why go through the bother of getting my gold out to buy something when all that happens is that the seller takes the gold I pay and puts it right back into the goldsmith's vault? That's two extra trips.

Consequently, people began using the receipts the goldsmith gave them to certify that they had deposited $100 worth (or whatever) of gold in his vault. At that point gold was no longer the only money—gold receipts were also money. However, as long as the total amount in the gold receipts directly represented the total amount of gold, it was still reasonable to say, since the receipts were 100 percent backed by gold, that gold was the money supply.

Gold Receipts Become Money   Once this process of using the receipts rather than the gold became generally accepted, the goldsmith found that he had substantial amounts of gold in his vault. All that gold, just sitting there! On a normal day only 1 percent of the gold was claimed by "depositors" and had to be given out. Usually on the same day an amount at least equal to that 1 percent came in from other depositors. What a waste! Gold sitting around doing nothing! So when a good friend came in, needing a loan, the goldsmith said, "Sure, I'll lend you some gold receipts as long as you pay me some interest." When the goldsmith made this loan, he created more gold receipts than he had covered in gold in his vault. He created money.

Pretty soon the goldsmith realized he could earn more from the interest he received on loans than he could earn from goldsmithing. So he stopped goldsmithing and went full-time into making loans of gold receipts. At that point the number of gold receipts outstanding significantly exceeded the amount of gold in the goldsmith's vaults. But not to worry; since everyone was willing to accept gold receipts rather than gold, the goldsmith had plenty of gold for those few who wanted actual gold.

It was, however, no longer accurate to say that gold was the country's money or currency. Gold receipts were the money. They met the definition of money. These gold receipts were backed partially by gold and partially by people's trust that the goldsmiths would pay off their deposits on demand. The goldsmith shops had become banks.

Banking Is Profitable   The banking business was very profitable for goldsmiths. Soon other people started competing with them, offering to hold gold for free. After all, if they could store gold, they could make a profit on the loans to other people (with the first people's money). Some even offered to pay people to store their gold.

---

[2]The banking history reported here is, according to historians, apocryphal (more myth than reality). But it so nicely makes the point that we repeat it anyhow.

The goldsmith story is directly relevant to banks. People store their cash in banks and the banks issue receipts—chequing accounts—which become a second form of money. When people place their cash in banks and use their receipts from the bank as money, those receipts also become money because they meet the definition of *money:* They serve as a medium of exchange, a unit of account, and a store of wealth. So money includes both cash that people hold and their deposits in the bank.

Which brings us back to why banks hold your cash for free. They do it, not because they're nice, but because when you deposit cash in the bank, your deposit allows banks to make profitable loans they otherwise couldn't make.

The Money Multiplier

With that background, let's go back to your $100, which the bank is now holding for you. You have a chequing account balance of $100 and the bank has $100 cash. As long as other people are willing to accept your cheque in payment for $100 worth of goods, your cheque is as good as money. In fact it is money in the same way gold receipts were money. But when you deposit $100, no money has been created yet. The form of the money has simply been changed from cash to a chequing account or demand deposit.

Now let's say Big Bank lends out 90 percent of the cash you deposit, keeping only 10 percent as **reserves** on hand (we just picked this number out of our heads: in prac- tice it could be anything)—that is, enough money to manage the normal cash inflows and outflows. This 10 percent is the **desired reserve ratio** (the proportion of their deposits they want to hold as cash, to keep as a reserve against withdrawals). This reserve ratio is determined by Big Bank on the basis of many factors, such as their forecast of how much cash they'll need on any day. Since there's a lot of guesswork involved in that forecast, in practice, Big Bank will probably end up holding their desired reserves plus some **excess reserves** (which we define as cash reserves above the desired level) that they hadn't planned on:

Reserves   Cash on hand and deposits at the central bank that a bank keeps to manage the normal cash inflows and outflows.

Desired reserve ratio   The propor- tion of its deposits that a financial institution desires to hold to satisfy its demand for cash.

Excess reserves   Reserves in excess of what banks desire.

$$\text{actual reserves} = \text{desired reserves} + \text{excess reserves.}$$

So, like the goldsmith, Big Bank lends out $90 to someone who needs a loan. That person the bank loaned the money to now has $90 cash and you have $100 in a demand deposit, so now there's $190 of money, rather than just $100 of money. The $10 in cash the bank holds in reserve isn't counted as money since the bank must keep it as reserves and may not use it as long as it's backing loans. Only cash held by the public is counted as money. By making the loan, the bank has created $90 in money.

Of course, no one borrows money just to hold it. The borrower spends the money, say on a new sweater, and the sweater store owner now has the $90 in cash. The store owner doesn't want to hold it either. She'll deposit it back into the bank. Since there's only one bank, Big Bank discovers that the $90 it has loaned out is once again in its coffers. The money operates like a boomerang: Big Bank lends $90 out and gets the $90 back again.

The same process occurs again. The bank doesn't make any money holding $90, so it lends out $81, keeping $9 (10 percent of $90) in reserve. The story repeats and repeats itself, with a slightly smaller amount coming back to the bank each time. At each step in the process, money (in the form of chequing account deposits) is being created.

Determining How Many Demand Deposits Will Be Created
What's the total amount of demand deposits that will ultimately be created from your $100? To answer that question, we continue the process over and over: 100 + 90 + 81 + 72.9 + 65.6 + 59 + 53.1 + 47.8 + 43.0 + 38.7 + 34.9. Adding up these numbers gives us $686. Adding up $686 plus the numbers from the next 20 rounds gives us $961.08. If we kept on adding and adding each round after that, eventually we'd get to the point at which no additional money would be created from your $100.

As you can see, that's a lot of adding. Luckily there's an easier way. Mathematicians have shown that you can determine the amount of money that will eventually be created by such a process by multiplying the initial $100 in money that was deposited by 1/r, where r is the desired reserve ratio (the percentage banks keep out of each round). In this case we assumed the reserve ratio is 10 percent. Dividing,

$$1/r = 1/.10 = 10$$

so the amount of demand deposits that will ultimately exist at the end of the process is

$$(10 \times \$100) = \$1,000.$$

The \$1,000 is in the form of chequing account deposits (demand deposits). The entire \$100 in cash that you were given, and which started the whole process, is in the bank as reserves, which means that \$900 (\$1,000 − \$100) of money has been created by the process.

Calculating the Money Multiplier   The ratio 1/r is called the **simple money multiplier.** It tells us how much money will ultimately be created by the banking system from an initial inflow of money. In our example, 1/.10 = 10. Had the bank kept out 20 percent each time, the money multiplier would have been 1/.20 = 5. If the reserve ratio were 5 percent, the money multiplier would have been 1/.05 = 20. The higher the reserve ratio, the smaller the money multiplier, and the less money will be created.

Banks are not the only holders of cash. Firms and individuals hold cash too, so in each round we must also make an adjustment in the multiplier for what people and firms hold. The math you need to formally calculate the money multiplier gets a bit complicated when firms and people hold cash. Since for our purposes a rough calculation is all we need, we will use an approximate money multiplier in which individuals' cash holdings are treated the same as reserves of banks. Thus the **approximate real-world money multiplier** in the economy is:

$$1/(r + c)$$

where r = the percentage of deposits banks hold in reserve and c is the ratio of money people hold in cash to the money they hold as deposits. Let's consider an example.[3] Say the banks keep 10 percent in reserve and the ratio of individuals' cash holdings to their deposits is 25 percent. This means the approximate real-world money multiplier will be

$$1/(.1 + .25) = 1/.35 = 2.9.$$

Simple money multiplier   Measure of the amount of money ultimately created by the banking system per dollar deposited, when people hold no cash. The mathematical expression is 1/r.

5   The money multiplier is the measure of the amount of money ultimately created per dollar deposited by the banking system. When people hold no cash it equals 1/r. When people hold cash the approximate money multiplier is 1/(r + c).

Approximate real-world money multiplier   Measure of the amount of money ultimately created by the banking system per dollar deposited, when cash holdings of individuals and firms are treated the same as reserves of banks. The mathematical expression is 1/(r + c).

The creation of money and the money multiplier are easy to understand if you remember that money (the financial asset created) is offset by an equal amount of financial liabilities of the bank. The bank owes its depositors the amount in their chequing accounts. Its financial liabilities to depositors, in turn, are secured by the loans (the bank's financial assets) and by the financial liabilities of people to whom the loans were made. Promises to pay underlie any modern financial system.

The initial money in the story about the goldsmiths was gold, but it quickly became apparent that it was far more reasonable to use gold certificates as money. Therefore gold certificates backed by gold soon replaced gold itself as the money supply. Then, as goldsmiths made more loans than they had gold, the gold certificates were no longer backed by gold. They were backed by promises to get gold if the person wanted gold in exchange for the gold certificate. Eventually the percentage of gold supposedly backing the money became so small that it was clear to everyone that the promises, not the gold, underlay the money supply.

That's why today, all that backs the modern money supply are banks' promises to pay. There's no gold backing up the Canadian money supply.

Faith as the Backing of Our Money Supply

You've already been introduced to the basis of financial accounting: the T-account presentation of balance sheets. The balance sheet is made up of assets on one side and

Creation of Money Using T-Accounts

---

[3]In the appendix we discuss the precise calculation of the money multiplier when individuals hold cash.

THE COMPLEX MONEY
MULTIPLIER AND REFORMS IN
BANKING

Life keeps getting tougher. In the old days (as recently as the 1980s), economics students only had to learn the simple money multiplier. Recent reforms in the Canadian banking system have made that impossible. In the late 1980s and early 1990s, the Bank of Canada eliminated required reserves. Required reserves were set as a complicated fraction of a chartered banks' deposits, with the fraction set higher than the bank would otherwise want to hold. Required reserves were supposed to provide a degree of liquidity to the banking system because they forced banks to hold more cash than they would like. Nonbank financial institutions such as credit unions and caisses populaires didn't face the same requirement: They weren't forced to tie up large sums of cash as reserves that weren't paying interest. Remember that financial institutions profit by lending out their excess reserves, so reserve requirements actually constrained the way that banks could behave. In fact, the chartered banks had been crying foul for some time, arguing they faced an unfair "reserve tax."

The government decided they were right. Under new legislation, members of the Canadian Payments Association (chartered banks and other financial intermediaries) simply need to maintain an average clearing balance of zero (on a daily basis) with the Bank of Canada over the specified time period. **Clearing** refers to the process in which claims drawn against different chartered banks and other financial intermediaries are satisfied by transferring funds between their accounts at the Bank of Canada.

If you insert a value for the reserve ratio of zero into the simple money supply multiplier, you get a multiplier approaching infinity (any number over a very small number tends to be a very large number). The real-world money multiplier is much lower than that because banks always want to hold a certain proportion of their deposits as reserves against the clearing process and the demand for currency from the public.

liabilities and net worth on the other. By definition the two sides are equal; they balance (just as the T-account must).

To cement the money creation process in your mind, let's discuss how banks create money using transactions that affect the balance sheet. To keep the analysis simple, we limit the example to the case where only banks create money. (In the appendix we do the more complicated example in which people also hold cash.)

Exhibit 2 shows the initial balance sheet of an imaginary Textland Bank, which we assume is the only bank in the country. As you can see, Textland has $500,000 in assets: $30,000 in cash, $300,000 in loans, and $170,000 in property. On the liabilities side, it has $150,000 in demand deposits and $350,000 in shareholder equity net worth. The two sides of the balance sheet are equal.

EXHIBIT 2   Textland Bank Balance Sheet   Beginning Balance

Assets		Liabilities and Shareholders' Equity	
Cash	$ 30,000	Demand deposits	$150,000
Loans	300,000	Net worth	350,000
Property	170,000		
Total assets	$500,000	Total liabilities and shareholders' equity	$500,000

The first thing to notice about this balance sheet is that if all holders of chequing accounts (demand deposits) wanted their cash, the bank couldn't give it to them. The cash it holds is only a portion—20 percent—of the total deposits:

$$\$30,000/\$150,000 = .20.$$

Banks rely upon statistical averages and assume that not all people will want their money at the same time. Let's assume Textland Bank has decided 20 percent is an appropriate reserve ratio.

Now let's say that John Finder finds $10,000 in cash. He deposits that $10,000 into Textland Bank. After he does so, what will happen to the money supply? The first step is seen in Transaction 1, which shows the effect of John Finder's deposit on the bank's account. The bank gains $10,000 in cash, but its liabilities also increase by $10,000, so, as you can see, the two sides of the balance sheet are still equal. At this point no additional money has been created; $10,000 cash has simply been changed to a $10,000 demand deposit.

EXHIBIT 2   *(continued)*   Transaction 1

Assets		Liabilities and Shareholders' Equity	
Cash (beginning balance)	$30,000	Demand deposits (beginning balance)	$150,000
Cash from John	$10,000	John's deposit	10,000
Total cash	$040,000	Total demand deposits	$160,000
Loans	300,000	Shareholders' equity.	350,000
Property	170,000		
Total assets	$510,000	Total liabilities and net worth	$510,000

Now let's assume the bank uses a reserve ratio of 20 percent, meaning it lends out 80 percent of what it takes in. Therefore it lends out 80 percent × $10,000 = $8,000 to Fred Baker, keeping 20 percent × $10,000 = $2,000 in reserve. The change in the bank's balance sheet is seen in Transaction 2. This step creates $8,000 in money. Why? Because John Finder still has $10,000 in his chequing account, while Fred Baker has $8,000 cash, so, combining John's chequing account balance with Fred's cash, the public has $8,000 in money. As you can see, loans have increased by $8,000 and cash in Textland Bank has decreased by $8,000.

EXHIBIT 2   *(continued)*   Transaction 2

Assets		Liabilities and Shareholders' Equity	
Cash (after Trans. 1)	$ 40,000	Demand deposits (after Trans. 1)	$160,000
Cash given to Fred	8,000	Shareholders' equity	350,000
Total cash	$ 32,000		
Loans (beginning balance)	300,000		
Loan to Fred	8,000		
Total loans	308,000		
Property	170,000	Total liabilities and	
Total assets	$510,000	shareholders' equity	$510,000

Fred Baker didn't borrow the money to hold onto it. He spends it buying a new oven from Mary Builder, who, in turn, deposits the $8,000 into Textland Bank (the only bank according to our assumptions). Textland's balance sheet now looks like Transaction 3.

EXHIBIT 2   **(continued)**   Transaction 3

Assets		Liabilities and Shareholders' Equity	
Cash (after Trans. 2)	$32,000	Demand deposits	$160,000
Cash from Mary	8,000	Mary's deposit	8,000
Total cash	$ 40,000	Total demand deposits	$168,000
Loans	308,000	Net worth	350,000
Property	170,000		
Total assets	$518,000	Total liabilities and	
		shareholders' equity	$518,000

EXHIBIT 3   **The Money-Creating Process**

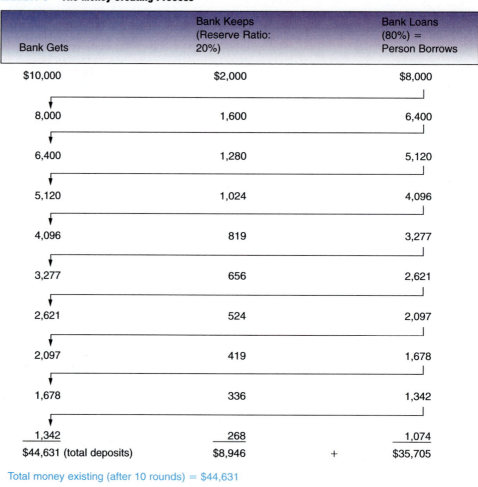

Bank Gets	Bank Keeps (Reserve Ratio: 20%)	Bank Loans (80%) = Person Borrows
$10,000	$2,000	$8,000
8,000	1,600	6,400
6,400	1,280	5,120
5,120	1,024	4,096
4,096	819	3,277
3,277	656	2,621
2,621	524	2,097
2,097	419	1,678
1,678	336	1,342
1,342	268	1,074
$44,631 (total deposits)	$8,946	+ $35,705

Total money existing (after 10 rounds) = $44,631

Mary Builder has a demand deposit of $8,000, and John Finder has a demand deposit of $10,000. But Textland Bank has excess reserves of $6,400, since it must keep only $1,600 of Mary's $8,000 deposit as reserves:

$$80\% \times \$8,000 = \$6,400$$

So the bank is looking to make a loan.

Now the process occurs again. Exhibit 3 shows the effects of the process for 10 rounds, starting with the initial $10,000. Each time it lends the money out, the money returns like a boomerang and serves as reserves for more loans. After 10 rounds we reach a point where total demand deposits are $44,631, and the bank has $8,946 in reserves. This is approaching the $50,000 we'd arrive at using the money multiplier:

$$[1/r](\$10,000) = [1/.2](\$10,000) = 5(\$10,000) = \$50,000.$$

If we carried it out for more rounds, we'd actually reach what the formula predicted.

Note that the process ends only when the bank holds all the cash, and the only money held by the public is in the form of demand deposits. Notice also that the total amount of money created depends on the amount banks hold in reserve.

To see that you understand the process, say that banks suddenly get concerned about the safety of their loans, and they decide to keep excess reserves—reserves in excess of what they desire to hold. What will happen to the money multiplier? If you answered that it will decrease, you've got it. Excess reserves decrease the money multiplier as much as do desired reserves. We mentioned this example because this is precisely what happened to the banking system in the early 1990s. Banks became concerned about the safety of their loans; they held large excess reserves, and the money multiplier decreased.

In summary, the process of money creation isn't difficult to understand as long as you remember that money is simply a bank's financial liability held by the public. Whenever banks create financial liabilities for themselves, they create financial assets for individuals, and those financial assets are money.

REGULATION OF BANKS AND THE FINANCIAL SECTOR

You just saw how easy it is to create money. The banking system and money make the economy operate more efficiently, but they also present potential problems. For example, say that for some reason suddenly there's an increase in money (that is, in promises to pay) without any corresponding increase in real goods and services. As the money supply increases without an increase in real goods to buy with that money, more money is chasing the same number of goods. Aggregate demand exceeds aggregate supply. The result will be a fall in the value of money (inflation), meaning real trade will be more complicated. Alternatively, if there's an increase in real goods but not a corresponding increase in money, there will be a shortage of money, which will hamper the economy. Either the price level will fall (deflation) or there will be a recession.

Societies have continually experienced these problems, and the financial history of the world is filled with stories of financial upheavals and monetary problems. For example, there are numerous instances of private financial firms who have promised the world, but their promises have been nothing but hot air. One instance occurred in the 1800s in Canada, when banks were allowed to issue their own notes (their own promises to pay). These notes served as part of the money supply. Sharp financial operators soon got into the process and created banks out in the boonies called *wildcat banks* because they were situated in places where only a wildcat would go. These wildcat banks issued notes even though they had no deposits, hoping that no one would cash the notes in. Many such banks defaulted on their promises, leaving holders of the notes with only worthless pieces of paper. Naturally the people who held the worthless notes tried to get rid of them as soon as they could—that way they would at least recover some of their losses. This provides us with an example of *Gresham's Law*—bad money drives out good money. What this basically says is that if you have two "pieces" of money, and you know that one of them really isn't worth its face value, you'll try to use that one first when you transact. That way you'll have kept the good money, and the bad money will have been traded to someone else, who will eventually learn that it's bad money, and try to pawn it off to the next unsuspecting soul. Merchants quickly caught on, and soon they began checking in a "book of notes" which listed whether the notes the buyer was offering were probably good or not.

Gresham's Law   Bad money drives out good money.

6   Financial systems are based on trust that expectations will be fulfilled. Banks borrow short and lend long, which means that if people lose faith in banks, the banks cannot keep their promises.

Anatomy of a Financial Panic

Another problem that can develop in the banking system is a financial panic. Banking and financial systems are based on promises and trust. People put their cash into other financial assets (such as demand deposits) and believe that these demand deposits are as good as cash. In normal times, demand deposits really are as good as cash. When times get bad, people become concerned about the financial firms' ability to keep those promises and they call upon the firms to redeem the promises. But banks have only their reserves (a small percentage of their total deposits) to give depositors. Most of the depositors' money is loaned out and cannot be returned quickly, even though the banks have promised depositors that their deposits will be given back "on demand." Put another way, banks borrow short and lend long.

When a lot of depositors lose faith in a bank and, all at one time, call on the bank to keep its promises, the bank cannot do so. The result is that the bank fails when depositors lose faith, even though the bank might be financially sound for the long run. Fear underlies financial panics and can undermine financial institutions.

Of course, it's possible for any one bank branch to run out of cash on a given day. That just means the bank manager did a poor job of forecasting the bank's cash requirements. Think about what would happen to you if, just before the Christmas break, you went to your campus bank to take out some cash for late-minute shopping—or your bus ticket home—only to find a sign in the window saying "Come Back in 1 Hour" (even the automatic teller machine is closed!). While that branch manager hustles to try to obtain some cash from other branches in town (assuming there are some), you might get worried about your account. If your branch finally opens, you might decide to close out your account. If everyone did that (or if rumours of financial collapse started to fly around campus), the branch would face more trouble. That's why, when a German bank found itself short of cash and had to close its doors, the bank manager stacked dozens of bars of gold behind the locked doors. While there wasn't any cash to be found in that branch, the pile of gold was meant to reassure depositors. It did, and that bank did not face financial ruin.

Government Policy to Prevent Panic

To prevent such panics, various levels of government guarantee the obligations of many financial institutions. The Canada Deposit Insurance Corporation (CDIC) was created in 1967. It provides a guarantee of up to $60,000 on deposits at all chartered banks and federally incorporated trust and mortgage loan companies. The Quebec Deposit Insurance Board, also established in 1967, guarantees deposits in credit unions and caisses populaires and other institutions in Quebec (but not deposits in chartered banks operating in Quebec). A number of provinces also offer protection to depositors in local area financial institutions. In most cases the guarantees work as follows: The financial institutions pay a small premium for each dollar of deposit to the government-organized insurance company. That company puts the premium into a fund used to bail out banks experiencing a run on deposits. These guarantees have two effects:

1. They prevent the unwarranted fear that causes financial crises. Depositors know that the government will see that they can get their cash back even if the bank fails. This knowledge stops them from responding to a rumour and trying to get their money out of a shaky financial institution before anyone else does.
2. They prevent warranted fears. Why should people worry about whether or not a financial institution is making reasonable loans on the basis of their deposits if the government guarantees the financial institutions' promises to pay regardless of what kind of loans the institutions make?

The Benefits and Problems of Guarantees

Guarantees prevent unwarranted fears. The illusion upon which banks depend (that people can get their money in the short run, even though it's only in the long run that they can all get it) can be met by temporary loans from the government. Guarantees can prevent unwarranted fears from becoming financial panics. The guarantee makes the illusion a reality. If people can indeed get their money in the long run, seeing to it that this illusion *is* reality isn't expensive to the government. As long as the bank has sufficient long-term assets to cover its deposits, the government will be repaid its temporary loan.

Unfortunately, covering the unwarranted fear can also mean preventing the war-

Institutions displaying this banner offer accounts that are insured by the CDIC. *CDIC.*

ranted fear from putting an effective restraint or discipline on banks' lending policies. If deposits are guaranteed, why should depositors worry whether banks have adequate loans to cover their deposits in the long run? Thus, when there's a bigger illusion than the short-run/long-run illusion, and depositors can't get their money in the long run (that is, their fears were warranted), guaranteeing deposits can be expensive indeed. The Canadian government found this out in the mid-1980s and early 1990s.

Costly Failures of the 1980s and 1990s   As we said, various levels of government have guaranteed the deposits of a variety of financial institutions. Since its inception, the CDIC has been called on to provide assistance to depositors in over 20 failed financial institutions. Two events were particularly costly, one in 1985, and the other in 1992.

In the late 1970s and early 1980s, a number of new financial institutions opened in Alberta and British Columbia, partially due to the resource boom that resulted from high commodity prices (particularly for oil). The western provinces offered attractive opportunities for investment, but when oil prices fell and the economy went into recession in 1982, several banks found themselves in financial difficulty. Bad loans and poor management practices led to the collapse of two small banks—the Northland Bank and the Canadian Commercial Bank. These banks went under even though the Bank of Canada intervened to provide short-term assistance through a coordinated effort that included many of the other chartered banks. Unfortunately the Bank of Canada's actions were misinterpreted as evidence that the Canadian financial system was weak, and public confidence in financial institutions fell like a rock. By 1985 this had led to the failure of a number of small financial institutions, as depositors fled to what they perceived to be safer havens. The CDIC eventually paid out the full value of deposits up to and even exceeding the stipulated $60,000 maximum. They settled claims on deposits above the $60,000 limit since the ill-conceived government bailout led some depositors to believe that their funds were safe—they believed the government was going to take care of the problem.

These events led to the Estey Commission whose 1986 report formed the basis of reforms to financial regulations. In 1987 a new position—the Superintendent of Financial Institutions—was created to ensure that financial institutions were undertaking safe and sound practices.

In 1992 there were other costly failures. The CDIC settled the claims of over a million depositors, totalling over $14.1 billion. Most of this went to cover the collapse of Central Guaranty Trust Company, which was Canada's fourth-largest trust company at the time. Over $10.6 billion went to almost 900,000 of its depositors. These failures put the CDIC in a difficult financial position, because the rates they had been charging for insurance just weren't high enough to cover their expenses: Losses almost doubled in just one year. A review of the deposit insurance program is now under way, with proposals for higher rates of insurance and a reduction in the maximum insurable deposit limit (to $30,000) among the most important of issues. The reforms should be much in the news in the 1990s.

We end this chapter with a final comment on the process of globalization. International trade and finance have become so sophisticated that tracing the flow of funds between countries is now the domain of forensic accountants (accountants who diagnose financial irregularities). When domestic banking regulations change, this affects the way that business is done vis-a-vis both the sources of funds (borrowing) and their uses (lending). Given the degree to which banking has been automated, and the potential for abuse, we should expect issues in international banking to dominate the regulatory agenda in the 1990s.

CHAPTER SUMMARY

- Money is a useful financial instrument.
- Money serves as a unit of account, a medium of exchange, and a store of wealth.
- There are various definitions of money: M1, M2, M2+, and M3.
- Since money is what people believe money to be, creating money out of thin air is easy. How banks create money out

of thin air is easily understood if you remember that money is simply a financial liability of a bank.
- The simple money multiplier is $1/r$.
- The approximate real-world multiplier is $1/(r + c)$.
- Financial panics are based on fear. They can be prevented by government, but only at a cost.

KEY TERMS

approximate real-world money
  multiplier   *(311)*
asset management   *(308)*
Bank of Canada   *(302)*
clearing   *(312)*
desired reserve ratio   *(310)*
excess reserves   *(310)*

liability management   *(308)*
M1   *(305)*
M2   *(305)*
M2+   *(306)*
M3   *(306)*
money   *(302)*
money substitutes   *(307)*

near banks   *(306)*
near money   *(307)*
reserve ratio   *(311)*
reserves   *(310)*
simple money multiplier   *(311)*

QUESTIONS FOR THOUGHT AND REVIEW

The number after each question represents the estimated degree of critical thinking required. (1 = almost none; 10 = deep thought.)

1. Money is to the economy as oil is to an engine. Explain. *(4)*

2. List the three functions of money. *(1)*

3. Why doesn't the government pay for all its goods simply by printing money? *(4)*

4. What are two components of M2 that are not components of M1? *(1)*

5. Assuming individuals hold no cash, calculate the simple money multiplier for each of the following reserve requirements: 5 percent, 10 percent, 20 percent, 25 percent, 50 percent, 75 percent, 100 percent. *(3)*

6. Assuming individuals hold 20 percent of their money in the form of cash, recalculate the approximate real-world money multipliers from Question 5. *(5)*

7. If bills (Bank of Canada notes) are backed by nothing but promises and are in real terms worthless, why do people accept them? *(4)*

8. If the government were to raise the reserve requirement to 100 percent, what would likely happen to the interest rate banks pay? Why? *(6)*

9. What was the cause of the 1985 banking crisis? What role did government guarantees play in that crisis? *(6)*

10. Is the current Canadian banking system susceptible to panic? If so, how might a panic occur? *(5)*

PROBLEMS AND EXERCISES

1. While Jon is walking to school one morning, he spots a $100 bill on the sidewalk in front of a vacant lot. Not knowing how to return it, Jon keeps the money and deposits it in his bank. (No one in this economy holds cash.) If the bank keeps 5 percent of its money in reserves:

   a. How much money can the bank now lend out?

   b. After this initial transaction, by how much is the money in the economy changed?

   c. What's the money multiplier?

   d. How much money will eventually be created by the banking system from Jon's $100?

2. Assume that there's only one bank in the country, that the desired reserve ratio is 10 percent, and that the ratio of individuals' cash holdings to their bank deposits is 20 percent. The bank begins with $20,000 cash, $225,000 in loans, $105,000 in physical assets, $200,000 in demand deposits, and $150,000 in shareholders' equity.

   a. An immigrant comes into the country and deposits $10,000 in a bank. Show this deposit's effect on the bank's balance sheet.

   b. The bank keeps enough of this money to satisfy its reserve requirement and loans out the rest to Ms. Entrepreneur. Show the effect on the bank's balance sheet.

   c. Ms. Entrepreneur uses the money to pay Mr. Carpenter, who deposits 84 percent of what he gets in the bank. Show the effect on the bank's balance sheet.

   d. Show the bank's balance sheet after the money multiplier is all through multiplying (based on the appendix).

3. Assume there is one bank in the country whose desired reserve ratio is 20 percent. It has $10,000 in cash; $100,000 in loans; $50,000 in physical assets; $50,000 in demand deposits; and $110,000 net worth. Mr. Aged withdraws $1,000 from the bank and dies on the way home without spending a penny. He is buried with the cash still in his pocket.

   a. Show this withdrawal's affect on the bank's balance sheet.

   b. What happened to the bank's reserve ratio and what must the bank do to meet reserve requirements?

   c. What is the money multiplier? (Assume no cash holdings.)

   d. What will happen to total money supply because of this event after the money multiplier is through multiplying?

4. Assume the reserve ratio is 15 percent. Textbook Bank's balance sheet looks like this:

Assets		**Liabilities**	
Cash	$ 30,000	Deposits	$150,000
Loans	320,000	Net worth	550,000
Property	350,000		
Total	$700,000	Total	$700,000

   a. How much is the bank holding in excess reserves?

   b. If the bank eliminates excess reserves by making new loans, how much new money would be created (assuming no cash holdings)?

   c. Assuming cash holdings are 20 percent of deposits, approximately how much new money would be created?

5. Categorize the following as components of M1, M2, M2+, all three, or none:

   a. Provincial government bonds.

   b. Chequing accounts at a trust company.

   c. Chequing accounts at a chartered bank.

   d. Stocks.

   e. Cash in your wallet.

   f. Savings accounts at chartered banks.

   g. Savings accounts at a credit union.

A Precise Calculation of the Money Multiplier When People Hold Cash

In the text we used the approximate money multiplier to determine what the effect of people holding cash will be. In this appendix we go through a similar example using a precise formula, first in an example, then in T-accounts.

Mathematicians have found a simple formula to determine the money multiplier when people hold cash. It's $(1 + c)/(r + c)$. The formula is the actual money multiplier when individuals hold cash.

Before we substitute in, it's important to call your attention to the definition of c. It's not the ratio of the money people keep to the total money they receive. It's the ratio of money people hold as cash to the money people hold as demand deposits. The two ratios are, however, related. If people deposit in the bank 80 percent of the money they receive, they're keeping 25 percent of the money *they deposit*. For example, if they receive $100 and keep $20, they're depositing $80.

The ratio of cash to money they receive is

$$20/100 = 20\%$$

Measuring c (the ratio of cash to money they deposit), we get

$$c = 20/80 = 25\%.$$

So in our example, $c = .25$.

With this formula we can calculate precisely how much the money multiplier would be when people hold cash. Say banks hold 10 percent of their deposits in reserve ($r = .10$) and individuals hold cash equal to 20 percent of the amount they deposit ($c = .25$). Substituting the numbers into the formula gives

$$(1 + .25)/(.1 + .25) = 3.57.$$

This tells us that when people hold 20 percent of their money as cash and 80 percent as chequing account deposits, and the banks hold 10 percent of their deposits as reserves, the complex money multiplier is 3.57. So in

our example in the text, from that initial $100, $357 in money would be created. Thus our approximate multiplier calculated in the text, 2.9, was too small. Why was it too small? Because it didn't take into account the fact that when people hold money as cash, the money they hold must also be included in the money supply; when banks hold money, it need not be included.

To cement the money creation process in your mind, let's go through the same example we did in the chapter, only this time allowing for individuals to hold cash.

Exhibit A1 shows the effects of the money multiplier process for 10 rounds, starting with the initial $10,000, with a reserve ratio of .2 and a ratio of money people hold in cash to the money they hold as deposits of .3. Each time it lends the money out, 77 percent of what it lends comes back to the bank like a boomerang and serves as reserves for more loans. After 10 rounds we reach a point where the public holds $5,961 in cash and total demand deposits are up to $19,949. Adding these two gives us a total money supply of $25,910. This is approaching the $26,000 we'd arrived at using the precise calculations of the money multiplier:

$$[(1 + c)/(r + c)](\$10,000) =$$
$$[(1 + .3)/(.2 + .3)]\,(\$10,000)$$
$$= 2.6(\$10,000) = \$26,000.$$

If we carried it out for a few more rounds, we'd actually reach what the formula predicted.

Note the $10,000 in currency notes is held jointly by the bank and the public. After 10 rounds the bank holds $3,979 in cash and the public holds $5,961 in cash. Thus, a total of $9,940 (approaching $10,000) is held in cash. However, the money supply, which includes both cash and chequing account deposits, has been increased to almost $26,000. The additional money is in the form of chequing account deposits.

EXHIBIT A1   The Money-Creating Process

Bank Gets	Bank Keeps (Reserve Ratio: 20%)	Bank Loans (80%) = Person Borrows	Demand Deposits (77% of What Person Gets)	Person Keeps (23% of What Person Gets)
			$ 7,700	$2,300
$7,700	$1,540	$6,160	4,743	1,417
4,743	949	3,794	2,921	873
2,921	584	2,337	1,799	538
1,799	360	1,439	1,108	331
1,108	222	886	682	204
682	136	546	420	126
420	84	336	259	77
259	52	207	159	48
159	32	127	98	29
98	20	78	60	18
	$3,979		$19,949 +	$5,961

13

Central Banks, the Bank of Canada, and Monetary Policy

There have been three great inventions since the beginning of time: fire, the wheel, and central banking.

~Will Rogers

After reading this chapter, you should be able to:

1 Recount a brief history of the Bank of Canada.

2 State what monetary policy is.

3 Provide a review of central bank independence.

4 Explain how monetary policy depends on international considerations.

5 List two tools of monetary policy and explain how they work.

6 Explain why changes in the bank rate provide a signal to the market.

7 Go through the effect of an open market operation on a bank, using T-accounts.

8 Explain how monetary policy works in the Keynesian model.

9 Explain the quantity theory of money and how monetary policy works in the Classical model.

10 List five problems often encountered in conducting monetary policy.

The preceding chapter ended with a discussion of financial panics that can occur when people lose faith in one financial asset and want to shift to another. Financial panics are no strangers to banking. In the 1800s, most market economies suffered a financial panic every 20 years or so. Initially a few people would suddenly fear they wouldn't be able to get their money out of their bank. They'd run down to the bank to get it. Others would see them getting their money and would do likewise. This was referred to as a *run on the bank.* As a result, their bank would have to close. If a bank closed, people would worry about other banks closing, and they'd run to *their* banks. That process could spread uncontrollably; banks would close and there would be a general financial panic. These panics led to considerable debate about what government should do to regulate and control the banking system.

Much of the debate about the Canadian banking system in the 1800s concerned whether there should be a central bank (a bank that could make loans to other banks in times of crisis and could limit those banks' expansionary loans at other times). Supporters of a central bank argued that a central bank would create financial stability, while opponents of a central bank argued that it would cause recessions and favour industrial interests over farming interests.

For a time, the development of the Canadian banking system closely followed what was happening in the United States. The Bank of Montreal was Canada's first bank, established in 1817 by a group of merchants in Montreal. In the next 50 years, over 20 banks opened their doors, and by Confederation there were almost 30 chartered banks. Each had the power to issue its own paper notes, which circulated as currency. When you wanted to buy something you could either use one of these bank notes, or you could write a cheque against your deposits in a chartered bank. Before the introduction of bank notes, "money" took several forms, ranging from playing cards (altered by the colonial authorities to act as currency) to gold and silver.

In the United States, banks expanded along regional lines, and there were few truly national banks. This is in stark contrast to the development of the Canadian banking system, which was characterized by centrally managed banks that spanned provincial borders. These differences between the U.S. and Canadian banking systems remain today: there are thousands of banks in the United States, each with relatively few branches, whereas Canada has relatively few banks, each with many branches.

Canadian banks provided the "lubrication" necessary for economic development. They gathered savings and lent them out to entrepreneurs and governments. Banks also provided the vehicle for foreign currency transactions, which were of vital importance to the development of the Canadian economy.

The Great Depression changed public confidence in financial institutions, and in 1933 the MacMillan Commission was charged with investigating whether Canada needed a central bank. Canadian politicians looked south of the border in their quest for a solution, since the United States created their central bank, the Federal Reserve Bank, in 1913. While many Canadians wondered whether Canada really needed a similar institution, critics of the Canadian financial system blamed the chartered banks for contributing to the Depression. Not surprisingly, the financial community lobbied against the introduction of a central body that would regulate their activities. The net result was that the MacMillan Commission recommended the establishment of a central bank for Canada, and in 1934 the Bank of Canada was officially created by the Bank of Canada Act.

The Bank of Canada was initially a private corporation that was later nationalized in 1938. It was given the powers to: replace the existing currency with Bank of Canada bank notes; force chartered banks to hold a certain proportion of their deposits as cash or on deposit at the Bank of Canada; make advances to the chartered banks when appropriate; and act as the federal government's banker.

HISTORY AND STRUCTURE OF THE BANK OF CANADA

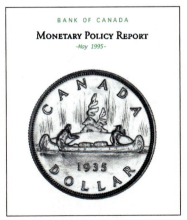

The *Monetary Policy Report* offers up-to-date information on Canadian monetary policy.

The Bank of Canada Is a Central Bank

Central bank   A bankers' bank; it conducts monetary policy and supervises the financial system.

1   The Bank of Canada was created in 1934 in response to a financial crisis that had begun in 1907.

Monetary policy   Policy of influencing the economy through changes in the money supply and credit availability.

2   Monetary policy is a policy that influences the economy through changes in the money supply and available credit.

Central Bank Independence

3   The price stability objective of the late 1980s and early 1990s triggered another round of debate over central bank independence in Canada.

Governor of the Bank of Canada   The head of the Bank of Canada, appointed by the federal cabinet for a seven-year term.

A **central bank** is a type of bankers' bank. If banks need to borrow money, they go to the central bank, just as when you need to borrow money, you go to a neighbourhood bank. If there's a financial panic and a run on banks, the central bank is there to make loans to the banks until the panic goes away. Since its IOUs are cash, simply by issuing an IOU it can create money. A central bank's duties also include assisting government with its financial affairs. A central bank serves as a financial advisor to government. As is often the case with financial advisors, the government sometimes doesn't like the advice and doesn't follow it.

Besides being a banker's bank and a financial advisor, the Bank of Canada also conducts monetary policy for the government. **Monetary policy** is a policy of influencing the economy through changes in the money supply and the availability of credit in the economy. You'll recall from the last chapter that credit simply represents savings made available to be borrowed, so when we say that monetary policy aims at affecting the availability of credit, we mean that the central bank attempts to make available an appropriate level of savings to the economy. Monetary policy is one of the two main macroeconomic tools (the other is fiscal policy) by which government attempts to control the aggregate economy. Unlike fiscal policy, which is controlled by the government directly, monetary policy is controlled by the Bank of Canada.

In many countries such as Germany, Great Britain, and France, the central bank is a part of their government, just as this country's Department of Finance is a part of the Canadian government. In Canada, the central bank is not part of the government in the same way as in some European countries. The Bank of Canada is a Crown corporation, not under the direct day-to-day control of the federal government.

The head of the Bank of Canada is the **Governor of the Bank.** The Governor is appointed by the federal Cabinet for a seven-year term. So far we've had six governors:

1934–54	Graham Towers
1955–61	James Coyne
1961–73	Louis Rasminsky
1973–87	Gerald Bouey
1987–94	John Crow
1994–	Gordon Thiessen

The Governor cannot be removed from office and, since mid-way through Rasminsky's terms, must agree to follow the government's direction or resign if he or she cannot support its policy. This was the result of the "Coyne Affair." Governor Coyne refused to expand the money supply at a time when the federal government was undertaking expansionary fiscal policies. This caused the interest rate to rise. Coyne was convinced that expanding the money supply (which would lower the interest rate) would make the recession of the late 1950s worse. He eventually resigned (just before the government had declared the Governor's seat to be vacant—they couldn't fire him so they decided to simply eliminate the position), and in the mid-1960s Rasminsky agreed that the government had the final say on whether to expand the money supply.

That is not to say that there's been harmony in the setting of monetary policy since 1961. The most recent conflicts arose between 1987 and 1994 when John Crow embarked on a policy that was aimed at stabilizing the price level. As we'll see shortly, in the long run, all that monetary policy can do is provide an anchor for the nation's unit of account. That is, all it can do is affect the price level. In the long run, it can't really affect employment or the level of output. Crow was convinced that monetary policy should take this long-run view even though monetary policy might have some short-run effects capable of perhaps reducing unemployment during a recession. The debate over price stability as the only objective for monetary policy was high-pitched and, as we'll see in the next chapter, it contributed to the recession of the early 1990s. While John Crow achieved price stability (we'll talk about what this means in a later chapter), it didn't help him win reappointment to a second term as Governor, and in 1994 Gordon Thiessen took over the job.

■n Canada the central bank is the Bank of Canada, and much of this chapter is about its structure. But there are many central banks. Let's briefly introduce you to some of the others.

Bundesbank   In Germany, the central bank is called the Bundesbank. It has a reputation as a fierce inflation fighter, in large part because of the historical legacy of the German hyperinflation of the late 1920s and early 1930s. It has a system of reserve requirements that constrain the ability of banks to expand the money supply. In the mid-1990s, to fight inflation, it maintained high interest rates relative to the rest of the world, causing international monetary disruption, which will be discussed in a later chapter.

The Bank of England   The Bank of England is sometimes called the Old Lady of Threadneedle Street (because it's located on that street). It does not use a required reserve mechanism. Instead, individual banks determine their own needed reserves, so any reserves they have would, in a sense, be excess reserves. Needless to say, bank reserves are much lower in England than they are in Germany.

How does the Old Lady control the money supply? With the equivalent of open market operations and with what might be called "tea control." Since there are only a few large banks in England, the Old Lady simply passes on the word at tea as to which direction they think the money supply should be going. Alas for sentimentalists, "tea control" is fading in England.

The Federal Reserve Bank   The central bank in the United States is called the Federal Reserve Bank. It's made up of 12 regional reserve banks, and is run by the Board of Governors. It uses reserve requirements and open market operations to control the ability of banks to create money. ("Open market operations" are explained later in this chapter.) The Chairman of the Board of Governors of the Federal Reserve is appointed by the President for a four-year term. The Federal Reserve Bank is affectionately known as the "Fed," and its actions have repercussion effects around the world, which we'll discuss in a later chapter.

The Bank of Japan   The Bank of Japan uses reserve requirements and open market operations to control the money supply. Reserve requirements are similar to those in the United States, but because banks are allowed a longer time to do their averaging, excess reserves are much lower in Japan than in the United States and Canada. Until the 1990s, the Bank of Japan held the Japanese interest rate far below the world rate, which caused an international outflow of savings and a corresponding trade surplus. In the early 1990s, Japanese interest rates were increased substantially, in part due to the actions of the Bank of Japan. By late 1995 interest rates began to fall again.

Clearly there's more to be said about each of these central banks, but this brief introduction should give you a sense of both the similarities and the diversities among the central banks of the world

John Crow's focus on price stability and his unwillingness to respond to double digit unemployment by "priming the monetary pumps" of the economy led to calls for a change in the structure of the Bank of Canada. Monetary policy is set by the Governor with the advice of his senior advisors. There is a Board of Directors that is made up of 12 nonspecialists in monetary economics, having a variety of backgrounds, but the Board has little say in the direction and the conduct of monetary policy. Proponents of change argue that there is too much power concentrated in the hands of unelected officials, and that those charged with operating the nation's monetary policy should be ultimately responsible to the people. They also suggest that the Board of Directors should be comprised of persons specializing in monetary policy and that the Directors receive a salary that would encourage their active participation in the design of monetary policy. There have also been calls for regional representation in the structure of the Bank of Canada, particularly during the recession of the early 1990s. As we'll see in a later chapter, Governor Crow raised Canadian interest rates in an effort to restrain inflationary pressures that were located primarily in central Canada. This had the desired effect of reducing demand in Ontario and Quebec, but it crippled many industries in regional areas that were already operating at the margin. Critics of the Bank of Canada want to see more public input into the design and implementation of monetary policy.

Opponents of change at the Bank of Canada point to the relationship between the Governor and the Minister of Finance. The Governor must take direction from the federal Finance Minister, or resign. The fact that Governor Crow was not forced to resign, they argue, shows the government's tacit agreement with Crow's policies. Furthermore, the critics suggest that if the Governor has to worry about electoral politics, he or she won't follow monetary policies that might reduce his chances of reelection or reappointment. If he has to worry about reelection to another term, he may not undertake the policies that are in the best interests of the nation. Having an independent central bank that is ultimately subservient to the Minister of Finance (if push comes to shove), it is argued, is the best of both worlds.

All of this does not mean that the Governor is impotent. As the government's banker, the Governor of the Bank of Canada can make running a budget deficit difficult for the government. He can exercise control over the amounts the government is allowed to borrow from the central bank, and the rates at which they can borrow. If policy/political disagreement became so grave that the Governor resigned, there would be serious implications for financial stability, particularly with respect to international investment. This would ultimately come back to haunt the government. Maintaining reputation and credibility are essential elements of any institutional arrangement, so if the Governor resigns, there's a price to pay in rebuilding the central bank's image in international markets.

Let's briefly touch on how international considerations affect the design and implementation of monetary policy in Canada. We'll see that exchange rates play a critical role in the process.

International Considerations

Exchange rate The rate at which one country's currency can be traded for another country's currency.

4 Canada relies heavily on international trade, so the Bank of Canada is always looking at how its policies affect the exchange rate and Canadian interest rates relative to those in the rest of the world.

We said that the dismissal or resignation of the Governor of the Bank of Canada could have disastrous effects on international investment. To understand why, we first need to talk a little bit about exchange rates. An **exchange rate** is simply the value of one nation's currency expressed in terms of another nation's currency. It tells us how much of one currency it takes to buy a unit of another currency. For example, the exchange rate between the United States dollar and the Canadian dollar tells us the value of a Canadian dollar in terms of U.S. dollars, and the value of a U.S. dollar in terms of Canadian dollars. Since there are two currencies involved, it's possible to measure exchange rates two different ways. That explains why, for example, you might turn on your TV and see that the Canadian dollar is trading for $0.75 U.S. dollars while today's newspaper says the exchange rate is $1.33. Why are the numbers different? The answer is simple: one is measuring how many Canadian dollars it takes to buy a U.S. dollar (1.33), while the other tells us how many U.S. dollars a Canadian dollar will buy (.75). If you look hard at these numbers you'll see that one is just the reciprocal (inverse) of the other: the reciprocal of 0.75 (3/4) is 1.33 (4/3).

We'll define the exchange rate to be *the domestic currency price of foreign exchange*—that is, it tells us how many Canadian dollars it takes to get a unit of the foreign currency. So, if we're looking at the Canadian dollar–U.S. dollar exchange rate, it tells us how many Canadian dollars it takes to buy one U.S. dollar (in our example, $1.33 buys one U.S. dollar). If we look at the Canadian dollar–Japanese yen exchange rate, it tells us how many dollars it takes to buy a yen. Similarly for the Canadian dollar–French franc exchange rate. Exhibit 1 presents information on exchange rates.

Why do exchange rates matter? For a country like Canada, international trade is important. The trade sector of the economy employs over 2 million people. Exchange rates matter because they allow people with different currencies to buy goods and services from each other. When Canadians want to buy foreign goods and services, they

EXHIBIT 1 **Foreign Exchange-Rate Table**

Source: The *Globe and Mail,* March 3, 1995.

Cross Rates

	Canadian dollar	U.S. dollar	British pound	German mark	Japanese yen	Swiss franc	French franc	Dutch guilder	Italian lira
Canada dollar	—	1.4036	2.2336	0.9624	0.014650	1.1351	0.2736	0.8592	0.000848
U.S. dollar	0.7125	—	1.5913	0.6857	0.010437	0.8087	0.1949	0.6121	0.000604
British pound	0.4477	0.6284	—	0.4309	0.006559	0.5082	0.1225	0.3847	0.000380
German mark	1.0391	1.4584	2.3209	—	0.015222	1.1794	0.2843	0.8928	0.000881
Japanese yen	68.26	95.81	152.46	65.69	—	77.48	18.68	58.65	0.057884
Swiss franc	0.8810	1.2365	1.9678	0.8479	0.012906	—	0.2410	0.7569	0.000747
French franc	3.6550	5.1301	8.1637	3.5175	0.053545	4.1488	—	3.1404	0.003099
Dutch guilder	1.1639	1.6336	2.5996	1.1201	0.017051	1.3211	0.3184	—	0.000987
Italian lira	1179.25	1655.19	2633.96	1134.91	17.275943	1338.56	322.64	1013.21	—

Mid-market rates in Toronto at noon, Mar. 2, 1995. Prepared by the Bank of Montreal Treasury Group.

	$1 U.S. in Cdn.$ =	$1 Cdn. in U.S.$ =	Country	Currency	Cdn.$ per unit	U.S.$ per unit
U.S./Canada spot	1.4036	0.7125	Fiji	Dollar	0.9853	0.7020
1 month forward	1.4062	0.7111	Finland	Markka	0.3144	0.2240
2 months forward	1.4087	0.7099	France	Franc	0.2736	0.1949
3 months forward	1.4106	0.7089	Greece	Drachma	0.00604	0.00431
6 months forward	1.4158	0.7063	Hong Kong	Dollar	0.1815	0.1293
12 months forward	1.4220	0.7032	Hungary	Forint	0.01258	0.00896
3 years forward	1.4431	0.6930	Iceland	Krona	0.02136	0.01522
5 years forward	1.4776	0.6768	India	Rupee	0.04473	0.03187
7 years forward	1.5356	0.6512	Indonesia	Rupiah	0.000634	0.000452
10 years forward	1.6156	0.6190	Ireland	Punt	2.2219	1.5830

need to trade Canadian dollars for foreign currency, which is then used to buy the foreign goods and services. When foreigners want to buy Canadian goods and services, they need to trade their currency for Canadian dollars. They then use those dollars to buy what they want from Canada.

The importance of all of this has to do with our previous definition of monetary policy. Recall we said monetary policy influences the economy through changes in the money supply and the availability of credit. From what we've just discussed, it's clear that monetary policy—*changes in the money supply*—will affect international trade, since the relative price of one nation's currency (the exchange rate) depends critically on how much of it is in circulation. For example, consider a world that includes only two countries, Canada and Germany. If the Canadian money supply rises while the German money supply remains fixed, the Canadian dollar will lose value against the mark—there are relatively more Canadian dollars around, so each is worth less than before.

If the dollar loses value, what will this do to international trade? What will it do to employment in industries that produce goods for export to other countries? The answer depends on many factors, including what happens to prices, interest rates, and incomes, both at home and abroad. So, if the Governor of the Bank of Canada is forced to resign, this might create increased levels of uncertainty in international markets, and the dollar could lose a lot of value (or gain value, if the market consensus was that the Governor had to go!). This has implications for where international investors want to place their funds; it could lead to changes in the pattern of international trade, thereby affecting the equilibrium level of income and employment in the Canadian economy.

All of this means that monetary policy cannot be set without consideration of international issues. We'll discuss this in much greater detail later in Chapters 15–17.

MONETARY POLICY

Monetary policy is probably the most used policy in macroeconomics. Although the Governor of the Bank of Canada must follow a directive from the Minister of Finance, in practice the Bank of Canada conducts and controls monetary policy, whereas fiscal policy is conducted directly by the government. Both policies are directed toward the same end: influencing the level of aggregate economic activity, hopefully in a beneficial manner. (In many other countries, institutional arrangements are different and the central bank is part of government, so both monetary and fiscal policy are directly conducted by the government, albeit by different branches of government.)

Actual decisions about monetary policy are made by the Governor in consultation with senior staff. The Board of Directors meets with the Governor on a regular basis. Minutes of their discussion are published in the *Bank of Canada Review,* published quarterly (with monthly supplements). The financial press and business community dissect every word uttered by the Governor. They're looking for information that will set the course of the economy over the near term.

The basic tools of monetary policy are:

1. The bank rate.
2. Cash management.

Let's discuss each in turn.

Tools of Monetary Policy

5   The primary tools of monetary policy are changes in the bank rate and cash management operations. Changes in the bank rate affect the term structure of interest rates. Cash management operations work by changing banks' excess reserves.

Bank rate   The rate of interest at which chartered banks can borrow from the Bank of Canada.

Students will find a wealth of data in the Bank of Canada Review.

Term structure of interest rates   The structure of yields on financial instruments with similar characteristics; it links short-term interest rates to long-term interest rates.

Arbitrage   The purchase of a product in a low-price market for resale in a high-price market.

The Bank Rate
The **bank rate** is the rate of interest at which chartered banks can borrow from the Bank of Canada. Until early 1980, the Bank of Canada set the bank rate at discrete intervals, usually when the U.S. discount rate (the rate at which U.S. banks can borrow from the Federal Reserve) changed. The timing was linked to keeping interest rate differentials across Canada and the United States stable enough so that the exchange rate didn't fluctuate wildly. How could that happen? International investors search for the best returns on their capital. If U.S. interest rates rise above Canadian rates, and other conditions are unchanged, international investors will sell Canadian dollars for U.S. dollars, putting downward pressure on the Canadian dollar (the exchange rate would change). If Canadian interest rates move above U.S. interest rates, capital will be attracted into Canada and the Canadian dollar will gain value, all other things being equal. If these capital flows become sensitive to interest rate differentials, it's not hard to see that this might cause wild swings in the exchange rate. We'll talk about why these swings might be bad for the economy in Chapters 16 and 17.

Changes in the bank rate are important because all other interest rates are related to the bank rate through what is known as the **term structure of interest rates**—the structure of yields on financial instruments with similar characteristics (like risk), but different terms, or length of time, to maturity. We know there is more than just one interest rate in the economy—there are hundreds of interest rates, each related to a particular financial claim: A Government of Canada 10-year bond carries with it a certain interest rate, and this differs from interest rates on 30-day commercial paper and a short-term Treasury bill. The term structure of interest rates describes a relationship between short-term and long-term interest rates. For example, it links short-term Government of Canada bond rates to long-term Government of Canada bond rates (remember the similar risk assumption), or short-term corporate bond rates to long-term corporate bond rates (which are more risky than Government of Canada bonds because there's little chance the federal government will default). **Arbitrage**—the buying and selling of similar goods and services across different markets—provides the link between interest rates on dissimilar assets (like Government of Canada bonds and corporate bonds). Exhibit 2 (a) illustrates the links between short-term and long-term bonds, while Exhibit 2 (b) shows the relationship between the 91-day Treasury bill rate and the 91-day commercial paper rate.

Changes in the bank rate affect the relationship between interest rates on short-term and long-term bonds. If this relationship becomes unstable or unpredictable, firms will hold off on capital-intensive projects that require investment financing, since they can't put firm numbers on their costs or revenues. (Recall our discussion of present values in the "Financial Institutions" chapter: When interest rates change, present value calculations change.) If investment plans are postponed or cancelled, the level of economic activity won't be as high—and output and employment could fall.

Today the bank rate is set to be a *penalty rate* of one-quarter of a percent above the average interest rate on Treasury bills auctioned during the week. It is a penalty

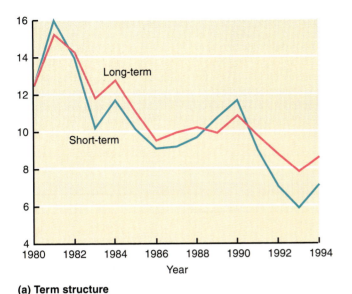

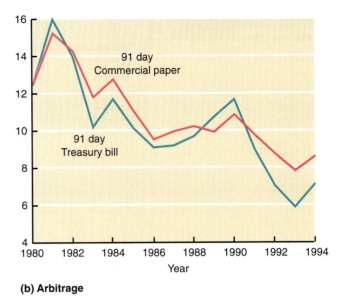

(a) Term structure

(b) Arbitrage

EXHIBIT 2   Relationships between Different Interest Rates

(a) The term structure ties short-term interest rates to long-term interest rates.
(b) Arbitrage between markets links interest rates to different financial assets.

rate because the borrower (a chartered bank) would be better off liquidating some of its Treasury bills (and losing only the interest on the Treasury bill) than directly borrowing funds from the Bank of Canada. In practice the bank rate is of little use since chartered banks have less-expensive ways of replenishing their cash holdings (they call in short-term loans—known as day-to-day loans—made to investment dealers). Today changes in the bank rate simply reflect the direction the Bank of Canada wants interest rates to follow.

6 Changes in the bank rate provide a signal to the market about where the Bank of Canada wants interest rates to go.

Cash Management   The second major tool of monetary policy in Canada involves **cash management.** Cash management operations are the main technique for operating monetary policy in Canada. They include a variety of **open market operations—** buying and selling of government bonds and bills—as well as **drawdowns and redeposits—**the transfer of government deposits between chartered banks (and others) and the Bank of Canada. All of these activities involve the same basic principle: give the chartered banks more, or less, cash and allow their entrepreneurial spirit to determine the effects on deposits. This directly affects the money supply, as banks lend out their excess reserves or, when they find themselves short of cash, call in loans.

Let's look at some examples.

Cash management   The main technique for operating monetary policy, including open market operations and drawdowns and redeposits; aimed at providing the chartered banks with more or less cash.

Open market operations   The Bank of Canada's day-to-day buying and selling of government securities.

Drawdown   The transfer of government deposits from the chartered banks and other financial institutions to the Bank of Canada.

Open Market Operations   Open market operations involve the purchase or sale of federal government securities such as Treasury bills and Government of Canada bonds. When the Bank of Canada buys bonds, it deposits the funds in federal government accounts at the chartered banks. From the last chapter you'll recall that chartered banks can create money by lending out their excess reserves. When the Bank of Canada pays the government for its bonds, chartered bank cash reserves rise. Chartered banks don't like to hold excess reserves, so they lend out the excess, thereby expanding the deposit base of the economy. The money supply rises. Thus, an open market purchase is an example of **expansionary monetary policy** (usually defined to be one that tends to raise income and reduce interest rates), since it raises the money supply (as long as the chartered banks strive to minimize their excess reserves).

Redeposits   The transfer of government deposits from the Bank of Canada to the chartered banks and other financial institutions.

Expansionary monetary policy   Monetary policy aimed at increasing the money supply and raising the level of aggregate demand.

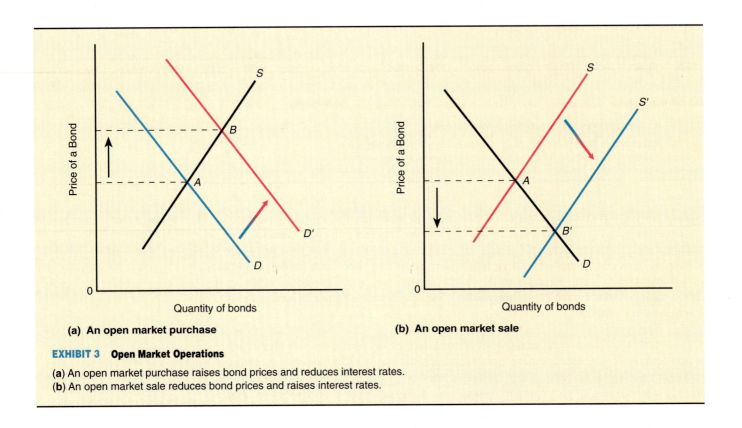

(a) **An open market purchase**

(b) **An open market sale**

EXHIBIT 3   Open Market Operations

(a) An open market purchase raises bond prices and reduces interest rates.
(b) An open market sale reduces bond prices and raises interest rates.

Contractionary monetary policy
Monetary policy aimed at reducing the money supply and thereby restraining aggregate demand.

An open market sale has the opposite effect. Here, the Bank of Canada sells bonds. In return for the bond, the Bank of Canada receives a cheque drawn against a chartered bank. The chartered bank loses demand deposits (since the Bank of Canada "cashes" the cheque and takes the money away from the chartered bank), and the money supply falls. That's an example of **contractionary monetary policy** (lowering income and raising interest rates).

What happens to bond prices and interest rates during this process? Exhibit 3 (a) illustrates the effects of an open market purchase. The Bank of Canada buys bonds, thereby raising the demand for bonds. Bond prices rise, and since we know that bond prices and interest rates are inversely related (when one goes up the other goes down), interest rates fall. That's what we'd expect of an expansionary monetary policy.

Exhibit 3 (b) shows us what happens to bond prices in an open market sale. From that you can figure out the change in interest rates. As the Bank of Canada sells bonds, the supply of bonds shifts right, leading to lower bond prices. What happens to interest rates? If you said they go up, you're on track.

This process takes place continuously. As the government's banker, the Bank of

Canada is always looking to buy and sell government bonds. In fact, every Tuesday there's a Treasury bill auction in which billions of dollars of new financial claims against the government are bought and sold. It's through this process that the Bank of Canada is able to provide funds to the federal government. This Bank of Canada process also has a major impact on Canadian interest rates, because those interest rates are, in large measure, a function of the bank rate. Through this major impact on Canadian interest rates, the value of the Canadian dollar against a host of other currencies is affected. That's because, other things equal, the most attractive location for capital is where interest rates are highest. The higher the Canadian interest rate, the more attractive is foreign investment in Canada and the higher the value of Canada's dollar.

> *To expand the money supply, the Bank of Canada buys bonds.*
> *To contract the money supply, the Bank of Canada sells bonds.*

Let's go through an example using T-accounts. Say there's only one chartered bank, Textland Bank, with branches all over the country. Textland is fully loaned out at a desired 10 percent desired reserve requirement. For simplicity, assume people hold no cash. (In reality, the desire to hold cash reduces a bank's reserves, and would thereby reduce the effects of an open market operation on the money supply, so our example just helps to make the point—but then you already knew that, since in reality, there's more than one bank.) Textland's beginning balance sheet is presented in Exhibit 4.

7 An open market operation changes reserves, which leads the banks to increase or decrease loans, which affects the income and price levels in the economy.

EXHIBIT 4   Textland Bank Balance Sheet   Beginning Balance

Assets		Liabilities and shareholders' equity	
Cash (reserves)	$ 300,000	Demand deposits	$3,000,000
Loans	2,000,000	Shareholders' equity	1,000,000
Treasury bills	400,000		
Property	1,300,000		
Total assets	$4,000,000	Total liabilities and net worth	$4,000,000

Now say the Bank of Canada sells $10,000 worth of Treasury bills to individuals. The person who buys them pays with a cheque to the Bank of Canada for $10,000. The Bank of Canada, in turn, presents the cheque to the chartered bank, getting $10,000 in cash from the bank. This step is shown in Transaction 1.

EXHIBIT 4   (continued)   Transaction 1

Assets		Liabilities and net worth	
Cash (reserves)	$300,000	Demand deposits	$3,000,000
Payment to Bank of Canada (person's Treasury bill purchase)	(10,000)	Deposit for cash (person's cheque)	(10,000)
Total cash	$ 290,000	Total deposits	$2,990,000
Loans	2,000,000	Shareholders' equity	1,000,000
Treasury bills	400,000		
Property	1,300,000		
Total assets	$3,990,000	Total liabilities and shareholders' equity	$3,990,000

As you can see, bank reserves are now $290,000, which is too low to meet the desired 10 percent requirements on demand deposits of $2,990,000. With a 10 percent desired reserve requirement, $2,990,000 in deposits would require $(1/10) \times$ $2,990,000 = $299,000, so the bank is $9,000 short of reserves. It must figure out a way to meet its desired reserve requirement. Let's say that it calls in $9,000 of its loans. After doing so it has assets of $299,000 in cash and $2,990,000 in demand deposits, so it looks as if the bank has met its desired reserve requirement.

If the bank could meet its desired reserve requirement that way, its balance sheet would be as shown in Transaction 2. Loans would decrease by $9,000 and cash would increase by the $9,000 necessary to meet the reserve requirement.

EXHIBIT 4   (continued)   Transaction 2

Assets			Liabilities and Shareholders' equity	
Cash (reserves)	$ 290,000		Demand deposits	$2,990,000
Loans (repaid)	9,000		Shareholders' equity	1,000,000
Total cash		$ 299,000		
Loans	2,000,000			
Loans called in	(9,000)			
Total loans		1,991,000		
Treasury bills		400,000		
Property		1,300,000		
			Total liabilities and	
Total assets		$3,990,000	shareholders' equity	$3,990,000

Unfortunately for the bank, meeting its desired reserve requirement isn't that easy. That $9,000 in cash had to come from somewhere. Most likely, the person who paid off the loans in cash did it partly by running down her chequing account, borrowing all the cash she could from others, and using whatever other options she had. Since by assumption in this example, people don't hold cash, the banking system was initially fully loaned out, and Textland Bank was the only bank, the only cash in the economy was in Textland Bank's vaults! So that $9,000 in cash had to come from its vaults. Calling in the loans cannot directly solve its reserve problem. It still has reserves of only $290,000.

But calling in its loans did *indirectly* help solve the problem. Calling in loans decreased investment which, because it decreased aggregate demand, decreased the income in the economy. (If you're not sure why this is the case, think back to the Keynesian model.) That decrease in income decreases the amount of demand deposits people want to hold. As demand deposits decrease, the bank's need for reserves decreases.

Contraction of the money supply in this example works in the opposite way to an expansion of the money supply discussed in the last chapter. Banks keep trying to meet their desired reserve requirement by getting cash, only to find that for the banking system as a whole the total cash is limited. Thus, the banking system as a whole must continue to call in loans until that decline in loans causes income to fall sufficiently to cause demand deposits to fall to a level that can be supported by the smaller reserves. In this example, with a money multiplier of 10, when demand deposits have fallen by $100,000 to $2,900,000, total reserves available to the system ($290,000) will be sufficient to meet the reserve requirement.

Drawdown The transfer of government deposits from the chartered banks and other financial institutions to the Bank of Canada.

Redeposits The transfer of government deposits from the Bank of Canada to the chartered banks and financial institutions.

Drawdown/Redeposits A **drawdown** is a transfer of government deposits from the chartered banks (and other financial institutions) to the Bank of Canada. A **redeposit** is a transfer in the opposite direction: from the Bank of Canada to the chartered banks (and others). Drawdowns and redeposits are the main tools for implementing monetary policy on a day-to-day basis, and they operate in a manner that is identical to an open market operation. Drawdowns reduce chartered bank reserves, leading to a contraction of the money supply. Redeposits provide the chartered banks with additional reserves that can be loaned out until actual bank reserves equal their desired

A REMINDER

MONETARY POLICY TOOLS

■he tools of monetary policy are:

1. Changing the bank rate.
2. Cash management operations, which include open market operations and drawdowns and redeposits.

Of these, the most important are cash management operations.

---

level. Through these techniques the Bank of Canada is able to exert control over the liquidity of the banking system, and, ultimately, over the money supply.

Both Keynesians and Classicals agree that monetary policy is important, but they differ in how they see monetary policy affecting the economy, and in their recommendations to the Bank of Canada about how to conduct monetary policy. These differences will become more apparent when we discuss macro policy in later chapters, but to provide a good foundation for those later discussions, let's now briefly consider these differences.

How Monetary Policy Works

Monetary Policy in the Keynesian Model In Keynesian terms, monetary policy can be seen as an alternative method of shifting the aggregate expenditures curve up or down, thereby controlling the level of income in the economy. Let's see how.

In Exhibit 5 (a) we see that when the Bank of Canada decreases the money supply (uses contractionary monetary policy), it increases the interest rate. Exhibit 5 (b) shows the effect of that increased interest rate on investment. As you can see, because the demand for investment is downward sloping, as discussed in an earlier chapter, the rise in interest rate decreases the quantity of investment.

A decrease in investment starts the income multiplier process and decreases income by a multiple of the amount that investment decreased. Exhibit 5 (c) shows the effect of a fall in investment on income. Thus, *contractionary* monetary policy tends to *decrease* the money supply, *increase* the interest rate, *decrease* investment, and *decrease* income and output:

$$\text{contractionary monetary policy } M\downarrow \;\rightarrow\; i\uparrow \;\rightarrow\; I\downarrow \;\rightarrow\; Y\downarrow$$

Expansionary monetary policy works in the opposite manner, as Exhibit 5 (d) shows. *Expansionary* monetary policy tends to *increase* the money supply, *decrease* the interest rate, *increase* investment, and *increase* income and output:

$$\text{expansionary monetary policy } M\uparrow \;\rightarrow\; i\downarrow \;\rightarrow\; I\uparrow \;\rightarrow\; Y\uparrow$$

The preceding discussion of how monetary policy works in theory is helpful, but it probably isn't very intuitive. Let's go through the reasoning again, only this time focusing on trying to provide an intuitive feel for what is happening. Say the Bank of Canada uses open market operations. As the Bank of Canada either injects or pulls out reserves, it influences the amount of money banks have to lend and the interest rate at which they can lend it. When banks have more reserves than desired, they want to lend. (That's how they make their profit.) To get people to borrow more from them, banks will decrease the interest rate they charge on loans. So expansionary monetary policy tends to decrease the interest rate banks charge their customers; contractionary policy tends to increase the interest rate banks charge customers. Expansionary monetary policy increases the amount of money banks have to lend, which tends to increase investment. Contractionary monetary policy decreases the amount of money banks have to lend, which tends to decrease investment.

If you still haven't got it, then think about the process in terms of the Keynesian **demand for money** and **supply of money.** As we saw in the last chapter, people want to hold money because it's useful to them as a medium of exchange and as a store of

8 In the Keynesian model, monetary policy works as follows:

$$M\uparrow \rightarrow \quad i\downarrow \rightarrow \quad I\uparrow \rightarrow \quad Y\uparrow$$
$$M\downarrow \rightarrow \quad i\uparrow \rightarrow \quad I\downarrow \rightarrow \quad Y\downarrow$$

Demand for money The total amount of money the public desires to hold at a point in time.

Supply of money The total amount of money in the economy at a point in time.

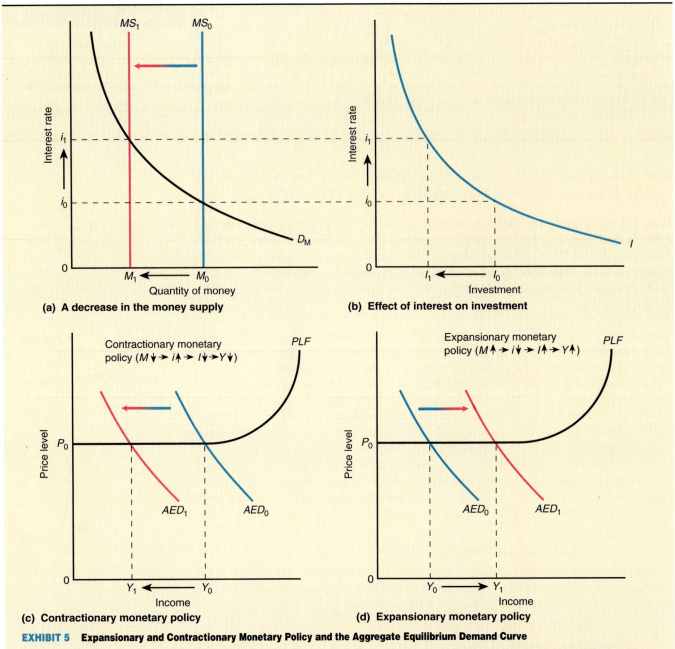

EXHIBIT 5   Expansionary and Contractionary Monetary Policy and the Aggregate Equilibrium Demand Curve

With a decrease in the money supply, the interest rate will rise from i_0 to i_1, as shown in (**a**). The rise in the interest rate results in a decrease in investment from I_0 to I_1, as shown in (**b**). The fall in investment shifts the aggregate equilibrium demand curve from AED_0 to AED_1. Income decreases from Y_0 to Y_1, as shown in (**c**), which decreases savings sufficiently so that savings equal investment. In (**d**), expansionary monetary policy is shown working the opposite way. It shifts the aggregate equilibrium demand curve upward, from AED_0 to AED_1. Income increases from Y_0 to Y_1.

wealth. But holding money isn't costless. *Money pays a lower return than other financial assets.* So how much money people want to hold depends on the interest rate on those other financial assets. The higher the interest rate on other financial assets, the greater the opportunity cost of holding money and the lower the quantity of money demanded. At lower interest rates, quantity of money demanded is larger because the opportunity cost of holding money is lower. Demand for money as a function of the interest rate is shown by the curve D_M in Exhibit 5 (a). That takes care of the demand side of the market.[1]

The supply of money in the Keynesian framework is determined when the Bank of Canada sets the amount of reserves in the system. Then the total amount of money in the economy is determined by the desired reserve requirement and the money multiplier. While it's not true in practice, we'll assume that the Bank of Canada can perfectly determine the amount of money supplied to the economy and that the amount of money supplied isn't influenced by the interest rate. That makes the supply of money perfectly vertical, as in Exhibit 5 (a).

The Keynesian theory of interest comes from combining the supply of money with the demand for money as in Exhibit 5 (a). The interest rate is determined where the quantity of money supplied equals the quantity of money demanded (i_0). If the supply of money falls, say from M_0 to M_1 as in Exhibit 5 (a), the interest rate will rise from i_0 to i_1. If the demand for money falls, the interest rate will rise. Keynes argued that, in the short run, the money market determines the interest rate. If interest rates rise, investment will fall, aggregate equilibrium demand will fall, and hence output will fall. That's contractionary monetary policy at work.

Keynesian Monetary Policy in the Circular Flow   Exhibit 6's familiar circular flow diagram shows how monetary policy works in the Keynesian model. In the Keynesian view, monetary policy works inside the financial sector to help equate the flow of savings with investment. When the economy is operating at too low a level of income and when savings exceeds investment, in the absence of monetary policy, income will fall. Expansionary monetary policy tries to channel more savings into investment so the fall in income is stopped. It does so by increasing the available credit, lowering the interest rate, and increasing investment and hence income.

Contractionary monetary policy is called for when savings is smaller than investment and the economy is operating at too high a level of income, causing inflationary pressures. In this case, monetary policy tries to restrict the flow of savings into investment. Thus, to control the economy, Keynesians tend to favour an activist monetary policy, with the Bank of Canada taking an active role in controlling the interest rate.

The Keynesian Emphasis on the Interest Rate   Because Keynesians see monetary policy working through the effect of interest rates on investment, they focus on the interest rate in judging monetary policy. They interpret a rising interest rate as a tightening of monetary policy. They interpret a falling interest rate as a loosening of monetary policy.

Keynesians believe the Bank of Canada should target interest rates in setting monetary policy. For example, if the interest rate is currently 6 percent and the Bank of Canada wants to loosen monetary policy, it should buy government securities (thereby forcing their price up) until the interest rate falls to 5 percent. If it wants to tighten monetary policy, it should sell government securities (forcing their price down) to make the interest rate go up to, say, 6.5 percent.

In the 1950s, the early Keynesians advocated keeping the interest rate low. More recently, Keynesians have advocated keeping the interest rate low enough to foster growth, but high enough to prevent inflationary pressures. As you can imagine, it's a fine line between the two, so whatever policy the Bank of Canada chooses usually has critics.

---

[1]If you're really on the ball, you might ask why *anyone* holds money if it means they have to forgo the interest they'd receive on a bond. The answer is that people need money to transact, so money must provide some benefit—some kind of a return—albeit not in the form of interest (when was the last time you used your credit card in a vending machine?). When choosing between interest-bearing and noninterest-bearing assets (bonds and money), people try to balance off the risk and return of their portfolio, taking all of these issues into account. How that's done is the stuff of a course devoted to money and banking, so we won't say any more about it here. Take another economics course!

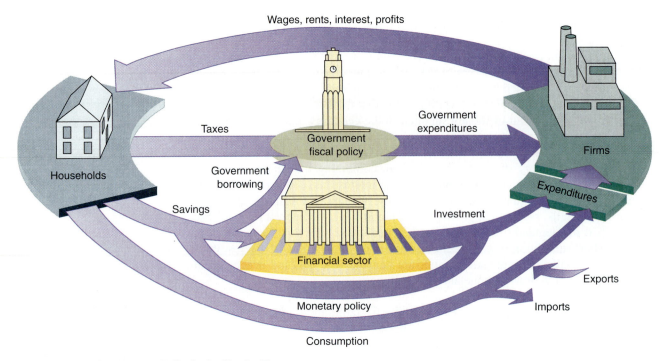

EXHIBIT 6   **Keynesian Monetary Policy in the Circular Flow**

If monetary and fiscal policy are needed, it is because the financial sector is, in some ways, clogged and is not correctly translating savings into investment. Monetary policy works to unclog the financial sector. Fiscal policy provides an alternative route for savings around the financial sector. A government deficit absorbs excess savings and translates it back into the spending stream. A surplus supplements the shortage of savings and reduces the flow back into the spending stream.

Discussions of whether interest rates are too high or too low and the effect of monetary policy on interest rates fill our newspapers' financial pages. These articles reflect the Keynesian focus on monetary policy.

Monetary Policy in the Classical Model   In the Classical model, monetary policy is best seen in the quantity theory of money. The Classical **Quantity Theory of Money** centres around the **equation of exchange:**

$$MV = PQ$$

Quantity theory of money   The price level varies in response to changes in the quantity of money.

where:

> M = Quantity of money
>
> V = Velocity
>
> P = Price level
>
> Q = Quantity of real goods sold.

Equation of exchange $MV = PQ$ (quantity of Money times Velocity of money equals the Price level times the Quantity of real goods sold).

Q is the real output of the economy (real GDP). P is the price level, so PQ is the economy's nominal output (nominal GDP—the quantity of goods valued at whatever price level exists at the time). Remember, real GDP equals nominal GDP divided by (deflated by) the price level, while nominal GDP equals nominal income.

9   In the Classical model, monetary policy works through the quantity theory:

$$MV = PQ$$

It has short-run effects on real output, Q, but in the long run it affects only the price level, P.

V, the **velocity of money,** is the number of times per year, on average, a dollar goes around to generate a dollar's worth of income. Put another way, velocity is the amount of income per year generated by a dollar of money. MV also equals nominal output. Thus, if there's \$100 of money in the economy and velocity is 20, nominal GDP is \$2,000. We can calculate V by dividing nominal GDP by the money supply. In Canada in 1994, nominal GDP was approximately \$750 billion, M was approximately \$57 billion (using M1), so velocity was about GDP/M = 13, meaning each dollar in the economy circulated enough to support approximately \$13 in total income.

Velocity of money   Number of times per year, on average, a dollar goes around to generate a dollar's worth of income; or amount of income per year generated by a dollar of money.

The equation of exchange is a *tautology,* meaning it's true by definition. What changes it from a tautology to a theory are certain assumptions the Classicals made about the variables in the equation of exchange.

First, Classical economists assumed velocity remains constant. They argued that money is spent only so fast; how fast is determined by the economy's institutional structure, such as how close to stores individuals live, how people are paid (weekly, biweekly, or monthly), and what sources of credit are available (can you go to the store and buy something on credit, that is, buy something without handing over cash?). This institutional structure changes slowly, they argued, so velocity won't fluctuate very much. Next year, velocity will be approximately the same as this year.

If velocity remains constant, the quantity theory can be used to predict how much nominal GDP will grow if we know how much the money supply grows. For example, if the money supply goes up 6 percent, using the quantity theory a Classical economist would predict that nominal GDP will go up by 6 percent.

The second Classical assumption concerned Q, real output. Classical economists assumed that Q was independent of the money supply. That is, the Classicals thought Q was **autonomous,** meaning real output was determined by forces outside the quantity theory.

This Classical assumption is sometimes called the **veil of money assumption,** which holds that real output is not influenced by changes in the money supply. Classical economists argued that in order to understand what is happening in the real economy, you must lift the veil of money.

This veil of money assumption made analyzing the economy a lot easier than it would have been had the financial and real sectors been interrelated and had real economic activity been influenced by financial changes. It allowed Classical economists to separate two puzzles: how the real economy works, and how the price level and financial sector work. Instead of having two different jigsaw puzzles all mixed up, each puzzle could be worked separately. They could analyze what happens in the real economy (in the production of real goods and services) separately from what happens to the money supply and price level. Classical economists recognized that there were interconnections between the real and financial sectors, but they argued that most of these interconnections involved short-run considerations. Classical economists were primarily interested in the long run.

In the long run, there is a strong intuitive reason why the real and nominal economies are separate. Say one day you walk into work and your salary has doubled—but all prices also have doubled. What difference will these changes make in your behaviour? Since no relative price has changed, it seems fair to say that your behaviour won't be affected very much. That's what the Classical economists were saying with the veil of money assumption.

With both V (velocity) and Q (quantity or output) unaffected by changes in M (money supply), the only thing that can change is P (price level). Classical economists said that M and P would change by equivalent percentages.

The final assumption of the Classical quantity theory was the *direction of causation.* Classical economists argued that changes in the money supply caused changes in the price level: In the quantity theory of money equation, the direction of causation went from left to right,

$$MV \rightarrow PQ$$

not the other way around. Thus, when a Classical economist was asked to predict what would happen to inflation, he or she would ask what's happening to the money supply's growth rate. If the money supply were continually increasing at an 8 percent rate, the Classical economist's prediction would be that inflation would be 8 percent.

We've covered a lot of ground, so let's briefly summarize how we went from the equation of exchange to the quantity theory. We start with the equation of exchange:

$$MV = PQ$$

To that we add three assumptions:

Autonomous   Determined by outside forces; for example, Classicals held that real output was determined by forces "autonomous" to the quantity theory of money.

Veil-of-money assumption   Real output is not influenced by changes in the money supply.

1. Velocity is constant.
2. Real output is independent of the money supply.
3. Causation goes from money supply to prices.

The result is the quantity theory of money. It holds that real output is set at levels desired by individuals, and that real output is independent of the wage and price level. An increase in money will not increase real output; it will simply increase the wage and price level.

So, how did Classical economists view monetary policy? They saw expansionary monetary policy as increasing the money supply, and in the long run they believed this would simply increase the price level:

$$MV = PQ$$

Thus, in the long run monetary policy has no effect on real economic variables such as income or employment. This view is consistent with the Classical proposition that there is a dichotomy between the real and nominal sectors. The Classical position on monetary policy is best seen in this theory.

The Classical Emphasis on Money Supply   The quantity theory of money framework and the long-run relationship between money and prices that Classicals emphasize lead them to focus on the money supply as the key variable in judging whether monetary policy is tight or loose. A large increase in the money supply indicates expansionary monetary policy; a large decrease in the money supply indicates contractionary monetary policy.

"Steady-as-You-Go" Policy   Because of the Classicals' focus on the long run, they favour a "steady-as-you-go" monetary policy, increasing the money supply just enough each year to allow for the normal real growth in the economy. That increase is to be maintained regardless of the state of the economy. Following that rule, Classicals claim, is most likely to provide the stable financial setting necessary for a market economy to operate. Thus, Classicals oppose the Keynesian policy of an activist monetary policy.

The reason for their steady-as-you-go policy proposal is that, in the short run, Classical economists are much less certain about the workings of monetary policy. They argue that in the short run it operates in numerous ways that are too hard to analyze because they're constantly changing. Classical economists just don't know how long monetary policy takes to work, by what channels it influences the real economy, and how, in the short run, it will influence prices versus real income—they argue that all this is unknowable. But what is knowable is that expansionary monetary policy will have some unknown strong effect in the short run and will raise the price level in the long run.

Classicals don't believe that monetary policy can ease or hinder the link between savings and investment because they believe the financial markets are already coordinating the flow from savings into investment as well as possible. True, sometimes savings and investment might get messed up a bit, but monetary policy, with its uncertain effect, will likely mess it up even more. Moreover, Classicals believe that since politicians focus on short-run effects, political pressures will generally be toward increasing the money supply. In the long run, these increases in the money supply will lead to an increase in the price level, so a Keynesian activist monetary policy that does not follow a predetermined rule will have an undesirable effect on inflation.

Real and Nominal Interest Rates   In support of their argument that the money supply rather than the interest rate should be considered in judging the looseness or tightness of monetary policy, Classicals point out the distinction between real and nominal interest rates. **Nominal interest rates** are the rates you actually see and pay. When a bank pays 7 percent interest, that 7 percent is a nominal interest rate. **Real interest rates** are rates adjusted for expected inflation.

Nominal interest rates   Interest rates you actually see and pay.

Real interest rate   Interest rate adjusted for expected inflation.

ADDED DIMENSION

THREE LETTERS

The relationship between the Prime Minister and the Bank of Canada is often more friendly than appears in the press. The Prime Minister and the Bank of Canada sometimes play good cop/bad cop. The central bank undertakes a politically tough decision. The Prime Minister screams and yells to the press about how awful the Bank of Canada is (off the record), while privately encouraging the Bank of Canada. The Bank of Canada takes the political heat since it doesn't have to face elections, while the Prime Minister seems like a nice guy (or gal).

It's Parliamentary folklore that each prime minister who takes up residence receives three letters from the outgoing prime minister. The letters are to be opened only in a dire economic emergency. Letter Number 1 says, "Blame it on the opposition." Letter Number 2, only to be opened if Letter Number 1 doesn't work says, "Blame it on the Bank of Canada." If Letter Number 2 doesn't work either, Letter Number 3 is to be opened. It says "Prepare three letters!"

For example, say you get 7 percent interest from the bank, but the price level goes up 7 percent. At the end of the year you have $107 instead of $100, but you're no better off than before, because the price level has risen—on average, things cost 7 percent more. What you would have paid $100 for last year now costs $107. (That's the definition of *inflation.*) Had the price level remained constant, and had you received 0 percent interest, you'd be in the equivalent position to receiving 7 percent interest on your $100 when the price level rises by 7 percent. That 0 percent is the *real interest rate.* It is the interest rate you would expect to receive if the price level remains constant.

The real interest rate cannot be observed because it depends on expected inflation, which cannot be directly observed. To calculate the real interest rate, you must subtract what you believe to be the expected rate of inflation from the nominal interest rate. For example, if the nominal interest rate is 7 percent and expected inflation is 4 percent, the real interest rate is 3 percent. The relationship between real and nominal interest rates is important both for your study of economics and for your own personal finances. Economists usually refer to the relationship between real and nominal interest rates as the Fisher equation, named after the economist Irving Fisher:

Nominal interest rate = Real interest rate + expected inflation rate.

Real and Nominal Interest Rates and Monetary Policy What does this distinction between nominal and real interest rates mean for monetary policy? It supports the Classical argument against using monetary policy to control the economy because it adds yet another uncertainty to the effect of monetary policy. Keynesians said that expansionary monetary policy lowers the interest rate and contractionary monetary policy increases the interest rate. However, if the expansionary monetary policy leads to expectation of increased inflation, Classicals point out that expansionary monetary policy can increase nominal interest rates (the ones you see). Why? Because of expectations of increasing inflation.

The distinction between nominal and real interest rates strengthens the Classical case that the best monetary policy is an unchanging policy. In the short run, monetary policy's effects are too uncertain; in the long run, they simply lead to changes in the price level.

Given the ambiguity of the short-run effect and the negative effect of the long run, monetary policy should not be used to influence the economy. Instead, according to Classical economists, the economy should be governed by a specific rule that sets the money supply at a predetermined level and either holds it there or increases it at a constant rate.

Earlier, after discussing fiscal policy's structure and mechanics, we presented the problems with using fiscal policy. Now that you've been through the structure and mechanics of monetary policy, let's consider the problems with using it too.

Problems in the Conduct of Monetary Policy

10 Five problems of monetary policy:
1. Knowing what policy to use.
2. Understanding what policy you're using.
3. Lags in monetary policy.
4. Political pressure.
5. Conflicting international goals.

Monetary base   The vault cash plus reserves that banks have at the Bank of Canada.

Knowing What Policy to Use   To use monetary policy effectively, you must know the potential level of income. Otherwise you won't know whether to use expansionary or contractionary monetary policy. Let's consider an example: late 1991. The economy's output had fallen earlier, and hence it fell below potential income. In late 1991, the economy seemed to be coming out of a recession. But these were significant debates about whether, because of restructuring, potential income had fallen, thus making increases in real output infeasible. The Bank of Canada had to figure out whether to use expansionary monetary policy to speed up and guarantee the recovery, or use contractionary monetary policy and make sure inflation didn't start up again. Initially the Bank of Canada tried to fight inflation, only to discover that, in fact, the economy wasn't coming out of the recession. In early 1992, the Bank of Canada switched from contractionary to expansionary monetary policy. It continued that policy through 1994. Inflation did not take off, so it appeared that potential income was higher than pessimists feared.

Understanding the Policy You're Using   To use monetary policy effectively, you must know whether the monetary policy you're using is expansionary or contractionary. You might think that's rather easy, but it isn't. In our consideration of monetary policy tools, you saw that the Bank of Canada doesn't directly control the money supply. It indirectly controls it, generally through cash market operations. It controls what's called the **monetary base** (the vault cash and reserves banks have at the Bank of Canada). Then the money multiplier determines the amounts of M1, M2, and other monetary measures in the economy.

That money multiplier is influenced by the amount of cash that people hold as well as the lending process at the bank. Neither of those is the stable number that we used in calculating the money multipliers. They change from day to day and week to week, so even if you control the monetary base, you can never be sure exactly what will happen to M1 and M2 in the short run. Moreover, the effects on M1 and M2 are sometimes different; one measure is telling you that you're expanding the money supply and the other measure is telling you you're contracting it.

And then, of course, there are changes in the interest rate—the measure of monetary policy that Keynesians focus on. If interest rates rise, is it because of expected inflation (which is adding an inflation premium to the nominal interest rate) or is it the real interest rate that is going up? There is frequent debate over which it is. Combined, these measurement problems make the Bank of Canada often wonder not only about what policy it should follow, but what policy it is following.

Lags in Monetary Policy   Monetary policy, like fiscal policy, takes time to work its way through the economic system. The Bank of Canada can change the money supply or interest rates; people don't have to borrow, however. An increased money supply may simply lead to excess reserves and have no influence on income. This problem can be especially difficult in a recession.

For example, in the 1930s the Great Depression was seen as being caused by the banks. This led early Keynesians to focus on fiscal policy rather than monetary policy as a way of expanding the economy. They likened expansionary monetary policy to pushing on a string. The same problem exists with using contractionary monetary policy. Banks have been very good at figuring out ways to circumvent cuts in the money supply, making the intended results of contractionary monetary policy difficult to achieve.

Political Pressure   While the Bank of Canada is partially insulated from political pressure by its structure, it's not totally insulated. Prime ministers place enormous pressure on the Bank of Canada to use expansionary monetary policy (especially during an election year) and blame the Bank of Canada for any recession. When interest rates rise, the Bank of Canada takes the pressure.

Conflicting International Goals Monetary policy is not conducted in a vacuum. It is conducted in an international arena and must be coordinated with other governments' monetary policies. Similarly, in the back of our minds we know that monetary policy affects the exchange rate and thereby the trade balance. Often the desired monetary policy for its international effects is the opposite of the desired monetary policy for its domestic effects. We'll come back to these issues in Chapters 16 and 17.

We could continue with a discussion of the problems of using monetary policy, but the above should give you a good sense that conducting monetary policy is not a piece of cake. It takes not only a sense of the theory; it also takes a feel for the economy. In short, the conduct of monetary policy is not a science. It does not allow the Bank of Canada to steer the economy as it might steer a car. It does work well enough to allow the Bank of Canada to *influence* the economy—much as an expert rodeo rider rides a bronco bull.

　　This chapter is not the end of our discussion of monetary policy. We'll see more of monetary policy when we discuss how to conduct macroeconomic policy in the next section. There you'll learn how monetary policy works in practice, the central role it plays in understanding inflation, and how it is integrated with fiscal policy. Before we turn to those issues, however, it is helpful to consider more deeply some of the theoretical and policy debates about macroeconomic policy. That is what we do in the next chapter.

CONCLUSION AND A LOOK AHEAD

CHAPTER SUMMARY

- The Bank of Canada is a central bank; it conducts monetary policy for Canada.
- Monetary policy influences the economy through changes in the money supply and credit availability.
- The basic tools of monetary policy are:
  1. The bank rate.
  2. Cash management, which includes open market operations and drawdowns and redeposits.
- Cash management operations are the Bank of Canada's most important tool:
  To expand the money supply, the Bank of Canada buys government securities.
  To contract the money supply, the Bank of Canada sells government securities.
- In the Keynesian model, contractionary monetary policy works as follows:

$$M\downarrow \rightarrow i\uparrow \rightarrow I\downarrow \rightarrow Y\downarrow$$

Expansionary monetary policy works as follows:

$$M\uparrow \rightarrow i\downarrow \rightarrow I\uparrow \rightarrow Y\uparrow$$

- As an indicator of monetary policy, Keynesians focus on interest rates; Classicals focus on money supply.
- Classical economists see the short-run effects of monetary policy as ambiguous. They favour a long-run monetary rule.
- The Bank of Canada uses an eclectic model that combines both Keynesian and Classical insights.
- Problems of monetary policy include knowing what policy to use, knowing what policy you are using, lags, political pressure, and conflicting international goals.

KEY TERMS

arbitrage *(328)*
autonomous *(337)*
bank rate *(328)*
cash management *(329)*
central bank *(324)*
Classical Quantity Theory
  of Money *(336)*
contractionary monetary policy *(330)*
demand for money *(333)*

drawdown *(332)*
equation of exchange *(336)*
exchange rate *(326)*
expansionary monetary policy *(329)*
Governor of the Bank
  of Canada *(324)*
monetary base *(340)*
monetary policy *(324)*
nominal interest rates *(338)*

open market operations *(329)*
real interest rates *(338)*
redeposit *(332)*
supply of money *(333)*
term structure of interest rates *(328)*
veil of money assumption *(337)*
velocity of money *(336)*

QUESTIONS FOR THOUGHT AND REVIEW

The number after each question represents the estimated degree of critical thinking required. (1 = almost none; 10 = deep thought.)

1. Is the Bank of Canada a private or a public agency?   *(5)*

2. The Bank of Canada wants to increase the money supply (which is currently 4,000) by 200. Assume that for each 1 percent the bank rate falls, banks borrow an additional 20. If the Bank of Canada decides to change the bank rate, how much should the Bank of Canada change the rate to increase the money supply by 200? Assume the money supply multiplier equals 3.0.   *(6)*

3. The Bank of Canada wants to increase the money supply (which is currently 4,000) by 200. Only now it decides to use open market operations. What should it do to achieve the desired change? Again, assume the money supply multiplier is equal to 3.0.   *(6)*

4. You can lead a horse to water, but you can't make it drink. How might this adage be relevant to expansionary (as opposed to contractionary) monetary policy?   *(7)*

5. The interest rate has just fallen. How might Classical and Keynesian economists draw different implications from that event?   *(7)*

6. Investment increases by 20 for each interest rate drop of 1 percent. The income multiplier is 3. If the money multiplier is 4, and each change of 5 in the money supply changes the interest rate by 1 percent, what open market policy would you recommend to increase income by 240?   *(6)*

7. If the nominal interest rate is 6 percent and inflation is 5 percent, what's the real interest rate?   *(3)*

8. "The effects of open market operations are somewhat like a stone cast in a pond." After the splash, discuss the first three ripples.   *(4)*

PROBLEMS AND EXERCISES

1. Suppose the Bank of Canada decides it needs to pursue an expansionary policy. Assume people hold no cash, the desired reserve requirement is 20 percent, and there are no excess reserves. Show how the Bank of Canada would increase the money supply by $2 million through open market operations.

2. Suppose the Bank of Canada decides that it needs to pursue a contractionary policy. It wants to decrease the money supply by $2 million. Assume people hold 25 percent of their money in the form of cash balances, the desired reserve requirement is 20 percent, and there are no excess reserves.

   a. Show how the Bank of Canada would decrease the money supply by $2 million through open market operations.

   b. Go to your local bank and find out how much excess reserves they hold. Recalculate a assuming all banks held that amount in excess reserves.

3. Some individuals have suggested raising the required reserve ratio for banks to 100 percent.

   a. What would the money multiplier be if this change were made?

   b. What effect would such a change have on the money supply?

   c. How could that effect be offset?

   d. Would banks likely favour or oppose this proposal? Why?

4. Using T-accounts, show the effect of an increase in the desired reserve ratio from 0.1 to 0.15 given the following initial position (Textland, again, is the only bank in town and no one holds cash).

Assets		Liabilities	
Reserves	$ 10,000	Demand Deposits	$100,000
T-bill holdings	5,000	Net Worth	85,000
Property	70,000		
Loans	100,000		

5. One of the proposals to reform monetary policy has been to ensure that the central bank's Board of Directors are specialists in monetary economics. What effect do you think that would have on the monetary policy process? Would it have made Governor Crow's job any easier? Why? Will it make Governor Theissen's job any easier? Explain.

Keynesian and Classical Theories of Interest and Their Implications for Monetary Policy

To understand the theoretical differences between Keynesian and Classical economists' theories of monetary policy, we must understand their alternative theories of interest. Unfortunately, these theories are complicated, confusing, and quite possibly confused—all at the same time.

The way these theories try to treat money is as simply another good—a good that has a supply and demand curve that can be analyzed separately from the other supply and demands. Having specified the analysis of the money market, both Keynesian and Classical theories then try to integrate it back into the aggregate analysis. There have been many articles written trying to do this on both the Keynesian and Classical sides, but the formal attempts to do so lead to one of two conclusions: (1) that money doesn't matter; or (2) that money matters but only as a third- or fourth-order effect on the economy.

If one believes money matters in a more substantive way, one is forced to make some ad hoc assumptions that money does matter (it is desired for its own sake). That approach doesn't come close to making money matter as much as it seems to in the real world.

In our view, money matters so much to the economy that its deep theoretical analysis must go beyond supply and demand analysis. Money is part of the institutional structure of our economy, and its effects are so substantial and interrelated with that institutional structure that it doesn't make a lot of sense to separate out the analysis of money independent of that institutional structure. Money is part of the macrofoundation of the economy. What this means is that output is not a function of money, i.e., $Q = F(M)$, but that the production function, F, is dependent on money and that production function cannot be specified independently of the existence of money. At the introductory level, we needn't worry about such high-level theoretical issues. We simply need to recognize that money does matter, and it matters a lot.

An analogy that Classical economists used might make this argument clear. They compared money's role in the economy to the role of oil in a gas engine. As inputs into running an engine go, oil plays a supplemental role. Gas, together with electrical sparks, would be seen as the primary input. Oil would likely be seen as a tangential input. Moreover, any formal analysis of how oil reduces friction and heat would be extraordinarily complicated. But try running an engine without oil, and you will see oil's importance, just as you will also see the importance of money if you try to run an economy without money.

That said, let us now review very briefly the Keynesian and the Classical theories of money. Keynesians believe the interest rate is primarily a monetary phenomenon, so they have a monetary theory of the rate of interest. For Keynesians, the interest rate is determined by the supply and demand for money. Classicals believe the interest rate is a real phenomenon, so they have a real theory of the rate of interest. In an earlier chapter you were introduced to the Keynesian and Classical theories of the interest rate. This appendix further develops their theories and discusses their implications for conducting monetary policy.

The Keynesian Supply and Demand for Money Theory of the Interest Rate

As we saw in the last chapter, money is a financial asset people want to hold. But how much do they want to hold? It shouldn't surprise you that economists' answer is that it depends upon the supply and demand for money.

The Supply of Money As we saw in Chapter 12, the Bank of Canada determines the money supply by setting the amount of reserves in the system. Then the total amount of money in the economy is determined by the desired reserve requirement and the money multiplier, assuming that the amount of money supplied isn't influenced by the interest rate. That makes the supply of money perfectly vertical, as in Exhibit A1.

The Demand for Money As we also saw in the chapter, people want to hold money because it's useful to them as a medium of exchange and as a store of wealth. But

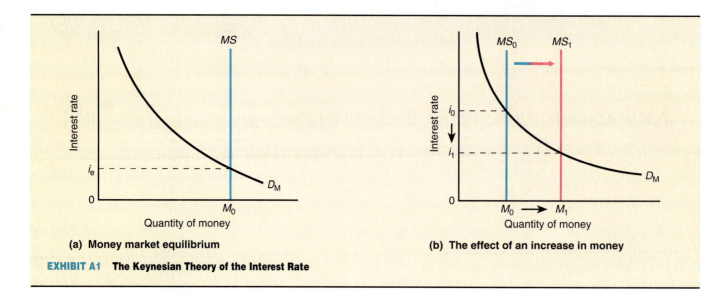

EXHIBIT A1   The Keynesian Theory of the Interest Rate

holding money isn't costless. *Money pays lower interest than other financial assets.* So how much money people want to hold depends on the interest rate on those other financial assets. The higher the interest rate on other financial assets, the greater the opportunity cost of holding money and the lower the quantity of money demanded. At lower interest rates, quantity of money demanded is larger because the opportunity cost of holding money is lower. Demand for money as a function of the interest rate is shown by the curve D_M in Exhibit A1.

The Keynesian theory of interest comes from combining the supply of money with the demand for money as in Exhibit A1. The interest rate is determined where the quantity of money supplied equals the quantity of money demanded (i_e). If the supply of money increases, say from M_0 to M_1 as in Exhibit A1 (b), the interest rate will fall from i_0. If the demand for money increases, the interest rate will rise. Keynes argued that, in the short run, the money market determines the interest rate.

The Classical Savings Investment Theory of the Interest Rate

The supply and demand for money isn't the only market that plays a role in determining the interest rate. The Classical view is that the interest rate is determined by the supply of savings and the demand for those savings for investment purposes. Money doesn't affect the interest rate, so it doesn't affect the real economy. It only

affects the price level. So the best monetary policy is a policy that provides stability of the price level. It's a long-run policy that emphasizes a constant predetermined growth rate of the money supply.

Implications of Keynesian and Classical Theories for Monetary Policy

In the Classical model, interest rate fluctuations keep savings equal to investment at the full-employment level of income. Changes in the interest rate equilibrate the savings/investment market.

That's not the way it works in Keynes's model. Income fluctuations, not interest rate fluctuations, bring the savings/investment market into equilibrium. As discussed in the text, this happens in the following way: Income fluctuates, which causes savings to fluctuate. That fluctuation in savings brings the savings/investment market into equilibrium.

So in Keynes's model, the real economy is affected by money. In the Classical model, money only affects the price level.

The implication of the Keynesian theory of interest for monetary policy is it's necessary to maintain an *active* discretionary monetary policy to keep the interest rate at a level that will maintain a savings/investment equilibrium at the target level of income. Classicals believe in a monetary rule.

14

Money, Inflation, and Macroeconomic Policy

*The first few months or year of inflation, like the first few drinks,
seem just fine. Everyone has more money to spend and prices aren't
rising quite as fast as the money that's available. The hangover
comes when prices start to catch up.*

~Milton Friedman

After reading this chapter, you should be able to:

1 Explain why sustained high inflation is inevitably accompanied
by a roughly equal increase in the money supply and expectations of inflation.

2 Differentiate between long-run and short-run Phillips curves.

3 State the differences between a Phillips curve and a price-level
flexibility curve.

4 Outline the Classical theory of inflation.

5 Explain why Classical economists favour a monetary rule.

6 Outline the Keynesian theory of inflation.

7 Distinguish the Keynesian and Classical views of the Phillips
curve trade-off.

8 Explain why a Keynesian would be more likely to support an
incomes policy than would a Classical economist.

Inflation and its relationship to unemployment were introduced earlier. Now that we've worked our way through macroeconomic theory and financial institutions, we're ready to consider these issues again and discuss the problems societies have had in trying to cope with inflation.

INFLATION

Inflation   A continual rise in the price level.

Inflation is a continuous rise in the price level. All economists agree on that. They also agree (1) that high inflation rates are inevitably accompanied by a roughly proportional increase in the money supply, and (2) that high inflation rates are associated with expectations of inflation of approximately that rate. Thus, most economists accept that when inflation is really high, say 40 percent, the money supply will be increasing by about 40 percent, and people will be expecting approximately 40 percent inflation.[1] Why do these rough equalities hold? Let's consider the money supply and inflation first.

The Money Supply and Inflation

1   High inflation rates are inevitably accompanied by high money growth and high inflationary expectations. The reason is that the velocity of money generally cannot increase enormously and people's expectations of the future are determined in large part by what is occurring now.

Say, for example, that the Canadian money supply growth rate is 10 percent. What will likely happen? From the quantity theory of money ($MV = PQ$), you can deduce that something else must also change. Assuming velocity, V, isn't decreasing enormously and real output, Q, isn't increasing enormously, that 40 percent increase in the money supply, M, must be accompanied by a rise in the price level, P, of about 40 percent. Otherwise there will be a shortage of goods. Alternatively, say prices are rising at a 40 percent rate but the money supply isn't growing at all. Unless velocity is increasing by 40 percent a year, firms will be unable to sell their goods at the higher prices because the amount of money people are spending won't buy the goods that firms are offering to sell at those higher prices. Given the shortage of aggregate demand, firms will be forced to stop increasing their prices.

Notice that so far we've said nothing about what's causing what to increase, which clearly is something policymakers would like to know. Determining the cause of inflation is important in determining how to fight it.

To distinguish cases in which price increases cause the money supply increases from cases in which money supply increases cause the price increases, inflation is divided into **cost-push inflation** (price increases cause money supply increases) and **demand-pull inflation** (money supply increases cause price increases). In a cost-push inflation, the central bank allows the money supply to rise in response to a hike in the costs of production—by doing so they engage in a process that's called **monetary validation.** When there's demand–pull inflation, the central bank is actively trying to reduce the unemployment rate and raise output by increasing the money supply. From the quantity theory we know that, in the long run, this only raises the price level—it has no effect on output or employment. We'll look at examples of each type of inflation shortly.

Cost-push inflation   Inflation resulting from the pressure exerted when a significant proportion of markets (or one very important market) experiences restrictions on supply.

Demand-pull inflation   Inflation resulting from the pressure exerted when the majority of markets in the economy experience increases in demand.

Monetary validation   Allowing the money supply to rise after a disturbance has increased the price level.

In an ongoing inflation, it's often impossible to distinguish whether it's cost-push or demand-pull. The reasons are expectations of inflation. Say the money supply is expected to increase. Firms will expect the demand for their goods to increase and will raise prices on the basis of that expectation. Then, even though price increases may come before money supply increases, it's the expected increase in the money supply that causes prices to rise. However, regardless of whether prices are being pulled by the money supply or are pushing the money supply, all economists agree that, for substantial inflation to continue, the money supply must rise.

Inflation and Expectations of Inflation

The second relationship that most economists agree exists is between inflation and expectations of inflation. The relationship is based on common sense. For example, if inflation is currently 2 percent, assuming no major change in policy, it is reasonable to expect that it will remain about 2 percent. So people's natural tendency is to base their expectations on what is or has recently been. Expectations based on what has been in the past are called **adaptive expectations.**

Adaptive expectations   Expectations of the future based on what has been in the past.

---

[1] Where economists disagree is on what causes what to increase. Is inflation causing the money supply to increase, or are increases in the money supply causing inflation? We'll address these issues shortly.

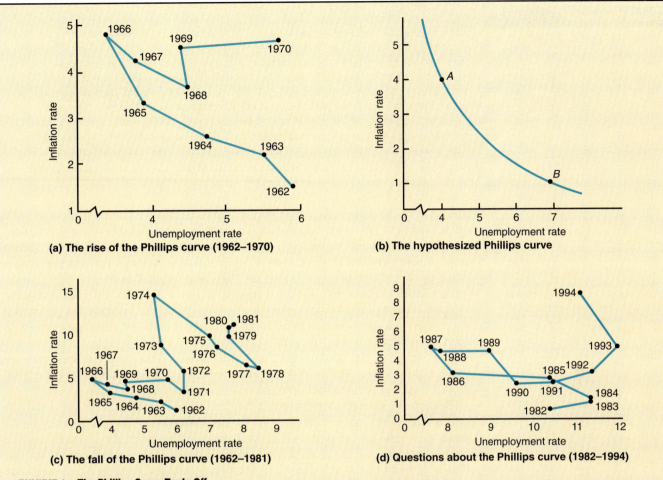

EXHIBIT 1   The Phillips Curve Trade-Off

Analyzing the empirical relationship between unemployment and inflation from 1962 to 1970—shown in (a)—led economists to believe there was the relatively stable Phillips curve which, for policy choices, could be represented by the smooth Phillips curve in (b). In the 1970s the empirical Phillips curve relationship between inflation and unemployment broke down, leading many economists to question the existence of any Phillips curve relationship that allowed policy makers to choose between inflation and unemployment. In (c) you can see how in the 1970s, no stable Phillips curve existed, while in (d) you can see how in the 1980s and 1990s, the evidence is mixed. Specifically, from 1985 to 1995, a Phillips curve relationship seemed to exist. This allows some economists to say a Phillips curve–type relationship exists and others to say it doesn't.
Source: *Statistics Canada*, CANSIM Database, March 1995.

Adaptive expectations aren't the only reasonable type. People likely will also base their expectations of inflation on their understanding of the economy, economists' predictions of inflation, and their own past experience. For example, if the money supply is increasing substantially, many economists will predict high inflation. To the degree that people believe economists, people will expect high inflation, even though it's not yet high. So the relationship between current inflation and expectations of future inflation is not perfect.

But, on average, most economists agree that expectations of inflation approximately equal the amount of inflation in the economy.

Perhaps the most vexing dilemma policymakers face in dealing with inflation is the inflation/unemployment policy dilemma: Whenever they try to fight inflation, unemployment seems to increase, and whenever they try to fight unemployment, inflation seems to increase. It is captured graphically in a curve, shown in Exhibit 1 (b), called the short-run Phillips curve. In it, unemployment is measured on the horizontal axis;

Inflation and Unemployment: The Phillips Curve Trade-Off

EXAMPLES OF COST-PUSH
AND DEMAND-PULL
INFLATION

There have been periods when it wasn't difficult to distinguish between cost-push and demand-pull inflations. For example, during the post-World War II period, which began in late 1945, there was large pent-up demand. Because of shortages of goods during the war, people had saved up buying power. After the war, most economists were expecting strong inflationary pressures from demand-pull forces. And that's what happened. There was general agreement that the period's inflation was demand-pull inflation.

But in the early 1970s, that stored-up buying power didn't exist. Then there was a significant supply shock—oil prices rose substantially, placing cost-push pressure on prices. That's why most economists call the inflation of the early 1970s cost-push inflation.

inflation is on the vertical axis. The Phillips curve tells us what combinations of inflation and unemployment are possible. It tells us that when unemployment is low, say 4 percent, inflation tends to be high, say 4 percent (point *A* on the short-run Phillips curve). It also tells us that if we want to lower inflation, say to 1 percent, we must be willing to accept high unemployment, say 7 percent (point *B* in Exhibit 1 (b)).

Phillips curve A representation of the relation between inflation and unemployment.

The **Phillips curve** was initially a representation of historical inflation and unemployment data. As economists looked at unemployment and inflation data over time, they noticed that there seemed to be a trade-off between inflation and unemployment. When unemployment was high, inflation was low; when unemployment was low, inflation was high. That empirical relationship seemed rather stable in the 1950s and 1960s. Exhibit 1 (a) shows this empirical relationship for Canada for the years 1962–70, when it became built into the way economists looked at the economy.

Because it seemed to represent a relatively stable trade-off, in the 1960s the Phillips curve played a central role in discussions of macroeconomic policy. Conservatives (often advised by Classical economists) generally favoured contractionary monetary and fiscal policy, which maintained high unemployment and low inflation (a point like *B* in Exhibit 1 (b)). Liberals (often advised by Keynesian economists) generally favoured expansionary monetary and fiscal policies which brought about low unemployment but high inflation (a point like A in Exhibit 1 (b)).[2]

The Breakdown of the Short-Run Phillips Curve   In the early 1970s, the empirical short-run Phillips curve relationship seemed to break down. When one looked at the data, there no longer seemed to be a trade-off between unemployment and inflation. Instead, when unemployment was high, inflation was also high. Exhibit 1 (c) shows the empirical relationship between inflation and unemployment from 1961 to 1981. Notice that the relatively stable relationship up until 1969 breaks down in the 1970s. In the 1970s, there doesn't seem to be any trade-off between inflation and unemployment at all. Something clearly changed in the 1970s. In the 1980s, inflation fell substantially, and beginning in 1986, a Phillips curve–type relationship began to reappear, as can be seen in Exhibit 1 (d).

To discover what changed in the 1970s, economists devoted much thought to explaining the theory underlying the Phillips curve. What caused inflation? How would inflation interact with unemployment if people acted in certain reasonable ways? As economists thought about these problems, they developed and refined their theories and models of both inflation and unemployment.

---

[2] We use the terms Keynesian economists and Classical economists to differentiate between economists who favour government intervention in the economy (the Keynesians), and those who propose a more laissez-faire role for government (the Classicals). We invite you to use other labels if you feel more comfortable with terms like "liberal" and "conservative," or "interventionist" and "noninterventionist." Getting bogged down in an intellectual debate about what Keynes or the Classical economists "really meant" isn't our primary objective—we're trying to describe two opposing schools of thought. While that means we sometimes fail to differentiate between the views of Neo-Keynesians and Post-Keynesians, or Classicists and proponents of Real Business Cycle models, we think it is the fairest way to present the material in an introductory economics course.

The Distinction between the Short-Run and Long-Run Phillips Curves As views of the Phillips curve changed, economists began distinguishing between a short-run Phillips curve and a long-run Phillips curve. The key element of that distinction is based on **expectations of inflation** (the rise in the price level that the average person expects). On each point on the **short-run Phillips curve**, expectations of inflation are constant and hence will not, generally, equal actual inflation. At each point on the **long-run Phillips curve**, expectations of inflation change so that they equal actual inflation. Economists used this distinction to explain why the short-run Phillips curve relationship broke down in the 1970s.

The reasons expectations are so central to the Phillips curve is seen by considering an individual's decision about what wage or price to set. Say you expect 0 percent inflation and you want a 2 percent wage or price increase. You'll raise your wage or price by 2 percent. Now say you expect 20 percent inflation and you want a 2 percent real wage increase. To get it, you must increase your wage by 22 percent. If everyone expects 20 percent inflation, everyone will raise their wage or price by 20 percent just to keep up.

This means that expectations of inflation play a significant role in inflation. When expectations of inflation are higher, the same level of unemployment will be associated with a higher rate of inflation. To capture this relationship, it makes sense to assume that the short-run Phillips curve moves up or down as expectations of inflation change.

The Shape of the Long-Run Phillips Curve To determine what the long-run Phillips curve would look like, economists asked themselves: What difference should expectations of inflation make to the target level of unemployment? Their answer was: none. If people expect 20 percent inflation and are raising their wages and prices 20 percent on average, the situation is just the same as if they expect 4 percent inflation and are raising their wages and prices 4 percent on average. Since their real incomes will be the same in both situations, their real decisions—how much labour to supply and demand—will be the same so employment will not change. People aren't fooled by expected inflation. Thus, economists theorized that the long-run Phillips curve would be a vertical line, as in Exhibit 2 (a). As you can see, in the long run, when expectations of inflation are fully built into people's wage- and price-setting decisions, there's no trade-off between inflation and unemployment.

This vertical long-run Phillips curve fits the empirical data for the 1970s and provides an explanation for why the short-run trade-off broke down. To see this, let's consider the years 1963 and 1970. Unemployment in both years was approximately 5.5 percent, but inflation in 1970 was over 3.3 percent while inflation in 1963 was less than 2 percent. Why the difference? Consider what happened in the interim: Inflation was consistently rising, so it's reasonable to assume that expectations of inflation were higher in 1970 than in 1963. Expectations of inflation explain the difference. When expectations are higher, actual inflation at each level of unemployment will be higher.

Moving from a Short-Run to a Long-Run Phillips Curve We can see how an economy moves from a short-run to a long-run Phillips curve by examining Exhibit 2 (b). Say, for example, that initially the economy is at point A. Expected inflation is zero, and unemployment is 5.5 percent—a level consistent with potential income. Since expected inflation is zero, the relative short-run Phillips curve is PC_1, which assumes zero-expected inflation. (Each short-run Phillips curve is consistent with one level of expected inflation.)

Now, say that the government expands aggregate demand with expansionary monetary policy. Initially, expectations of inflation remain constant, so the economy moves along the initial short-run Phillips curve, PC_1. Unemployment falls from 5.5 percent to 4 percent and inflation rises from 0 percent to 6 percent (point B).

Expectations of inflation The rise in the price level that the average person expects.

Short-run Phillips curve A curve showing the trade-off between inflation and unemployment when expectations of inflation are constant.

Long-run Phillips curve A curve showing the trade-off (or complete lack thereof) between inflation and unemployment when expectations of inflation equal actual inflation.

2 The long-run Phillips curve is vertical; it takes into account the feedback of inflation on expectations of inflation. The short-run Phillips curve does not take this feedback into account.

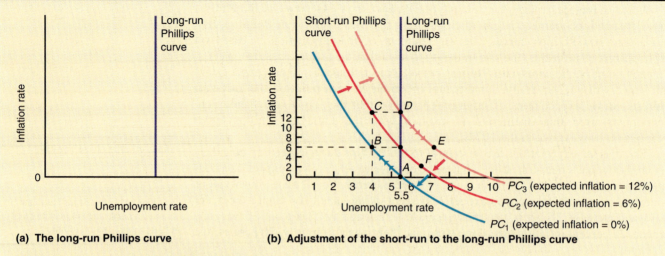

(a) The long-run Phillips curve

(b) Adjustment of the short-run to the long-run Phillips curve

EXHIBIT 2   The Long-Run and Short-Run Phillips Curve

In the long run, when expectations of rates of inflation are met, changes in rates of inflation have no effect on the level of unemployment, making the long-run Phillips curve perfectly vertical as shown in (a). If the government tries to expand the economy beyond its potential income, it can do so in the short run but not in the long run. For example, say the economy starts at point A in (b) and the government runs expansionary policy pushing the economy to point B. At point B, actual inflation, 6 percent, exceeds expected inflation, 0 percent. Because actual exceeds expected, expectations of inflation will rise, shifting the short-run Phillips curve up in the direction of PC_2. It will continue shifting up (to point C, for example) until expected inflation once again equals actual inflation (point D). The long-run Phillips curve is such that at all points expected inflation equals actual inflation. Once the economy has high inflation, one way to eliminate it is for the government to run contractionary policy, pushing the economy to point E where expected inflation exceeds actual inflation. As expectations of inflation fall, the short-run Phillips curve will shift back down to PC_2 and PC_1.

Induced recession   A deliberate attempt by government to rid the economy of inflationary expectations.

If the rise of inflation to 6 percent caused no change in individuals' expectations, the economy could remain at point B. But generally people change their expectations to match the actual inflation. As they do, the short-run Phillips curve shifts, since each short-run Phillips curve represents the trade-off for a given level of inflationary expectation. In this case the short-run Phillips curve shifts to PC_2. This means that people who wanted a 2 percent raise are now asking for a 2 + 6, or 8, percent raise. If the government wanted to maintain the 4 percent unemployment rate, it would have to use far more expansionary policies and accept 12 percent inflation (point C). But if the government did so, the short-run Phillips curve would shift up to PC_3, and the same expectation adjustment would occur. The short-run Phillips curve will continue to shift up as long as actual inflation exceeds expected inflation.

Now, the economy is on PC_3 where inflationary expectations are 12 percent. The only way for the government to stop this upward spiral is to back off on its unemployment goal, and to accept the level of unemployment consistent with potential income—5.5 percent unemployment in our example. If it does so, the economy will arrive at point D—with expected inflation of 12 percent equalling actual inflation of 12 percent and the unemployment rate at 5.5 percent. If you connect points A and D you will see that they are both points on a vertical line—the long-run Phillips curve—in which expectations of inflation equal actual inflation.

Notice that the economy has arrived at a new equilibrium, but it is an equilibrium with 12 percent inflation. The attempt to achieve the lower level of unemployment has left a legacy of 12 percent expected inflation. A good exercise is to ask yourself how the government can rid itself of that inflation. The answer is an **induced recession**— a deliberate attempt by government to rid the economy of inflationary expectations. The government would decrease the money supply growth to, say, 6 percent, which would cause unemployment to rise above 5.5 percent but inflationary expectations to fall, shifting the short-run Phillips curve down. The economy would follow a loop from point D to E to F to A as shown in Exhibit 2 (b). The adjustment would stop when expectations of inflation equalled actual inflation again (point A).

In summary, policies that decrease unemployment below the level of unemployment consistent with an economy's potential income will lead to increasing inflation, expectations of inflation, and, hence, to accelerating inflation. To rid the economy of those expectations of inflation, the government must be prepared to accept an unemployment rate above that consistent with potential income—it must induce a recession. The most well-known induced recession in Canada occurred in the early 1980s, when inflation had reached 12 percent. In response, the Bank of Canada cut the money supply growth, causing a recession and high unemployment. This recession brought down inflation and inflationary expectations.

By the 1980s, most economists accepted the view that there was a short-run trade-off but no long-run trade-off. Once again, however, economists' beliefs were challenged by empirical observation. As unemployment fell from 11.8 percent in 1983 to about 7.5 percent in 1989, the inflation rate increased too! Then, in 1992 and 1993 the trade-off reappeared, with unemployment rising as the Bank of Canada achieved its objective of price stability. The inflation rate remains low into the mid-1990s, but the unemployment rate is slow to respond. Because of these new observations, the inflation/unemployment trade-off is likely to be much in debate in the 1990s.

The Phillips curve analysis we just presented looks very much like a backwards price level flexibility curve, and in some ways the reasoning that leads to both of them is similar. But there's a big difference that distinguishes them. The *price level* is on the vertical axis of the macro policy model, and *inflation*—the change in the price level— is on the vertical axis of the Phillips curve analysis. It was because the price level was on the vertical axis that we could add the *AED* curve (which was based on reasoning relevant to the price level) to the price-level flexibility curve (since it refers to the price level) and create the macro model. That's an advantage of the macro policy model.

But the macro policy model also has disadvantages. Specifically, to talk about an ongoing inflation in the macro policy model we have to talk about an ongoing movement along the vertical axis—an ongoing shift from one price level to higher price levels; to talk about inflation in the Phillips curve analysis we simply have to refer to a point on the vertical axis. Thus the Phillips curve analysis can accommodate discussions of expectations of inflation into the analysis much better—which is why we use it.

The difference between the two can be seen by considering the price-level flexibility curve as a photograph, and the Phillips curve as a moving picture. By quickly flipping through a whole number of still photos, you can make the photos become a moving picture (that's how they make cartoon videos). But to see the movement, you need a large number of them to flip through. So to talk about an ongoing inflation rather than simply a one-time jump in the price level using the price-level flexibility curve requires us to assume that the steps will be repeated. But whether the steps can be repeated again and again depends very much on whether the rises in the price level will become expected. Will they? Well, that depends, and there are continual debates about whether a particular one-time price-level rise will generate an ongoing inflation. Shock inflation—rises in the price level that have particular one-time causes—is far less likely to generate an ongoing inflation than a rise in the average level of wage settlements. And both depend on whether the government follows a policy of accommodation or not.

When you consider this still-photo graphic limitation of the macro policy model, you can see one of the reasons why there is considerable debate about what is the level of potential income. In the macro policy model, we simply assumed that the government expanded demand and that this led to a one-time rise in the price level—that we could stop the analysis there. In certain cases we can, but in others we can't. That's what the Phillips curve analysis is telling us.

For example, consider Exhibit 3. Say the *AED* curve shifts up—that will increase output from Y_0 to Y_1 and the price level from P_0 to P_1. Output expands and real income rises (unemployment falls). But the Phillips curve analysis tells us that if that rise in

The Phillips Curve and the Price-Level Flexibility Curve

3   A Phillips curve describes the relationship between the *rate of inflation* and the *rate of unemployment*, while a price-level flexibility curve describes the relationship between the *price level* and the *level of output*.

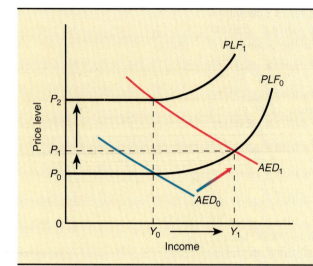

EXHIBIT 3   The Macro Policy Model

If aggregate demand rises so that the aggregate equilibrium demand curve shifts to AED_1, real output will increase from Y_0 to Y_1, and the price level will rise from P_0 to P_1. If, however, the rise in the price level becomes expected, the PLF curve will shift up, say, from PLF_0 to PLF_1. If this happens, output will fall back—in this case, all the way back to Y_0. Moreover, if the inflation remains expected, the PLF curve will continue to shift up.

the price level becomes fully expected, the price-level flexibility curve will shift up to PLF_1, and the price level will rise not just to P_1, but to P_2, and that the rises will continue. So simply choosing a higher price level is not an option for the government; they are creating an ongoing inflation if they expand and an accelerting inflation if they continue to try to expand real income beyond Y_0. So the lesson from the Phillips curve for the macro policy model is that the economy's actual potential income is not as high as the PLF curve suggests, but instead is back much closer to the range where the price level starts rising. This is a central debate in macro policy—those economists who believe most rises in the price level will become built into inflationary expectations favour less expansionary macro policy than do economists who believe that many changes in the price level will be seen as one-time increases, and not become built into inflation expectations.

THEORIES OF INFLATION AND THE PHILLIPS CURVE TRADE-OFF

Most economists accept the existence of a short-run Phillips curve and the rough equality between expectations of inflation, increases in the money supply, and the actual rate of inflation. In a theory, however, one must blur out a number of aspects of reality to focus on those aspects one believes are most important. That's what Keynesians and Classicals do with their theories of inflation.

Keynesians blur the relationship between inflation and money in order to focus on the institutional process of setting prices and on cost-push pressures as the underlying causes of the inflationary process. According to Keynesians, the money supply increases with inflation, but these increases aren't the cause of inflation; the money supply increases occur because government tries to see that inflation (the rise in the price level) doesn't lead to unemployment and cost-push pressures. When government increases aggregate demand to see that the price increases don't lead to unemployment, it ratifies the inflation. According to Keynesians, money supply increases are a necessary, but not a causal, link in the inflation process.

Classicals blur the price-setting process and the cost-push pressures in order to focus on demand-pull pressure and the relationship between increases in the money supply and inflation. When Classicals see inflation, they see the government increasing the money supply. Both theories shed light on inflation. Let's now consider them a bit more carefully.

The Classical Theory of Inflation

4   The Classical theory of inflation is summarized by the sentence: Inflation is everywhere and always a monetary phenomenon.

The Classical theory of inflation can be summed up in one sentence: *Inflation is everywhere and always a monetary phenomenon.* If the money supply doesn't rise, the price level won't rise. Forget all the other stuff. It obscures the connection between money and inflation. (This focus on money is why Classicals were called *monetarists* in the 1960s and 1970s.)

The Quantity Theory of Money and Inflation That connection between money and inflation is relatively simple and can be seen in the quantity theory: When the money supply rises, prices go up; if the money supply doesn't continue to rise, inflation won't continue. Consider the quantity theory of money:

$$MV = PQ$$

Classicals assume velocity, V, and real output, Q, are relatively constant. They also consider the price level, P, relatively flexible. According to Classical theory, any inflation is caused by demand-pull pressures—which are generated by increases in the money supply. Therefore,

$$\text{Change in } M = \text{Change in } P$$

Gordon Theissen, Governor of the Bank of Canada, summarizes that view:

> While the Bank of Canada has a number of functions, our main responsibility is monetary policy. Monetary policy has to do with controlling the amount of money in circulation and the speed at which it grows. The expansion of money has an influence on interest rates, and the Canadian dollar, and these in turn affect savings, investment, demand, and production. But the main result of monetary policy over time shows up in prices—specifically in the rate at which prices increase, in other words, in the rate of inflation.[3]

Classical Modifications of the Quantity Theory The quantity theory of money embodies the central element of the Classical theory of inflation. There are many modifications which explain why the connection between money and inflation in the short run isn't perfectly tight. One important modification is that Classicals believe that people are often fooled into thinking an increase in nominal demand caused by an increase in the money supply is actually an increase in real demand. The result will be a short-run expansionary effect on the real economy, as suggested in this chapter's opening quotation from Milton Friedman.

Examples of Money's Role in Inflation Let's consider two examples, the first from the United States. In 1971, the Federal Reserve increased the money supply significantly; as a result, U.S. income rose and unemployment fell. In response, in 1972 inflation fell slightly, as did unemployment. However, in 1974 and 1975 both U.S. inflation and unemployment rose substantially. Here's an example of expansionary monetary policy increasing real output as prices are slow to respond to increases in aggregate demand. But in the long run the expansionary monetary policy caused inflation. Classical economists also believe that people can be fooled in the opposite direction—thinking that a decrease in nominal demand is actually a decrease in real demand. This makes it difficult to stop an ongoing inflation because the initial short-run effect is on real output. The effect on inflation occurs in the long run.

Now look at an example from Canada from the 1980s, when significant inflation—over 10 percent—had become built into the economy. In late 1979 and the early 1980s, the Bank of Canada decreased money supply growth significantly. This led to a leap in unemployment from 7.5 to nearly 12 percent, but initially no decrease in inflation. By 1984, however, inflation had fallen to about 4 percent, and it remained low for several years.

Now let's consider a couple of more recent examples. In the early 1990s, the German central bank felt Germany's inflation rate was too high. It cut the money supply growth considerably. Initially, the impact was on output, and the tight money pushed the German economy into a recession. It remained in recession through early 1994, but the forecasts for 1995 were for growth, albeit slow.

Another example is Russia in the early 1990s. The Russian government was short

---

[3] "Monetary Policy and Financial Markets," *Bank of Canada Review,* Winter 1994–95, p. 71.

The Classical view that printing money causes inflation is seen in the 18th-century satirical drawing, by James Gilray, of William Pitt spewing paper money out of his mouth while gold coins are locked up in his stomach. *Bleichroeder Print Collection, Baker Library, Harvard Business School.*

of revenue and was forced to print money to finance its debt. As a result, inflation blew up into hyperinflation, and the Russian ruble became almost worthless.

Despite these and many other examples, the simple view connecting inflation with money supply growth lost favour in the late 1980s and early 1990s as formerly stable relationships between certain measurements of money and inflation broke down. Part of the reason for this was the enormous changes in financial institutions that were occurring because of technological changes and changing regulations. Another part was the increased global interdependence of financial markets, which increased the flow of money among countries. In the 1990s it seemed that, for low inflation, the random elements (called noise) in the relationship between money and inflation overwhelmed the connection. For large inflation of the type experienced by many developing and transition economies, the connection was still evident.

Classical Policy to Fight Inflation   In terms of policy, monetary policy is powerful, but unpredictable in the short run. Its short-run effects are unknown, partially because we're not sure how quickly expectations respond to changes in the money supply. And, even once expectations change, it takes time for those expectations to be incorporated into economic institutions like contracts. If you just signed a three-year deal with your employer that gives you a 2 percent raise each year, new information on the money supply will change your expectations of inflation, and you'll want more than that 2 percent raise each year. But you're stuck in the current contract—you won't be able to change your behaviour until the next contract is negotiated. Because of this unpredictability, classical economists argue that monetary policy cannot, and should not, be used to control the level of output in the economy. Thus, paradoxically, monetarists favour a laissez-faire monetary policy.

Classicals, or monetarists as they are sometimes called because of their focus on money, believe that in the long run money affects only the price level. Since the short-run effects are unpredictable and in the long run only the price level is affected, Classicals say that monetary policy should follow a **monetary rule** (a prescribed monetary policy that's to be followed regardless of what's happening in the economy). They argue that:

5   Classical economists favour a monetary rule because they believe the short-run effects of monetary policy are unpredictable and the long-run effects of monetary policy are on the price level, not on real output.

Monetary rule   A prescribed monetary policy to be followed regardless of what is happening in the economy.

ADDED DIMENSION

THE KEEPER OF THE
CLASSICAL FAITH: MILTON
FRIEDMAN

By most accounts, Milton Friedman was a headstrong student. He didn't simply accept the truths his teachers laid out. If he didn't agree, he argued strongly for his own belief. He was very bright and his ideas were generally logical and convincing. He needed to be both persistent and intelligent to maintain and promote his views in spite of strong opposition.

Throughout the Keynesian years of the 1950s and 1960s, Friedman stood up and argued the Classical viewpoint of economics. He kept Classical economics alive. He was such a strong advocate of the quantity theory of money that, during this period, Classical economics was called monetarism. Friedman was the leader of the monetarists.

Friedman argued that fiscal policy simply didn't work. It led to expansions in government's size. He also opposed an activist monetary policy. The effects of monetary policy, he said, were too variable for it to be useful in guiding the economy. He called for a steady growth in the money supply and argued consistently for a laissez-faire policy by government.

He has made his mark in both microeconomics and macroeconomics. In the 1970s, his ideas caught hold and helped spawn a renewal of the Classical school of economics. He was awarded the Nobel prize in economics in 1976.

1. The money supply should be increased by a determined percentage, say 3 percent per year, to allow for changes in productivity and real growth.
2. Monetary policy should not be used in the short run to try to steer the economy.

Classicals believe that monetary policy should be used only to achieve long-run objectives, the most important of which is price stability.

There are many alternative ways in which short-run Classical theory of inflation makes adjustments for changes in velocity, real output, and inflationary expectations, but the core of their theory is inevitably that *inflation is everywhere and always a monetary phenomenon.* That core connection between money and inflation is pleasant for students because it makes it possible to present succinctly the Classical view.

The Classical View of the Phillips Curve Trade-Off   The Classical view of the trade-off centres around the **natural rate of unemployment** (the rate of unemployment to which the economy naturally gravitates).[4] This natural rate of unemployment is independent of the inflation rate and expectations of inflation. It is the unemployment rate that will exist in long-run equilibrium when expectations of inflation equal the actual level of inflation. The long-run Phillips curve is vertical at this natural rate of unemployment.

Unemployment rates below the natural unemployment rate would lead to actual inflation higher than expected inflation, which would bring about a future increase in expectations of inflation, and an upward shift of the short-run Phillips curve. This Classical view is shown in Exhibit 4.

At unemployment rates to the left of the long-run Phillips curve (unemployment rates below the natural rate), actual inflation is above expectations of inflation so the short-run Phillips curve will shift upward (shown by the upward arrows in Exhibit 4). To the right of the long-run Phillips curve (at unemployment rates higher than the natural rate), actual inflation is below expectations of inflation and the short-run Phillips curve will shift downward (shown by the downward arrows in the exhibit).

Maintaining an unemployment rate below the natural rate would cause an ever-increasing acceleration of inflation. Such an accelerating inflation is unsustainable because it destroys the benefits of money. It would cause hyperinflation and a breakdown of the economy. Eventually the government must give up its attempt to lower

Milton Friedman won the Nobel prize in 1976 for work on monetary theory. Friedman is the macroeconomist who most strongly argued the monetarist view. © *The Nobel Foundation.*

Natural rate of unemployment
Classical term for the unemployment rate in long-run equilibrium when expectations of inflation equal the actual level of inflation.

---

[4] The natural rate concept is the Classical equivalent of what this book calls the *target rate of unemployment.* The Keynesian equivalent for the target rate is the *nonaccelerating inflation rate of unemployment (NAIRU).*

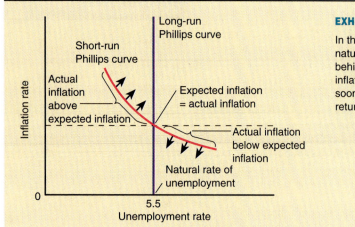

EXHIBIT 4   The Classical View of the Phillips Curve Trade-Off

In the Classical view, the long-run Phillips curve is vertical at the natural rate of unemployment. Because expectations of inflation lag behind actual inflation, there exists a temporary trade-off between inflation and unemployment. But the trade-off is an illusion, and as soon as expectations catch up with actual inflation, the economy will return to the natural rate of unemployment.

Stagflation   Combination of high inflation and high unemployment.

the unemployment rate below the natural rate. But even after giving up its attempt to achieve an unemployment rate below the natural rate, the government will have left a legacy of high inflation. The combination of high and accelerating inflation and high unemployment is known as **stagflation.**

Exhibit 5 graphs the Classical explanation of how stagflation occurs. Say the economy starts at an equilibrium of zero actual inflation, zero expected inflation, and 5.5 percent unemployment, which, let's suppose, happens to be the natural rate of unemployment. Now government comes along and expands the economy with expansionary monetary or fiscal policy to point A on the short-run Phillips curve, so that there will be 3 percent inflation and 4 percent unemployment. The 3 percent actual inflation exceeds 0 percent expected inflation, which causes a shift up in expectations of inflation. This increase in expectations causes the short-run Phillips curve to shift up from PC_1 to PC_2.

After expectations of inflation have shifted up fully, instead of being able to achieve 4 percent unemployment with a 3 percent inflation rate, it would take a 6 percent inflation rate to maintain unemployment at 4 percent (point B). Let's say the government is willing to accept 6 percent inflation and uses expansionary monetary or fiscal policy to try to maintain unemployment at 4 percent, which is 1.5 percent below the natural rate. Expectations of inflation would shift up to 6 percent and the short-run Phillips curve would shift up to PC_3. Now the government finds that to keep the economy at 4 percent unemployment would require an even more expansionary policy and an inflation rate of 9 percent (point C). And even that 9 percent is only temporary; as long as the unemployment rate is less than the natural rate, actual inflation will be above expected inflation, the short-run Phillips curve will be shifting up, and inflation will be accelerating.

That's what Classicals said happened in the 1970s. Government, following Keynesians' advice, expanded the economy and reduced unemployment below the natural rate, causing expectations of inflation to rise and the short-run Phillips curve to shift up. Inflation stopped rising only when the government accepted the natural rate of unemployment as inevitable. In the Classical view, government expansionary policy caused stagflation.

The Keynesian Theory of Inflation

Keynesians would agree with much of what the Classicals have to say but believe that they aren't focusing on the important institutional and structural aspects of inflation. Keynesians argue that when firms and individuals set prices, they do not take into account the effect of their pricing decisions on the price level. Since generally firms, rather than consumers, set prices, those prices quickly adjust upward in response to an

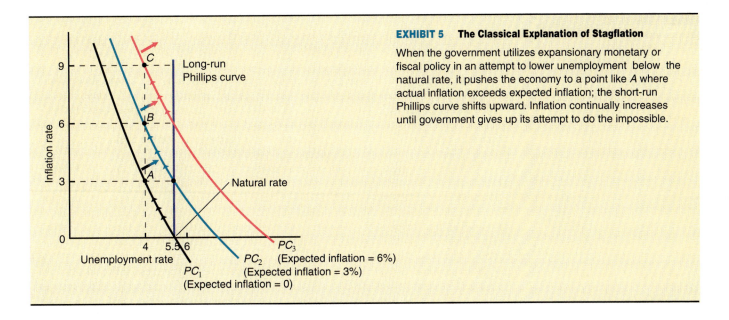

EXHIBIT 5   The Classical Explanation of Stagflation

When the government utilizes expansionary monetary or fiscal policy in an attempt to lower unemployment below the natural rate, it pushes the economy to a point like A where actual inflation exceeds expected inflation; the short-run Phillips curve shifts upward. Inflation continually increases until government gives up its attempt to do the impossible.

increase in demand, but are much slower to adjust downward in response to a decrease in demand.

The revenue that firms receive is divided among profits, wages, and rent. All this income is ultimately paid to individual owners of the factors of production. Firms are simply intermediaries between individuals as owners of the factors of production and individuals as consumers. Keynesians argue that, given the institutional structure of our economy, it's often easier for firms to increase wages, profits, and rents to keep the peace with their employees and other factors of production than it is to try to hold those costs down. Firms then pay for that increase by raising the prices they charge consumers. That works as long as, in response to the rising price level, the government increases the money supply so that the demand is there to buy the goods at the higher prices.

Let's consider an example: A zuka firm is happy with its competitive position in the zuka market. It expects 0 percent inflation. Productivity (output of zukas per unit input) is increasing 2 percent, the same as the increase in productivity in the economy as a whole, so the firm can hold its nominal price of zukas constant even if it increases wages by 2 percent. Since the price level isn't expected to change, holding the price of zukas constant should maintain the firm's share of the zuka market. The firm offers workers a 2 percent increase.

The firm meets its workers to discuss the 2 percent offer. At that meeting it becomes clear to the firm that its workers will push for a 4 percent pay increase. What should the firm do? In a highly competitive market in which supply and demand forces alone determine wages and prices, there's no question what it would do; it would increase wages only 2 percent and hold its price constant. Real-world firms, however, often meet workers' demands under the expectation that other firms will do so too. Meeting these demands helps maintain morale and prevents turnover of key workers. This occurs whether or not there are unions. The result is an upward push on nominal wages and prices.

This upward push on nominal wages and prices can exist only if the labour and product markets are not highly competitive. In a highly competitive market, even small amounts of unemployment and excess supply would cause wages and prices to fall. Keynesians believe that most real-world markets are not highly competitive in this fashion. While they agree that some competition exists, they argue that in most sectors of the economy, competition works slowly. The invisible handshake, as well

6   The Keynesian theory of inflation holds that highly institutional and structural aspects of inflation, such as increases in the money supply, are important causes of inflation.

**THE DISTRIBUTIONAL
EFFECTS OF INFLATION**

If inflation is a distributional fight, who wins and who loses? The winners are people who can raise their wages or prices and still keep their jobs and sell their labour or goods. The losers are people who can't.

The composition of these groups changes over time. For example, at one time people on government assistance and pensions lost out during inflations since government assistance and pensions were, on the whole, set at fixed rates. Inflation lowered recipients' real income. But government assistance payments and many pensions are now indexed (automatically adjusted to compensate for low rates of inflation), so their recipients are no longer losers. Their real income became independent of inflation.

Similarly, it's sometimes said that bondholders are hurt by inflation, since the value of the money with which the bonds are redeemed falls during inflation. That's true, but whether bondholders lose depends on how the interest rate on bonds adjusts to the expected inflation rate. In recent years, the nominal interest rate has adjusted quickly to expectations of inflation. When that happens, it is unclear how much bondholders have lost. If nominal interest rates adjust quickly to expectations of inflation, the real interest rate may remain as high as it otherwise would have been.

For example, in the 1950s, bondholders received 2 percent interest; inflation was low, so 2 percent interest was close to a 2 percent real interest rate. In the early 1970s, interest rates on bonds were 8 percent, in large part because people expected 6 percent inflation. Six percent compensated bondholders for inflation, leaving them the same 2 percent real return they had received in the 1950s. So we must be careful in generalizing about distributional effects of inflation.

What we can say about the distributional consequences of inflation is that people who don't expect inflation and who are tied in to fixed contracts denominated in unindexed monetary values will likely lose in an inflation. However, these people are rational and probably won't let it happen again. They'll be prepared for a subsequent inflation.

as the invisible hand, influences wages and prices. The result is that even when there is substantial unemployment and considerable excess supply of goods, existing workers can still put an upward push on nominal wages, and existing firms can put an upward push on nominal prices.

The Insider/Outsider Model and Inflation   To get a better picture of how existing workers can push up wages despite substantial unemployment, let's consider a Keynesian model which divides the economy into insiders and outsiders. Insiders are workers who have good jobs with excellent long-run prospects, and current business owners. Both receive above-equilibrium wages, profits, and rents. If the world were competitive, their wages, profits, and rents would be pushed down to the equilibrium level. To prevent this from happening, Keynesians argue, insiders develop sociological and institutional barriers that prevent outsiders from competing those above-equilibrium wages, profits, and rents away. Because of those barriers, outsiders (often minorities) must take dead-end, low-paying jobs or attempt to undertake marginal businesses that pay little return for many hours worked. Even when outsiders do find better jobs or business opportunities, they are first to be fired and their businesses are the first to suffer in a recession. Thus, outsiders have much higher unemployment rates than insiders.

In short, Keynesians see an economic system that's only partially competitive. In their view, the invisible hand is often thwarted by other invisible forces. Such partially competitive economies are often characterized by insiders' monopolies. Insiders get the jobs and are paid monopoly wage levels. Outsiders are unemployed at those higher wages. Imperfect competition allows workers (and firms) to raise nominal wages (and prices) even as unemployment (and excess supply of goods) exists. Then, as other insiders do likewise, the price level rises. This increase in the price level lowers workers' real wages. In response, workers further raise their nominal wages to protect their real wages. The result is an ongoing chase in which the insiders protect their real wage, while outsiders (the unemployed) suffer. (If the ideas of *nominal* and *real* are unclear to you, a review of earlier chapters may be in order.)

Within this imperfectly competitive system, both wages and prices develop their own inertia that causes inflation to take on a life of its own. Keynesians believe that to understand inflation you must understand the psychology of the individuals with wage- and price-setting power, including both firms and organizations of workers.

Thus, Keynesians see the nominal wage- and price-setting process as generating inflation. As one group pushes up its nominal wage or price, another group responds by doing the same. More groups follow until finally the first group finds its relative wage or price hasn't increased. Then the entire process starts again. Once the nominal wage and price levels have risen, government has two options: It can either ratify the increase by increasing the money supply (the monetary validation underlying cost-push inflation), thereby accepting the inflation; or it can refuse to ratify it, causing unemployment.

The Role of Unemployment in Keynesian Theories of Inflation

What role does unemployment play in the inflation process for Keynesians? They see the fear of unemployment as a way of "disciplining" workers to accept lower pay. The reality that there are a number of unemployed people out there waiting to take the jobs of employed workers who ask for too high a wage increase helps prevent existing workers from raising their wage. Thus, unemployment helps fight inflation. But unemployment is not a complete retardant of inflation because many workers and firms have insulated themselves from unemployment through implicit or explicit contracts providing them with job and market security regardless of the level of unemployment. This means that the unemployment costs of fighting inflation are borne heavily by minorities and other outsiders. Insiders are more protected and have less to fear from unemployment. The resulting unemployment is not "natural" in the sense that it reflects people's choices; it is simply the amount of unemployment that is necessary to create competitive pressure on insiders and thereby limit their attempts at further monopolization.

Another difference between Keynesians and Classicals is that Keynesians are far less likely to see a specific level of unemployment as the "natural rate" of unemployment. Because they believe that aggregate supply and aggregate demand are interrelated, they are far more cautious about specifying a single rate of unemployment toward which the aggregate economy gravitates. For them the target rate of unemployment can shift around; it is to be empirically determined, not theoretically deduced.

7A The Classical view of the Phillips curve trade-off centers around the natural rate of unemployment. Any attempt to maintain unemployment at a rate below the natural rate is unsustainable because doing so would cause accelerating inflation.

The Keynesian View of the Phillips Curve Trade-Off

As we've stated, Keynesians see an economy of imperfectly competitive markets. Keynesians believe that, in the short run, social forces (the invisible handshake, which creates a type of implicit contract between buyers and sellers) and explicit contracts play a large role in price determination. Because of these social forces, there is no reason that, in the short run, expected inflation must precisely equal actual inflation. Keynesians argue that if the economy is kept close to the existing level of inflation (say within 2 or 3 percent), these social forces can hold inflationary expectations in check at their existing level and prevent them from being built into higher inflationary demands, and thereby shifting up the short-run Phillips curve. Thus, within a limited range of inflation rates around the actual inflation rate, many Keynesians believe that the short-run Phillips curve can be relatively stable, and not shift up even though actual inflation exceeds expected inflation. They argue that the trade-off existing up to 1970 was not an illusion and that the relationship did exist in the late 1980s. There can be a long-run trade-off between inflation and unemployment, as there was up until 1970. In a sense, Keynesians are saying that the long run never comes.

The reason many Keynesians believe there can be a long-run trade-off between inflation and unemployment is not that they believe people are irrational; it is that they

7B Keynesians believe that institutional factors play a major role in determining inflation, and that expected inflation need not precisely equal actual inflation. Within a range of output levels, a trade-off is possible.

believe people are reasonable. Keynesians argue that, given the cost of rationality, it would be unreasonable for most people to make explicit calculations about inflation's effect on their incomes. People have a general feeling, but that is all they have. Consequently people's calculations about their relative wage and prices based on the price level are inexact. Three or four percent inflation per year is about .008 percent per day, meaning that $1,000 will lose about 8¢ in value each day. That 8¢ is hardly noticeable. Price indices are more inexact than that. Therefore, say many Keynesians, low inflation levels (2 or 3 percent) will be accepted by individuals without leading them to immediate increases in their nominal wages or prices.

Keynesians argue that people will rationally respond quite differently to a 2 percent decrease in their real wage caused by a 2 percent decrease in their nominal wage than they would to a 2 percent decrease in their real wage caused by a 2 percent increase in the price level. This argument accounts for the Keynesian explanation of the reasonably stable trade-off that existed before 1970.

How then do these Keynesians explain the 1970s? The answer is that the economy experienced a combination of unfortunate events, including oil price shocks and overly expansionary government policies. These events caused inflation to exceed what psychologists called the *just-noticeable difference.*

Just-noticeable difference A threshold below which our senses don't recognize that something has changed.

The **just-noticeable difference** is the threshold where our senses realize that something has changed. For example, say it gets 2°C warmer; most people won't notice. But if it gets 10°C warmer, most people will notice. Thus, the just-noticeable difference is a change of somewhere between 2°C and 10°C. Keynesians argue that, in the 1970s, inflation exceeded that threshold. As it did, inflation became built into people's expectations and everyone who previously had wanted a 4 percent wage hike now asked for a 9 percent hike, while firms that wanted a 3 percent price increase raised their prices by 8 percent to account for the expected higher price level due to inflation. The entire short-run Phillips curve shifted up, as suggested by the Classicals. But that happened only because the economy was pushed too far; it doesn't negate the existence of a continuing trade-off between inflation and unemployment within certain limits.

Thus, there is a central difference between the Keynesian and Classical views of the Phillips curve. The Keynesian view allows that, within a limited range, there is a long-run trade-off between inflation and unemployment. That's why Keynesians generally support a more expansionary policy than do Classical economists, and also why they support more activist monetary and fiscal policies. In the Keynesian view, government macroeconomic policy can do good; in the Classical view, it cannot.

Similarities and Differences between Keynesian and Classical Theories

The preceding discussion highlighted differences between Keynesian and Classical theories of inflation. Keynesians see inflation as an institutional phenomenon; Classicals see it as a monetary phenomenon.

Classicals and Keynesians on Supply Shocks The distinction between the Keynesian and Classical theories of inflation comes out most clearly when we consider the effects of a supply-price shock, such as a sudden increase in the price of oil. Keynesians see such a supply-price shock as a cost-push pressure, likely to lead to significant inflationary pressures as people try to maintain their relative income at their previous level.

Classical economists see a supply-price shock as simply a relative price change. They argue that as long as the government does not increase the money supply, other relative prices will fall and there will be little inflationary pressure from a supply-price shock. So they advocate maintaining a monetary rule and not increasing the money supply to accommodate higher prices.

Classicals and Keynesians on Recent Inflation To see these differences, let's compare how Classicals and Keynesians explain the inflation that's been occurring in the early 1990s.

First, the facts, which we present in Exhibit 6. As you can see, in the early 1990s

EXHIBIT 6   **Inflation, Money Supply Growth, and Unemployment**

Year	Inflation (GDP deflator)	Rate of Growth of Money Supply			Unemployment Rate
		M1	M2+	M3	
1990	3.1%	−0.7%	11.5%	10.4%	8.1%
1991	2.7	4.6	8.7	6.5	10.4
1992	1.4	5.5	5.6	5.1	11.3
1993	1.1	10.8	3.9	4.9	11.3
1994	0.7	11.7	2.1	3.6	10.4

Source: CANSIM Database, Statistics Canada, March 1995.

inflation remained low, while unemployment fluctuated. Different measures of the money supply were changing at different rates. There were no major price shocks during this time, but there were significant changes in financial institutions. The monetarists argued that, once one accounted for financial institutional changes, the core relationship between changes in the money supply and inflation could be seen.

Thus, the period, while not perfectly consistent with the Classical view, was not a refutation of it. Classicals claimed that if the Bank of Canada held constant an appropriate measure of the money supply, inflation could be totally stopped.

Keynesians would say that the inflation was relatively low because the unemployment rate was being kept higher than the economy could handle, and that the remaining inflation was a combination of supply shock inflation and inflation caused by existing institutions. They would claim that holding down the appropriate measure of the money supply was impossible (since one couldn't decide what the appropriate measure was), but that even if one could hold it down, holding it down further would only cause more unemployment since the inflation was inherent in the institutions.

Similarities in the Keynesian and Classical Views   These differences between the theories shouldn't obscure the similarities. Once the economy reaches its potential output, both Keynesians and Classicals see inflation as an excess demand phenomenon: too much money chasing too few goods. The differences in views occur when the economy is not at its potential output. Keynesians believe inflation is still possible; Classicals believe it is not.

The two different theories of inflation lead to two different sets of policies to fight inflation and the unemployment/inflation dilemma.

Classicals say to stop inflation one must reduce the rate of growth of the money supply. Control the money supply and you will control inflation.

Keynesians agree that controlling the money supply will ultimately control inflation, but they argue that it will do so in an inefficient and unfair manner. They argue that tight monetary policy usually causes unemployment among those least able to handle it. Keynesians ask, "Why should this group bear the cost of fighting inflation?" Their argument is that putting a brick wall in front of a speeding car will stop the car, but that doesn't mean that's how you should stop a car. Instead, Keynesians are more likely to favour the use of supplemental policies in conjunction with contractionary monetary policy. Let's consider both views more carefully.

One way to escape a stagflation is embodied in the Classical analysis of the natural rate of unemployment. If you got into the problem by actual inflation exceeding expected inflation because you tried to hold unemployment below the natural rate, you can get out of inflation by having actual inflation below expected inflation. To do that you must maintain the unemployment rate higher than the natural rate. In essence, you run a planned recession. Exhibit 7 graphs this method of getting out of stagflation.

KEYNESIAN AND CLASSICAL POLICIES TO FIGHT STAGFLATION

The Classical Approach to Fighting Stagflation

DIETING AND FIGHTING INFLATION

The debate on what to do about inflation has an analogy to dieting. Fasting will cause you to lose about a pound a day. Want to lose 30 pounds? A Classical dietitian would say, "Fast. Thirty pounds equals 105,000 calories. When you've managed to complete a period in which you've eaten 105,000 fewer calories than are necessary to maintain your present weight, you'll have lost 30 pounds." A Keynesian dietitian would offer a variety of diets or would explore your soul to discover why you want to overeat, and would perhaps suggest a liquid protein plan. The Keynesian diet would also involve your taking in 105,000 fewer calories than if you'd continued to overeat. But, Keynesians argue, you can't stick with a diet unless you've discovered what makes you want to overeat.

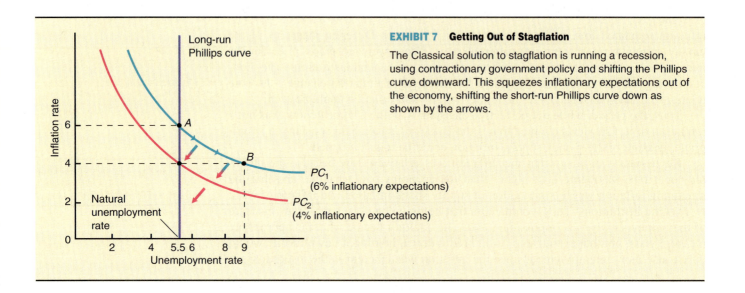

EXHIBIT 7   Getting Out of Stagflation

The Classical solution to stagflation is running a recession, using contractionary government policy and shifting the Phillips curve downward. This squeezes inflationary expectations out of the economy, shifting the short-run Phillips curve down as shown by the arrows.

Say that initially the economy was in equilibrium at 6 percent inflation and 5.5 percent unemployment, and that the natural rate of unemployment was 5.5 percent (point *A*). Say that the government runs contractionary aggregate policy so that the unemployment rate increases to 9 percent and inflation falls to 4 percent (point *B*). As expectations of inflation fall, the short-run Phillips curve shifts down from PC_1 (6 percent inflationary expectation) to PC_2 (4 percent inflationary expectation).

As long as the actual unemployment rate remains above the natural rate of unemployment, the Phillips curve trade-off will keep falling as expectations of inflation keep falling in response to lower-than-expected inflation. If government policies hold unemployment above the natural rate, eventually expectations of inflation will fall to zero. At that point, the government can stop squeezing inflation out of the economy and it can be allowed to return to the natural rate of unemployment. This is the Classical solution to stagflation: contractionary monetary and fiscal policies squeezing the inflationary expectation out of the economy. True, it involves suffering, but the economy must atone for the expansionary sins of the Keynesians.

For Classicals, however, since people's expectations are rational and the rate of increase in the money supply determines the rate of inflation, the suffering need not be that great if the government is firm. If a strict monetary rule can be adopted and people can know that, no matter what, the government won't exceed the monetary growth rate specified in the rule, expectations of inflation will fall quickly.

The Keynesian Approach to Fighting Stagflation

Inducing a recession to rid the economy of expected inflation isn't a pleasant policy, so it isn't surprising that a Keynesian alternative has often been tried. The Keynesian alternative is to use a supplemental policy that directly holds down inflation. Such a policy is often called an *incomes policy*. An **incomes policy** is a policy that places direct pressure on individuals to hold down their nominal wages and prices. Because it holds down inflation, an incomes policy can help to eliminate expectations of inflation, thereby reducing the cost in unemployment necessary to fight inflation.

An example of an incomes policy is a program of temporary *wage and price controls,* which directly prohibit inflation. Keynesians argue that when people see that inflation is at a lower level, they'll expect less inflation, the Phillips curve will shift down, and the controls can be repealed. With wage and price controls, expectations of inflation are eliminated without a recession.

It seems a highly desirable alternative, and in October 1975 Prime Minister Trudeau instituted wage and price controls. The Anti-Inflation Board was responsible for administering the program. Initial results were encouraging as inflation fell substantially in 1976. But in 1978 as controls were being lifted, inflation jumped. By 1982 unemployment was 11 percent and inflation was over 10 percent.

What went wrong? One problem was bad timing. About the time controls were removed, an oil price shock generated more inflation. A second problem was that the fall in the inflation rate allowed aggregate policy to be more expansionary than it otherwise would have been. Temporary wage and price controls can only temporarily hold down inflation. If controls are expected to have a long-run effect, they must be long-run controls—but no one expected the 1975–78 wage and price controls to be long run. Thus, temporary controls change nothing in the underlying reality. Using controls often tempts government to be too expansionary.

It's unclear what the inflation rate in the absence of these controls would have been. Supporters of temporary wage and price controls argue that the controls stopped a bad situation from getting worse. Opponents of temporary price controls as a way to reduce expectations of inflation argue that, inevitably, such price controls will be used to camouflage expansionary policy and thus should be avoided.

A more recent example comes from Mexico. In early 1995 the Mexican peso underwent a significant depreciation, relative to other currencies. The decline in the value of the peso raised the cost of imported goods, since it took more pesos to buy the necessary foreign currency than before. In an attempt to restrain the inflationary pressures that would follow the depreciation (as producers passed on higher costs to consumers), the Mexican government introduced wage and price controls. Whether these controls will work or not remains to be seen, but given the Canadian experience, one can expect to see a substantial jump in the Mexican inflation rate when the controls are removed.

CONCLUSION

The Classical and Keynesian views of inflation and the Phillips curve trade-off reflect two consistent world views. Keynesians see a world in which sociological and institutional factors interact with market forces, keeping the economy in a perpetual disequilibrium when considered in an economic framework. Classicals see a world in which market forces predominate. They consider institutional and sociological factors insignificant, and view the overall economy as one in continual equilibrium. These two worldviews carry over to their analyses of the central policy issue facing most governments as they decide on their monetary and fiscal policies: the trade-off between inflation and unemployment.

These different worldviews are why there are major disagreements about policy. Classicals believe the best policy is laissez-faire; Keynesians believe an activist policy is needed. Given their contrasting worldviews, the debate will likely continue for a long time.

Incomes policy   A policy placing direct pressure on individuals to hold down their nominal wages and prices.

8A   Classicals see monetary growth and competitive markets determining the level of inflation and unemployment. No role for an incomes policy remains.

8B   Keynesians see institutional and social forces determining the level of inflation and unemployment, and hence see a role for an incomes policy.

CHAPTER SUMMARY

- High inflation is inevitably accompanied by roughly pro-portional increases in the money supply and expectations of inflation.
- The short-run Phillips curve differs from the long-run Phillips curve because, on the long-run Phillips curve, expected inflation must equal actual inflation, and hence much of the short-run trade-off disappears.
- The Classical theory of inflation blurs out the institutional process of setting prices and focuses on the relation between money and inflation.
- Classical economists favour a monetary rule that is to be followed regardless of economic conditions.

- The Keynesian theory of inflation blurs out the relation-ship between inflation and money and focuses on the institutional process of setting prices.
- In the Classical theory of inflation, the only equilibrium is on the long-run Phillips curve.
- In the Keynesian theory of inflation, a short-run Phillips curve trade-off can persist into the long run as long as inflation doesn't exceed a certain range.
- Classicals argue that the only way to stop inflation is to stop increasing the money supply. Keynesians argue that supplemental policies (such as an incomes policy) are needed.

KEY TERMS

adaptive expectations   *(346)*
cost-push inflation   *(346)*
demand-pull inflation   *(346)*
expectations of inflation   *(349)*
incomes policy   *(363)*

induced recession   *(350)*
inflation   *(346)*
just-noticeable difference   *(360)*
long-run Phillips curve   *(349)*
monetary rule   *(354)*

monetary validation   *(346)*
natural rate of unemployment   *(355)*
Phillips curve   *(348)*
short-run Phillips curve   *(349)*
stagflation   *(356)*

QUESTIONS FOR THOUGHT AND REVIEW

The number after each question represents the estimated degree of critical thinking required. (1 = almost none; 10 = deep thought.)

1. Distinguish cost-push from demand-pull inflation.   *(2)*
2. Draw a short-run and a long-run Phillips curve.   *(2)*
3. How would a Keynesian explain the relatively stable inflation/unemployment trade-off existing before 1969?   *(5)*
4. How would a Classical economist explain the relatively stable inflation/unemployment trade-off existing before 1969?   *(9)*

5. What policy implications would a Classical draw from the quotation at the beginning of the chapter?   *(4)*
6. What policy implications would a Keynesian draw from the quotation at the beginning of the chapter?   *(6)*
7. What implication does the insider/outsider view of the economy have for macroeconomic policy?   *(6)*
8. What arguments would a Classical economist give in opposing an incomes policy?   *(3)*
9. Demonstrate graphically how an induced recession will eliminate stagflation.   *(4)*
10. The Phillips curve is nothing but a figment of econo-mists' imagination. True or false?   *(9)*

PROBLEMS AND EXERCISES

1. People's perception of inflation often differs from actual inflation.
   a. List five goods that you buy relatively frequently.
   b. Looking in old newspapers (found in the library on microfiche), locate sale prices for these goods since 1950, finding one price every five years or so. Determine the average price rise of each of these five goods from 1950 until today.
   c. Compare that price rise with the rise in the Consumer Price Index.

2. Congratulations! You've just been appointed finance minis-ter of Inflationland. Inflation has been ongoing for the past five years at 5 percent. The target rate of unemployment, 5 percent, is also the actual rate.
   a. Demonstrate the economy's likely position on both short-run and long-run Phillips curves.
   b. The prime minister tells you she wants to be reelected. Devise a monetary policy strategy for her that might help her accomplish her goal.

c. Demonstrate that strategy graphically, including the likely long-run consequences.

3. In the early 1990s, Argentina stopped increasing the money supply and fixed the exchange rate of the Argentine austral at 10,000 to the dollar. It then renamed the Argentine currency the "peso" and cut off four zeros so that one peso equaled one dollar. Inflation slowed substantially. After this was done, the following observations were made. Explain why these observations did not surprise economists.

a. The golf courses were far less crowded.

b. The price of goods in dollar-equivalent pesos in Buenos Aires, the capital of the country, was significantly above that in Toronto.

c. Consumer prices—primarily of services—rose relative to other goods.

d. Luxury auto dealers were shutting down.

4. Grade inflation is widespread. Students' grades are increasing, but what they are learning is decreasing. Some economists argue that grade inflation should be dealt with in the same way that price inflation should be dealt with—by cre-ating a fixed standard and requiring all grades to be specified relative to that standard. One way to accomplish this is to index the grades professors give: specify on the grade report both the student's grade and the class average, and deflate (or inflate) the professor's grade to some common standard.

a. Discuss the advantages and disadvantages of such a proposal.

b. What relationship does it have to economists' proposals for fixed exchange rates?

5. In 1990 Japan's money supply growth rate fell from 11–12 percent to 3–4 percent. What effect would you expect this decline to have on:

a. Japanese real output?

b. Japanese unemployment?

c. Japanese inflation?

6. Compare and contrast the Classical and the Keynesian theories of inflation. Would a Keynesian economist ever be appointed to run the Bank of Canada? Explain why or why not.

15

International Trade

One of the purest fallacies is that trade follows the flag. Trade follows the lowest price current. If a dealer in any colony wished to buy Union Jacks, he would order them from Britain's worst foe if he could save a sixpence.

~Andrew Carnegie

After reading this chapter, you should be able to:

1 List Canada's primary trading partners.

2 Explain the principle of absolute advantage.

3 Explain the principle of comparative advantage.

4 List three determinants of the gains from trade.

5 Explain three policies countries use to restrict trade.

6 Discuss why countries impose trade restrictions.

7 Summarize why economists generally oppose trade restrictions.

8 Discuss the Canada–United States Free Trade Agreement and show how tariff reduction leads to greater economic efficiency.

9 Briefly discuss the problems facing the World Trade Organization.

Many goods we use every day aren't made in Canada: cars, clothes, televisions—the list is endless. These goods are imported from other countries. Almost every day we hear calls from some sector of the economy to restrict foreign imports in order to save Canadian jobs and protect Canadian workers from unfair competition. Economists generally oppose these restrictions; economists favour free trade. In this chapter we consider why countries trade, why economists generally favour free trade, and why, despite what economists tell them, countries impose trade restrictions.

Before we consider these issues, let's look at some numbers relevant to international trade to get a sense of the nature and dimensions of international trade.

PATTERNS OF TRADE

Increasing but Fluctuating World Trade

In terms of dollar amounts, the fluctuations in international trade over the years are staggering. In constant 1980 Canadian dollars, world trade fell from $286 billion in 1928 to $129 billion in 1935. It then rose again, to well over $2.4 trillion in the early 1990s. The conclusion: International trade has been growing, but with significant fluctuations in that growth. Sometimes international trade has grown rapidly; at other times it has grown slowly or has even fallen.

In part, fluctuations in world trade result from fluctuations in world output. When output rises, international trade rises; when output falls, international trade falls. Fluctuations in world trade are also in part explained by trade restrictions that countries have imposed from time to time. For example, decreases in world income during the Depression caused a large decrease in trade, but that decrease was exacerbated by a worldwide increase in trade restrictions during the 1930s.

Differences in Importance of Trade

The importance of international trade to countries' economies differs widely, as we can see in Exhibit 1, which presents the importance of the shares of exports and imports for various countries. Among the countries listed, the Netherlands has the highest amount of exports compared to GDP; the United States has the lowest.

The Netherlands' imports are also the highest as a percentage of GDP. The United States and Japan have the lowest. The relationship between a country's imports and its exports is no coincidence. For most countries, imports and exports roughly correspond, though in any particular year that correspondence can be rough indeed. For Canada in recent years, merchandise exports have generally significantly exceeded merchandise imports. But that situation can't continue forever, as we'll discuss.

Total trade figures provide us with only part of the international trade picture. We must also look at what types of goods are traded and with whom that trade is conducted. Exhibit 2 breaks Canadian international trade down into its various components. Notice that Canada both imports and exports significant amounts of manufactured goods. This isn't unusual, since much of all international trade is in manufactured goods.

EXHIBIT 1   Relation of Exports and Imports to GDP in Selected Countries, 1993

	GDP*	Exports*	Percent of GDP	Imports*	Percent of GDP
United States	$5,951	$442	7%	$544	9%
Canada	537	124	23	118	22
Netherlands	260	129	50	118	45
Germany	1,398	378	27	355	25
United Kingdom	921	187	20	211	23
Italy	1,012	169	17	170	17
France	1,080	213	20	230	21
Japan	2,468	340	14	233	9

*Numbers in billions of U.S. dollars.
Source: *The World FactBook,* 1993.

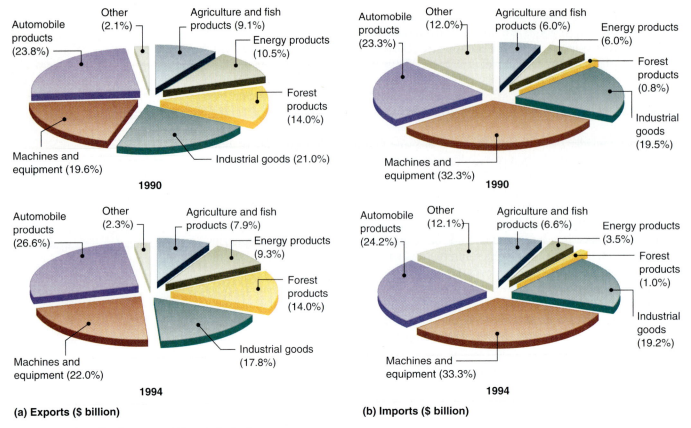

(a) Exports ($ billion)   **(b) Imports ($ billion)**

EXHIBIT 2   Canadian Imports and Exports by Sector

These pie charts show the relative shares of each sector in exports and imports. Notice how much of Canada's trade's in machinery and equipment and automobile products.
Source: *Canadian Economic Observer*, Table 18, March 1995.

1   The primary trading partners of Canada are the United States, Western Europe, and Japan.

Exhibit 3 shows the regions with which Canada trades. Exports to the United States made up the largest percentage of total Canadian exports in 1994, as did Canadian imports from the United States. Over 80 percent of Canadian exports went to the United States while Canadian imports from the United States represented only 75 percent of total imports. With numbers like these, it's not hard to see why economic events in the United States have such an important impact on the Canadian economy.

WHY DO NATIONS TRADE?

International trade exists for the same reason that all trade exists: Country A has something that Country B wants and Country B has something that Country A wants. Both countries can be made better off by trade.

The Principle of Absolute Advantage

Trade between countries in different types of goods is relatively easy to explain. For example, trade in raw materials and agricultural goods for manufactured goods can be easily explained by the **principle of absolute advantage:**

> *A country that can produce a good at a lower cost than another country is said to have an absolute advantage in the production of that good. When two countries have absolute advantages in different goods, there are gains from trade to be had.*

2   The principle of absolute advantage states that a country that can produce a good at a lower cost than another country has an absolute advantage in the production of that good.

The principle of absolute advantage explains trade of, say, oil from Saudi Arabia for food from Canada. Saudi Arabia has millions of barrels of easily available oil, but growing food in its desert climate and sandy soil is expensive. Canada can grow food cheaply in its temperate climate and fertile soil, but its oil isn't as easily available or as cheap to extract. Because it can produce a certain amount of oil with fewer

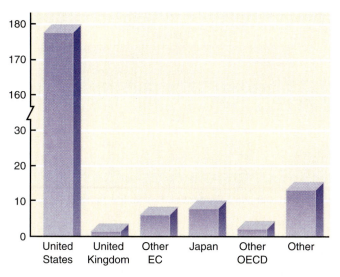

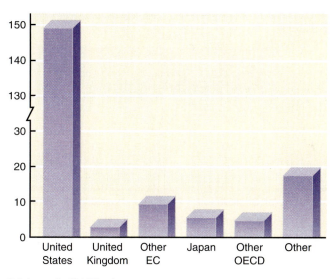

(a) Exports ($ billion)

(b) Imports ($ billion)

EXHIBIT 3

Canadian exports (**a**) and imports (**b**) are dominated by trade with the United States.
Source: *Statistics Canada*, CANSIM Database, March 1995.

resources, Saudi Arabia has an absolute advantage over Canada in producing oil. Because it can produce a certain amount of food with fewer resources, Canada has an absolute advantage over Saudi Arabia in producing food. When each country specializes in the good it has an absolute advantage in, both countries can gain from trade.

In Exhibit 4, we consider a hypothetical numerical example which demonstrates how the principle of absolute advantage can lead to gains from trade. For simplicity, we assume constant opportunity costs (that means the production possibility curve is a straight line, as you'll recall from Exhibit 1 of Chapter 1) .

Exhibits 4 (b) and (d) show the choices for Canada; Exhibits 4 (a) and (c) show the choices for Saudi Arabia. In Exhibits 4 (a) and (b) you see that Canada and Saudi Arabia can produce various combinations of food and oil by devoting differing percentages of their resources to producing each. Comparing the two tables and assuming the resources in the two countries are comparable, we see that Saudi Arabia has an absolute advantage in the production of oil and Canada has an absolute advantage in the production of food.

For example, when Canada and Saudi Arabia devote equal amounts of resources to oil production, Saudi Arabia can produce 10 times as much as Canada. When Canada devotes 60 percent of a given amount of resources to oil production, it gets 60 barrels of oil. But when Saudi Arabia devotes 60 percent of that same amount of resources to oil production, it gets 600 barrels of oil. The information in the tables is presented graphically in Exhibits 4 (c) and (d). These graphs represent the two countries' production possibility curves without trade. Each combination of numbers in the table corresponds to a point on the curve. For example, point *B* in each graph corresponds to the entries in row *B*, columns 2 and 3, in the relevant table.

Let's assume that, without any international trade, Canada has chosen point *C* (production of 60 barrels of oil and 400 tonnes of food) and Saudi Arabia has chosen point *D* (production of 400 barrels of oil and 60 tonnes of food).

Now I. T. (International Trader), who understands the principle of absolute advantage, comes along and offers the following deal to Saudi Arabia:

> If you produce 1,000 barrels of oil and no food (point *A*) and give me 500 barrels of oil while keeping 500 barrels for yourself, I guarantee you 120 tonnes of food, double the amount of food you're now getting. I'll put you on point *G*, which is totally above your current production possibility curve. You'll get more oil and more food. It's an offer you can't refuse.

International trade means that huge amounts of goods are shipped through ports. Here exports are being loaded onto a South Korean shipping line. © *Bob Daemmrich/The Image Works.*

Saudi Arabia

Percentage of resources devoted to oil	Oil produced (barrels)	Food produced (tonnes)	Row
100	1,000	0	A
80	800	20	B
60	600	40	C
40	400	60	D
20	200	80	E
0	0	100	F

(a) Saudi Arabia's Production Possibility Table

Canada

Percentage of resources devoted to oil	Oil produced (barrels)	Food produced (tonnes)	Row
100	100	0	A
80	80	200	B
60	60	400	C
40	40	600	D
20	20	800	E
0	0	1,000	F

(b) Canada's Production Possibility Table

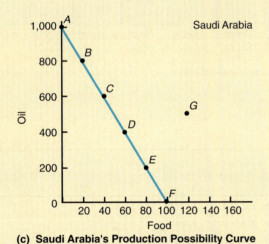

(c) Saudi Arabia's Production Possibility Curve

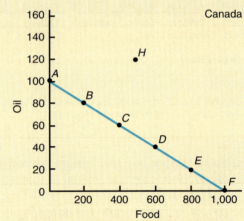

(d) Canada's Production Possibility Curve

EXHIBIT 4   Absolute Advantage: Canada and Saudi Arabia

Looking at tables (**a**) and (**b**), you can see that if Saudi Arabia devotes all its resources to oil, it can produce 1,000 barrels of oil, but if it devotes all of its resources to food, it can produce only 100 tonnes of food. For Canada, the story is the opposite: devoting all of its resources to oil, Canada can only produce 100 barrels of oil—10 times less than Saudi Arabia—but if it devotes all of its resources to food, it can produce 1,000 tonnes of food—10 times more than Saudi Arabia. Assuming resources are comparable, Saudi Arabia has an absolute advantage in the production of oil, and Canada has an absolute advantage in the production of food.

The information in the tables is presented graphically in (**c**) and (**d**). These are the countries' production possibility curves without trade. Each point on each country's curve corresponds to a row on that country's table.

I. T. then flies off to Canada, to whom he makes the following offer:

> If you produce 1,000 tonnes of food and no oil (point *F*) and give me 500 tonnes of food while keeping 500 tonnes for yourself, I'll guarantee you 120 barrels of oil, double the amount you're now getting. I'll put you on point *H*, which is totally above your current production possibility curve. You'll get more oil and have more food. It's an offer you can't refuse.

Both countries accept; they'd be foolish not to. So the two countries' final consumption positions are as shown in Exhibit 5. For arranging the trade, I. T. makes a handsome profit of 380 tonnes of food and 380 barrels of oil.

I. T. has become rich because he understands the principle of absolute advantage. Unfortunately for I. T., the principle of absolute advantage is easy to understand, which means that he will quickly face competition. Other international traders come in and offer the countries even better deals than I. T. offered, squeezing his share. With free entry and competition in international trade, eventually I. T.'s share is squeezed down to his costs plus a normal return for his efforts.

Now obviously this hypothetical example significantly overemphasizes the gains a trader makes. Generally the person arranging the trade must compete with other

EXHIBIT 5   Distribution of Production among Canada, Saudi Arabia, and I. T.

	Oil (barrels)	Food (tonnes)
Total production	1,000	1,000
Canadian consumption	120	500
Saudi consumption	500	120
I. T.'s profit	380	380

traders and offer both countries a better deal than the one presented here. But the person who first recognizes a trading opportunity often makes a sizable fortune. The second and third persons who recognize the opportunity make smaller fortunes. Once the insight is generally recognized, the possibility of making a fortune is gone. Traders still make their normal returns, but the instantaneous fortunes are not to be made without new insight. In the long run, benefits of trade go to the countries, not the traders.

I. T. realizes this and spends part of his fortune on buying a Greek island, where he retires to contemplate more deeply the nature of international trade so he can triple his remaining fortune. He marries, has a daughter whom he names I. T. Too, and dies. But before he dies he teaches his daughter about international trade and how new insights can lead to fortunes. His dying words to his daughter are, "Keep searching for that new insight."

Many years pass. I. T. Too grows up, and one day, while walking along the beach, contemplates the possibilities of trade between Germany and Algeria in automobiles and food. No other traders have considered trade between these two countries because Germany is so much more productive than Algeria in *all* goods. No trade is currently taking place because Germany has an absolute advantage in production of both autos and food. Assuming the resources in the two countries are comparable, this case can be seen in Exhibit 6.

But I. T. Too is bright. She remembers what her father taught her about opportunity costs back in her first economics lesson. She reasons as follows: Germany's opportunity cost of producing an auto is 2/1. That means Germany must give up 2 tonnes of food to get 1 additional auto. For example, if Germany is initially producing 60 autos and 80 tonnes of food, if it cuts production of autos by 20, it will increase its food output by 40. For each car lost, Germany gains 2 tonnes of food. When Algeria cuts its production of autos by 4, it gains 1 tonne of food. Algeria's opportunity cost of producing another auto is 1/4. It must give up 1 tonne of food to get an additional 4 autos.

I. T. Too further reasons that if Algeria needs to give up only 1/4 unit of food to get an auto while Germany needs to give up 2 tonnes of food to produce 1 auto, there

The Principle of Comparative Advantage

EXHIBIT 6   Germany's Comparative Advantage over Algeria in the Production of Autos and Food

	Percent of resources devoted to autos	Autos produced	Food produced (tonnes)		Percent of resources devoted to autos	Autos produced	Food produced (tonnes)
A	100%	100	0	A	100%	20	0
B	80	80	40	B	80	16	1
C	60	60	80	C	60	12	2
D	40	40	120	D	40	8	3
E	20	20	160	E	20	4	4
F	0	0	200	F	0	0	5
(a) Germany				**(b) Algeria**			

EXHIBIT 7   **Final Consumption for Both Countries**

	Autos	Food (tonnes)
Total production	68	104
German consumption	61	82
Algerian consumption	5	5
I. T. Too's profit	2	17

are potential gains to be made, which can be split up among the countries and herself. Then, like her father before her, she can make the countries offers they can't refuse. She walks the beach mulling the following: "*Absolute advantage* is not necessary for trade; *comparative advantage* is." A smile comes over her face; she understands.

Flying happily over the Mediterranean Sea, she formulates her insight precisely. She calls it the **principle of comparative advantage:** *As long as the relative opportunity costs of producing goods (what must be given up in one good in order to get another good) differ among countries, there are potential gains from trade, even if one country has an absolute advantage in everything.*

It is comparative advantage, not absolute advantage, that forms a basis of trade. If one country has a comparative advantage in one good, the other country must, by definition, have a comparative advantage in the other good.

Having formulated her idea, she applies it to the Germans and Algerians. She sees that, unexpectedly, Germany has a comparative advantage in producing food and Algeria has a comparative advantage in producing cars. With this insight firmly in mind, she leaves her island, flies to Germany, and makes the Germans the following offer:

> You're currently producing and consuming 60 autos and 80 tonnes of food (row C of Exhibit 6 (a)). If you'll produce only 48 autos but 104 tonnes of food and give me 22 tonnes of food, I'll guarantee you 13 autos for those 22 tonnes of food. You'll have more autos (61) and more food (82). It's an offer you can't refuse.

She then goes to Algeria and presents the Algerians with the following offer:

> You're currently producing 4 tonnes of food and 4 automobiles (row E of Exhibit 6 (b)). If you'll produce only automobiles (row A) and turn out 20 autos, keeping 5 for yourself and giving 15 of them to me, I'll guarantee you 5 tonnes of food for the 15 autos. You'll have more autos (5) and more food (5). It's an offer you can't refuse.

Neither Germany nor Algeria can refuse. They both agree to I. T. Too's offer. The final position appears in Exhibit 7.

I. T. Too then proceeds to visit various other countries, making similar offers. They accept the offers because it's in their interest to accept them. Countries (and people) trade because trade benefits them.

As was the case with her father, her initial returns are the greatest. Then, as other people recognize the principle of comparative advantage and offer the countries better deals than hers, her share shrinks until her return just covers her opportunity cost and the costs of transporting the goods. But because the principle of comparative advantage is more difficult to understand than the principle of absolute advantage, the competing traders enter in much more slowly. Her above-normal returns last longer than did her father's, but eventually they're competed away. When the gains decline to only normal levels, she sells out and retires.

Competitiveness, Exchange Rates, and Comparative Advantage

As discussed in Chapter 5, generally a low value of the dollar encourages exports from a country and discourages imports; a high value of the dollar discourages exports and encourages imports. An example of the importance of exchange rates can be seen by considering Canada and Japan: in the mid-1980s a dollar bought almost 150 yen, but in the mid-1990s the Canadian dollar bought only 70 yen. That change halved the

Principle of comparative advantage
As long as the relative opportunity costs of producing goods differ among countries, there are potential gains from trade, even if one country has an absolute advantage in everything.

3 The principle of comparative advantage states that as long as the relative opportunity costs of producing goods differ among countries, there are potential gains from trade, even if one country has an absolute advantage in everything.

ADDED DIMENSION

WHO FORMULATED
THE PRINCIPLE OF
COMPARATIVE
ADVANTAGE?

■n case you were wondering, I. T. Too didn't really formulate the principle of comparative advantage. It first appeared in a book called *Principles of Economics* written by an extraordinarily bright stockbroker, David Ricardo, in 1817. Thus, it's often called the *Ricardian principle of comparative advantage.*

As with many other principles of economics, the true lineage of this principle is subject to dispute. Ideas are often "in the air" long before they get into print, and the person to whom history attributes them may not be the person who formulated them. After some superb detective work, in 1976 William Thweat discovered that Ricardo's good friend, economist James Mill, and not Ricardo himself, was the first to write about comparative advantage and so deserves to be called the discoverer of the principle of comparative advantage. Not all historians agree with Thweat, but all agree that it was one of those two, not I. T. Too.

absolute advantage of Japan and significantly discouraged Canadian consumption of Japanese products. The resurgence of the Canadian auto industry is in large part due to that change in the exchange rate.

The principle of comparative advantage is powerful. It determines when there are gains from trade to be made. It doesn't determine how those gains from trade will be divided up among the countries involved and among traders like I. T. Too. We can, however, offer some insights into how those gains are likely to be divided up. We've already noted the first insight:

> The more competition that exists in international trade, the less likely it is that the trader gets the gains of trade; more of the gains from trade will go to the citizens in the two countries.

This insight isn't lost upon trading companies. Numerous import/export companies exist whose business is discovering new possibilities for international trade. Individuals representing trading companies go around hawking projects or goods to countries. For example, in 1989 at the end of the Iran–Iraq war, what the business world calls the *import/export contingent* flew in to Iraq with offers of goods and services to sell. Many of these same individuals had been in Saudi Arabia when the oil price rose in the 1970s, and in Asia when China opened its doors to international trade in the 1980s. In the early 1990s, this same group flocked to the countries of the former Soviet Union.

Selling Canadian goods is often easy for such Canadian traders. The problem generally is arranging financing. The goods must be paid for in the currency of the country doing the exporting, not in the currency of the country doing the importing. Often firms that are doing the selling must also arrange financing for the trade. Thus, foreign exchange arrangements are important.

A second insight is:

> Once competition prevails, smaller countries tend to get a larger percentage of the gains from trade than do larger countries.

The reason, briefly, is that more opportunities are opened up for smaller countries by trade than for larger countries. The more opportunities, the larger the relative gains. Say, for instance, that Canada begins trade with Mali, a small country in Africa. Enormous new consumption possibilities are opened up for Mali—prices of all types of goods will fall. Before international trade began, cars were probably extraordinarily expensive in Mali, while fish were cheap. With international trade, the price of cars in Mali falls substantially, so Mali gets the gains. Because the Canadian economy is so large compared to Mali's, the Canadian price of fish doesn't change noticeably. Mali's fish are just a drop in the bucket. The price ratio of cars to fish doesn't change much for Canada, so it doesn't get much of the gains from trade. Mali gets almost all the gains from trade.

Dividing Up the Gains from Trade

4   Three determinants of the gains from trade are:
1. The more competition, the less the trader gets.
2. Smaller countries get a larger proportion of the gain than larger countries.
3. Countries producing goods with economies of scale get a larger gain from trade.

TRADE ALLOWS COUNTRIES TO CONSUME OUTSIDE THEIR PRODUCTION POSSIBILITY CURVES

The previous example of I.T. and his daughter gave you a good feel for comparative advantage using tables, but knowing us as you do, you didn't really expect to escape without some graphs, did you? The gains from trade can be illustrated by demonstrating that two countries can consume outside of their production possibility curves, given the chance to trade.

Let's assume there are two countries, Canada and the Netherlands, both able to produce tulips and wheat. Given their endowments of resources and technologies, we can plot their production possibility curves in (a). Canada can produce 30 bushels of wheat, or 3 tonnes of tulips (or somewhere in between). The opportunity cost of 1 tonne of tulips in Canada is 10 bushels of wheat: to get one more tonne of tulips, we need to give up 10 bushels of wheat. The Netherlands can produce 36 bushels of wheat, or 18 tonnes of tulips (or somewhere in between). In the Netherlands, the opportunity cost of a tonne of tulips is 2 bushels of wheat: to get one more tonne of tulips they need to produce 2 fewer bushels of wheat. Without trade, each country is limited to consuming combinations of tulips and wheat bounded by their (respective) production possibility curves.

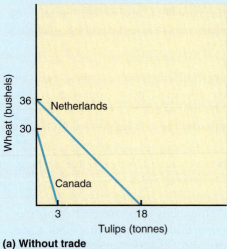

(a) Without trade

Each country has to consume some combination of wheat and tulips bounded by their production possibility curve.

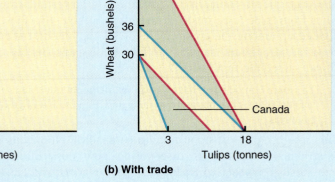

(b) With trade

Trade expands the set of goods available for consumption.

To demonstrate the gains from trade, suppose the world price of a tonne of tulips is 4 bushels of wheat (for our purposes we don't need to explain how this world price is set. This means that Canada could trade 4 bushels of wheat for one tonne of tulips, while the Netherlands could trade 1 tonne of tulips for 4 bushels of wheat. For example, if Canada produced only wheat it could trade that for 7.5 tonnes of tulips (30 divided by 4), whereas if the Netherlands produced only tulips, it could trade those tulips for 72 bushels of wheat (4 × 18). If we plot two new lines on (b) to illustrate how each country can expand its consumption opportunities from trade, it's clear that each country can now consume somewhere in the shaded areas outside of their original production possibility curves. The gains to trade accrue from being able to trade what is domestically produced at a world price that differs from domestic opportunity costs.

There's an important catch to this gains-from-trade argument. The argument holds only "once competition among traders prevails." That means that Mali residents are sold cars at the same price (plus shipping costs) as Canadian residents. International traders in small countries often have little competition from other traders and keep large shares of the gains from trade for themselves. In the preceding examples, Germany and Algeria didn't get a large share of the benefits. It was I. T. Too who got

Many countries place restrictions on imports and allow a trader to sell foreign goods in a country only if the trader finds someone to buy an equal amount of the country's exports. Such restrictions are called *countertrade restrictions.* Thus, to sell your goods to a foreign country, you may find yourself selling that country's goods to your own country. For example, a Canadian hospital supply firm that sells its goods to China might sell Chinese textiles in Canada, while a Canadian heavy equipment firm that sells machinery to Africa might sell African coffee beans in Canada.

To meet the needs of these various firms, "countertrading" firms have sprung up, which buy the countertrade goods (at a discount, of course) and sell them in Canada

most of the benefits. Since the traders often come from the larger country, the smaller country doesn't get the benefits of the gains from trade; the larger country's international traders do.

A third insight is:

Gains from trade go to the countries producing goods that exhibit economies of scale.

Trade allows an increase in production. If there are economies of scale, that increase can lower the average cost of production of a good. Hence an increase in production can lower the price of the good in the producing country. The country producing the good with the largest economies of scale has its costs reduced by more, and hence gains more from trade than does its trading partner.

TRADE RESTRICTIONS

In the previous examples, I. T. Too had a relatively easy time persuading the countries to trade. All she had to do was show them that there were gains from trade to be made. Like any good trader, she didn't emphasize the potential difficulties that trade presents. In reality, international trade creates significant problems. That's why almost no country in the world allows free trade, but instead imposes a variety of trade restrictions. We briefly consider the nature of those policies to reduce trade.

Varieties of Trade Restrictions

Countries can use a variety of policies to restrict trade. These include tariffs, quotas, voluntary restraint agreements, embargoes, regulatory trade restrictions, and nationalistic appeals. We'll consider each in turn.

Tariffs   **Tariffs,** also called *customs duties,* are taxes governments place on internationally traded goods—generally imports. Tariffs are the most-used and most familiar type of trade restriction. Tariffs operate in the same way a sales tax does: They make imported goods relatively more expensive than they otherwise would have been, and thereby encourage the consumption of domestically produced goods.

Tariff   A tax governments place on internationally traded goods—generally imports. Tariffs are also called *customs duties.*

You can see this if you consider the domestic demand and supply of textiles in Exhibit 8. At a world price of P_W, Canada ends up importing Q_2–Q_1 units, since domestic suppliers only want to sell Q_1 units while domestic consumers want Q_2 units. If the government placed a tariff on imported textiles, consumers would face a higher price, and import less. You can see this at price P_T, which is higher than the world price by the amount of the tariff: imports have fallen to Q_4–Q_3. Domestic production has increased from Q_1 to Q_3 and domestic consumption has fallen from Q_2 to Q_4.

Many countries implemented tariffs during the Great Depression in the mistaken view that tariffs would protect domestic workers. In Canada, moderate tariff protection gave way to protectionism, and tariffs were increased by an average of 50 percent. In the United States, tariffs increased the price of imported goods by about 60 percent. Other countries responded with similar tariffs, leading to trade wars; international trade plummeted, unemployment worsened, and the international depression deepened. These effects of the tariff convinced many, if not most, economists that free trade is preferable to trade restrictions. The dismal failure of these tariffs was the main

5   Three policies used to restrict trade are (1) tariffs (taxes on internationally traded goods), (2) quotas (quantity limits placed on imports), and (3) regulatory trade restrictions (government-imposed procedural rules that limit imports).

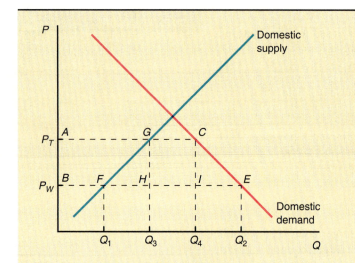

EXHIBIT 8   A Tariff

The imposition of a tariff raises price from P_W to P_T. Domestic production rises, from Q_1 to Q_3 helping suppliers, but domestic consumption falls (from Q_2 to Q_4) hurting consumers.

General Agreement on Tariffs and Trade (GATT) International agreement not to impose trade restrictions except under certain limited conditions. Replaced by the World Trade Organization (WTO) in 1995.

reason the **General Agreement on Tariffs and Trade (GATT),** an international conference to reduce trade barriers, was established immediately following World War II. Since then, periodic rounds of negotiations have resulted in a continued decline in worldwide tariffs. GATT was replaced in 1995 by the World Trade Organization, which continues many of GATT's functions.

Quotas Limitations on how much of a good can be shipped to a country.

Quotas **Quotas** are quantity limits placed on imports. Their effect in limiting trade is similar to a tariff's effect. One big difference is in who gets the revenue. With a tariff, the government gets the revenue; with a quota, revenues usually accrue to producers of the protected good. For example, if Canada places quotas on imported foreign textiles, Canadian textile producers will receive the proceeds of the resulting higher price.

You can see this by returning to Exhibit 8. A quota limiting imports to Q_4–Q_3 would force the domestic price to respond—it would rise to P_T to be consistent with the quota. But now area *CGHI* would be received by producers rather than the government. The difference between the domestic price at P_T and the world price P_W is a **quota rent.** It's possible for the government to affect the amount of the quota rent that accrues to producers through auctioning off **import licenses**—in essence giving the holder the right to import goods—but the administrative costs of holding auctions would probably exhaust the quota rent. Thus, while a quota has efficiency losses that are identical to those of a tariff, a welfare comparison of tariffs and quotas depends critically on whether the government can recapture all of the quota rents.

Quota rent A payment received by domestic producers who supply a good that is subject to an import quota.

Import license A license the government requires a firm to purchase giving it the legal right to import a good.

A second big difference is that under a quota, any increase in domestic demand will be met by the less-efficient domestic producers (who would otherwise lose in the competition) since a quota places strict numerical limitations on what can be imported. Under a tariff, part of any increase in domestic demand will be met by more efficient foreign producers since a tariff places a tax on imports but does not restrict their quantity. Needless to say, foreign producers prefer quotas to tariffs.

Voluntary Restraint Agreements Imposing new tariffs and quotas was specifically ruled out by GATT, but foreign countries knew that GATT was voluntary and that, if a domestic industry brought sufficient political pressure on its government, GATT would be forgotten. (The same problem is faced by GATT's successor, the World Trade Organization.) To avoid the imposition of new tariffs on their goods, countries often voluntarily restrict their exports. That's why Japan has agreed informally to limit the number of cars it exports to North America.

The effect of such voluntary restraint agreements is identical to the effect of quotas: They directly limit the quantity of imports, increasing the price of the good

Trade restrictions, in practice, are often much more complicated than they seem in textbooks. Seldom does a country say, "We're limiting imports to protect our home producers." Instead the country explains the restrictions in a more politically acceptable way. Consider the fight between the European Union and the United States over U.S. meat exports. In 1988 the EU, in line with Union-wide internal requirements, banned all imports of any meat from animals treated with growth-inducing hormones, which U.S. meat producers use extensively. The result: the EU banned the meat exported from the United States.

The EU claimed that it had imposed the ban only because of public health concerns. The United States claimed that the ban was actually a trade restriction, pointing out that its own residents ate this kind of meat with confidence because a U.S. government agency had certified that the levels of hormones in the meat were far below any danger level.

The United States retaliated against the EU by imposing 100 percent tariffs on Danish and West German hams, Italian tomatoes, and certain other foods produced by EU member nations. The EU threatened to respond by placing 100 percent tariffs on $100 million worth of U.S. walnuts and dried fruits, but instead entered into bilateral meetings with the United States. Those meetings allowed untreated meats into the EU for human consumption and treated meats that would be used as dog food. In response, the United States removed its retaliatory tariff on hams and tomato sauce, but retained its tariffs on many other goods.

Which side is right in this dispute? The answer is far from obvious. As we said, trade restrictions are more complicated in reality than in textbooks.

and helping domestic producers. For example, when Canada and the United States encouraged Japan to impose "voluntary" quotas on exports of its cars to North America, Toyota benefitted from the quotas because it could price its limited supply of cars higher than it could if it sent in a large number of cars, so profit per car would be high. Since they faced less competition, North American car companies also benefitted. They could increase their prices because Toyota had done so.

Embargoes   An **embargo** is an all-out restriction on import or export of a good. Embargoes are usually established for international political reasons rather than for primarily economic reasons.

Embargo   All-out restriction on import or export of a good.

An example was the NATO embargo on trade with Iraq. NATO leaders hoped that the embargo would so severely affect Iraq's economy that Saddam Hussein would lose political power. It did make life difficult for Iraqis, but it didn't bring about the downfall of the Hussein government.

Regulatory Trade Restrictions   Tariffs, quotas, and embargoes are the primary direct methods to restrict international trade. There are also indirect methods that restrict trade in not-so-obvious ways; these are called **regulatory trade restrictions** (government-imposed procedural rules that limit imports). One type of regulatory trade restriction has to do with protecting the health and safety of a country's residents. For example, a country might restrict import of all vegetables grown where certain pesticides are used, knowing full well that all other countries use those pesticides. The effect of such a regulation would be to halt the import of vegetables.

Regulatory trade restrictions   Government-imposed procedural rules that limit imports.

A second type of regulatory restriction involves making import and customs procedures so intricate and time consuming that importers simply give up. For example, France requires all imported VCRs to be individually inspected in Toulouse. Since Toulouse is a provincial city, far from any port and outside the normal route for imports after they enter France, this inspection process can take months.

Some regulatory restrictions are imposed for legitimate reasons; others are designed simply to make importing more difficult and hence protect domestic producers from international competition. It's often hard to tell the difference. A good example of this difficulty occurred in 1988 when the European Union disallowed all imports of meat from animals that had been fed growth-inducing hormones, as the accompanying box details.

Nationalistic Appeals   Finally, nationalistic appeals can help to restrict international trade. "Buy Canadian" campaigns and Japanese xenophobia[1] are examples. Many Canadians, given two products of equal appeal except that one is made in Canada and one is made in a foreign country, would buy the Canadian product. To get around this tendency, foreign and Canadian companies often go to great lengths to get a made-in-Canada classification on goods they sell in Canada. For example, components for many autos are made in Japan but shipped to Canada and assembled in Quebec and Ontario so that the finished car can be called a Canadian product.

Canadians aren't the only nationalistic people on the international trade scene. Preference for Japanese goods is deeply ingrained in Japanese culture. Faced with international demands that Japan reduce its trade surplus and with threats of retaliation if it doesn't, the Japanese government has attempted to change its people's cultural bias and to encourage consumption of foreign goods.

Reasons for Trade Restrictions

6   Reasons for restricting trade include:

1. Unequal internal distribution of the gains from trade.
2. Haggling by companies over the gains from trade.
3. Haggling by countries over trade restrictions.
4. Specialized production: learning by doing and economies of scale.
5. Macroeconomic aspects of trade.
6. National security.
7. International politics.
8. Increased revenue brought in by tariffs.

As you can see, there are many ways to restrict trade. But if trade makes sense, as it did in our example of I. T., why do countries restrict trade? Reasons for restricting trade include:

1. Unequal internal distribution of the gains from trade.
2. Haggling by companies over the gains from trade.
3. Haggling by countries over trade restrictions.
4. Specialized production: learning by doing and economies of scale.
5. Macroeconomic aspects of trade.
6. National security.
7. International politics.
8. Increased revenue brought in by tariffs.

We consider each of these obstacles to free trade in turn.

Unequal Internal Distribution of the Gains from Trade   In the first example of trade discussed in this chapter, I. T. persuaded Saudi Arabia to specialize in the production of oil rather than of food, and persuaded Canada to produce more food than oil. That means, of course, that some Canadian oil workers will have to become farmers, and in Saudi Arabia some farmers will have to become oil producers.

Often people don't want to make radical changes in the kind of work they do—they want to keep on producing what they're already producing. So when these people see the same kinds of goods that they produce coming into their country from abroad, they lobby to prevent the foreign competition. Often they're successful. A good example is the "voluntary" quotas placed on Japanese cars discussed earlier. These quotas saved domestic jobs, but forced consumers to pay higher prices for cars. Economists have estimated that it cost consumers about $100,000 for each job saved. Exhibit 9 lists economists' estimates of the cost to consumers of saving a job in some other industries.

The Costs of Change   Had I. T. been open about the difficulties of trading, he would have warned the countries that change is hard. It has very real costs that I. T. didn't point out when he made his offers. But these costs of change are relatively small compared to the gains from trade. Moreover, they're short-run, temporary costs, whereas gains from trade are permanent, long-run gains. Once the adjustment has been made, the costs will be gone but the benefits will still be there.

For most goods, the benefits for the large majority of the population so outweigh

---

[1] *Xenophobia* is a Greek word meaning "fear of foreigners." Pronounce the X like Z.

EXHIBIT 9   Cost of Saving Jobs, Selected Industries

Industry	Cost of Production (per job saved)
Specialty steel	$1,000,000
Colour TVs	420,000
Ceramic tiles	135,000
Clothing	36,000–82,000
Agriculture	20,000 (per farmer)
Dairy	1,800 (per cow)

Source: GATT, 1993.

---

the small costs to some individuals that, decided on a strict cost/benefit basis, international trade is still a deal you can't refuse. With benefits so outweighing costs, it would seem that transition costs could be forgotten. But they can't.

Benefits of trade are generally widely scattered among the entire population. In contrast, costs of free trade often fall on specific small groups of people who loudly oppose the particular free trade that hurts them. Though the benefits of free trade to the country at large exceed the costs of free trade to the small group of individuals, the political push from the few (who are hurt) for trade restrictions exceeds the political push from the many (who are helped) by free trade. The result is trade restrictions on a variety of products. You'll likely see TV ads supporting such restrictions under the heading "saving Canadian jobs." But you'll see few ads in favour of free trade to keep prices low for consumers.

It isn't only in Canada that the push for trade restrictions focuses on the small costs and not on the large benefits. For example, the European Union places large restrictions on food imports from nonmember nations. If the EU would remove those barriers, food prices in EU countries would decline significantly. For example, meat prices would probably fall by 65 percent. Consumers would benefit, but farmers would be hurt. The farmers, however, have the political clout to see that the costs are considered and the benefits aren't. The result: The EU places high duties on foreign agricultural products.

Trade Adjustment Assistance   Trade restrictions make the international trader's life more difficult but they also open up new possibilities. To see these possibilities, let's go back to I. T. Too. She has died and her son, I. T. Too II, has frittered away the entire family fortune and now must rely on his wits. Like his ancestors, he has good insights. He analyzes the problem as follows:

> Trade will make most members of society better off, but will make a particular subgroup in society worse off. Because of the country's political dynamics, this subgroup can prevent free trade. If I structure a program so that it transfers some of society's gains to individuals who are made worse off by trade, I can eliminate their opposition and thereby make society better off.

Such programs are called **trade adjustment assistance programs.** Using this analysis, he presents the countries with the following deal:

> Given that adjustment costs of trade are small, here's what I'll do. I'll pay the adjustment costs of those people who are hurt by the trade—costs I've calculated to be only 1/20 of the gains. I'll then have eliminated the opposition to free trade. For doing this, all I want for myself is 1/10 of the gains from trade, leaving 17/20 of the gains going to society. Now isn't this a deal you can't refuse?

Unfortunately for I. T. Too II, it's a deal most countries can refuse. Here's why.

Governments have tried to use trade adjustment assistance to facilitate free trade, but they've found that it's enormously difficult to limit the adjustment assistance to those who are actually hurt by international trade. As soon as people find that there's assistance for people injured by trade, they're likely to try to show that they too have

Trade adjustment assistance programs Programs designed to compensate losers for reductions in trade restrictions.

been hurt and deserve assistance. Losses from free trade become exaggerated and magnified. Instead of only 1/20 of the gains from trade being needed for trade adjustment assistance, much more is demanded—often even more than the gains.

Telling people who claim to be hurt that they aren't really being hurt isn't good politics. That's why offering trade adjustment assistance as a way to relieve the pressure to restrict trade is a deal many governments can refuse. I. T. Too II must return home to go on public welfare and contemplate further the nature of international trade.

Haggling by Companies over the Gains from Trade   Many naturally advantageous bargains aren't consummated because each side is pushing for a larger share of the gains from trade than the other side thinks should be allotted. This is another example of the prisoner's dilemma.

To see how companies haggling over the gains of trade can cause restriction on trade, let's reconsider the original deal that I. T. proposed. I. T. got 380 tonnes of food and 380 barrels of oil. Canada got an additional 100 tonnes of food and 60 barrels of oil. Saudi Arabia got an additional 100 barrels of oil and 60 tonnes of food.

Suppose the Saudis had said, "Why should we be getting only 100 barrels of oil and 60 tonnes of food when I. T. is getting 380 barrels of oil and 380 tonnes of food? We want an additional 300 tonnes of food and another 300 barrels of oil, and we won't deal unless we get them." Similarly Canada might have said "We want an additional 300 tonnes of food and an additional 300 barrels of oil, and we won't go through with the deal unless we get them." If either the Canadian or the Saudi Arabian company that was involved in the trade for their country (or both) takes this position, I. T. might just walk—no deal. The potential for gains from trade is there, but tough bargaining positions can make it almost impossible to achieve them.

Such bargaining problems occur often. The side that drives the hardest bargain gets the most gain from the bargain, but it also risks making the deal fall through. Such strategic bargaining goes on all the time. **Strategic bargaining** means demanding a larger share of the gains from trade than you can reasonably expect.[2] If you're successful, you get the lion's share; if you're not successful, the deal falls apart and everyone is worse off.

Strategic bargaining Demanding a larger share of the gains of trade than you can reasonably expect.

Haggling by Countries over Trade Restrictions   Another type of trade bargaining that often limits trade is bargaining between countries. Trade restrictions and the threat of trade restrictions play an important role in that kind of haggling. Sometimes countries must go through with trade restrictions that they really don't want to impose just to make their threats credible.

Once one country has imposed trade restrictions, other countries attempt to get those restrictions reduced by threatening to increase their own restrictions. Again, to make the threat credible, sometimes countries must impose or increase trade restrictions simply to show they're willing to do so.

Ultimately, strategic bargaining power depends on negotiators' skills and the underlying gains from trade that a country would receive. A country that would receive only a small portion of the gains from trade is in a much stronger bargaining position than a country that would receive significant gains. It's easier for the former to walk away from trade.

The United States is currently using such strategic bargaining in its attempt to get Japan to lower its restrictions on imports of U.S. goods. The U.S. Congress often threatens to restrict imports from Japan significantly if Japan doesn't ease its trade restrictions against U.S. goods. Since Japan depends heavily on exports to the United States, she takes such threats seriously. For example, in the late 1980s Japan's prime minister went on TV and asked Japanese people to buy U.S. goods. Japan also

---

[2] Here's an example: You're buying a house. You're willing to pay $80,000, but you'd prefer to pay less. The seller is asking $85,000, but you believe the seller will accept considerably less. So what do you offer? There's no one right strategy. If you offer $75,000 and refuse to go higher, you're using strategic bargaining.

changed some of its laws governing industrial organization to make selling goods in Japan easier for U.S. companies. Why do Canadians care about U.S.–Japanese trade? Because international trade affects all countries, and when two of your major trading partners are involved in a trade dispute, you have to think about how that's going to affect your economy.

Specialized Production: Learning by Doing and Economies of Scale   Our discussion of absolute and comparative advantage took it as given that one country was more productive than another country in producing certain goods. But when one looks at trading patterns, it's often not at all clear why particular countries have a productive advantage in certain goods. There's no inherent reason for Switzerland to specialize in the production of watches or for South Korea to specialize in the production of cars. Much in trade cannot be explained by inherent resource endowments.

If they don't have inherent advantages, why are countries and places often so good at producing what they specialize in? Two important explanations are that they *learn by doing* and that *economies of scale* exist.

Learning by Doing   You become better at a task the more often you perform it due to **learning by doing.** Take mechanical watches in Switzerland. Initially production of such watches in Switzerland may have been a coincidence; the person who started the watch business happened to live there. But then people in the area became skilled in producing watches. Their skill made it attractive for other watch companies to start up. As additional companies moved in, more and more members of the labour force became skilled at watchmaking, and word went out that Swiss mechanical watches were the best in the world. That reputation attracted even more producers so Switzerland became the mechanical watchmaking capital of the world. Had the initial watch production occurred in Austria, not Switzerland, Austria might be the watch capital of the world. (Battery-powered watches are another story.)

Learning by doing   Becoming more proficient at doing something by actually doing it; in the process, learning what works and what doesn't.

When there's learning by doing, it's much harder to assign comparative advantage to a country. One must always ask: Does country A truly have a comparative advantage, or does it simply have more experience? Once country B gets the experience, will country A's comparative advantage disappear? If it will, then country B has a strong reason to limit trade with country A in order to give its own workers time to catch up as they learn by doing.

Economies of Scale   In determining whether an inherent comparative advantage exists, a second complication is **economies of scale.** There are economies of scale when costs per unit output fall as output increases. Many manufacturing industries (such as steel and autos) exhibit economies of scale. The existence of significant economies of scale means that it makes sense (i.e., it lowers costs) for one country to specialize in one good and another country to specialize in another good. But who should specialize in what is unclear. Producers in a country can, and generally do, argue that if only the government will establish barriers, they'll be able to lower their costs per unit and eventually sell at lower costs than foreign producers.

Economies of scale   A decrease in per-unit cost as a result of an increase in output.

A number of countries follow trade strategies to allow them to take advantage of economies of scale. For example, in the 1970s and 1980s Japan's government consciously directed investment into automobiles and high-tech consumer products, and significantly promoted exports in these goods to take advantage of economies of scale.

Most countries recognize the importance of learning by doing and economies of scale. A variety of trade restrictions are based on these two phenomena. The most common expression of the learning-by-doing and economies-of-scale insights is the **infant industry argument,** which countries use to justify many trade restrictions. They argue, "You may now have a comparative advantage, but that's simply because you've been at it longer, or are experiencing significant economies of scale. We need trade restrictions on our _____ industry to give it a chance to catch up. Once an infant industry grows up, then we can talk about eliminating the restrictions."

Infant industry argument   With initial protection, an industry will be able to become competitive.

Macroeconomic Aspects of Trade   The comparative advantage argument for free trade assumes full employment. When countries don't have full employment, imports can decrease domestic aggregate demand and increase unemployment. Exports can stimulate aggregate domestic demand and decrease unemployment. Similarly imports can decrease domestic economic activity. Thus, when an economy is in a recession, there is a strong macroeconomic reason to limit imports and encourage exports. These macroeconomic effects of free trade play an important role in the public's view of imports and exports. When a country is in a recession, pressure to impose trade restrictions increases substantially.

National Security   Countries often justify trade restrictions on grounds of national security. These restrictions take two forms:

1. Export restrictions on strategic materials and defense-related goods.
2. Import restrictions on defense-related goods. For example, in a war we don't want to be dependent on oil from abroad.

For a number of goods, national security considerations make sense. For example, NATO countries restrict the sale of certain military items to countries that are likely to be fighting NATO some day. The problem is where to draw the line about goods having a national security consideration. Should countries protect domestic agriculture? All high-technology items, since they might be useful in weapons? All chemicals? Steel? The national security argument has been extended to a wide variety of goods whose importance to national security is indirect rather than direct. When a country makes a national security argument for trade, one must be careful to consider whether a domestic political reason may be lurking behind that argument.

International Politics   International politics frequently provides another reason for trade restrictions. The United States forbids trade with Cuba to punish that country for trying to extend its Marxist political and economic policies to other Latin American countries. Until 1991, the United States restricted exports to and imports from the Union of South Africa because it disapproved of South Africa's racist apartheid policies. U.S. grain exports to the Soviet Union were stopped in 1979 to protest the Soviet invasion of Afghanistan. The list can be extended, but you get the argument: Trade helps you, so we'll hurt you by stopping trade until you do what we want. So what if it hurts us too? It'll hurt you more than us.

Increased Revenue Brought In by Tariffs   A final argument made for one particular type of trade restriction—a tariff—is that tariffs bring in revenues. In the 19th century, tariffs were the government's primary source of revenue. They've receded in importance as a revenue for developed countries because those countries have instituted other forms of taxes. However, tariffs remain a primary source of revenue for many developing countries. They're relatively easy to collect and are paid by people rich enough to afford imports. These countries justify many of their tariffs with the argument that they need the revenues.

Why Economists Generally Oppose Trade Restrictions

Each of the preceding arguments for trade restrictions has some validity, but most economists discount them and support free trade. The reason is that, in their considered judgement, the harm done by trade restrictions outweighs the benefits.

Economists' first argument for free trade is that, viewed from a global perspective, free trade increases total output. From a national perspective, economists agree that particular instances of trade restriction may actually help one nation, even as most other nations are hurt. But they argue that the country imposing trade restrictions can benefit *only if the other country doesn't retaliate* with trade restrictions of its own. Retaliation is the rule, not the exception, however, and when there is retaliation, trade restrictions cause both countries to lose.

A second reason most economists support free trade is that trade restrictions reduce international competition. International competition is desirable because it

7   Economists generally oppose trade restrictions because: (1) from a global perspective, free trade increases total output; (2) trade restrictions lead to retaliation; and (3) international trade provides competition for domestic companies.

forces domestic companies to stay on their toes. If trade restrictions on imports are imposed, domestic companies don't work as hard, and they become less efficient. For example, in the 1950s and 1960s the United States imposed restrictions on imported steel. U.S. steel industries responded to this protection by raising their prices and channelling profits from their steel production into other activities. By the 1970s the U.S. steel industry was a mess, internationally uncompetitive, and using outdated equipment to produce overpriced steel. Instead of making the steel industry stronger, restrictions made it a flabby, uncompetitive industry.

Economists dispose of the infant industry argument by reference to the historical record. In theory the argument makes sense. But very few of the infant industries protected by trade restrictions have ever grown up. What tends to happen instead is that infant industries become dependent on the trade restrictions and use political pressure to keep that protection. As a result, they often remain immature and internationally uncompetitive. Most economists would support the infant industry argument only if the trade restrictions included definite conditions under which the restrictions would end.

Most economists agree with the national security argument for export restrictions on goods that are directly war related. Selling bombs to Iraq, with whom NATO was at war in early 1991, doesn't make much sense (although it should be noted that some members of NATO did exactly that throughout the 1980s when they supported Iraq in its war with Iran).

Economists point out that the argument is often carried far beyond goods directly related to national security. For example, in the 1980s the United States restricted exports of sugar-coated cereals to the Soviet Union for reasons of national security. Sugar-frosted flakes may be great, but they were unlikely to help the Soviet Union start a war.

Another argument that economists give against the national security rationale is that trade restrictions on military sales can often be evaded. Countries simply have another country buy the goods for them. Such third-party sales—called *transshipments*—are common in international trade and limit the effectiveness of any absolute trade restrictions for national security purposes.

Economists also argue that by fostering international cooperation, international trade makes war less likely—a significant contribution to national security.

Economists' final argument against trade restrictions is: Yes, some restrictions might benefit a country, but almost no country can limit its restrictions to the beneficial ones. Trade restrictions are addictive—the more you have, the more you want. Thus, a majority of economists take the position that the best response to such addictive policies is "just say no."

Most politicians feel a strong push from constituents to impose trade barriers. Even politicians who accept free trade in principle support restrictions in practice. They have, however, found it possible to support a limited type of free trade in which a few countries agree to have free trade with each other. A **free-trade association** (or *customs union*) is a group of countries that allows free trade among its members and, as a group, puts up common barriers against all other countries' goods.

Common Markets   The **European Union (EU)** is one of the most famous free-trade associations. All barriers to trade among the EU's 15 member countries were removed in 1992. During the 1990s, more European countries can be expected to apply to join the EU. In 1989, Canada and the United States entered into the Canada–U.S. **Free Trade Agreement** (FTA was signed in 1987 and came into effect on January 1, 1989). In 1993, the United States and Canada agreed to enter into a similar free-trade union with Mexico, creating the **North American Free Trade Agreement** (NAFTA). Early in 1995 Chile was invited to join NAFTA, and a host of Central and South American countries (as well as several Caribbean nations) are lining up to join—they don't want to be left on their own. Under the FTA and NAFTA, tariffs and other trade barriers among these countries will be reduced throughout the 1990s. It's too early to tell if

Free Trade Associations

Free trade association   Countries that allows free trade among its members and puts up common barriers against all other countries' goods.

European Union (EU)   Union of European countries that allow free trade among countries.

Free Trade Agreement (FTA)   Deal signed by Canada and the United States aimed at reducing barriers to trade. It took effect on January 1, 1989.

North American Free Trade Agreement (NAFTA)   Trade deal signed by Canada, Mexico, and the United States aimed at reducing barriers to North American trade; went into effect January 1, 1994.

NAFTA will be a success, but we can look at some preliminary results of the Canada–U.S. Free Trade Agreement.

8 The Canada–U.S. Free Trade Agreement and NAFTA aim at eliminating tariff and nontariff barriers to trade. Canada has an incentive to secure access to the larger American market and in doing so, it has the opportunity to benefit from its comparative advantages. As free trade agreements come into full force there will be adjustments in labour markets—these make for good press, so one needs to be careful when assessing the benefits and costs of free trade.

The Canada–U.S. Free Trade Agreement   The Free Trade Agreement was signed by Canada and the United States in 1987. It set into motion a series of changes to bilateral trade in which tariff and nontariff barriers would be removed gradually over a ten-year period beginning in 1989. Canada entered into the agreement primarily because protectionist sentiment in the United States had been on the rise for a decade. Since most of our trade is with the United States, it was in our best interests to try to negotiate an agreement that would, for the most part, shelter us from import restrictions coming out of the U.S. Congress.

Canada had other reasons for entering into the agreement. With a relatively small domestic market of only 28 million people, manufacturers wanted secure access to a larger market. This would allow them to take advantage of gains in productive efficiency through the use of larger production facilities. It would also allow them to expand into new product lines that just weren't financially feasible given the size of the Canadian market.

Media attention on the deal focused on the costs of labour market adjustments that were predicted to occur from the loss of tariff protection to uncompetitive domestic industries (like textiles). The recession of the early 1990s didn't help proponents of the FTA, and at almost every turn there were calls to scrap the deal because it was seen as the cause of high unemployment. In retrospect, the high value of the Canadian dollar and high interest rates were probably the fundamental contributing factors to adjustments in the labour market, but there's no doubt that structural changes resulting from the deal added to job losses.

Critics of the deal argued that Canadian manufacturers would eventually shut down because U.S. production facilities were already operating on a much larger scale than their Canadian counterparts. The critics suggested that Canada would end up exporting natural resources and importing manufactured goods—some suggested that the deal should be changed to allow Canada to retain tariff protection in the manufacturing sector. The problem with this argument is that *both* U.S. and Canadian tariffs were going to be dramatically reduced (and eventually eliminated), and while some Canadian manufacturers would lose, others would gain; the key is that not everyone would lose.

Tariff Reduction: The Winners and Losers   Let's examine how a reduction in tariffs might affect two firms in a Canadian industry—say textiles. Exhibit 10 provides a view of the market, where a tariff raises prices above the world price, P_W to P_T. The elimination of the tariff would allow domestic prices to fall to the world price. Canadian textile imports would rise, and consumers would be better off.

The Free Trade Agreement reduces tariffs of both countries, causing problems for producing firms. We can see this if we think about two textile firms operating with different costs of production—perhaps due to the use of different technologies. Suppose the world price of cloth is $1.50 per metre, and the tariff raises the domestic price to $2.00 per metre. Say firm A, Walcloth, operates with costs of $1.50 per metre while firm B, Zellcloth, operates with costs of $1.75 per metre. The tariff ensures that both firms earn positive profits: $0.50 per metre for Walcloth; $0.25 per metre for Zellcloth. When the tariff is eliminated and cloth prices fall to the world price of $1.50 per metre, Walcloth will just break even, whereas Zellcloth will make losses ($0.25 per metre) and eventually leave the industry (they can't cover their costs per metre). So, when the tariff is removed and the domestic price falls to the world price, the marginal (high cost) firm will shut down. Domestic cloth production will fall.

Under any trade agreement there will be winners and losers. Policymakers spend a great deal of effort in attempting to identify the benefits and the costs of alternative trade arrangements. Unfortunately, economists' empirical estimates of the gains to free trade vary considerably, and sometimes there's little agreement on how the economy will respond to changes in trade policy. For example, estimates of the gains

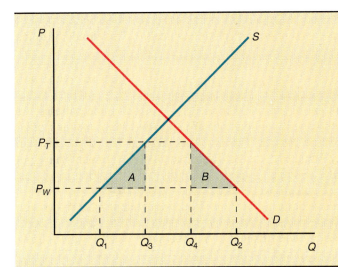

EXHIBIT 10   **The Benefits of Tariff Reduction**

The elimination of a tariff will reduce prices to P_W and imports will rise from $Q_4 - Q_3$ to $Q_2 - Q_1$. Society will recapture areas A and B. An inefficient firm whose costs exceed P_W will be forced out of business.

to Canada under the Canada–U.S. FTA varied by as much as 50 percent (from 2.5 percent to 5 percent of output). And, with respect to NAFTA, estimates of the gains to Mexico vary between 1.6 percent and 5.0 percent of Mexican output; for Canada the gains were calculated to be somewhere between 0.7 percent to 6.75 percent of Canadian output; and for the United States, gains were expected to be between 0.5 percent and 2.55 percent of U.S. output. When there's this much uncertainty in the numbers, it is difficult to design a set of economic policies that will mitigate the deleterious effects of structural change. At this point, the invisible handshake and the invisible foot enter decision making. After significant debate, policymakers arrive at a compromise between the invisible hand and the invisible foot, resulting in an invisible handshake. (The FTA debate played a significant role in the 1988 federal election, and when the Tories were given a second mandate, opponents of the deal—mainly Liberals and New Democrats—admitted defeat.)

Faulty Reasoning   Many economists pointed to a fundamental flaw in the economic reasoning of the opponents of the deal—the critics appeared to deny the principle of comparative advantage. From earlier in this chapter, we know that if Canada has a comparative advantage in the export of raw materials, we should seize that opportunity. Yet opponents of the deal went so far as to talk about scrapping it. For instance, some Canadians saw it as a U.S. attempt to get its hands on Canada's fresh water—that is, they predicted Canada's fresh water would be one of the natural resources that Canada would end up exporting. The critics appeared to argue that we should sacrifice economic efficiency for *short-term* employment. We say *short-term* employment because any industry that requires protective barriers for its existence won't survive the process of globalization. Competitive pressures will eventually lead to the production of the same products, at lower cost, somewhere else. World demand for our uncompetitive goods would be attracted to foreign soil, and Canada would be left with an inefficient industry with no market for the product. Firms would shut down, contributing further to the unemployment problem.

Many opponents of the deal argued that competition would put pressure on Canadian social programs—specifically, our health care system—to change. Universal medical coverage in Canada is the norm—not so in the United States. While there's an ongoing debate over the reform of the U.S. health care system, it's hard to say what will happen there. While it's true that the Canadian health care system faces a number of fiscal challenges, for now there's no serious talk about eliminating universality. But that could change quickly if the federal government decides to proceed with block–funding arrangements in which they provide the provinces with a pool of funds out of which to run provincial programs (including health). This should be much in the news in the 1990s.

Adjustment and Disputes We don't want to give the impression that everyone will benefit from the Free Trade Agreement. There have been, and will continue to be, adjustment costs as workers are displaced as a result of shifts in trade patterns. As tariff protection falls and uncompetitive industries are allowed to fail, labour market adjustment is inevitable. (Some put the figures at as high as 461,000 Canadian manufacturing jobs already.) While both the U.S. and Canadian governments have put into place a number of programs that attempt to deal with these transition problems, whether or not they will work remains to be seen.

The most pressing issues relating to the Free Trade Agreement have to do with how disputes are settled. Trade tribunals have already dealt with a number of complaints, and in 1994 there was a major dispute over Canadian wheat. As the following newspaper article suggests, Canada stands ready to retaliate against U.S. tariffs and quotas:

U.S. WATCHDOGS STEP UP WHEAT WAR

Panel seeks cap on Canadian durum exports worth $300-million this year

By Barrie McKenna
Parliamentary Bureau

OTTAWA—The wheat war between Canada and the United States got a little uglier yesterday after a ruling by a U.S. panel of trade watchdogs that Canadian wheat shipments are hurting U.S. farmers and should face sanctions.

The six-member International Trade Commission voted unanimously to urge the U.S. government to impose emergency quotas or tariffs on Canadian wheat.

Several commissioners recommended capping Canadian wheat imports at 900,000 metric tonnes a year, or roughly one-third of what Canada exports now.

The vote ends a six-month ITC investigation ordered by U.S. President Bill Clinton under the controversial Section 22 of the U.S. Agricultural Adjustment Act. The United States will lose the right to use Section 22, which allows the imposition of emergency trade sanctions, if it ratifies the new General Agreement on Tariffs and Trade next year.

The commission's final recommendations are expected to be sent to Mr. Clinton later this month.

Growers of Canadian durum would be hurt most if sanctions are imposed because prices would likely fall.

Robert Roehle, a spokesman for the Canadian Wheat Board, said farmers have substantially increased their durum acreage in recent years in response to strong demand from the United States.

"If that market is cut off and restricted, it means durum has to find somewhere else to go and presumably it's going to be at a lower price," he said.

The ITC's decision doesn't bind the United States to take any particular course of action and is really only the latest step in a long process that both sides say they still want resolved through negotiation.

Mr. Clinton can choose to ignore the ITC, doctor its findings or accept them intact, a senior Canadian official said yesterday.

"The buck stops at the White House," he said. "At some point, the President has to make a decision whether to take action or not."

While the White House chews on the ITC report, both sides are expected to continue talking. The focus of the sometimes-acrimonious negotiations has been a U.S. plan to cap Canadian wheat imports at one million tonnes and impose a tariff on the rest that would vary depending on the volume shipped.

The investigation by the ITC, an independent government agency, is only one half of a two-pronged U.S. attack on Canadian wheat.

The next major deadline in the wheat feud is Aug. 1. That's the day a 90-day waiting period expires stemming from a U.S. complaint to GATT authorities that Canada unfairly subsidizes exports of wheat, barley and other grains.

The United States could choose at that time to slap stiff tariffs or quotas on imports from Canada.

But under GATT rules, Canada has the right to fire back with sanctions of its own on Sept. 1, or 30 days later. Canadian officials have already warned they are eyeing tariffs on a basket of U.S. goods of equal value, including chicken, wine, baked goods, pasta, canned fruit and canned tomatoes.

Canadian grain farmers are expected to ship 2.5-million tonnes of wheat worth roughly $300-million to the United States in the current crop year. That's up from $210-million worth last year.

The biggest surge has come in durum wheat exports to the United States, which hit $95-million last year and are up 172 per cent since 1988.

Canadian officials have never denied that exports are way up, but they blame last year's floods in the U.S. Midwest and U.S. export subsidies for raising domestic prices and pushing up demand there.

The United States, meanwhile, has accused Canada of using hidden subsidies—particularly in transportation— to undercut U.S. crops and disrupt the market.

With a report from Canadian Press.

Source: The *Globe and Mail*, July 9, 1994.

DUMPING

GATT allows countries to impose trade restrictions on imports if they can show that the goods are being dumped. *Dumping* is selling a good in a foreign country at a lower price than in the country where it's produced. On the face of it, who could complain about someone who wants to sell you a good cheaply? Why not just take advantage of the bargain price? The first objection is the learning-by-doing argument. To stay competitive, a country must keep on producing. Dumping by another country can force domestic producers out of business. Having eliminated the competition, the foreign producer has the field to itself and can raise the price. Thus, dumping can be a form of predatory pricing.

The second argument against dumping involves the short-term macroeconomic and political effects it can have on the importing country. Even if one believes that dumping is not a preliminary to predatory pricing, it can displace workers in the importing country, causing political pressure on that government to institute trade restrictions. If that country's economy is in a recession, the resulting unemployment will have substantial macroeconomic repercussions, so pressure for trade restrictions will be amplified.

Economists have mixed reactions to free-trade associations. They see free trade as beneficial, but are concerned about the possibility that these regional free-trade associations will impose significant trade restrictions on nonmember countries. Some economists believe that bilateral negotiations between member nations will replace multilateral efforts among members and nonmembers. Whether the net effect of these negotiations is positive or negative remains to be seen.

Devastating trade wars took place during the 1930s. As a result, international trade fell by over 75 percent. This decline contributed to the worldwide Great Depression. Following that experience, countries organized to try to promote free trade among themselves. The most visible result—the General Agreement on Tariffs and Trade (GATT), established in 1947—had as its central goal the elimination of tariffs.

GATT created a mechanism for the 96 subscribing countries (in 1994 membership grew to over 120 countries) to establish multilateral regulations for eliminating trade barriers. Member countries met every five years to work toward this end. Initially GATT focused on tariffs on manufactured goods, but increasingly included services and agricultural goods as trade in these activities expanded. In 1995 GATT was replaced by the **World Trade Organization.**

One of the goals of GATT was to equalize a country's trade barriers so that it did not discriminate against one specific country. The term **most-favoured nation** refers to a country that will be charged as low a tariff on its exports as any other country. Thus, if the United States lowers tariffs on goods imported from Japan, which has most-favoured nation status with the United States, it must lower tariffs on those same types of goods imported from any other country with most-favoured nation status.

Trade negotiations are never easy. Here's the type of problem that continually occurs: In the 1988 Round (as GATT meetings were called), a dispute arose over agricultural policy. The United States argued that the EU's subsidies to farmers should be reduced, and that tariffs on farm exports from the United States to the EU should be reduced or eliminated. When the EU hesitated to go along with these proposals, there was a temporary breakdown of the talks. Eventually, in 1994 an agreement on the 1988 round of the GATT meeting was concluded. Such breakdowns demonstrate the fragility of all free-trade agreements. They can quickly be replaced by trade wars which hurt all countries. This is one of the greatest challenges facing the World Trade Organization—achieving consensus without creating an environment hostile to the expansion of world trade.

International trade has always been important for Canada. With international transportation and communication becoming easier and faster, and with other countries'

The World Trade Organization

World Trade Organization (WTO) World body charged with reducing impediments to trade; it replaced GATT in 1995.

Most-favoured nation   Country that will pay as low a tariff on its exports as will any other country.

9   Creating an environment conducive to international trade is the greatest challenge facing the World Trade Organization.

CONCLUSION

ADDED DIMENSION

STRATEGIC TRADE POLICIES

The problem with strategic trade policies is that they can backfire. One rule of strategic bargaining is that the other side must believe that you'll go through with your threat. Thus, strategic trade policy can lead a country that actually supports free trade to impose trade restrictions, just to show how strongly it believes in free trade.

Even though most economists support free trade, they admit that in bargaining it may be necessary to adopt a strategic position. A country may threaten to impose trade restrictions if the other country does so. When such strategic trade policies are successful, they end up eliminating or reducing trade restrictions.

When should trade restrictions be used, and when should they not be used? For strategic purposes? Economic theory does not tell us. That question is part of the practice of the art of economics. (It should be pointed out that economic game theorists are adding insights into the issue and that the field of strategic trade policies is a hot area of research.)

economies growing, the Canadian economy will inevitably become more interdependent with the other economies of the world. As international trade becomes more important, the push for trade restrictions will likely increase. Various countries' strategic trade policies will likely conflict, and the world will find itself on the verge of an international trade war which would benefit no one.

Concern about that possibility leads most economists to favour free trade. As often happens, economists advise politicians to follow a policy that is politically unpopular—to take the hard course of action. Whether politicians follow economists' advice or whether they follow the politically popular policy will play a key role in determining the course of the Canadian economy in the 1990s.

CHAPTER SUMMARY

- Canada's primary trading partners are the United States, Western Europe, and Japan.

- According to the principle of absolute advantage, a country that can produce a good more cheaply than another country is said to have an absolute advantage in the production of that good. When two countries have absolute advantages in different goods, there are gains from trade to be had.

- According to the principle of comparative advantage, as long as the relative opportunity costs of producing goods (what must be given up in one good in order to get another good) differ among countries, there are potential gains from trade, even if one country has an absolute advantage in everything.

- Three insights into the terms of trade include:

1. The more competition exists in international trade, the less the trader gets and the more the involved countries get.

2. Once competition prevails, smaller countries tend to get a larger percentage of the gains from trade than do larger countries.

3. Gains from trade go to countries that produce goods that exhibit economies of scale.

- Trade restrictions include: tariffs, quotas, embargoes, voluntary restraint agreements, regulatory trade restrictions, and nationalistic appeals.

- Reasons that countries impose trade restrictions include: unequal internal distribution of the gains from trade; haggling by companies over the gains from trade; haggling by countries over trade restrictions; learning by doing and economies of scale; macroeconomic aspects of trade; national security; international political reasons; and increased revenue brought in by tariffs.

- Economists generally oppose trade restrictions because of their knowledge of history and their understanding of the advantages of free trade.

- Free Trade Agreements benefit member countries in the long run, but in the short run it is difficult to foresee how changes in trade policy will affect an economy—and even more difficult to design policies to lubricate the adjustment process.

KEY TERMS

economies of scale *(381)*
embargo *(377)*
European Union (EU) *(383)*
Free Trade Agreement (FTA) *(383)*
free-trade association *(383)*
General Agreement on Tariffs and
  Trade (GATT) *(376)*
import licenses *(376)*
infant industry argument *(381)*

learning by doing *(381)*
most-favoured nation *(387)*
North American Free Trade
  Agreement (NAFTA) *(383)*
principle of absolute advantage *(368)*
principle of comparative
  advantage *(372)*
quota *(376)*
quota rent *(376)*

regulatory trade restrictions *(377)*
strategic bargaining *(380)*
tariff *(375)*
trade adjustment assistance
  programs *(379)*
World Trade Organization
  (WTO) *(387)*

QUESTIONS FOR THOUGHT AND REVIEW

The number after each question represents the estimated degree of critical thinking required. (1 = almost none; 10 = deep thought.)

1. With which countries does Canada trade most? *(2)*

2. Are these countries the ones you would expect Canada to trade with, based on the law of comparative advantage? Why? *(7)*

3. Textland can produce, at most, 40 olives, 20 pickles, or some combination of olives and pickles such as the 20 olives and 10 pickles it's currently producing. Happyland can produce, at most, 120 olives, 60 pickles, or some combination of olives and pickles such as the 100 olives and 10 pickles it's currently producing. Is there a basis for trade? If so, offer the two countries a deal they can't refuse. *(6)*

4. Would your answer to Question 3 differ if you knew that there were economies of scale in the production of pickles and olives rather than the production possibilities described in the question? Why? If your answer is yes, which country would you have produce which good? *(9)*

5. Widgetland has 60 workers. Each worker can produce 4

widgets or 4 wadgets. It's considering producing only widgets. Wadgetland also has 60 workers. Each can produce 3 widgets or 12 wadgets. Its residents consume wadgets but never buy widgets. Is there a basis for trade? If so, offer the countries a deal they can't refuse. *(7)*

6. Why do smaller countries usually get most of the gains from trade? What are some reasons why a small country might not get the gains of trade? *(6)*

7. Demonstrate diagrammatically how the effects of a tariff differ from the effects of a quota. *(6)*

8. If you were economic advisor to a country that was following your advice about trade restrictions and that country fell into a recession, would you change your advice? Why, or why not? *(7)*

9. The Canadian trade balance improved significantly in early 1991. What would you say is the primary reason for that improvement? *(6)*

10. Mexico exports many vegetables to the United States. These vegetables are grown using chemicals that are not allowed in U.S. vegetable agriculture. Should the United States restrict imports of Mexican vegetables? Why, or why not? *(7)*

PROBLEMS AND EXERCISES

1. Suppose that two countries, Machineland and Farmland, have the following production possibility curves:

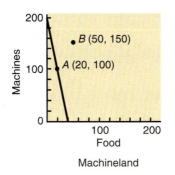

Machineland

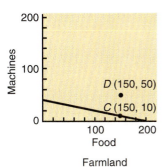

Farmland

a. Explain how these two countries can move from points *A* and *C*, where they currently are, to points *B* and *D*.

b. If possible, state by how much total production for the two countries has risen.

c. If you were a trader, how much of the gains from trade would you deserve for discovering this trade?

d. If there were economies of scale in the production of both goods, how would your analysis change?

2. The world price of textiles is P_w as in the accompanying figure of the domestic supply and demand for textiles. The government imposes a tariff, *t*, to protect domestic producers.

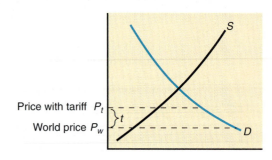

Price with tariff P_t

World price P_w

a. Shade in the gains to producers from this tariff.

b. Shade in the revenue to government.

c. Shade in the costs to producers.

d. Are the gains greater than the costs? Why?

3. Let's suppose in 1997 the hourly cost to employers per German industrial worker will be $26.90. The hourly cost to employers per Canadian industrial worker will be $15.89, while the average hourly cost per Taiwanese industrial worker will be $5.19.

a. Give three reasons why firms produce in Germany rather than in a lower-wage country.

b. Germany has just entered into an agreement with other EU countries that allows people in any EU country, including Greece and Italy, which have lower wage rates, to travel and work in any EU country, including high-wage countries. Would you expect a significant movement of workers from Greece and Italy to Germany right away? Why or why not?

c. Workers in Thailand are paid significantly less than workers in Taiwan. If you were a company CEO, what other information would you want before you decide where to establish a new production facility?

4. Peter Sutherland, the director-general of GATT in 1994, published a pamphlet on the costs of trade protection. He subtitled the pamphlet "The Sting: How Governments Buy Votes on Trade with the Consumer's Money."

a. What does he likely mean by this subtitle?

b. If a government is out to increase votes with its trade policy, would it more likely institute tariffs or quotas? Why?

5. One of the basic economic laws is "the law of one price." It says that, given certain assumptions, one would expect that if free trade is allowed, the price of goods in countries should converge.

a. Can you list what three of those assumptions likely are?

b. Should the law of one price hold for labour also? Why or why not?

c. Should it hold for capital more so or less so than for labour? Why or why not?

16

International Finance: The Basics

A foreign exchange dealer's office during a busy spell is the nearest thing to Bedlam I have struck.

~Harold Wincott

After reading this chapter, you should be able to:

1 Describe the balance of payments and the merchandise trade balance.

2 Explain why a country might have simultaneously a merchandise trade surplus and a balance of payments deficit.

3 Discuss how real-world exchange rates are set.

4 Explain why many developing countries have nonconvertible currencies.

5 Differentiate fixed, floating, partially floating, and nonconvertible exchange rates, and discuss the advantages and disadvantages of each.

6 Give a brief history of the gold standard.

As we have emphasized throughout the book, Canadian economic questions must be considered in an international setting. Earlier chapters introduced international financial issues such as exchange rates and the balance of payments, but we didn't cover those topics in any detail. This chapter expands on those discussions and presents the central issues of international finance.

THE BALANCE OF PAYMENTS

1A The balance of payments is a country's record of all transactions between its residents and the residents of all foreign countries.

The best door into an in-depth discussion of international financial issues is a discussion of **balance of payments** (a country's record of all transactions between its residents and the residents of all foreign nations).[1] These include buying and selling of goods and services (imports and exports) and interest and profit payments from previous investments, together with all the capital inflows and outflows. Exhibit 1 presents the 1990 and 1994 balance of payments accounts for Canada. It records all payments made by foreigners to Canadian citizens and all payments made by Canadian citizens to foreigners in those years.

In the balance of payments accounts, flows of payments into Canada have a plus sign. Goods Canada exports must be paid for in dollars; they involve a flow of payments into Canada, so they have a plus sign. Similarly, Canadian imports must be paid for in foreign currency; they involve a flow of dollars out of Canada and, thus, they have a minus sign. Notice that the bottom line of the balance of payments is $0. By definition, the bottom line (which includes *all* supplies and demands for currencies, including those of the government) must add up to zero.

As you can see in Exhibit 1, the balance of payments account is broken down into the *current account,* the *capital account,* and the *official settlements balance.* The **current account** (lines 1–10) is the part of the balance of payments account in which all short-term flows of payments are listed. It includes exports and imports, which are what one normally means when one talks about the trade balance. The **capital account** (lines 11–13) is the part of the balance of payments account in which all long-term flows of payments are listed. If one buys a German stock, or if a Japanese company buys a Canadian company, the transaction shows up on the capital account.

Current account   The part of the balance of payments account that lists all short-term flows of payments.

Capital account   The part of the balance of payments account that lists all long-term flows of payments.

Official settlements account   The part of the balance of payments account that records the amount of a currency or other international reserves a nation buys.

The government can influence the exchange rate by buying and selling currencies, or by buying and selling other international reserves, such as gold and U.S. dollars. Such buying and selling is recorded in the **official settlements balance,** line 17 of Exhibit 1. To get a better idea of what's included in the three accounts, let's consider each of them more carefully.

The Current Account

1B The merchandise trade balance is the difference between the value of goods a nation exports and the value of goods it imports.

Merchandise trade balance   The difference between the goods a nation exports and the goods a nation imports.

At the top of Exhibit 1, the current account is composed of the merchandise (or goods) account (lines 1–3), the services account (lines 4–6), the net investment income account (line 7), and the net transfers account (line 8).

Starting with the merchandise account, notice that in 1990 Canada imported $137 billion worth of goods and exported $146 billion worth of goods. The difference between the two is sometimes called the **merchandise trade balance.** Looking at line 3, you can see that Canada had a merchandise trade surplus of $9 billion in 1990 and $17 billion in 1994.

The merchandise trade balance is often discussed in the press as a summary of how Canada is doing in the international markets, but it's not a good summary. Trade in services is just as important as trade in merchandise, so economists pay more attention to the combined balance on goods and services. Notice that in 1990 the merchandise trade surplus was more than offset by a deficit in the balance on services, while in 1994 the merchandise surplus was larger than the service deficit. The service accounts include tourist expenditures and insurance payments by foreigners to Canadian firms. For instance, when you travel in the United States, you spend U.S. dollars, which you must buy with Canadian dollars; this is an outflow of payments or a negative contribution to the services account.

---

[1] These records are not very good. Because of measurement difficulties, many transactions go unrecorded and many numbers must be estimated, leaving a potential for large errors.

EXHIBIT 1   **The Balance of Payments Account, 1990 and 1994 ($ billions)**

	1990		1994	
Current Account				
Merchandise				
1. Exports	$146		$219	
2. Imports	−137		−202	
3. Trade balance		$9		$17
Services				
4. Exports	23		30	
5. Imports	−34		−41	
6. Trade balance		−11		−11
Investments and Transfers				
7. Net investment income	−23		−32	
8. Net transfers	0		1	
9. Investment and transfer balance		−23		−31
10. **Balance of Current Account**		−25		−25
Capital Account				
11. Net capital inflows (Canadian liabilities to nonresidents)	38		37	
12. Net capital outflows (Canadian claims on nonresidents)	−11		−12	
13. **Balance of Capital Account**		27		25
14. **Balance of Current and Capital Accounts**		2		0
15. Statistical discrepancy		−2		−2
16. **Balance of Current and Capital Accounts (adjusted)**		0		−2
Official Settlements				
17. **Balance of Official Settlements**		0		+2
18. **Balance of Current and Capital Accounts and Official Settlements**		0		0

Source: *Statistics Canada*, CANSIM Database, March 1995.

There is no reason that the goods and services sent into a country must equal the goods and services sent out in a particular year, even if the current account is in equilibrium, because the current account also includes payments from past investments and net transfers. When you invest, you expect to make a return on that investment. The payments to foreign owners of Canadian capital assets is a negative contribution to the Canadian balance of payments. The payment to Canadian owners of foreign capital assets is a positive contribution to the Canadian balance of payments. These payments on investment income are a type of holdover from past trade and services imbalances. So even though they relate to investments, they show up on the current account.

As you can see, Canadians make substantial payments to foreigners for the services of foreign capital. Net investment income flows of $23 billion were made in 1990; in 1994 this jumped to $32 billion. As we'll see in Chapter 18 when we discuss government deficits and debts, these payments are mainly to foreigners who hold Canadian securities. When foreigners receive interest payments on their investments in Canada, these funds enter as a net outflow of investment income (hence the minus signs).

The final component of the current account is net transfers, which include foreign aid, gifts, and other payments to individuals not exchanged for goods or services. If you send $100 to your aunt in Australia, it shows up with a minus sign here. Over the last few years these sums have been below a billion dollars, with the exception of 1994, when just over a billion dollars were received by Canadians.

Adding up the pluses and minuses on the current account, we arrive at line 10, the current account balance. Notice that in both 1990 and 1994 Canada ran a $25 billion deficit on the current account. That means that, in the current account, the supply of dollars greatly exceeded the demand for dollars. If the current account represented the total supply of and demand for dollars, the value of the dollar would have fallen. But it doesn't. There are also the capital account, the official settlements balance, and statistical discrepancies.

The Capital Account

The capital account measures the flow of payments between countries for assets such as stocks, bonds, and real estate. As you can see in Exhibit 1, in 1990 there was a significant inflow of capital into Canada in excess of outflows of capital from Canada. Capital inflows (payments by foreigners for Canadian real and financial assets—sometimes referred to as Canadian liabilities to nonresidents since we owe them those funds) were $27 billion more than capital outflows (payments by Canadian citizens for foreign assets—also known as Canadian claims on nonresidents, or what foreigners owe Canadians). In 1994, there was a net inflow of $25 billion (line 13).

To buy these Canadian assets foreigners needed dollars, so these net capital inflows represent a demand for dollars. In both these years the demand for dollars to buy capital goods was more than sufficient to balance supply of dollars on the current account. In 1990 they were over by $2 billion (capital account of +27 plus the current account of −25), and in 1994 they were roughly equal (due to rounding—capital account of +25 plus current account of −25).

Thus it would seem that the government would have to intervene in the foreign currency market and sell dollars in 1990 (*sell* because the demand (capital account) for dollars was higher than the supply of dollars (current account)). That wasn't the case, however. The reason is statistical discrepancies, as we see in line 15. In 1990 there was a −$2 billion discrepancy. These discrepancies arise because many international transactions, especially on the capital account, go unrecorded and hence must be estimated. With these discrepancies taken into account, in the absence of government policy there would have been little upward pressure on the value of the dollar. Because of the importance of capital flows, when you think about what's likely to happen to a currency's value, it's important to remember both the demand for dollars to buy goods and services and the demand for dollars to buy assets.

There is, of course, a difference between demand for dollars to buy currently produced goods and services and demand for dollars to buy assets. Assets earn profits or interest, so when foreigners buy Canadian assets, they earn income from those assets just for owning those assets. The net investment income from foreigners' previous asset purchases shows up on line 7 of the current account. It's the difference between the income Canadian citizens receive from their foreign assets and the income foreigners receive from their Canadian assets. If assets earned equal returns, one would expect that when foreigners own more Canadian capital assets than Canadian citizens own foreign capital assets, net investment income should be negative. And when Canadian citizens own more foreign capital assets than foreigners own Canadian capital assets, net investment income should be positive. Why is this? Because net investment income is simply the difference between the returns on Canadian citizens' assets held abroad and foreign citizens' assets held in Canada.

In the 1980s, the inflow of capital into Canada greatly exceeded the outflow of capital from Canada, and this trend has continued into the 1990s. As a result, Canada has become a net debtor nation: the amount foreigners own in Canada now exceeds the amount Canadian citizens own abroad. So one would expect that Canadian net investment income would be negative. And, looking at Exhibit 1, line 7, we see that was exactly the case in both 1990 and 1994.

2 Since the balance of payments consists of both the capital account and the trade account, if the capital account is in surplus and the trade account is in deficit, there can still be a balance of payments surplus.

The Official Settlements Balance

We're not quite finished with Exhibit 1, since in 1994 the statistical discrepancies don't take the sum of the current account and the capital account to zero (they do in 1990). In 1994 there was an excess supply of dollars of $2 billion.

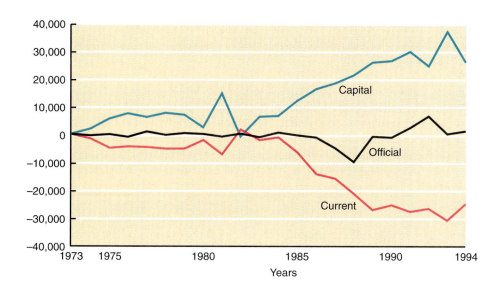

EXHIBIT 2 **Canadian Capital Account, Current Account, and Official Settlements Balance**

This exhibit demonstrates that international flow in goods and services and in capital changed significantly in the early 1980s.
Source: *Statistics Canada*, CANSIM Database, March 1995.

The current account and the capital account measure the supply of and demand for dollars. A *balance of payments deficit* will put downward pressure on the value of a country's currency while a *balance of payments surplus* will put upward pressure on the value of the currency. If a country wants to prevent that from happening, it can buy or sell its own currency. The official settlements balance records the amount of dollars that Canada bought (a negative entry means the Bank of Canada is selling dollars and buying foreign currencies while a positive entry means the Bank of Canada is buying dollars and selling foreign currencies). As you can see on line 17 of Exhibit 1, in 1994 the government entered into the foreign exchange market and bought 2 billion Canadian dollars (alternatively they sold $2 billion worth of foreign currencies and gold). When a government buys its own currency to hold up the currency's price, we say that the government has supported its currency. It's holding the value of its currency higher than it otherwise would have been. If it sells its currency, it's attempting to depress the value of the currency.[2]

Exhibit 2 shows the capital account, current account, and official settlements balances since 1973. It appears that in 1984 there was a significant change in Canada's balance of payments. As we'll see shortly, this was the result of a substantial depreciation of the Canadian dollar against most other currencies of the industrialized countries.

Now let's return to the point made at the beginning of the chapter: As long as a currency is freely exchangeable for another currency, the current account, capital account, official settlements balance, and statistical discrepancy must sum to zero. Why is this? Because that's what it means to be freely exchangeable. Whenever anybody wants, they can take their currency and trade it for another. The supply must equal the demand.

Another way to see this is to think about buying hot dogs at a football game. Hungry spectators give the concession operator $2.00 in return for each hot dog. At the end of the game, if we measure flows in goods and services (hot dogs) and financial assets (money), they'd exactly offset one another. The value of hot dog sales ("current account") just equals the value of the payments made for the hot dogs ("capital account").

The concepts *balance of payments* and *surplus* or *deficit* refer to the balance of payments, not counting a country's official settlements balance. Thus, if a currency is freely exchangeable, any deficit in the balance of payments must be offset by an equal

---

[2] Support for the dollar can also come from foreign central banks. In fact, many of the industrialized nations coordinate their intervention activities.

surplus in the official reserve transactions, and any surplus must be offset by an equal deficit. This means that the supply of and demand for a freely exchangeable currency must sum to zero by definition.

EXCHANGE RATES

The balance of payments has two sides: the flow of goods or assets, and the flow of money to pay for those goods. International finance is more complicated than domestic finance because international finance always involves two financial transactions: the exchange of a real good or asset for money, and the exchange of money of one country for the money of another country. For international trade to take place, one must be able to exchange currencies. If either of these financial transactions is difficult or costly, trade is impeded.

As we will discuss later, a number of countries' currencies cannot be freely exchanged today. These countries have what are called **nonconvertible currencies.** International trade is greatly impeded by that lack of free exchange. The former Soviet Union is an example of a country whose currency did not trade freely. In the 1980s, as the Soviet Union attempted to expand its international trade, it looked for ways to make its currency (the ruble) convertible (exchangeable) into other currencies.

Nonconvertible currencies
Currencies that cannot be freely exchanged with currencies of other countries.

Thinking about the problem of trade with nonconvertible currencies gives one a deeper appreciation of the role of money in an economy. Money makes an economy operate efficiently—but only if everyone agrees to the monetary convention. You accept dollars because you know that someone else will accept dollars who in turn knows that someone else will accept dollars. Dollars have no inherent value, but they acquire value because our government declares that dollars are legal tender and that it will accept only dollars in payments of taxes, and because people believe that dollars have value. Hence dollars do have value.

In the international sphere there is no legally mandated monetary convention, so a foreign exchange market in which one currency can be exchanged for another must be set up. That foreign exchange market is a system of formal or informal international monetary markets governed by a set of internationally agreed-upon conventions. These conventions provide the framework within which international financial affairs are conducted.

Supply, Demand, and Fundamental Analysis of Exchange Rates

Supply and demand are the two central forces of economics, and so it shouldn't be surprising that our initial discussion of the determination of exchange rates uses supply and demand curves.

At first glance, the analysis of foreign exchange rates seems simple: You have an upward-sloping supply curve and a downward-sloping demand curve. But what goes on the axes? Obviously price and quantity, but what price? And what quantity? Because you're talking about the relative prices of currencies—that's basically what exchange rates are—you have to specify which currencies you're using.

In Exhibit 3, we present the supply and demand for French francs in terms of dollar prices. Notice that the quantity of francs goes on the horizontal axis and the dollar price of francs goes on the vertical axis.

The first point to recognize is that when you are comparing the currencies of only two countries, the supply of one currency is equal to the demand for the other currency. To demand one currency, you must supply the other. In Exhibit 3 we are assuming that there are only two countries: Canada and France. This means that the supply of francs is the equivalent of a demand for dollars. The demand for dollars comes from the French who want to buy Canadian goods or assets. To do so, they supply francs to buy dollars. Let's consider an example showing why. Say a French person wants to buy an IBM computer made in Canada. She has francs, but IBM wants dollars. So, in order to buy the computer, she or IBM must somehow exchange francs for dollars. She is *supplying* francs and *demanding* dollars.

The supply curve of francs is upward sloping because the more dollars French citizens get for their francs, the cheaper Canadian goods and assets are for them. Say, for example, that the dollar price of one franc rises from 15¢ to 20¢. That means that the price of a dollar to a French person has fallen from 6.67 francs to 5 francs. For a

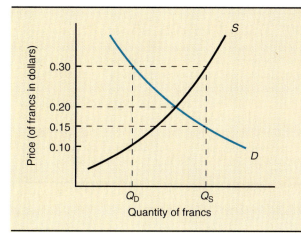

EXHIBIT 3   The Supply and Demand for Francs

As long as one keeps "quantities and prices of what" straight, the standard, or fundamental, analysis of the determination of exchange rates is easy. Exchange rates are determined by the supply and demand for a country's currency. Just remember that if you're talking about the supply and demand for francs, the price will be measured in dollars and the quantity will be in francs, as in this exhibit. If you're talking about the supply of and demand for dollars, the quantity will be in dollars, but the price of dollars will be measured in another currency. Otherwise the price of a dollar would be a dollar.

French person, a good that cost $100 now falls in price from 667 francs to 500 francs. Canadian goods are cheaper, so the French buy more Canadian goods and more dollars, which means they supply more francs.

The demand for francs comes from Canadians who want to buy French goods or assets. The demand curve is downward sloping because the lower the dollar price of francs, the more francs Canadian citizens want to buy, for the same reasons we just described.

Equilibrium is where the quantity supplied equals the quantity demanded. In our example, equilibrium occurs at a dollar price of 20¢ for one franc. If the price of francs is above or below 20¢, quantity supplied won't equal the quantity demanded and there will be pressure for the exchange rate to move to equilibrium. Say, for example, that the price is 30¢. The quantity of francs supplied will be greater than the quantity demanded. People who want to sell francs won't be able to sell them. To find buyers, they will offer to sell their francs for less. As they do, the price of francs falls.

The supply/demand framework directly relates to the balance of payments. When quantity supplied equals quantity demanded, the balance of payments is in equilibrium. If the currency is overvalued, there will be a deficit in the balance of payments; if the currency is undervalued, there will be a surplus in the balance of payments. Thus, in Exhibit 3 when the price of francs is 30¢, quantity of francs supplied exceeds the quantity demanded so France is running a balance of payments deficit. When the price of francs is 15¢, the quantity of francs demanded exceeds the quantity supplied, so France is running a balance of payments surplus.

Supply/Demand, Traders, and Exchange Rates   It would appear from Exhibit 3 that the determination of exchange rates is a relatively simple process: All one need do is determine the supply and demand curves and decide where equilibrium occurs. And in some ways, it is relatively easy. But in other ways it isn't; if it were as simple as determining supply and demand curves and equilibrium, the quotation at the head of this chapter about the bedlam in a foreign exchange dealer's office wouldn't have been appropriate, and governments would not agonize over exchange rates as they do. There's more to the story of exchange rates than is told in those two curves.

The reason is that the curves in Exhibit 3 reflect long-run considerations; they reflect the effect of normal market forces on the supply and demand for currency. It was normal market forces that we used to justify the shapes of the curves. An analysis of curves based on normal market forces like that in the discussion of Exhibit 3 is often called **fundamental analysis** because the forces described there are the forces one arrives at by applying normal or fundamental economic analysis to the exchange rates. The normal market forces are the forces that will determine exchange rates in the long run—say in two, three, or four years.

3   In the short run, fundamental analysis only influences the value of a currency. Expectations of traders are far more important in determining short-run exchange rates than are fundamentals.

Fundamental analysis   Analysis of curves describing fundamental forces that will be operating in the long run.

DETERMINING THE CAUSES OF FLUCTUATIONS IN THE DOLLAR'S VALUE

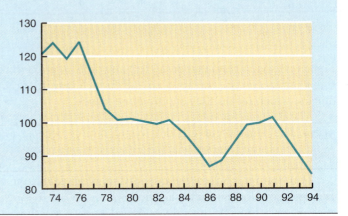

A s you can see on the graph, the dollar's value has fluctuated considerably since 1973. The **G-10 index** is a weighted average of the value of the Canadian dollar against the currencies of the other nations in the Group of Ten (the United Kingdom, the United States, Germany, Italy, France, Switzerland, Japan, Sweden, the Netherlands, and Belgium). Since it is a weighted average, large fluctuations in the value of any one currency will be reduced by the averaging process. A good exercise to see if you understand movements in the value of the dollar is to try to choose which factors caused the fluctuation.

Let's start with 1973. During that time Canada had relatively large inflation compared to other countries, so the value of the dollar fell. The sudden fluctuations in 1973–1977 probably reflected expectational bubbles—in which speculators were more concerned with short-run than long-run fundamentals—while the dollar's low value in 1979 and 1980 reflected high inflation, relatively low real interest rates, and the booming economy.

In 1984 the dollar lost value against most of the world's currencies. This stimulated trade, and combined with relatively high Canadian interest rates, the capital account balance rose significantly. Payments to foreigners for the use of their capital also rose around 1984, and the current account deficit climbed to its current level. The path of the official settlements balance began to change in 1982. Speculative attacks on the Canadian dollar in the mid–1980s and early 1990s were resisted by Bank of Canada intervention in foreign currency markets.

The rise of the dollar in the late 1980s reflected higher interest rates and the falling Canadian inflation rate, although the rise was much more than expected and probably reflected speculation, as did the sudden fall in the dollar's value in 1994.

As you can see, after the fact we economists are pretty good at explaining movements in exchange rates. Alas, before the fact we aren't so good because often speculative activities make the timing of the movements unpredictable.

Most movements in exchange rates that are discussed in the newspapers are influenced by these normal market forces, but are not determined by them. Thus, the short-run analysis of exchange rates (what will happen to the exchange rate in the next week, month, or year) is not directly based on fundamental analysis but upon a variety of effects that influence traders' decisions whether to buy, sell, or hold a currency. Those decisions depend much more on a variety of forces that cause *shifts* in the supply and demand curves for a country's currency than on forces governing the shapes of the supply and demand curves.

In the real world, shifts in the supply of, and demand for, currencies are extremely important, and the exchange rate fluctuations necessary to keep the balance of payments in equilibrium in the short run are large. As we will see, such large shifts in exchange rates cause problems and lead to attempts to reduce exchange rate fluctuations. But before we consider this problem, let's consider the forces that cause supply of, and demand for, currencies to shift.

Forces that Cause Shifts in the Supply of and Demand for Currencies   The major forces that can cause shifts include changes in a country's income, changes in a country's prices, changes in interest rates, and changes in expectations. Let's consider each in turn.

Changes in a Country's Income   The demand for imports depends on the income in a country. When a country's income falls, demand for imports falls. Hence demand for foreign currency to buy those imports falls, which means that the supply of the country's currency to buy the foreign currency falls. That's why, in our presentation of the Keynesian model, we said that imports depend on income.

Changes in a Country's Prices   Canada's demand for imports and foreign countries' demand for Canadian exports depend on prices of Canadian goods compared to prices of foreign competing goods. If Canada has more inflation than other countries, foreign goods will become cheaper, Canadian demand for foreign currencies will tend to increase, and foreign demand for dollars will tend to decrease. This rise in Canadian inflation will shift the dollar supply outward and the dollar demand inward.

Changes in Interest Rates People like to invest their savings in assets that will yield the highest return. A rise in Canadian interest rates relative to those abroad will increase demand for Canadian assets as long as that rise is a rise in the real interest rate—that is, as long as the rise isn't accompanied by a rise in inflation. As a result of a rise in the Canadian interest rate, demand for dollars will increase, while simultaneously the supply of dollars will decrease as fewer Canadians sell their dollars to buy foreign assets. A fall in the Canadian interest rate or a rise in foreign interest rates will have the opposite effect.

Changes in Expectations If the value of a currency falls, the holders of that currency and of assets denominated in that currency lose; if the value of a currency rises, the holders of that currency and of assets denominated in that currency gain. So everyone tries to hold currencies whose value will rise and get rid of currencies whose value will fall. Thus, expectations of whether a currency will rise or fall can cause large shifts in the supply and demand. Expectations can even be self-fulfilling. For example, the expectation of a rise in the dollar's value will increase the demand for dollars and decrease the supply, which will cause a rise in the value of the dollar. The dollar rises because it is expected to rise.

Given that these large shifts in the supply and demand for currencies are constantly occurring, one might expect that there would be enormous shifts in exchange rates. But that doesn't often happen. Usually exchange rates are rather stable for two reasons. First, government enters into exchange markets to maintain stability. When people buy, the government sells; when people sell, the government buys. Government action counters the shifts.

A second reason is that foreign exchange traders and speculators stabilize the rates. Traders know that eventually market forces will be strong and will lead to fundamental forces that will control the exchange rates, and they base their expectations on those fundamentals. Which of these two reasons is more important is debatable. Since that debate centres on whether private traders or government are better at stabilizing exchange rates, we need to look behind the supply and demand curves for currencies—at the traders who make the markets work.

Stability and Instability in Foreign Exchange Markets

Exchange Rate Markets, Traders, and the Spread
International currency traders are interested in making money. They buy and sell currencies. If they buy low and sell high, they make a profit. If they buy high and sell low, they lose money. The currency trader is constantly on the phone offering to buy a currency at one rate and to sell it at another rate.

The **spread** is the difference between the price at which they buy a currency and the price at which they sell it. To see how the spread works, let's consider a trader of francs and dollars. She might post the following rates:

Spread The difference between the price at which traders buy and sell a currency.

Today's Rates	
Sell: $1	4.5 francs
Buy: $1	4.4 francs
Sell: 1 franc	23¢
Buy: 1 franc	22¢

The spread is 1¢ for every franc traded, and 10 centimes (100 centimes equals one franc) for every dollar traded. The greater the spread, the greater the profit per transaction but the smaller the number of transactions that are likely to go through that trader. Traders become known as aggressive or nonaggressive. Aggressive traders

ARBITRAGE

International currency traders often deal in a variety of currencies, and when they do they must be continually on the lookout for discrepancies among the exchange rates for various countries. For example, let's say a trader opens an office with several windows and sets up the following exchange rates:

> Window 1: $1 = 4.5 francs or 1 franc = 22.5¢
> Window 2: $1 = 707.9 won or 1 won = 0.14¢
> Window 3: 1 won = 0.005 francs or 1 franc = 200 won.

Enter Mr. Arbitrage, who's always keeping his eye on international currency traders. Mr. Arbitrage goes up to window 1 and says, "I'll buy $1,000 worth of French francs." He receives 4,500 francs. He then goes to window 3 and says, "I'd like to buy Korean won for these 4,500 French francs, please." Handing over 4,500 francs, he receives 900,000 won. He then goes to window 2 and says, "I'd like to exchange these 900,000 won for dollars, please." He hands over 900,000 won, for which he receives $1,260. Next he takes the $1,260 back to window 1 and says, "I'd like to buy French francs, please." At this point the currency trader should know that she's goofed: In setting the exchange rates she has forgotten the principle of arbitrage.

Arbitrage is the buying of a good in one market at a low price and selling that good in another market at a higher price. It limits the exchange rates a currency trader can set in various markets and still make a profit. Specifically, the roundabout exchange rates must be identical to the direct exchange rates. Recognizing this, she changes the exchange rate between won and francs so that 1 won = 0.0063 francs and no arbitrage profits are to be made.

Our little story and example make it look as if arbitrage is simple. But remember, there are hundreds of currencies, and with even as few as 50 currencies there are many thousands of possible roundabout exchange rates. Real-world arbitragers have computers that constantly monitor these exchange rates. If they find a difference, they buy and sell quickly, keeping the people who set exchange rates on their toes to set all exchange rates so that arbitragers can't make money by arbitrating markets. All of this happens in the span of minutes.

Foreign exchange markets have become sophisticated and the spread is small. Computers, programmed to spot any potential for arbitrage, monitor exchange rates and keep exchange rates among currencies in line so that roundabout trading does not bring about long-term profits for arbitragers. Arbitragers, like others in a competitive market, cover their costs (which include normal profits) but don't make so much profit that they attract others into the business.

---

have the smallest spread. They buy high and sell cheap, relying on volume for their profit.

How does an international currency trader choose what rates she will set? The answer is that she must choose a rate that brings her about the same amount of dollars that other people want to buy. That is, she must choose a rate for which the quantity of dollars supplied roughly equals the quantity of dollars demanded.

Thus, after a trader sets her rates, she will see how many dollars her advertised rates are bringing in, and how many dollars are going out. If fewer dollars are coming in than going out, she'll raise the price of dollars in terms of French francs. Instead of 4.5 francs to the dollar, she'll make it 4.6 francs to the dollar. Dollars become more expensive in terms of francs; francs become cheaper in terms of dollars. International traders hope that if everything goes right, that change will bring the two currencies into equilibrium. Traders set exchange rates to equate supply and demand for dollars.

The Short-Run Determination of Exchange Rates   Most currency traders will have taken an introductory economics course, so they'll look at the factors that cause shifts in supply and demand and think about the general long-run direction of exchange rates. As stated before, they call the analysis of the long-run determinants of exchange rates *fundamental analysis*. But traders recognize that in the very short run the quantities of currencies supplied and demanded aren't significantly influenced by exchange rates,

Foreign exchange traders often have millions of dollars riding on small movements in exchange rates. © *David H. Wells/The Image Works.*

but are significantly influenced by expectations. They expect that supply and demand for currencies will shift enormously, which means the equilibrium price will fluctuate widely. Traders' time horizon is the very short run (minutes, hours, or days). Thus, you'll seldom hear currency traders talking about fundamentals of exchange rate determination. They're far more concerned with the short-run factors that shift demand, especially expectations.

Currency traders are active in markets for most of the major currencies. The spreads are extremely narrow. The traders are constantly buying or selling—listening for trade figures, rumours on the street, and interest rate policy changes by governments. They don't limit themselves to buying and selling for customers. They can buy for their own accounts, speculating on whether a currency is about to go up or down. Often a trader has millions of dollars riding on whether a currency will go up or down a single percentage point.

Traders see only a small part of a currency's supply and demand—the part that flows through their offices as they buy and sell. Given their very limited observations, they have to guess what's going on. They're making judgements not about shifts in demand, but about their belief about other traders' beliefs about . . . . Rumours can, and do, drive international currency markets wild.

Predicting how much of a foreign currency all the people in a country will want in the short run is a complicated task. If a currency trader predicts wrong, she gets stuck with some currencies that nobody wants. When the spread is wide, she can afford a few losses, but when the bid/ask spread is narrow, she must predict very carefully and must try to make sure that she chooses a rate for which the supply of, and demand for, various currencies flowing through her office are equal.

So far we haven't discussed government's role in exchange rate determination. Where does government policy come in?

Every country has goals for its exchange rate and trade balance, and uses monetary and fiscal policies to achieve those goals. Through these policies governments can influence income and, hence, the current account and interest rates and, hence, the capital account. This means that, through monetary and fiscal policies, government can indirectly affect a country's balance of payments and, hence, exchange rates.

Government's Role in Determining Exchange Rates

LIMITS ON TRADERS' SPECULATION

When many Canadian banks first got seriously involved in international currency markets in the 1970s, traders had relatively loose limits on the speculative positions they could take. A speculative position is the net amount of a currency a trader holds from buying or selling currency for his or her own account in the hope that its value will rise or fall.

Speculative positions can be either long or short. Holding a currency in the hope that its price will rise is a long position; selling a currency you don't have but will buy when you must supply it, in the hope that its price will have fallen, is a short position.

Some traders have lost millions of dollars in the span of a couple of minutes. A long time ago one of us was offered a job forecasting exchange rates at a major bank. He was informally told that he could make one mistake—any more than that and he'd be history (not surprisingly he didn't take the job).

In response to such problems, most banks instituted stringent controls over the positions that traders can take. Most traders aren't allowed to have unauthorized positions at the end of each trading day.

Who are these foreign exchange traders? Usually they're not Ph.D. economists or even MBAs; such people often don't have the guts or personality to be traders. Instead traders are often people who are directly out of high school or college, people who have been discovered to have an ability to make split-second correct decisions (to buy or sell); who have few regrets ("If only I'd . . ."); and who want to earn about $60,000 a year to start. They're a bungee-type group. (Bungee is a sport in which you tie one end of an elastic rope to a rock or a tree and the other end to your feet and dive off a cliff, hoping the rope will stop you right before you hit the ground. If you're successful, you yo-yo up and down for two or three minutes.) Bungee is a trader's hobby. We prefer gardening.

In addition to monetary and fiscal policies, countries can use other economic policies to influence the exchange rate. A government might simply pass a law flatly specifying what the exchange rate will be. Alternatively, a government can directly affect its currency's exchange rate by means of capital control policies and exchange rate policies. Still another possibility is for it to use trade policies, such as quotas and tariffs, to influence the trade balance. Let us look more specifically at setting exchange rates by legal mandate, exchange rate policies, and capital control policies.

4 Developing countries often have nonconvertible currencies to avoid making economic adjustments that international considerations would otherwise force upon them.

Exchange Rates Set by Law: Nonconvertible Currency and Capital Controls A government can simply pass a law outlawing international currency trading and prohibiting the buying and selling of foreign currencies except at a rate determined by the government. Many developing countries set their exchange rates in this manner. When governments do so, they make international trade difficult, because their currencies can't be freely exchanged with other currencies—that is, their currencies are *nonconvertible*.

Nonconvertible currencies' exchange rates don't fluctuate in response to shifts in supply and demand. Often the only legal way to deal in such currency is to buy it from the government and sell to the government. It is illegal to trade nonconvertible currencies privately or even to carry large amounts of nonconvertible currency out of the country. Such prohibitions against currency flowing freely into and out of a country are called **capital controls.** If one country's currency can't be exchanged for another's at anything reflecting a market price, it's very difficult to buy each other's goods.

Capital controls A government's prohibitions on its currency freely flowing into and out of the country.

If nonconvertible currencies make trade so difficult, why do countries use them? The answer is: to avoid making the economic adjustments that international considerations would otherwise force upon them. Say that a country is running a large balance of payments deficit and the value of its currency is falling. This fall is pushing up the price of imports, causing inflation, and making its assets cheaper for foreigners. Foreigners can come in and buy up the country's assets at low prices.

The country can avoid this political problem simply by passing a law that fixes the exchange rate at a certain level. This action indirectly limits imports, since most foreign firms won't sell their goods at the official exchange rate. They don't want the country's currency at the official exchange rate. It also limits exports since the price of a country's exports is held high. The government can and often does give favoured firms special dispensation to import or export. Thus, having a nonconvertible currency enables the government to control what can and can't be imported and exported. Generally when there's a nonconvertible currency, there is a large incentive for people to trade currencies illegally in a black market.

Exchange Rate Policy and Government Intervention in the Currency Market

Even if a government doesn't establish a nonconvertible currency, it can still directly affect the exchange rate. The government can buy and sell currencies, just like an individual trader. If it buys or sells enough of a particular currency, it can affect that currency's relative price (its exchange rate). So an **exchange rate policy** is a policy in which the government buys and sells a currency in order to affect its price.

Exchange rate policy Deliberately affecting a country's exchange rate in order to affect its trade balance.

Say the Bank of Canada wants to raise the value of the Canadian dollar. If it buys lots of dollars (paying for them with other currencies), it will increase the demand for dollars, which will push the price of dollars up. If it wants to lower the price of dollars (in terms of other currencies), it can sell dollars and buy other currencies.

Think back to the Canadian balance of payments as summarized in Exhibit 1. When Canada bought $2 billion worth of dollars in 1994 (selling foreign currencies and gold in return), it was using exchange rate policy to support the value of the dollar.

In the autumn of 1993, there was a typical example of Canadian intervention. The value of the dollar had been falling relative to the U.S. dollar, and that fall accelerated, bringing the exchange rate up to about 1.33 Canadian dollars per U.S. dollar. While some fall in the value of the Canadian dollar was seen as desirable since Canada was coming out of recession, the Bank of Canada felt that the fall was too fast. It feared the market was being disorderly. The Bank of Canada entered into the exchange markets, buying Canadian dollars and maintaining an "orderly market." The amount it bought compared to total transactions was small, but the mere presence of the Bank of Canada in the market changed expectations and reduced pressure on the value of the dollar to fall.

The actual intervention is generally too small to move the market, but the expectations that the intervention generates are often large enough. It's like a rolling snowball that grows as it collects snow from the snowy ground. This autumn 1993 intervention was typical: The Bank of Canada will let the value of the dollar fall, but if it can stop the fall, it won't let the value of the dollar fall "too fast."

Since Canada can create all the dollars it wants, it's easier for Canada to push the value of its currency down by selling dollars than to hold it up. In contrast, it's easier for another country (say, Japan) to push the value of the dollar up (by pushing the value of the yen down). Thus, if the two countries can decide which way they want their exchange rates to move, they have a large incentive to cooperate. Of course, cooperation requires an agreement on the goals. One role of the various international economic organizations discussed in Chapter 5 is to provide a forum for reaching agreement on exchange rate goals and a vehicle through which cooperation can take place.

The Effect of Exchange Rates on the Balance of Goods and Services and Balance of Payments

A government's exchange rate goal can be an end in itself, or it can be a means to an end. An increase in a country's exchange rate—that is, a decline in its currency's value relative to that of another country's currency—pushes the price of imports up and the price of exports down. Thus, it tends to decrease the *quantity* of imports coming into a country and to increase the *quantity* of exports going out of a country. It also makes a country's assets cheaper to foreigners. These changes in quantity *eventually* improve the balance of trade and hence the balance of payments.

We emphasize the words *eventually* and *quantity* to highlight a paradox that often occurs when exchange rates change. Often initially a rise in the exchange rate doesn't decrease the balance of trade deficit and the balance of payments deficit; it increases

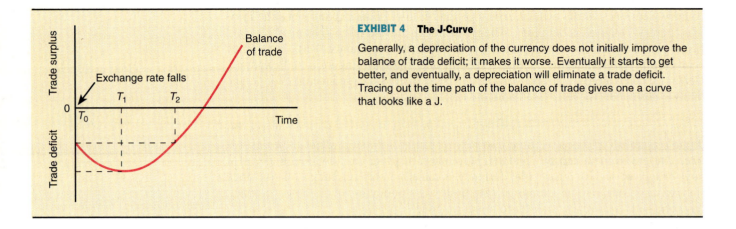

EXHIBIT 4   The J-Curve

Generally, a depreciation of the currency does not initially improve the balance of trade deficit; it makes it worse. Eventually it starts to get better, and eventually, a depreciation will eliminate a trade deficit. Tracing out the time path of the balance of trade gives one a curve that looks like a J.

J-curve Curve describing the rise and fall in the balance of trade deficit following a fall in the exchange rate.

them. This phenomenon has occurred so often that it has acquired a name, the **J-curve.** We'll explain why it's called that in a moment.

Why do trade deficit increases initially occur when a country's exchange rate rises? To answer that question, remember that a country's imports and exports are determined by two variables: price multiplied by quantity. When a country's exchange rate rises, the *quantity* of imports tends to decrease and the *quantity* of exports tends to rise, but the *price* of imports tends to rise and the *price* of exports tends to fall. In the short run these price effects tend to predominate over the quantity effects, so the balance of payments and balance of trade deficits become larger. Eventually, however, the quantity effects tend to predominate over the price effects, so the balance of trade and balance of payments deficits get smaller.

If one were graphing what happens to the balance of trade and balance of payments after an exchange rate rises, the graph would look something like Exhibit 4. The rise in the exchange rate occurs at time T_0, and initially the balance of trade and hence the balance of payments worsen. The balance of trade keeps worsening until time T_1, whereupon it starts to improve. At time T_2, it's back where it was at the start, and thereafter it substantially improves. The curve looks like a "J"—hence the name the *J-curve*.

Let's go through a numerical example to place the J-curve concept into your deep memory. Say that at an exchange rate of 0.4/1 (each German mark costs $0.4), Canada is importing 40 Mercedes at $50,000 (125,000 German marks) each, and is exporting to Germany 200,000 videos at $9 (22.5 German marks) each. Imports are $2,000,000 (40 x $50,000) and exports are $1,800,000 ($9 x 200,000). Canada thus has a $200,000 trade deficit with Germany.

Now say that the value of the dollar falls (the exchange rate rises) to 0.44/1 (each German mark now costs $0.44) and the price of Mercedes to Canadian citizens goes to $55,000 (125,000 German marks now costs $55,000). In response, the quantity imported falls to 39. The price of videos falls to $8.20, and the quantity exported rises to 210,000. Let's now calculate the trade balance:

$$\text{Imports (\$55,000} \times \text{39)} = \$2,145,000$$
$$\text{Exports (\$8.20} \times \text{210,000)} = \underline{\$1,722,000}$$
$$\text{Trade deficit} \qquad\qquad\quad \$\ 423,000$$

In response to a *fall* in the relative value of the dollar, the trade deficit has increased from $200,000 to $423,000.

This result was dependent on the numbers we chose. Experience suggests that eventually, the quantity effect is much larger than this example indicates, and a fall in the value of a currency improves a country's trade balance, but that *eventually* can be as long as five to seven years. This possibility presents policymakers with a serious long-run/short-run dilemma in using exchange rate policy to achieve government's balance of trade and payments goals. Escaping that dilemma is one reason that many developing countries use nonconvertible currencies. Politically, often they can't afford to make their balance of payments deficit larger in the short run in order to achieve a long-run improvement.

The J-curve phenomenon—which suggests that normal market forces don't operate to keep the exchange rate in short-run equilibrium—is the reason that in our earlier discussion we separated the short-run determination of the exchange rate from the long-run determination of exchange rates. Fundamental analysis only works in the long run. In the short run, normal market forces don't determine exchange rates.

Understanding the limited, and possibly even perverse, short-run effect of normal market forces on achieving equilibrium is important to understanding why most governments don't leave determination of the exchange rate to the market, but instead play varying roles in its determination. We now turn to a consideration of three alternative exchange rate regimes and how they affect short-run determination of exchange rates.

FLEXIBLE, PARTIALLY FLEXIBLE, AND FIXED EXCHANGE RATES

When governments do not enter into foreign exchange markets at all, but leave the determination of exchange rates totally up to currency traders, the country is said to have a **perfectly flexible exchange rate.** The price of its currency is allowed to rise and fall as market forces dictate.

5 **Flexible exchange rate** Determination of exchange rates is left totally up to the market.

When governments sometimes buy or sell currencies to influence the exchange rate, while at other times they let private market forces operate, the country is said to have a **partially flexible exchange rate.** A partially flexible exchange rate is sometimes called a *dirty float,* or a *managed float,* because it isn't purely market determined or government determined.

Partially flexible exchange rate The government sometimes affects the exchange rate and sometimes leaves it to the market.

If the government chooses a particular exchange rate and offers to buy and sell currencies at that price, it is imposing a **fixed exchange rate.** For example, suppose the Bank of Canada says it will buy francs at 20¢ and sell dollars at 5 francs. In that case, we say that the country has a fixed exchange rate of 0.2 dollars to the franc (or, alternatively, 5 francs to the dollar).

Fixed exchange rate The government chooses an exchange rate and offers to buy and sell currencies at the rate.

How does the Bank of Canada operate a fixed exchange rate? It has to let the money supply change in response to changes in the demand for dollars so that the foreign currency price of a dollar doesn't change. For example, say the demand for dollars falls because foreigners don't see Canada as an attractive place to invest. That would put pressure on the Canadian dollar to lose value. To stop that from happening—to operate a fixed exchange rate—the Bank of Canada buys the dollars that foreigners no longer desire. The Bank of Canada pays for those dollars by running down its **foreign exchange reserves**—its holdings of U.S. dollars, Japanese yen, and other foreign currencies that it has obtained through its foreign currency activities. This leads to a reduction in the supply of Canadian dollars so that, when all is said and done, the value of the dollar remains at its previous level. Exhibit 5 demonstrates this process.

Nonconvertible exchange rate The government does not allow the free exchange of its currency with currencies of other nations.

Foreign exchange reserves The pool of foreign currencies and gold used by the central bank when it intervenes to affect the external value of the dollar.

Since the Bank of Canada can't print new U.S. dollars to use whenever it wants to buy back some Canadian dollars, there's a limit to the central bank's ability to resist a depreciation. That's true for everyone who trades in the market. In principle, any trader could establish a fixed exchange rate by guaranteeing to buy or sell a currency at a given rate. Any "fix," however, is only as good as the guarantee, and to fix an exchange rate the trader/Bank of Canada may require many more resources than she has. To maintain a fix they must borrow other currencies to prevent the price of their currency from falling. A case in point: In the late 1980s the Canadian dollar came under heavy speculative attack from foreign currency traders—and the Bank of Canada had to borrow 2 billion U.S. dollars from the Federal Reserve to use to buy back Canadian dollars. Eventually the pressure eased, but the Bank of Canada was left owning billions of dollars in foreign currencies that it had used to support the Canadian dollar.

A good way to give you an idea of how the various systems work is to present a brief history of international exchange rate systems.

History of Exchange Rate Systems

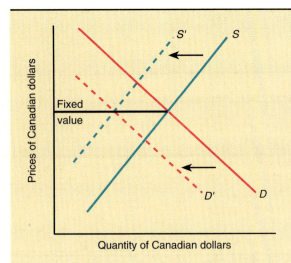

EXHIBIT 5   Foreign Exchange Market Intervention

When the demand for dollars falls, the Bank of Canada can keep the exchange rate fixed by reducing the supply of dollars to *S'*. It does this through buying dollars and selling foreign currencies and gold. It takes those dollars out of circulation, thereby maintaining a constant value of the dollar.

Gold standard   The system by which the value of a country's currency is fixed in relation to the price of gold and under which the country must maintain a stockpile of gold sufficiently large that it can pay in gold for as much of its currency as anyone wants to sell.

The Gold Standard: A Fixed Exchange Rate System   Governments played a major role in determining exchange rates until the 1930s. Beginning with the Paris Conference of 1867 and lasting until 1933 (except for the period around World War I), most of the world economies had a system of relatively fixed exchange rates under what was called a **gold standard.**

Under a gold standard, the amount of money a country issued had to be directly tied to gold, either because gold coin served as the currency in a country (as it did in the United States before 1914) or because countries were required by law to have a certain percentage of gold backing their currencies. Gold served as currency or backed all currencies. Each country participating in a gold standard agreed to fix the price of its currency relative to gold. That meant a country would agree to pay a specified amount of gold upon demand to anyone who wanted to exchange that country's currency for gold. To do so, each country had to maintain a stockpile of gold. When a country fixed the price of its currency relative to gold, it fixed its currency's price in relation to other currencies as a result of the process of arbitrage.

Under the gold standard, a country made up a difference between the quantity supplied and the quantity demanded of its currency by buying or selling gold to hold the price of its currency fixed in terms of gold. How much a country would need to buy and sell depended upon its balance of payments deficit or surplus. If the country ran a surplus in the balance of payments, it was required to sell its currency—that is, buy gold—to stop the value of its currency from rising. If a country ran a deficit in the balance of payments, it was required to buy its currency—that is, sell gold—to stop the value of its currency from falling.

The gold standard enabled governments to prevent short-run instability of the exchange rate. If there was a speculative run on its currency, the government would buy its currency with gold, thereby preventing the exchange rate from falling.

But for the gold standard to work, there had to be a method of long-run adjustment; otherwise countries would run out of gold and would no longer be able to fulfil their obligations under the gold standard. That long-run adjustment mechanism was called the **gold specie flow mechanism.** Here's how it worked: Since gold served as reserves to a country's currency, a balance of payments *deficit* (and hence an upward pressure on the exchange rate) would result in a flow of gold out of the country and hence a decrease in the country's money supply. That decrease in the money supply would contract the economy, decreasing imports, lowering the country's price level, and increasing the interest rate, all of which would work toward eliminating the balance of payments deficit.

Similarly a country with a balance of payments *surplus* would experience an inflow of gold. That flow would increase the country's money supply, increasing

Gold specie flow mechanism   Long-run adjustment mechanism under the gold standard in which flows of gold and changes in the price level bring about equilibrium.

income (and hence imports), the price level (making imports cheaper and exports more expensive), and lowering the interest rate (increasing capital outflows). These would work toward eliminating the balance of payments surplus.

Thus, the gold standard determined a country's monetary policy and forced it to adjust any international balance of payments disequilibrium. Adjustments to a balance of payments deficit were often politically unpopular; they led to recessions, which, because the money supply was directly tied to gold, the government couldn't try to offset with expansionary monetary policy.

The gold adjustment mechanism was called into play in the United States when the Federal Reserve, in late 1931 in response to a shrinking U.S. gold supply, decreased the amount of money in the U.S. economy, deepening the depression that had begun in 1929. The government's domestic goals and responsibilities conflicted with its international goals and responsibilities.

That conflict led to partial abandonment of the gold standard in 1933. At that time the United States made it illegal for individual U.S. citizens to own gold. Except for gold used for ornamental and certain medical and industrial purposes, all privately owned gold had to be sold to the government. Dollar bills were no longer backed by gold in the sense that U.S. citizens could exchange dollars for a prespecified amount of gold. Instead dollar bills were backed by silver, which meant that any U.S. citizen could change dollars for a prespecified amount of silver. In the late 1960s that changed also. Since that time, for U.S. residents, dollars have been backed only by trust in the soundness of the U.S. economy.

Gold continued to serve, at least partially, as international backing for U.S. currency. That is, other countries could still exchange dollars for gold. However in 1971, in response to another conflict between international and domestic goals, the United States totally cut off the relationship between its dollars and gold. After that a U.S. dollar could be redeemed only for another U.S. dollar, whether it was a U.S. citizen or a foreign government who wanted to redeem the dollar.

The Bretton Woods System: A Fixed Exchange Rate System

As World War II was coming to an end, the United States and its allies met to establish a new international economic order. After much wrangling they agreed upon a system called the **Bretton Woods system,** named after the resort in New Hampshire where the meeting was held.

The Bretton Woods system established the International Monetary Fund (IMF) to oversee the international economic order. The IMF was empowered to arrange short-term loans between countries. The Bretton Woods system also established the World Bank, which was empowered to make longer-term loans to developing countries. Today the World Bank and IMF continue their central roles in international financial affairs.

The Bretton Woods system was based upon mutual agreements about what countries would do when experiencing balance of payments surpluses or deficits. It was essentially a fixed exchange rate system. For example, under the Bretton Woods system, the exchange rate of the U.S. dollar for the British pound was set at slightly over U.S. $4 to the pound.

The Bretton Woods system was not based on a gold standard. When countries experienced a balance of payments surplus or deficit, they did not necessarily buy or sell gold to stabilize the price of their currency. Instead they bought and sold other currencies. To ensure that participating countries would have sufficient reserves, they established a stabilization fund from which a country could obtain a short-term loan. It was hoped that this stabilization fund would be sufficient to handle all short-run adjustments that did not reflect fundamental imbalances.

In those cases where a misalignment of exchange rates was determined to be fundamental, the countries involved agreed that they would adjust their exchange rates. The IMF was empowered to oversee an orderly adjustment. It could authorize a country to make a one-time adjustment of up to 10 percent without obtaining formal approval from the IMF Board of Directors. After a country had used its one-time adjustment, formal approval was necessary for any change greater than 1 percent.

6 The gold standard is the system by which the value of a country's currency is fixed in relation to the price of gold. Its heyday was from 1867 until about 1933.

Bretton Woods system An agreement that governed international financial relationships from the period after World War II until 1971, named for Bretton Woods, New Hampshire, where the agreement was reached at a meeting of international officials.

The Bretton Woods system reflected the underlying political and economic realities of the post–World War II period in which it was set up. European economies were devastated; the U.S. economy was strong. To rebuild, Europe was going to have to import U.S. equipment and borrow large amounts from the United States. There was serious concern over how high the value of the dollar would rise and how low the value of European currencies would fall in a free market exchange. The establishment of fixed exchange rates set limits on currencies' relative movements; the exchange rates that were chosen helped provide for the rebuilding of Europe.

In addition, the Bretton Woods system provided mechanisms for long-term loans from the United States to Europe that could help sustain those fixed exchange rates. The loans also eliminated the possibility of competitive depreciation of currencies, in which each country tries to stimulate its exports by lowering the relative value of its currency.

Special Drawing Rights (SDRs) A type of international money consisting of IOUs of the IMF.

One difficulty with the Bretton Woods system was a shortage of reserves and international liquidity. To offset that shortage, the IMF was empowered to create a type of international money called **Special Drawing Rights (SDRs).** But SDRs never became established as an international currency and the U.S. dollar soon began serving as a **reserve currency** (a currency in which countries hold their liquid financial assets) for individuals and countries. To get the dollars to foreigners, the United States had to run a deficit in the current account. Since countries could exchange the dollar for gold at a fixed price, the use of dollars as a reserve currency meant that, under the Bretton Woods system, the world was on a gold standard once removed.

Reserve currency A currency in which countries hold reserves.

The number of U.S. dollars held by foreigners grew enormously in the 1960s. By the early 1970s, those dollars far exceeded in value the amount of gold the United States had. Most countries accepted this situation; even though they could legally demand gold for their dollars, they did not. But Charles de Gaulle, the nationalistic president of France, wasn't pleased with the U.S. domination of international affairs at that time. He believed France deserved a much more prominent position. He demanded gold for the dollars held by the French central bank, knowing that the United States didn't have enough gold to meet his demand. As a result of his demands, on August 15, 1971, the United States ended its policy of exchanging gold for dollars at $35 per ounce of gold. With that change, the Bretton Woods system was dead.

The Present System: A Partially Flexible Exchange Rate System International monetary affairs were much in the news in the early 1970s as countries groped for a new exchange rate system. The makeshift system finally agreed upon involved partially flexible exchange rates. Most Western countries' exchange rates are allowed to fluctuate, although at various times governments buy or sell their own currencies to affect the exchange rate.

Under the present partially flexible exchange rate system, countries must continually decide when a balance of payments surplus or deficit is a temporary phenomenon and when it is a signal of a fundamental imbalance. If they believe the situation is temporary, they enter into the foreign exchange market to hold their exchange rate at what they believe is an appropriate level. If, however, they believe that the balance of payments imbalance is a fundamental one, they let the exchange rate rise or fall.

While most Western countries' exchange rates are partially flexible, certain countries have agreed to fixed exchange rates of their currencies in relation to rates of a group of certain other currencies. For example, European Union countries maintained almost fixed exchange rates among their currencies until 1993, although this group of EU currencies could float relative to other currencies. Other currencies are fixed relative to the U.S. dollar.

Deciding what is, and what is not, a fundamental imbalance is complicated, and such decisions are considered at numerous international conferences held under the auspices of the IMF or governments. A number of organizations such as G-5 (Group of Five) and G-7 (Group of Seven), which were introduced in Chapter 5, focus much

ADDED DIMENSION

TURMOIL WITHIN THE EURO-
PEAN EXCHANGE RATE
MECHANISM

In the 1980s, it all looked so easy. After economic union in 1992 would come monetary union. A single European central bank would take over for individual banks, and a single currency—the ECU (European Currency Unit)—would replace the domestic currencies of Europe and would challenge the dollar as the reserve currency of the world economy.

But, as often happens with grand plans, there's a big jump between the plan and the reality. Let's consider the history of that case, and the case itself, again, now that we've discussed exchange rates.

The problems began when Germany, the dominant EU economy, changed its focus from EU unity to German reunification and the financing of that reunification. To bring about the reunification, the German government ran large deficits, which forced the German interest rate up as the Bundesbank refused to monetize the deficit. The high relative interest rate increased demand for the deutsche mark, putting pressure on other EU countries to keep their exchange rates within the agreed-upon band. After using all their reserves to defend their currencies, the only remaining tool available to them to keep within the range was contractionary monetary policy. (They had already agreed that goods could flow freely among member countries, and that no capital controls were allowed.)

But many of these countries were in a recession; contractionary monetary policy would worsen the recession. Sensing a contradiction, speculators entered the market, increasing the upward pressure on the mark. The result was inevitable. First Britain, Spain, and Italy, and finally France, broke their EU commitment to a fixed exchange rate, and let their currencies float to a lower level relative to the mark. Speculators made billions, and the idea of the EU having a single monetary policy and a single currency ended, at least for the near future.

Eventually, in the autumn of 1993, the countries agreed to a wide 15 percent band within which EU countries would confine their currencies, but, given the experience of the early 1990s when domestic concerns overwhelmed EU concerns, this band was seen as a fixed exchange rate limit that would probably be broken as it imposed constraints on countries' domestic monetary policies.

of their discussion on this issue. Often the various countries meet and agree, formally or informally, on acceptable ranges of exchange rates. Thus, while the present system is one of partially flexible exchange rates, the range of flexibility is limited.

Now that we've summarized the history of exchange rate systems, let's consider the advantages and disadvantages of each of the three exchange rate systems.

Advantages and Disadvantages of Alternative Exchange Rate Systems

Fixed Exchange Rates   The advantages of a fixed exchange rate system are:

1. Fixed exchange rates provide international monetary stability.
2. Fixed exchange rates force governments to make adjustments to meet their international problems.

The disadvantages of a fixed exchange rate system are:

1. Fixed exchange rates can become unfixed. When they're expected to become unfixed, they create enormous monetary instability.
2. Fixed exchange rates force governments to make adjustments to meet their international problems. (Yes, this is a disadvantage as well as an advantage.)

Let's consider each in turn.

Fixed Exchange Rates and Monetary Stability   To maintain fixed exchange rates, the government must choose an exchange rate and have sufficient reserves to support that rate. If the rate it chooses is too low, its exports lag and the country continually loses reserves. If the rate it chooses is too high, it is paying more for its imports than it needs to and is building up reserves, which means that some other country is losing reserves.

ADDED DIMENSION

INTERNATIONAL TRADE PROBLEMS FROM SHIFTING VALUES OF CURRENCIES

Major fluctuations in exchange rates can cause problems for international trade. Say, for instance, that a firm decides to build a plant in Canada because costs in Canada are low. But say the value of the dollar then rises significantly; the firm's costs rise significantly too, making it uncompetitive.

Or let's take a recent real-world example: Korean companies decided to make a major drive to sell Korean VCRs in Canada. They decided on a low-price strategy, which was justified by their cost advantage. Their export drive was a success, but the value of the Korean won relative to the dollar rose significantly. The result was that in 1989 Korean VCR companies were losing money on each VCR they sold in Canada. They kept the price low, hoping that the won would fall in value. (In other words, their average variable costs were less than the price; their average total costs were greater than the price.)

A country that is continually gaining or losing reserves must eventually change its fixed exchange rate.

The difficulty is that as soon as the country gets close to its reserves limit, foreign exchange traders begin to expect a drop in the value of the currency, and they try to get out of that currency because anyone holding that currency when it loses value will lose money. False rumours of an expected depreciation or decrease in a country's fixed exchange rate can become true by causing a "run on a currency," as all traders sell that currency. Thus, at times fixed exchange rates can become highly unstable because expectation of a change in the exchange rate can force the change to occur. As opposed to small movements in currency values, under a fixed rate regime these movements occur in large, sudden jumps.

Fixed Exchange Rates and Policy Independence   Maintaining a fixed exchange rate places limitations on a central bank's actions. In a country with fixed exchange rates, the central bank must ensure that the international supply of and demand for its currency are equal at the existing exchange rate.

Say, for example, that Canada and the Bahamas have fixed exchange rates: $1 B = $1 C. The Bahamian central bank decides to run an expansionary monetary policy, lowering the interest rate and stimulating the Bahamian economy. The lower interest rates will cause financial capital to flow out of the country, and the higher income will increase imports. Demand for Bahamian dollars will fall. To prop up their dollar and to maintain the fixed exchange rate, the Bahamas will have to buy their own currency. They can do so only as long as they have sufficient reserves of other countries' currencies.

Because most countries' international reserves are limited, a country with fixed exchange rates is limited in its ability to conduct expansionary monetary and fiscal policies. It loses its freedom to stimulate the economy in response to a recession. That's why, when a serious recession hits, many countries are forced to abandon fixed exchange rates. They run out of international reserves, and choose expansionary monetary policy to achieve their domestic goals over contractionary monetary policy to achieve their international goals.

The British newspaper is one of the best sources for up-to-date news on international finance.

Flexible Exchange Rates   The advantages and disadvantages of flexible exchange rates are the reverse of those of fixed exchange rates.

The advantages are:

1. Flexible exchange rates provide for orderly incremental adjustment of exchange rates, rather than large, sudden jumps.
2. Flexible exchange rates allow government to be flexible in conducting domestic monetary and fiscal policies.

The disadvantages are:

1. Flexible exchange rates allow speculation to cause large jumps in exchange rates that do not reflect market fundamentals.
2. Flexible exchange rates allow government to be flexible in conducting domestic monetary and fiscal policies. (This too is a disadvantage as well as an advantage.)

Let's consider each in turn.

Flexible Exchange Rates and Monetary Stability   Advocates of flexible exchange rates argue as follows: Why not treat currency markets like any other market and let private market forces determine a currency's value? There is no fixed price for TVs; why should there be a fixed price for currencies? The opponents' answer is based on the central role that international financial considerations play in an economy and the strange shapes and large shifts that occur in the short-run supply and demand curves for currencies.

As you saw in the discussion of the J-curve, short-run changes in the exchange rate do not necessarily improve the balance of payments. This suggests that the short-run supply of and demand for currencies may be a little bit strange. As opposed to sloping up and sloping down nicely (as normal supply and demand curves do), short-run supply and demand curves for currencies often slope in a way that makes the invisible hand push the wrong way: Supply curves are likely to bend backward, and demand curves are likely to fall backward.

With supply and demand curves that slope the wrong way and shift around all the time, there's no guarantee that a rise in the exchange rate will help achieve equilibrium. As you saw with the J-curve, it can take the economy further from equilibrium. If equilibrium is to be achieved, it must be achieved because speculators enter in and buy an undervalued currency in expectation of its future rise. Thus, two arguments against flexible exchange rates are that they don't necessarily help achieve equilibrium in the short run, and that they allow far too much fluctuation in exchange rates, making trade difficult.

Flexible Exchange Rates and Policy Independence   The policy independence arguments for and against flexible exchange rates are the reverse of those given for fixed exchange rates. Individuals who believe that national governments should not have flexibility in setting monetary policy argue that flexible exchange rates don't impose the discipline on policy that fixed exchange rates do. Say, for example, that a country's goods are uncompetitive. Under a fixed exchange rate system, the country would have to contract its money supply and deal with the underlying uncompetitiveness of its goods. Under a flexible exchange rate system, the country can maintain an expansionary monetary policy, allowing inflation simply by allowing the value of its currency to fall.

Advocates of policy flexibility argue that it's stupid for a country to go through a recession when it doesn't have to; flexible exchange rates allow countries more flexibility in dealing with their problems. True, policy flexibility may lead to inflation, but inflation is better than a recession.

Partially Flexible Exchange Rates   Faced with the dilemma of choosing between these two unpleasant policies, most countries have opted for a policy in between the two: partially flexible exchange rates. With such a policy they try to get the advantages of both a fixed and a flexible exchange rate.

When policymakers believe there is a fundamental misalignment in a country's exchange rate, they will allow private forces to determine it—they allow the exchange rate to be flexible. When they believe that the currency's value is falling because of speculation, or that too large an adjustment in the currency is taking place, and that that adjustment won't achieve their balance of payment goals, they step in and fix the exchange rate, either supporting or pushing down their currency's value.

If policymakers are correct, this system of partial flexibility would work smoothly and would have the advantages of both fixed and flexible exchange rates. If policymakers are incorrect, however, a partially flexible system has the disadvantages of both fixed and flexible systems.

Which view is correct is much in debate. Most foreign exchange traders that we know tell us that the possibility of government intervention increases the amount of private speculation in the system. In private investors' view, their own assessments of what exchange rates should be are better than those of policymakers. If private investors knew the government would not enter in, private speculators would focus on fundamentals and would stabilize short-run exchange rates. When private speculators know government might enter into the market, they don't focus on fundamentals; instead they continually try to outguess government policymakers. When that happens, private speculation doesn't stabilize; it destabilizes exchange rates as private traders try to guess what the government thinks.

Many of our economics colleagues who work for the Fed and the Bank of Canada aren't convinced by private investors' arguments. They maintain that some government intervention helps stabilize currency markets. We don't know which group is right.

CONCLUSION

Even though you've stayed with us through the chapter's in-depth introduction to international finance, you still won't be able to predict exchange rates. Nobody can do that. But at least we hope you know why you can't. The most honest prediction that one can make is that exchange rates are likely to be highly volatile—unpredictable in the short run and even unpredictable in the long run as new short-run phenomena develop. To make even a reasonable guess about what will happen in such markets, you will likely need a psychologist (who can tell you what other people are thinking, what other people think you're thinking, what other people think you think you're thinking, and so on), and perhaps also a psychiatrist to handle the mental marshmallow you might become if you get into international currency markets.

Being an international currency trader isn't for most people. When our students suggest that they'd like to become international currency traders, we suggest they go into a more pleasant, less stressful field—like, say, air traffic control.

Our story has a moral, however. The moral is that in many so-called economic phenomena, noneconomic criteria play a significant role in what happens; in the short run they swamp the long-run economic forces. Economists can predict which types of markets will have these fluctuations (foreign exchange markets are definitely one type), but they can't predict exactly how prices will fluctuate in these markets.

CHAPTER SUMMARY

- The balance of payments is made up of the current account, the capital account, and the official settlements balance.
- Canada is one of the largest debtor nations in the world.
- Exchange rates in a perfectly flexible exchange rate system are determined by the supply of and demand for a currency.
- When a country sets an exchange rate by law, it has a non-convertible currency.
- It is easier technically for a country to bring the value of

- its currency down than it is to support its currency.
- In many so-called economic phenomena, noneconomic criteria play a significant role in what happens.
- Often, in the short run, a rise in a country's exchange rate can increase a balance of payments and balance of trade deficit. In the long run, a rise tends to improve those balances.
- Perfectly flexible, partially flexible, and fixed exchange rates all have advantages and disadvantages.

KEY TERMS

balance of payments *(392)*
Bretton Woods system *(407)*
capital account *(392)*
capital controls *(402)*
current account *(392)*
exchange rate policy *(403)*
fixed exchange rate *(405)*

foreign exchange reserves *(405)*
fundamental analysis *(397)*
gold specie flow mechanism *(406)*
gold standard *(406)*
J-curve *(404)*
merchandise trade balance *(392)*
nonconvertible currency *(396)*

official settlements balance *(392)*
partially flexible exchange rate *(405)*
perfectly flexible exchange rate *(405)*
reserve currency *(408)*
Special Drawing Rights
  (SDRs) *(408)*
spread *(399)*

QUESTIONS FOR THOUGHT AND REVIEW

The number after each question represents the estimated degree of critical thinking required. (1 = almost none; 10 = deep thought.)

1. If a country is running a balance of trade deficit, will its current account be in deficit? Why? *(3)*

2. When someone sends 100 British pounds to a friend in Canada, will this transaction show up on the capital or current account? Why? *(3)*

3. Support the statement: "It is best to offset a capital account surplus with a current account deficit." *(7)*

4. Support the statement: "It is best to offset a capital account deficit with a current account surplus." *(5)*

5. Which is likely to have the larger spread:

South Korean won or Canadian dollars? Why? *(7)*

6. What are the advantages and disadvantages of a nonconvertible currency? *(5)*

7. What is the J-curve and why might its existence provide an argument for a country having a nonconvertible currency? *(6)*

8. Explain how an international financial adjustment would occur under a gold standard. *(6)*

9. Which is preferable: a fixed or a flexible exchange rate? Why? *(7)*

10. Explain how high interest rates in Germany placed downward pressure on other EU countries' currencies and ended the European fixed exchange rate system. *(8)*

PROBLEMS AND EXERCISES

1. Draw the fundamental analysis of the supply and demand for British pounds sterling in terms of dollars. Show what will happen to the exchange rate with those curves in response to each of the following events:
   a. The U.K. price level rises.
   b. The Canadian price level rises.
   c. The U.K. economy experiences a boom.
   d. The U.K. interest rates rise.

2. At an exchange rate of Rs20 to $1 (Rs is the sign for rupees), Pakistan is exporting 100,000 bales of cotton to Canada at $5 (or Rs100) each. It's importing 60 cars from Canada at $10,000 (Rs200,000) each. Now say that the value of the rupee falls to Rs22 to $1. Pakistan's exports rise to 103,000 bales of cotton while car imports fall to 58.
   a. What has happened to the merchandise trade balance?
   b. What will likely happen in the long run?
   c. What would happen if Pakistani exporters raised their price for cotton so that they were getting the same revenue as before the rupee's fall in value?
   d. How would that response affect what would happen in the long run?

3. Will the following be suppliers or demanders of Canadian dollars in foreign exchange markets?
   a. A Canadian tourist in Latin America.
   b. A German foreign exchange trader who believes that

the Canadian dollar exchange rate will fall.
   c. A Canadian foreign exchange trader who believes that the Canadian dollar exchange rate will fall.
   d. A Costa Rican tourist in Canada.
   e. A Russian capitalist who wants to protect his wealth from expropriation.
   f. A British investor in Canada.

4. You've been hired as an economic advisor to Yamaichi Foreign Exchange Traders. What buy or sell recommendations for Canadian dollars would you make in response to the following news?
   a. Faster economic growth in the EU.
   b. Expectations of higher interest rates in Canada.
   c. Canadian interest rate rises, but less than expected.
   d. Expected loosening of Canadian monetary policy.
   e. Higher inflationary predictions for Canada.

5. State whether the following will show up on the current account or the capital account:
   a. IBM's exports of computers to Japan.
   b. IBM's hiring of a British merchant bank as a consultant.
   c. A foreign national living in Canada repatriates money.
   d. Ford Motor Company's profit in Hungary.
   e. Ford Motor Company uses that Hungarian profit to build a new plant in Hungary.

17

International Dimensions of Monetary and Fiscal Policies

The actual rate of exchange is largely governed by the expected behaviour of the country's monetary authority.

~Dennis Robertson

After reading this chapter, you should be able to:

1 Explain why there is significant debate about what Canadian international goals should be.

2 State why domestic goals sometimes conflict with international goals.

3 Explain the paths through which monetary policy affects exchange rates and the trade balance.

4 Explain the paths through which fiscal policy affects exchange rates and the trade balance.

5 Summarize the reasons why governments try to coordinate their monetary and fiscal policies.

6 State the potential problem of internationalizing a country's debt.

In Canada, it's impossible to talk about macroeconomic policy without talking about international issues. That's what we do in this chapter: We discuss the effect that monetary and fiscal policies have on international macroeconomic goals, plus the effect that certain international phenomena have on domestic macroeconomic goals of low inflation, low unemployment, and high growth.

The discussion in this chapter is not totally new to you. Earlier chapters have introduced you to many international concepts and the last chapter provided you with what you'll need to examine the international dimensions of fiscal and monetary policies. It's time to put those discussions together and consider the issues more carefully. This discussion will provide you with the necessary international base for understanding the macroeconomic policy you'll be reading about in the newspapers.

THE AMBIGUOUS INTERNATIONAL GOALS OF MACROECONOMIC POLICY

Macroeconomics' international goals are less straightforward than its domestic goals. There is general agreement about the domestic goals of macroeconomic policy: We want low inflation, low unemployment, and high growth. There's far less agreement on what a country's international goals should be.

Most economists agree that the international goal of Canadian macroeconomic policy is to maintain Canada's position in the world economy. But there's enormous debate about what achieving that goal means. Do we want a high or a low value of the dollar? Do we want a trade surplus? Or would it be better to have a trade deficit? Or should we not even pay attention to the **trade balance** (the difference between what we export and what we import)? Let's consider the exchange rate goal first.

Trade balance   The difference between a country's exports and its imports.

The Exchange Rate Goal

As we've already seen, an **exchange rate** is the rate at which one country's currency can be traded for another country's currency. We discussed exchange rates at length in the last chapter; for now, let's briefly review the three types of exchange rates that exist. We've covered a lot of this material already, but experience has shown us that some students need to see it again, and again, and . . . .

Fixed and Flexible Exchange Rates   Countries can have fixed exchange rates, flexible exchange rates, or a partially flexible exchange rate. With a **fixed exchange rate,** the exchange rates are set and governments are committed to buying and selling currencies at a fixed rate. With a **flexible exchange rate,** the exchange rate is set by market forces (supply and demand for a country's currency). With a **partially flexible exchange rate,** the government sometimes buys and sells currencies to influence the price directly, and at other times the government simply accepts the exchange rate determined by supply and demand forces. In the 1990s, Canada uses a partially flexible exchange rate.

In this chapter, to keep the analysis at a manageable level, we assume that the country in question has a flexible exchange rate. Thus, it accepts that its exchange rate will be determined by the forces of supply and demand. But that doesn't mean that the country can't indirectly influence the exchange rate through monetary and fiscal policies' effects on the economy and on the supply and demand for dollars. It is that indirect effect that we focus on in this chapter.

Exchange rate   The rate at which one country's currency can be traded for another country's currency.

Fixed exchange rate   An exchange rate established by a government that chooses an exchange rate and offers to buy and sell currencies at that rate.

Flexible exchange rate   An exchange rate the determination of which is left totally up to the market.

Partially flexible exchange rate   Exchange rate where the government sometimes buys and sells currencies to influence the price directly and at other times simply accepts the exchange rate determined by supply and demand forces.

Does Canada Want a High or a Low Value of the Dollar?   There is a debate over whether Canada should have a high or a low value of the dollar. A high value of the dollar makes foreign currencies cheaper, lowering the price of imports. Lowering import prices places competitive pressure on Canadian firms and helps to hold down inflation. All of this benefits Canadian residents' living standard. But a high value of the dollar encourages imports and discourages exports. In doing so, it can cause a trade deficit which can exert a contractionary effect on the economy by decreasing aggregate demand for Canadian output. So a high value of the dollar has a cost to Canadian residents.

A low value of the dollar has the opposite effect. It makes imports more expensive (including both imported raw materials and imported final goods) and exports cheaper, and it can contribute to inflationary pressure. But, by encouraging exports and discouraging imports, it can cause a trade surplus and exert an expansionary effect on the economy.

Thus, depending on the state of the economy, there are arguments for both high and low values of the dollar. Hence there's often a divergence of views about what the exchange rate goal should be. Because of that divergence of views, many economists argue that a country should have no exchange rate policy because exchange rates are market-determined prices that are best left to the market. These economists question whether the government should even worry about the effect of monetary policy and fiscal policy on exchange rates. According to them, government should simply accept whatever exchange rate exists and not consider it in its conduct of monetary and fiscal policies.

1A Exchange rates have conflicting effects and, depending on the state of the economy, there are arguments for both high and low values of the dollar.

The Trade Balance Goal

A deficit in the trade balance means that, as a country, we're consuming more than we're producing. Imports exceed exports, so we're consuming more than we could if we didn't run a deficit. A surplus in the trade balance means that exports exceed imports—we're producing more than we're consuming. Since consuming more than we otherwise could is kind of nice, it might seem that a trade deficit is preferred to a trade surplus.

But wait. A trade deficit isn't without costs, and a trade surplus isn't without benefits. We pay for a trade deficit by selling off Canadian assets to foreigners—by selling Canadian companies, factories, land, and buildings to foreigners, or selling them financial assets such as Canadian dollars, stocks, and bonds. All the future interest and profits on these assets will go to foreigners, not Canadian citizens. That means eventually, some time in the future, we will have to produce more than we consume so we can pay them their profit and interest on *their* assets. Thus, while in the short run a trade deficit allows more current consumption, in the long run it presents problems.

As long as a country can borrow, or sell assets, a country can have a trade deficit. But if a country runs a trade deficit year after year, eventually the long run will arrive and the country will run out of assets to sell and run out of other countries from whom to borrow. When that happens, the trade deficit problem must be faced.

The debate about whether a trade deficit should be of concern to policymakers involves whether these long-run effects should be anticipated and faced before they happen.

Opinions differ greatly. Some say not to worry. We should accept what's happening and not concern ourselves about a trade deficit. These "not-to-worry" economists argue that the trade deficit will end when Canadian citizens don't want to borrow from foreigners any more and foreigners don't want to buy any more of our assets. They argue that the inflow of financial capital (money coming into Canada to buy our assets) from foreigners is financing new investment which will make the Canadian economy strong enough in the long run to reverse the trade deficit without serious disruption to the Canadian economy. So why deal with the trade deficit now when it will take care of itself in the future?

Others argue that, yes, the trade deficit will eventually take care of itself, but the economic distress accompanying the trade deficit taking care of itself will be great. By dealing with the problem now, Canada can avoid a highly unpleasant solution in the future.

Both views are reasonable, which is why there's no consensus on what a country's trade balance goal should be.

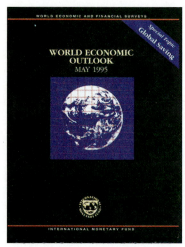

World Economic Outlook—This IMF publication provides useful economic surveys of problems facing the world economy.

1B Running a trade deficit is good in the short run but presents problems in the long run; thus there is debate about whether we should worry about a trade deficit or not.

International versus Domestic Goals

In the real world, when there's debate about a goal, that goal generally gets far less weight than goals about which there's general agreement. Since there's general agreement about our country's domestic goals (low inflation, low unemployment, and high growth), domestic goals generally dominate the Canadian political agenda. The problem is that domestic goals sometimes conflict with international goals. While Canada might not want to incur a trade deficit (since it means we're selling off Canadian assets to foreigners), we know it will allow us to enjoy higher levels of consumption than would be the case under a trade surplus. Given that employment and inflation are intricately linked to international trade, it's difficult to separate domestic goals from international goals.

Often a country responds to an international goal only when the international community forces it to do so. For example, when in the 1980s Brazil couldn't borrow any more money from other countries, it reluctantly made resolving its trade deficit a key goal. Similarly, when other countries threatened to limit Japanese imports, Japan took steps to increase the value of the yen and decrease its trade surplus. When a country is forced to face certain economic facts, international goals can become its primary goals. As countries become more economically integrated, these pressures from other countries become more important.

To say that achieving international goals is not the determining factor in the choice of macroeconomic policies isn't to say that economists don't consider the effects of monetary and fiscal policies on international goals. They watch these carefully.

In Canada in the late 1980s and early 1990s, the merchandise trade balance with the rest of the world was positive (we were exporting more merchandise than we were importing) yet our nonmerchandise (services) and investment trade has been in deficit for more than 20 years, leading to a Canadian trade deficit. You can understand Canadian macroeconomic policy during that period only after you look at how international factors affect the Canadian economy. To follow the debates about macroeconomic policy, you must be familiar with how monetary and fiscal policies affect the exchange rate and the trade balance. Those effects often can significantly influence the choice of policies. We begin by considering the effect of monetary policy.

Monetary policy affects exchange rates in three ways: (1) through its effect on the interest rate, (2) through its effect on income, and (3) through its effect on price levels and inflation.

The Effect on Exchange Rates via Interest Rates

Expansionary monetary policy pushes down the Canadian interest rate, which decreases the financial capital inflow into Canada, decreasing the demand for dollars, pushing down the value of the dollar, and raising the exchange rate via the interest rate path (remember our previous definition of the exchange rate—how much domestic currency it takes to buy a unit of the foreign currency). Contractionary monetary policy does the opposite. It raises the interest rate, which tends to bring in financial capital flows from abroad, increasing the demand for dollars, increasing the value of the dollar, and reducing the exchange rate.

To see why these effects take place, consider a person in Japan in the late 1980s, when the Japanese interest rate was about 2 or 3 percent. He or she reasoned, "Why should I earn only 2 or 3 percent return in Japan? I'll save (buy some financial assets) in Canada where I'll earn 8 percent." If the Canadian interest rate goes up due to contraction in the money supply, other things equal, the advantage of holding one's financial assets in Canada will become even greater and more people will want to save here. People in Japan hold yen, not dollars, so in order to save in Canada they must buy dollars. Thus, a rise in Canadian interest rates increases demand for dollars and, in terms of yen, pushes the Canadian exchange rate down (remember the exchange rate tells you how many Canadian dollars it takes to buy foreign currency, so if the dollar gains value, the exchange rate falls).

It's important to recognize that it's the relative interest rate that governs the flow

2 Domestic goals are hard to distinguish from international goals because trade plays such an important role in the Canadian economy.

THE EFFECTS OF MONETARY AND FISCAL POLICIES ON INTERNATIONAL GOALS

Monetary Policy's Effect on Exchange Rates

of financial capital. In the early 1990s, Japan tightened its money supply, raising interest rates there to 6 percent. This relative increase in the Japanese interest rate decreased the demand for dollars and thus raised the Canadian exchange rate.

Another example of how important relative international interest rates are involves Germany and the European Union (EU). In 1992, the EU was heading toward a monetary union in which all member countries would use a common currency. As a stepping stone, the EU countries had exchange rates set within a narrow band. Because of fiscal problems caused by German reunification, the German central bank, the Bundesbank, felt it had to raise its interest rates. That rise put upward pressure on the mark, and destroyed the fixed exchange rate system and the upcoming monetary union. Many economists are willing to say that relative interest rates, because of their importance in the short run, are *the primary* short-run determinant of exchange rates.

The Effect on Exchange Rates via Income   Monetary policy also affects income in a country. As the money supply rises, income expands; when the money supply falls, income contracts.[1] This effect on income provides another way the money supply affects the exchange rate. As we saw earlier, when income rises, imports rise while exports are unaffected. To buy foreign products, Canadian citizens need foreign currency which they must buy with dollars. So when Canadian imports rise, the supply of dollars to the foreign exchange market increases as Canadian citizens sell dollars to buy foreign currencies to pay for those imports. This raises the dollar exchange rate (the dollar loses value). This effect through income and imports provides a second path through which monetary policy affects the exchange rate: Expansionary monetary policy causes Canadian income to rise, imports to rise, and the Canadian exchange rate to rise via the income path. Contractionary monetary policy causes Canadian income to fall, imports to fall, and the Canadian exchange rate to fall via the income path.

The Effect on Exchange Rates via Price Levels   A third way in which monetary policy can affect exchange rates is through its effect on prices in a country. Expansionary monetary policy pushes the Canadian price level up. As the Canadian price level rises relative to foreign prices, Canadian exports become more expensive, decreasing Canadian competitiveness, and goods Canada imports become cheaper. This increases demand for foreign currencies and decreases demand for dollars. Thus, via the price path, expansionary monetary policy pushes down the dollar's value for the same reason that an expansion in income pushes it down.

Contractionary monetary policy puts downward pressure on the Canadian price level and slows down any existing inflation. This tends to decrease the Canadian price level relative to foreign prices, making Canadian exports more competitive and the goods Canada imports more expensive. Thus, contractionary policy pushes the value of the dollar up via the price path.

The Net Effect of Monetary Policy on Exchange Rates   Notice that all these effects of monetary policy on exchange rates are in the same direction. Expansionary monetary policy pushes a country's exchange rate up; contractionary monetary policy pushes a country's exchange rate down. Summarizing these effects, we have the following relationships for expansionary and contractionary monetary policy:

---

[1] When there's inflation, it's the rate of money supply growth relative to the rate of inflation that's important. If inflation is 10 percent and money supply growth is 10 percent, the rate of increase in the real money supply is zero. If money supply growth falls to, say, 5 percent while inflation stays at 10 percent, there will be a contractionary effect on the real economy.

Expansionary policy

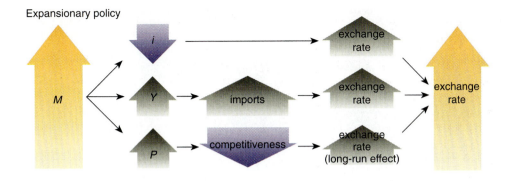

Contractionary policy

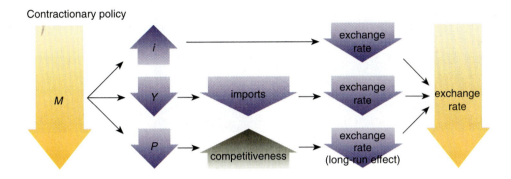

There are, of course, many provisos to the relationship between monetary policy and the exchange rate. For example, as the price of imports goes up, there is some inflationary pressure from that rise in price and hence some pressure for the price level to rise as well as fall. Monetary policy affects exchange rates in subtle ways, but if an economist had to give a quick answer to what effect monetary policy would have on exchange rates it would be:

Expansionary monetary policy raises exchange rates. It decreases the relative value of a country's currency.

Contractionary monetary policy reduces exchange rates. It increases the relative value of a country's currency.

3A Monetary policy affects exchange rates through the interest rate path, the income path, and the price path.

When a country's international trade balance is negative (in deficit), the country is importing more than it is exporting. When a country's international trade balance is positive, the country is exporting more than it is importing.

Monetary policy affects the trade balance in three ways: through income, through the price level, and through the exchange rate.

Monetary Policy's Effect on the Trade Balance

The Effect on the Trade Balance via Income Expansionary monetary policy increases income. When income rises, imports rise, while exports are unaffected. As imports rise, the trade balance shifts in the direction of deficit. So, via the income path, expansionary monetary policy shifts the trade balance toward a deficit.

Contractionary policy works in the opposite direction. It decreases income. When income falls, imports fall, while exports are unaffected, so the trade balance shifts in the direction of surplus. Thus, via the income path, expansionary monetary policy increases a trade deficit; contractionary monetary policy decreases a trade deficit.

The Effect on the Trade Balance via Price Levels A second way monetary policy affects the trade balance is through its effect on a country's price level. Expansionary monetary

For international trade to take place, currencies must be convertible into other currencies. Here we see a Japanese currency trader taking bids on buying and selling currencies. *Fujifotos/The Image Works.*

policy pushes a country's price level up. This decreases its competitiveness and increases a trade deficit. So, via the price path, expansionary monetary policy increases a trade deficit (the trade balance falls).

Contractionary monetary policy works in the opposite direction. It tends to push a country's price level down; this fall makes exports more competitive and imports less competitive. Both these effects tend to decrease a trade deficit. So, via the price path, contractionary monetary policy decreases a trade deficit (the trade balance rises).

Monetary policy's effect on the price level is a long-run, not a short-run, effect. It often takes a year for changes in the money supply to affect prices, and another year or two for changes in prices to affect imports and exports. Thus, the price path is a long-run effect. Price level changes don't significantly affect the trade balance in the short run.

The Effect on the Trade Balance via Exchange Rates

A third path through which expansionary monetary policy influences the trade balance is the exchange rate. Expansionary monetary policy decreases the interest rate which tends to push the dollar exchange rate up, increasing Canadian competitiveness. This decreases a trade deficit and hence works in a direction opposite to the effects of income changes and price level changes on the trade balance. Like the price effect, the exchange rate path on the trade balance is a long-run effect. This path doesn't have a significant effect in the short run.

Contractionary monetary policy works in the opposite direction. It reduces the exchange rate, increasing the relative price of Canadian exports and lowering the relative price of imports into Canada. Both effects tend to increase a trade deficit (the trade balance falls).

The Net Effect of Monetary Policy on the Trade Balance

Since the effects are not all in the same direction, talking about the net effect of monetary policy on the trade balance is a bit more ambiguous than talking about its net effect on a country's exchange rate. However, only one of these paths—the income path—is a short-run effect. Thus, in the short run the net effect of monetary policy is relatively clear: Expansionary monetary policy tends to increase a trade deficit; contractionary monetary policy tends to decrease it. Since, in the long run, the price path effect and the exchange rate effect tend to offset each other, the short-run effects of monetary policy through the income path often carry over to the long-run effect.

Summarizing these three relationships, we have the following relationships for expansionary and contractionary monetary policy:

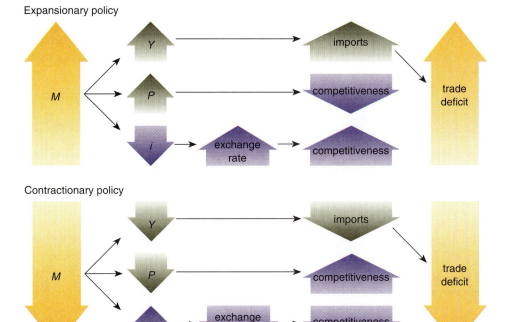

While many complications can enter the trade balance picture, most economists would summarize monetary policy's short-run effect on the trade balance as follows:

3B Monetary policy affects the trade deficit through the income path, the price-level path, and the exchange rate path.

Expansionary monetary policy makes a trade deficit larger.

Contractionary monetary policy makes a trade deficit smaller.

Now we'll consider fiscal policy's effect on exchange rates. Fiscal policy, like monetary policy, affects exchange rates via three paths: via income, via price, and via interest rates. Let's begin with its effect through income.

Fiscal Policy's Effect on Exchange Rates

The Effect on Exchange Rates via Income Expansionary fiscal policy expands income and therefore increases imports, increasing a trade deficit and raising the exchange rate. Contractionary fiscal policy contracts income, thereby decreasing imports and reducing the exchange rate. These effects of expansionary and contractionary fiscal policies via the income path are similar to the effects of monetary policy, so if it's not intuitively clear to you why the effect is what it is, it may be worthwhile to review the slightly more complete discussion of monetary policy's effect presented previously.

The Effect on Exchange Rates via Prices Let's turn to the effect of fiscal policy on exchange rates through prices. Expansionary fiscal policy increases aggregate demand and increases prices of a country's exports; hence it decreases the competitiveness of a country's exports, which pushes the exchange rate up. Contractionary fiscal policy works in the opposite direction. These are the same effects that monetary policy had. And, as was the case with monetary policy, the price path is a long-run, not a short-run, effect.

The Effect on Exchange Rates via Interest Rates Fiscal policy's effect on the exchange rate via the interest rate path is different from monetary policy's effect. Let's first consider the effect of expansionary fiscal policy. Whereas expansionary monetary policy lowers the interest rate, expansionary fiscal policy raises interest rates because the government sells bonds to finance that deficit. The higher interest rate causes foreign capital to flow into Canada, which pushes down the Canadian dollar exchange rate. Therefore expansionary fiscal policy's effect on exchange rates via the interest rate effect is to push a country's exchange rate down (the dollar gains value).

Contractionary fiscal policy decreases interest rates since it means that the number of bonds that must be sold to finance a deficit decreases. Lower Canadian interest rates cause capital to flow out of Canada, which pushes the Canadian dollar exchange rate up.

4A Fiscal policy affects exchange rates through the income path, the interest rate path, and the exchange rate path.

The Net Effect of Fiscal Policy on Exchange Rates Of these three effects, the interest rate effect and the income effect are both short-run effects. These two work in opposite directions to each other, so the net effect of expansionary fiscal policy on the exchange rate is ambiguous (although most economists would probably agree that the net effect is likely to lead to an appreciation of the domestic currency). Let's summarize these three effects.

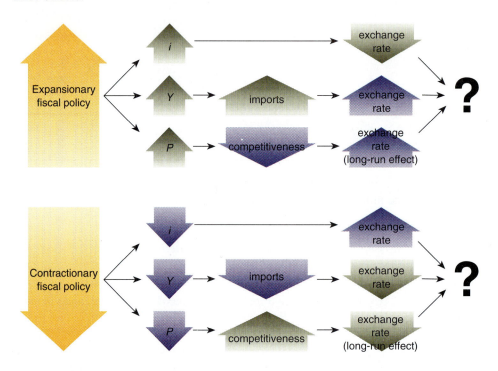

Fiscal Policy's Effect on the Trade Deficit

Fiscal policy works on the trade deficit primarily through its effects on income and prices. (Since fiscal policy's effect on the exchange rate is unclear, there is no need to consider its effect through exchange rates.)

The Effect on the Trade Deficit via Income Let's begin by looking at the income path. As with expansionary monetary policy, expansionary fiscal policy increases income. This higher income increases imports, which increases the size of the trade deficit.

Contractionary fiscal policy decreases income and decreases imports. Hence it decreases the size of a trade deficit. These are the same effects as those of monetary policy.

The Effect on the Trade Deficit via Prices The effect via the price route is also similar to effects of monetary policy. Expansionary fiscal policy pushes up the price level, increasing the price of a country's exports and decreasing its competitiveness. Hence it increases the trade deficit.

Contractionary fiscal policy pushes down the price level, decreasing the price of a country's exports, increasing its competitiveness, and decreasing the trade deficit. This effect via price is a long-run effect, as it is with monetary policy.

The Net Effect of Fiscal Policy on the Trade Deficit   Since these two effects work in the same direction, fiscal policy's net effect on the trade balance is clear:

Expansionary fiscal policy increases a trade deficit.

Contractionary fiscal policy decreases a trade deficit.

Summarizing these two effects schematically, we have:

4B   Fiscal policy affects the trade balance through the income path and the price path.

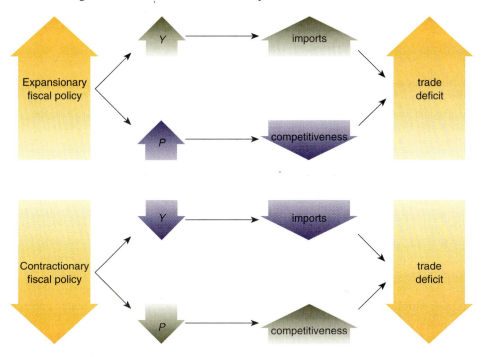

Exhibit 1 summarizes the primary net short-run effects of both expansionary monetary and fiscal policies on international goals. (The effects of contractionary policy work in the opposite direction.)

So far, we've focused on the effect of monetary and fiscal policies on international goals. But often the effect is the other way around: International phenomena change and have significant influences on the domestic economy and on the ability to achieve domestic goals.

In the example, say that Japan ran contractionary monetary policy. That would raise the value of the yen and increase the Japanese trade surplus, which means it would decrease the value of the Canadian dollar and increase the Canadian trade deficit, both of which would affect Canadian domestic goals. Japan's actions would also affect the U.S. economy, and there would be further repercussion effects through our trade links with the United States. We saw this in late 1993 and 1994 when the United States and Japan couldn't agree on how to coordinate their policies to allow greater U.S. access to the Japanese market. International pressures led to a fall in the value of the U.S. dollar, and given our close ties to the United States, the Canadian dollar lost value in tandem. The monetary and fiscal policies of other countries can have significant effects on the Canadian domestic economy. This has led to significant pressure for countries to coordinate their economic policies—but that's easier said than done.

Unless forced to do so because of international pressures, most countries don't let international goals guide their macroeconomic policy. But for every effect that monetary and fiscal policies have on a country's exchange rates and trade balance, there's an equal and opposite effect on the combination of other countries' exchange rates and

INTERNATIONAL PHENOMENA AND DOMESTIC GOALS

5   Governments try to coordinate their monetary and fiscal policies because their economies are interdependent.

International Monetary and Fiscal Coordination

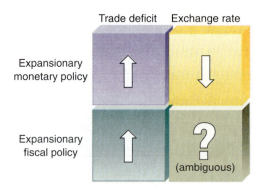

EXHIBIT 1   The Effect of Expansionary Monetary and Fiscal Policy on International Goals

In the short run, expansionary monetary policy tends to increase a trade deficit and decrease the exchange rate. Expansionary fiscal policy tends to increase the trade deficit. Its effect on the exchange rate is ambiguous.

trade balances. When one country's exchange rate goes up, by definition another country's exchange rate must go down. Similarly, when one country's balance of trade is in surplus, another's must be in deficit. This interconnection means that other countries' fiscal and monetary policies affect Canada, while Canadian fiscal and monetary policies affect other countries, so pressure to coordinate policies is considerable.

Because of this interdependence, many economists argue that all countries must work together to coordinate their monetary and fiscal policies. For example, if Japan has a trade surplus and the United States has a trade deficit, the United States can run contractionary monetary policy or Japan can use expansionary monetary policy to help expand U.S. exports to Japan and thereby reduce the U.S. trade deficit. Why would Japan do something like that? Because, if it doesn't, the United States might threaten to directly limit Japanese exports to the United States through trade sanctions. So Japan must take U.S. desires into account in conducting its monetary and fiscal policies.

Coordination Is a Two-Way Street

Coordination, of course, works both ways. If other countries are to take the Canadian economy's needs into account, Canada must take other countries' needs into account in determining its goals. Say, for example, the Canadian economy is going into a recession. This domestic problem calls for expansionary monetary policy. But expansionary monetary policy will increase Canadian income and Canadian imports and lower the value of the dollar. Say that, internationally, Canada has agreed that it must work toward eliminating a Canadian trade deficit in the short run. Does it forsake its domestic goals? Or does it forsake its international commitment?

There's no one right answer to those questions. It depends on political judgements (how long until the next election?), judgements about what foreign countries can do if Canada doesn't meet its international commitments, and similar judgements by foreign countries about Canada. The result is lots of international economic parleys (generally in rather pleasant surroundings) to discuss these issues. Nicely worded communiques are issued which say, in effect, that each country will do what's best for the world economy as long as it's also best for itself.

Crowding Out and International Considerations

6   While internationalizing a country's debt may help in the short run, in the long run it presents potential problems, since foreign ownership of a country's debts means the country must pay interest to those foreign countries. And, don't forget, one day that debt will come due.

As a final topic in this chapter, let's reconsider the issue of *crowding out* that we considered in an earlier chapter, only this time we'll take into account international considerations. Say a government is running a budget deficit, and that the central bank has decided it won't accommodate the deficit. This happened in the 1980s with the Bank of Canada and the federal government. What will be the result?

The basic idea of crowding out is that the budget deficit will cause the interest rate to go up. But wait. There's another way to avoid the crowding out that results from financing the deficit: Foreigners could buy the debt at the existing interest rate. This

The world has become much more inter-dependent in recent years. In this picture you see cars made in Germany being unloaded for sale in North America. © *David Wells/The Image Works.*

is called *internationalizing the debt,* and is what has been happening to the Canadian economy now for some time.

In the past twenty years, there were massive inflows of financial capital from abroad. These inflows held down the Canadian interest rate even as the federal government ran large budget deficits. Thus, those large deficits didn't push up interest rates too much because foreigners, not Canadian citizens, were buying Canadian debt.

But, as we discussed, internationalization of the Canadian debt is not costless. While it helps in the short run, it presents problems in the long run. Foreign ownership of Canadian debt means that Canada must pay foreigners interest each year on that debt. To do so, Canada must export more than it imports, which means that Canada must consume less than it produces at some time in the future to pay for the trade deficits it's running now.

In addition, foreign borrowing can cause problems for exchange rate and interest rate management. If foreigners become concerned about domestic political or economic stability, they will be much less willing to invest in the country. To assuage their fears, the central bank will be forced to allow interest rates to rise—by an amount we can call a risk premium—to attract foreign investors. This can lead to destabilizing financial speculation, further exacerbating the difficulties facing domestic policy-makers.

As you can see, the issues become complicated quickly.

Despite the complications, the above discussion gives you an understanding of many of the events that may have previously seemed incomprehensible. To show you the relevance of what we have said above about crowding out and international considerations, let's look at two situations that occurred in the early 1990s.

The first concerned Germany and the EU (discussed above). For political reasons, Germany was running loose fiscal policy. Fearing inflation from this loose fiscal policy, the Bundesbank ran tight monetary policy, forcing both the German interest rate and the German exchange rate up. This disrupted the movement toward a European Monetary System and a common European currency—the ECU—as other European countries refused to go along. Here we see domestic goals superseding international goals.

The second concerns Japan in 1993 and 1994. Japan was experiencing a recession, in part because its tight monetary policy had pushed up interest rates and hence pushed up the exchange rate for the year. Other countries, especially the United States and European countries, put enormous pressure on Japan to run expansionary fiscal policy which would keep the relative value of the yen high, but simultaneously increase Japanese income, and hence Japanese demand for imports.

There are many more examples, but these two should give you a good sense of the relevance of the issues.

CONCLUSION: SELECTING POLICIES TO ACHIEVE GOALS

Throughout this chapter we have organized the discussion around policies. Another way to organize the discussion would have been around goals, and to show how alternative policies will achieve those international goals.

The following table does this, and will serve as a useful review of the chapter.

International Goal	Policy Alternatives
Lower exchange rate	Contractionary foreign monetary policy Expansionary domestic monetary policy Contractionary domestic fiscal policy Expansionary foreign fiscal policy
Lower trade deficit	Contractionary domestic fiscal policy Expansionary foreign fiscal policy Contractionary domestic monetary policy Expansionary foreign monetary policy

EXHIBIT 2   **Selecting Policies to Achieve Goals**

You can see in the table why coordination of monetary and fiscal policies is much in the news, since a foreign country's policy can eliminate or reduce the need for domestic policy.

This brief chapter in no way exhausted the international topics. Countries use many policies in pursuit of their international goals. But this chapter has, we hope, made you very aware of the international dimensions of our economic goals, and of how monetary and fiscal policies affect those goals. That awareness is necessary to discuss the real-world macroeconomic policies that we turn to in the next chapters.

CHAPTER SUMMARY

- The international goals of a country are often in dispute.
- Domestic goals are difficult to separate from international goals; countries often respond to an international goal when forced to do so by other countries.
- Expansionary monetary policy tends to raise a country's exchange rate and increase its trade deficit.
- Contractionary fiscal policy has an ambiguous effect on a country's exchange rate but tends to decrease its trade deficit.

- For every effect that monetary and fiscal policies have on a country's exchange rate and trade balance, there is an equal and opposite effect on the combination of foreign countries' exchange rates and trade balances.
- International capital inflows can reduce crowding out.
- Internationalizing a country's debt means that at some time in the future the country must consume less than it produces.

KEY TERMS

exchange rate   *(415)*
fixed exchange rate   *(415)*

flexible exchange rate   *(415)*
partially flexible exchange rate   *(415)*

trade balance   *(415)*

The following are three replacement diagrams for MACROECONOMICS, First Canadian Edition, By Colander and Sephton.

We apologize for the inconvenience.

1. Please refer to Exhibit 4 on page 194.

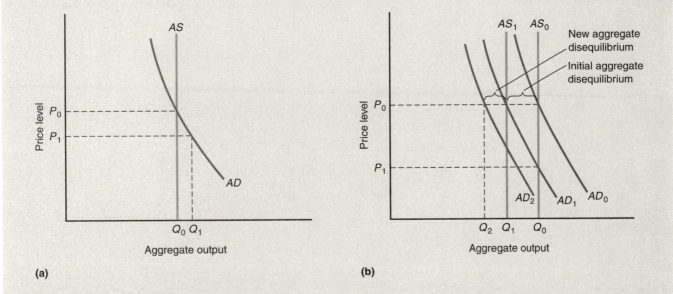

(a)

(b)

EXHIBIT 4

The *AD* curve shown in (a) tells us how much additional quantity will be forthcoming if there is a fall in the price level, other things, including the supply of output, constant. It tells us that if the price level fell from P_0 to P_1 the quantity of output demanded would increase from Q_0 to Q_1. The *AS* curve shown in (a) is a curve that tells us how much less quantity will be supplied if there is a fall in the price level. It is generally considered to be either upward sloping (if nominal wages are fixed) or perfectly vertical (if nominal wages change proportionately with prices). Throughout the chapter, we assume wages change proportionately with prices, which is why we draw the *AS* curve perfectly vertical.

In (b) we show the reasoning why the *AS/AD* analysis involving interdependencies between aggregate supply and aggregate demand is more complicated than micro supply and demand analysis. When the *AD* curve shifts (say from AD_0 to AD_1) unless there is instantaneous price level adjustment, the *AS* curve will shift in response to a shift in the *AD* curve (say, from AS_0 to AS_1). But, when the *AS* curve shifts, there will be further shift in the *AD* curve (say, from AD_1 to AD_2). After both of these shifts there is still a disequilibrium of Q_2 to Q_1. The existence of this interdependence means that the shapes of the curves alone do not determine the new equilibrium. The nature of these interdependent shifts—the dynamic interdependencies—must be specified before one can decide where the new equilibrium will be.

2. Please refer to Exhibit 1 on page 424.

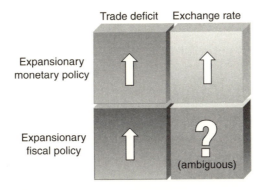

EXHIBIT 1   The Effect of Expansionary Monetary and Fiscal Policy on International Goals

In the short run, expansionary monetary policy tends to increase a trade deficit and increase the exchange rate. Expansionary fiscal policy tends to increase the trade deficit. Its effect on the exchange rate is ambiguous.

3. Please refer to Exhibit 2 on page 426.

International Goal	Policy Alternatives
Higher exchange rate	Contractionary foreign monetary policy Expansionary domestic monetary policy Contractionary domestic fiscal policy Expansionary foreign fiscal policy
Lower trade deficit	Contractionary domestic fiscal policy Expansionary foreign fiscal policy Contractionary domestic monetary policy Expansionary foreign monetary policy

EXHIBIT 2   Selecting Policies to Achieve Goals

Please make the following corrections in your text as well:

- page 54   - in boxed diagram, "historeses" should read "hysteresis".

- page 247   - in diagram (b) the label should read "AS/AD".

- page 150   - diagram label (a) should read "1870-1994", and diagram label (b) should read "1871-1994".

QUESTIONS FOR THOUGHT AND REVIEW

The number after each question represents the estimated degree of critical thinking required. (1 = almost none; 10 = deep thought.)

1. Look up the current Canadian exchange rate relative to the yen. Would you suggest raising it or lowering it? Why? *(7)*

2. Look up the current Canadian trade balance. Would you suggest raising it or lowering it? Why? *(7)*

3. What effect on the Canadian trade deficit and exchange rate would result if Japan ran an expansionary monetary policy? *(4)*

4. What would be the effect on the Canadian trade deficit and the Canadian exchange rate if Japan ran a contractionary fiscal policy? *(4)*

5. If modern Classicals are correct and expansionary monetary policy immediately increases inflationary expecta-

tions and the price level, how might the effect of monetary policy on the exchange rate be different than that presented in this chapter? *(9)*

6. What effect will a combination of expansionary fiscal policy and contractionary monetary policy have on the exchange rate? *(5)*

7. How would a Classical economist differ from a Keynesian economist in their policies for dealing with an oil price shock? Why? *(8)*

8. If Canada were to complain of Japan's use of an export-led growth policy, would Canada be justified? Why? *(8)*

9. What effect would you expect a fall in the price of oil to have on the economy? Why? *(6)*

10. How is the Bundesbank's running a tight monetary policy in the early 1990s an example of domestic goals superseding international goals? *(0)*

PROBLEMS AND EXERCISES

1. Draw the schematics to show the effect of contractionary fiscal policy on exchange rates.

2. Draw the schematics to show the effect of expansionary monetary policy on the trade deficit.

3. You observe that over the past decade a country's competitiveness has been continually eroded and its trade deficit has risen.

   a. What monetary or fiscal policies might have led to such results? Why?

   b. You also observe that interest rates have steadily risen along with a fall in the exchange rate. What policies would lead to this result?

   c. What policy might you suggest to improve the country's competitiveness? Explain how that policy might work.

4. Congratulations! You have been appointed an adviser to the IMF. A country that has run trade deficits for many years now has difficulty servicing the accumulated international debt and wants to borrow from the IMF to meet its obligations. The IMF requires that the country set a target trade surplus.

   a. What monetary and fiscal policies would you suggest the IMF require?

   b. What would be the likely effect of that plan on domestic inflation and growth?

   c. How do you think the country's government will respond to your proposals? Why?

5. Congratulations! You've been hired as an economic advisor to Textland, a country that has perfectly flexible exchange rates. State what monetary and fiscal policy you might suggest in each of the following situations, and explain why you would suggest those policies.

   a. You want to lower the interest rate, decrease inflationary pressures, and lower the trade deficit.

   b. You want to lower the interest rate, decrease inflationary pressures, and lower a trade surplus.

   c. You want to lower the interest rate, decrease unemployment, and lower the trade deficit.

   d. You want to raise the interest rate, decrease unemployment, and lower the trade deficit.

18

Deficits and Debt

*Any government, like any family, can for a year spend a little more
than it earns. But you and I know that a continuance of that habit
means the poorhouse.*

~Franklin D. Roosevelt

After reading this chapter, you should be able to:

1 Define the terms deficit and debt.

2 Explain why, in an expanding economy, a government can run a
limited, but continual, deficit without serious concern about the
consequences.

3 Define opportunity cost, and explain its relationship to economic reasoning.

4 Differentiate between a real deficit and a nominal deficit.

5 Explain why, even though the real federal budget deficit of
Canada is much lower than the nominal federal deficit, there is
still reason for concern about deficits across all levels of government in Canada.

6 Explain how internally held debt differs from externally held
debt.

7 Explain why there are alternative reasonable views about the
deficit.

In our discussion of macroeconomic policies and problems, two concepts come up continually: deficits and debt. Is the Canadian budget deficit something we have to worry about? Is the $550+ billion federal government debt going to be an unbearable burden on our grandchildren? These and similar questions are sufficiently important to warrant a separate chapter that explores the government budget deficit and debt.

Before we begin the exploration, let's briefly consider the definitions. A **deficit** is a shortfall of revenues under payments; it is a flow concept. If your income (revenues) is $20,000 per year and your expenditures (payments) are $30,000 per year, you are running a deficit. If revenues exceed payments, you are running a surplus. This means that a *government budget deficit* occurs when government expenditures exceed government revenues.

Debt is accumulated deficits minus accumulated surpluses; it is a stock concept. For example, say you've spent $30,000 a year for 10 years and have had annual income of $20,000 for 10 years. So you've had a deficit of $10,000 per year. At the end of 10 years, you will have accumulated a debt of $100,000:

$$10 \times \$10,000 = \$100,000.$$

(Spending more than you have in income means that you need to borrow the extra $10,000 per year from someone, so in later years much of your expenditure will be on interest on your previous debt.)

Let's begin with a consideration of the historical record of deficits in Canada. Exhibit 1 (a) graphs the Canadian budget balance since 1950. As you can see, for many years the Canadian budget has been significantly in deficit. But that hasn't always been the case. Before the 1950s, the Canadian government ran a budget surplus sometimes (mainly in peacetime) and a budget deficit at other times (mainly during wartime). After World War II—that is, after 1945—that changed, and since the mid-1960s Canada has run consistent deficits (with the exception of a tiny surplus in 1969–70).

Because debt is accumulated deficits, and Canada has had a deficit almost every year since the mid-1960s, you would expect Canada's debt to have increased substantially in the last 30 years. Exhibit 1 (b) shows that is indeed the case.

Why was there a change in the late 1960s and early 1970s? A reason many economists suggest is the change in social programs that took place at that time. In 1965 the Canada and Quebec Pension Plans were introduced, followed by Medicare and the Canada Assistance Plan in 1966. Changes to Unemployment Insurance followed in 1971—leading to radical changes in government spending. Tax revenues didn't rise sufficiently to cover spending, and the deficit went from $294 million in 1966–67 to well over $30 billion in 1993–94.

Other economists point to the inflation resulting from the energy crisis of the early 1970s as the main culprit. As we'll see shortly, inflation affects the way we measure debt and deficits. When oil prices and inflation started to rise significantly in 1973, the federal government indexed the tax system to eliminated **bracket creep**—the process of moving to higher and higher tax brackets as a result of inflationary increases in income. What this meant was that *nominal,* but not *real,* incomes rose as a result of inflation. When the federal government raised the income levels associated with different rates of taxation, they gave up the revenues those higher levels of income would have generated. In conjunction with the facts that (1) the government indexed its expenditures to rise with inflation, and (2) higher inflation led to higher nominal interest rates and thereby a higher cost of servicing the debt, many economists argue it's little wonder that deficits and debt are so high.

To see an example of bracket creep, consider three tax brackets: 15 percent for incomes below $20,000, 20 percent for incomes between $20,000 and $30,000, and 25 percent for incomes above $30,000. If you made $25,000 in one year, you'd pay 20 percent in income taxes. If in the second year there was 100 percent inflation and your income was indexed for inflation, you should have made $50,000 that year. But, this level of income puts you into the 25 percent tax bracket. That means the propor-

1 A deficit is a shortfall of incoming revenue under outgoing payments. A debt is accumulated deficits minus accumulated surpluses.

Deficit   A shortfall per year of incoming revenue under outgoing payments.

Debt   Accumulated deficits minus accumulated surpluses.

CANADIAN GOVERNMENT DEFICITS AND DEBT: THE HISTORICAL RECORD

Policy Regimes, the Deficit, and the Debt

Bracket creep   When an inflationary rise in income pushes you into a higher tax bracket.

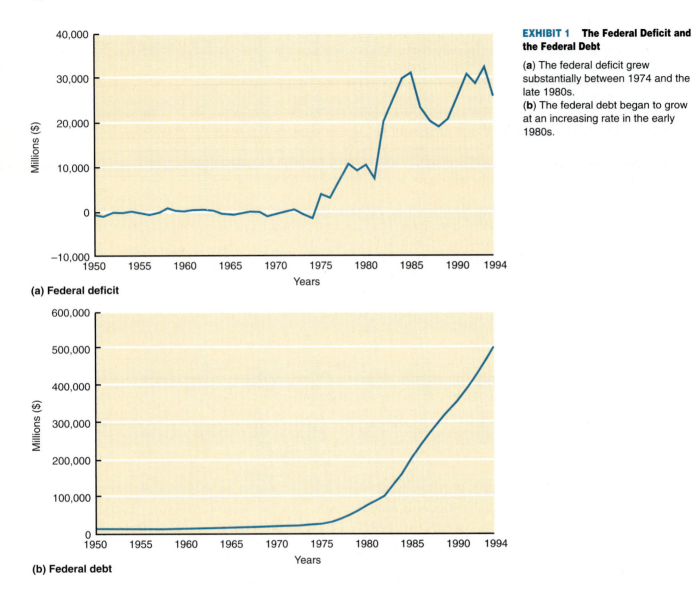

EXHIBIT 1   The Federal Deficit and the Federal Debt

(a) The federal deficit grew substantially between 1974 and the late 1980s.
(b) The federal debt began to grow at an increasing rate in the early 1980s.

(a) Federal deficit

(b) Federal debt

Indexed tax system   One in which the income levels associated with different levels of taxation are allowed to change as a result of inflation.

tion of your income you pay in tax has risen, but only because there was inflation. Many economists and politicians see that as being regressive, so the Liberal government of the day **indexed the tax system**—essentially changing the income levels at each level of taxation. So, continuing with our example, in year two the income tax rates would be 15 percent for incomes below $40,000, 20 percent for incomes between $40,000 and $60,000, and 25 percent for incomes above $60,000. With adjustments to the income thresholds, you'd remain in the 20 percent tax bracket.

Some economists argued that this was a major structural shift in Canadian tax policies that led to increasing deficits and debt. It wasn't until the late 1980s that full indexation of income taxes (and program spending) was abolished.

The introduction of Keynesian economics and its use of discretionary fiscal policy also contributed to deficit expansion. Before World War II, Classical economics dictated that government budget deficits were bad and that, except in wartime, they should be avoided. And that was the policy the Canadian government followed. That was changed by Keynesian economics, which prescribed deficits to stimulate the economy and achieve a higher level of output. According to Keynesian economics, deficits were not necessarily bad. You had to look at the state of the economy to decide whether a deficit was good or bad.

Because Keynesian economics removed the stigma connected with deficits, some economists argue that government budget deficits are the result of Keynesian policies.

Others argue that view is too simplistic. They point out that Keynesian economics never said that all deficits are good—it only said that deficits aren't necessarily bad, and when the economy is in a recession deficits might actually be good.

The argument that Keynesian economics accounts for the deficit is weakened by the fact that, in the 1980s, when there was a second change in policy regimes (Keynesian economics was discarded and replaced with a modern conservative economic policy regime), the deficit did not disappear. In fact, the deficit grew. The modern conservative policy regime has led to an even larger deficit than existed in the Keynesian policy regime.

The modern conservative regime focused on the need for tax cuts whenever they could possibly be implemented. This supply-side Classical focus on tax cuts as the key to economic prosperity with little concern about the deficit is why you are now likely to see role reversals—Keynesians arguing against a deficit and Classicals arguing in favour of government running a deficit!

Politics and the Deficit

The changing view of groups of economists who differ with each other about deficits and debt have had little impact on the lay public's view about deficits and debt. The lay public doesn't like either. In response, politicians say that they too don't like deficits and debt and that they're greatly concerned about the deficit problems.

Some politicians suggested that Parliament adopt a balanced budget rule that would make it impossible for the government to run a deficit. Support for such an amendment grew in the early 1990s as budget deficits surpassed $35 billion. Even economists who support a balanced budget rule agree that the reason for not running a budget deficit is not the immediate economic consequences of a deficit. The reason is political. They believe that a balanced budget requirement would work like a lock on the refrigerator and that the political structure of Canada lacks self-control in spending and hence needs that lock. If you unlock a refrigerator, people without self-control will grow fat. Similarly, without the discipline of a mandatory balanced budget, government and politicians without self-control won't make the hard choices. Instead they'll say, "We can have both CDs and cheeseburgers. We'll pay for them by running a deficit."

Many provincial governments have introduced or are considering introducing balanced budget legislation, but it's too early to tell what effects such legislation might have. For example, New Brunswick adopted a balanced budget rule in 1994–95, Manitoba is set to introduce legislation in 1995–96, and similar shifts in tax and spending policies are already underway in Alberta. In the case of Manitoba, provincial cabinet ministers will face fines if the province runs a deficit: 20 percent of their pay for the first year of a deficit and 40 percent if there is a deficit the following year. While the legislation in Manitoba contains certain exceptions (natural disasters, wars, and a decline in revenues in excess of 5 percent), policymakers have a strong personal incentive to be fiscally responsible.

Judging by events since the 1940s, there's substance to the political argument that most democracies lack self-control in spending and taxing decisions. Most political observers agree that democracy tends to put off difficult decisions. People want lots of goods and services from government, but nobody wants to pay for them with taxes. For them, running a deficit (buy now, pay later) allows democracies to buy current goods and services but delay paying and hence to avoid the hard choices for the present.[1] It will be interesting to see whether the balanced-budget legislation in Manitoba affects self-control. Perhaps the federal government will adopt similar rules. . . .

The problem with annually balancing the budget is that it will actually exacerbate swings in the economy. To see this, consider what would happen if autonomous spending fell—say net exports went down. This would reduce income, and thereby tax rev-

---

[1] The fact that democracy has problems doesn't mean that some other form of government is preferable to democracy. As Winston Churchill said, democracy is the worst form of government, except for all the other forms.

This lithograph, entitled "Legislative assault (on the budget)," appeared in a French newspaper in 1835. *Bleichroeder Print Collection, Baker Library, Harvard Business School.*

enues. The balanced budget rule would require a reduction in government spending, and income would fall again! The same effects would arise when there were expansionary pressures raising income: Taxes would rise and government spending would rise in an attempt to balance the budget, and these effects would further raise income. Balancing the budget over some prespecified time interval won't help moderate fluctuations in economic activity. Balancing the budget over the business cycle would help moderate such fluctuations, but the difficulty is that no two business cycles are the same. The expansions and contractions don't last the same time across different business cycles, so in practice, some kind of time frame is necessary to tie fiscal policy to the balanced budget objective.

ECONOMISTS' WAY OF LOOKING AT DEFICITS AND DEBT

Where do economists come out in the debate about the deficit? On most sides of the issue. But the reasons for their differences are quite unlike the reasons lay people and politicians differ. Why? Because there are a number of technical aspects behind the deficits and debt that most economists understand, and most lay people (and politicians) don't. Thus, to understand economists' views on deficits and debt, you've got to understand these technical aspects behind applying the definitions of "deficits" and "debt." We'll now examine these technical aspects and see how understanding them changes our ideas about problems deficits and debt pose for society.

Arbitrariness in Defining Deficits

The definitions of *deficits* and *debt* are simple, but their simplicity hides important aspects—aspects that will help you understand current debates about deficits and debt. Thus, it's necessary to look carefully at some ambiguities in the definitions. Let's start with deficits.

Deficits are a shortfall of revenues compared to expenditures. So whether you have a deficit depends on what you include as a revenue and what you include as an expenditure. How you make these decisions can make an enormous difference in whether you have a deficit.

For example, consider the problem of a firm with revenues of $8,000 but no expenses except a $10,000 machine expected to last five years. Should the firm charge the $10,000 to this year's expenditures? Should it split the $10,000 evenly among the five years? Or should the firm use some other approach? Which method the firm chooses makes a big difference in whether its current budget will be in surplus or deficit.

This accounting issue is central to the debate about whether we should be concerned about the budget deficit. Say, for example, that government promises to pay an individual $1,000 ten years from now. How should government treat that promise? Since the obligation is incurred now, should government count as an expense now an amount that, if saved, would allow government to pay that $1,000 later? Or should government not count the amount as an expenditure until it actually pays out the money?

The same ambiguity surrounds revenues. For example, say you're holding government bonds valued at $100,000, which pay $10,000 interest per year, while you're spending $10,000 per year. You might think your budget is balanced. But what if the market value of the bonds (the amount you can sell them for) rises from $100,000 to $120,000? Should you count that $20,000 rise in value of the bonds as a revenue? Using an opportunity cost approach that economists use, a person holding bonds should count the rise in the bond's market value as revenue, which means that your income for the year is $30,000, not $10,000. Similarly the government that issued the bond should count the rise in the market value of the bond it issued as an expenditure and count any fall in the market value of a bond it issued as income.[1]

Many such questions must be answered before we can determine whether a budget is in deficit or surplus. Some questions have no right or wrong answer. For others there are right or wrong answers that vary with the question being asked. For still others, an economist's "right way" is an accountant's "wrong way." In short, there are many ways to measure expenditures and receipts so there are many ways to measure deficits.

To say that there are many ways to measure deficits is not to say that all ways are correct. Pretending to have income that you don't have is wrong by all standards. Similarly, inconsistent accounting practices—sometimes to measure an income flow one way and sometimes another—are wrong. Standard accounting practices rule out a number of "creative," but improper, approaches to measuring deficits. But even eliminating these, there remain numerous reasonable ways of defining deficits, which accounts for much of the debate.

The point of the previous discussion is that deficits are simply a summary measure of a budget. As a summary, a deficit figure reduces a complicated set of accounting relationships down to one figure. To understand whether that one summary measure is something to worry about, you've got to understand the accounting procedures used to calculate it. Only then can you make an informed judgement about whether a deficit is something to worry about.

Debt is accumulated deficits. If you spend $1,000 more than you earn for each of three years, you'll end up with a $3,000 debt. (To make things simple, we assume that spending includes paying interest on the debt.)

Debt is also a summary measure of a country's financial situation. As a summary measure, debt has even more problems than deficit. Unlike a deficit (which is the difference between outflows and inflows and hence provides at least a full summary measure), debt by itself is only half of a picture. The other half of the debt picture is assets. For a country, assets include its skilled workforce, its natural resources, its factories, its housing stock, and its holdings of foreign assets. For a government, assets include the buildings and land it owns but, more importantly, it includes a portion of the assets of the people in the country, since government gets a portion of all earnings of those assets in tax revenue.

To get an idea why the addition of assets is necessary to complete the debt picture, consider two governments: one has debt of $3 trillion and assets of $500 trillion; the other has $1 trillion in debt but only $1 trillion in assets. Which is in a better position?

Deficits as a Summary Measure

2   The deficit is simply a summary measure of the financial health of the economy. To understand that summary you must understand the methods that were used to calculate it.

The Need to Judge Debt Relative to Assets

---

[1] Since a fixed-rate bond's price varies inversely with the interest rate in the economy, a rise in the interest rate creates an income for bond issuers and an expense for bondholders. Reviewing the reasons why in relation to the present value formula is a good exercise.

The government with more debt is, because its debt is significantly exceeded by its assets. The example's point is simple: To judge a country's debt, you must view its debt in relation to its assets.

Arbitrariness in Defining Debt

Like income and revenues, assets and debt are subject to varying definitions. Say, for example, that an 18-year-old is due to inherit $1 million at age 21. Should that expected future asset be counted as an asset now? Or say that the government buys an aircraft for $1 billion and discovers that it doesn't fly. What value should the government place on that aircraft? Or say that a country owes $1 billion, due to be paid 10 years from now, but inflation is ongoing at 100 percent per year. The inflation will reduce the value of the debt when it comes due by so much that its current real value will be $1 million—the approximate present value of $1 billion in 10 years with 100 percent inflation. It will be like paying $1 million today. Should the country list the debt as a $1 billion debt or a $1 million debt?

As was the case with income, revenues, and deficits, there's no unique answer to how assets and debts should be valued. So even after you take assets into account, you still have to be careful when deciding whether or not to be concerned about debt.

Difference between Individual and Government Debt

Another important fact about debt is that all debt is not the same. In particular, government debt is different than an individual's debt. There are three reasons for this.

First, government is ongoing. There's no real need for government ever to pay back its debt. An individual's lifespan is limited; when a person dies, there's inevitably an accounting of assets and debt to determine whether anything is left to go to heirs. Before any part of a person's estate is passed on, all debts must be paid. The government, however, doesn't ever have to settle its accounts.

Second, government has an option for paying off a debt that individuals don't have. Specifically, it can pay off a debt by creating money. As long as people will accept a country's currency, a country can always exchange its interest-bearing debt for money (non-interest-bearing debt). By doing so, it pays off its debt.

Internal government debt
Government debt owed to its own citizens.

Third, much of a government debt is **internal government debt** (government debt owed to its own citizens). Paying interest on the debt involves a redistribution among citizens of the country, but it does not involve a net reduction in income of the average citizen. For example, say that a country has a $600 billion debt, all of which is internal debt. Say also that the government pays $30 billion interest on its debt each year. That means the government must collect $30 billion in taxes so people are $30 billion poorer; but it pays out $30 billion in interest to them, so on average, people in the country are neither richer nor poorer because of the debt.[2]

External government debt
Government debt owed to individuals in foreign countries.

External government debt (government debt owed to individuals in foreign countries) is different, being more like an individual's debt. Paying interest on it involves a net reduction in domestic income. Canadian taxpayers will be poorer; foreign holders of Canadian bonds will be richer. Later we'll see that Canadian debt held by foreigners has risen substantially over the last 15 years. The implications for fiscal and monetary policies are significant, as we'll see shortly.

These three differences between government debt and individual debt must be continually kept in mind when considering governments' debt problems.

Deficits, Debt, and Debt Service Relative to GDP

Let's now apply some of these insights. In Exhibits 1 (a) and (b), we saw that Canadian government debt and deficits have been increasing since the mid-1960s. Let's now consider the question from a slightly different perspective, taking into account government's ability to handle debt and deficits. That different perspective is to look at deficits and debt relative to GDP, as in Exhibits 2 (a) and (b). As you can see, relative to GDP, recent federal deficits look much smaller. As a percentage of GDP, deficits haven't shown the same alarming trend as when they're considered in

---

[2] There are, of course, distributional effects. The people who pay the taxes are not necessarily the same people who receive the interest.

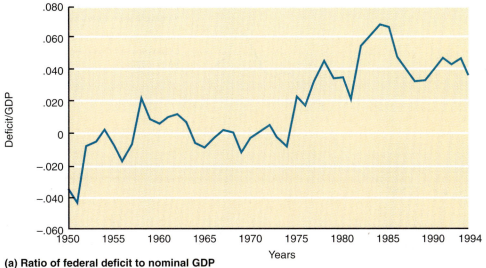

(a) Ratio of federal deficit to nominal GDP

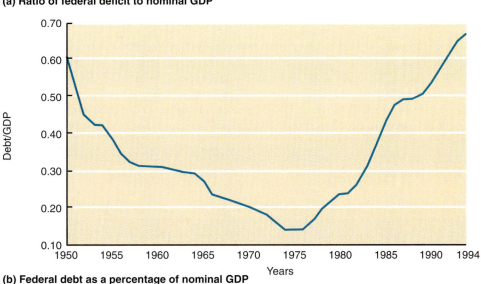

(b) Federal debt as a percentage of nominal GDP

EXHIBIT 2   Debt and Deficit as a Share of GDP

(a) The deficit to GDP ratio jumped up in the early 1970s.
(b) The debt to GDP ratio has risen consistently over the last 20 years.

absolute terms. And it's the same with the federal debt. Relative to GDP, debt has not been continually increasing. Instead, from after World War II to the mid-1970s, the debt/GDP ratio actually decreased. In the mid-1990s it stabilized at somewhat under 70 percent of GDP.

Why measure deficits and debt relative to GDP? Because the ability to pay off a deficit depends upon a nation's productive capacity. Government's ability to bring in revenue depends upon GDP. So GDP serves the same function for government as income does for an individual. It provides a measure of how much debt, and how large a deficit, government can handle.

Considering deficits and debt relative to GDP should ease our concern about the large Canadian deficit and growing Canadian debt. Although the absolute size of the deficits is much larger today than earlier, their relative importance compared to GDP is not. Similarly for debt. Though the debt has been increasing continuously, the problem it presents hasn't necessarily increased.

Considering debt relative to GDP is still not quite sufficient. Economists are also concerned about the interest rate paid on the debt. How much of a burden a given amount of debt imposes depends on the interest rate that must be paid on that debt. The interest rate on debt times the total debt is the **debt service** a country must pay each year. Money spent on debt service cannot be spent on buying new goods and services.

Debt service   The interest rate on debt times the total debt.

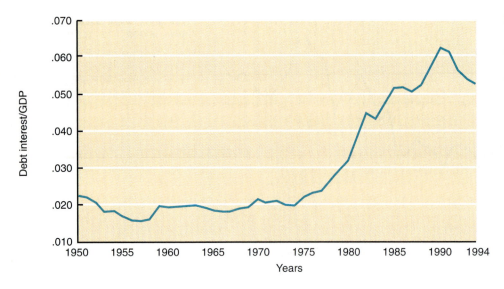

EXHIBIT 3   **Interest Payments on Federal Debt relative to Nominal GDP**

Interest payments on the federal debt were over six percent in the early 1990s.

Over the past 50 years, the interest rate has fluctuated considerably. When it has risen, the debt service has increased; when it has fallen, debt service has decreased. Exhibit 3 shows the federal interest rate payments relative to GDP. As interest rates fell in the early 1990s, the ratio of interest payments on the federal debt to nominal GDP declined to about 5 percent. Thus, this measure of the debt problem suggests that the debt is more of a problem than the debt/GDP measure, but less of a problem than when we simply looked at debt.

Let's now turn to a consideration of how growth in GDP reduces problems posed by deficits and debt service.

Two Ways GDP Growth Reduces Problems Posed by Deficits

GDP can grow either because there's real growth or because there's inflationary growth. Both types of growth play major roles in economists' assessment of deficits. So we must consider how both types of GDP growth affect deficits and debt.

Structural deficit   Proportion of the budget deficit that would exist even if the economy were at its potential level of income.

Structural Deficits, Cycles, and Growth   In our earlier discussion of fiscal policy, we pointed out that the level of income in the economy affected the deficit. As income increases, tax revenue increases and the deficit declines. This means that in a cyclical downturn, the deficit increases, and in a cyclical upturn, the deficit decreases. In talking about the problem of total debt, economists generally focus on the **structural deficit**—the deficit that would remain when the cyclical elements have been netted out (when the economy is at its potential income). In theory, determining the structural deficit is easy to do; in practice, it is difficult since there is significant debate about where potential income is and how much it is increasing from one year to the next. Despite this, in discussing the deficit problem, economists focus on the structural deficit; the cyclical component of the deficit will solve itself.

Real Growth and the Deficit   When a society experiences real growth, it becomes richer, and, being richer, it can handle more debt. Since 1961, real growth in Canada has averaged over 3 percent per year, which means that Canadian debt can grow at a rate of 3 percent without increasing the debt/GDP ratio. But for debt to grow, government must run a deficit, so a constant debt/GDP ratio in a growing economy is consistent with a continual deficit. Of course, for those who believe that total Canadian government debt is already too large relative to GDP, this argument (that the debt/GDP ratio can remain constant) is unsatisfying. They'd prefer the debt/GDP ratio to fall.

Is the current Canadian debt/GDP ratio too high? That's a difficult question. Canada can afford its current debt, in the sense that it can afford to pay the interest on that debt. In fact, it could afford a much higher debt/GDP ratio since Canadian government bonds are still considered one of the safest assets in the world. No one is worried about the Canadian government defaulting. So technically the current debt can be handled, and can probably be increased by billions of dollars without problem.

But, of course, that debt requires interest to be paid on it. In 1994, the Canadian government paid out approximately $39 billion in interest. A larger debt would require even higher interest payments. The $39 billion in interest payment is government revenue that can't be spent on education or welfare; it's a payment for past expenditures. Ultimately the interest payments are the burden of the debt. That's what people mean when they say a deficit is burdening future generations. That burden is the interest payments future generations will have to make to the holders of Canadian debt.[3]

Summarizing: Real growth makes it possible for a country to run a deficit without increasing the debt/GDP ratio. Since that ratio is a key ratio for judging economists' concern about debt, real growth lessens concern about the deficit.

We now turn to inflation's effect on deficits and debt.

Inflation, Debt, and the Real Deficit   Inflation's subtle effect on deficits and debt requires careful consideration. The first key point is that inflation wipes out debt. How much does it wipe out? Consider an example. Say a country has a $500 billion debt and inflation is 4 percent per year. That means that the real value of all assets denominated in dollars is declining by 4 percent each year. If you had $100 and there's 4 percent inflation in a year, that $100 will be worth 4 percent less at the end of the year—the equivalent of $96 had there been no inflation. By the same reasoning, when there's inflation the value of the debt is declining 4 percent each year. Four percent of $500 billion is $20 billion, so with an outstanding debt of $500 billion, 4 percent inflation will eliminate $20 billion of the debt each year.

The larger the debt and the larger the inflation, the more debt will be eliminated with inflation. For example, with 10 percent inflation and a $2 trillion debt, $200 billion of the debt will be eliminated by inflation each year. With 4 percent inflation and a $4 trillion debt, $160 billion of the debt will be eliminated.

If inflation is wiping out debt, and the deficit is equal to the increases in debt from one year to the next, inflation also affects the deficit. Economists take this into account by defining two types of deficits: a nominal deficit and a real deficit.

A **nominal deficit** is the deficit determined by looking at the difference between expenditures and receipts. It's what most people think of when they think of the budget deficit; it is the value that is generally reported.

A **real deficit** is the nominal deficit adjusted for inflation's effect on the debt. It is the nominal deficit *minus* the decrease in the value of the government's total outstanding debts due to inflation. Thus, to calculate the real deficit one must know the nominal deficit, the rate of inflation, and the total outstanding government debt. Let's consider some examples.

In our first example, assume:

$$\text{Nominal deficit} = \$40 \text{ billion}$$
$$\text{Inflation} = 4\%$$
$$\text{Total debt} = \$500 \text{ billion.}$$

The definition of *real deficit* states:

$$\textit{Real deficit} = \textit{Nominal deficit} - (\textit{Inflation} \times \textit{Total debt}).$$

3 Since in a growing economy a continual deficit is consistent with a constant ratio of debt to GDP, and GDP serves as a measure of the government's ability to pay off the debt, a country can run a continual deficit.

4 Real deficit = Nominal deficit − (Inflation × Total debt).

Nominal deficit The deficit determined by looking at the difference between expenditures and receipts.

Real deficit The nominal deficit adjusted for inflation's effect on the debt.

[3] This statement about the burden of the debt doesn't contradict our earlier statement that government's internal debt doesn't directly decrease income in a country. With internal debt, those interest payments are paid to someone in the country. Thus, the burden of the debt isn't the loss of income to society. The burden is the prior commitment of government revenue to paying interest on government bonds. If collecting those tax revenues necessary to pay off bondholders has negative incentive effects and reduces income, then the debt indirectly lowers income in the economy.

Substituting in the numbers gives us:

$$\text{Real deficit} = \$40 \text{ billion} - (4\% \times \$500 \text{ billion})$$
$$= \$40 \text{ billion} - \$20 \text{ billion}$$
$$= \$20 \text{ billion.}$$

Though the nominal deficit is $40 billion, the real deficit is only $20 billion.

In our second example, assume:

$$\text{Nominal deficit} = \$40 \text{ billion}$$
$$\text{Inflation} = 10\%$$
$$\text{Total debt} = \$500 \text{ billion.}$$

The only change from the first example is the inflation rate. But look what happens to the real deficit:

$$\text{Real deficit} = \$40 \text{ billion} - (10\% \times \$500 \text{ billion})$$
$$= \$40 \text{ billion} - \$50 \text{ billion}$$
$$= -\$10 \text{ billion.}$$

In this case, the country is not running a real deficit. After adjusting for inflation, the $40 billion nominal deficit becomes a −$10 billion deficit (a $10 billion real surplus)!

In our third example, assume:

$$\text{Nominal deficit} = \$40 \text{ billion}$$
$$\text{Inflation} = 4\%$$
$$\text{Total debt} = \$1 \text{ trillion.}$$

In this example we've changed both the inflation rate and the amount of total debt. Now see what happens:

$$\text{Real deficit} = \$40 \text{ billion} - (4\% \times \$1 \text{ trillion}) = \$0 \text{ billion.}$$

The $100 billion deficit becomes a balanced budget. As you can see, the real deficit can differ significantly from the nominal deficit.

Inflation, Debt, and Nominal Deficits   This distinction between the nominal deficit and the real deficit is not an illusion. Inflation wipes out debt, and that fact must be considered when evaluating the effect of a deficit. Inflation is an important reason why the Canadian debt/GDP ratio initially declined in the postwar period. When inflation increases, the debt/GDP ratio can decrease even when the nominal deficit is large.

You may be somewhat hesitant to accept the preceding argument about how inflation eliminates debt and can change a nominal deficit into a real surplus. The first time we were presented with the argument, we were dubious. Somehow, inflation as a way of reducing debt's burden sounds too good to be true. If you are hesitant, it's with good reason. While the argument that inflation wipes out debt is correct, your fears are not groundless. Inflation is not a costless answer to eliminating debt.

To see that it isn't, let's carefully consider how inflation eliminates the debt. Say you bought Canadian bonds having a 4 percent annual interest rate with the expectation that the price level would remain constant. That's not a bad return; in each year you expect $4 for each $100 you loaned the government, and as each bond matures you expect to get $100 back. Now let's say that inflation is 6 percent per year. For each year of the loan the dollars with which the government pays you back are worth 6 percent less than the dollars you loaned the government, so instead of getting 4 percent more, you're losing 2 percent—the 4 percent interest you get minus the 6 percent inflation.

For you (the holder of debt), inflation isn't a costless way to eliminate a debt. It's very costly to creditors, who lose what the government gains. The government's gain from an inflation is the bondholder's loss from inflation. So the effect of inflation on

INFLATION AND INDEXED BONDS

Here's a proposal that some economists have suggested could significantly reduce the nominal Canadian deficit. Currently most bonds are fixed-interest bonds. They pay back a stated number of dollars in a given period. For example, at 10 percent interest a $1,000 five-year bond pays $100 interest each year for five years, and pays back another $1,000 at the end of five years.

Some economists have proposed the following: Make the amount that is to be paid back, the $1,000, indexed to inflation. Thus, if price level rises 40 percent, the amount paid back would be $1,400 rather than $1,000. Bonds that pay back an amount dependent on inflation are called *indexed bonds*.

Let's now ask: What would happen if Canada were to issue indexed bonds? Since bondholders are compensated for inflation, the interest on bonds would fall. If 5 percent inflation were the expected rate and the nominal interest rate were 8 percent, the real interest rate would be 3 percent—so the interest rate on bonds would be 3 percent instead of 8 percent, Canadian debt service would fall from about $40 billion to somewhere around $15 billion, and the measured Canadian deficit would decrease significantly.

Most economists oppose having the government issue indexed bonds. Yes, they agree, it would lower the measured deficit, but it would not change real Canadian debt. At the same time, indexing would introduce new complexities of government finance as the inflation index came under even more scrutiny because so much money would be riding on it.

Whether or not you favour the proposal, it is a superb proposal from an academic perspective. It helps us recognize the difference between real and nominal deficits. What's so interesting about the proposal is that it has already been in effect since 1991! Real-return bonds are long-term bonds whose nominal yield is indexed to the Consumer Price Index. Institutional investors and portfolio managers have shown great interest in this bond program, and as of early 1994 there were over $2.8 billion outstanding real-return bonds. Retail markets are now showing an interest in real-return bonds.

How does the return on a real-return bond compare to the return on an instrument that is not indexed? The following table lists the yield on real-return bonds and the yield on long-term Government of Canada bonds, along with the inflation rate. Which would you prefer?

Month	Yield on a Real-Return Bond	CPI Inflation Rate	Yield on a Long-Term Government of Canada Bond
Jan '94	3.52%	1.31%	7.16%
Feb '94	3.79	0.23	7.53
Mar '94	4.10	0.15	8.33
Apr '94	4.16	0.23	8.22
May '94	4.29	−0.15	8.58
June '94	4.70	0.00	9.27
July '94	4.70	0.15	9.46
Aug '94	4.69	0.15	8.87
Sept '94	4.63	0.15	9.07
Oct '94	4.67	−0.15	9.36
Nov '94	4.80	−0.08	9.26
Dec '94	4.92	0.22	9.13

Source: *Statistics Canada*, CANSIM Database, March 1995

debt is no illusion; it is simply a transfer of money from bondholders to the government.

Nominal and Real Interest Rates and Deficits Such transfers of income do not make bondholders (creditors) very happy. Yes, the government's real debt is being reduced by inflation, but it's being reduced by bondholders' losses. And bondholders aren't helpless people. What can they do about it? For the fixed-interest-rate bonds they already hold, they can do nothing. When they bought the bonds, the contract was set. But they can do something about future bonds. The next time a bond salesman suggests buying government bonds, purchasers will likely take any expected inflation into account. Instead of buying a bond with a 4 percent interest rate, they will require an additional 6 percent to compensate them for the 6 percent expected inflation, for a total of 10 percent.

Expectations of inflation push up the nominal interest rate and cause bondholders to demand an inflation premium on their bonds. Expected future inflation causes the real interest rate to be different from the nominal interest rate. Thus, in the absence of inflation the nominal interest rate might be 4 percent. With 6 percent inflation, the nominal interest rate might be 10 percent—4 percent real interest rate plus 6 percent expected inflation.

If the nominal interest rate is 6 percent higher than the real interest rate, bondholders have fully adjusted their 6 percent expectations of inflation into their bond purchases. In this case they won't lose if there's 6 percent inflation. Bondholders do not lose when they correctly expect inflation and build that expectation into their financial dealings. But if bondholders don't lose when they make a full adjustment for expected inflation, government can't win.

With Full Adjustment in Expectations, Creditors Don't Lose

To see that, with full interest rate adjustment for inflation, creditors don't lose, it is helpful to divide the government's deficit into two components: a spending-on-current-needs component and a debt service component.

Let's say the government has a total debt of $500 billion, total expenditures of $140 billion, and a nominal deficit of $40 billion. Let's also assume that initially there's no expected inflation. Because there's no expected inflation, a 4 percent nominal interest rate will also be the real interest rate, and the nominal deficit will equal the real deficit. This means that the government is paying $20 billion a year in interest ($500 billion debt × 4 percent interest). The debt service component of the deficit is $20 billion, leaving $120 billion to finance spending on current needs.

Now assume that there's an unexpected 6 percent inflation but the interest rate remains 4 percent. That 6 percent inflation decreases real debt by $30 billion (6 percent × $500 billion). Using the real deficit formula, you can calculate that the government is actually running a real deficit of $10 billion:

$$\text{Real deficit} = \$40 \text{ billion} - (6\% \times \$500 \text{ billion})$$

$$= \$40 \text{ billion} - \$30 \text{ billion}$$

$$= \$10 \text{ billion}$$

But what happens if the 6 percent inflation were fully expected? In that case, the nominal interest rate on the debt, assuming it's all short term, will rise from 4 to 10 percent to account for the expected inflation. Debt service will be $50 billion (10 percent × $500 billion), $30 billion more than government would have had to pay had there been no inflation adjustment to the interest rate. That $30 billion increase in the debt service expenditures just equals the $30 billion that the inflation wiped out.

This $30 billion increase in the debt service component of the deficit decreases the $120 billion current-spending component of the budget to $90 billion. So when nominal interest rates go up, simply in order to maintain the nominal deficit at its current level government must either reduce spending on current needs or it must raise taxes and collect more in revenues. It's paying extra interest to bondholders to compensate them for their loss due to inflation.

This distinction between nominal and real is necessary to make a judgement about a given nominal deficit. When there's high expected inflation and a large debt, much of the nominal deficit is a debt service component which is simply offsetting the decrease in the debt due to inflation.

This insight into debt is directly relevant to the budget situation in Canada. For example, back in 1991 the nominal Canadian deficit was about $30 billion, while the real deficit was about half of that—$18 billion (interest rates were about 12 percent and the debt was about $400 billion). But that low real deficit was not costless to the government. When inflationary expectations were much lower, as they were in the 1950s, government paid 3 or 4 percent on its bonds. In 1991 it paid rates that were

INTERNATIONAL COMPARISONS OF GOVERNMENT DEBT

One way to get a handle on whether the Canadian government debt is "too high" is to compare it to the debt of some other countries, as is done in the bar chart. Since debt is defined slightly differently in different countries, and since fluctuation in GDP can change ratios, these percentages should be interpreted as measures of magnitude only.

In the chart you can see that Canada comes out in the high end of these ten countries. Of course, there is no economic law stating that the other countries are right, or that the economic situation might not change, making these current ratios unsustainable. Still, it's nice to know that Canada is not alone in its deficit and debt problems.

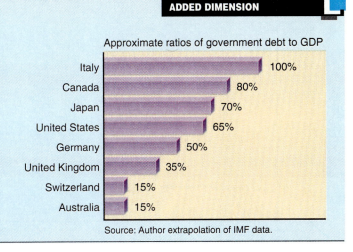

Approximate ratios of government debt to GDP

Italy	100%
Canada	80%
Japan	70%
United States	65%
Germany	50%
United Kingdom	35%
Switzerland	15%
Australia	15%

Source: Author extrapolation of IMF data.

about 9 percent more than it paid in the 1950s. With its $400 billion debt, in 1991 Canada was paying about $36 billion more in interest than it would have had to pay if no inflation had been expected and the nominal interest rate had been 3 percent rather than 12 percent. That reduced the amount it could spend on current services by $36 billion. This means that much of the 1991 nominal Canadian deficit existed because of the rise in debt service necessary to compensate bondholders for the expected inflation.

As inflationary expectations and nominal interest rates fell in the 1990s, the difference between the real and nominal deficit decreased. Still, a 2 percent gap between nominal and real interest rates and a $500 billion debt would mean that $10 billion of any deficit is due to the inflation premium raising the nominal interest rate.

We've covered a lot of material, so before we move on let's review four important points:

1. Deficits are summary measures of the state of the economy. They are dependent on the accounting procedures used.
2. It is the financial health of the economy, not the deficit, with which we should be concerned.
3. Deficits and debt should be viewed relative to GDP to determine their importance.
4. The real deficit is the nominal deficit adjusted for the inflation reduction in the real debt:

$$\text{Real deficit} = \text{Nominal deficit} - (\text{Inflation} \times \text{Debt})$$

Summary to This Point

Considering real deficits rather than nominal deficits and viewing the deficit and debt relative to GDP should have lessened your concern about the size of the Canadian deficit. Given inflation, the real deficit is lower than the nominal deficit, and given real growth we can stand an increase in total debt without the burden becoming intolerable.

SOME REASONS FOR CONCERN ABOUT CANADA'S BUDGET DEFICITS AND DEBT

But wait a minute. So far we've only discussed the *federal* deficit and the *federal* debt. Provinces and municipalities also run deficits by borrowing to spend in excess of their revenues, and, when they do, this raises the total amount of government debt in the economy. Exhibit 4 (a) shows deficits of all levels of government in Canada and compares them to the federal figures. The debts of the federal government are compared to total debt of all levels of government in Canada (this adds provincial and local government deficits to the federal figures) in Exhibit 4 (b). The deficit and debt problems

The Federal Deficit and Debt Are Only Part of the Picture

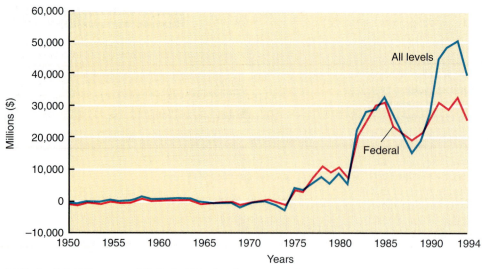

(a) Federal deficit versus deficit at all levels of government

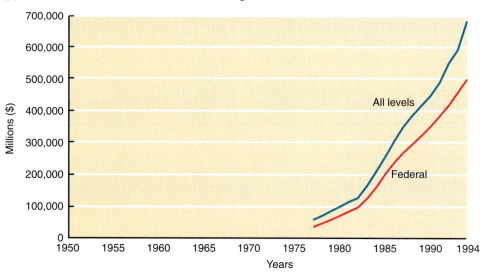

(b) Federal debt versus debt at all levels of government

EXHIBIT 4   Federal Deficit and Debt in Perspective

(a) Some economists argue the federal deficit is lower than that at all levels of government because the federal authorities leave "off-loaded" programs to the provinces, forcing the provinces to "spend beyond their means".

(b) Federal debt remains the largest componant of all levels of government debt in Canada.

5 Even though the real deficit is lower than the nominal deficit, there is still cause for concern because the provinces also run deficits. Government spending at all levels of government exceeds revenues so the federal numbers give only part of the picture.

are clearly more serious than we would have guessed from looking at just the federal books. Exhibit 5 shows the total figures as a proportion of GDP. Total government debt in Canada almost equals nominal GDP, and it shows a much different trend since 1990 than the federal picture viewed alone.

Until the early 1980s many provinces alternated between periods of budget surplus and deficit. (That's why the deficit for all levels of government was below that of the federal government in Exhibit 4 (a) until 1990—the provinces and municipalities had been running a net surplus. The recession of 1981–82 led to rising provincial deficits as governments weathered the economic downturn, and one would have thought that during the expansion of 1982–90, provincial (and federal) governments would adopt less expansionary policies in an attempt to build a surplus out of which to fund programs during the next recession. Unfortunately the political will to raise taxes and cut spending during that period just didn't appear. The refrigerator was unlocked (if you don't know what we mean, go back and read the beginning of this chapter again) and budget deficits, and hence debts, rose. The recession of 1990–91 saw a shift in the total provincial and municipal budget balances towards deficits.

Many provinces argue that they were forced to undertake higher levels of spending because the federal government "off-loaded" programs in its attempt to reduce the federal deficit and debt. While to some extent this justifies the recent growth in

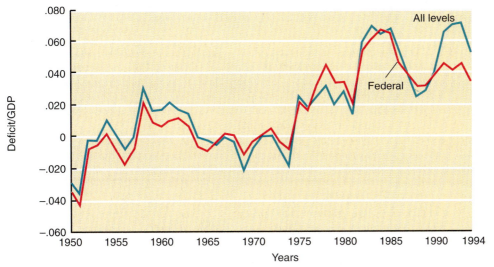

(a) Comparing deficit to GDP ratios: Federal versus all levels of government

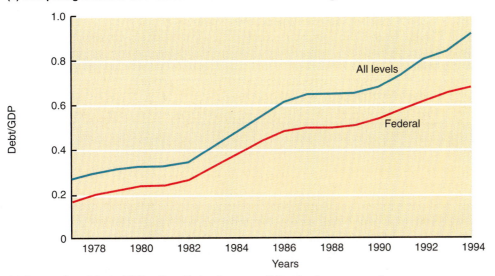

(b) Comparing debt to GDP ratios: Federal versus all levels of government

EXHIBIT 5   Federal Debt/GDP and Deficit/GDP in Perspective

(a) demonstrates the upward trend in deficit/GDP ratios since the 1970s. **(b)** shows that the gap between debt/GDP all all levels of government and the federal government has been widening for nearly twenty years.

provincial deficits and debts, it does not explain why Ontario, for instance, failed to adopt the traditional Keynesian stance that would have generated a budget surplus during the 1980s. Either way you look at it, total Canadian deficits and debts rose significantly over this period.

In mid-1994 the inflation rate hovered around zero yet interest rates rose almost continuously over the year. Media accounts attributed these anomalies to (1) uncertainty regarding the Quebec election and the chance that Quebec would separate from Canada, and (2) the rising deficits and debts of the Canadian economy.

Higher and higher government deficits require an ever increasing amount of borrowing, and this reduces the pool of capital available to government and private enterprise. Firms that wish to fund expansion by issuing debt instruments are forced to pay higher rates of return. In many cases the internal rate of return on the project the firm wants to fund just can't match the kinds of rates that the government offers when they issue bonds and treasury bills. Thus, private sector investment is **crowded out**— higher levels of government spending raise interest rates, which in turn reduce the level of private investment.

But there's another form of crowding out that results from the appreciation of the domestic currency that results from higher levels of government spending. As the dollar gains value, it becomes more expensive for foreigners to buy our goods and ser-

A Different Type of Crowding Out

Crowding out   The offsetting effect on private expenditures caused by the government's sale of bonds to finance expansionary fiscal policy.

OTTAWA WANTS TO CUT RELIANCE ON FOREIGN INVESTORS

Wants to cut reliance on foreign investors, change way it sells CSBs to Canadians

BY ALAN FREEMAN

Parliamentary Bureau

OTTAWA—The federal government plans a new retail debt program that could involve issuing Canada Savings Bonds on a year-round basis as well as other financial products designed to compete with the chartered banks.

"We're trying to introduce a number of new instruments into the marketplace," said David Walker, parliamentary secretary to Finance Minister Paul Martin.

"There seems to be a lot of good will out there that Canadians would like to participate more in the debt reduction in this country," he said following an appearance before the House of Commons finance committee, which approved the government's borrowing authority for the 1995–96 fiscal year.

The government announced plans for a new retail debt program in last month's budget, but didn't provide details. Mr. Martin said only that the aim of the program was to reduce Canada's reliance on foreign investors, who at the end of fiscal 1993–94 held 26 per cent of the federal government's outstanding market debt of $411-billion at the end of last March.

Canada Savings Bonds have traditionally been the government's major retail debt product, but their importance has declined sharply in recent years. They now account for only about 8 per cent of Ottawa's outstanding debt, compared with 19 per cent in 1982–83.

In November, the government sold $7.5-billion of CSBs, but after accounting for redemptions of past series, net purchases were $5.7-billion.

As a first step to updating the CSB as a financial product, last fall's campaign for the first time included guaranteed minimum interest rates for the first

three years of the 1994 issue.

Offering CSBs year-round would be an even more fundamental change. The bonds are now issued once a year on Nov. 1, for about a two- to three-week sales period.

Mr. Walker said there is also a lot of dissatisfaction that the CSB program, which operates mainly through the chartered banks, hasn't been run as effectively as it could be.

The new debt products could continue to be offered through brokerage firms and credit unions as well as through the banks but the government may decide to do more direct marketing. "Do we set up an 800 number and do it ourselves?"

Mr. Walker also complained that the CSB system as run by the Bank of Canada is "clumsy" administratively and has to be updated.

Alan Freeman, *Globe and Mail*, March 14, 1995.

---

vices, and our exports fall. Our imports rise since we can buy goods from the rest of the world more cheaply than before the dollar gained value. Thus, higher levels of government spending lead to higher deficits and debt levels, an appreciated currency, and private sector spending takes "two hits"—one directly to investment through higher interest rates, and one directly to net exports as the dollar gains value.

Does It Matter Who Holds Government Debt?

6 Who holds government debt matters—internally held debt simply involves a redistribution of income within Canada while externally held debt is a burden to society.

We know that when the government borrows money it eventually has to pay it back. If it doesn't, no one will hold its bonds and Treasury bills, because there's no way to tell if you'll ever see your money again. But that doesn't mean the government can't issue new bonds and Treasury bills to raise the money to use to repay the monies it borrowed in the past. In fact, that's pretty much what it does today.

Problems arise when we think about who is holding our debt. As we've already seen, when our debt is held internally—that is, when Canadians hold Canadian government debt—there's a redistribution involved, but the funds stay within Canada. Not so when foreigners hold the debt. The interest payments we make to foreigners who hold our debt flow out of the country, and the real returns reside with the foreigners. This represents a loss to the Canadian economy, so it does matter who holds government debt.

Exhibit 6 illustrates that nonresident holdings of Government of Canada debt has increased substantially over the last 20 years. Not surprisingly, this is related to our huge current account deficit that is primarily due to service flows to foreigners for the use of their funds—that is, the interest payments that we make to foreigners who hold Canadian debt.

There are a number of issues that tie into who holds our debt. To attract foreign capital, Canadian and provincial government debt must offer higher rates of return

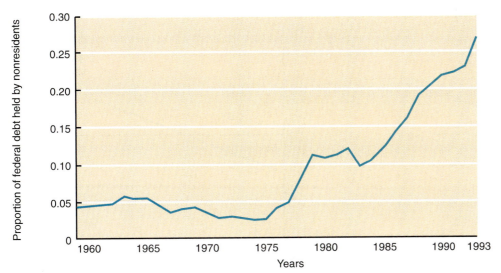

EXHIBIT 6   Federal Debt Held by Nonresidents

Federal debt held by nonresidents has grown significantly over the last 20 years.

than debt offered on similar instruments issued by other governments. This means that political uncertainty in Canada can affect our interest rates, since foreign investors require a premium to take on the associated risk. Similarly with respect to changes in exchange rates: Government debt in Canada has to offer a rate of return that compensates investors for anticipated changes in the value of the dollar relative to a number of other currencies. When interest rates and exchange rates no longer satisfy international investors, the Bank of Canada nudges those rates in the desired direction through monetary policy. Some economists argue that, to a great extent, the Bank of Canada has lost discretion over interest rates *because* a large portion of the debt is externally held. This observation might help to explain why Canadian interest rates were so high despite the absence of inflation during 1994 and 1995.

Continuing deficits and rising levels of debt have significant implications for Canada's future. The government will have to raise taxes and cut spending to pay off the debt. We know this will reduce the level of demand in the economy, leading to lower levels of output and employment. In its 1995 budget, the federal government announced its intention to substantially reduce government spending through eliminating 45,000 public service jobs and cutting department expenditures. Much of the political rhetoric at the time was aimed at assuaging the fears of international investors who began to wonder whether Canada was an attractive investment haven.

We've spent a lot of time looking at the deficit and the debt. Now we want to ask if we can use the deficit to tell us whether fiscal policies are becoming more or less expansionary—that is, we want to know the **stance of fiscal policy.** For example, let's say your campus radio station wants you to comment—live—on the next federal budget. Going over the documents, would you be able to say that fiscal policy has become more expansionary if the deficit figures went up?

If you said no, then kudos to you—you read the chapter on fiscal policy and it stuck with you. If you said yes, then a review of tax and fiscal policies is in order. The basic reason a flat "no" is wrong is that the government deficit can change as a result of a shift in an autonomous component of demand. For example, say autonomous investment fell. This would reduce income and tax revenues, and the deficit would rise. If you said that fiscal policy had become more expansionary, you'd be wrong, since government spending and taxation variables hadn't changed. A good measure of the stance of fiscal policy is the structural deficit—it's the deficit we'd get if we adjusted the figures for the business cycle.

To cement this in your mind, consider Exhibit 7 (a). It shows the government

Is the Deficit a Good Measure of the Stance of Fiscal Policy?

Stance of fiscal policy   Expansionary or contractionary changes in government spending and/or taxes.

7   Because the deficit has many dimensions and each is widely debated, there are many alternative reasonable views about the deficit.

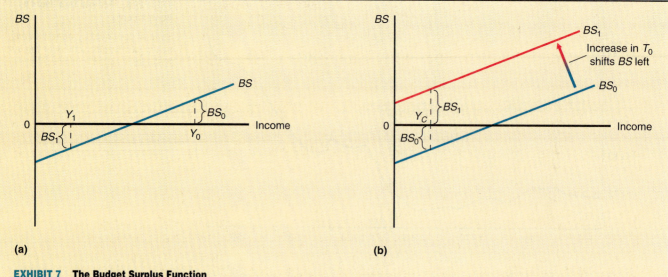

EXHIBIT 7   The Budget Surplus Function

(a) Reduction in income from Y_0 to Y_1 could change a budget surplus to a budget deficit, but fiscal policy variables T_0, G_0, and t have not changed. The budget surplus is a bad measure of the stance of fiscal policy.
(b) Holding income at a cyclically adjusted value Y_C, we can see how changes in fiscal policy affect the budget surplus. If BS_0 shifts to BS_1, when autonomous taxes rise, the budget surplus rises, signalling contractionary fiscal policy.

budget surplus as a function of income, using the tax and expenditure functions of Chapter 11:

$$\text{Government spending}\quad G = G_0$$

$$\text{Taxes}\qquad\qquad\qquad T = T_0 + tY$$

$$\text{Budget surplus:}\qquad\quad BS = T - G$$

$$BS = [T_0 - G_0] + tY$$

Clearly a change in equilibrium income (due to a reduction in autonomous investment, for example) will change the budget surplus independently of changes in fiscal policy variables T_0, G_0, or t (the tax rate). A better measure of the stance of fiscal policy would be to control for changes in income over the business cycle and look at how the budget surplus changes as fiscal policy variables change. Exhibit 7 (b) provides a view of how this would be done, holding income fixed at some cyclically adjusted value. Then, the budget surplus measured at that controlled level of income would tell us whether fiscal policy has become more expansionary (reducing the budget surplus), or less expansionary (raising the budget surplus).

CONCLUSION

There are many accounting problems associated with measuring the government deficit that we haven't dealt with, since they're more the stuff of an accounting course. What you should get from what we've done is a clear understanding of how deficits and debts matter. You should also be clear about some of the adjustments economists make to the figures. We recognize that the measured deficit will be at the centre of the debate about government spending and taxes, but we hope we've impressed on you the fact that it's the financial health of the economy that's important, not the deficit per se.

Few economists believe the deficit will bring imminent doom—some even believe the deficit doesn't matter. The majority of economists believe the deficit will cause serious problems in the long run unless appropriate measures are taken to restore the integrity of government finances. We'll discuss several proposals for reform in the next chapter.

CHAPTER SUMMARY

- A deficit is a shortfall of incoming revenues under outgoing payments. Debt is accumulated deficits.
- A budget deficit should be judged in light of economic and political conditions.
- The deficit is a summary measure of a budget. Whether a deficit is a problem depends on the budgeting procedures that measure it.
- A country's debt must be judged in relation to its assets.
- To judge the importance of deficits and debt, economists look at them relative to GDP.
- A real deficit is nominal deficit adjusted for the effect of inflation.

- When expectations of inflation have fully adjusted, inflation involves no transfer from creditors to debtors.
- Government spending can cause an appreciation that crowds out net exports.
- Internally held debt isn't a burden to society—it just redistributes income between Canadians.
- Externally held debt represents a burden to society—foreigners receive the benefits.
- The structural deficit is a good measure of the stance of fiscal policy.
- There are various reasonable views about the Canadian budget deficit.

KEY TERMS

bracket creep *(429)*
crowded out *(443)*
debt *(429)*
debt service *(435)*

deficit *(429)*
external government debt *(434)*
indexing the tax system *(430)*
internal government debt *(434)*

nominal deficit *(437)*
real deficit *(437)*
stance of fiscal policy *(445)*
structural deficit *(436)*

QUESTIONS FOR THOUGHT AND REVIEW

The number after each question represents the estimated degree of critical thinking required. (1 = almost none; 10 = deep thought.)

1. Your income is $40,000 per year; your expenditures are $45,000. $10,000 of your $45,000 expenditure is for tuition. Is your budget in deficit or surplus? Why? *(6)*

2. "The deficit should be of concern." What additional information do you need to undertake a reasonable discussion of that statement? *(5)*

3. "The debt should be of concern." What additional information do you need to undertake a reasonable discussion of that statement? *(5)*

4. Inflation is 20 percent. Debt is $2 trillion. The nominal deficit is $300 billion. What is the real deficit? *(2)*

5. How would your answer to Question 4 differ if you knew that expected inflation was 15 percent? *(5)*

6. If the government were to issue inflation-adjusted bonds, the deficit would fall. Would you suggest such a policy? Why? *(6)*

7. "Bracket creep will reduce the deficit." How would you argue against this statement? *(7)*

8. "An increase in the budget surplus means fiscal policy has become less expansionary." Do you agree? Why? *(6)*

9. In what sense would balanced budget legislation be a gimmick? *(7)*

10. "Since the tax system is no longer fully indexed to inflation, the deficit should fall." Would you disagree with this statement? Why? *(8)*

PROBLEMS AND EXERCISES

1. Calculate the real deficit in the following cases.

    a. Inflation is 10 percent. Debt is $3 trillion. Nominal deficit is $220 billion.

    b. Inflation is 2 percent. Debt is $1 trillion. Nominal deficit is $50 billion.

    c. Inflation is −4 percent. (Price level is falling.) Debt is $500 billion. Nominal deficit is $30 billion.

2. Using the latest figures available from your library, calculate the real budget deficits for Canada, the United States, Britain, France, Brazil, and Nigeria.

3. Assume a country's nominal GDP is $600 billion, government expenditures less debt service are $145 billion, and revenue is $160 billion. The nominal debt is $360 billion. Inflation is 3 percent while real interest rates are 3 percent. Expected inflation is fully adjusted.

    a. Calculate debt service payments.

    b. Calculate the nominal deficit.

    c. Calculate the real deficit.

    d. What would you expect to happen if expectations of inflation fall? Why?

4. Assume a country's real growth is 2 percent per year, while its real deficit is rising by 5 percent per year. Can a country continue to afford such deficits ad infinitum? What problems might this country face in the future?

5. You've been hired by Creative Accountants, consultants to Textland. Your assignment is to make suggestions about how to structure Textland's accounts so that the current deficit looks as small as possible. Specifically, Textland wants to know how to treat the following:

    a. Government pensions.

    b. Sale of land.

    c. Proceeds of a program to allow people to prepay taxes at a 10 percent discount.

    d. Expenditures on new helicopters.

19

The Art of Macro Policy

*The worst episodes of recent monetary history—the great infla-
tions—
have been marked by the subjection of central bankers to overriding
political pressures.*

~R. S. Sayers

After reading this chapter, you should be able to:

1 Summarize the conflicting goals of macro policy.

2 Explain why macroeconomic policy is an art, not a science.

3 Distinguish a policy model from a theoretical model.

4 Explain why modern macro policy focuses on credibility.

5 State the main points of agreement between Keynesians and
Classicals.

6 Explain why the macroeconomic debate in the early 1990s was
based on supply-side macro policies.

7 Discuss the debate over the appropriate objectives of macro
policy: stable prices, low unemployment, or both?

8 Explain why governments want to reform the unemployment
and welfare programs.

9 Explain how a return to fixed exchange rates might benefit
Canada.

10 Take a hypothetical situation and develop a reasonable macroeconomic strategy for dealing with that situation.

In earlier chapters we introduced you to the terminology, the institutions, and the theory of the macroeconomy. It's now time to put it all together.

- What should government do if the economy seems to be falling into a recession?
- What should government do if inflation seems to be increasing?
- What should government do if the economy seems to be falling into a recession but, simultaneously, inflation seems to be increasing?
- What should government do if there's a large trade deficit at the same time that it's worried about a recession?
- What should government do if its currency's value is falling and there's concern about inflation?

Policymakers face these and similar questions every day. In this chapter, using the terminology, knowledge of institutions, theory, and insights we developed in previous chapters, we'll try to come to grips with these difficult real-world issues.

The first two sections provide some context for discussing these questions by considering the conflicting goals of macroeconomic policy. These two sections summarize and review similarities and differences between Keynesians and Classicals described in earlier chapters. (Remember, when we talk about Keynesians and Classicals, we mean interventionists and noninterventionists.) The first section updates some recent theoretical developments relevant for policy and discusses the interaction between theory and policy. The second section considers the similarities and differences between Keynesians and Classicals on macro policy.

The third section of the chapter reviews recent Canadian economic experience and investigates three topical issues in Canadian macroeconomic policy. The final section presents you with a hypothetical case and shows how the understanding you've gained in earlier chapters can let you function as an economic advisor to a government.

THE LIMITS OF MACROECONOMIC THEORY AND POLICY

1 Too contractionary a policy will cause unemployment and recession. Too expansionary a policy will accelerate inflation and expand trade deficits.

One reason why macroeconomic policy is so complicated is that it involves conflicting goals. As we saw in the chapter on inflation, the low inflation goal often conflicts with the low unemployment/high growth goal. And as we saw in a previous chapter, international trade balance and exchange rate goals often conflict with one another and with domestic goals. Thus, the government finds itself and the economy on a tightrope. Too expansionary a policy will accelerate inflation and expand trade deficits. But the government also knows that if it's too contractionary, it will cause a recession.

To maintain the economy on this tightrope, governments use trade policies and monetary and fiscal policies as a balance bar. (They also use some others that deal with regulation which we'll discuss in the microeconomics section of the course.) If the economy seems to be falling into inflation, governments can use contractionary monetary and fiscal policies; if it seems to be falling into recession, they can use expansionary monetary and fiscal policies. If they face both problems simultaneously, they must choose between the two and hope for the best.

The Limits of Macroeconomic Policy

In thinking about these goals, we must recognize that there are limits to what can be achieved with macroeconomic policy. Economists often tell governments that they're asking for too much. These governments are like a patient who asks his doctor for a health program that will enable him to forget about a training program, eat anything he wants, and run a four-minute mile. Some things just can't be done, and it's important for governments to recognize the inevitable limitations and trade-offs, at least with the monetary and fiscal policy tools currently available. Good economists are continually pointing out those limits.

But, like the patient who doesn't like to hear there are limits, governments often go to other advisors who offer more upbeat advice. Economists are often put in the position of the stick-in-the-mud who sees only problems, not potentials.

EXHIBIT 1   **Macroeconomic Policy Dilemmas**

	Option	Advantages	Disadvantages
Monetary policy	Expansionary	1. Interest rates may fall. 2. Economy may grow. 3. Decreases unemployment.	1. Inflation may worsen. 2. Exchange rate may rise. 3. Capital outflow. 4. Trade deficit may increase.
	Contractionary	1. Exchange rate may fall. 2. Helps fight inflation. 3. Trade deficit may decrease. 4. Capital inflow.	1. Risks recession. 2. Increases unemployment 3. Slows growth. 4. May help cause short-run political problems. 5. Interest rates may rise.
Fiscal policy	Expansionary (borrow and spend)	1. Maybe growth will continue. 2. May help solve short-run political problems. 3. Decreases unemployment.	1. Budget deficit worsens. 2. Hurts country's ability to borrow in the future. 3. Trade deficit may increase. 4. Upward pressure on interest rate.
	Contractionary (reduce deficit)	1. May help fight inflation. 2. May allow a better monetary/fiscal mix. 3. Trade deficit may decrease. 4. Interest rates may fall.	1. Risks recession. 2. Increases unemployment. 3. Slows growth. 4. May help cause short-run political problems.

This stick-in-the-mud image isn't appropriate. We economists are often dynamic, innovative, positive sorts of people (would you believe?) who've just been cast in a difficult role of pointing out that there are no free lunches.

What makes economists' stick-in-the-mud role so difficult is that the trade-offs are often uncertain, meaning that once in a while the "promise-them-everything" advisors turn out to be right. Here's an example:

In 1987 and 1988, most economists were convinced that there was serious potential for inflation. Based on this concern, they warned against monetary and fiscal policies that would exacerbate the inflationary problem. But due in part to some unexpected falls in the prices of oil and raw materials, that inflation didn't occur, even though the government listened instead to a set of "full-speed-ahead" advisors. Because the inflation didn't occur, the advisors who said "Full-speed ahead" could point to this period and correctly say that they were right.

With policy effects so uncertain, most economists are hesitant to make unambiguous predictions about policy. But they do have a sense of the effects of certain policies and the trade-offs each involves. Exhibit 1 summarizes those trade-offs.

When advising governments about real-world macro policy, economists are very aware that economic relationships aren't certain, and that conducting macroeconomic

2 Economic relationships are not certain, which makes macroeconomic policy an art rather than a science.

policy is an art, not a science. In practicing the **art of macro policy,** Keynesians and Classicals have different styles, and before we talk about some real-world episodes, it's helpful to contrast those styles. We begin by reviewing some recent policy-relevant theoretical developments in macroeconomics.

In the 1980s and 1990s, there have been a lot of theoretical developments in thinking about macroeconomic problems, but most of those developments have had only tangential effects on macro policymakers. The reason is that those new developments lead to the conclusion that the aggregate economy is enormously complicated. Once one takes full account of that complexity, it's unclear, theoretically, what policies, if any, should be followed.

Recent theoretical work that often goes under the name **rational expectations** has focused on building dynamic feedback effects into macro models. Rational expectations are expectations about the future based on the best current information. Such expectations are important because if people expect a policy, and make adjustments in anticipation of it, the policy will have a different effect than if they didn't expect it. Affecting the expectations becomes the channel through which policy actions affect the economy.

The influence of the rational expectations work is woven into much of the discussion in this book. It is why, for example, when we discuss monetary policy, we talk about Bank of Canada posturing—*seeming to be* absolutely resolute about fighting inflation—in addition to *being* resolute. If people believe the Bank of Canada will do nothing but fight inflation, people will react differently than if they do not believe that. One central banker nicely summarized this distinction when he differentiated "bark policy" from "bite policy." If the central bank barks loudly and convincingly enough, it doesn't have to bite.

In this book Keynesian economics is interpreted as a theory in which, because of interdependencies of individuals' expectations, what is individually rational is not necessarily collectively rational. This interpretation is influenced by the work on rational expectations. It is a modern interpretation of Keynesian economics that makes it theoretically sound, even if all individuals have rational expectations. In modern macroeconomic theory, the key Keynesian insight is that the aggregate economy involves enormous interdependencies.

What is undermined by rational expectations is what has sometimes been called **mechanistic Keynesianism**—the belief that the simple multiplier models (or even complex variations) actually describe the aggregate adjustment process and lead to a deterministic solution that policymakers can exploit in a mechanistic way.

Modern macroeconomists do not believe the economy works this way, and even the most complicated models leave out most interdependencies to make those models tractable. When one adds back these interdependencies, the solutions to the models are indeterminate. Once one takes into account these many interdependencies, one recognizes that Keynesian models, at best, describe tendencies toward an exaggeration of external real shocks to the economy. This more limited interpretation of Keynes's insight is the modern interpretation of Keynesian theory.

The last three paragraphs summarize about 5,000 articles and lots of fancy math that have been done over the past 10 years. This chapter is policy-oriented, so we can summarize that work briefly because, while recent theoretical developments have been influential in the interpretation given to macro models, they have not had a significant effect on macro policy. These developments have simply brought home the fact that if you build dynamic feedback effects into an aggregate model, you can come up with just about any result. Slightly different assumptions in models lead to substantially different results and policy recommendations. These models describing that complexity are grist for tenure for academic economists but are of little use to policymakers. Policymakers don't want complexity. They want models that come to definite conclusions, because policymakers don't have the luxury of waffling on issues.

The Difference between Theoretical Models and Policy Models

Art of macro policy   An art practiced by economists who advise governments about real-world macro policy. In the practice of that art, economists recognize that economic relationships aren't certain and that conducting macroeconomic policy is not a science.

Rational expectations   Expectations about the future based on the best current information, used in theoretical economic work that focuses on building dynamic feedback effects into macro models.

Mechanistic Keynesianism   The belief that the simple multiplier models (or even complex variations) actually describe the aggregate adjustment process and lead to a deterministic solution that policymakers can exploit in a mechanistic way.

Most theoretical work of macroeconomists involves abstract models that omit institutional context to try to capture those aspects of economic behaviour that transcend institutions. However, most actions by individuals do not transcend institutions. So it should not be surprising that those theoretical models don't come to policy conclusions until the institutional context is added back. And adding back institutional context involves judgement—judgement about which reasonable people may differ.

This differing institutional judgement explains why no conclusion can be reached regarding whether the Keynesian model or the Classical model is the best guide for policy. Once one adds the institutional context back, both Classical and Keynesian macro models become reasonable guides, depending on the situation, and that's how policymakers use them—as guides, not as directives.

The introductory Keynesian and Classical models presented in the text are the ones in the back of policymakers' minds. They use them not as mechanical guides, but, with judgement, as working models, as descriptions of empirical regularities that they assume will be maintained—unless something else comes up. Policymakers do not care whether these models can be deductively derived from micro principles, or even whether they involve logical inconsistencies; what they care about is that these models fit with their intuition, describe observed reality, and predict reasonably well.

Let us give an example. Some farmers use the following rule of thumb: When the cows lie down, it is going to rain. The larger the percentage of their cows that lie down, the higher the probability of rain. If this rule of thumb usually works, it is a good rule of thumb. People who use this rule to predict don't care about the cows' decision-making process. They care about observable empirical regularity that they can base policy decisions on (such as whether to harvest the hay immediately, or wait a day).

Academic cowonomists would have a different focus. They would look into the cow's decision-making process and would try to explain the cow's lying-down decision in cost/benefit terms consistent with a cow's utility function.

What we are saying is that there are two fundamentally different types of models used in economics: policy models and theoretical models. A policy model is a working tool that captures empirical regularities that may be caused by features of the current institutional framework or by inherent economic tendencies; for short-run policy, policymakers don't care which, as long as the model leads to the best prediction.

An academic theoretical model has a different purpose. Academic economists care passionately about whether an empirical regularity reflects inherent economic tendencies or the current institutional framework. Which of these is the cause of an empirical regularity has significant long-run policy relevance, and that is an academic economist's focus. By separating out institutionally determined effects from institution-transcendent economic tendencies, their models can be used to predict whether a policy can be used indefinitely, or whether it only works temporarily—until institutions change. The recent Classical and Keynesian theoretical work on microfoundations is an attempt to make that separation for macroeconomics.

When teaching this subject, the instructor must discuss both types of models. That presents a problem, because on the one hand, the theoretical models are highly abstract and mathematically too complicated to present to anyone but specialists. On the other hand, the policy-oriented observational models are not really models at all—they are simply empirical generalizations, and they often fail to bring out the differences between those empirical regularities based on institutional constraints that will likely change and those that transcend existing institutions.

Let's now briefly consider the influence of some of this modern theoretical work on macro policy and some of the ideas underlying it.

As we stated before, modern Classical economics is centred around rational expectations. The essence of the modern Classical policy argument based on rational expectations is the following: Say the government uses an activist monetary and fiscal

The Interface between Theoretical and Policy Models

3 Theoretical models are abstract; they try to capture certain aspects of economic behaviour that transcend institutions. Policy models combine individuals' actions that transcend institutions and individual actions that depend on institutions; they try to capture empirical regularities.

People Aren't Stupid

policy. People aren't stupid; they'll soon come to expect that activist monetary and fiscal policy will be used and, in anticipation, will change their behaviour. But if they change their behaviour, the government's estimates of what is going to be the effect of policy, based on past experience, will be wrong.

Let's consider an example. Say everyone knows government will run expansionary fiscal policy if the economy is in a recession. In the absence of any expected policy response by government, people would have lowered their prices when they saw a recession coming. Expecting government expansionary policy, however, they won't lower their prices. Thus, an activist policy creates its own problems, which can be avoided by establishing a set of rules that limit government's policy responses. Modern Classical economics has formalized that insight.

As we can see from this discussion, the key element of modern Classical ideas about policy is that you must consider the effects of policy on people's behaviour, and that those effects place limits on policy options. Specifically, the fact that the economy is falling into a recession is not a sufficient reason for the government to run expansionary monetary and fiscal policies. Some modern Classicals go further than that, arguing that if all people have rational expectations and the economy is competitive, there's no room for any activist monetary policy.

Modern Keynesians generally agree with this modern Classical argument about expectations. But they argue that it doesn't rule out activist monetary and fiscal policies in all instances. As we discussed above, they argue that many fluctuations in the economy are due to a collective irrationality, which leaves room for government to correct that irrationality.

Credibility and Macro Policy

A good way to see how modern Classical and Keynesian ideas have affected macroeconomic policy, or at least the thinking about that policy, is the discussion in the 1994 and 1995 *Federal Budget Speeches.* There's little or no mention of an activist fiscal policy and sizes of multipliers. Instead, the central theme is that fiscal policy should be based on ". . . reasonable economic assumptions, not rosy forecasts. We believe it is more important to meet a target than declare an illusion and then fall short of it" (1994 *Budget Speech,* p. 2). *Credibility* is a key issue with the federal government.

Similarly with statements made by the Governor of the Bank of Canada—for example, in his 1993 Annual Report. It contains a joint statement with the government of Canada that begins:

> High levels of economic growth and employment on a sustained basis are the primary objectives of monetary and fiscal policies. The best contribution that monetary policy can make to these objectives is to preserve confidence in the value of money by achieving and maintaining price stability.

The economists who wrote the joint statement wanted to emphasize that one cannot think of macroeconomic policy without thinking about what effect expectations of macroeconomic policy will have. The policy must be credible, systematic, and consistent. The joint statement emphasizes that you cannot think of policy choices in one time period as not affecting individuals' behaviour in another time period.

An analogy to raising a child might make the point clear. Say that your child is crying in a restaurant. Do you hand out a piece of candy to stop the crying or do you maintain your "no candy" rule? Looking only at the one situation, it might make sense to give the candy, but doing so will undermine your credibility and consistency, and therefore has an additional cost. This emphasis on credibility is the primary effect modern theoretical work has had on macroeconomic policy. In conducting macro policy, one must consider the effect that expectations of that policy will have on the economy generally, not only in a particular case.

4   Modern economists focus on credibility because they see macro policy operating through expectations as much as through the real channels emphasized in the traditional models.

THE KEYNESIAN/CLASSICAL POLICY DEBATE

Debates about economic theory often mask debates about economic policy. Economists use theories to guide their reasoning, but before they can translate the results of a theory into a policy prescription, they must add a sense of institutions and history, adjusting the model to fit reality. Keynesians and Classicals differ not only in the theoretical models they prefer, but also, and probably more importantly, in their sense of institutions and history.

The Classical View of Government Policy

As you saw in earlier chapters, Classicals have a profound distrust of government and the political process. They tend to believe that, even if theoretically the government might be able to help solve a recession, there's a serious question whether, given the political process, it will do so. Politics will often guide government to do something quite different than "further the general good." In the Classical view, real-world government intervention is more likely to do harm than good.

Classicals see democratic government as being significantly controlled by special interest groups. While, in theory, government might be an expression of the will of the people, in practice it's not. Thus, government is not a legitimate method of correcting problems in the economy. True, government sometimes does good, but this is the exception. Overall the costs of government action outweigh the benefits.

In the Classical view, politicians often are guided by politics, not by society's best interest. Therefore any policy that increases the government's role is highly suspect and should be avoided. Modern Classical models reflect this view and focus on a model that highlights a laissez-faire policy for government.

The Keynesian View of Government Policy

Keynesians tend to have more faith in government not only being able to recognize what's wrong, but also in being willing to work to correct it. Thus, for a Keynesian it's worthwhile to talk about a model that highlights an activist role for government.

Keynesians tend to see government as an expression of the will of the people. Thus, they see it as a legitimate method of correcting problems in the economy. True, government is sometimes misled by interest groups who direct government to do their own bidding rather than follow the general interest, but this is simply a cost of government. In the Keynesian view, the benefits of government generally outweigh the costs.

Who's Right on Policy?

Notice that these differences between Keynesians and Classicals are based on judgement calls requiring a knowledge of the workings of the market and the social institutions that tie our country together. They're judgements upon which reasonable individuals may differ. Between the two extremes are innumerable shades of Keynesians and Classicals. There's no objective way of deciding which group is right or wrong.

Flip-Flopping Views of the Deficit

Now that we've considered the complex interaction between policy and theoretical models, let's consider how that interaction can lead to confusion about policy positions. Specifically, let's consider the recent flip-flopping of Keynesian and Classical views on the deficit.

Historically, as we saw in earlier chapters, Classical economists opposed budget deficits whereas Keynesian economists supported them. Both positions were simplifications—but reasonable simplifications. In the 1980s, however, many modern Classicals put forward a view of the deficit quite outside the Classical tradition. Modern Classicals said that deficits didn't matter. This switch occurred about the time that many Keynesians were arguing that the government budget deficit was too large and should be reduced. Thus, the 1980s saw Classicals and Keynesians flip-flop their positions on the budget deficit.

Why Modern Classicals Flipped   One reason for the modern Classical switch in position was the rediscovery of a theoretical argument for ignoring the effects of deficits. That argument was called the *Ricardian equivalence theorem,* named for David Ricardo, an early Classical economist who first developed the argument. The **Ricardian equivalence theorem** states that it makes no difference whether government spending is financed by taxes or by a deficit. The effect of an increase in government spending is the same in either case: a transfer of resources from the private sector to the government with *no* net effect on the aggregate economy.

Ricardian equivalence theorem
Proposition that it makes no difference whether government spending is financed by taxes now or by a deficit (taxes later).

The Classical view of government as a tool that individuals use to enrich themselves has been around for a long time, as can be seen in this 19th-century lithograph. *Bleichroeder Print Collection, Baker Library, Harvard Business School.*

The reasoning for the Ricardian equivalence theorem is based on rational expectations. If the government runs a deficit, at some time in the future that deficit must be paid off—meaning that, eventually, taxes will be higher than if there were no deficit. Rational individuals will take those future taxes into account in their decisions and will spend less now, just as they would have spent less on themselves now if current taxes had been raised. So individuals with rational expectations will save more now to pay for future taxes, and therefore will be unaffected by a government deficit.

Earlier Classical economists didn't emphasize the Ricardian equivalence theorem because they saw it as primarily a *theoretical* argument of little practical relevance. They opposed deficits because of their concern that government would waste the money. Modern Classicals focused more on formal theory, so they gave this argument more weight.

A second reason for the flip-flop was a change in the political realities. Even for those modern Classicals who didn't believe that tax cut incentives would stimulate the economy, or didn't believe in the Ricardian equivalence theorem, there was a major reason to support tax cuts. Tax cuts would limit new government programs. It was as if you had a spendthrift spouse who spent money faster than you could earn it. You've tried many strategies to get the spouse to stop spending, but nothing has worked. So you adopt the final strategy: earn less money and spend it immediately yourself so the bills pile up higher and higher and that your spouse won't have anything to spend.

Thus, some modern Classicals supported supply-side tax cuts because of the limitation they placed on government social programs. And it worked. In the 1980s, large cuts occurred in many social programs—cuts that many had believed were impossible. The modern Classical support for tax cuts also helped to put in office conservative candidates who opposed government activism and helped to keep out of office candidates in favour of government activism.

Why the Keynesians Flipped   The argument that one didn't have to worry about deficits was at the centre of the Keynesian policy revolution. Indeed, because he made that argument, Alvin Hansen, a Harvard economist who was instrumental in introducing Keynesian economics to the United States in the late 1930s (and later to Canada through his students), had been called a radical communist. Most 1930s Classical economists opposed Keynesianism precisely because it led to deficits. A balanced budget placed a constraint on government that was consistent with Classicals' judgement about governments.

Part of the early Keynesians' support of the federal deficit was based upon the political position that allowing budget deficits would allow an expansion of government programs. By the 1980s, government programs had expanded about as much as was politically feasible, so that reason to favour deficits ended.

Many Keynesians also felt that the large deficit was forcing government to hold down the economy with its other tool, monetary policy. Heavy reliance on monetary policy to slow the Canadian economy in the 1980s and 1990s, while government ran large deficits, is one reason Keynesians have argued for a more contractionary fiscal policy. They believed that a more contractionary fiscal policy would allow the Bank of Canada to run a more expansionary monetary policy, lowering interest rates, increasing investment, and increasing growth. In short, crowding out would be reduced. Thus, even though Keynesians supported a more expansionary aggregate policy than Classicals, they criticized the monetary/fiscal mix: They supported a somewhat less expansionary fiscal policy but a much more expansionary monetary policy. They believed that if the deficit were reduced, monetary policy could provide a stronger stimulus to the economy without generating inflation.

Not all Keynesians flip-flopped, but enough of them did so that it was no longer an acceptable simplification to say that Keynesians generally supported deficits and expansionary fiscal policy. So, in the 1990s, we find both Classicals and Keynesians divided in their views of the deficit.

With that update on modern theoretical developments and their relevance for policy, let's consider the three central problems of macroeconomics—inflation, unemployment, and growth—and see where Keynesians and Classicals tend to come out in their judgements about what to do about each of these. Exhibit 2 provides a summary comparison.

As you can see in Exhibit 2, there are some differences, but those differences reflect differences in emphasis, interpretation, and judgement as much as they reflect differences in theory.

Similarities and Differences between Keynesians and Classicals on Macro Policy

Similarities and Differences between Keynesians and Classicals on Fiscal Policy Classicals tend to worry slightly more about inflation than do Keynesians. Thus, Classicals tend to be more willing to believe that a higher unemployment rate is consistent with potential income than is a Keynesian. Moreover, Classicals see expansionary monetary and fiscal policy as having far less effect on real income and unemployment. All Classicals see expansionary monetary policy as inflationary. However, they are divided on their view of expansionary fiscal policy's effect on inflation. The monetarist school of Classical thought says the deficit isn't important for inflation; some modern Classicals say that the deficit doesn't make any difference, since people with rational expectations offset any effect of the deficit. But the majority Classical position is that expansionary fiscal policy can contribute to inflationary pressures because it increases aggregate demand, while aggregate supply doesn't change. The result is inflation.

These theoretical differences between Keynesians and Classicals and among different subgroups of Classical economists on the expansionary effect of fiscal policy aren't too important in practice, since, in the real world, fiscal policy is a difficult tool to use. The reason these theoretical differences are not too important in practice is political reality. A country's fiscal policy generally reflects political considerations as much as or more than economic stabilization considerations. Due to these political considerations, economists of all persuasions tend to believe that governments usually lean toward expansionary fiscal policy, regardless of economists' advice.

If expansionary aggregate policy (a deficit) is needed, fiscal policy generally turns expansionary. Tax cuts or spending increases are politically popular, and if the need for them is recognized in time, usually we can count on expansionary fiscal policy.

Turning the other way—contractionary fiscal policy—isn't so easy. When the prime minister says "Elect me and we'll get rid of the GST," and the House of

EXHIBIT 2   A Comparison of Classical and Keynesian Policies

Problem	Keynesian Policy	Classical Policy
Inflation	• *Cause: Inflation is a combination institutional and monetary problem* • Use contractionary monetary and fiscal policy • Supplement above policy with policies to change wage–and price–setting institutions—possibly consider a temporary income policy • Some small amount of inflation may be good for economy, and it is not worth trying to push inflation to zero if it involves significant unemployment	• *Cause: Inflation is a monetary problem* • Avoid inflation by relying on strict monetary rule—use contractionary monetary policy • Be careful about expanding output too high and causing inflation • Push inflation to zero by following strict monetary rule
Slow Growth	• *Cause: Slow growth is a combination institutional and aggregate demand problem* • Use expansionary monetary and fiscal policy • Supplement above policy with policies to establish incentives for growth	• *Cause: Growth rate reflects people's desires; probable cause of slow growth is too much regulation, too high tax rates, and too few incentives for growth* • Remove government impediments to growth; go back to laissez-faire policy
Recessionary Unemployment	• *Cause: Recessionary unemployment is a combination institutional and aggregate demand problem* • Use expansionary monetary and fiscal policy	• *Cause: Recessionary unemployment was probably caused by earlier government policies which were too expansionary, causing inflation* • If unemployment is very high, use expansionary monetary and fiscal policy. Generally, however, government policies should focus on the long run.

Commons committee says "We'll replace it with a tax that covers everything, including food," it's not hard to see why contractionary fiscal policy is hard to implement. Former U.S. President Bush used to say, "Read my lips: No new taxes," and the U.S. Congress said, "No cuts in government programs." With those pronouncements—presto! It's rather difficult to have contractionary fiscal policy. The fiscal policy steering wheel is consistently being pulled toward being inflationary.

Both Keynesians and Classicals agree about the political difficulties of using fiscal policy to slow inflation. Thus, much of the debate about what types of macroeconomic policy to use generally focuses on monetary policy.

Similarities and Differences between Keynesians and Classicals on Monetary Policy   The majority Keynesian and Classical views on monetary policy agree that expansionary monetary policy can stimulate the economy in the short run (although some modern Classicals argue that people with rational expectations will immediately push up prices, so expansionary monetary policy can only cause inflation, even in the short run). But Keynesians and Classicals disagree about the long run, and hence they disagree on the effectiveness of expansionary policy. Classicals tend to see the long-run effect of monetary policy as exclusively on inflation; Keynesians believe that the inflationary effect of monetary policy is dependent on how close the economy is to its potential income. Because of this difference, Keynesians tend to advocate more activist policies, while Classicals tend to advocate more laissez-faire policies.

Theoretically these differences show up in their views on the aggregate supply curve. Keynesians see the aggregate supply curve as dependent upon expected demand. Thus, an increase in nominal demand can increase real output. Classicals see aggregate supply as independent of expected aggregate demand. Unless expansionary monetary policy fools suppliers into thinking there's been an increase in real demand, it can only cause inflation.

Most Keynesians and Classicals agree that in the short run, expansionary monetary policy can stimulate growth and keep the economy out of a recession. But it can do so only at the cost of creating inflationary pressure. That inflationary pressure leads to increased rates of inflation in the long run, as it breaks down institutional constraints on firms raising wages and prices and as it becomes built into expectations. Therefore, the initial inflationary side effects of expansionary monetary policy are often hidden. This hiding of costs creates enormous political pressure for expansionary monetary policy. With politicians' short-run time horizon, a push for expansionary monetary policy is almost inevitable, especially around election time. Given the Bank of Canada's quasi-independence, there is debate about whether the Bank of Canada responds to that pressure as well.

The debate about whether or not to use expansionary monetary policy arises because of disagreement about whether moderate expansionary pressures will always lead to inflation in the long run. This difference in views means that there's a range of inflation and unemployment where it's not clear whether expansionary or contractionary monetary policy should be used. The economy is often in this range. On the one hand, to use expansionary policy in that range is to take a chance that inflationary expectations will get built into expectations and institutions. On the other hand, to use contractionary policy can lead to a slow-growth, high-unemployment economy.

Amid these debates between Keynesians and Classicals we shouldn't lose sight of the convergence of views. There's more agreement about policy than disagreement. Both Keynesians and Classicals generally agree that:

1. Expansionary monetary and fiscal policies have short-run stimulative effects on income.

2. Expansionary monetary and fiscal policies have potential long-run inflation effects.

3. Monetary policy is politically easier to use than fiscal policy.

4. Expansionary monetary and fiscal policies tend to increase a trade deficit.

5. Expansionary monetary policy places upward pressure on the exchange rate.

6. Expansionary fiscal policy has an ambiguous effect on the exchange rate.

In the actual conduct of policy, these agreements often mean that various economists' advice is similar, whether it's Keynesian or Classical advice.

Another way to see the consistency of policy advice is to consider macro policy in terms of the three ranges of price-level flexibility that we presented in earlier chapters. We reproduce those ranges in Exhibit 3. In range *A,* where unemployment is very high and the economy is a long way from potential output, both Classicals and Keynesians agree that expansionary macro policy is called for. In range *C,* where the aggregate demand exceeds potential income, both Keynesians and Classicals agree that contractionary macro policy is called for. The debate concerns range *B,* where unemployment may be too high but, simultaneously, there are inflationary pressures that could lead to an accelerating inflation. Because there is agreement about policy in ranges *A* and *C,* the economy is generally in range *B.*

Agreement about Macroeconomic Policy

5   Both Keynesians and Classicals generally agree that:

a. Expansionary monetary and fiscal policies have short-run stimulative effects on income.

b. Expansionary monetary and fiscal policies have potential long-run inflation effects.

c. Monetary policy is politically easier to implement than fiscal policy.

d. Expansionary monetary and fiscal policies tend to increase a trade deficit.

e. Expansionary monetary policy places upward pressure on the exchange rate.

f. Expansionary fiscal policy has an ambiguous effect on the exchange rate.

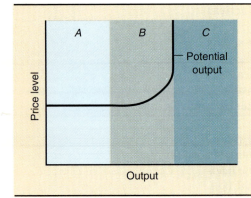

EXHIBIT 3   The Three Ranges of Price Level Flexibility

Most economists see the economy as having three ranges of price level flexibility. In range *A*, when the economy is significantly below potential income, most economists agree that expansionary policy is useful. In range *C*, when the economy is above its potential income, most economists favour contractionary policy. In range *B*, the intermediate range, there is debate about policy. The economy is generally thought to be in range *B* so there is generally debate about what is the appropriate policy.

RECENT HISTORY OF MACROECONOMIC POLICY

The period 1982–1990 set the stage for the recent history of macro policy. This was a period of substantial growth in the economy. Brian Mulroney was prime minister during most of this time. His Liberal successor, Jean Chretien, was elected in 1993 after Kim Campbell failed to deliver an economic agenda that voters could distinguish from Mulroney's.

In the first half of Mulroney's term the economy kept on its path of growth, but in the fall of 1990 the string of good luck ended. Due to a Middle East military conflict, oil prices rose substantially, leading many to fear that inflationary pressures would result in an inflationary spurt like that of the mid- and late 1970s. Those fears of policymakers and businesspeople, and, as we'll see shortly, the policies of the new Governor of the Bank of Canada, led to contractionary monetary policy and a fall in investment, and led to the 1990 recession.

The 1990 Recession

Going into the 1990s, the consensus view was that fiscal policy was expansionary, not for macroeconomic reasons, but for political reasons. This was unlikely to change significantly, so if inflationary pressures were going to be nipped in the bud, monetary policy had to provide the contractionary effect.

In 1990, regardless of how one measured monetary policy—by interest rates or by money supply—Bank of Canada policy was contractionary, and there was significant debate about whether it should have loosened up policy to avoid a recession. The tight monetary policy had stronger-than-desired effects as banks limited loans. The arguments for loosening were countered by the fear that, if the Bank of Canada did loosen up, or even showed weakness in its resolve to fight inflation, inflation would take off. Whether that would have happened is unclear; what is clear is that there were problems with the anti-inflationary policy the Bank of Canada followed.

The Bank of Canada's resolve to fight inflation was strengthened by international pressures. In September 1990, as concern about the Middle East political situation grew, the G-7 countries met and decided to coordinate their monetary policies. All would maintain relatively contractionary policies, so that the 1974 and 1979 experiences, in which an oil price rise led to serious world-wide inflation, wouldn't be repeated. The G-7 would come down on the side of fighting inflation. Many economists felt that this would be the path to a serious recession, which would lead the Bank of Canada and other countries' central banks to change their policies from contractionary to expansionary, as they had in the past.

The policy most economists advocated for Canada was to reduce the deficit by tightening up somewhat on fiscal policy—but not too much, for fear of furthering recessionary pressures. This contractionary fiscal policy was meant to be counteracted by expansionary monetary policy. The combination of policies would lower the interest rate some, decreasing the value of the dollar, which, in the long run, would stimulate Canadian exports.

The recession lingered on through all of 1991 despite some signs that it was ending. When it was clear that the recovery was slow in coming and that inflation was remaining low, the Bank of Canada loosened monetary policy significantly. Interest rates fell to their lowest level in 30 years. Their fall pushed down the value of the Canadian dollar and that decrease, combined with the recession, temporarily raised Canadian net exports. Simultaneously, recessions in the EU and Japan refocused international concern away from inflation.

The Sort-Of Recovery, 1992—and the Debate about Supply-Side Macro Policies

The pickup in the economy did not occur fast enough for Kim Campbell. Entering the election of 1993 with the economy in the doldrums, she lost the election to the Liberals, who ran on a platform of getting the economy going again.

Precisely how Jean Chretien planned to do this was unclear, not because he lacked an understanding of the economic problems facing the country, but because the situation the economy was in made traditional policies contradictory. That may be one reason why people had no difficulty coming to terms with the Liberal Party's "book of promises," the so-called Red Book. The goals were beyond the normal macroeconomic tools of monetary and fiscal policy. Traditional methods weren't working. It was time for something new.

Pointing out the limitations of normal macro policies would not have gotten him elected, so instead, Chretien promised to do everything. After he was elected, he had to figure out how to achieve those contradictory goals, or at least how to appear to be doing so.

The dilemma Chretien faced provides a good statement of the modern confusion about macroeconomic policy. The difficulty was the following: To expand the economy and create jobs, both Keynesian and Classical economics tell us to run deficits and increase the money supply (although Classical economics says this will only work temporarily). But the political imperatives of the 1990s were to *decrease the size of the deficit* and to prevent inflation by not increasing the money supply.

The Allure of Supply-Side Policies

Within this new situation, the difference between the Classical and Keynesian theories becomes of minor importance, since both theories say that to stimulate the economy you must do what is politically infeasible. It is at this point that supply-side policies enter in.

Supply-side policies expand potential output by creating supply-side incentives, by lowering tax rates, or by modifying the composition of government spending and taxes to stimulate supply. Because they expand potential output, they allow the economy to grow; that growth decreases the budget deficit and creates jobs. Thus, supply-side policies offer the hope of having it all—growth, prosperity, and low unemployment. It isn't surprising that Conservative, Liberal, and Reform politicians have all been attracted to such policies.

6   Traditional macro policies offer trade-offs. To expand the economy, one must run deficits and increase the money supply. Doing so causes inflation. Supply-side policies offer hope of expanding potential output and hence having it all—growth, prosperity, and low unemployment—without deficits.

Supply-side policies   Policies that focus on incentive effects of taxes and advocate lower tax rates or modifying the composition of government spending and taxes to stimulate supply, expand potential output, and allow the economy to grow, with the result that the growth decreases the budget deficit and creates jobs—that is, creates growth, prosperity, and low unemployment.

Classical supply-side economics
Economics that focuses on incentive effects of taxes and argues that low tax rates are central to an economy's success.

Classical Supply-Side Economics   **Classical supply-side economics** focuses on incentive effects of taxes. It argues that low tax rates are central to an economy's success. Classical supply-side economics developed not in the economics profession, but in the popular press, in Jude Wanniski's book *The Way the World Works*. Wanniski, a former newspaper reporter, prides himself on never having taken an economics course. He bases his arguments on some ideas of economist Arthur Laffer, who argued that the economy's problem was that tax rates were too high and that if rates were cut, the economy would expand.

Classical supply-side rhetoric worked well for Mulroney, but not so well for Campbell. The deficits kept mounting as the supply-side incentives didn't create the needed increase in the growth of potential output and didn't end the political push for more and more government spending. But that did not undermine its political appeal because supply-side policies were the only set of policies in town that promised everything.

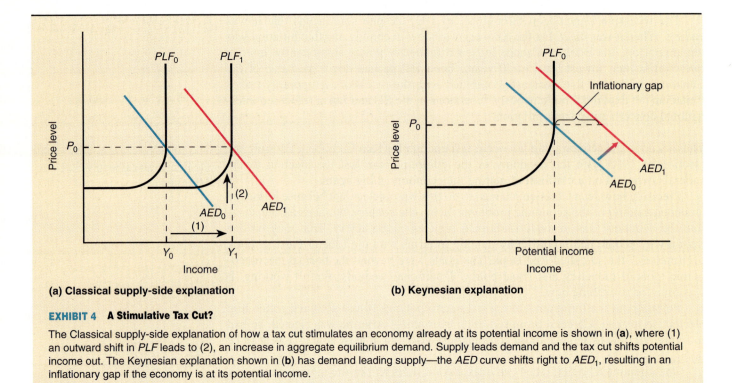

EXHIBIT 4   A Stimulative Tax Cut?

The Classical supply-side explanation of how a tax cut stimulates an economy already at its potential income is shown in (**a**), where (1) an outward shift in *PLF* leads to (2), an increase in aggregate equilibrium demand. Supply leads demand and the tax cut shifts potential income out. The Keynesian explanation shown in (**b**) has demand leading supply—the *AED* curve shifts right to AED_1, resulting in an inflationary gap if the economy is at its potential income.

Differences between Classical Supply-Side and Keynesian Explanations of How a Tax Cut Stimulates the Economy   At first glance, Wanniski's supply-side argument may look very much like a Keynesian argument for fiscal policy in which cutting taxes stimulates the economy via the multiplier effect. But there's an important difference between the Keynesian and supply-side views. The supply-side explanation of how the tax cut would stimulate the economy is by microeconomic incentives. It focuses on tax rates, not tax revenues.

The supply-side argument goes as follows: If the government cuts tax rates, people will have greater incentive to work, to save, and to invest. As they do all these things, output will increase, not because of expectations of increased demand, but because of the incentive effects of lower tax rates on supply. (The price-level flexibility curve, and hence potential income, will shift out.) Since supply creates its own demand, aggregate equilibrium demand will also increase. The economy will expand because of greater incentives to work. Exhibit 4 (a) shows the supply-side view. A decrease in taxes directly shifts the PLF curve out and, since supply creates its own demand, also shifts the aggregate equilibrium demand curve out. In the supply-side view, range *C* of the price-level flexibility curve is the best estimate of potential income, which means the tax rate cut increases potential income too.

The Keynesian explanation of the effect of a cut in taxes, shown in Exhibit 4 (b), differs. The Keynesian theoretical explanation holds that a tax cut increases income and expected aggregate equilibrium demand. If the level of potential income is greater than the actual level of income, producers will increase output because of that increased expected demand, which further increases aggregate equilibrium demand. If, however, the economy is initially at potential income, the tax cut shifts aggregate equilibrium demand, but not the PLF, because supply can't increase beyond potential income. The result will be either shortages or inflation.

The Keynesian explanation of a tax cut's effect is the multiplier process: In it, *demand* leads *supply* and potential income is unaffected. In the supply-side explanation, *supply* leads *demand* and potential income is increased. The differences are important because the supply-side explanation has specific policy implications. The supply-side explanation says that a deficit financed by a tax cut will not be inflationary. Politically, this is a desirable argument: society can have its free lunch.

DISTINGUISHING THE
KEYNESIAN AND CLAS-
SICAL SUPPLY-SIDE
ARGUMENTS

We can see the theoretical difference between the Keynesian and Classical supply-side explanations by considering the following thought experiment: Assume the government replaced the income tax (a tax in which the total amount a person pays changes with the amount of income she earns) with a poll tax (a tax in which the total amount an individual pays is constant regardless of his income). Also assume that the poll tax generated as much revenue as the income tax, and that marginal propensities to consume were equal for all income groups. What would be the effect on the aggregate economy?

Classical supply-siders would say that the aggregate output would increase enormously since the reward for additional work would be increased significantly. For Classical supply-siders, a cut in tax rates, not a cut in tax revenues, is what stimulates the economy.

A Keynesian would say that a shift from an income tax to a poll tax would have no effect on the economy. Why? Because tax revenues wouldn't change; only the method of assessing the taxes would change. In the Keynesian model, it is the amount of tax collected, not the tax rate, that affects the economy. A change in the tax rates, tax revenue remaining constant, would have no effect.

In reality, tax revenues are almost invariably changed by changing tax rates, so the effect of a tax cut is difficult to discover, and that's why there is so much debate about which side is right.

Economists and Classical Supply-Side Economics Most economists were not convinced by the supply-side arguments. While all agreed that there are supply-side effects on incentives to save on labour supply and effort, the majority see the time dimension needed for these supply-side policies to take effect—two to four years—as longer than the focus of short-run macro policy. Therefore, most economists saw the supply-side arguments as involving significant political rhetoric without much substance for short-run aggregate policy.[1] Setting tax rates could stimulate the economy in the short run through expectations. If the economy were below its potential income (and remember, it's unclear where potential income is) and if the tax cuts positively affected expectations, tax cuts could lead to a boom because people believed they would work. Some economists supported supply-side policies on these grounds.

Other economists supported supply-side policies for a different reason. They argued that since much of government spending was a waste, some way had to be found to reduce it. Cutting taxes thereby created a large deficit, making it impossible for the government to spend more, while at the same time introducing positive long-run supply-side incentive effects. Compared with the alternatives, many economists believed that the supply-side policies offered the best hope for the economy, even if they might not achieve the short-run benefits claimed in the political rhetoric through the path that supply-siders claimed.

Keynesian Supply-Siders Chretien's supply-side policy was based on a variation of the Classical supply-side policy, but it had definite Keynesian overtones, so we call it **Keynesian supply-side policy.** A Keynesian supply-side policy goes beyond the traditional Keynesian demand-side analysis that has been so far discussed. The Keynesian version of supply-side economics focuses on the composition of government spending and taxes. It says that composition can be modified to expand supply and potential output, decreasing the deficit at the same time that it expands the economy. Thus, the policy does not look at the level of total taxes and spending; instead it focuses on the composition of total taxes and spending.

Here's how it is supposed to work: You design a policy that combines tax cuts with tax increases; you call the tax cuts "investments in productivity," and you don't discuss the tax increases. Similarly, you combine spending cuts with spending

Keynesian supply-side policy Policy that goes beyond the traditional Keynesian demand-side analysis and focuses on the composition of government spending and taxes, modifying that composition to expand supply and potential output, decreasing the deficit at the same time that it expands the economy.

---

[1] On the provincial level, where substitution effects from one province to another are likely, supply-side arguments have many more supporters among economists.

increases; you call the spending increases "supply-enhancing" spending, and you call the spending cuts "supply-enhancing" cuts.

If you're a good orator, and lucky, you can make the policy sound attractive and, perhaps, even pull it off, if you are fortunate enough to have inflation remaining low, expectations holding up private demand, and monetary policy holding the interest rate down. How? By affecting expectations, and thereby stimulating private investment and consumption. As we discussed earlier, there is a self-fulfilling nature to the economy. If you can convince people the economy is going to be great, and get them to act on that conviction, the economy will be great. The policy works through expectations and beliefs, and then through economic channels—not directly through economic channels.

In late 1993, 1994, and 1995, this policy worked for Chretien. The economy picked up and started to expand, creating the usual debates about how close to potential income the economy was and how much inflation would be generated. In 1994, the Bank of Canada started tightening monetary policy slightly to ward off speculation against the Canadian dollar resulting from the fall election in Quebec and international concerns over debts and deficits. Economists were divided on whether this was the right policy or not.

The above may sound like an unsympathetic discussion of Chretien's policy, but it should be kept in mind that he had almost no other options. Both Keynesian and Classical theory said that the political demands—cut the deficit, hold inflation down, expand growth, and increase jobs—could not be achieved through traditional policies.

The problem some economists have with this Keynesian supply-side policy is three-fold:

1. The government is deciding which activities are, and are not, supply-enhancing. Past experience is not heartening about the government's ability to make those decisions.

2. Politically, getting the tax and spending changes to follow the structure that has actually been decided upon is difficult. Politics, not economics, usually guides those decisions.

3. Supply-side effects of compositional changes in taxes and spending are second-order, long-term effects. In the short run, the aggregate effects of the budget deficit will predominate.

These three reasons leave a number of economists, even those who generally support the goals Chretien advocated, wary of the long-run success of his Keynesian supply-side policies. While such policies sound good politically and reconcile the otherwise irreconcilable goals, it is unclear how long the high expectations could support the economy. Like the Classical supply-side proposals, the Keynesian supply-side proposals were seen by the majority of economists as political rhetoric without much substance for short-run aggregate policy, except through the expectational path.

TOPICAL ISSUES IN CANADIAN MACRO POLICY

Price stability A period during which the overall price level does not suffer from excessive volatility.

Now we want to put our macro theory to work and look at topical issues in Canadian macroeconomic policy. First we want to look at **price stability** as the be-all and end-all of monetary policy. The Bank of Canada embarked on its price stability goal in 1988, and by 1994 inflation had been wrestled to the ground. The problem is that the unemployment rate rose substantially during this period. We want to review the issues relating to price stability and discuss proposals that might help us achieve both stable prices and full employment in the future.

The second issue we'll look at concerns proposals for changes to the unemployment insurance and welfare programs. In the last chapter we saw that federal and provincial deficits rose significantly as a result of the recession of the early 1990s and that debt service costs are becoming significant. In an attempt to be more fiscally responsible, federal and provincial governments are changing the social safety nets that Canadians have come to rely on. We want to look at some of the changes to these social programs.

THE MONETARY CONDITIONS
INDEX

The monetary conditions index (MCI) is a weighted sum of the changes in the short-term interest rate (the 90-day commercial paper rate) and the G-10 trade-weighted exchange rate from a given base period. The Bank has been using the MCI as an operational target of policy for several years.* In an open economy like Canada's, which operates with a flexible exchange rate, monetary policy actions influence aggregate demand through both the interest rate and the exchange rate. Therefore, the central bank cannot ignore exchange rate movements when determining its policy stance.

The weighting for the interest rate versus the exchange rate is 3 to 1 and is based on a number of empirical studies that estimate the effect of changes in real interest rates and the real exchange rate on real aggregate demand over six to eight quarters. The relative weights mean that a 1 percentage point change (100 basis points) in the real interest rate is judged to have about the same effect over time on aggregate demand as a 3 percentage point change in the real effective exchange rate. Because of the lags in publishing the price indexes to calculate the G-10 real effective exchange rate, the Bank tends to focus on a nominal MCI over short horizons.

A change in the MCI simply gives a measure of the degree of tightening or easing in monetary conditions. No meaning should be attached to a particular level of the MCI since it is constructed as a change from an arbitrary base date (currently January 1987 = 0). While the MCI is better conceptually than short-term interest rates as an operational target, this does not imply that monetary policy operations can be tied to any simple mechanical rule related to the MCI. First, the MCI does not (nor do interest rates for that matter) provide a nominal anchor for policy. Second, desired changes in monetary conditions vary in response to movements in aggregate demand and supply. Consequently, the monetary conditions consistent with the target path for inflation control are constantly reevaluated. For example, an increase in the relative prices of primary commodities produced in Canada tends to lead to an increase in aggregate demand and thus to an increase in the desired MCI.

It is important to note that on a day-to-day basis, the Bank does not try to maintain a precise MCI level by adjusting interest rates in response to every exchange rate wiggle. Only if the exchange rate moved to a new trading range would the Bank try to offset its effect on aggregate demand by encouraging an offsetting movement in interest rates. In addition, there are occasions when Bank actions cannot be devoted to achieving the desired MCI because of the need to cope temporarily with disorderly markets.

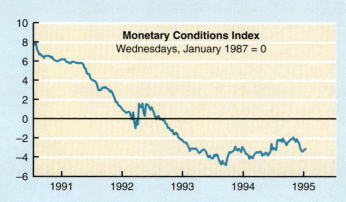

* An operational target is a variable that the central bank can influence fairly directly when it changes the setting of its instrument variable. In Canada, the instrument is the size of the central bank's balance sheet.

Source: Monetary Policy Report, May 1995 Bank of Canada: Ottawa.

Finally, we'll see whether a return to a fixed exchange rate regime would benefit Canada in the long run. Recent proposals for changing our exchange rate system suggest that a fixed exchange rate regime might be a panacea for all of our troubles—but remember, TANSTAAFL.

There is legitimate debate over the appropriate conduct of monetary and fiscal policies—should they focus on attaining price stability, or should policy aim at reducing

Price Stability, Full Employment, or Both?

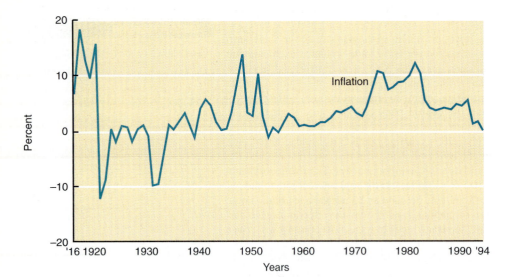

EXHIBIT 5   Inflation in Canada

This exhibit provides a clear picture of the historical pattern of inflation in Canada.

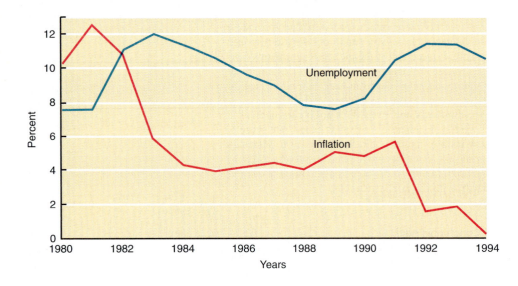

EXHIBIT 6   Unemployment and Inflation Rates in Canada

Economists try to explain why inflation has fallen over the last fifteen years while unemployment has cycled around ten percent.

7 Monetary policy focused on price stability in the late 1980s and early 1990s. With stable prices, the market can predict the value of money. Given that fiscal policies are politically constrained, this may be the most appropriate goal for monetary policy.

the unemployment rate? From our previous work on the relationship between inflation and unemployment we saw that there's usually a trade-off—we can't reduce inflation while at the same time reducing the unemployment rate. Has the Bank of Canada's policy of achieving price stability forced us to accept high rates of unemployment? Is a return to inflation the only solution for the unemployment problem? Is there any way to achieve full employment and price stability?

Exhibit 5 shows us the inflation rate in the Canadian consumer price index. The major inflationary bouts were in response to the two World Wars (1914–1918 and 1939–1945) and the oil price shocks of the 1970s. Exhibit 6 focuses on the period from 1980 to 1994, and includes the Canadian unemployment rate. This figure clearly demonstrates the empirical observation that when inflation rises, unemployment falls, and vice versa. Closer inspection of Exhibit 6 also suggests that a low and stable rate of inflation may allow the unemployment rate to fall. From 1984 to 1988, the rate of inflation was fairly constant, yet the unemployment rate fell from over 12 percent to 8 percent in four years. We know there were a number of other factors that might have led to a lower unemployment rate, such as the expansion of export industries in response to the depreciated Canadian dollar, but Exhibit 6 tells us that a stable rate of inflation might be good for the economy.

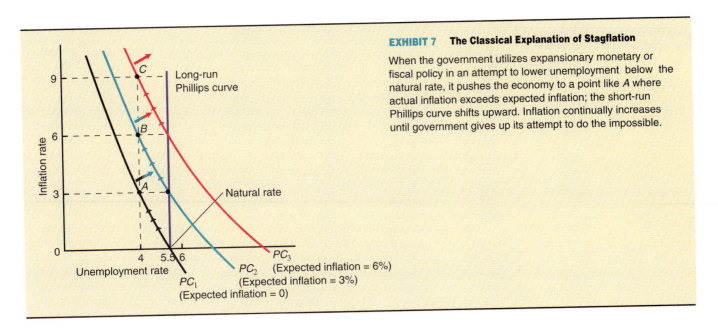

EXHIBIT 7   The Classical Explanation of Stagflation

When the government utilizes expansionary monetary or fiscal policy in an attempt to lower unemployment below the natural rate, it pushes the economy to a point like *A* where actual inflation exceeds expected inflation; the short-run Phillips curve shifts upward. Inflation continually increases until government gives up its attempt to do the impossible.

Price stability became the focus of monetary policy when the former Governor of the Bank of Canada, John Crow, gave his Hanson Memorial Lecture at the University of Alberta in 1988. At that time Governor Crow said:

> Monetary policy should be conducted as to achieve a pace of monetary expansion that promotes stability in the value of money. This means pursuing a policy aimed at achieving and maintaining stable prices.

This was a clear statement of the stance of monetary policy: the Bank of Canada was going to focus on attaining price stability at the expense of all other objectives. The Bank had relatively little concern for the impact its policies would have on unemployment, especially as it related to regional diversity.

Governor Crow argued that in the long run, the value of money was the only economic variable the central bank could control. We can see Governor Crow's logic by using Phillips curves. Exhibit 7 illustrates that while expansionary monetary policy can cause a temporary reduction in the unemployment rate, in the long run this can be maintained only through a continual process of monetary expansion: in other words, a series of rightward shifts in the short-run Phillips curve. This creates an ongoing inflation that conveys the wrong signals to the marketplace.

We know that inflation confuses the distinction between changes in relative prices and changes in the general price level. Resources are employed in what appear to be their best uses, but after the market disentangles price information into changes in the price level and changes in relative prices, workers, firms, and international investors may recognize that they had made expectations errors. This was behind Governor Crow's view that while monetary policy might be capable of creating short-run changes in real output, it does so only through frustrating the informative role of the price system. Since this involves the wasteful use of scarce resources, it was viewed as an inappropriate goal of monetary policy.

We need to remember that the price stability debate took place during a period in which the fiscal policy refrigerator was unlocked. Federal and provincial deficits were growing, leading to ever-increasing debt servicing costs. Political rhetoric on deficit and debt reduction was commonplace, yet little effort was made in reforming taxation and spending programs. Provincial premiers sought cheaper sources of funds and attempted to persuade the Bank of Canada to buy provincial debt rather than being forced themselves to float their bond issues in the international marketplace, where competition would force them to offer higher rates of return to attract internationally mobile financial capital. Governor Crow refused, arguing that the monetization (the

DOES PRICE STABILITY MEAN ZERO INFLATION?

Governor Crow's desire to maintain a stable value of our money suggests that price stability really means zero inflation. Why then have the Bank of Canada and the Federal Minister of Finance announced target rates of inflation below 3 percent as being acceptable? Does price stability mean zero inflation?

There are a number of ways of answering this question. The "lubricant view" suggests that markets need a small rate of inflation to restore equilibrium. This is because when nominal wages (or any other price for that matter) are downwardly rigid due to contracts that set wages over several periods (or if it is costly for firms to change prices), a small inflation will reduce the real cost of hiring workers (or buying goods). This returns real wages (or the real prices of goods and services) to their equilibrium values. Empirical evidence on this view is somewhat mixed, with some analysts finding evidence of significant downward wage and price rigidity while others do not.

When we measure the inflation rate we need to be aware of the fact that different price indexes will generate different rates of inflation. Is the price stability goal a function of the consumer price index, or is it a function of the gross domestic product price deflator? Recent work at the Bank of Canada has shown that the CPI contains an inflationary bias because of various factors such as discrete changes in indirect taxes and the prices of regulated goods that are included in the CPI. When these prices change, the measured CPI inflation rate may be positive for some time as the price adjustments work through the marketplace. For this reason, the Bank of Canada now looks at both the inflation rate in the CPI and in an index of unregulated prices to get a feel for the course of inflation.

Finally, there may be regional differences in inflation rates that would make it difficult to achieve a zero rate of inflation on a national basis. In addition, the incentive to inflate is always a factor in financing government spending, since government has an interest in borrowing today and repaying tomorrow using cheaper dollars. Through creating a small rate of inflation, the government ensures that the real value of its liabilities is falling through time. All of these arguments suggest that price stability should be interpreted as a low and stable rate of inflation. When inflation is relatively constant and low (whatever level that means), the market is more likely to be able to predict the value of money.

central bank buying the new debt issued by government by increasing the money supply) of provincial debt would lead to even more expansionary fiscal policies. It was as if the premiers wanted to go on a diet, but only if Governor Crow agreed to keep the refrigerator door closed but unlocked. There was a definite conflict between the goals of fiscal and monetary policies. This schism was most apparent when there were proposals for the Bank of Canada Act to be rewritten to include price stability as the *only* objective of monetary policy.

Canada went through another recession in 1990–91, putting upward pressure on the unemployment rate and downward pressure on the inflation rate. Critics of the Bank of Canada argued vehemently against the goal of price stability, since they believed expansionary monetary policy could have been used to reduce the employment effects of the downturn. Indeed, some economists argue that the 1990–91 recession was the first "made-in-Canada" recession. They contend that for the first time in recent memory, global factors such as shocks to commodity prices and the behaviour of the U.S. economy played little role in the Canadian downturn. They believe the recession resulted from the Bank of Canada's single-mindedness towards beating inflation to the ground.

Calls for a change in the stance of monetary policy were heard loudest in the Prairies and Atlantic Canada. The Bank of Canada's high interest rate policy targeted the overheating Ontario economy, yet it placed a great burden on the regionally depressed areas of the country. With the combination of low harvests and internationally depressed commodity prices, farmers in the West found it increasingly difficult to remain on the land. High interest rates made it all but impossible to weather the storm. Similar criticisms held in the Atlantic economy, particularly with respect to agriculture and aquaculture. With already lower-than-average wages, price stability in the form of high interest rates made it difficult for individuals and firms to survive, let alone flourish.

EXHIBIT 8   Canadian Monetary Policy Objectives

STATEMENT OF THE GOVERNMENT OF CANADA AND THE BANK OF CANADA ON MONETARY POLICY OBJECTIVES

High levels of economic growth and employment on a sustained basis are the primary objectives of monetary and fiscal policies. The best contribution that monetary policy can make to these objectives is to preserve confidence in the value of money by achieving and maintaining price stability. In February 1991, the government and the Bank of Canada jointly announced a series of targets for reducing inflation and reaching price stability in Canada. By the end of 1995, the goal was to reduce inflation to the mid-point of a range of 1 to 3 percent.

It is now time to specify the objective that will steer monetary policy beyond 1995 and to provide a medium-term guide for Canadians in making their economic decisions. There is general agreement that economies function better when the rate of increase in prices is so low as to not distort the key decisions of businesses and households. There is less agreement on the precise rate at which this occurs. It is a long time since Canada has had inflation as low as it is now, and more experience in operating under these conditions would be helpful before an appropriate longer-term objective is determined. Moreover, some time is needed to enable Canadians to adjust to the improved inflation outlook.

Accordingly, the government and the Bank of Canada have agreed to extend the inflation reduction targets from 1995 to 1998 and to maintain the objective of holding inflation inside the range of 1 to 3 per cent (mid-point 2 per cent) during that time. In addition, the present approach under the targets for dealing with major price shocks, stemming from unexpected developments, and with indirect tax changes that result in sharp changes to the consumer price index will continue. It is important to ensure that these influences remain clearly temporary and that they do not lead to a sustained change in the outlook for inflation.

On the basis of the experience with low inflation over the period, a decision will be made by 1998 on the target range for the consumer price index that would be consistent with price stability and, therefore, with the long-run monetary policy goal of preserving confidence in the value of money in Canada.

Source: *Bank of Canada Review*, Winter 1993–94.

During the 1990–91 recession, there were calls for expansionary fiscal policies to offset the effects of Governor Crow's single-minded price stability policies, yet the financing constraints of the ever-growing federal and provincial debt left little room for governments to react. Governor Crow gained a reputation of being overly concerned with the rate of inflation at the expense of the unemployed, and some economists and politicians began to wonder how an unelected official could have so much control over the state of the economy. There were calls for a reorganization of the Bank of Canada to provide more regional representation. Proposals for the reform of the Bank included several aimed at allowing a majority of the Board of Directors of the Bank to force Governor Crow to adopt policies that were less concerned with achieving price stability.

By 1991, the federal government and the Bank of Canada jointly announced targets for the rate of inflation, acknowledging that the design of monetary policy is an inexact science. They announced an acceptable band for the rate of inflation, set between 1 and 3 percent. This was an attempt to show international investors that fiscal and monetary policies were coordinated so as to encourage growth in an environment where the value of money could be predicted with a reasonable degree of certainty.

Throughout the early 1990s, critics of the Bank of Canada called for Governor Crow's resignation at every available opportunity. Media attention given to the price stability objective led to a great deal of unrest. With the 1993 election decided only three months before the end of Governor Crow's seven-year term, it came as no surprise that Senior Deputy Governor Gordon Theissen was named the next Governor of the Bank of Canada late in 1993. The federal government and Governor Theissen immediately announced that price stability remained the basic objective of monetary policy, and that price stability should be viewed in terms of a low and stable rate of inflation rather than a zero rate of inflation. Exhibit 8 contains the press release; it discusses the immediate and future course of monetary policy.

Was the price stability goal the best objective for monetary policy? Should the central bank have been more concerned with reducing unemployment? While we do not have enough experience in a low and steady inflationary environment at this point in time to answer this question, we do know that inflation imposes costs on the economy through misallocating resources. Those who would argue against price stability are really saying that it is better to have a resource employed inefficiently rather than not employed at all. The problem with this view is that resources are scarce: once used for one purpose, it is difficult to reassign them to another task. This applies equally to physical capital as it does to human capital. Should a plant manager operate her facility for one shift every day for 52 weeks when the demand for the product could be satisfied by a double shift every day over 26 weeks? Should the government create low-skill temporary public works projects rather than provide workers, particularly the young, with the opportunity to train for highly-skilled positions? If you lean towards answering yes to both questions, you may have a rather myopic view of the role of government, and that was Governor Crow's point. Political realities tend to force the fiscal authorities to look to short-run solutions that may not be in the best long-run interests of the nation. With a price stability objective, the central bank was focusing on the long-run—in a way, forcing a degree of credibility upon the public purse.

Reforming Unemployment Insurance and Social Assistance Programs

8 Rising debts and deficits have forced governments to be more fiscally responsible. Towards that end many social programs are undergoing significant change, with a focus on self-sufficiency.

Unemployment insurance A federal government program aimed at replacing earnings of those who are temporarily out of work.

Growing government debts and deficits have led to changes to the network of social programs in Canada. In fact, one of the reasons the Chretien government was elected was its promise to review and revise social programs to make them more effective and more cost-efficient. We now turn to a discussion of proposals for the reform of two important areas of social policy in Canada: unemployment insurance and social assistance.

Unemployment Insurance The **Unemployment Insurance** Program provides protection for Canadians who have lost their jobs and are searching for work. Benefits are provided to those who are laid off from work, as well as individuals who face temporary absences from the labour force due to illness, pregnancy, work-sharing, and job creation and training programs. In 1992, almost 4 million Canadians received benefits of one kind or another under the program. It is funded by contributions from employees and employers. In early 1994, the premium for employees was $3.07 for every $100 of insurable earnings. Employers paid 1.4 times the employee rate. Exhibit 9 demonstrates that unemployment benefits have grown significantly over the past ten years. As of the end of 1993, the unemployment insurance fund was over $6 billion in deficit.

The unemployment insurance program has perhaps played more of the role of a tool of regional stabilization policy than the temporary insurance program it was initially meant to be. The large number of repeat users suggests that the program is used to stabilize income over the year rather than as a pure form of insurance. This has led to proposals for the reform of unemployment insurance. In February 1994, the Minister of Finance introduced a budget which contained background information on some of the changes. These included reducing the premium rate paid in support of the program from $3.07 per $100 to an even $3.00, as well as changing the period over which benefits would be paid. The federal government predicts these changes will allow business to create another 40,000 jobs by the end of 1996, and this is only the beginning. Eligibility rules were revised to make it more difficult to secure benefits. The previous rules regarding the effect of regional unemployment rates on the duration of benefits was revised to place more emphasis on steady employment rather than seasonal or intermittent employment. The new system would still allow claimants in depressed regions to qualify for more benefits than claimants in areas with low unemployment, but the changes were targeted at those who gain temporary employment and

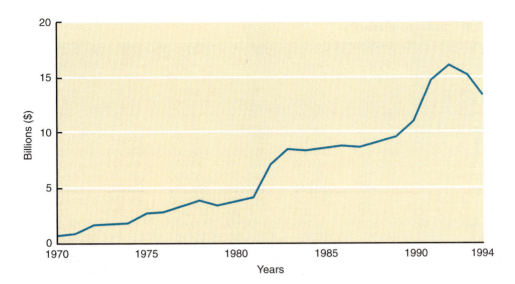

EXHIBIT 9   Unemployment Insurance Benefits

Payments to those collecting unemployment insurance benefits have risen significantly over the last twenty-five years.

leave their jobs after securing sufficient time to be eligible for benefits. This form of "job-sharing" is discouraged under the proposals for reform.

Social Assistance   Canada offers one of the most generous **social assistance programs** in the world. Each province designs and administers its own program, with funding assistance from the federal government. There are both long-term and short-term programs. In some provinces, municipalities are responsible for providing short-term assistance while the province funds those on long-term assistance. Benefit levels vary across the provinces and may be associated with the specific needs of the individual or family unit vis-a-vis medical needs and the composition of the family. Exhibit 10 shows how the number of beneficiaries has changed since 1986. Ontario, Quebec, and British Columbia consistently represent over 75 percent of total beneficiaries and total expenditures.

Social assistance programs
Government programs aimed at providing earnings and services to meet basic needs.

There is widespread agreement among economists that social assistance programs may discourage recipients from returning to the job market. Job skills and individual ability can suffer significant depreciation over sustained periods of passive social assistance. As time passes, it becomes increasingly difficult to return to the labour force. For some who are given an opportunity to work, the change is too drastic because they have been unable to maintain the skills they had, and they are unprepared to cope with the requirements of new technology. This may lead to the cycle of temporary employment, layoff, unemployment benefits, and eventually back to social assistance.

The push is on to create new assistance programs that will provide opportunities for upgrading education and training so that individuals can secure lasting employment and remain off social assistance. The basic idea is to allow people to develop new skills that will both make them more attractive to potential employers and give them the confidence they need to make the adjustment back to the labour force. Ideally, income security programs should provide adequate training and support, and in doing so, remove the disincentive to work.

As of 1994–1995 there were a number of national and provincial programs aimed at reforming social assistance programs. The Self-Sufficiency project provides temporary income subsidies to encourage income assistance recipients to move off social assistance and accept employment. The project attempts to provide a national view of how effective a financial subsidy might be in the decision to return to the labour force. The province of New Brunswick introduced the NB Works program to determine how retraining and education affect those on social assistance who appear to have the greatest potential for successful reentry to the labour force. Other programs and services have been introduced across the country to determine how we can make the transition

EXHIBIT 10   Canada Assistance Plan[1]

General assistance beneficiaries[2] (including dependents)					
	1986	1987	1988	1989	1990	1991
Newfoundland	47,000	50,500	47,900	44,800	47,900	51,800
Prince Edward Island	9,200	9,300	8,900	8,300	8,600	10,300
Nova Scotia	72,100	73,000	73,800	75,600	78,900	86,200
New Brunswick	68,800	73,700	70,600	67,700	67,200	71,900
Quebec	693,900	649,600	594,000	559,300	555,900	594,900
Ontario	485,800	518,400	533,500	588,200	675,700	929,900
Manitoba	62,600	60,600	62,700	63,000	66,900	71,700
Saskatchewan	62,700	62,100	60,300	57,200	54,100	53,400
Alberta	126,600	150,500	149,800	151,700	148,800	156,600
British Columbia	255,700	247,700	241,100	230,000	216,000	244,000
Yukon	1,400	1,200	1,100	900	1,000	1,200
Northwest Territories	7,100	8,300	9,300	9,400	10,000	10,300
Canada	1,892,900	1,904,900	1,853,000	1,856,100	1,931,000	2,282,000

General assistance expenditures (total federal-provincial[3]) ($ millions)					
	1986	1987	1988	1989	1990	1991
Newfoundland	$ 85.2	$ 108.0	$ 107.8	$ 109.3	$ 119.2	$ 142.5
Prince Edward Island	22.4	23.2	24.6	24.9	27.5	33.1
Nova Scotia	143.3	165.2	178.5	204.9	219.9	249.3
New Brunswick	206.7	229.3	235.0	227.5	236.2	261.1
Quebec	2,221.9	2,146.7	2,118.1	2,121.5	2,144.0	2,408.6
Ontario	1,479.5	1,642.8	1,831.5	2,124.4	2,425.1	3,639.2
Manitoba	156.8	179.8	177.8	219.1	206.3	242.3
Saskatchewan	190.7	215.5	215.0	200.1	189.3	201.5
Alberta	481.7	543.4	593.0	655.7	683.5	710.3
British Columbia	879.0	859.7	895.1	878.4	872.3	966.6
Yukon	2.2	—	1.3	6.1	2.8	3.6
Northwest Territories	11.0	12.0	16.2	14.4	20.3	24.7
Canada	$5,880.4	$6,125.7	$6,393.9	$6,786.3	$7,146.3	$8,882.8

[1]Fiscal years ending March 31st.

[2]Beneficiaries as of March 31st of each fiscal year.

[3]Total federal-provincial expenditures are estimates. They have been calculated by doubling the federal amount paid for claims received each year.
Source: *Canada Year Book*, 1994, p. 262.

from social assistance to gainful employment can be made as effectively as possible. All of these activities are part of a larger review of how Canada's social safety net can be modernized and made more efficient.

More recently there have been a number of changes and proposals for reform of unemployment insurance and social assistance programs. In Ontario and New Brunswick, able-bodied recipients of social assistance payments will lose some of their benefits if they fail to search for employment. And, nationally, there have been proposals to legally limit overtime to 100 hours per year in an attempt to give the unemployed a chance at a full-time job (that's the invisible foot in action!). All of these proposals will be much in the news in the 1990s.

Is the Solution a Return to Fixed Exchange Rates?

Several Canadian economists have recently argued for a return to a fixed exchange rate regime. One, Richard Harris of Simon Fraser University, suggests this is the key to making the transition to a global economy. From our earlier discussions we know that a fixed exchange rate has several implications for economic policy. The first and most obvious is that the Bank of Canada would lose control over the domestic money supply: it would be required to allow the money stock to rise and fall in response to shifts in demand in order to maintain a constant value of the dollar. We know this places undue pressure on Canadian inflation rates in that they will follow those of our major trading partners—for all intents and purposes, the United States. To see this, think back to the Quantity Theory of Money: if, in an attempt to keep the exchange rate fixed, our money supply is rising in the same proportion as that of our trading partners, there's inflation. This would seem to suggest that we abandon the goal of

NEW BRUNSWICK BEGINS REWEAVING SOCIAL SAFETY NET

Volunteers between 50 and 65 Years Old to Get Annual Salary for Community Work

By Edward Greenspon
Parliamentary Bureau

Ottawa—One of the first in a set of new experimental social programs was unveiled in Ottawa yesterday—which could provide some work for New Brunswickers over the age of 50 and some political relief for Liberals in the province.

Under the federal-provincial scheme, 1,000 workers between 50 and 65 will receive a guaranteed minimum salary of $12,000 a year in exchange for at least six months of community work. All will be volunteers.

Human Resources Development Minister Lloyd Axworthy described the initiative as a working model for his redesign of the country's social safety net.

"I think this gives us a real opportunity to test out some new concepts," he said in announcing the $80-million, five-year program.

The program, called NB Job Corps, embraces several principles the government is trying to introduce in reforming the country's $70-billion system of social programs.

It provides a financial incentive for people to leave so-called passive income support programs—in which unemployment insurance or welfare is paid and nothing required of the recipient—in favour of working at such tasks as cleaning up beaches, helping in libraries, or planting trees. At $1,000 a month, the benefits are far more generous than the $7,000 to $8,000 a year maximum offered under New Brunswick's welfare scheme.

Those enrolled in the program also will be allowed to work at other jobs without having to forfeit their Job Corps cheque and will be allowed to retain medical benefits awarded to welfare recipients. New Brunswick Premier Frank McKenna said that existing rules that require those receiving benefits to give back everything extra they may earn perpetuates dependence on public assistance.

In reality, though, nobody is expecting this particular program to move people from public assistance to private-sector employment. Applicants will have to demonstrate that long-term job retraining is not a realistic goal because of skills levels, age, geography, or other limitations.

Participants will be paid for a full year even if they are enrolled in the program for only six months. They will be allowed to engage in normal seasonal jobs, such as fishing or forestry, when they aren't doing community work. Mr. McKenna said he hopes to expand the program beyond 1,000 workers if it is successful.

Mr. Axworthy indicated that this particular pilot project is aimed at areas of high seasonal employment and won't necessarily apply nationally. Other programs with different aims will be announced in the coming weeks.

"What happens in New Brunswick may well also be applicable in northern Ontario or in the interior of British Columbia. That's what we'll find out.

We're not going to solve all the problems just by Job Corps," Mr. Axworthy said.

Mr. McKenna, who was in Ottawa for the announcement, touted the initiative as "a harbinger of social programs," which he thinks will be based on a bargain that in exchange for income support, there will be some obligation to train or work.

"We're taking at face value with this program what we're told repeatedly by activists and by people around welfare-unemployment that what we really want is to work. We're providing an opportunity to work."

Federal support for the New Brunswick idea comes at a critical time for Mr. McKenna. His province, which is heavily reliant on seasonal employment, was hit hard by Ottawa's recent tightening of qualifications for unemployment insurance.

There have been several major protests in the province and both provincial and federal Liberals have been feeling the political heat.

Just last week, Mr. McKenna complained to Prime Minister Jean Chrétien

in Moncton that the federal UI changes would end up adding $200 million to the province's welfare bill.

While yesterday's announcement does not remove the UI irritant, which will grow more serious as seasonal jobs draw to a close in September, it does give both Mr. McKenna and Liberal MPs in the area something positive to show their constituents.

Federal money for the program will come from a two-year $800-million fund set aside by Ottawa in last month's budget for such pilot projects. But it appears that New Brunswick may have jumped the queue in tapping into this money before criteria are fully set for its use.

Both Mr. Axworthy and Mr. McKenna went out of their way yesterday to point out that they have been discussing this program since last fall. In an interview after the announcement, the New Brunswick Premier said he couldn't comment on whether Ottawa was trying to help him out by acting on his proposal now "because I don't know the thinking on the federal side."

Mr. McKenna, who helped extricate Mr. Chrétien from a dicey situation over comments about welfare reform during the autumn election campaign and who signed on quickly to the federal anti-tobacco smuggling policy, has a long record of profiting from good relations with Ottawa. Under the Conservatives, he was able to secure federal support for an ambitious training program called NB Works in which Ottawa contributes more than $100,000 for each successful graduate.

Mr. Axworthy and Mr. McKenna stressed that the Job Corps program is voluntary and that nobody will be forced to work for their welfare money.

While an approach that imposes penalties for refusing work is intellectually defensible, according to Mr. McKenna, the question is academic. Governments will probably exhaust the funds they have available for voluntary programs before they run out of volunteers for them, he said.

Source: *The Globe and Mail,* Thursday, March 24, 1994, pp. A1, A5.

price stability. Does this mean the costs we paid to achieve a low and stable inflation rate were in vain? If the government decides to follow this course of action, what can we expect? Will this solve our unemployment and inflation problems? Is this the key to economic renewal?

As with almost any economic question, the answer is "it depends." We know that the Canadian economy benefited from importing U.S. manufacturing methods in the 1950s through the 1970s. When the Bretton Woods system of fixed exchange rates collapsed in the early 1970s, exchange rate fluctuations made it increasingly difficult to glean information on relative prices from the data we observed. When this happens, workers, firms, and international investors find it difficult to decide how to best maximize their welfare, profits, and returns.

Think of an American firm trying to decide whether or not it should maintain its branch plant in southern Ontario. If the demand for its product and its production costs are relatively insensitive to exchange rate fluctuations, the decision to move or to stay will depend on factors like barriers to trade. If the goods a U.S. firm produces in U.S. plants face a hefty tariff to cross into Canada, the firm might want to establish a branch plant in Canada to service that market. On the other hand, if trade barriers are of little concern, fluctuations in exchange rates will dominate the firm's decision. There's little merit to continuing to produce in a relatively small market, especially when the U.S. dollar value of Canadian dollar profits is not known with any degree of precision. A fixed exchange rate system would help firms and investors make the calculations necessary for trade and development. This is particularly true in the context of the U.S–Canada Free Trade Agreement (FTA) and the U.S.–Canada–Mexico North American Free Trade Agreement (NAFTA). If Canada is going to compete in this environment, we need to reduce as many of the uncertainties to trade as possible. Only then will firms decide to locate here rather than Mexico, the United States, or possibly Chile (Chile was invited to join NAFTA starting in 1996 but the negotiations are far from complete as of late 1995).

This suggests we need to fix the value of the Canadian dollar against the U.S. dollar. By doing so, we implicitly accept the rate of inflation in the United States. If an inflationary process begins in the United States, Canada will be forced to inflate at the same rate to keep the exchange rate constant. This abandonment of the price stability objective might at first seem unreasonable, yet think of the alternative. If U.S. inflation spills over into Canada, the Bank of Canada will raise short-term interest rates in an attempt to maintain stable prices. Internationally mobile capital will flow into Canada, given the higher rate of return on Canadian dollar-denominated assets. The appreciating Canadian dollar reduces our exports and encourages our imports (without taking into account changes in domestic and foreign prices). Our trade balance falls, and employment in export industries falls. The costs of servicing government debt rise with higher interest rates, leading to higher deficits in government spending and in the current account, and to lower employment. But remember, there won't be any inflation in Canada!

Now think what would happen if we didn't try to maintain stable prices and, instead, operated a fixed exchange rate against the U.S. dollar. The U.S. inflation would require higher rates of monetary expansion in Canada to keep the exchange rate fixed: our inflation rate would rise. Our interest rates would not be out of line with those in the United States, so nothing would happen to our exports and imports (remember our inflation rate will equal that in the United States, so the relative prices of our goods should be the same as before the U.S. inflation). Yes, there would be some resource misallocation resulting from trying to distinguish between changes in the general price level and changes in relative prices, but that would be common to both Canada and the United States. The only difference is that fluctuations in exchange rates would not affect trade.

The key to the fixed exchange rate as the panacea for all our ills is the belief that a fundamental change has occurred in the "wealth generation process," that is, in the way Canadians generate income from the resource endowments we enjoy. If the economy is truly more dependent now on international trade, exchange rate misalign-

9 A return to fixed exchange rates would reduce uncertainty associated with the globalization of trade. If the wealth generation process has changed, fixed exchange rates might be beneficial for Canada.

ment can have disastrous effects on our economy. This is especially true within the current environment dominated by bilateral and multilateral trade agreements. A fixed exchange rate system would at least minimize errors made as a result of excessive exchange rate volatility.

What would be the implications of fixing the exchange rate? Some critics argue that Canada would lose its sovereignty over economic policy and social programs. Proponents of fixed exchange rates counter that we now have different social programs from those in the United States, funded by a very different tax system from that in the United States, so there is little to be feared from a return to fixed exchange rates in the social policy area. Critics also argue that Canadian economic policy would be more dependent on U.S. monetary policy, but it might be reasonably argued that Canada could always move back to a floating exchange rate, or revalue/devalue if it believed the United States was embarking on an ill-conceived path. While operating under a fixed exchange rate system, our monetary policy would, in effect, be dictated by the U.S. Federal Reserve Board, but we would retain the right to restore the status quo when we thought it desirable to do so. At least we would minimize the costs of exchange rate misalignment to the domestic economy.

This debate is far from over and promises to be fertile ground for economic research as we attempt to quantify how exchange rate misalignment has affected the Canadian economy over the past 20 years. Only once we put some numbers to the analysis can we determine whether it is to our benefit to return to a fixed exchange rate regime. If this does happen, we need to be sure that we don't forget the lessons the Bretton Woods system taught us.

Now that we've discussed some topical issues in macroeconomic policy, let's switch gears and consider a hypothetical example that raises some of the same issues. Only this time you don't have hindsight to assist you.

In this example, you've been appointed head of the Xanadu central bank. You have the following information about the economy:

- The current interest rate is 10 percent.
- The unemployment rate is 8 percent.
- The government is running a budget deficit of 1 billion xanadi (the Xanadu currency), which is 2 percent of its GDP.
- The country has a trade deficit of 2 billion xanadi.
- Inflation is 6 percent.
- Your central bank has almost no international reserves so you can do little to affect the exchange rate in the market.

Prime Minister Xorcist, who appointed you, is running for reelection. He tells you that, to win, he must lower the unemployment rate and reduce the interest rate. He also remembers, from the introductory economics course he took with you when you were teaching at Xanadu U., that increasing the money supply will accomplish these goals.

How do you respond? You tell him that yes, in the short run, expansionary monetary policy will accomplish his goals, but that it will have some side effects. Specifically it will likely increase the trade deficit, push up Xanadu's exchange rate, and boost inflation.

"Why?" he asks. First, you tell him that imports depend upon income, so when income increases, imports will increase, so the trade deficit will worsen. Then you explain that lower interest rates will mean fewer people will want to hold their money in xanadi. That will lower demand for xanadi, while higher income and higher imports will increase demand for foreign currencies. The result will be a rise in Xanadu's exchange rate. This rise will cause import prices to rise, while the increased money supply will contribute directly to inflation.

The prime minister will likely respond that he wants you to expand the money supply while avoiding the side effects. How can you do that? You'll have to do something to stop imports from increasing as income increases. You'll have to introduce an

10   By remembering the relationships among economic variables, one can conduct a reasonable analysis for dealing with any economic situation, but it may not be politically desirable.

CONGRATULATIONS! YOU ARE NOW A POLICY ADVISOR

Import control law A law preventing people from importing.

Capital control law A law preventing people from investing abroad.

Foreign exchange control law A law preventing people from buying foreign currency.

import control law that prevents people from importing. Similarly, you'll need a **capital control law** that prevents people from investing abroad, and a **foreign exchange control law** that prevents people from buying foreign currency. And of course you'll have to do something to prevent inflation, which means price controls. In short, with import controls, price controls, capital controls, and exchange controls, you can for a short time prevent the effects. The prime minister tells you, "But those policies will be unpopular!" You answer, "Yes, but don't you remember the other lesson we learned in economics at Xanadu U.? There's no such thing as a free lunch." At that point the prime minister fires you, and you go into exile.

After being reelected, the prime minister calls you and apologizes for canning you. He says that the economist he hired in your place was able to increase the money supply, but he didn't know what he was doing: the delayed response of net exports to changes in the exchange rate appears to be throwing the economy "off track." He offers to hire you at twice your normal consulting fee and tells you to restore the economy to its pre-election condition. You tell him that isn't possible—even though you like the idea of making twice as much money. You remind him that he missed the lecture on the J-curve back at Xanadu U., and that there's not much you can do. You hold out for five times your normal consulting fee, tell him you'll do your best, cut back on the money supply, and tell him to wait for the J-curve effect to respond to the appreciating domestic currency. You invest your earnings offshore, and retire just before the next election.

Dealing with such difficult trade-offs is what real-world macro policy is all about.

CONCLUSION

As you can see, real-world monetary and fiscal policies are not cut and dried. Working with these policies is an art, not a science, and involves politics and psychology as well as economics. But the messiness of real-world policy doesn't mean that one can forget the simplified theories and relationships of economic models. Far from it. Real-world policy problems require a much deeper understanding of the models so that one can see through the messiness and design a policy consistent with the general principles embodied in those models.

CHAPTER SUMMARY

- The goals of macro policy often conflict with one another.
- Macroeconomic policy is an art, not a science.
- A policy model has a different focus than a theoretical model.
- Modern macroeconomists emphasize the need for policy to be credible.
- Modern Classicals and Keynesians have flip-flopped in their views of a deficit.
- Keynesians tend to favour activist policy; Classicals tend to favour laissez-faire policy.
- Keynesian and Classical economists agree about many aspects of macroeconomic policy.
- Monetary policy has been used far more often than fiscal policy over the past 50 years.

- Macro policy is chosen through a combination of economic and political considerations.
- Supply-side policies are policies that expand potential output by creating incentives for individuals to increase output, either by lowering tax rates or changing the composition of spending and taxes.
- Often short-run solutions to problems create even worse long-run problems. If monetary policy really does only have long-run effects on the economy, then price stability might be the most appropriate objective of monetary policy.
- Growing debts and deficits have led to the reform of many of Canada's social programs.
- A return to fixed exchange rates may be beneficial for Canada.

KEY TERMS

art of macro policy   *(452)*

capital control law   *(475)*

Classical supply-side
  economics   *(461)*

foreign exchange control law   *(475)*

import control law   *(475)*

Keynesian supply-side policy   *(463)*

mechanistic Keynesianism   *(452)*

price stability   *(464)*

rational expectations   *(452)*

Ricardian equivalence theorem   *(455)*

social assistance programs   *(471)*

supply-side policies   *(461)*

unemployment insurance   *(470)*

QUESTIONS FOR THOUGHT AND REVIEW

The number after each question represents the estimated degree of critical thinking required. (1 = almost none; 10 = deep thought.)

1. What is the difference between a mechanistic Keynesian view and a modern Keynesian view?   *(3)*

2. How do policy models and theoretical models differ? (3)

3. What is the relationship between rational expectations and the modern macro emphasis on credibility?   *(4)*

4. Keynesians and Classicals are in direct opposition on macroeconomic policy. True or false? Why?   *(5)*

5. Why did Keynesians and Classicals flip-flop in their view of the deficit?   *(5)*

6. Distinguish between Keynesian supply-side policy and Classical supply-side policy.   *(5)*

7. What are the arguments in favour of price stability?   *(5)*

8. Why is the government discouraging repeat users of unemployment insurance?   *(4)*

9. How might the policy advice given to Prime Minister Xorcist have changed if he hadn't needed to run for reelection for three more years?   *(6)*

10. Would a return to fixed exchange rates solve all our problems? Why?   *(8)*

PROBLEMS AND EXERCISES

1. Find the current rules for obtaining unemployment insurance benefits in your area. Are they more or less stringent than the national average? Can you explain why?

2. Find the current unemployment, inflation, and growth rates.
   a. What fiscal policy is government using to deal with the problems?
   b. What monetary policy is government using?
   c. Name the current prime minister, Governor of the Bank of Canada, and minister of finance. What are their political affiliations (if any)?
   d. How might the policies be different if individuals from another party were in power?

3. In a recent article, two economists proposed that countries implement a plan of mandatory forced savings of 4 percent of a person's income per year.

   a. Explain the likely effect of this plan on interest rates and savings.
   b. Discuss the macroeconomic implications of the plan.
   c. Discuss the administrative problems of the plan.

4. As Europe's unemployment rates rose to over 10 percent in the early 1990s, a number of proposals were put forward for work-sharing, in which individuals work one day less per week and have their pay reduced by from 10 to 20 percent. Do you think such proposals could play a significant role in reducing unemployment in Europe? Why or why not?

5. Contact your local social assistance office and find out what your entitlement would be. Are there any restrictions on your outside activities? Do you have to provide community services in return for social assistance, or be willing to take a job if one is offered?

20

Growth and the Macroeconomics of Developing and Transitional Economies

Rise up, study the economic forces which oppress you. . . . They have emerged from the hand of man just as the gods emerged from his brain. You can control them.

~Paul LaFargue

After reading this chapter, you should be able to:

1 Distinguish between growth and development.

2 Explain why there might be a difference in normative goals between developing, transitional, and developed countries.

3 Explain why economies at different stages in development have different institutional needs.

4 Explain what is meant by "the dual economy."

5 Distinguish between a regime change and a policy change.

6 Explain why the statement that inflation is a problem of the central bank issuing too much money is not sufficient for developing and transitional countries.

7 Distinguish between convertibility on the current account and full convertibility.

8 Explain the "borrowing circle" concept and why it was successful.

Throughout this book we have emphasized that macro policy is an art in which one takes the abstract principles learned in *positive economics*—the abstract analysis, and models, that tell us how economic forces direct the economy—and examines how those principles work out in a particular institutional structure to achieve goals determined in *normative economics*—the branch of economics that considers what goals we should be aiming for. In this chapter we see another aspect of that art.

Most of this book has emphasized the macroeconomics of Western industrialized economies, Canada in particular. That means we have focused on their goals and their institutions. In this chapter we shift focus and discuss the macroeconomic problems of *developing economies* and *transitional economies*. As discussed in Chapter 5, a **developing economy** is an economy that has a low level of GDP per capita and a relatively undeveloped market structure, and has never had an alternative, developed, economic system. As discussed in Chapter 3, a **transitional economy** is an economy that has had an alternative, developed, socialist economic system, but is in the process of changing from that system to a market system.

Economists use the terms developing and transitional, rather than growing, to emphasize that the goals of these countries involve more than simply an increase in output; these countries are changing their underlying institutions. Put another way, these economies are changing their production function; they are not increasing inputs given a production function. Thus *development* refers to an increase in productive capacity and output brought about by a change in the underlying institutions, and *growth* refers to an increase in output brought about by an increase in inputs.

The distinction can be overdone. Institutions, and hence production functions, in developed as well as in developing countries are continually changing, and output changes are essentially a combination of both changes in production functions and increases in inputs. For example, in the 1990s the major Western economies have been **restructuring** their economies—changing the underlying economic institutions—as they work to compete better in the world economy. As they restructure, they change their methods of production, their laws, and their social support programs. Thus, in some ways, they are doing precisely what developing and transitional countries are doing—developing rather than just growing. Despite the ambiguity, the distinction between growth and development can be a useful one if you remember that the two blend into each other.

The reason economists separate out developing and transitional economies is that these economies have (1) different institutional structures and (2) a different weighting of goals than do Western developed economies. These two differences—in institutional structure, and in goals—change the way in which the lessons of abstract theory are applied and discussed.

The chapter begins with a consideration of how the goals of developing countries differ from the goals of developed countries. Then we turn our attention to how the institutions differ. In the process of that discussion, we consider the general conduct of macro policy in developing countries, and some case studies that bring to life important aspects of the macroeconomic problems they face.

When discussing macro policy within Western developed economies, we did not dwell on questions of normative goals of macroeconomics. Instead, we used generally accepted goals in Canada as the goals of macro policy—achieving low inflation, low unemployment, and an acceptable growth rate—with a few caveats. You may have noticed that the discussion focused more on what might be called stability goals—achieving low unemployment and low inflation—than it did on the acceptable growth rate goal. We chose that focus because growth in Western developed countries is desired because it holds unemployment down, and because it avoids difficult distributional questions, as much as it is desired for its own sake. Our economy has sufficient productive capacity to provide its citizens, on average, with a relatively high standard of living. The problem facing Western societies is as much seeing that all members of those societies share in that high standard of living as it is raising the standard.

Developing economy   An economy that has a low level of GDP per capita and a relatively undeveloped market structure, and has never had an alternative, developed economic system.

Transitional economy   An economy that has had an alternative, developed, socialist economic system, but is in the process of changing from that system to a market system.

1   Growth occurs because of an increase in inputs, given a production function; development occurs through a change in the production function.

Restructuring   Changing the underlying economic institutions (of an economy).

DIFFERING GOALS OF DEVELOPED, DEVELOPING, AND TRANSITIONAL COUNTRIES

ADDED DIMENSION

THE NORTH/SOUTH CONFLICT

Consider the map of the world and you will see that most of the developed nations are in the Northern hemisphere and most of the developing nations are in the Southern hemisphere. This has led to a characterization of the normative questions about growth as the "North/South conflict." Roughly, "North" refers to North America and Western Europe (together with Japan and Australia). "South" refers to Latin America and Africa.

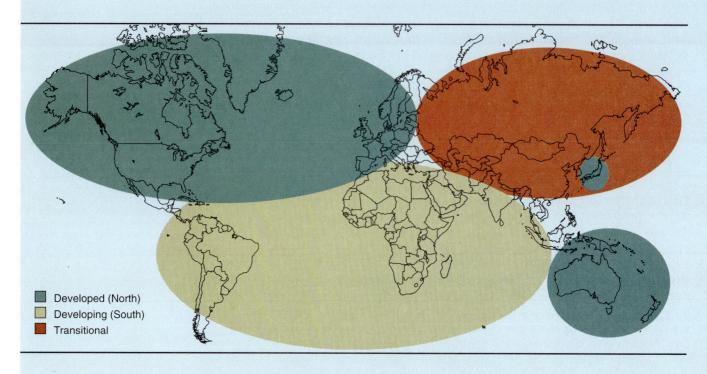

■ Developed (North)
■ Developing (South)
■ Transitional

The South's Position

In this conflict, the "South" takes the following position:

Economic growth uses natural resources or, more precisely, modifies the forms certain resources take. Much of the modification of resources that occurs due to current Northern production processes is, in the South's view, undesirable. For example, in many production processes we start with beautiful raw materials—forests, mountains, and pristine rivers—

Growth and Basic Needs

2 There are differences in normative goals between developing and developed countries because their wealth differs. Developing countries face true economic needs whereas developed countries' economic needs are considered by most people normatively less pressing.

Economic Growth as an Appropriate Goal for Developing Countries

Basic needs Adequate food, clothing, and shelter for the people in a society.

In the developing countries, the weighting of goals is different. Growth—an increase in the economies' output—and development—a transition of the economies' institutions so that the economies can achieve higher levels of output—are primary goals. When people are starving and the economy isn't fulfilling people's **basic needs**—adequate food, clothing, and shelter—a main focus of macro policy will be on how to increase the economy's growth rate through development so that the economy can fulfil those basic needs.

When Classical economics developed, its focus was almost totally on economic growth. Early developers of that Classical economics—Adam Smith, Thomas Malthus, and David Ricardo—took growth as economics' central area of concern. As Western market economies grew, the focus of macroeconomics changed from issues of long-run growth to issues of short-run stability. The macroeconomic models developed in this book reflect that change in focus. Keynesian economics, specifically, has a short-run focus, and has little relevance to long-term growth. That part of Classical

and we end up with trash heaps—dumps and polluted cesspools. In short, current production processes create too many of what society considers waste products in order to create goods that people don't really need, but which, instead, reflect needs created for them by society. The South asks: "Do Northern industrialized economies really need closets filled with this year's fashions—to be thrown out and replaced with next year's fashions? Or would something simpler—less resource-intensive—suffice?" Alternatively, think of automobiles. Do Western consumers really need air-conditioned automobiles at the cost of the depletion of the ozone layer?

The normative value judgements that must be made to answer these questions posed by the South are enormous, and we do not intend to deal with them here. But that does not mean that such judgements are not important. It is, in our view, legitimate to question whether further growth along the lines that Western economies are currently following is a goal to which the majority of people in Western society would subscribe, if they thought seriously about the issue.

The South points out that even if Northern societies have chosen the growth path, that path may still be suspect when one considers the normative issue of growth from an international perspective. Western economic growth imposes costs on the rest of the world. The world has a population of about 5.5 billion. The population of the industrialized countries is less than 1 billion, or 17 percent of the world's population, yet the industrialized nations use 60 percent of the world's resources and create many of the waste products that influence the entire atmosphere of the world. The South argues that if we had a worldwide democratic government and a vote were taken on whether the majority of all people felt that physical growth in Western economies was a worthwhile goal, that growth would not be supported.

The North's Response

The Northern response to this philosophical question is varied. One response is to feel somewhat guilty about the North's success and use of the world's resources, and to establish aid programs to try to assuage that guilt. A number of international development programs have been started to try to offset the costs, but these programs are not large.

A second response is that the world isn't a democracy, and so in reality the question is moot. It doesn't matter what is right in some abstract philosophical sense. What matters simply is "what is."

A third response is that the South has the argument backwards. True, the North uses resources, but it is also creating new technologies. Technological changes are occurring faster than resource depletion, and with modern technological improvements in waste disposal, wastes are decreasing, not increasing. These pro-economic-growth economists argue that economic growth of Northern industrial countries is good not only for people in Northern countries; it is good for the entire world.

economics that we concentrated on in earlier chapters was a response to Keynes, which means that the Classical economics we presented earlier concerned more short-run than long-run issues. We left out a discussion of Classical long-run economics, which did focus on growth. (See the accompanying box for a brief discussion of Classical long-run economics.)

In summary, the goals of developed and developing countries differ; for developing countries, growth in economic output is a more generally agreed-upon goal than it is for developed countries. The central policy question facing these developing countries is: What set of macro policies will lead to growth?

Developing and transitional countries differ from developed countries not only in their goals, but also in their macroeconomic institutions. These macroeconomic institutions are qualitatively different from institutions in developed countries. Their governments are different; their financial institutions—the institutions that translate savings into investment—are different; their fiscal institutions—the institutions through which

INSTITUTIONAL
DIFFERENCES

CLASSICAL ECONOMISTS AND LONG-RUN GROWTH

How did Classical economists advise countries to grow? They advised: (1) keep the government out of the economy; (2) channel income to entrepreneurs and capitalists who consume little and who have a fetish for investing; (3) channel income away from landowners, who use it on servants and good living, not on growth-creating activities; and (4) channel income away from government that spends it on who-knows-what (but certainly not on growth-creating activities).

They also generally opposed programs to raise wages of workers because (1) workers would use the raises to have more children (the Malthusian doctrine), and (2) high wages would make the economy internationally uncompetitive in a fixed exchange rate system as then existed.

Early Classical economists—Adam Smith, Thomas Malthus, and David Ricardo—were strongest in their support of these propositions. Later Classical economists—John Stewart Mill and Alfred Marshall—were less adamant in their support and often advocated contrary policies. Likely reasons for the change include changing institutions and increased wealth in the economy.

Democracy entered into society together with capitalism, and as the democratic nature of government became part of the institutional structure, the Classical arguments against government intervention were modified. Similarly, as industrialists lost their investment fetish and started to enjoy life (i.e., as they (or their children) started to consume some of their profits, not invest), it made less sense to channel income to industrialists to bring out investment and growth. Also, with the development of financial markets, savings from others, such as landowners or workers, could be channelled into investment and hence into growth. And finally, as society got richer, other goals besides growth became more important. In short, as Western institutions changed and Western wealth grew, so, too, did Classical economists' proposed policies.

---

3 Economies at different stages of development have different institutional needs because the problems they face are different. Institutions that can be assumed in developed countries cannot necessarily be assumed to exist in developing countries.

government collects taxes and spends its money—are different; and their social and cultural institutions are different. Because of these differences, the way in which one discusses macroeconomic policy is different.

One of the differences concerns very basic market institutions—such as Western-style property rights and contract law. In certain groups of developing countries, most notably sub-Saharan Africa, these basic market institutions don't exist; instead, communal property rights and tradition structure economic relationships. In the transitional economies, where the government previously owned large portions of the economy, ownership is often unclear. Decades ago, before the government owned large portions of the economy, there was private ownership, and claims based on those old conditions are surfacing, often placing clouds on current "ownership" and control. How can one talk about market forces in such economies?[1] On a more mundane level, consider the issue of monetary policy. Talking about monetary policy via open market operations (the buying and selling of bonds by the central bank) is not all that helpful when there are no open market operations, as there are not in many developing countries.

Let's now consider some specific institutional differences more carefully.

Political Differences and Laissez-Faire

Views of how activist macroeconomic policy should be are necessarily contingent on the political system an economy has. One of the scarcest commodities in developing countries is socially-minded leaders. Not that developed countries have any over-abundance of them, but at least in most developed countries there is a tradition of politicians seeming to be fair and open-minded, and a set of institutionalized checks and balances that limits leaders using government for their personal benefit. In many developing countries, those institutionalized checks and balances on governmental leaders often do not exist.

---

[1] One can, of course, talk about economic forces. But, as discussed in Chapter 1, economic forces only become market forces in a market institutional setting.

Let's look at a few examples. First, consider Saudi Arabia, which, while economically rich, maintains many of the institutions of a developing country. It is an absolute monarchy in which the royal family is the ultimate power. Say a member of that family comes to the bank and wants a loan that, on economic grounds, doesn't make sense. What do you think the bank loan officer will do? Grant the loan, if the banker is smart. Thus, despite the wealth of the country, it isn't surprising that many economists believe the Saudi banking system reflects that political structure, and may find itself in serious trouble in the 1990s.

Another example is Lebanon, which has so many competing political factions fighting for power that even to talk about macro policy proposals that assume a central government, let alone a government out to do good, is misplaced. The government in Lebanon is mainly concerned with continued existence; a primary institutionalized check on government leaders is a bullet.

A third example is the new transitional countries of the former Soviet Union. They face enormous political instability problems, and in the early- and mid-1990s the largest growth industry there was the private protection agency business. In such an institutional setting, government policy often has little to do with economics or what's good for the economy, and any proposed macroeconomic policy must take that into account.

A final example is Nigeria, which had enormous possibilities for economic growth in the 1980s because of its oil riches. It didn't develop. Instead, politicians fought over the spoils, and bribes became a major source of their income. Corruption was rampant, and the Nigerian economy went nowhere. We will stop there, but, unfortunately, there are many other examples.

Because of the structure of government in many developing countries, many economists who, in Western developed economies, favour activist government policies may well favour Classical laissez-faire policies for the same reasons that early Classical economists did—because they have a profound distrust of the governments. That distrust, however, must have limits. As we discussed in Chapter 4, even a laissez-faire policy requires some government role in setting the rules. So there is no escaping the need for socially-minded leaders.

A second institutional difference between developed and developing countries is the dual nature of developing countries' economies. Whereas it often makes sense to talk about Western economies as a single economy, it does not for most developing countries. Their economies are generally characterized by a duality—a traditional sector and an internationally oriented modern market sector.[2]

Often, the largest percentage of the population participate in the traditional economy. It is a local-currency, or no-currency, sector in which traditional ways of doing things take precedence. The second sector—the internationally oriented modern market sector—is often indistinguishable from Western economies. Activities in the modern sector are often conducted in foreign currencies, rather than domestic currencies, and contracts are often governed by international law. This **dual economy** aspect of developing countries creates a number of policy dilemmas for them and affects the way they think about macroeconomic problems.

For example, take the problem of unemployment. Many developing countries have a large, subsistence farming economy. Subsistence farmers aren't technically unemployed, but often there are so many people on the land that, in economic terms, their marginal product is minimal or even negative, so for policy purposes one can consider the quantity of labour that will be supplied at the going wage to be unlimited. But to call these people unemployed is problematic. These subsistence farmers are

The Dual Economy

4 "The dual economy" refers to the existence of the two sectors in most developing countries: a traditional sector and an internationally oriented modern market sector.

Dual economy Tendency of developing countries to have two somewhat unrelated economies—one an internationally based economy, the other a traditional, often nonmarket, economy.

---

[2] We discuss these two economies as if they were separate but, in reality, they are interrelated. Portions of the economy devoted to the tourist trade span both sectors, as do some manufacturing industries. Still, there is sufficient independence of the two economies that it is reasonable to treat them as separate.

simply outside the market economy. In such cases one would hardly want, or be able, to talk of an unemployment problem in the same way we talk about it in Canada.

Fiscal Structure of Developing and Transitional Economies

A third institutional difference concerns developing and transitional countries' fiscal systems. To undertake discretionary fiscal policy—running a deficit or surplus to affect the aggregate economy—the government must be able to determine expenditures and tax rates, with a particular eye toward the difference between the two. As discussed above, discretionary fiscal policy is difficult for Western developed countries to undertake; it is almost impossible for developing and transitional economies. Often, the governments in these economies don't have the institutional structures with which to collect taxes (or, when they have the institutional structure, it is undermined by fraud and evasion), so their taxing options are limited; that's why they often use tariffs as a primary source of revenue.

In the traditional sector of many developing and transitional countries, barter or cash transactions predominate, and such transactions are especially difficult to tax. For example, consider Bulgaria, which at the beginning of the 1990s was attempting to transform from a centrally planned economy to a market economy. Initially it had no agency for tax collection since all previous economic activity was under the control of the state. Under its old institutional structure, revenues automatically flowed into the state. As the country shifted to a market economy, that changed dramatically. With no experience in tax collection, and with no tradition of paying taxes, initially all the fiscal policy discussion concerned how to collect enough to finance the basic core of government in order to keep it functioning.

Similar problems exist with government expenditures. Many expenditures of developing countries are mandated by political considerations—if the government doesn't make them, it will likely be voted out of office. Within such a setting, to talk about Keynesian fiscal policy—choosing a deficit for its macroeconomic implications—even if it might otherwise be relevant, is not much help since the budget deficit is not a choice variable, but instead is a result of other political decisions.

5   A regime change is a change in the entire atmosphere within which the government and the economy interrelate; a policy change is a change in one aspect of government's actions.

The political constraints facing developing and transitional countries can, of course, be overstated. The reality is that developing countries do institute new fiscal regimes. Take, for example, Mexico. In the early 1980s, Mexico's fiscal problems seemed impossible to solve, but in the late 1980s and early 1990s, Carlos de Salinas, a U.S.-trained economist, introduced a fiscal austerity program and an economic liberalization program that lowered Mexico's deficit and significantly reduced its inflation. But such changes are better called a **regime change**—a change in the entire atmosphere within which the government and the economy interrelate—rather than a **policy change**—a change in one aspect of government's actions, such as monetary policy or fiscal policy.

Regime change   A change in the entire atmosphere within which the government and the company interrelate.

Policy change   A change in one aspect of government's actions, such as monetary policy or fiscal policy.

Financial Institutions of Developing and Transitional Economies

We spent three chapters discussing the complex financial systems of developed countries because you had to understand those financial systems in order to understand macro policy. While some parts of that discussion carry over to developing countries, other parts don't, since financial systems in developing countries are often quite different than those in developed countries.

The primary difference arises from the dual nature of developing countries' economies. In the traditional part of developing economies, the financial sector is embryonic; trades are made by barter, or with direct payment of money; trades requiring more sophisticated financial markets, such as mortgages to finance houses, just don't exist.

In the modern international part that isn't the case. Developing countries' international financial sectors are sometimes as sophisticated as Western financial institutions. When one walks into a currency trading room in Bulgaria or Nigeria, one will see a room similar to a room that one would see in Toronto, London, or Frankfurt. That modern financial sector is integrated into the international economy (with pay rates that often approach or match those of the West). This dual nature of developing countries' financial sectors imposes constraints on the practice of monetary policy and changes the regulatory and control functions of central banks.

Let's consider an example of a transitional economy—Bulgaria, where one of us spent some time trying to understand the banking system and teaching Bulgarian professors about Western banking. Before going over there, he had expected to teach about money and banking the same way he had done in the West, explaining how the quantity of high-powered money serves as a basis for loans, and how the money multiplier works. Then, he had expected to explain how the banks made decisions on long-term loans, and how those decisions were related to central bank policy.

He soon discovered that much of this was not directly relevant for Bulgaria. While Bulgarian private banks had many long-term loans on the books, when he was there they were making almost no new long-term loans, and those that already existed were, in large part, worthless. The reason was that the Bulgarian private banks had been created out of the former Bulgarian National Bank. In the transition, that single bank was broken up into the Central Bank and a number of private banks, with the private banks carrying on their books some portion of the loans of the single bank from which they were created. These loans had little value; as part of the planned economy, the bank had systematically extended whatever credit was needed to the companies it served. These firms simultaneously extended **inter-firm credit** (loans from one firm to another) to other firms so that monetary payment for whatever they wanted was easy to obtain. This is what is meant by the **soft budget constraint.** By this is meant that, since firms could get loans without difficulty, financial constraints—the need to pay for inputs—place little constraint on firms' decisions in centrally planned economies. With the end of the central planning and an attempt to switch their economies from centrally planned to market economies, the soft budget constraint came to a hard end.

The private banks that evolved from the government bank inherited the loans of their predecessor banks, and it was these long-term loans that they carried on their books. The loans were uncollectible. Even if the firms to whom the loans were made were still viable, those viable firms had so many trade credits extended to other unviable firms that viable firms couldn't pay off the loans. Most firms couldn't even afford to pay the interest, and the only reason they didn't default was that the banks kept lending them the money to pay the interest. Luckily or unluckily, depending on where you stood, the real interest rate was negative, and inflation was wiping out many of these loans. (For whom was this unlucky? Remember: inflation makes the society neither richer nor poorer, so someone was losing. Who? Holders of cash whose wealth was being wiped out.)

New long-term loans weren't being made for three reasons. The first was that the central bank was attempting to restrict credit in order to restrain the inflationary pressures. Thus, private banks had a hard time getting loans from the central bank. An important reason why the central bank was concerned about making too much credit available was, in turn, a second reason why new long-term loans weren't being made. Since the private banks had never made loans based on sound lending principles (remember the soft budget constraint), they had no loan officers or procedures to determine who should get loans.

Third, even if they had such a system, there was little demand for what we'd call sound long-term loans. These were two reasons for their low demand. First, the Bulgarian economy was in a serious downward spiral. With expectations of a downward economic spiral, sound long-term investment doesn't make much sense. Second, the interest rate charged by the Bulgarian banks was about 50 percent. Such high nominal interest rates have a tendency to discourage loans. But, you must remember, the inflation was around 60 percent, making the real interest rate minus 10 percent. A negative real interest rate should, according to simple economic theory, encourage firms to take out loans. That wasn't taking place. Why? It seems that once inflation and nominal interest rates get that high, they are accompanied by enormous uncer-

An Example of the Different Roles of Financial Institutions in Transitional Economies

Inter-firm credit   Loans form one firm to another.

Soft budget constraint   Loose financial constraints on firms' decisions in centrally planned economies.

tainty about future inflation and, in particular, about relative prices of products. To make a business plan work with a 60 percent rate of inflation and a 50 percent nominal interest rate, you must build a 50 or 60 percent price rise into your business plan, making your profitability analysis on the basis of an expected rise in prices.

When businesspeople were asked why they didn't do that, the answer turned out to lie in the fact that the business texts that they were using to guide them didn't include such an inflation adjustment—their texts did break-even analysis (an analysis of whether an investment makes sense or not) at fixed prices. (Remember, these were people new to business, and they were looking to the Western textbooks to guide them). Even those who understood that the break-even analysis could be adjusted for expected inflation didn't want their success or failure to be dependent on an inflation rate over which they had no control. Entrepreneurial types generally like control, and the inflation made them feel controlled rather than in control. In short, they felt the financial situation was too uncertain to take a chance, and so they didn't want to invest.

To say that there was no demand for solid productive investment loans is not to say there was no demand for loans. There was a large demand for long-term loans, but most of that demand was connected to high-risk investments in which the borrower received most of the return in the unlikely event that the project turned out to be successful, and the bank bore all the loss in the likely event the project was unsuccessful. The end result was that the banks were making almost no long-term loans.

Despite the fact that the banking system was not making any long-term loans, it provided significant short-term loans (one to two weeks), called trade credits, to facilitate inter-firm trade. This necessary function for a working economy is provided primarily by firms in Western economies. When a firm orders a product from another firm, the bill is sent payable in about 30 days—weeks after the product is sent. Accounts payable and accounts receivable representing short-term loans from one firm to another are parts of every Western firm's balance sheet. The Bulgarian firms were unwilling to extend such trade credits to other Bulgarian firms; they wanted payment guaranties before they would sell to another firm. (In Canada, firms want such guaranties when the firms they are dealing with are close to bankruptcy.) The Bulgarian banking system was providing this guarantee function. It extended large amounts of **trade credits** making inter-firm trade possible.

Trade credits Short-term loans to facilitate inter-firm trade.

This trade-credit role of banking is hardly mentioned in modern Western money and banking books, and is not even discussed in the financial and monetary institutions chapters of this book. It is, however, an absolutely necessary function for an economy to work. In developed countries, one takes the fulfilment of that function for granted; in Bulgaria one couldn't. (This function of banking was not always taken for granted in Canada; academic discussion of banking in the early 1800s often included discussion of this vital role and how to maintain sufficient "elasticity" in the money supply to meet the trade-credit needs. Western institutions simply became so good at fulfilling this function that we don't discuss it.)

The above is one of many institutional examples of differences that exist and that change the nature of the macro problem. What's important is not so much the specifics of the example but, rather, the general point it brings home. Economies at different stages of development have different institutional, and policy, needs. Institutions with the same names in different countries can have quite different roles. Such institutions can differ in subtle ways, making it important to have specific knowledge of a country's institutions before one can understand its economy and meaningfully talk about policy for them.

Monetary Policy in Developing and Transitional Countries

Now that we've discussed some of the ways in which financial institutions differ in developing and transitional countries, let's consider some issues of central banking and monetary policy for those economies.

The first thing to note about central banking in developing and transitional countries is that its primary goal is often different than a central bank's primary goal in developed countries. The reason is that, while all central banks have a number of

EXHIBIT 1   Inflation Rates of Selected Developing and Developed Countries

Inflation is a problem of many developing countries, especially in Latin and South America. Notice the generally lower rates of inflation in the developed as compared to the developing countries.
Source: *U.N. Statistical Yearbook*, various years.

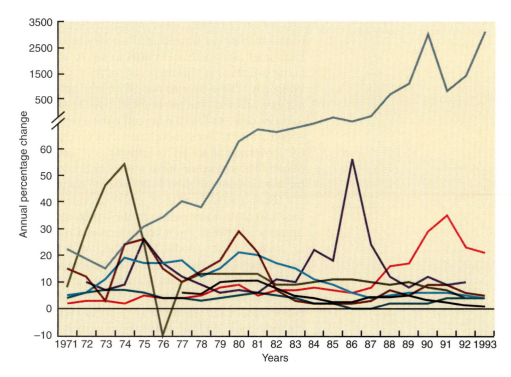

goals, at the top of them all is the goal of keeping the economy running. In the 1990s, Western central banks have the luxury of assuming away the problem of keeping the economy running—inertia, institutions, and history hold Western industrial economies together, and keep them running. Central banks in developing and transitional countries can't make that assumption.

What this means in practice is that central banks in developing and transitional countries have far less independence than do central banks in developed countries. With a political and fiscal system that generates large deficits and cannot exist without those deficits, the thought of an independent monetary policy goes out the window.

A second difference concerns the institutional implementation of monetary policy. In a developing or a transitional country, a domestic government bond market seldom exists. So if the government runs a deficit and is financing it domestically, the central bank usually must buy the bonds, which means that it must increase the money supply.

Monetary Policy and Inflation   The above institutional background gives us some insight into the significant inflation problem many developing and transitional countries face. The extent of that inflation can be seen in Exhibit 1.

It shows recent inflation rates for various countries. Notice that for a number of developing countries, the Canadian inflation rate wouldn't be seen as inflation at all, but only as background noise in the price level. For example in the 1990s inflation in Brazil has averaged over 1,000 percent per year. Thus, talking about inflation as a macroeconomic problem of developing countries would seem to make sense. But it cannot be talked about as a simple economic problem; it must be talked about as a macro-political problem.

Let us explain. In Canada, there's significant debate about the cause and nature of inflation. The cause and nature of developing and transitional countries' inflation is clear. Economists of all persuasions agree that large inflations can continue only if the central bank issues large amounts of money. So the cause of developing countries' inflation is that the central bank is issuing too much money. But, as discussed above, the central bank knows that. The real policy debate is not about the economic cause but is about the political cause—does the central bank have a choice about issuing so much money? That debate concerns issues related to the political consequences of *not* issuing too much money.

6   Central banks recognize that printing too much money causes inflation, but often feel compelled to do so for political reasons. Debate about inflation in developing countries generally concerns those political reasons, not the relationship between money and inflation.

As we discussed above, often, in developing countries, the government's sources of tax revenue are limited, and the low level of income in the economy makes the tax base small. A government attempting to collect significantly more taxes might risk being overthrown. Similarly its ability to cut expenditures is limited. If it cuts expenditures, it will be overthrown. With new tax sources unavailable and with no ability to cut expenditures, the government uses its only other option to meet its obligations—it issues debt. And, if the central bank agrees with the conclusion that the government is correct in its assessment that it has no choice, then if the central bank doesn't want the government to be overthrown, it has no choice but to monetize that debt. Sometimes the central bank's choices are even more limited; dictatorships simply tell the central bank to provide the needed money, or be eliminated.

The problem for transitional economies is slightly different. As socialist countries, they had their taxes built into their pricing structure. Their government received the difference between the revenue received for the goods they sold and the cost to them to produce those goods. Their "tax" was that difference. As they moved toward a market economy, this source of revenue was eliminated and they had no taxing institutions—such as Revenue Canada—in place to implement new taxes and to supply that revenue. Moreover, people had no tradition of paying taxes and, hence, avoided and evaded taxes whenever they could. With the legal system in transition, the government could do little to force individuals to pay taxes.

Inflation tax   An implicit tax on the holders of cash and the holders of any obligations specified in nominal terms.

The Inflation Tax

Issuing money to finance budget deficits may be a short-term solution but it is not a long-term solution. It is an accounting identity that real resources consumed by the economy must equal the real resources produced or imported. If the government deficit doesn't increase output, the real resources the government is getting because the central bank is monetizing its debt must come from somewhere. Where do those real resources come from? From the **inflation tax**: an implicit tax—on the holders of cash and the holders of any obligations specified in nominal terms. Inflation works as a type of tax on these individuals.

Let's consider that inflation tax in relation to the transitional economies. With the end of central planning, there was an enormous monetary overhang—large stores of currency in excess of real goods in the economy at market prices. This monetary overhang existed because most individuals had stored their financial wealth in the currency of their country. This currency represented the enormous past obligations of the former socialist governments—obligations that far exceeded the governments', or the economies', ability to meet them.

As they moved to a market economy without an acceptable tax base there was no way for these governments to meet their current obligations, let alone their past obligations. Something had to give; accounting identities are unforgiving. Either the government must default, or prices must rise enormously.

The central banks generally chose to keep the governments operating (which isn't surprising, since they were often branches of the government). To do that they increased the money supply enormously, causing hyperinflation in many of these countries. These hyperinflations soon took on a life of their own. The expectation of accelerating inflation created even more inflationary pressure as individuals tried to spend any money they had quickly, before the prices went up. This increased velocity, nominal demand for goods, and inflationary pressures. These hyperinflations wiped out (taxed away) the monetary overhang, allowing most of those transitional countries to rein in their inflation, getting it down to double digits (less than 100 percent per year). This was possible because, with the overhang wiped out, the inflation tax only had to make up for the government budget deficit; it no longer had to be used to eliminate past obligations.

One problem with the use of an inflation tax is that in an inflation, the government is not the only recipient of revenue; any issuer of fixed-interest-rate debt denominated in domestic currency also gains. And the holder of any fixed-interest-rate debt denominated in domestic currency loses. This income redistribution caused by an inflation can temporarily stimulate real output, but it can also undermine the country's financial institutions.

The point of the above discussion is that the central banks know that issuing large quantities of money will cause inflation. What they don't know, and what the policy discussions are about, is which is worse: the inflation or the unpleasant alternatives. Should the central bank bail out the government? There are legitimate questions about whether countries' budget deficits are absolutely necessary or not. It is those assessments in which the debate about developing countries' inflation exists; the debate is not about whether the inflation is caused by the issuance of too much money.

Opponents of any type of bailout point out that any "inflation solution" is only a temporary solution that, if used, will require ever-increasing amounts of inflation to remain effective. Proponents of bailouts agree with this argument, but argue that inflation buys a bit more time, and the alternative is the breakdown of the government and the economy. Because of the unpleasant alternative, the fact that inflation is only a temporary solution doesn't stop developing and transitional countries' leaders from using it. They don't have time for the luxury of long-run solutions, and are often simply looking for policies that will hold their governments together for a month at a time.

Another difference between the monetary policies of developed and developing countries concerns the policy options they consider for dealing with foreign exchange markets. Developed countries are generally committed to full exchange rate convertibility on both the current and capital accounts. With full exchange rate convertibility, individuals can exchange their currency for any other country's currency without significant government restrictions.

Transitional and developing countries often do not have fully convertible currencies. Individuals and firms in these countries face restrictions on their ability to exchange currencies—sometimes general restrictions and sometimes restrictions depending on the purpose for which they wish to use the foreign exchange.

Various Types of Convertibility   Since convertibility plays such a central role in developing countries' macro policies, let's review the various types of convertibility. Canada has **full convertibility.** That means that Canadian law does not prevent individuals from changing dollars into any currency they want for whatever legal purpose they want. (There are, however, reporting laws about movements of currency.) Most Western developed countries have full convertibility.

A second type of convertibility is **convertibility on the current account.** This system allows people to exchange currencies freely to buy goods and services, but not to buy assets in other countries.

The third type of convertibility is **limited capital account convertibility.** This system allows full current account convertibility and partial capital account convertibility. There are various levels of restrictions on what types of assets one can exchange, so there are many types of limited capital account convertibility.

Almost no developing country allows full convertibility. Why? One reason is that they want to force their residents to keep their savings, and to do their investing, in their home country, not abroad. Why don't their citizens want to do that? Because when there is a chance of a change in governments—and government seizure of assets—as there often is in developing countries, rich individuals generally prefer to have a significant portion of their assets abroad, away from the hands of their government.

These limits on exchange rate convertibility explain a general phenomenon found in most developing countries—the fact that much of the international part of the dual economy in developing countries is "dollarized." Contracts are framed in, and accounting is handled in, U.S. dollars, not in the home country's currency. Dollarization exists almost completely in the international sectors of countries that have nonconvertible currencies, and largely in the international sectors of countries

Focus on the International Sector and the Exchange Rate Constraint

Full convertibility   System where there is no law preventing individuals from changing their domestic currency into any currency they want for whatever legal purpose they want.

7   Full convertibility means one can exchange one's currency for whatever legal purpose one wants. Convertibility on the current account limits those exchanges to buying goods and services. Limited capital account convertibility allows partial capital account convertibility.

where the currency is convertible on the current account, but not on the capital account. This dollarization exists because of nonconvertibility, or the fear of nonconvertibility. Thus, ironically, nonconvertibility increases the focus on dollarized contracts in the international sector, and puts that sector beyond effective control by the central bank.

Nonconvertibility does not halt international trade—it merely complicates it, since it adds another layer of uncertainty and bureaucracy to the trading process. Each firm that is conducting international trade must see that it will have sufficient foreign exchange to carry on its business. Developing and transitional governments will often want to encourage this international trade, while preventing outflows of their currencies for other purposes.

Exchange rate policy   Deliberately affecting a country's exchange rate in order to affect its trade balance.

When developing countries have partially convertible exchange rates, **exchange rate policy**—buying and selling foreign currencies in order to help stabilize the exchange rate—often is an important central bank function. This is such an important function because trade in most of these countries' currencies is thin—there are not a large number of traders or trades. When trading is thin, large fluctuations in exchange rates are possible in response to a change in a few traders' needs. Even the uncertainties of the weather can affect traders. Say an expected oil tanker is kept from landing in port because of bad weather. The financial exchange—paying for that oil—that would have taken place upon landing does not take place, and the supply/demand conditions for a country's currency could change substantially. In response, the value of the country's currency could rise or fall dramatically unless it were stabilized. The central bank often helps provide exchange rate stabilization.

Conditionality and the Balance of Payments Constraint

In designing their policies, transitional and developing countries often rely on advice from the International Monetary Fund (IMF). One reason is that the IMF has economists who have much experience with these issues. A second reason is that, for these countries, the IMF is a major source of temporary loans that they need to stabilize their currencies.

These loans usually come with conditions that the country meet certain domestic monetary and fiscal stabilization goals. Specifically, these goals are that government deficits be lowered and money supply growth be limited. Because of these requirements, IMF's loan policy is often called **conditionality**—the making of loans that are subject to specific conditions.

Conditionality   Making loans that are subject to specific conditions.

Balance of payments constraint   Limitation on expansionary domestic macro policy due to a shortage of international reserves.

Even a partially flexible exchange rate regime presents the country with the **balance of payments constraint**—limitations on expansionary domestic macroeconomic policy due to a shortage of international reserves. Attempts to expand the domestic economy with expansionary monetary policy continually push the economy to its balance of payments constraint. To meet both its domestic goals and international balance of payments constraints, many developing countries turn to loans from the IMF, not only for the exchange rate stabilization reasons discussed above, but also for a more expansionary macro policy than would otherwise be possible. Because of the IMF's control of these loans, macro policy in developing countries is often conducted with one eye toward the IMF, and sometimes with a complete bow.

MACRO INSTITUTIONAL POLICY IN DEVELOPING COUNTRIES

The above discussion may have made it seem as if conducting domestic macro policy in developing countries is almost hopelessly dominated by domestic political concerns and international constraints. If by macro policy one means using traditional monetary and fiscal policy tools as they are used in standard ways, that's true. But macro policy, interpreted broadly, is much more than using those tools. It is the development of new institutions that expand the possibilities for growth. It is creating a new production function, not operating within an existing one. Macro policy, writ large to include the development of new institutions, can have enormous effects. To undertake such policies requires an understanding of the role of institutions, the specific nature of the problem in one's country, and creativity.

Macro institutional policies   Policies to change the underlying macro institutions and thereby increase output.

Let's consider a recent World Bank report on the developmental success of "The Asian Tigers" to see how economists view what might be called **macro institutional**

policies—policies to change the underlying macro institutions and thereby increase output. The report asked what were the causes of these countries' high growth rates, and whether their success provides lessons for other developing countries.

The report concluded that the most important reason for these countries' success was that they "got the economic fundamentals right, with low inflation, sound fiscal policies, high levels of domestic savings, heavy investment in education; and they kept their economies more open to foreign technology than most other developing countries." In a sense, what the World Bank concluded was that these high growth rates were not a miracle at all, but simply the result of sound economic policies.

While economists will disagree with particulars of many of these fundamentals, almost all would agree with the general argument: Macro policy in developing countries involves getting the infrastructure right—creating a climate within which individual initiative is directed toward production.

Let's now consider some of these fundamentals more carefully.

Growth depends on investment, and investment depends on saving. This saving can come from domestic sources, or it can come from international sources, either in the form of foreign private investment or foreign aid.

Because it is difficult to generate domestic savings, developing countries often look abroad for savings to finance investment. But many of the firms in these countries are unable to borrow abroad because they lack creditworthiness. This leads the governments of many of these developing countries to guarantee loans by private firms, thereby creating large government debt overhangs, all denominated in U.S. dollars, leaving the monetary policy with a serious external debt problem.

Had the loans that led to this debt gone for productive investments that paid a return greater than the principal and interest on the loans, these investments would have been helpful. But in reality, as a result of political corruption and economic mismanagement, the investments were often unproductive. Returns on the investments didn't even cover the interest payments, let alone the principal. The situation was worsened by tight U.S. monetary policy that simultaneously raised interest rates, increasing the interest burden of these floating-rate loans, and raised the value of the U.S. dollar, increasing the developing countries' indebtedness far beyond their expectations. In short, the governments that had guaranteed the loans found themselves responsible for repaying the loans without the wherewithal to do so. They found themselves in a debt crisis.

In the early 1990s, the total debt of Latin American countries was about $400 billion, much of it owned by U.S. banks, while all the developing countries combined had about U.S. $1.4 trillion in outstanding debt. That meant that they had to have a large annual trade surplus simply to pay the interest of about U.S. $100 billion a year on their debt. Some countries' annual interest was more than they could afford to pay from their export earnings. But if they paid only the interest on the debt and did not make payments on the principal, the debt would remain as large as ever. And as long as that debt remained unpaid, there would be no new incoming foreign investment to devote to development. The developing countries found themselves trapped by debt, and that trap became known as the debt crisis.

In the late 1980s, when the debt situation looked hopeless, some economists urged the developing countries simply to repudiate their debt—to say it was guaranteed by corrupt former officials, that fraud was involved, and that it was time to start over. This would have allowed the countries to make a new start, declaring that they owe nothing. For obvious reasons this strategy was extraordinarily tempting, and in the late 1980s a number of Latin American countries threatened to repudiate their debt, and some partially did so.

Apart from the moral argument that a debt should be repaid, the major argument against repudiation is that it will destroy the country's ability to get loans in the future. The counter-argument is that the country already has so much debt that it won't be able to get new credit anyway, so why worry about obtaining future loans? If they

Generating Saving and Investment and the Lingering Shadow of the Debt Crisis

The Debt Repudiation Strategy

repudiate their debt, they won't need much in the way of loans since they can use the interest they were paying on the debt to finance internal development. Moreover, if all the developing countries were to collectively repudiate their debts, forming a debtors' cartel, the banks would be unable to single out one or two countries that had repudiated and, according to many observers, would start making loans to them again in a year or two.

Whether or not that repudiation strategy made sense, the threat of it made lots of sense, and worry about total repudiation increased banks' willingness to give developing countries leeway in repaying loans. This worry also made those existing loans to developing countries, which can be sold on the secondary market just like bonds, sell for far less than par—some for only about 15 to 30¢ on the U.S. dollar. (Each dollar of the loan amount is sold at anywhere between 15 and 30¢.) Thus countries could buy their debt back at only a portion of what they had borrowed.

In the 1990s, the fall in the value of the U.S. dollar and the fall in international market rates of interest assisted developing countries so that by 1993 the debt, while still a problem, was no longer considered a crisis. The value of developing country debt rose substantially, making significant profits for those who bought it at 15¢ to 30¢ on the U.S. dollar.

Unfortunately there were new debt problems in the making, and many economists saw the debt incurred by Russia and other former republics of the Soviet Union as being unrepayable, and hence a new international debt crisis of the late 1990s is a potential problem.

How the Debt Crisis Was Managed   There's a saying in banking, "If you owe the bank a million, you're in trouble; if you owe the bank a billion, your trouble is the bank's trouble." When a lender will go broke if a borrower defaults, the lender will try as hard as it can to work something out. Accordingly, the 1980s were years of intense negotiation designed to prevent developing countries from defaulting on their loans. The U.S. government, other Western governments, and the International Monetary Fund were active in these negotiations.

In the late 1980s, default was prevented by (1) restructuring the debt, (2) lending developing countries even more money to pay the interest on the debts, (3) writing off some of the old loans (essentially forgiving them), and (4) lowering the interest rate on the remaining loans.

The Debt Restructuring Strategy   Since the process by which these debts were reduced shows the role of the IMF in developing countries' economies, let's consider portions of it a bit more carefully.

The fall in the value of developing countries' debt led to an alternative strategy— the debt restructuring strategy—which achieved the same goals as debt repudiation would have—a decrease in the debt—but without a bankruptcy or repudiation of the debt. The basic plan that was followed, called The Brady Plan, involved banks accepting a reduction in indebtedness of the developing country (at, say 40¢ on the U.S. dollar) in trade for either a U.S. government or IMF guarantee of the "restructured" debt. These restructuring plans were instituted in the early 1990s and, by the mid-1990s, the developing countries were once again in a reasonably strong debt position and banks were making new, unguaranteed loans to them.

Generating Domestic Savings   Because of the problems of international debt, generating domestic saving is, in many ways, preferable to borrowing from abroad. But it is a difficult strategy—poor people don't have much discretionary income, and hence can't save much, and rich people are concerned about confiscation of their wealth, and hence save abroad, either legally or illegally. Moreover, for the small middle class that does exist, there are few financial instruments that effectively channel savings into investment. Macro monetary policy in such countries involves setting up such institutions. Let's now consider two case studies that give some insight into these issues.

A Real-Names Policy   Macro policies in developing countries often deal with setting up laws and institutional structures to handle attempts to circumvent policies that restrict freedom of movement, rather than conducting macro policy given an unchanging institutional structure. Thus, our first case study involves an attempt by the South Korean government to control the way its citizens save money. It was called a "real-names" policy.

The Wall Street Journal reported the South Korean real-names policy as follows: "President Kim Young Sam staged a surprise raid on [South] Korea's underground economy, introducing a real-names financial transaction system." (*The Wall Street Journal,* August 13, 1993, p. A4.)

The background that led to the policy is as follows: As in most developing countries, businesspeople are concerned about holding too much of their wealth in South Korea because of taxes and fear of government confiscation. Having wealth means they may have to explain how they got it, and the ways they got it may not always have been legal. Moreover, many politicians had significant wealth, and it is unclear how they came to have that wealth.

They could have simply put their money outside South Korea, and many of them did. But South Korea, like most developing countries, limits the flow of domestic capital abroad. Moreover, South Korea's economy is one of the success stories of development, and the rates of return on South Korean investments were high. This led many South Koreans to want to invest in South Korea, but they didn't want it to be known that it was their money. They managed to solve these conflicting goals by investing their money in South Korea using fictional names to hide their holdings. The "real-names" policy made that fictional name strategy illegal.

Making that strategy illegal sounds like a good policy, but it has a problem. Consider the economic effect of the law. It will drive South Koreans to hold more of their money abroad rather than at home, and will tend to depress investment, and hence income, in the South Korean economy. Soon after the introduction of the policy, the South Korean government lowered economic growth estimates by 25 percent.

If the policy depresses the economy, why did Kim Young Sam institute it? One of the reasons was political pressure from the middle class to control the excesses of the rich. During his election campaign, Kim Young Sam had promised to institute this popularly favoured policy if he won the presidency. After he was elected he backed off, but the expectation that he might actually implement the policy led to a withdrawal of funds from South Korea and into other countries.

Those expectations that he would institute the law were destabilizing. To stop the destabilizing effects of those expectations, he had to really institute the policy. That said, it should also be said that the law very likely won't be all that effective. The reason is that there is a high threshold level specified by the law. It only applies to accounts of more than 50 million won (about $90,000 Canadian in April 1995). This lessens the impact on a number of small businesspeople using the fictitious name accounts, letting the President seem as if he is a reformist while still assuring South Korean businesspeople that he will support them. Still, more than a thousand high-ranking government officials reported wealth of U.S. $1.3 million or more, and a Chief Justice of the South Korean Supreme Court resigned after it was revealed that he had $3.5 million. Such are the ironies of macro policies in developing countries.

The Borrowing Circle   Our next case study considers the development of an institution in one of the poorest countries of the world—Bangladesh. There, Mohammed Yunus, a U.S.-trained economist, created a bank—the Grameen Bank—that made market-rate-interest loans to poor village women. According to reports, the loans had a 97 percent payback rate, and Yunus made a profit.

How did he do it? As we discussed above, most banks in developing countries are internationally oriented. They use the same structure that Western banks use. This leaves the traditional part of many developing countries' economies without an effective way to translate savings into investment, leaving many entrepreneurial individuals without ways to develop their ideas.

Yunus recognized that Western financial institutional structures were not well suited to the traditional sectors of developing countries. He further recognized that the

aking productive loans in developing countries involves more than simply lending money. It involves changing cultural norms and creating a market economy. Thus, when the Grameen Bank makes a loan, it has the borrower promise to abide by the following 16 decisions, in an effort to change the culture and ways of life of the borrower.

The 16 Decisions

1. The four principles of Grameen Bank—discipline, unity, courage, and hard work—we shall follow and advance in all walks of our lives.
2. We shall bring prosperity to our families.
3. We shall not live in dilapidated houses. We shall repair our houses and work towards constructing new houses as soon as possible.
4. We shall grow vegetables all the year round. We shall eat plenty of them and sell the surplus.
5. During the planting seasons, we shall plant as many seedlings as possible.
6. We shall plan to keep our families small. We shall minimize our expenditures. We shall look after our health.
7. We shall educate our children and ensure that they can earn enough to pay for their education.
8. We shall always keep our children and the environment clean.
9. We shall build and use pit latrines.
10. We shall drink tube-well water. If it is not available, we shall boil water or use alum.
11. We shall not take any dowry in our sons' weddings, neither shall we give any dowry in our daughters' weddings. We shall keep the centre free from the curse of dowry. We shall not practice child marriage.
12. We shall not inflict any injustice on anyone, neither shall we allow anyone to do so.
13. For higher income we shall collectively undertake bigger investments.
14. We shall always be ready to help each other. If anyone is in difficulty, we shall all help.
15. If we come to know of any breach of discipline in any centre, we shall all go there and help restore discipline.
16. We shall introduce physical exercise in our centres. We shall take part in all social activities collectively.

purpose of financial institutions is to direct resources to those with good ideas who can back up their promises to pay back their loans in the future with increased output.

What Yunus did was to reconsider the fundamental role of banking in an economy—to make it possible for people with "good" ideas to develop those ideas by providing them with funds to develop their ideas—and to devise a structure that allowed such lending to take place.

He saw that Western banking institutions did not provide the answer for Bangladesh. By basing their lending decisions on the amount of collateral a borrower had, they essentially made it impossible for most people in Bangladesh to get loans. But Yunus also recognized that the collateral function served a useful purpose: it forced people to make the hard decision about whether they really needed the loans, and to work hard to see that they could pay the loans back, even if the going got tough. If you eliminate the role of collateral, something else must replace it.

The ingenious solution he came up with was the **borrowing circle** concept. Recognizing that the invisible handshake was extremely strong in Bangladesh, he made use of that handshake in his bank's lending practices. He offered to make loans to any woman who could find four friends who would agree that they would, if necessary, help her pay the loan back. If the borrower defaulted, the others could not borrow until the loan was repaid. The invisible handshake replaced the traditional collateral.

Notice a couple of things about the concept:

· It used economic insights creatively, and it recognized the essence of the problem, not the superficial aspects.

8 The "borrowing circle" concept replaced traditional collateral with guarantees by friends of the borrower. It was successful because the invisible handshake in Bangladesh, where the borrowing circle originated, was very strong.

Borrowing circle Loan system in which collateral is not required. Instead, the borrower must find friends to guarantee the repayments. It is enforced by preventing the friends from getting loans themselves unless the loan they guaranteed is paid back.

- It relied on an individual rather than governmental initiative. Yunus made a profit, and the individuals getting the loans made profits. Thus it encouraged development without a plan.

- It created a new institution that fit the social structure, rather than importing outside institutions.

- It was directed at the traditional economy, rather than the international economy, and the successful loans improved the lot of millions.

This simple concept worked. In ten years it developed into a large bank that has made more than 1,600,000 loans. The loans have been taken out to buy such things as a cow or material to make a fishing net—not large items, but items to use in precisely the types of activity that generate bottom-up development.

Mr. Yunus's work has received enormous accolades (some have suggested he should get a Nobel Prize), and even developed countries are looking into the borrowing circle concept as a way of getting credit to the poor. For example, the **Canadian International Development Agency** supports lending circles through supporting the Canadian Cooperative Association and other development supporters. While the concept was extraordinarily simple, Yunus's borrowing circle concept made use of economic insights but simultaneously reflected an understanding of and concern about the cultural and social dimensions of the economy. It is the type of macro policy most needed in developing countries.

Canadian International Development Agency (CIDA) Federal agency charged with providing assistance to developing countries in becoming self-sufficient.

The above two case studies are quite different from each other, but they both involved attempts to change institutions to make them more efficient at translating saving into investment. Such attempts at changing institutions are characteristic of macro policy in developing and transitional countries.

Examples of macro policy in developing countries like the above exist, but not as often as we would like to report. They are most likely to be found in Asian countries, although in the early 1990s there were some bright spots in Latin America. These cases show that creative macro institutional policies play an important role in development, and that the future of developing countries can be brighter than the present.

CONCLUSION

Whether their futures will be brighter depends on the imagination, drive, and creativity of their policymakers. It doesn't surprise us that the originator of this Bangladeshi plan (whom, in case you haven't guessed, we greatly admire) studied economics, because economic thinking directs one to solutions that combine economic insight with existing institutions. It doesn't promise easy answers, but it does allow one to see the type of institutions that are sustainable. The economic way of thinking can lead to institutional change and economic takeoff.

CHAPTER SUMMARY

- Economists separate out developing and transitional economies because these economies have different institutional structures and different weighting of goals than do Western economies.

- Many developing economies have serious political problems which make it impossible for government to take an active, positive role in the economy.

- Many developing countries have dual economies—one a traditional, nonmarket economy, and the other an internationalized market economy.

- Inflation in developing countries is usually related to the printing of too much money; the debate is about the political reasons why this occurs, and the viability of the alternatives.

- Most monetary policies in developing countries focus on the international sector and are continually dealing with the balance of payments constraint.

- Most developing countries have some type of limited convertibility.

- Macro policies in developing and transitional countries are more concerned with institutional policies and regime changes than are macro policies in developed countries.

- The debt crisis of the 1980s was resolved by a combination of write-downs and restructuring.

- The borrowing cycle is an example of an innovative macro institutional policy designed to better translate savings into investment.

KEY TERMS

balance of payments constraint   *(490)*
basic needs   *(480)*
borrowing circle   *(494)*
Canadian International Development
   Agency (CIDA)   *(495)*
conditionality   *(490)*
convertibility on the current
   account   *(489)*

developing economy   *(479)*
dual economy   *(483)*
exchange rate policy   *(490)*
full convertibility   *(489)*
inflation tax   *(488)*
inter-firm credit   *(485)*
limited capital account
   convertibility   *(489)*

macro institutional policies   *(490)*
policy change   *(484)*
regime change   *(484)*
restructuring   *(492)*
soft budget constraint   *(485)*
trade credits   *(486)*
transitional economy   *(479)*

QUESTIONS FOR THOUGHT AND REVIEW

*The number after the questions represents the estimated
degree of critical thinking required. (1 = almost none;
10 = deep thought.)*

1. Do different economic theories apply to developing countries than to developed countries?   *(2)*

2. What is the difference between development and growth?   *(2)*

3. What are three ways in which the institutions of developing countries differ from those in developed countries?   *(2)*

4. Why do governments in developing countries often seem more arbitrary and oppressive than governments in devel-

oped countries?   *(3)*

5. What is meant by "the dual economy"?   *(2)*

6. How does a regime change differ from a policy change?   *(2)*

7. What was the soft budget constraint?   *(2)*

8. What is the inflation tax?   *(2)*

9. Why doesn't the fact that the "inflation solution" is only a temporary solution stop many developing countries from using it?   *(4)*

10. What is conditionality, and how does it relate to the balance of payments constraint?   *(4)*

PROBLEMS AND EXERCISES

1. Could the borrowing circle concept be adopted for use in Canada?

    a. Why or why not?

    b. What modifications would you suggest if it were to be adopted?

2. Choose any developing country and answer the following questions about it:

    a. What is its level of per capita income?

    b. What is its growth potential?

    c. What is the exchange rate of its currency in relation to the Canadian dollar?

    d. What policy suggestions might you make to the country?

3. Bulgarian private banks rarely made long-term loans, but made substantial short-term loans in the early 1990s.

    a. List three reasons why long-term loans were not made

and two reasons why short-term loans were extended.

    b. Contrast this with banking practices in Canada.

4. It has been argued that development economics has no general theory; it is instead the application of common sense to real-world problems.

    a. Do you agree or disagree with that statement? Why?

    b. Why do you think this argument about that lack of generality of theories is made for developing countries more than it is made for developed countries?

5. In 1993 and 1994 President Fujimori of Peru instituted a set of policies that turned the Peruvian economy around. Research the following questions:

    a. How did he engineer this turnaround?

    b. Why has the U.S. government limited aid to Peru?

    c. What monetary and fiscal policy did he use?

    d. How would you judge his policies?

Glossary

A

activist economists   Economists who believe that the government can come up with some policy proposals that will positively impact the economy.

adaptive expectations   Expectations of the future based on what has been in the past.

aggregate consumption function   The name of all consumption functions of all individuals in society.

aggregate demand curve *(AD)*   A schedule, graphically represented by a curve, that shows how a change in the price level will change output demanded, other things (including supply) held constant.

aggregate demand (expenditure) management policy   Policy aimed at changing the level of income in the economy by a combination of a change in autonomous expenditures and the multiplied induced expenditures resulting from that change.

aggregate demand shock   A shift in the aggregate demand curve.

Aggregate Production/Aggregate Expenditures *(AP/AE)* **Model**   Keynesian model giving *aggregate supply* the name *aggregate production* and focusing on total production changes, not on changes in output caused by price-level changes. Emphasizes the difference between the Keynesian focus and the Classical focus on quantity of aggregate supply and demand changes resulting from changes in the price level.

aggregate equilibrium demand curve (AED)   A curve which reflects the net effect of the forces of aggregate demand and aggregate supply in an AS/AD model of the economy.

aggregate expenditures   The summation of all four components of expenditures: aggregate of consumption (spending by consumers), investment (spending by business), spending by government, and net foreign spending on Canadian goods (the difference between Canadian exports and Canadian imports). It is expressed by the equation $AE = C + I + G + (X - M)$.

aggregate production curve   In the Keynesian model, the 45-degree line on a graph with real income measured on the horizontal axis and real production on the vertical axis. Alternatively called the *aggregate income curve*.

aggregate supply/aggregate demand macro models   Macro-economic models in which the shapes of the curves depend on macro relationships, not substitution, and which have the price level, not relative price, on the vertical axis.

aggregate supply curve *(AS)*   A schedule graphically represented by a curve, which shows how a change in the price level will change the quantity of output supplied, other things (including expectations and aggregate demand) constant.

approximate real-world money multiplier   Measure of the amount of money ultimately created by the banking system per dollar deposited, when cash holdings of individuals and firms are treated the same as reserves of banks. The mathematical expression is $1/(r + c)$.

arbitrage   The purchase of a product in a low-price market for resale in a high-price market.

art of economics   The relating of positive economics to normative economics—the application of the knowledge learned in positive economics to the achievement of the goals determined in normative economics.

art of macro policy   An art practiced by economists who advise governments about real-world macro policy. In the practice of that art, economists recognize that economic relationships aren't certain and that conducting macroeconomic policy is not a science.

Asian tigers   Group of Asian countries that have achieved economic growth well above the level of other developing countries.

asset management   How a bank handles its loans and other assets.

automatic stabilizer   Any government program or policy that will counteract the business cycle without any new government action.

autonomous consumption   Consumption that is unaffected by changes in disposable income.

autonomous   Determined by outside forces; for example, Classicals held that real output was determined by forces "autonomous" to the quantity theory of money.

average propensity to consume (apc)   Consumption divided by disposable income.

average propensity to save (aps)   Savings divided by disposable income.

B

balance of payments   A country's record of all transactions between its residents and the residents of all foreign countries.

balance of payments constraint   Limitation on expansionary domestic macro policy due to a shortage of international reserves.

balance of trade   The difference between the value of goods a nation exports and the value of goods it imports.

balance of trade deficit   When a nation imports more than it exports.

balance of trade surplus   When a nation exports more than it imports.

Bank of Canada   Canada's central bank, its liabilities serve as cash in Canada.

bank rate   The rate of interest the Bank of Canada charges on loans to chartered banks.

base year   The year against which all comparisons are made.

basic needs   Adequate food, clothing, and shelter for the people in a society.

bond   Promissory note that a certain amount of money plus interest will be paid back in the future.

boom   In the business cycle, a very high peak representing a big jump in output.

borrowing circle   Loan system in which collateral is not required. Instead, the borrower must find friends to guarantee the repayment. It is enforced by preventing the friends from getting loans themselves unless the loan they guaranteed is paid back.

bracket creep   When a rise in income pushes you into a higher tax bracket.

Bretton Woods system   An agreement that governed international financial relationships from the period after World War II until 1971, named for Bretton Woods, New Hampshire, where the agreement was reached at a meeting of international officials.

business   The private producing unit in our society.

business cycle   The upward or downward movement of economic activity that occurs around the growth trend.

C

Canadian International Development Agency (CIDA)   Federal agency charged with providing assistance to developing countries in becoming self-sufficient.

capacity utilization rate   Rate at which factories and machines are operating compared to the maximum rate at which they could be used.

capital account   The part of the balance of payments account that lists all long-term flows of payments.

capital consumption allowance   Also known as depreciation, the amount by which the capital stock is estimated to have fallen in a year.

capital control law   A law preventing people from investing abroad.

capital controls   A government's prohibitions on its currency freely flowing into and out of the country.

capital market   Financial market in which financial assets having a maturity of more than three years are bought and sold.

capitalism   An economic system based upon private property and the market. It gives private property rights to individuals and relies on market forces to coordinate economic activity.

capitalists   Businesspeople who have acquired large amounts of money and use it to invest in businesses.

cash flow accounting system   An accounting system entering expenses and revenues only when cash is received or paid out.

cash management   The main technique for operating monetary policy, including open market operations and drawdowns and redeposits; aimed at providing the chartered banks with more or less cash.

CD *(certificate of deposit)*   Piece of paper certifying that you have a sum of money in a savings account in the bank for a specified period of time.

central bank   A bankers' bank; it conducts monetary policy and supervises the financial system.

change in aggregate demand   A shift of the entire demand curve.

change in the aggregate quantity demanded   A movement along the *AD* curve.

classical economists   Economists who generally oppose government intervention.

Classicals   Economists who generally oppose government intervention.

Classical laissez-faire economists   Economists who believe that any government policies will probably make things worse, and consequently that the best policy is government disinvolvement with the economy—lowering taxes and keeping the government out of the market as much as possible.

Classical long-run aggregate supply curve   Vertical aggregate supply curve formed if price level rises but real output doesn't change.

Classical supply-side economics   Economics that focuses on incentive effects of taxes and argues that low tax rates are central to an economy's success.

coincidental indicators   Indicators that tell us what phase of the business cycle the economy is currently in.

commercial paper   Short-term IOU of a large corporation.

comparative advantage   The ability to produce a good at a lower opportunity cost (forgone production of another good) than another country or resource can.

competition   Ability of individuals to freely enter into business activities.

competitiveness   A country's ability to produce goods and services more cheaply than other countries.

conditionality   Making loans that are subject to specific conditions.

Consumer Price Index (CPI)   Index of inflation measuring prices of a fixed "basket" of consumer goods, weighted according to each component's share of an average consumer's expenditures.

consumer sovereignty   The right of the individual to make choices about what is consumed and produced.

consumer surplus   The additional amount that consumers would be willing to pay for a product above what they actually pay.

consumption function   Representation of the relationship between consumption and disposable income as a mathematical function ($C = C_o + mpcY_d$, where C = consumption expenditures, C_o = autonomous consumption, mpc = marginal propensity to consume, and Y_d = disposable income).

contractionary monetary policy   Monetary policy aimed at reducing the money supply and thereby restraining aggregate demand.

contractual intermediaries   Financial institution that holds and stores individuals' financial assets.

convertibility on the current account   System that allows people to exchange currencies freely to buy goods and services, but not to buy assets in other countries.

corporation   Business that is treated like a person, legally owned by its stockholders. Its stockholders are not personally liable for the actions of the corporate "person."

cost-push inflation   Inflation resulting from the pressure exerted when a significant proportion of markets (or one very important market) experiences restrictions on supply.

countercyclical fiscal policy   Fiscal policy in which the government offsets any shock that would create a business cycle.

credible systematic policies   Policies that people believe will be implemented regardless of consequences.

crowding in   Positive effects of government spending on other components of spending.

crowding out   The offsetting effect on private expenditures caused by the government's sale of bonds to finance expansionary fiscal policy.

cultural norms   Standards people use when they determine whether a particular activity or behaviour is acceptable.

current account   The part of the balance of payments account that lists all short-term flows of payments.

cyclical unemployment   Unemployment resulting from fluctuations in economic activity.

D

debt   Accumulated deficits minus accumulated surpluses.

debt service   The interest rate on debt times the total debt.

deficit   A shortfall per year of incoming revenue under outgoing payments.

demand   Schedule of quantities of a good that will be bought per unit of time at various prices.

demand curve   Curve that tells how much of a good will be bought at various prices.

demand for money   The total amount of money the public desires to hold at a point in time.

demand-pull inflation   Inflation resulting from the pressure exerted when the majority of markets in the economy experience increases in demand.

demerit goods or activities   Things government believes are bad for you, although you may like them.

depository institutions   Financial institution whose primary financial liability is deposits in chequing or savings accounts.

depreciation   Decrease in an asset's value.

depression   A large recession.

desired reserve ratio   The proportion of its deposits that a financial institution desires to hold to satisfy its demand for cash.

developing economy   An economy that has a low level of GDP per capita and a relatively undeveloped market structure, and has never had an alternative, developed economic system.

diffusion index   An average that captures changes across a variety of sectors over time. Used to illustrate how the business cycle affects different industries.

discouraged workers   People who do not look for a job because they feel they don't have a chance of finding one.

disequilibrium adjustment story   Story of how the economy adjusts from disequilibrium to equilibrium.

disintermediation   Borrowing directly from an individual without going through an intermediary bank.

disposable income   Income remaining after paying taxes.

disposable personal income   Personal income minus personal income taxes and payroll taxes.

diversification   Spreading of risks by holding many different types of financial assets.

domestic income   Total income earned by residents and businesses in a country.

downturn   Segment of the business cycle characterized by the economy starting to fall from the top of the cycle.

drawdown   The transfer of government deposits from the chartered banks and other financial institutions to the Bank of Canada.

dual economy   Tendency of developing countries to have two somewhat unrelated economies—one an internationally based economy, the other a traditional, often nonmarket, economy.

durable goods   Goods expected to last more than one year.

dynamic externalities   Effects of adjustment decisions that are not taken into effect by the decision maker.

E

economic decision rule   If benefits exceed costs, do it. If costs exceed benefits, don't do it.

economic forces   The forces of scarcity (when there isn't enough to go around, goods must be rationed).

economic institution   Physical or mental structures that significantly influence economic decisions.

economic policy   An action (or inaction) taken, usually by government, to influence economic events.

economic reasoning   Making decisions on the basis of costs and benefits.

economic system   The set of economic institutions that determine a country's important economic decisions.

economic theory   Generalizations about the working of an abstract economy.

economics   The study of how human beings coordinate their wants.

economies of scale   A decrease in per-unit cost as a result of an increase in output.

economy   The institutional structure through which individuals in a society coordinate their diverse wants or desires.

effective demand   Aggregate demand that exists after suppliers cut production in response to aggregate supply exceeding aggregate demand.

efficiency   Achieving a goal as cheaply as possible.

embargo All-out restriction on import or export of a good.

entrepreneurship Labour services that involve high degrees of organizational skills, concern, and creativity.

equation of exchange $MV = PQ$ (quantity of **M**oney times **V**elocity of money equals the **P**rice level times the **Q**uantity of real goods sold).

equilibrium A concept in which the dynamic forces cancel each other out.

equilibrium price The price toward which the invisible hand (economic forces) drives the market.

European Union (EU) An economic and political union of European countries that allow free trade among countries.

excess demand Quantity demanded is greater than quantity supplied.

excess reserves Reserves in excess of what banks desire to hold.

excess supply Quantity supplied is greater than quantity demanded.

exchange rate The rate at which one country's currency can be traded for another country's currency.

exchange rate policy Deliberately affecting a country's exchange rate in order to affect its trade balance.

expansion Upturn that lasts for more than two consecutive quarters of a year.

expansionary monetary policy Monetary policy aimed at increasing the money supply and raising the level of aggregate demand.

expectations of inflation The rise in the price level that the average person expects.

expected inflation Inflation people expect to occur.

export-led growth policy A policy that increases autonomous exports or decreases autonomous imports, thereby increasing autonomous expenditures.

exports Goods produced in the home country but sold to foreign countries.

external government debt Government debt owed to individuals in foreign countries.

externality A result of a decision that is not taken into account by the decision maker.

F

factors of productions Resources, or inputs, necessary to produce goods.

fallacy of composition The false assumption that what is true for a part will also be true for the whole.

feudalism Political system divided into small communities in which a few powerful people protect those who are loyal to them.

financial assets Assets, such as stocks or bonds, whose benefit to the owner depends on the issuer of the asset meeting certain obligations called *financial liabilities*.

financial institution A business whose primary activity is buying, selling, or holding financial assets.

financial liabilities Liability incurred by the issuer of a financial asset to stand behind the issued asset.

financial market Institution that brings buyers and sellers of financial assets together.

fine tuning Countercyclical fiscal policy designed to keep the economy always at its target or potential level of income.

firm Economic institution that transforms factors of production into consumer goods.

first dynamic law of supply and demand When quantity demanded is greater than quantity supplied, prices tend to rise; when quantity supplied is greater than quantity demanded, prices tend to fall.

fiscal policy Deliberate change in either government spending or taxes to stimulate or slow down the economy.

fixed exchange rate An exchange rate established by a government that chooses an exchange rate and offers to buy and sell currencies at that rate.

flexible exchange rate An exchange rate the determination of which is left totally up to the market.

foreign exchange control law A law preventing people from buying foreign currency.

foreign exchange market Market in which one country's currency can be exchanged for another country's.

foreign exchange reserves The pool of foreign currencies and gold used by the central bank when it intervenes to affect the external value of the dollar.

free rider Person who participates in something for free because others have paid for it.

Free Trade Agreement (FTA) Trade deal signed by Canada and the United States aimed at reducing barriers to trade. It took effect on January 1, 1989.

free trade association Group of countries that allows free trade among its members and puts up common barriers against all other countries' goods.

frictional unemployment Unemployment caused by new entrants to the job market and people who have left their jobs to look for and find other jobs.

full convertibility System where there is no law preventing individuals from changing dollars into any currency they want for whatever legal purpose they want.

full employment An economic climate in which almost everyone who wants a job has one.

fundamental analysis Analysis of curves describing fundamental forces that will be operating in the long run.

funded pension system Pension system in which money is collected and invested in a special fund from which payments are made.

G

GDP deflator Index of the price level of aggregate output of the average price of the components in GDP relative to a base year.

General Agreement on Tariffs and Trade (GATT) International agreement not to impose trade restrictions except under certain limited conditions. Replaced by World Trade Organization (WTO) in 1995.

general purpose transfers Payments from the federal government to provincial and local governments meant to reduce disparities between "have" and "have not" provinces.

global corporations Corporations with substantial operations on both the production and sales sides in more than one country. Another name for multinational corporation.

globalization The cross-border spread of goods and services, factors of production, firms, and markets.

gold specie flow mechanism Long-run adjustment mechanism under the gold standard in which flows of gold and changes in the price level bring about equilibrium.

gold standard The system by which the value of a country's currency is fixed in relation to the price of gold and under which the country must maintain a stockpile of gold sufficiently large that it can pay in gold for as much of its currency as anyone wants to sell.

government budget deficit Situation when government expenditures exceed government revenues.

government budget surplus Situation when government revenues exceed expectations.

Governor of the Bank of Canada The head of the Bank of Canada, appointed by the federal cabinet for a seven year term.

gross domestic product (GDP) Aggregate final output of residents and businesses in an economy in a one-year period.

gross national product (GNP) Aggregate final output of citizens and businesses of an economy in a one-year period.

Group of Five Group that meets to promote negotiations and coordinate economic relations among countries. The Five are Japan, Germany, Britain, France, and the United States.

Group of Seven Group that meets to promote negotiations and coordinate economic relations among countries. The Seven are Japan, Germany, Britain, France, Canada, Italy, and the United States.

growth-compatible institutions Institutions that foster growth.

H

households Groups of individuals living together and making joint decisions.

human capital People's knowledge.

hyperinflation Inflation that hits triple digits (100 percent) or more.

I

idealogy Values that are held so deeply that they are not questioned.

import control law A law preventing people from importing.

import license A license the government requires a firm to purchase giving it the legal right to import a good.

imports Goods produced in foreign countries but sold in the home country.

income Payments received plus or minus changes in value of one's assets in a specified time period.

income adjustment mechanism Chase between aggregate supply and aggregate demand.

incomes policy A policy placing direct pressure on individuals to hold down their nominal wages and prices.

index number An average that captures change over time, usually in relation to a base year figure of 100. Used to construct price indexes like the consumer price index.

indexed tax system One in which the income levels associated with different level of taxation are allowed to change as a result of inflation.

induced consumption Consumption that changes as disposable income changes.

induced recession A deliberate attempt by government to rid the economy of inflationary expectations.

Industrial Products Price Index (PPI) An index or ratio of a composite of prices of a number of important raw materials.

Industrial Revolution Period (1750–1900) during which technology and machines rapidly modernized industrial production.

inefficiency Getting less output from inputs which, if devoted to some other activity, would produce more output.

infant industry argument With initial protection, an industry will be able to become competitive.

inflation A continual rise in the price level.

inflation tax An implicit tax on the holders of cash and the holders of any obligations specified in nominal terms.

inflationary gap The difference between equilibrium income and potential income when equilibrium income exceeds potential income.

input What you put in to achieve output.

inter-firm credit Loans from one firm to another.

interest The income paid to savers—individuals who produce now but do not consume now.

interest groups Individuals and others who band together to encourage and protect government spending in certain areas of the economy.

intermediate products Products of one firm used in some other firm's production of another firm's product.

internal government debt Government debt owed to its own citizens.

international effect Given a fixed exchange rate, when the price level in a country goes down, the price of its exports decreases relative to the price of foreign goods.

International Monetary Fund (IMF) A multinational international financial institution concerned primarily with monetary issues.

interpretative Keynesian model Keynesian model that is an aid in understanding complicated disequilibrium dynamics.

intertemporal price-level effect If the price level falls but is expected to rise in the future, people will decide to purchase some goods now that they would have purchased in the future.

investment Expenditures by business on plants and equipment.

invisible foot Political and legal forces that play a role in deciding whether to let market forces operate.

invisible hand Economic forces, that is, the price mechanism; the rise and fall of prices that guides our actions in a market.

invisible handshake Social and historical forces that play a role in deciding whether to let market forces operate.

invisible hand theory The insight that a market economy will allocate resources efficiently.

J

J-curve Curve describing the rise and fall in the balance of trade deficit following a fall in the value of the dollar.

just-noticeable difference A threshold below which our senses don't recognize that something has changed.

K

Keynesian economists   Economists who generally favour government intervention in the aggregate economy.

Keynesians   Economists who generally favour government intervention in the aggregate economy.

Keynesian equation   Equation that tells us that income equals the multiplier times autonomous expenditures (Y = (*Multiplier*) (*Autonomous Expenditures*).

Keynesian supply-side policy   Policy that goes beyond the traditional Keynesian demand-side analysis and focuses on the composition of government spending and taxes, modifying that composition to expand supply and potential output, decreasing the deficit at the same time that it expands the economy.

Keynes Law   Demand creates its own supply.

L

L   Broad definition of "money" that includes almost all short-term assets.

labour force   The number of people in the economy willing and able to find work.

laissez-faire   Economic policy of leaving coordination of individuals' wants to be controlled by the market.

laissez-faire economists   Economists who believe that most government policies would probably make things worse, and favour (relative) government disinvolvement in the economy.

law of aggregate demand   As the price level falls the quantity of aggregate demand will increase, holding everything else constant.

law of demand   More of a good will be demanded the lower its price, other things constant. Also can be stated as: Less of a good will be demanded the higher its price, other things constant.

law of supply   More of a good will be supplied the higher its price, other things constant. Also can be stated as: Less of a good will be supplied the lower its price, other things constant.

leading indicators   Indicators that tell us what's likely to happen 12 to 15 months from now.

learning by doing   Becoming more proficient at doing something by actually doing it; in the process, learning what works and what doesn't.

liability management   How a bank attracts deposits and what it pays for them.

limited capital account convertibility   System that allows full current account convertibility and partial capital account convertibility.

limited liability   The liability of a stockholder (owner) in a corporation; it is limited to the amount the stockholder has invested in the company.

liquidity   Ability to turn an asset into cash quickly.

long-run Phillips curve   A curve showing the trade-off (or complete lack thereof) between inflation and unemployment when expectations of inflation equal actual inflation.

long-run potential income   The level of income the economy is capable of producing if it does not experience cumulative circles of declining production.

long-run shift factors   Shift factors that are unlikely to change substantially in the short run, but in the long run they can change significantly.

long-run supply   Level of supply consistent with an economy's potential income; it is the maximum amount of output that can be produced, given the institutional structure of the economy.

low-income cut-off   The income level at which families spend at least 20 percent more than the average family on the necessities of life. Used by Statistics Canada to define low-income families.

M

M1   Component of the money supply that consists of cash in the hands of the public and chequing account balances.

M2   Component of the money supply that consists of M1 plus personal savings deposits and non-personal notice deposits at the chartered banks.

M2+   Components of the money supply that include M2 plus deposits at non-bank financial institutions.

M3   The broadest definition of money in terms of deposits held by Canadian chartered banks.

macro institutional policies   Policies to change the underlying macro institutions and thereby increase output.

macroeconomic externality   Externality that affects the levels of unemployment, inflation, or growth in the economy as a whole.

macroeconomics   The study of inflation, unemployment, business cycles, and growth primarily from the whole to the parts, focusing on aggregate relationships and supplementing its analysis with microeconomic insights.

macro policy model   A model which combines intermediate adjustments with initial shifts, and shows what the final result will be without explaining each step along the way. It provides a simplified presentation of macro policy issues.

marginal benefit   Additional benefit above what you've already derived.

marginal cost   The change in cost associated with a change in quantity.

marginal propensity to consume (*mpc*)   Percentage change in consumption that accompanies a percentage change in income.

marginal propensity to expend (*mpe*)   The additional spending that will be translated into the income stream when all induced expenditures are included.

marginal propensity to save (*mps*)   Percentage saved from an additional dollar of disposable income.

market demand curve   The horizontal sum of all individual demand curves.

market force   Economic force to which society has given relatively free rein so that it has been able to work through the market.

mechanistic Keynesian model   Model picturing the economy as representable by a mechanistic, timeless model with a determinant equilibrium, with little or no discussion of the fleetingness of that equilibrium.

mechanistic Keynesianism   The belief that the simple multiplier models (or even complex variations) actually describe the aggregate adjustment process and lead to a deterministic solution that policy makers can exploit in a mechanistic way.

mercantilism   Economic system in which government doles out the rights to undertake economic activities.

merchandise trade balance   The difference between the goods a nation exports and the goods a nation imports.

merit goods or activities   Things government believes are good for you, although you may not think so.

microeconomics   The study of individual choice, and how that choice is influenced by economic forces.

microfoundations of macro   The decisions of individuals that underlie aggregate results.

MITI   Japanese agency, the Ministry of International Trade and Industry, that guides the Japanese economy.

model   Framework for looking at the world.

monetary base   The vault cash plus reserves that banks have at the Bank of Canada.

monetary policy   Policy of influencing the economy through changes in the money supply and credit availability.

monetary rule   A prescribed monetary policy to be followed regardless of what is happening in the economy.

monetary validation   Allowing the money supply to rise after a disturbance has increased the price level.

money   A highly liquid financial asset that's generally accepted in exchange for other goods and is used as a reference in valuing other goods.

money market   Financial market in which financial assets having a maturity of less than three years are bought and sold.

money substitutes   Mediums of payment other than money, including credit cards.

monopoly power   Ability to prevent others from entering a business field, which enables a firm to raise its price.

mortgage   A special name for a secured loan on real estate.

most-favoured nation   Country that will pay as low a tariff on its exports as will any other country.

movement along a demand curve   Method of representing a change in the quantity demanded. Graphically, a change in quantity demanded will cause a movement along the demand curve.

movement along the supply curve   Method of representing a change in the quantity supplied. Graphically, a change in quantity demanded will cause a movement along the supply curve.

multiplier   Key aspect of the Keynesian model that differentiates it from the Classical model. It is a number that tells us how much income will change in response to a change in autonomous expenditures.

N

national income accounting   A set of rules and definitions for measuring economic activity in the aggregate economy.

national income accounting identity   The relationship between output and income: Whenever a good or service is produced, somebody receives an income for producing it.

natural rate of unemployment   Classical term for the unemployment rate in long-run equilibrium when expectations of inflation equal the actual level of inflation.

near banks   Deposit taking institutions such as trust and mortgage loan companies, credit unions, and *caisses populaires*.

near money   Financial assets that can be easily converted into money—very liquid interest earning assets such as Canada Savings Bonds.

neomercantilism   An economic system in which the government explicitly guides the economy.

Net Domestic Income at Factor Cost (NDI)   An income measure we arrive at using the factor incomes approach to national income accounting.

net domestic product (NDP)   GDP adjusted to take account of depreciation.

net exports   A country's exports minus its imports.

net foreign factor income   Income from foreign domestic factor sources minus foreign factor incomes earned domestically.

Net National Income (NNI)   A measure of a nation's output that excludes depreciation but includes net foreign income. The total income earned by citizens and businesses of a country, less depreciation.

net private investment   Gross investment minus depreciation.

Nimby   A short way to express "**N**ot **I**n **M**y **B**ack **Y**ard" when a community objects to a proposed development in its neighborhood.

nominal concepts   Economic concepts specified in monetary terms (current dollars) with no adjustment for inflation.

nominal deficit   The deficit determined by looking at the difference between expenditures and receipts.

nominal GDP   GDP calculated at existing prices.

nominal interest rates   Interest rates you actually see and pay.

nominal output   Output as measured, without any adjustments.

nonconvertible currencies   Currencies that cannot be freely exchanged with currencies of other countries.

nondurable goods   Goods that last less than one year.

nonprofit business   Business that does not try to make a profit. It tries only to make enough money to cover its expenses with its revenues.

nontariff barriers   Indirect regulatory restrictions on exports and imports.

normative economics   The study of what the goals of the economy should be.

North American Free Trade Agreement (NAFTA)   Trade deal signed by Canada, Mexico, and the United States aimed at reducing barriers to North American trade; went into effect January 1, 1994.

O

objective   Term applied to "analysis," meaning that the analysis keeps your subjective views—your value judgments—separate.

off-budget expenditure   An expenditure that is not counted in the budget as an expenditure.

official settlements account   The part of the balance of payments account that records the amount of a currency or other international reserves a nation buys.

Okun's law   Rule of thumb economists use to translate the unemployment rate into changes in income: "A one percent fall in the unemployment rate equals a 2.5 percent increase in income."

Okun's rule of thumb   Another name for Okun's Law: A one-percent change in the unemployment rate will cause income in the economy to change in the opposite direction by 2.5 percent.

open market operations   The Bank of Canadas day-to-day buying and selling of government securities.

opportunity cost   The benefit forgone, or the cost, of the best alternative to the activity you've chosen. In economic reasoning, the cost is less than the benefit of what you've chosen.

other things constant   An assumption that places a limitation on the implications that can be drawn from any supply/demand analysis. The elements of the particular analysis are considered under the assumption that all other elements that could affect the analysis remain constant (whether they actually remain constant or not).

output   The result of an activity.

P

paradox of thrift   Individuals attempting to save more cause income to decrease: thereby, they end up saving less.

partial equilibrium analysis   Analysis of a part of a whole; it initially assumes all other things remain equal.

partially flexible exchange rate   Exchange rate where the government sometimes buys and sells currencies to influence the price directly and at other times simply accepts the exchange rate determined by supply and demand forces.

partnership   Business with two or more owners.

passive deficit   Portion of the deficit that exists because the economy is operating below its potential level of output.

path-dependent equilibrium   Equilibrium that is influenced by the adjustment process to that equilibrium.

perfectly flexible exchange rates   Exchange rate system in which the government does not intervene in foreign currency markets to affect the value of the dollar.

personal income (PI)   National income plus net transfer payments from government minus amounts attributed but not received.

Phillips curve   A representation of the relation between inflation and unemployment.

planning   Deciding, before the production takes place, what will be produced, how to produce it, and for whom to produce it.

policy change   A change in one aspect of government's actions, such as monetary policy or fiscal policy.

policy regime   The general set of rules, whether explicit or implicit, governing the monetary and fiscal policies a country follows.

positive economics   The study of what is, and how the economy works.

potential income   Income level achieved at some previous point plus a normal growth factor.

potential output   Output that would materialize at the target rate of unemployment and the target level of capacity utilization.

present value   Method of translating a flow of future income or savings into its current worth.

price ceiling   A government-imposed limit on how high a price can be charged.

price floor   A government-imposed limit on how low a price may be.

price level   A composite price of all goods.

price level flexibility curve (PLF)   A curve which reflects the net effect of the forces of aggregate supply in an AS/AD model of the economy.

price-level interest rate effect   A decrease in the price level will increase the real money supply.

price stability   A period during which the overall price level does not suffer from excessive volatility.

primary financial market   Market in which newly issued financial assets are sold.

principle of absolute advantage   A country that can produce a good at a lower cost than another country has an absolute advantage in the production of that good.

principle of comparative advantage   As long as the relative opportunity costs of producing goods differ among countries, there are potential gains from trade, even if one country has an absolute advantage in everything.

principle of increasing marginal opportunity cost   In order to get more of something, one must give up ever-increasing quantities of something else.

private good   A good that, when consumed by one individual, cannot be consumed by other individuals.

private property rights   Control of an asset or a right given to an individual or a firm.

producer surplus   The difference between the price at which producers would have been willing to supply a good and the price they actually receive.

production possibility curve   A curve measuring the maximum combination of outputs that can be obtained from a given number of inputs.

production possibility table   Table that lists a choice's opportunity costs.

productive efficiency   Getting as much output for as few inputs as possible.

profit   A return on entrepreneurial activity and risk taking.

progressive tax   Average tax rate increases with income.

proletariat   The working class.

proportional tax   Average tax rate is constant with income.

protectionist policies   Policies that favour domestic products over foreign-produced products.

public goods   Goods whose consumption by one individual does not prevent their consumption by other individuals.

purchasing power parity   Method of comparing income by looking at the domestic purchasing power of money in different countries.

Q

quantity demanded   A specific amount that will be demanded per unit of time at a specific price. Refers to a point on a demand curve.

quantity supplied   A specific quantity of a good offered for sale at a specific price. Refers to a point on a supply curve.

quantity theory of money   The price level varies in response to changes in the quantity of money.

quota rent   A rent received by domestic producers who supply a good that is subject to an import quota.

quotas   Limitations on how much of a good can be shipped into a country.

R

rational expectations   Expectations about the future based on the best current information, used in theoretical economic work that focuses on building dynamic feedback effects into macro models.

rationing   Structural mechanism for determining who gets what.

real business cycle theory   Real business cycle theories are economic cycles as the result of real shifts in the economy. Shocks to technology and tastes affect the supply side, leading to business cycles.

real concepts   Concepts adjusted for inflation.

real deficit   The nominal deficit adjusted for inflation's effect on the debt.

real GDP   Nominal GDP adjusted for inflation.

real interest rate   Interest rate adjusted for expected inflation.

real output   The total amount of goods and services produced, adjusted for price level changes.

real wage   The ratio of the wage rate to the price level.

recession   A downturn that persists for more than two consecutive quarters of a year.

recessionary gap   The difference between equilibrium income and potential income when potential income exceeds equilibrium income.

redeposits   The transfer of government deposits from the Bank of Canada to the chartered banks and other financial institutions.

régime change   A change in the entire atmosphere with which the government and the company interrelate.

regressive tax   Average tax rate decreases with income.

regulatory trade restrictions   Government-imposed procedural rules that limit imports.

relative price   The price of a good relativethe price level.

reserve currency   A currency in which countries hold reserves.

reserve ratio   Ratio of cash or deposits a bank holds at the central bank to deposits a bank keeps as a reserve against withdrawals of cash.

reserve requirement   The minimum percentage of deposits that a bank desires to hold as cash reserves.

reserves   Cash and deposits at central bank that a bank keeps on hand that is sufficient to manage the normal cash inflows and outflows.

restructuring   Changing the underlying economic institutions (of an economy).

Ricardian equivalence theorem   Proposition that it makes no difference whether government spending is financed by taxes now or by a deficit (taxes later).

Rosy Scenario policy   Government policy of making optimistic predictions and never making gloomy predictions.

S

Say's law   Supply creates its own demand.

second dynamic law of supply and demand   In a market, the larger the difference between quantity supplied and quantity demanded, the greater the pressure on prices to rise (if there is excess demand) or fall (if there is excess supply).

secondary financial market   Market in which previously issued financial assets can be bought and sold.

services   Activities done for other people not involving the production or sales of goods. Examples include cutting hair, teaching, and lawn-mowing.

services balance   The difference between the services a nation exports and the services a nation imports.

shift factors of aggregate demand   Shift factors of aggregate demand cause movements along the aggregate supply curve rather than shift the aggregate supply curve.

shift factors of aggregate supply   Factors that shift the aggregate supply curve rather than cause movements along the aggregate supply curve.

shift factors of demand   Something, other than the good's price, that affects how much of the good is demanded.

shift in demand   If how much of a good is demanded is affected by a shift factor, there is said to be a shift in demand. Graphically, a shift in demand will cause the entire demand curve to shift.

shift in supply   If how much of a good is supplied is affected by a shift factor, there is said to be a shift in supply. Graphically, a shift in supply will cause the entire supply curve to shift.

short-run decision   Firm is constrained in regard to what production decisions it can make.

short-run potential income   The level of income to which the economy gravitates in the short-run because of cumulative circles of declining production.

short-run Phillips curve   A curve showing the trade-off between inflation and unemployment when expectations of inflation are constant.

short-run shift factors   Shift factors that change significantly in the short run and that can be expected to cause short-run fluctuations in income.

simple money multiplier   Measure of the amount of money ultimately created by the banking system per dollar deposited when people hold no cash. The mathematical expression is $1/r$.

social assistance programs   Government programs aimed at providing earnings and services to meet basic needs.

social capital   The habitual way of doing things that guides people in how they approach production.

socialism   Economic system that tries to organize society in such a way that all people contribute what they can and get what they need, adjusting their own wants in accordance with what's available.

soft budget constraint   Loose financial constraints on firms' decisions in centrally planned economies.

sole proprietorship   Business with only one owner.

Soviet-style socialism   Economic system that uses central planning and government ownership of the means of production to answer the questions: what, how, and for whom.

Special Drawing Rights (SDRs)   A type of international money consisting of IOUs of the IMF.

special purpose transfers   Payments from the federal government to provincial and local governments for funding social spending on health care, welfare, and post-secondary education.

spread   The difference between the price at which traders buy and sell a currency.

stage of production Any of the various levels, such as manufacturing, wholesale, or retail, on which businesses are organized.

stagflation Combination of high inflation and high unemployment.

stance of fiscal policy Expansionary or contractionary changes in government spending and/or taxes.

state socialism Economic system in which government sees to it that people work for the common good until they can be relied upon to do that on their own.

stock A partial ownership right to a company.

strategic bargaining Demanding a larger share of the gains of trade than you can reasonably expect.

structural deficit Proportion of the budget deficit that would exist even if the economy were at its potential level of income.

structural readjustment Phenomenon of economy trying to change from what it had been doing to doing something new instead of repeating what it had done in the past.

structural unemployment Unemployment resulting from changes in the economy itself.

subjective Term applied to "analysis," meaning that the analysis reflects the analyst's views of how things should be.

supply A schedule of quantities of goods that will be offered to the market at various prices.

supply/demand models Microeconomic models in which the shapes of supply and demand curves are based on the principle of substitution and opportunity cost.

supply of money The total amount of money in the economy at a point in time.

supply price shocks Shocks that cause a rise in nominal wages and prices.

supply-side policies Policies that focus on incentive effects of taxes and advocate lower tax rates or modifying the composition of government spending and taxes to stimulate supply, expand potential output, and allow the economy to grow, with the result that the growth decreases the budget deficit and creates jobs—that is, creates growth, prosperity, and low unemployment.

T

target rate of unemployment Lowest sustainable rate of unemployment economists believe is possible under existing conditions.

tariff A tax governments place on internationally traded goods—generally imports. Tariffs are also called *customs duties*.

tax-based income policies Policies in which the government tries to directly affect the nominal wage- and price-setting institutions.

term structure of interest rates The structure of yields on financial instruments with similar characteristics; it links short-term interest rates to long-term interest rates.

third dynamic law of supply and demand When quantity supplied equals quantity demanded, prices have no tendency to change.

trade adjustment assistance programs Programs designed to compensate losers for reductions in trade restrictions.

trade balance The difference between a country's exports and its imports.

trade credits Short-term loans to facilitate inter-firm trade.

transfer payments Payments by government to individuals that are not in payment for goods or services.

transitional economy An economy that has had an alternative, developed, socialist economic system, but is in the process of changing from that system to a market system.

U

unemployment insurance A federal government program aimed at replacing earnings of those who are temporarily out of work.

unemployment rate The percentage of people in the labour force who can't find a job.

unexpected inflation Inflation that surprises people.

unfunded pension system Pension system in which pensions are paid from current revenues.

upturn Period characterized by the economy starting to come out of the trough, or lowest point on the business cycle.

V

value added The contribution that each stage of production makes to the final value of a good.

veil-of-money assumption Real output is not influenced by changes in the money supply.

velocity of circulation Number of times per year, on average, a dollar goes around to generate a dollars' worth of income; or amount of income per year generated by a dollar of money.

velocity of money Number of times per year, on average, a dollar goes around to generate a dollar's worth of income; or amount of income per year generated by a dollar of money.

W

wage and price controls Legal limits on prices and wages.

wealth effect If the price level falls, people feel wealthier because each of their dollars will buy more than they did before, so people will increase their spending until aggregate goods demanded equals aggregate supply.

welfare capitalism Economic system in which the market operates but government regulates market significantly.

welfare loss Loss to society caused by a policy inducing a wedge between marginal private and marginal social costs and benefits.

World Bank A multinational, international financial institution that works with developing countries to secure low-interest loans.

World Trade Organization (WTO) World body charged with reducing impediments to trade; it replace GATT in 1995.

Index

A

Activist economists, **185**
Adaptive expectations, **346**
AD curve, 215
  shifts in, 210–211
AED curve, 215–216, 218, 257, 351
  shifts in, 210–211
AED/PLF model, 192, 195–216
Aggregate adjustment, 212–214
Aggregate consumption function, **223**
Aggregate demand curve (AD), **193**, 208
Aggregate demand (expenditure)
  management policy, **253**
Aggregate equilibrium demand curve
  (AED), **195**
  shift factors, 198–203
Aggregate Equilibrium Demand/Price
  Level Flexibility model. See
  AED/PLF model
Aggregate expenditures, **220**–228
Aggregate income, 228–232
  determining with the Keynesian
    equation, 229–230
  income adjustment mechanism,
    231–232
  the multiplier, 230–231
  solving for equilibrium graphically,
    229
Aggregate income curve, **219**
Aggregate Production/Aggregate
  Expenditures model. See AP/AE
  model
Aggregate production curve, **219**
Aggregate supply, short-run shift factors
  of, 212
Aggregate supply/aggregate demand
  macro models, **192**
Aggregate supply curve (AS), **193**
  determining the shape of, 211
  slope of the short-run, 211–212
Alberta, University of, 467
Anglo-Canadian Telephone Co., 88
AP/AE model, **218**, 237–242, 245–248
  and the AS/AD model, 237–239
  and the Keynesian model, 240–241
  and the macro policy model, 239–240
  mechanistic and interpretive
    Keynesians, 241–242
Approximate real-world money
  multiplier, **311**
Arbitrage, **328, 400**
Arkwright, Richard, 72
Art of economics, 24
Art of macro policy, **452**
AS/AD curve, from the AP/AE model,
  245–248
AS/AD model, 192–197, 245–248
  and the macro policy model, 214–215
AS curve, 211, 216
  slope of the long-run, 212
Asian tigers, **76**
Asset management, **308**
Asset prices, and the economy, 295–296
Assets, 86
Astor, Lady Nancy, 20
Atlantic Canada Opportunities Agency
  (ACOA), 98
Automatic stabilizer, **272**
Autonomous, **337**
Autonomous consumption, **221**

Autonomous expenditures, 233–236
  and the Keynes model, 234–236
  shifts in autonomous consumption,
    233
  shifts in government expenditures, 234
  shifts in the investment function,
    233–234
Average propensity to consume (apc),
  222–223
Average propensity to save (aps) **225**
Axworthy, Lloyd, 473

B

Balance of payments, **392**–395
  the capital account, 394
  the current account, 392–394
  the official settlements balance,
    394–395
Balance of payments constraint, **490**
Balance of trade, **111**
Balance of trade deficit, **111**
Balance of trade surplus, **111**
Balance sheet, 86
Bank of Canada, **302**–303, 323–340,
    353, 445, 461, 464, 467–470
  as a central bank, 324
  central bank independence, 324–326
  international considerations, 326–327
Bank of Canada Act, 323, 468
Bank of Canada Review, 353, 469
Bank of England, 325
Bank of Japan, 325
Bank of Montreal, 88
Bank of Nova Scotia, 88
Bank rate, **328**
Banks, 308–318
  backing the money supply, 311
  creating money, 308–310
  creation of money using T-accounts,
    311–315
  money multiplier, 310–311
  regulation of, 315–318
Bar graph, 32
Base year, **152**
Basic needs, **480**
Bay Street, 291
BCE Inc., 88
Becker, Gary, 57
The Bettmann Archives, 121, 186
Black markets, in currency, 112
Bonds, **285,** 291–294
Boom, **138**
The Borrowing circle, 493, **494**–495
Bouey, Gerald, 324
Bracket creep, **429**
Brascan Ltd., 88
Bretton Woods system, **407**–408
Bryce, Robert B., 189–190, 218
Buchanan, James, 52
Bundesbank, 325, 409
Bush, President George, 458
Business, **82**–90
  categories of, 84
  consumer sovereignty, 84
  entrepreneurship, 82–83
  forms of, 89–90
  goals of, 87–89
  sizes of, 87
  stages of, 84–87

Business—*cont.*
  trials and tribulations of starting,
    83–84
Business cycles, **136**–140
  leading and coincidental indicators,
    138–140
  phases of, 137–138
  and the stock market, 140
Business Week, 99

C

Caisses populaires, 283
California Institute of Technology, 250
Cambridge University, 189
Campbell, Kim, 461
Canada Assistance Plan, 429
Canada Pension, 84
Canada Safeway Ltd., 88
Canada Savings Bonds (CSBs), 444
Canada treasury bills, 288
Canadian Business, 99
Canadian Cancer Society, 88
Canadian Consumer Price Index, 152
Canadian economy, 80–82. See also
    Canadian international trade
  diagram of, 80–82
  geographic economic information, 80
  geography of, 83
Canadian Imperial Bank of Commerce,
  88
Canadian International Development
  Agency (CIDA), **495**
Canadian international trade, 111–114.
  See also Canadian economy
  debtor and creditor nations, 111–112
  determinants of the trade balance,
    112–113
  economists' view of trade restrictions,
    113–114
Canadian Pacific Ltd., 88
Canadian Payments Association, 312
Canadian Unemployment Assistance Act,
  23
Capacity utilization rate, **139**
Capital account, **392,** 394
Capital consumption allowance, **173**
Capital control law, **475**
Capital controls, **402**
Capital gains and losses, 293
Capitalism, 63–64
  difference from Soviet-style socialism,
    66–67
Capitalists, 70–72
Capital market, **287**–288
Capital market assets, 289
Car, insuring, 296
Carlyle, Thomas, 34, 48
Carnegie, Andrew, 366
Cash management, **329**
CBC, 99
Ceausescu, Elena, 62
Ceausescu, Nicolae, 62
Central bank, **324**
Ceteris paribus. See Other things
  constant
Chartered banks, 282
Chenery, W.E., 292
Chicago, University of, 57

Chretien, Jean, 144, 267, 461, 463–464,
  473
Chrysler Canada Ltd., 88
Churchill, Winston, 20, 189
CIA World Fact Book, 65, 116
Circular flow, Keynesian monetary
  policy in, 335–336
Clark, W. Clifford, 218
Clarke, Peter, 189, 255
Classical economists, **186,** 218, 249–251,
  253, 266, 297
  and long-run growth, 482
Classical model, 212–214, 233, 355
  monetary policy in, 336–338
Classicals, 16, 129, **143,** 144, 146–147,
  198, 205
Classical supply-side economics, **461**
Classical supply-siders, 463
Classical theory
  compared to Keynesian theory,
    360–361
  to fight stagflation, 361–363
  of inflation, 352–357
  of interest, 343–344
Clearing, **312**
Clinton, Bill, 144, 386
CNN, 99
Coincidental indicators, **139**
Colander, David, 190, 218
The Coming of Keynesianism to America
  (Landreth and Colander), 190
Commercial paper, **285,** 289
Comparative advantage, **14,** 107
Competition, **96**
Competitiveness, **112**–113
Conditionality, **490**
Consumer Price Index (CPI), **151**
  index numbers and, 153
Consumer sovereignty, **84**
Consumption, 134
Consumption function, **221**
Contractionary fiscal policy, 253,
  257–259
Contractionary monetary policy, **330,**
  421
Contractions, 137
Contractual intermediaries, **282,** 284
Convertibility on the current account,
  489
Coordinate space, 29
Corey, Jane, 83–84
Corey, Lee, 83–84
Corey Feed Mills Ltd., 83–84
Corporation, **89**
Cost-of-living adjustments (COLA), 153
Cost-push inflation, **156,** 346
  examples of, 348
Countercyclical fiscal policy, **261**
Countertrade, 375
Coyne, James, 324
Crow, John, 324–326, 467–470
Crowding in, **268**
Crowding out, **268, 443**
  and international considerations,
    424–426
CTV, 99
Cultural norms, **8**
Currencies, shifting values of, 410
Current account, **392**

Currie, Lauchlin, 191
Customs duties, **375**
Cyclical unemployment, **141**

D

Debt, **94**, **429**
Debt crisis, generating saving and
   investment in, 491
The Debt reduction strategy, 491–492
Deficit, **429**
Deficits and debt, 429–441
   arbitrariness in defining, 432–434
   deficits as a summary measure, 433
   difference between individual and
      government debt, 434
   different type of crowding out,
      443–444
   federal, 441–442
   and GDP growth, 436–440
   government debt, 444–445
   judge debt relative to assets, 433–434
   as measures of fiscal policy, 445–446
   and policy regimes, 429–431
   politics and, 431–432
   relative to GDP, 434–436
Demand, **35**–42
   the demand table, 38–39
   from demand table to demand curve,
      39
   individual and market demand curves,
      39–40
   law of, 35–38
   shifts in, 40–42
Demand curve, **35**
   things to remember, 42
Demand curves, 36, 46
Demand for money, **333**
Demand-pull inflation, **155**, **346**
   examples of, 348
Demerit goods or activities, **98**
Depository institutions, **282**
Depreciation, **171**
Depression, **138**
Desired reserve ratio, **310**
Developing countries
   the dual economy, 483
   economic growth as goal, 480–481
   financial institutions of, 484
   fiscal structure, 484
   growth and basic needs, 480
   monetary policy in, 486–489
Developing economies, 105
Developing economy, **479**
Diffusion index, **138**
Discouraged workers, **146**
Disintermediation, **289**
Disposable income, **220**
Disposable personal income, **177**
Diversification, **285**
Domar, Evsey, 255
Domestic savings, generating, 492–495
Dow Jones Industrial Average, 102
Downturn, **138**
Downward-sloping curve, 31
Drawdown, **329**, **332**
Dual economy, **483**
Dummy corporations, 115
Durable goods, **170**
The Dutch disease, 141
Dynamic externalities, 278–279

E

Economic decision rule, **10**
Economic forces, **17**, 20
Economic insights, 20–23
   invisible hand theory, 20–21
   microeconomics and macroeconomics,
      21–22
   theories and stories, 21
Economic institutions, 7–8, 22–23
Economic policy, **8**
Economic policy options, 23–25
   objective policy analysis, 24
   policy and the invisible forces, 24–25

Economic reasoning, **6**, 8–19
   economics and passion, 10
   economics and the invisible forces,
      17–19
   marginal costs and benefits, 8–10
   opportunity cost, 10–11
   the production possibility curve,
      12–17
   the production possibility table, 11–12
Economics, **7**
   milestones in, 69
   in perspective, 28
Economic steering wheel, 254
Economic system, **62**–76
   capitalism, 63–64
   from capitalism to socialism, 73–74
   difference between socialism and
      capitalism, 66–67
   evolving, 67
   from feudalism to mercantilism, 70
   from feudalism to socialism, 75–76
   feudal society, 68–70
   from mercantilism to capitalism,
      70–73
   planning, politics, and markets, 62–63
   socialism in practice, 64–66
   socialism in theory, 64
Economic terminology, 7, 19–20
Economic theory, **7**
Economies of scale, **381**
The Economist, 99
Economy, **7**
   finding more information about, 99
ECU, 120, **409**
Embargo, **377**
Empirical evidence, interpreting, 135
Entrepreneurship, 16, **82**–83
Equation of exchange, **336**
Equilibrium, **50**–52
Equilibrium price, **50**–52
Equity capital, 89
European Currency Unit. See ECU
European exchange rate mechanism, 409
European Union (EU), **119**–121, 125,
   377, **383**–387, 409, 418
Excess demand, **48**
Excess reserves, **310**
Excess supply, **48**
Exchange rate, **326**, **415**
Exchange rate constraint, and the
   international sector, 489
Exchange rate policy, 264, **403**, 489–490
Exchange rates, 396–405. See also
   Monetary policy
   advantages and disadvantages of
      alternative systems, 409–412
   flexible, partially flexible, and fixed,
      405–409
   government role in determining,
      401–405
   stability and instability in foreign
      markets, 399–401
Expansion, **138**
Expansionary fiscal policy, 253
Expansionary monetary policy, **329**, 421
Expansions, 137
Expectations of inflation, **349**
Expected inflation, **157**
Export-led growth policy, 263
Exports, **106**
External government debt, **434**
Externality, **96**–97

F

Factor market, 80
Factors of production, **42**
Fallacy of composition, **194**
Fear of hunger, 141
Federal Employment and Social
   Insurance Act, 142
Feudalism, **68**–70
Financial assets, **281**
Financial institutions, 281, **282**–298
   contractual intermediaries, 284

Financial institutions—cont.
   depository institutions, 282–284
   financial assets, 288–294
   financial assets and liabilities,
      281–282
   financial markets, 286–288
   investment intermediaries, 285–286
   types of, 285
   value of a financial asset, 294–296
Financial liabilities, **281**
Financial panic, anatomy of, 315–316
The Financial Post, 99
The Financial Post 500, 88
The Financial Times, 99
Fine tuning, **261**
Firms, **42**
First dynamic law of supply and
   demand, 48–49, 53
Fiscal policy, **253**–274. See also
      Government
   aggregate demand management,
      255–256
   alternatives to, 261–262
   applying the models and questionable
      effectiveness of, 259–261
   autonomous consumption policy, 264
   building Keynesian policy into
      institutions, 272
   directed investment policies, 262–263
   effect on exchange rates, 421–422
   effect on trade deficit, 422–423
   financing the deficit, 268–269
   government budget and traded
      deficits, 264–266
   government changing taxes and
      spending, 271
   government spending multiplier,
      256–257
   in graphs, 257–259
   Keynesian, 253–255
   and the Keynesian model, 273–274
   level of potential income, 270–271
   in perspective, 272–273
   size of government debt, 271
   some real-world examples, 266–267
   tax/transfer multiplier, 256–257
   trade policy and export led-growth,
      263–264
Fixed currency exchange rates, 189
Fixed exchange rates, **405**–409, **415**
   and monetary stability, 409–410
   and policy independence, 410
   return to, 472–475
Flexible exchange rate, **405**–411, **415**
Forbes, 99
Ford, Henry, 46
Ford Motor Company, 102
Ford Motor Company of Canada, Ltd.,
   88
Foreign exchange control law, **475**
Foreign exchange market, **108**
Foreign exchange reserves, **405**–409
Foreign Investment Review Agency
   (FIRA), 113
Fortune, 99
Freeman, Alan, 444
Free rider, **97**
Free Trade Agreement (FTA), **118**,
   383–387
Free Trade Association, **383**–387, 474
Free trade policies, 24
Frictional unemployment, **142**
Friedman, Milton, 24, 345, 355
Full convertibility, **489**
Full employment, **142**, 147–148,
   465–470
Fundamental analysis, **397**

G

Galbraith, John Kenneth, 301
Gardner, George, 56
GATT, **114**, **376**, 386–387
GDP, 111, **162**, 166–177, 215, 266–267,
   367, 434–443, 475

GDP—cont.
   calculating, 163–166
   comparing among countries, 177–178
   economic welfare over time, 178
   the expenditures approach, 168–173,
      176
   the income approach, 175–176
   measurement errors, 180–181
   misinterpretation of subcategories, 181
   national income accounting identity,
      166–168
   from nominal net domestic income,
      176–177
   real and nominal, 173–175
GDP deflator, 151, **152**–154, 174
General Agreement on Tariffs and Trade.
   See GATT
General Motors, 46
General Motors of Canada Ltd., 88
General purpose transfers, **94**
The General Theory of Employment,
   Interest, and Money (Keynes), 250,
   255, 263
George Weston Ltd., 88
Gilray, James, 354
Global corporations, **104**, 115–117
Globalization, **118**
The Globe and Mail, 99, 102, 444, 473
GNP, **162**
Gold specie flow mechanism, **406**
Gold standard, **406**
Goods market, 80
Government, **94**–99. See also Fiscal
      policy
   limits of action, 99
   as a referee, 94–99
Government budget deficit, **94**
Government budget surplus, **94**
Governor of the Bank of Canada, **324**
Grameen Bank, 493
Graphs
   language of, 29–33
   presenting real-world data in, 32–33
Greenspon, Edward, 473
Gresham's law, 315
Grey markets, in currency, 112
Gross Domestic Product. See GDP
Gross Domestic Product deflator. See
   GDP deflator
Gross National Product. See GNP
Gross profit, 86
Group of Five, **114**
Group of Seven, **114**
Group of Ten, 398
Growth, 132–136, 159
   benefits and costs of, 132–133
   causes of, 133–136
Growth-compatible institutions, **133**
Guarantees, benefits and problems,
   316–318

H

Haberler, Gottfried, 217
Hanson Memorial Lecture, 467
Hargreaves, James, 72
Harris, Richard, 472
Harvard Business School, 11, 292, 354,
   456
Hayek, Frederick, 191
Historeses, 54
House, buying, 296–297
Households, **90**–93
   people power, 92
   social, cultural, and and ideological
      sensibilities of, 92–93
   as suppliers of labour, 91–92
   type and income, 90–91
Hudson's Bay Co., 88
Human capital, **135**
Hyperinflation, **158**

I

Ideology, 92
The Image Works, 56, 401, 420

Imasco Ltd., 88
Import control law, **475**
Import license, **376**
Imports, **106**
Income adjustment mechanism, 218, 249
Income statement, 86
Indexed tax system, **430**
Index number, **152**
Indicators, 139
Induced consumption, **221**
Induced recession, **350**
Industrial economies, 105
Industrialists, 70–72
Industrial Products Price Index (PPI), 151, **153**
Industrial Revolution, **72**, 140–142
Inefficiency, **15**
Infant industry argument, 381
Inflation, **150**–159, **346**–363
    costs of, 157–159
    distributional effects of, 358
    and expectations of, 346–347
    expected and unexpected, 157
    Keynesian theory of, 356–366
    measurement of, 151–154
    the money supply and, 346
    occurrence of, 155–156
    the Phillips curve and the price-level flexibility curve, 351–352
    real and nominal concepts, 154–155
    theories of and the Phillips curve, 352–356
    and unemployment: the Phillips curve trade-off, 347–351
Inflationary gap, **259**
Inflation tax, **488**
Input, **11**, 16
Institutional differences, 481–490
    political differences and laissez-faire, 482–483
Interest groups, **93**
Interest rates
    changes in, 233
    and the economy, 295–296
    Keynesian emphasis on, 335–336
Inter-firm credit, **485**
Intermediate products, **164**
Internal government debt, **434**
International competitors, 117–125
    developing countries as competitors, 125
    the European Union, 119–121
    "Japan, Inc.", 121–124
    "Japan, Inc." versus Canada, 124–125
International considerations, and crowding out, 424–426
International economic institutions, **115**
International economic statistics, 105–108
    comparative advantage and trade, 106–108
    differing economic problems, 106
    economic geography, 106
International effect, 209–210
International Monetary Fund (IMF), **114**–115
International policy and institutions, 114–117
    global corporations, 115–117
International Trade Commission (ITC), 386
Interpolation assumption, 31
Interpretive Keynesian model, 241–242
Intertemporal price-level effect, 209
Intervals, 29
Inverse relationship, 31
Investment, **226**
Invisible foot, **18**–19
Invisible hand, **18**–19
Invisible handshake, **18**–19
Invisible hand theory, 20–21

J
J-curve, **404**

Journal of Economic Perspectives, 205
Just-noticeable difference, **360**

K
Kay, James, 72
Keynes, John Maynard, 24, 184–185, 189, 191, 218, 233, 249–251, 255
Keynes, John Neville, 24
Keynesian business cycles, 278–279
Keynesian/Classical policy debate, 454–460
    Classical view of government policy, 455
    flip-flopping views of the deficit, 455–457
    Keynesian view of government policy, 455
Keynesian economists, **186**, 218, 250–251, 266, 297
Keynesian equation, **229**–230
Keynesian fiscal policy, 253–255, 268–274
Keynesian model, 208, 212–214, 218–228, 240–242, 253, 265, 332, 355
    aggregate expenditures in, 220–228
    aggregate production in, 219–220
    algebraic, 276–277
    examples of, 236
    and fiscal policy, 273–274
Keynesian monetary policy, in the circular flow, 335–336
Keynesian multiplier model, 266
Keynesian policy, 255
The Keynesian Revolution in the Making 1924–1936 (Clarke), 189
Keynesians, 129, 137, **143** 144, 146–147, 162, 185, 189, 198, 205, 255
The Keynesian spiral, 278–279
Keynesian supply-side policy, **463**
Keynesian theory
    compared to Classical theory, 360–361
    to fight stagflation, 361–363
    of inflation, 356–366
    of interest, 343–344
Keynes law, **220**
Kim Young Sam, 493
Knight, Frank, 191

L
Labour Force Survey, **145**
LaFargue, Paul, 478
Laissez-faire, **72**, **186**
Laissez-faire economists, **185**
Laissez-faire policy, 129
Landreth, Harry, 190
Law of aggregate demand, 208
Law of demand, 35–38
Law of supply, **43**
Leading indicators, **139**
Learning by doing, **381**
Lerner, Abba, 61, 254–255
Liability, 86
Liability management, **308**
Limited capital account convertibility, **489**
Limited liability, **89**
Linear curve, 31
Line graph, 32
Liquidity, **287**
Lloyd George, David, 189
Long-run Phillips curve, **349**
Long-run potential income, **190**
Low-income cutoff, **90**

M
M1, **305**–306
M2, **305**–307
M2+, **306**
M3, **306**
Mackenzie King, 93
MacKintosh, W.A., 218
MacLean's, 99

MacMillan Commission, 323
Macroeconomic externality, **97**–98
Macroeconomic policy, 415–417, 450–476
    agreement about, 459–460
    and credibility, 454
    differences between theoretical and policy models, 452
    dilemmas, 451
    the exchange rate goal, 415–416
    interface between theoretical and policy models, 453
    international versus domestic goals, 416–417
    and Keynesians and Classicals, 457–459
    limits of, 450–451
    the 1990 Recession, 460–461
    the sort-of recovery, 461
    supply-side policies, 461–464
    the trade balance goal, 416
Macroeconomics, 21–**22**, 54
Macro institutional policy, in developing countries, **490**–495
Macro model, analytic, 205–216
Macro policy, topical issues in Canadian, 464–475
Macro policy model, **192**–203, 245–248
    complications of, 203–205
    macro policy in, 201–202
    the rudiments of the AS/AD model, 192–195
    some practices using, 202–203
    using, 200–201
Magee, Stephen, 19
Malthus, Thomas, 28, 187, 482
Mao Zedong, 75
Marginal benefit, **9**
Marginal cost, **9**
Marginal propensity to consume (mpc), **222**–223
Marginal propensity to expend (mpe), **260**
Marginal propensity to save (mps), **225**
Market demand curve, 39–40
Market force, **18**
Market forces, 20
Markets, rise of, 72
Market supply curve, 45–46
Marshall, Alfred, 5, 46, 156, 482
Marshallian economics, 46
Martin, Paul, 444
Marx, Karl, 28, 73–75
Math anxiety, dealing with, 123
Maturity, 288
Maturity date, 292
Maximum points, 32
McKenna, Frank, 473
The McNeil-Lehrer Report, 99
Mechanistic Keynesianism, **452**
Mechanistic Keynesian model, **241**–242
Medicare, 429
Mencken, H.L., 103
Mercantilism, 70–71
Merchandise trade balance, **111**, **392**
Merit goods or activities, **99**
Microeconomics, 21–22
Middle-income economies, 105
Mill, John Stuart, 28, 482
Minimum points, 32
Ministry of International Trade and Industry (MITI), **123**–124
Model, **51**
Modern Classicals, 242
Modern macroeconomics, 185–192
    classical view of the Great Depression, 188–189
    emergence of classical economics, 186–187
    emergence of Keynesian economics, 189–192
    quantity theory of money, 188
Monetarist economists, 129
Monetary and fiscal coordination, international, 423–424

Monetary base, **340**
The Monetary conditions index (MCI), 465
Monetary policy, **324**, 327–340. See also Exchange rates
    effect on exchange rates, 417–419
    effect on the trade balance, 419–421
    how it works, 333–339
    problems in the conduct of, 339–340
    tools of, 328–333
Monetary rule, **354**
Monetary validation, **346**
Money, **188**, **302**–307
    alternative definitions of, 305–307
    functions of, 302–305
Money market, **287**–288
Money market assets, 288
Money multiplier
    precise calculation of, 320
    and reforms in banking, 312
Money price, 37
Money substitutes, **307**
Monopoly power, **96**
Mortgage, **296**
Most-favoured nation, **387**
Movement along the demand curve, **41**–42
Movement along the supply curve, **47**–48
The Multiplier, **230**–231
Municipal bonds, 288–289

N
NAFTA, **120**–121, 125, **383**–387, 474
National income, limitations of, 178–181
National income accounting, **162**–166
    and double-entry bookkeeping, 168
National income accounting identity, 166, **167**–168
NATO, 377, 383
Natural rate of employment, 148
Natural rate of unemployment, **355**
Natural resources, 16
NB Job Corps, 473
Near money, **307**
Neo-Classical economists, 129
Neo-Classical political economists, 52
Neo-Keynesian economists, 129
Neomercantilist, 122
Net domestic income at factor cost (NDI), **175**
Net domestic product (NDP), **173**
Net exports, **226**
Net foreign factor income, **163**
Net national income (NNI), **175**
Net private investment, **171**
Net worth, 86
New Classical economists, 129
New Keynesian economists, 129
Newsweek, 99
Nike, 54
NIMBY, **63**
Nobel prize, 355
Nominal concepts, **162**
Nominal deficit, **437**
Nominal GDP, **173**
Nominal interest rates, **338**
Nominal output, 154
Nonaccelerating inflation rate of unemployment (NAIRU), 148, 355
Nonconvertible currencies, **396**
Nonconvertible exchange rate, **405**–409
Nondurable goods, **170**
Nonlinear curves, 31
Nonprofit business, **87**–88
Noranda Inc., 88
Normative economics, 24
North American Free Trade Agreement. See NAFTA
North Atlantic Treaty Organization. See NATO
The North/South conflict, 480
Not in my back yard. See NIMBY

O

Objective, **24**
Objective policy analysis, 24
Official settlements balance, **392**
Okun, Arthur, 19
Okun's law, **270**
Okun's rule of thumb, **147**
OPEC, 55–56, 105, 115, 156
Open market operations, **329**
Opportunity cost, **10–11**, 20
The Organization of Economic
　　Cooperation and Development
　　(OECD), 115
Organization of Petroleum Exporting
　　Countries. See OPEC
The Oshawa Group Ltd., 88
Other things constant, **36**–37, 44, 54,
　　208, 250
Output, **11**, 16

P

Panic, government policy to prevent, 316
Paradox of thrift, **236**
Partial equilibrium analysis, 37
Partially flexible exchange rate,
　　405–409, 411–412, **415**
Partnership, **89**
Passive deficit, **265**
Path dependency, 54
Path-dependent equilibrium, 241
Peak, 138
Perfectly flexible exchange rates,
　　405–409
Perks, 88
Personal income (PI), **177**
Phillips curve, 347, **348**–356, 362–363
Pie chart, 32
Pigou effect. See The Wealth effect
Pitt, William, 354
Planning, **66**
PLF curve, 205, 216
Policy, and the invisible forces, 24–25
Policy change, **484**
Political differences, and laissez-faire,
　　482–483
Positive economics, **24**
Post-Keynesian economists, 129
Potential income, **190**
Potential output, **139**
Power Corp. of Canada, 88
Present value, **294**–295
Price ceiling, **56**–57
Price floor, **57**
Price-level flexibility, and
　　macroeconomic theory, 249–251
Price level flexibility curve (PLF),
　　195–198, 215–216
　　shift factors, 200
Price-level interest rate effect, 208–209
Price stability, **464**, 465–470
Primary financial market, **286**–287
Principle of absolute advantage, **368**
Principle of comparative advantage,
　　371–**372**
Principle of increasing marginal
　　opportunity cost, **15**
Principles of Economics (Ricardo), 373
Private good, **97**
Private property rights, **63**
Production possibility curve, **12**–17
Production possibility table, **10**–11
Productive efficiency, **15**
Profit, **84**
Progressive tax, **98**
Proletariat, **73**–74
Proportional tax, 98
Protectionist policies, **118**
Provigo Inc., 88
Provincial bonds, 288–289
Public choice economists, 52
Public goods, **97**

Q

Quantity demanded, **35**

Quantity supplied, **43**
Quantity theory of money, **188**, **336**
Quota rent, **376**
Quotas, **108**, **376**

R

Rasminsky, Louis, 324
Rational expectations, **452**
Rationing, **17**–18
R.B. Bennett, 93, 142, 255
Real business cycles, 278–279
Real business cycle theory, **250**
Real concepts, **162**
Real deficit, **437**
Real GDP, **173**
Real interest rate, **338**
Real output, **154**
Real wage, **186**
Recessionary gap, **257**
Redeposits, **329**
Regime change, **484**
Regional multipliers, 265
Regressive tax, 98
Regulatory trade restrictions, **377**
Relative price, **37**, 44–45, **192**
Relative price adjustment, 215
Reserve currency, **408**
Reserve ratio, **311**
Reserves, **310**, 312
Resources, 16
Restructuring, **479**
Retained earnings, 291
Reuters, 121
Revenue Canada, 180
Ricardian equivalence theorem, **455**
Ricardo, David, 28, 187, 373, 455, 482
Robertson, Dennis, 191
Roehle, Robert, 386
Rogers, Will, 79, 322
Rogers Cantel Mobile Communications
　　Inc., 88
Roosevelt, Franklin D., 428
Rosy scenario policy, **262**
Royal Bank of Canada, 88

S

Salaries, 88
Say, Jean Baptiste, 187
Sayers, R.S., 449
Say's law, **187**, 220, 249
Schultze, George, 252
Secondary financial market, **287**
Second dynamic law of supply and
　　demand, **49**
Semi-durable goods, **170**
Services, **170**
Services balance, **111**
Shareholders, 76
Shareholder's equity, **86**
Shift factors, 44
Shift factors of demand, **37**
Shift in demand, 41–42
Shift in supply, 47–48
Short-run AS curve, 215–216
Short-run Phillips curve, **349**
Short-run potential income, **190**
Short-run supply, shift factors of, 212
Short-term Canada bonds, 288
Simon Fraser University, 472
Simple money multiplier, **311**
Slope, 31
　　of linear curves, 31
　　of nonlinear curves, 31–32
Smith, Adam, 19, 28, 71–73, 186, 482
Social assistance programs, **471**
　　reforming, 470–472
Social capital, **135**
Socialism, **64**
Socialist economies, 106
Socrates, 131
Soft budget constraint, 485
Sole proprietorship, **89**
Soviet-style socialism, **65**
　　difference from capitalism, 66–67

Special drawing rights (SDRs), **408**
Special purpose transfers, **94**
Spread, **399**
Stage of production, **84**
Stagflation, **356**
Stakeholders, 76
Stalin, Joseph, **75**
Stamp, Sir Josiah, 161
Stance of fiscal policy, **445**
Standard & Poor's, 102
State socialism, **75**
Statistics Canada, 137, 145–146, 149,
　　152, 170–172, 180, 393
Steady-as-you-go policy, 338–339
Stock, **89**, **289**
Stock exchange, 89
Strategic bargaining, **380**
Structural deficit, **265**, **436**
Structural readjustment, **143**, **204**
Structural unemployment, **141**
Subjective, **24**
Supply, 42, **43**–48
　　individual and market supply curves,
　　　　45–46
　　law of, 43–45
　　shifts in, 45–48
　　the supply table, 45
　　from supply table to supply curve, 45
Supply and demand, 48–54
　　in action, 54
　　changes in, 52–54
　　dynamic laws of, 50
　　equilibrium, 50–52
　　first dynamic law of, 48–49
　　graphical marriage of, 50
　　second dynamic law of, 49
　　third dynamic law of, 49–50
Supply curve, things to remember, 48
Supply/demand models, **192**
Supply of money, **333**
Supply-side arguments, distinguishing
　　the Keynesian and Classical, 463
Supply-side policies, **461**

T

TANSTAAFL, 9, 465
　　law, 133
Target rate of employment, 147–148
Target rate of unemployment, **139**
Tariff, **375**
Tariff tax, **108**
Tarshis, Lorrie, 190
Technology, 16
Teleglobe Inc., 88
TELUS Corp., 88
Term structure of interest rates, **328**
Thatcher, Margaret, 144
Theissen, Gordon, 353
Thiessen, Gordon, 324–325
Third dynamic law of supply and
　　demand, **49**–50
Time, 99
Time dimension, 38
Toronto-Dominion Bank, 88
Toronto Stock Exchange, 102, 139, 291
Towers, Graham, 324
Trade, 367–388
　　competitiveness, exchange rates, and
　　　　comparative advantage, 372–373
　　differences in importance of, 367–358
　　dividing up the gains from trade,
　　　　373–375
　　free trade associations, 383–387
　　increasing but fluctuating world trade,
　　　　367
　　international versus domestic,
　　　　108–111
　　the principle of absolute advantage,
　　　　368–371
　　the principle of comparative
　　　　advantage, 371–372
　　reasons for trade restrictions, 378–382
　　varieties of trade restrictions, 375–378

Trade—*cont.*
　　why economists oppose trade
　　　　restrictions, 382–383
Trade adjustment assistance programs,
　　379
Trade balance, **415**
Trade credits, **486**
Trade restrictions
　　reasons for, 378–382
　　why economists oppose, 382–383
Trader speculation, limits on, 402
Trade war, 114
Transfer payments, **94**, **172**, **256**
Transitional countries
　　financial institutions, 484
　　fiscal structure, 484
　　monetary policy in, 486–489
　　roles of financial institutions, 485–486
Transitional economy, 106, **479**
Treasury bill, 288
Trough, 138
Trudeau, Pierre, 363
Tullock, Gordon, 52

U

U.N. Statistical Yearbook, 487
The Underground economy, 180
Unemployment, 140–150, 159
　　categories of, 144
　　measurement of, 145–147
　　microeconomic categories of, 147–150
　　and potential income, 147
　　responsibility for, 143–145
Unemployment Insurance, **470**
　　reforming, 470–472
Unemployment Insurance Program, 144
Unemployment rate, **139**
Unexpected inflation, **157**
United Nations, 115
United States Federal Reserve Bank,
　　325, 353
University Review, 254
Upturn, 138
Upward-sloping curve, 31

V

Value added, **165**
Variables, 30
Veil-of-money assumption, 337
Velocity of money, **336**
Venture, 99

W

Wage flexibility, and macroeconomic
　　theory, 249–251
The Wall Street Journal, 99, 493
Wall Street Week, 99
Wal-Mart, **84**
Walras, Leon, 46
Walrasian economics, 46
Watt, James, 72
The Wealth effect, 208
The Wealth of Nations (Smith), 28, 71,
　　186
Welfare capitalism, 73, **74**–75
Wells, David H., 401
Whitney, Eli, 72
Wilshire Index, 102
Wincott, Harold, 391
World Almanac, 116
World Bank, **114**–115
The World FactBook, 367
World Trade Organization (WTO), **114**,
　　387
Wormhole effect, 250

Y

Young, Allyn, 191
Yunus, Mohammed, 493–495

Z

Zero inflation, 468